AMNE ADVERSO

Roman Legal Heritage in European Culture

Amne Adverso

Roman Legal Heritage in European Culture

Laurent Waelkens

Leuven University Press

Original title: Civium causa. Handboek Romeins recht.
Authorized translation from the Dutch language editon published by Acco, Leuven.
Translated from Dutch by Line Leys (KU Leuven, Law Faculty)

ISBN 978 94 6270 054 3
D / 2015 / 1869 / 46
NUR: 686

Cover: Anton Lecock
Lay-out: Frederik Danko

Dedicated to the memory of Robert Feenstra (1920-2013)

Table of contents

Preface

Nihil nisi historia, everything is history. The alignment of the houses and university buildings of Leuven is the upshot of centuries of living and striving. The university itself faces the future, but does it thanks to its embedment in the rich past of the Low Countries, at the fault line of the tectonic plates of European culture, in-between the Continent and the Atlantic world, the Roman south and the Nordic countries. We are mostly happy prisoners of our past. In Western music, major scale chords were developed because they were well adapted to gothic vaults. Even now, long after the gothic period, they make us feel solemn. But when aiming to change the future or looking for an egress, it is more successful to study and adapt history than to shake it vigorously. Lawyers who are the judges of the *pax europaea* have to be aware of the old Roman law. It determined European culture in the past and is still a strong presence today. Sometimes, it makes a reappearance, the way musical feelings do. Onlookers of a car crash with some minor material damage begin to discuss torts, guilt, fault and liability although they are not involved in the settlement of the case. This is an example of old legal culture bubbling up again. Does this mean that Roman law is food for psychologists? No. It really does come in handy to deal with deep-seated conflicts. An affable English banker sells secured bonds to a German savings bank. They later turn out to be junk bonds and the German bank feels cheated. Are English bankers unfair or indifferent to decent legal culture? No. On the Continent, good faith applies to all obligations; in England it does not apply to strict obligations. Both good faith and strict obligations stem from Roman law, but the legal transplant of the Roman obligations on the Continent differed from that in England. It is impossible to clear up this situation and reconcile both viewpoints without Roman law. Another example: a Greek man has been collecting his deceased father's pension and is incensed about being labelled a fraudster by Westerners. He is a *romaios*, an heir of Rome, and he received this money from his government. Greece did not experience the evolution of Roman law in the West during the Age of Enlightenment and in 1831 it sought alignment with the imperial Roman law of 1453. Can such a Roman citizen refuse what the emperor grants him? This is Roman law as well, although it sounds strange to Western ears. One has to take account of the different reception of Roman law in the different regions of Europe. Roman law cannot be studied as a fixed body of rules.

In Leuven, Roman law has been taught since 1425. Philip the Good, who became the ruler of the Low Countries at that time, wanted to unify the law of this region according to the legal model of Constantinople that had been taught at the university of Bologna since the twelfth century. Like the East, the West had always preserved Roman law. However, it had been given a particular twist in the early Middle Ages. As a consequence of the confrontation with the Levant during the Crusades, Roman law became the first subject that was studied at a 'university'. The second subject was theology, because the religion of the Levant was just as different from that of the West as its law. Roman law was also at the origin of the university of Leuven. This academic law was highly valued by rulers, bishops, citizens, traders, scholars and thinkers. In the fifteenth and sixteenth centuries, Roman law flourished once again because of the immigration of tens of thousands of Greeks who fled Constantinople. They brought us the concept of a nation with a centralised administration and a religion controlled by the monarch. In response to this royal absolutism, the Roman civil rights were recast into unassailable private rights and freedoms during the Age of Enlightenment. At this time, legal scholars were using this law as the basis for their development of the supranational *ius commune* of the Modern Era. After the Napoleonic wars, Roman law was once again appealed to in order to stabilise European culture around a civil society. At this time, the study of Roman law was paired with that of national civil law. In the latter half of the nineteenth century, the law of Germany served as the main touchstone. In Leuven, Roman law was also studied at that time as the basis of the Code civil. In the twentieth century, a pandemonium broke out that once again questioned all law. From 1950 onwards, thousands of legal experts sought the formula for a *pax europaea* that furthered cooperation between European countries. Because of this, legal scholars in Leuven began to see the study of Roman law as the comparative legal history of the European *ius commune*. This means that our Research Department of Roman Law and Legal History studies all aspects and periods of the reception of Roman law in Europe and takes account of the diverse ways in which it was transplanted into European legal systems. The reception in the Middle Ages and Modern Times is examined, as are medieval canon law, the differing reception in the Occident and the Levant, the impact of the Renaissance, the influence of theology on the law of the Early Modern Era or financial law... The Department of Roman Law and Legal History of KU Leuven has become a merry band of researchers from five different countries who are working on extremely varied projects. In other words: Roman law is an old study, but it has not ossified and is in need of constant modernisation.

This publication is the textbook of Roman law that is used by starting undergraduates in the English-language study programmes in Leuven. It is based on my Dutch-language *Civium causa*, 3d edition, Leuven 2014. The English title is an expression of the Leuven method of studying Roman law: *Amne adverso*, 'looking upstream'. Roman sources cannot be read against the background of current ideas. One has to travel upstream, just like the explorers who journeyed up the Nile to discover its sources. Justinianic *proprietas* cannot be taken to mean 'property' if the latter notion only originated in Early Modern Times, nor can the ancient Roman *matrimonium* be considered to indicate the medieval concept of matrimony. In Cicero's works, one can neither read about the good faith that the canonists thought up in the Middle Ages, nor about the general theory of obligations that was first written down by Donellus. It is especially fascinating to discover how the same Roman legal sources were interpreted differently in every country and historical period and how different traditions grew out of the same soil. For roughly the last thirty years, I have approached Roman law *amne adverso*. I have often been told that my views were not in line with the scholarly tradition of Max Kaser et al. To be unruly is also expressed *amne adverso* in Latin. May this second meaning of a different view on Roman law be a cheerful wink in the title.

This textbook offers an introduction into the history of Roman legal thought and its institutions. Its scope and depth are limited by the role of Roman law in the curriculum of the Law Faculty. It remains a coursebook, which is simple at the beginning and more complicated at the end and raises important matters at least twice. During the last centuries the study of Roman law has been oriented mainly towards private law and to a lesser extent towards public law and criminal law. For a long time, the emphasis in this science lay on ancient legal thought rather than on its reception in the Middle Ages and the Modern Era. We wanted the situation to be different, but science requires the work of many. It is clear that the transplant of Roman law, which was different everywhere, still does not get the attention it deserves. Perhaps the subtitle of this book should have been 'provisional notes', but is not everything in life provisional and limited? Even a rough outline of the Roman law should give the reader a sharper insight into the legal problems with which he finds himself confronted. For jurists, legal history is both a form of comparative law and the only way to assess the future. The history of Roman law is part of this. It does not have to sound dogmatic. It does not have to defend gothic chords, but has to lead to the harmony of the *pax europaea.*

Many controversies that cropped up in the course of the history of law have been summarised in this book. And yet it does not contain footnotes or references. Every now and then, I provide a bibliography, but there are no sparring matches with confreres and authors of previous centuries. The sparse references wish to remind the reader that he himself needs to dig a little deeper every now and then, that one witness is no witness and that one cannot remain critical without engaging in comparisons with the work of others. Wherever I am too *amne adverso,* I try to fit the divergent opinions into a scientific context by referring to other publications in which I have examined sources and interpretations in greater depth.

I am thankful to the many people who have inspired me to write this book. They are, first of all, my students – who continuously fill me with the fear of misinterpreting the legal history and of presenting them with fanciful tales – and my colleagues from different countries who have provided new insights, as well as those who are at the basis of new doctrine thanks to the special scientific process of *vituperantia.* In the Dutch linguistic region, I am obliged to the Circle of Dutch-language Romanists, which encourages cooperation. This group of experts in Roman law will notice that in my quest for renewal I took advantage of the roads they have already travelled. I am also grateful to the Alma Mater of Leuven for investing so much in Roman law. Thank you to Line Leys, who translated the text from Dutch when she was an assistant at the Leuven Department of Roman Law and Legal History, and to our research fellow James Mearns who proofread the manuscript in his capacity as a native speaker.

This book is dedicated to the memory of my Doktorvater Robert Feenstra. From 1945 onwards he used his extraordinary knowledge of Roman law to introduce himself in all European law faculties, where he promoted cooperation and internationalization, and eventually the *pax europaea.* He showed me the way out of the classical Roman law of the nineteenth and twentieth centuries and promoted the study of the historical Roman law which determined the European legal culture of all epochs.

Laurent Waelkens,
Leuven, Candlemas 2015.

Introduction
The science of Roman law

Roman law is the oldest course at the university. In Bologna legal education started in the eleventh century; Leuven began to teach Roman law in 1425. Why? And why is the subject still taught and studied today? What do Romanists occupy themselves with?

§1. The purpose of the study of Roman law

There are four principal reasons to study Roman law: (1) the comprehension of academic thought, of which Roman legal thought is a component, (2) the search for the roots of common European legal thought, (3) the fact that the study of Roman law has been used since the nineteenth century as an antidote to the thought of the Enlightenment and (4) that it helps jurists to reach a better understanding of other people.

1. A component of academic thought

People think according to a formula. In every era, this formula changes. The academic method of thought was developed in Western Europe in the Middle Ages and the Modern Period and grew from a soil consisting of the fusion of four old cultures: Roman societal thought, Jewish-Christian theological thought, Greek scientific thought and Oriental mathematical thought.

The universities emerged in the eleventh century. Their development was furthered by the First Crusade, in which many Westerners were confronted for the first time with the Levant. The Latin West and the Greek Levant had grown from the same roots, namely the Roman Empire and Christianity, but had branched in different directions since the fifth century. In Constantinople the crusaders discovered city-dwellers who led rich lives despite the barren Greek landscape and lived Christianity in another way. Apparently, agriculture was not the only source of wealth: societal structures also contributed to prosperity. And what about the Greek rites? Did they give the Levant an advantage as well? Confronted with the Greek world, Westerners began to question their *latinitas*. In the universities, people began to reflect deeply on what was at that time considered as the basis of this *latinitas*: old Roman societal logic and Jewish-Christian culture. Old Roman logic was first and foremost societal thought; legal thought. Rome became great through its societal structures and its capacity to let individuals and peoples work together by means of law. Jewish-Christian thought focused first and foremost on the transcendental search for meaning. In the first centuries of the Common Era the Roman search for meaning and the Jewish-Christian search for justice had clicked together. In the twelfth century, it was mainly these two old modes of thought or *facultates* which people were studying in order to fathom out our culture. In Constantinople they discovered other patterns of thought which were typical of the *graecitas* of the Levant: Greek logic, as well as mathematical and scientific thought. Greek logic had only penetrated sporadically into Latin culture through Neo-Platonism and Boethius. In the thirteenth century the study of Aristotle was added to academic thought. After the fall of Constantinople (1453) the West was flooded by influential Greeks, who caused another intellectual revolution. From then on their mathematics as well as their technical and scientific thought – their active way of dealing with nature – began to play a role at the universities. In the universities of the Early Modern Era these components were used to brew a critical mode of thought which would become very successful and would furnish the poor West with a dominant culture. Western academic thought differs from any other model. This is evident not only from comparisons with Chinese thought or Bantu philosophy, but also from juxtapositions with Russia or the Ottoman countries, which do not have an old academic tradition. Within Western Europe, it is also very different from other complex forms of thought such as musical logic or Jewish theology.

Universities study their own mode of thought. This is not just food for philosophers. Fathoming out a blended whisky is impossible without knowledge of its single malts. Therefore, the main ingredients of our mode of thought, such as mathematics, logic, natural sciences, or theology are studied separately. So is Roman law. Together with the Jewish-Christian tradition, it is part of the basic broth of typical Western thought which was present in both the *latinitas* and the *graecitas*. The other ingredients were blended in with these. It is no coincidence that these courses are the oldest at the university and that in large universities the study of Roman law deserves a place in a critical research environment. In order to remain critical, we must analyse Roman legal logic and study its fortunes before we instil academic thought into our students.

Within the West itself, the recipe for thought differs from country to country. Greek logic is more common in Portugal than in Ireland. Aristotelianism was repressed to a greater extent in Italy than north of the Alps. You will get further with theology in Northern Germany than in England. The component of Roman law was also dosed differently in different regions. It is for this reason that we need it to understand the *ius commune*, the common law of Europe.

2. The comprehension of the *ius commune*, the common law of Europe

Roman law is more than a component of our academic thought. It can first and foremost be found in the legal systems of Western Europe and the Levant. The Roman Empire became strong during the Republic through its legal system. In the imperial period there was peace, the highest good for jurists, for centuries. Even in regions beyond the Empire's borders attention was paid to the 'reception' of Roman law. In this manner, the West and the former Greco-Roman Empire acquired a certain *ius commune*, a common law of Europe that was ' received' from Roman law.

The 'reception' of legal norms is a variant of acculturation. In order to improve their chances of survival, everyone copies patterns of behaviour from people who seem to be in a stronger position. Children imitate their parents and friends, and adults look a bit further, but everyone easily adopts the techniques and values of others to survive in a hostile environment. Just as farmers quietly copy the methods of neighbours with larger yields, all people adopt patterns of thought. Until recently, Great Britain was the greatest power of all time. Fifty years after the fall of the Empire, we are still adopting English societal values, standards and views. English is considered a world language and imposes a thought structure through its linguistic structure. English philosophy starts from perception rather than from an ideal world. The principal operating systems have computers reason according to English logic, to the exclusion of for example a Japanese or Kantian way of thought. Acculturation is not always well thought-through. After the World War, the US liberated us and put us back on our feet. We were keen to adopt such a powerful culture, including its summer drinks and Californian swimming pools which become so different in our cooler climes. Chinese entrepreneurs successfully copy not only Western production techniques, but also Western clothes, which are not adapted to their climate. Jurists also adopt values from neighbours which they deem stronger. In law, young branches such as labour law and consumer law are strongly inspired by the Anglo-American legal culture. Also jurists sometimes have an irrational preference for foreign procedures which do not represent a real improvement.

In Europe the Roman Empire served as a model for centuries. In 476 the Western Empire fragmented into smaller domains, which were further subdivided during the period of feudalism. As a consequence, the law evolved in a different manner in each of these regions, but Roman elements survived. The medieval monarchs wanted to be Roman emperors, so for their warriors they introduced the rights and freedoms which had made the Roman armies invincible. The Latin bishops promoted the Roman culture in which they had thrived and the law under which they could organise their charitable activities. They promoted the spread of Latin culture everywhere, even far beyond the borders of the old Empire. The crusaders associated the beauty of Constantinople with Roman culture, experienced the freedom of its inhabitants and wanted to bring this world back to Europe. In the high Middle Ages, the study of Roman law at the universities led to a specific reception in which the old legal sources were interpreted in a similar manner at different institutions. This led to the development of Western *ius commune*. The Middle Ages ended on a sad note. Between 1350 and 1450 the population decreased because of epidemics. However, this was beneficial to the development of the *ius commune* as well. In this dark century conservatism prevailed and furthered the similar reception of Roman law throughout Western Europe.

In the fifteenth and sixteenth centuries the European nations originated, again under the influence of Constantinople. European monarchs strove to become Roman emperors and to introduce a central Roman administration that was controlled by sovereign courts. In order to combat particularism, they appealed to jurists who had been educated at the universities and had, by consequence, enjoyed a training in Roman law. This led to a new wave of reception and a *ius commune* that was supported by the monarchical courts, which became the embodiment of monarchical absolutism. Their case law caused the law of the different nations to grow apart. Legal education, however, remained similar in many countries. In the seventeenth century the jurists countered royal absolutism and nationalism by shifting conflict management and the setting of norms from royal case law to other fora such as legal doctrine, the forum of conscience and the private sphere. Civil law became private law and was rethought starting from the Western European context. In this manner another new *ius commune* was developed, the *ius commune* of Modern Times, that of natural law and private law. Citizens who wanted to curtail the power of monarchs appealed to the legal tradition that could be a counterweight to monarchical autonomy. Private law was laid down in law codes, which were more difficult to alter than the case law of the sovereign councils. While the civil codes were being developed, Roman law cropped up once more as well. In the nineteenth century the German jurists searched for a civil law which could be shared by all the German nations, like a common dictionary. For this purpose they explored their *ius commune*, which would lead them to the Roman law of the nineteenth century.

There is, in other words, a common law of Europe that encompasses the typical Western sense of justice, which is supported by fundamental rights and freedoms and a specific doctrine of sovereignty. It was adopted from Roman law and its study. In order to appreciate this Western *ius commune* and reach a precise explanation of the differences between countries, one has to consider the reception of Roman law. Further on in this book, we will see that the *ius commune* has a monarchical and a canonical tradition. The relations between these two strongly differ per country. Some jurists mainly emphasise the differences between the legal systems of different Western countries, but from the moon one cannot confuse them with Mongolian or Tibetan law, nor can one perceive differences in colour which preclude European integration.

This law that is common to the West can be found between Tromsø and Cádiz, Riga and the Carpathian Mountains. Its outer borders were drawn by the Latin church and the universities. Between Vilnius and Minsk the legal culture changes; there is a rift between the legal thought of Transylvania and that of Moldavia and Walachia; and the Ottoman tradition is separated from the Western reception and its academic tradition by a border that runs through the Balkans. There, we hit a glass wall, despite the fact that the cultures on the other side have also been strongly marked by Roman law, namely by the Greco-Roman law that was developed in Constantinople. In order to understand these countries and facilitate negotiations with the jurists of the eastern EU Member States, we urgently have to extend the study of the *ius commune* and its reception to include the legal history of the Levant. Ongoing attempts to have this extension happen from Leuven are fraught with difficulties. The reader should therefore not expect this book to contain revelations which will drastically improve dealings with the former Eastern Empire.

3. The Historical School as *causa efficiens* of the study of Roman law

The eighteenth century saw the emergence of the conviction that statute law was the highest source of law; that this law emanated from the people, was clarified by reasonable, elected citizens in a parliament, and was then written down. This view had gradually grown among the jurists of Spanish late Scholasticism, in the School of Natural Law, among the English political thinkers of the Modern Era, and was at the centre stage in the Enlightenment. For the Enlightened thinkers, the law was an expression of reason. It was to be understood by means of the rules of epistemology. Starting from their experience of reason, the German idealists often wrote about law and society. After the civil revolutions of the late eighteenth century and the dissolution of the Holy Roman Empire (1806), the reasonable will of the people became a central notion in public law. What, however, is the reasonable character of a legal norm? The 'triumph of reason' in the seventeenth and eighteenth centuries consisted of the penetration of Greek logic into academic thought. This was a new method, which did not generate content. Nevertheless, jurists also began to deduce legal concepts from their own thought. Their activities turned into a search for 'Vernunftrecht' and the corresponding ambition to draw up a universal model of society that was rationally sound. This then begs the question whether this enterprise entailed the danger that enlightened minds would decide in a totalitarian manner what was written in the will of the people.

In the German legal science a counter-movement already began among legal historians in the eighteenth century. German scholars began to look for the will of the people in 'Germanic' legal history. Around 1800 F.C. von Savigny strongly emphasised the need for legal historical research in order to understand the will of the people. His effort to deepen the law through legal history led to the emergence of the 'Historic School'. Savigny reacted against his contemporaries who preached the triumph of reason in law, such as the French revolutionaries or the German idealists. For Savigny, law was the result of the development of the 'Volksgeist', the spirit of the people. It could not be understood without the study of this 'Volksgeist', nor should it be ossified through its codification. In order to reach pure legal concepts, legal historical research had to be employed to remove the ballast that had been added to them by history. Savigny stressed the necessity of studying the old territorial laws, case law, the Weistümer, etcetera. His most famous student of German legal history was Jacob Grimm. The influence of the Historical School soon led to the establishment of a chair of legal history in every law faculty.

In this return to history which was coloured by Romanticism, one would expect an emphasis on native German law. Savigny, however, was fascinated by Roman law. In his search for Roman influence, he unveiled the legal doctrine of the medieval law faculties. He was the first to recognise the scope of medieval reception. With his 'Geschichte des römischen Rechtes im Mittelalter', he became the founding father of the scientific study of medieval Roman law. Tying in with the humanist tradition and the nineteenth-century study of classical Antiquity, he also showed a great interest in the Roman law of Antiquity and drew links between law and classical studies. Soon, the Historical School aroused such an interest in the study of Roman law that in addition a chair of Roman law was established in every law faculty.

In his reaction against Vernunftrecht Savigny turned legal history into an integral part of legal thought. Legal history and the historical interpretation have since then been fields of study in large law faculties, where they serve as an antidote to excessive legal positivism and a surfeit of legal theory.

Friedrich Carl von Savigny (Frankfurt/Main 1779 – Berlin 1861) descended from a family from Upper Lorraine which had left France after the Peace of Alès (1629). He was born to wealthy parents. In 1790, however, he had already lost all five of his brothers and sisters. His father died in 1791; his mother in 1792. Left on his own with his patrimony, he grew up in Wetzlar with a friend of his father's. In 1795, he enrolled at the university of Marburg, where he concluded his law studies in 1800 with a brilliant doctoral thesis. In the meantime, he had studied in Göttingen for a semester and had taken two educational trips to Jena in 1800. Later in the same year Savigny became a professor in Marburg. From Leipzig he asked to be found a house which the twenty-one-year-old insisted should be sufficiently large, among other things because he would bring roughly three thousand books... In 1802 he published his great work on the law of possession, in which he emphasised that all law is legal history. In 1804 he married Kunegonde Brentano and took her with him on a study tour during which he visited twenty-six large manuscript libraries in Germany, Italy and France long before the existence of railroads. In 1807 he became a professor in Landshut. In 1810 he was called to Berlin on the occasion of the foundation of its university. There, he published his 'Geschichte des römischen Rechtes im Mittelalter' between 1815 and 1831 (second edition 1834-1851). In 1842 he retired as a professor and became the Minister of Justice of Prussia. Between 1839 and 1849, he worked on his most famous publication, 'System des heutigen römischen Rechts', in which he mirrored nineteenth-century civil law in the long history of Roman law. Savigny opposed the codification of civil law. For him, law was too much of a living entity to be set down in formulas.

4. The study of Roman law as 'Dogmengeschichte'

The fourth reason to study Roman law is to understand our fellow men. Law faculties train students to reach such an understanding. Courses like philosophy or psychology are not the only ones that are useful to this end: so is legal history. Why do witnesses to an accident discuss liability? Why do television viewers judge the behaviour of a foreign head of state? Why do newspapers anticipate judicial decisions? They do so because their perceptions interact with the legal convictions which they carry in their heads.

Our culture is stored in our heads. The German philosopher Hegel (1770-1831) described a fascinating explanatory model in his 'Phänomenologie des Geistes' (1807). Everyone adopts elements from the 'objektive Geist', a kind of collective world of ideas, which is spread over thousands of heads and with which we come into contact through many channels, like conversations, reading, patterns of authority, etcetera. Everyone processes this body of ideas for himself and consequently develops a 'subjektive Geist'. These individual views in their turn influence the 'objektive Geist', which is, as a result, always evolving (Hegelian dialectics). In his 'Geist des römischen Rechts' (1852-1862) Jhering described how Roman law, originally a temporal and local legal system, developed into an important cultural element, an essential constituent of the 'objektive Geist' of our law. We all carry a large quantity of Roman law in our head, which got there through the history of ideas, and we are all regularly at loggerheads with these ideas in our 'subjektive Geist'.

In order to better understand our fellow men, we have to consider the history of ideas. As long as the Latin component of our mental world remains important, Latin studies will help us to understand our fellow men and society. As long as the juridical component remains so prevalent in societal and moral thought, legal history will remain a useful tool to understand our fellow men. If Roman law is as ubiquitous as Jhering alleges, its study will help us to gain an insight into human thought. It is typical of European jurists that they enquire into the world of ideas of the persons subject to the law, into motives, interpretations, foundations and coherence. The assessment of the development of ideas is part of the study of Roman law and plays a role in the analysis of both our own dogmas and those of our law. This history of ideas is also useful to the practice of good legal theory.

Conclusion: the methodology of Roman law

The study of Roman law is relevant for present-day jurists. It is not just the Roman law of Antiquity that needs to be studied, but also what happened to this law during the long period of reception. Without this reception, Roman law has barely any meaning as a legal course. However, the trouble begins immediately. The Roman law of Antiquity proves almost inaccessible. Only a limited amount of texts have been handed down, and these have been interpreted for centuries by jurists who were trained to resolve conflicts and prepare a better future, not to sojourn in Antiquity. Medieval, modern and nineteenth-century readers used contemporary notions to read the old Roman sources and studied these sources with the intention of solving concrete problems and preparing their students for the future. The civil lawyers of the nineteenth century read Gaius and the Digest in the Latin of the nineteenth century and used the legal notions of the French Revolution when doing so. They discovered a Republic that met the dreams of the Modern Era. They found marriage and divorce in classical Antiquity, even though marriage dates from the twelfth century and divorce from the sixteenth. They described classical ownership, even though ownership is a thirteenth-century notion, and classical real rights identical to those that were developed in the seventeenth century. They found obligations with the characteristics of those in canon law and laws that were like modern acts of parliament. They projected the nineteenth-century gender gap of civil law onto the old distinction between those who fought and those who did not. A simple example will elucidate this. In Gaius one reads about the *tutela* of women and children. In military courts, women and children needed a legal representative. For women, this legal representation ceased to exist in later types of procedure, but the legal representation of children evolved into guardianship which was characterised by the typical liability of those who did not take good care of their wards. Nineteenth-century readers discovered *tutela mulierum* in Gaius and read it as... guardianship over women.

Is it even possible to penetrate as far as the classical sources of our law, or does such research always get bogged down in history? A good research method is that of Speke, who discovered the source of the Nile in 1857-1859. He neither philosophised about the stream, nor read the Nubian sagas. He simply travelled upstream to take a look himself. If you want to study legal history, you have to undertake a similar journey upstream into the legal past. When you see the origin of a legal notion, you know that you can no longer encounter it beyond this point. For example, the primacy of law appears in the eighteenth century, while public and private law have their origin in the seventeenth, and subjective rights in the sixteenth. In older texts, you must not find them. You will notice that in the Middle Ages, civil law and canon law are unmixed. Many Europeans who travel further back than the twelfth century, have to forget their native language. Having passed the first universities, you are journeying towards the ideas of Augustine, but nevertheless they are becoming quieter and quieter. In the feudal period, you witness the development of ownership, which means that you cannot encounter this notion prior to feudalism. You cross Carolingian confessional books full of moral innovations. In the sixth and fifth centuries you suddenly come in sight of the imperial chancelleries. Going further, you leave their modernisations behind you. When you reach Gaius in the second century, you only have a few clues left to understand him. While travelling through time, you have also noticed that the Latin language was always understood in different ways. You feel like a dialectologist who cycles from one village to the next and feels the language change. In the sixteenth century many simple words hide a reference to a higher notion, as if Aristotle had disseminated his theory of actuality and potentiality. In the Middle Ages words harbour values. The Latin of Antiquity in contrast is packed with the myriad of verb forms and personal pronouns with which the Romans indicated relations between people in as precise a manner as possible.

In other words, you will only gain a limited view of the law of Antiquity through the science of Roman law. Instead, you will be continuously confronted with what happened to Roman law on the road between Antiquity and the twenty-first century. That is where the research area lies. A Romanist examines when and how institutions were based on notions of Roman law and pays attention to the interpretation of old legal notions in the period under consideration. You cannot hope to study a fixed legal system from times gone by. Rather, you will continuously look at notions which are on the move. You will be overtaken by some notions, and meet others that travel in the opposite direction. It is there that you will try to gain an insight into the development of the law and the institutions as well as into the history of ideas. Just as the history of philosophy is part and parcel of philosophy and the interpretation of the Bible is inextricably bound up with its content, Roman law cannot be separated from its history. Jurists of all centuries have contributed to 'our' Roman law and *ius commune*. This handbook deals with this Roman law. In between certainties and convictions, and looking at the bickering among scientists, the reader must try to learn something, not in order to understand Antiquity, but in order to gain an insight into his own time. Is this new method better than that used by previous generations? Earlier Romanists were asked to rouse their students' interest in civil law. The current method is geared to a greater extent towards the *ius commune*. In a few decades' time, it will become clear that this was the Roman law of the legal historians of the early twenty-first century, who had to support the study of European law and further human rights.

In this handbook, civil law is still at the centre stage. Up to this time, it is the subject about which there is the greatest amount of secondary literature. Other branches of law, such as public law, institutions, procedure and some criminal law will also be discussed.

§2. Roman law as a science

Roman law was the first course at the university and has by now been taught for more than nine centuries. Historians claim that the first university was that of Paris, but when this university was founded by Anselm of Aosta (later of Canterbury, 1033-1109), Roman law was already being studied in Bologna under the impulse of Anselm's teacher Lanfranc of Pavia (1005/10-1089). This tradition gives the teaching of Roman law colour and character. It is a legal science, which appeals to auxiliary sciences like classical literary studies, palaeography, history and philosophy.

1. Legal science

Roman law always fell within the domain of the law faculties. Between 1425 and 1797 Roman law was the only subject taught at the law faculty of Leuven. Philip the Good introduced the study of Roman law in the Netherlands in 1425 in order to reform the local law. At that time 'Roman' referred to the European *ius commune*. Today, Roman law is still not a specialist field within classical studies. It is research into the foundations of law. Some current Romanists lack some practical legal experience, but this does not make their profession any less juridical. It was a juridical profession in the past as well. Romanists of all historical periods took an active part in legal life. Lanfranc of Pavia, the great promoter of the study of the Digest, became bishop of Canterbury and president of the English *Curia regis*. Jacobus Balduini (✝1235), the most sophisticated glossator, reformed the law of the Republic of Genoa in his capacity as 'podestà'. Guillaume Durand (1230/1-1296), the greatest proceduralist of all times, was the rector of Romagne during the Italian crusades. Viglius (1507-1577), who published the Greek version of the Institutes of Justinian, led the government of the Netherlands. Grotius (1583-1645) served as ambassador of Sweden in Paris. Savigny (1779-1861), the champion in all disciplines of Roman law, was Prussia's minister of justice from 1842 until the revolution of 1848. Even Mommsen (1817-1903), the last publisher of the *Corpus iuris*, had a career as liberal politician under his belt. This involvement in legal life was not always beneficial to Roman law itself. Active jurists have a tendency to let their agenda influence their research and active Romanists often read Roman law in such a manner that they could utilise it to improve the present. Roman law was used to integrate new institutions such as civil law. Even today, it is central to the comparative legal history that is necessary to coordinate the different European legal systems. As a course, Roman law is in danger in faculties where it no longer offers an independent view of law or does not make a large enough contribution to the education of jurists...

2. The charms of classical philology

No Roman law without Latin. Scholars of Roman law are always immersed in texts and commentaries which were written in Latin until around 1800. As secondary literature, both Latin authors from Antiquity and treatises from the Middle Ages and the Modern Era are important. Translations of these old sources into modern languages are available and secondary sources are being translated as well. These, however, are snapshots in time which represent the state of the art of science in the year of the translation. They do make it possible to read the original Latin more quickly. Knowledge of Greek is necessary to examine the influence of Constantinople. Those who study the Roman law of the Levant are also confronted with the demotic and Coptic scripts of Egypt and with the ancient languages of the Near East. Arabic is important because the Greco-Roman law of Constantinople was also handed down through Arabic culture.

Latin is a very structured language and the majority of texts are clear and precise. It was a living language for many centuries, which means that it underwent further development. The same texts were interpreted throughout the centuries, each time in a different temporal context. Eight centuries of teaching about these texts in a changing world meant that lecturers had to find some elbow room by dealing with grammar and the meaning of legal terms in a creative manner. The meaning of these words changed often. *Natura* meant birth in Antiquity, but came to signify nature in the Middle Ages, in view of Creation. *Aequitas* first meant equality, but later came to mean equity. *Proprietas* signified close involvement with an object in Antiquity, but turned into ownership thereof in the Modern Era. *Dominium* was originally fatherhood, later domain and then private ownership. In the science of Roman law, one meets with completely different interpretations of Latin texts. For the comprehension of the rest of this book, it is important that this point be understood. Therefore, we will first provide some examples of evolving Latin.

In the first case, a personal pronoun is misunderstood in a controversy.

D. 9.2.11.5. – Item cum eo, qui canem irritauerat et effecerat, ut aliquem morderet, quamuis eum non tenuit, Proculus respondit Aquiliae actionem esse: sed Iulianus eum demum Aquilia teneri ait, qui tenuit et effecit ut aliquem morderet: ceterum si non tenuit, in factum agendum.

Classical translation. – Proculus also gave as his opinion that if someone provoked a dog and had in this manner brought about that it bit someone, the action under the Lex Aquilia was applicable, even though he did not hold the dog. Julian, however, says that he is only liable under the Lex Aquilia if he held the dog and brought about that it bit someone; that, however, if he held it, an action tailored to the facts should be brought.

Sebastian LOHSSE, *'Canem vel servum tenuit.* D. 9.2.11.5 and the applicability of the *actio legis Aquiliae* in cases involving inanimate objects used for killing?', *The Legal History Review* 70 (2002), p. 251-264, however, claims that 'hold him' could denote the victim as well as the dog. In his interpretation, he does not take the form of the personal and demonstrative pronouns in Latin into account: *aliquem* can never be *eum*. Personal pronouns, which represent relations between people, were much more important in Roman Antiquity than today.

In a second example, the mood of the verb is not taken into consideration.

D. 43.26.18. – Unusquisque potest rem suam, quamuis non possideat, precario dare ei qui possideat.

Traditional translation. – Anyone can give an object that belongs to him, even though he does not possess it, by precarium to someone who does possess it.

However, *possideat* is a conjunctive and a relative clause in the conjunctive expresses a goal. One therefore has to translate the clause as 'so that he gains possession', but that does not make sense for most Romanists. It is for this reason that the conjunctive is not read. Possession as a real right, however, is a notion of the Modern Era. In Antiquity, people would have read 'so that he be granted possessory protection'. The many personal pronouns indicate the importance of interpersonal relations in Latin.

In a third case, the meanings of words have been altered.

C. 8.52.2 (319 AD). – Consuetudinis ususque longaeui non uilis auctoritas est, uerum non usque adeo sui ualitura momento ut aut rationem uincat aut legem.

Traditional translation. – The authority of custom and long usage is not small, but their importance shall not be so great that they prevail over reason or the law.

This is a thirteenth-century interpretation, which remained important until the French Revolution. In the hierarchy of norms, customary law is situated below monarchical law and the 'reason' of scholars. However, *usus* did not mean custom, but acquisitive prescription in Antiquity. *Ratio* did not signify reason, but rather account or budget. *Lex* did not signify the law, but any legal obligation and in the Code of Justinian any legal precedent. The decision of Constantine's prefecture simply meant: if you are in the habit of not paying a tax, you are never exempted from it, not even by prescription. Concerning this interpretation, see L. WAELKENS,

'*Consuetudo contra rationem*, La signification de C. 8,53,2', in: *Studi in omaggio di Ennio Cortese*, Rome 2001, p. 466-473. The antique meaning reads as follows:

C. 8.52.2 (319 AD). Consuetudinis ususque longaeui non uilis auctoritas est, uerum non usque adeo sui ualitura momento ut aut rationem uincat aut legem.	Translation L.W. – The authority of custom and acquisitive prescription is not small, but will not be of such importance that it removes a tax rule or a legal precedent.

This great variation in the interpretation of legal concepts is food for thought. Especially in long texts in which readers do not pay close attention to grammar and vocabulary, interpretations can differ enormously. As an example, we give C. 5.27.5, a judgment of the imperial chancellery from 477, which was read for centuries as a text stating that children became legitimate through the subsequent marriage of their parents, but in which we see a fifth-century indictment of gender inequality in the law of succession.

C. 5.27.5. – *Imperator Zeno A. Sebastiano pp.* Diui Constantini, qui ueneranda christianorum fide romanum muniuit imperium, super ingenuis concubinis ducendis uxoribus, filiis quin etiam ex isdem uel ante matrimonium uel postea progenitis suis ac legitimis habendis, sacratissimam constitutionem renouantes iubemus eos, qui ante hanc legem ingenuarum mulierum (nuptiis minime intercedentibus) electo contubernio cuiuslibet sexus filios procreauerunt, quibus nulla uidelicet uxor est, nulla ex iusto matrimonio legitima proles suscepta, si uoluerint eas uxores ducere, quae antea fuerant concubinae, tam coniugium legitimum cum huiusmodi mulieribus ingenuis, ut dictum est, posse contrahere, quam filios utriusque sexus ex earundem mulierum priore contubernio procreatos, mox quam nuptiae cum matribus eorum fuerint celebratae, suos patri et in potestate fieri et cum his, qui postea ex eodem matrimonio suscepti fuerint, uel solos, si nullus alius deinde nascatur, tam ex testamento uolentibus patribus etiam ex integro succedere quam ab intestato petere hereditatem paternam: pactis, quae matrimonii tempore super dotalibus uel ante nuptias donationis rebus subsecuta fuerint, etiam ad ipsorum personas pertinentibus, ut una cum fratribus suis postea ex isdem parentibus forte progenitis, aut soli, si nullus alius sit procreatus, dotis et ante nuptias donationis pro tenore legum nec minus pactorum emolumenta recipiant. 1. Hi uero,	Translation Fred H. Blume. – *Emperor Zeno to Sebastianus, Praetorian Prefect.* In revising the constitution of the divine Constantine, who strengthened the Roman power through the venerable Christian faith, and who by said constitution provided that free born concubines might be made wives and that sons born to people thus married, before or subsequent to such marriage should be considered as legitimate, we order that unmarried men having no children from a legitimate marriage, but who previous to this law, had children of either sex from an alliance without marriage, with free born women, may, if they have no children from a legal marriage, marry such women who previously were their concubines, and may not only contract with them, as has been said, a legal marriage, but the children also, of either sex, born of these same women prior to marriage, shall, as soon as the marriage with their mother is celebrated, be considered as the legitimate children of the father and shall be in his power, and may, together with those who are subsequently born of this marriage, or alone, if no other children are so born, take their father's property if left to them by will, and claim it if their father dies intestate. The agreements made concerning dowry and prenuptial gifts at the time of the marriage shall also be for their benefit, so that they, together with their brothers (and sisters) subsequently born, receive the benefit of the dowry and the prenuptial gift according to

qui tempore huius sacratissimae iussionis necdum prolem aliquam ex ingenuarum concubinarum consortio meruerunt, minime huius legis beneficio perfruantur, cum liceat easdem mulieres sibi prius iure matrimonii copulare non extantibus legitimis liberis aut uxoribus ac legitimos filios utpote nuptiis procedentibus procreare, nec debeant, quos ex ingenua concubina dilato post hanc legem matrimonio nasci uoluerint, ut iusti ac legitimi postea uideantur, magnopere postulare. < A. 477 d. x k. mart. post consulatum Armati.>

the tenor of the law and of the agreement made. 1. But persons who at the time of the enactment of this imperial sanction had no offspring of an alliance with freewomen, shall not enjoy the benefit of this law, since they are permitted, if they have no wife or legitimate children, to marry such women and have children of a legal marriage, and they cannot ask that children born to them of a free concubine, after delaying marriage with her subsequent to the enactment of this law, should be considered legitimate. Given February 20 (477).

According to this translation, there would have been a one-off regularisation of illegitimate children in 477. On this traditional interpretation see for example G. LUCCHETTI, *La legimitazzione dei figli naturali nelle fonti tardoimperiali e giustinianee*, Milan 1990. We read this judgment in a different manner. The children born to a Roman woman were her legal heirs, while a man had to live in *nuptiae* or *matrimonium* with the mother of his biological children in order to make them his heirs. A man demanded that his future biological children would become his heirs, irrespective of his relationship with their mother. The chancellery decided not to revise its case law. It also indicated that the claimant did not have sufficient interest. The text deals with one couple, but the plural form indicates that the chancellery considered its judgment to be a precedent. In addition, it is characteristic of this text that it contains all of the different terms for relationships between two people, which will be discussed further in this book. This is Roman law at its most beautiful. See L. WAELKENS, 'La légitimité de C. 5,27,5', in: B. D'ALTEROCHE, F. DUMOULIN-AUZARY, O. DESCAMPS and F. ROUMY (eds.), *Mélanges en l'honneur d'Anne Lefebvre-Teillard*, Paris 2009, p. 1031-1041. This is our translation:

C. 5.27.5. – *Imperator Zeno A. Sebastiano pp.* Diui Constantini, qui ueneranda christianorum fide romanum muniuit imperium, super ingenuis concubinis ducendis uxoribus, filiis quin etiam ex isdem uel ante matrimonium uel postea progenitis suis ac legitimis habendis, sacratissimam constitutionem renouantes

Translation L.W. – Revising the constitution of the unassailable Constantine, who strengthened the Roman authority with the honourable Christian faith, about the freeborn concubines who had to become wives and whose sons, born to them before or after the marriage [*matrimonium*] had to be considered as their own [*sui (heredes)*] and as intestate heirs,

iubemus eos, qui ante hanc legem ingenuarum mulierum (nuptiis minime intercedentibus) electo contubernio cuiuslibet sexus filios procreauerunt, quibus nulla uidelicet uxor est, nulla ex iusto matrimonio legitima proles suscepta, si uoluerint eas uxores ducere, quae antea fuerant concubinae, tam coniugium legitimum cum huiusmodi mulieribus ingenuis, ut dictum est, posse contrahere,

we find that they who before the present sentence have fathered children of either sex in a voluntary *contubernium* [relationship with slaves] with free women (where a wedding was inconceivable) and who apparently still do not have a wife, who have not had any acknowledged [*legitima*] progeny during a legally valid marriage [*matrimonium*], can if they want to live as husband and wife [*uxores*] with those who previously were their concubines either [*tam*] live together in a relationship with the aforementioned freeborn women which is acknowledged by the law [*coniugium legitimum*],

quam filios utriusque sexus ex earundem mulierum priore contubernio procreatos, mox quam nuptiae cum matribus eorum fuerint celebratae, suos patri et in potestate fieri et cum his, qui postea ex eodem matrimonio suscepti fuerint, uel solos, si nullus alius deinde nascatur, tam ex testamento uolentibus patribus etiam ex integro succedere quam ab intestato petere hereditatem paternam:

or [*quam*] [we find that] the children of both sexes who were begot earlier by these women in a previous *contubernium*, will become the father's own children [*sui (heredes)*] and come under his authority as soon as the wedding [*nuptiae*] has taken place, and that together with the children who later come of this marriage or alone if no other children are born, they can claim the paternal succession, both integrally through a will on the basis of the wish of their fathers and as intestate heirs,

pactis, quae matrimonii tempore super dotalibus uel ante nuptias donationis rebus subsecuta fuerint, etiam ad ipsorum personas pertinentibus, ut una cum fratribus suis postea ex isdem parentibus forte progenitis, aut soli, si nullus alius sit procreatus, dotis et ante nuptias donationis pro tenore legum nec minus pactorum emolumenta recipiant.

the pacts which had been concluded at the moment of the marriage [*matrimonium*] concerning dotal goods or concluded before the wedding [*nuptiae*] concerning goods which would be gifted, are also due to the parties [*personas*] of these, so that [*ut*] they, together with their brothers if these were born later to the same parents, or alone if no one else was begot, will receive the proceeds of the dowry and of the gifts for the wedding, calculated according to both the case law and the pacts,

Hi uero, qui tempore huius sacratissimae iussionis necdum prolem aliquam ex ingenuarum concubinarum consortio meruerunt, minime huius legis beneficio perfruantur, cum liceat easdem mulieres sibi prius iure matrimonii copulare non extantibus legitimis liberis aut uxoribus ac legitimos filios utpote nuptiis procedentibus procreare,

but that those who, at the time that our decision is sanctioned have not yet obtained any progeny from their material cohabitation [*consortium*] with freeborn concubines, wil not benefit from this judgment [*huius legis*] in any way, since they are at liberty to have intercourse with these women according to matrimonial law [*iure matrimonii*] – because in their case their are neither free heirs nor wives [*uxores*] – and can easily beget lawful heirs by concluding a wedding [*nuptiae*] beforehand,

nec debeant, quos ex ingenua concubina dilato post hanc legem matrimonio nasci uoluerint, ut iusti ac legitimi postea uideantur, magnopere postulare.

and that they must not plead with the court that those who they would like to see born to a freeborn concubine – with whom the marriage [*matrimonium*] has already been postponed until after this judgment – be considered as lawful and as legal successor.

3. Palaeography and textual criticism

With the exception of inscriptions, all texts dating from before the invention of the art of printing (1450) have a manuscript tradition. This means that they were written by hand, but also that each copy of the same document is different and has a separate history. During the copying process, changes were made because the copyist interpreted illegible passages or was absent-minded. The use of goose quills meant that copyists could only trace straight lines and light curves, as these pens could not be used to draw small circles. For this reason, some letters in medieval uncial script are very similar. An 'f' is an 's' with an extra horizontal stroke; the only difference between a 't' and a 'c' is a small corner. Reading *munus* or *minus* is sometimes a matter of counting vertical strokes. Mistakes arose in the internal dictation of the copyists, who repeated dictated texts to themselves. Antique texts do not feature any punctuation marks; all the letters are joined. It is only at a later stage that words were separated from each other and that punctuation marks were added. The author, in other words, had most certainly not written the text in this manner. Some passages were lost or were rendered illegible by sunlight, water or fire. Differences between manuscripts were not only caused by copyists. Jurists like to correct the texts of their predecessors. A jurist has to take great pains to leave a text unaltered. A legal scholar who wants to provide an authentic reconstruction of a text, always introduces changes.

When working with manuscripts, we have recourse to palaeography for the script and to codicology for the external character of the books and documents. There are almost no legal manuscripts from Antiquity, because the script changed in the ninth century and almost all of the old manuscripts were 'transliterated'. The new uncial script and standardised abbreviations required only half the amount of expensive parchment to record the same text. Literary and theological manuscripts were copied and the excess parchment was recycled. This period of systematic 'transliteration' in the libraries was a disaster for the science of law, as it was often not deemed necessary to copy an age-old and unknown collection of case law before recycling the parchment it was written on. Only a very small number of manuscripts of Roman law have survived this period. The most famous one is the sixth-century *littera florentina* of the Digest, which has been preserved in the Florentine Biblioteca Medicea Laurenziana since 1406. The library of the chapter of Verona holds a palimpsest of the Institutes of Gaius: its parchment was recycled in a careless manner and the old text became visible through the new one. The majority of Roman law manuscripts are medieval. There are thousands of manuscripts from that period, spread over hundreds of libraries. In the thirteenth century prestigious copies of the Digest, the Code of Justinian and his Institutes were made. Many manuscripts of Roman law are, however, working documents, study materials, comments, glossaries, lecture notes, *peciae* (cahiers) that were hired out to students, etcetera. We know of the existence of some six hundred and fifty manuscripts of Roman law in the Biblioteca Apostolica Vaticana, but it is highly likely that this library also holds several hundreds of Roman law manuscripts that have not yet been inventoried. The Royal Library in Brussels and the University of Ghent have beautiful manuscripts of Roman law. Manuscripts of canon law are also of importance to the study of Roman law, and are more well-known than those of Roman law. Leuven saw its beautiful collection of manuscripts of Roman law go up in flames in 1914, and its new acquisitions in 1940. The university currently owns only a few legal manuscripts.

Bibliography. – A good introduction to palaeography is given by A. DAIN, *Les manuscrits*, 3d ed., Les Belles Lettres, Paris 1975, 223 p. An overview of the manuscripts of Roman law that have been preserved is provided by G. DOLEZALEK, *Verzeichnis der Handschriften zum römischen Recht*, 4 vol., Frankfurt/Main 1972. Readers who have never seen manuscripts can discover them on the internet. See for example the manuscript library of the abbey of Sankt Gallen at http://www.cesg.unifr.ch/virt_bib/manuscripts.htm.

Those who deal with texts from before 1450 which have since then been printed, are haunted by a second problem of the manuscript tradition: the textual edition. Before the old sources were printed, they were reread and corrected by an editor. It is, however, possible that this editor used a bad manuscript or did not look at a sufficient number of variants. He may have emended the text because he did not understand it. It is also possible that he bent illegible or illogical passages to his will or misjudged the composition of the manuscript. Remarks or additions of earlier editors were sometimes incorporated into the text by the next editor. Supposed additions were omitted or altered. Scaliger (1540-1609), a humanist of Italian descent who settled in Leyden, was a zealous reconstructor of passages that were missing from classical texts, but when new manuscripts of the texts in question were found, it often turned out that his emendations were wrong.

Example. – The manuscript of Gaius found in Verona, which was published for the first time in the nineteenth century, contains the following passage in Gaius 4.73: '[Cum autem quaeritur quantum in peculio sit ante de]ducitur quod patri dominoue quique in eius potestate sit a filio seruoue debet et quod superset, hoc solum peculium esse intelligitur. Aliquando tamen, id quod ei debet filius seruusue qui in potestate patris dominue sit, non deduitur ex peculio, uelut si is cui debet in huius peculio sit.' The word *debet* is emendated and turned into *debetur* by all of the editors of this text because it is preceded by an *a* + ablative. They then read *quique* as a dative, which is certainly impossible. *Debet a* is an expression used in bookkeeping that refers to the debiting of a *credit a*. A further explanation can be found in L. WAELKENS, 'Gaius IV, 73: debet ou debetur?', *The Legal History Review* 68 (2000), p. 347-356.

Around 1500 the market of the scholarly book became a European one. Publishers hired humanists to correct their editions. The most important source for jurists was the *Corpus iuris*. In the fifteenth century a good Italian version was printed by Torti in Venice and in the sixteenth century the best edition of the medieval *Corpus iuris* was that of Hugues Desportes from Lyon. In 1523 the *crisis Digestorum*, the critical edition of the Digest on the basis of the Florentine manuscript, began with the Parisian edition of Louis Blauwblomme. Important editions were those of Torelli (Florence 1553) and Denis Godefroy (Lyon 1583). In the later editions of Godefroy the critical work of François de Maulde (Modius, 1556-1597) from Leuven was incorporated. Legal books were printed in small editions and were often republished by several printers. One can therefore also find differences between old editions.

The publication of texts of Roman law was always part of the science of Roman law. New critical editions of the *Corpus iuris* were published until the nineteenth century (the last one was that of Mommsen and Krüger, Berlin, around 1870), but even today first editions of texts of Roman law appear regularly. Every Romanist occasionally publishes a commentary that he found in a manuscript or a corrected version of a printed source.

Texts of Roman law must be read critically, with the influence of the manuscript tradition and the techniques of edition in mind. Old editions were drawn up on the basis of the knowledge of Roman law during the publisher's lifetime, but we read them with the current scientific knowledge at the back of our minds and try to comprehend their original meaning. This is not easy! At the beginning of the twentieth century, scholars attempted to purify the texts of Roman law from later insertions (interpolations). Today, this hunt for interpolations is deemed unscientific, even though there is no new information to corroborate this view. Who is right?

4. Historical criticism

Roman law encompasses many centuries. Every institution and every fact must be placed in its historical context. External history always plays a part. A text which has been established with certainty still has to be investigated by means of historical criticism. With the spirit of the times at the back of your mind, you search for a significant meaning in the relevant geographical, sociological, economic and philosophical milieu. Like musicians, many Romanists tend to interpret their manuscripts in a modern manner. This is 'Hineininterpretierung', the appraisal of old situations by means of current ideas. It is better to analyse institutions from the perspective of a preceding situation than from that of the succeeding one. Do not speak of ownership over a slave in classical Antiquity: ownership is a notion of the Modern Era. Do not write about the relations between the Church and the state in classical Antiquity: the Church originated in the eleventh century and the state in the seventeenth. Do not project nineteenth-century Pan-Germanism onto the migration of the Germanic peoples in the fifth century. Do not try to find the medieval sense of guilt in Antiquity and do not take umbrage at the unequal treatment of people with regard to whom everyone considered differential treatment as the ideal course of action.

Do not accept facts that have not been established. Jurists are not the only ones who are afraid of considering matters from their own convictions: so are historians. Take into account nevertheless that historiography is always biased. Every science has its own logic. For doctors, there is no life after death. For theologians, the reverse is the beginning of all wisdom. Jurists attempt to make the world a better place by resolving conflicts, while graduates of arts faculties try to attain the same goal by improving communication. The individual approach, as opposed to the societal one, leads to large differences. A publication by a historian is not necessarily useful for a legal historian. Historians of classical Antiquity analyse the military and political power of Rome, whereas legal historians looks for the active ingredient of the *pax romana*.

Legal historians sometimes overlook demographical data. The culture of fifty million Romans was not shaken by that of fifteen thousand Vandals. On the other hand, the influence of the tens of thousands of Greeks who fled from Constantinople to the West in 1453 was larger than that of the hundreds of monks who copied manuscripts in the Middle Ages.

5. The history of philosophy

The study of Roman law as 'Dogmengeschichte' requires that attention be paid to the history of philosophy, in particular that of logic, linguistics and moral philosophy. Jurists do not think like philosophers, but philosophy can be of help when interpreting Roman texts. Philosophers have more sources. Plotinus, Ambrosius and Augustine are more well-known than the jurists of their time. Their works allow one to get a first impression of the thought of those centuries. The thirteenth-century jurists were familiar with Scholasticism and Grotius lived in the same intellectual environment as Descartes. The philosophers of these eras show what these contexts were like. Do not, however, reverse the roles. In their personal education, jurists come into contact with the literary and philosophical world before they become acquainted with the science of law. Some scholars are misled by their own past and look for the origin of legal conceptions in philosophical notions. Philosophy remains law's younger sister. The church fathers were influenced by Roman legal logic; Descartes translated the doctrine of subjective rights into philosophy; the fundamental rights and freedoms which the Spanish Scholastics passed on to the Enlightened philosophers were drawn from legal thought.

§3. The external framework of the science

As an old, venerable science, Roman law has a tradition and maintains decorum. There is a cult of libraries and antiquarian bookshops, journals, conferences and societies, meetings and correspondence. As in any other science, meetings are central. New ideas are passed on orally and one mainly reads the publications of colleagues whom one has heard. A Babel-like confusion characterises the entire process of reading and communication.

Under the influence of Savigny every law faculty got its own Romanist. Some of these faculties established institutes with lavish libraries. In the nineteenth and the first half of the twentieth centuries the Germans set the tone. Roman law played a large part in the unification of German civil law. In its heyday the German approach influenced the entire Western world. Italy is still steering a German course, as are Spain, Eastern Europe, South America... A more historical approach, in which Roman law and its reception are studied together, has become successful in Western Europe. The French jurists dedicate themselves to this approach. One of the great promoters of this type of Roman law was the professor of Leyden R. Feenstra (1920-2013). The American S. Kuttner (1906-1997) was the greatest contributor to the study of the reception of Roman law via canon law.

Large universities possess enough books to overwhelm Romanists. Some specialised libraries, such as that of the Max-Planck-Institut für Rechtsgeschichte in Frankfurt, the institute for legal history of the University of Milan and the Robbins Collection in Berkeley are very impressive. However, reading too much is not beneficial, because not all of these publications are innovative. A copy of Gaius' Institutes or the Digest is enough to keep one occupied for years. Further on in this book we will list some basic literature.

A large part of the science takes place in journals like the 'Zeitschrift der Savigny-Stiftung für Rechtsgeschichte' (Munich-Cologne-Weimar), 'The Legal History Review'

(Boston-Leyden), the 'Revue historique de droit français et étranger' (Paris), the 'Revue international des droits de l'Antiquité' (Brussels-Liège), *Studia et documenta historiae et iuris* (Lateran University), 'Rivista internazionale di diritto commune' (Rome), 'IVRA – Rivista internazionale di diritto romano ed antico' (Naples) or 'Orbis iuris romani' (Bratislava). Online journals such as 'Roman legal tradition' (United Kingdom and United States of America) or the 'International review of Roman law' (Spain) are a recent development. These journals are the fresh food market of science, where legal historians find out what their colleagues are doing, read about new developments and discuss new books.

Romanists can find lectures and discussions in fora such as the Deutsche Rechtshistorikertag, the Société d'Histoire du Droit (Paris), the annual conference of the Société Internationale des Droits de l'Antiquité, good doctoral schools, the Roman law groups of London and Edinburgh, the Accademia Romanistica Constantina in Spello (for Roman law from the fourth to sixth centuries), the Société Jean Bodin (comparative legal history) or the Scuola internazionale di diritto commune in Erice (medieval Roman law). Research projects concerning Roman law are conducted at several universities. The most important thereof is perhaps the Volterra project of University College London. Roman law is also dealt with in some academies, like the Austrian or Dutch Academies of Sciences, the Academies of Göttingen and München and the Accademia dei Lincei in Rome.

Bibliography. – An overview of research centres for legal history can be found in M. Duynstee, R. Feenstra and L. Waelkens, *Repertorium bibliographicum institutorum et sodalitatum iuris historiae,* Kortrijk 2000.

The internet also offers quite a lot of sources of and information about Roman law. Collections of texts are the most interesting documents online. However, the danger of limiting oneself to messing around and looking at pictures online is as great in the field of Roman law as in any other branch. It is therefore best to know the basic works from the library in order to find one's way around the texts consulted online.

Chapter I

Overview of the external history and the sources of Roman law

The external history of Roman law spans the period between 600 BC and the present and concerns widely diverse institutions throughout history. The early Republic, the medieval Church and the sovereign courts of the Early Modern Era have little in common, except that they contributed to the inculcation of principles of Roman law in our society. Below, we will provide an overview of the development of Roman law.

Bibliography. – For a general view of the history of ancient Rome the best works are still M. CRAWFORD, *The Roman Republic*, Harvard 1993; H. BENGSTON, *Grundriss der Römischen Geschichte mit Quellenkunde*, I, *Republik und Kaiserzeit bis 284 n.Chr.*, Munich 1982 and A. DEMANDT, *Die Spätantike, Römische Geschichte* von *Diocletian bis Justinian, 284-565 n. Chr.*, Munich 1989. An excellent handbook on the specific legal history of Roman Antiquity is F. WIEACKER, *Römische Rechtsgeschichte*, I, *Einleitung, Quellenkunde, Frühzeit und Republik*, Munich 1989; II, *Die Jurisprudenz vom frühen Prinzipat bis zum Ausgang der Antike im weströmischen Reich und die oströmische Rechtswissenschaft bis zur justinianischen Gesetzgebung. Ein Fragment*, posthumously published by J.G. WOLF and others, Munich 2006. J. GAUDEMET, *Institutions de l'Antiquité*, Paris 1982 is a well-organised work that discusses all of the important ancient legal systems. A good resource in English is P. STEIN, *Roman Law in European History*, Cambridge 1999. Those who are looking for an extensive bibliography concerning ancient Roman law can still find what they need in J. GILISSEN (ed.), *Introduction bibliographique à l'histoire du droit et à l'ethnologie juridique*, Brussels 1965-1982. A recommended bibliography in Dutch is J.E. SPRUIT, *Bibliografie Romeins recht, Wegwijzer tot de bronnen, hulpmiddelen en literatuur*, De Walburg Pers, Zutphen 1981 and in English O.F. ROBINSON, *The sources of Roman law, Problems and methods for ancient historians*, London 1997. At the moment, the most beautiful study of the origins of the medieval *ius commune* is E. CORTESE, *Il diritto nella storia medievale*, 2 vol., Rome 1995. *Ius Romanum Medii Aevi*, Milan, since 1961 is an excellent series that focuses on the medieval sources of Roman law: some forty little volumes by diverse authors each describe one aspect of the external history of the Roman law of the Middle Ages. The series treats both the history of sources, like the Theodosian Code, and the reception of Roman law in individual countries. The sources and bibliography of the Roman law of the Middle Ages, the Early Modern Period and the Modern Period have been neatly arranged in H. COING (ed.), *Handbuch der Quellen und Literatur der neueren europäischen Privatrechtsgeschichte*, 10 vols., Munich 1973-1888. An overview of the *ius commune* of the Early and Late Modern Periods can be found in H. COING, *Europäisches Privatrecht*, I, Älteres Gemeines Recht (1500 bis 1800), Munich 1985; II, *19. Jahrhundert, Überblick über die Entwicklung des Privatrechts in den ehemals gemeinrechtlichen Ländern*, Munich 1989. A classic work concerning the external history of canon law was written in Latin by A. VAN HOVE, *Prolegomena*, Mechlin 1945.

§1. The Kingdom and the early Republic (7th century BC – 367 BC)

1. The Kingdom

Rome was founded around 650 BC near the last ford of the Tiber before it flows into the Mediterranean. *Roma* is the Etruscan word for 'river' and the Roman script was derived from Etruscan writing. It is said that three old tribes (*tribus*), the Ramnenses, the Titienses and the Luceres, merged at that time and transformed their settlements on the Palatine, Esquiline and Quirinal Hills into a single city, which had the Capitoline Hill as its centre. As the words *tribus, tribunal* or *tribuere* are no longer reminiscent of this trinity, this triad may be the result of popular etymology. Very little is known about this early period. There were seven successive *reges* (army leaders, 'kings'), the last of whom was deposed in 509 BC, a Senate and *curiae*. How power was divided or what the sources of law looked like is unknown. As old law, some Romanists mention the *mores maiorum*, ancestral customs to which later Romans piously referred. To some extent these can be compared with the indeterminate customs from which some European legal historians think their laws stem. Voltaire called this 'le mythe du bon sauvage', the myth that a society could develop out of the friendly behaviour of unsullied primitive men. Law originates from the settling of conflicts. In the Roman law of classical Antiquity, there was no law outside of the courts. Maybe this was also the case during the Kingdom.

At the end of the first century BC a certain Granius Flaccus claimed to have found something in the archives of the Capitol: a collection of case law that had been compiled by the jurist Papirius at the end of the Kingdom. The document itself was not preserved, but twenty-three references to Papirius' collection have been found in the works of other Roman writers. In the nineteenth century they were published by Dirksen as the *Leges Regiae,* the 'Decrees of the Kings' or 'Laws of the Kings'. At the end of the century Mommsen, having been deceived by an Italian antiquarian who continuously produced new inscriptions, claimed that the *ius papirinianum* was a forgery. However, it is a rule of textual criticism that one must present strong arguments in order to reject a text which scholars have accepted as authentic. Currently, editions of the Decrees of the Kings contain more than the abovementioned twenty-three fragments because other texts concerning the law under the Kings have been inserted. Dionysius of Halicarnassus, for example, wrote an apologia for Emperor Augustus in which the latter's imperial prerogatives were projected onto Romulus. Many excerpts were included as Decrees of the Kings in modern editions, even though they were not judicial decisions. Other Decrees of the Kings were taken from Plutarch, Pliny and Festus.

Some of the decisions recorded in the Decrees of the Kings played a part in legal practice for centuries. If a *paterfamilias* transferred his son to a different family three times, he lost his authority over that son. Five centuries later, this rule would still be applied when a son was emancipated. If a couple confirmed its relationship by means of a *confarreatio,* they created community property. If a husband sent his wife away without proof of adultery, poisoning or the forgery of keys, he lost one half of his goods to his wife and the other half to the court. The most famous Decrees of the Kings are two decisions attributed to Romulus. If a pregnant woman died, her unborn child had to be cut out of her body and, if necessary, buried separately. Did the unborn child have a right to life in these days, or did its environment have a right to the baby? The answer to this question cannot be inferred from the text. A man who found his adulterous wife *in flagrante delicto* and killed her immediately was excusable, as were other family members who did not stop the manslaughter. These judgments concerning unborn life and the manslaughter of an adulterous wife recur in later sources and still play a part in our current criminal law. The fact that this law of the first Roman village crops up two thousand years later in the law of powerful European countries illustrates the importance of the reception of Roman law.

Many Romanists emphasise the religious character of some Decrees of the Kings because they feature the word *sacer*, which they translate as 'sacred'. A son who hit his father became *sacer* and should be dedicated to the gods: in other words, he should be sacrificed on an altar. However, it seems very strange that the Roman Empire would be willing to lose a soldier because he was aggressive. This type of interpretation is to be treated with caution. Latin has both perfect and imperfect adjectives. *Sacer* is an imperfect adjective of *sanciri* (to sanction), the juridical word 'par excellence'. It is best translated as 'liable, to be brought before the court'. The *sacerdotes* were not priests, but judges. The word's association with priests stems from Judaism and early Christianity. These religions' spiritual leaders doubled as judges and were designated with this term. Let us avoid rashly classifying as religious anything that we do not fully understand but find primitive nonetheless. Religious matters are outside the province of legal science and are also studied in a scientific manner.

Bibliography. – The Decrees of the Kings were republished by V. GUIFFRÈ, *Les lois des Romains*, Naples 1977, which features an updated bibliography and a translation of the Greek texts. Other editions can be found in, among others, the *Fontes Iuris Romani Anteiustiniani* (FIRA) I,3-18, Florence 1941 (reprinted in 1968) and in P.F. GIRARD and F. SENN, *Textes de droit romain*, Paris 1967. The Decrees of the Kings can be found online.

Legal acts like the *mancipatio* and institutions like the *familia* are said to stem from the Kingdom, but these are conjectures. The *mancipatio* which we know from later sources was a kind of play performed on the *forum*, where one could find an official scale-holder who assayed coins. Before this scale-holder, a Roman could transfer a good from one family to another. In the presence of witnesses, the transferee stated that the person or good was his, awaited the agreement or silence of the transferor and then struck a copper coin against the scale. Henceforth the person or good belonged to his family.

2. The early Republic (509 BC-367 BC)

In 509 BC the 'patricians', the Etruscan section of the population of Rome, seized power. It is not clear which new institutions they established. From then on, the *respublica*, the military regime, is mentioned. *Populus* was derived from an old Etruscan word for army. Its adjective was *poplicus* and, later, *publicus*. The word bears a resemblance to Pericles' democracy, in which *demos* also referred to the army. The early Roman Republic was still a far cry from the republic and democracy of the humanists. The Roman Republic would be thoroughly reorganised in 367 BC (see below) and would continue to exist until the second century AD. During the early Republic, Rome was still the kind of city state that we know from Thucydides. It was, however, already a strong city state in 509 BC. Its first treaty with Carthage dates from 508-507. The patricians, whom we consider to have been Etruscans but whom others identify as Sabines, ruled over the other ethnic groups, which mainly consisted of Latin plebeians. The latter seceded from the patricians and became a new enemy. Subsequently, the patricians discovered that they had to collaborate with these plebeians if Rome was to be successful. During this collaboration in the republican period, one of the most important cornerstones of Roman legal thought was laid: the *peraequatio iuris*. In the army, those who fought for Rome were not only given privileges vis-à-vis non-warriors, but also equal rights vis-à-vis their brothers in arms, irrespective of their ethnic origin. All warriors would share in the new Rome. This principle became the basis of the legions' strike power. Strength in union through law became one of the foundations of Roman society.

The sources remain scarce, but the Latin historians do seem to have known the institutions of the early Republic somewhat better than those of the Kingdom. The city state was governed from the Capitoline, originally by patrician praetors and military tribunes, and later by consuls. They received their power from the *comitia curiata*, the meetings of the *curiae*. The plebeians were governed from the Aventine Hill by aediles. From 496 BC onwards they were protected against the patricians by plebeian tribunes. Their leaders were appointed by the *concilia plebis*. Patricians and plebeians jointly organised the army through a consultative body, the meetings of which were the *comitia centuriata*. In these assemblies they discussed not only military matters and the organisation of the army, but also all measures and taxes in favour of the army. In 449 BC the *comitia centuriata* approved the Twelve Tables, a series of agreements which were chiselled into twelve stone tables and exhibited on the Forum. They listed the privileges of warriors, which were the same for all ethnic groups and were guaranteed by the military courts. These texts had been drawn up after deliberation with the *decemuiri*, lower officers who were the spokesmen of the soldiers. The humanists would later turn these *decemuiri* into 'ten wise men'.

The Twelve Tables were a large step forwards for Roman law. Some historians see them as the first codification of civil law, but in doing so they are confusing Roman Antiquity with the eighteenth century. In either case, the Twelve Tables were a monument of *ius ciuile*. *Ciues* were brothers in arms and *ius ciuile* was the law that was developed in order to resolve conflicts between these brothers in arms while taking into account their warriors' privileges. The word 'citizens', which we use as the translation of *ciues*, also refers to citadels and fortified cities. The Twelve Tables were voted in under a military regime, by a committee which was only competent for military matters. *Ius ciuile*, however, did not remain limited to military men on campaigns. Many veterans kept their civil status and could bring conflicts before the military courts. We will return to the *status libertatis* and the *ciuitas*, the military status and the law that applied between military men, later on in this book. It is out of these two notions that universal civil rights would develop. The status of soldiers was at the basis of the efficiency of the Roman armies, but would also mark the history of Europe.

The stone tables of the Forum were destroyed by the Gauls in 390 BC. They were replaced with bronze copies, which were lost as well. Six centuries later, however, the Twelve Tables were still cited by jurists. In the Early Modern Period, many scholars tried to reconstruct the Twelve Tables on the basis of these citations. A former student of the university of Leuven, Jacob Reyvaert (1534-1568), compiled a decent edition of these citations in 1563. In 1814 the Institutes of Gaius, which brought to light a new series of references to the Twelve Tables, were discovered. This brought the number of known excerpts to one hundred and nineteen. No new fragments have been found since. Dirksen compiled a new edition in the nineteenth century. It was corrected by Schöll, whose edition of 1866 is now used as the standard text.

The largest part of the Law of the Twelve Tables deals with civil procedure. The Capitoline and the Aventine Hills did not recognise each other's case law for a long time. For *ciues*, a common system was devised. Every soldier who was involved in a conflict with a fellow warrior could go to the military praetor and would be allowed to commence legal proceedings irrespective of his ethnic origin. The army oversaw the execution of the judgements. If a patrician lost a case against a plebeian and refused to pay, the plebeian could have the patrician's status reduced to that of a slave and sell him *trans Tiberim* (a fixed expression which originally meant 'on the other side of the Tiber', 'across the border' and therefore 'as a prisoner of war'). Another series of measures concerned the family and the division of the goods of a warrior after his death. Here, we find the origin of the *familia*: *ciues* were allowed to invoke their privileges for other people. This was accepted if the *ciues* and his *familiares* appeared in court as a group having community of property. The law of succession occupies an important position in the Twelve Tables. When a warrior died, the family's community property was always divided. Note that in the fifth century BC there were female heirs as well and that women could also acquire assets under civil law. The Twelve Tables also mention the most original of all civil rights, the right to draw up a will. Furthermore, the Twelve Tables contain an entire series of measures pertaining to peaceful coexistence in daily life. Many of these concern farmers and neighbours and they give the impression that the patricians had control over the immovable property. The four-day Etruscan funerals which annoyed the plebeians were curbed, but respect for the dead was guaranteed. Not everything became possible: a relationship between a patrician and a plebeian remained without legal effect for the time being. In addition, we find that the Twelve Tables contained rules of criminal law by means of which a mutual respect between both groups was enforced. Some of these measures already heralded classical criminal law. A person who accused someone of theft had to prove the presence of an intent to steal. This importance of intent in the fifth century BC is certainly remarkable.

The Law of the Twelve Tables is a juridical work and many of its provisions are interpreted in a dubious manner. *Ciues* who treated each other badly, risked *infamia*. This word is often misread as infamy. In the early Republic, *infamia* consisted of the revocation of civil rights with regard to the *familia*. The word is more closely related to *familia* than to *fati*. The most famous text of the Twelve Tables concerns injuries to limbs. If someone inflicts such an injury on someone else, *talio esto*. Most scholars read this as 'an eye for an eye and a tooth for a tooth'. If someone injured another person, retaliation consisted of inflicting the same injury on the perpetrator. In military law, however, such a provision seems odd. Losing one soldier because of an injury is a serious matter. That the military court would allow a second soldier to be put out of action through retaliation if this injury resulted from a private conflict, seems implausible. And yet this is the traditional interpretation of the principle of *talio*. This reading stems from Augustine, who was continuously trying to reconcile Biblical and

Roman culture. He found the principle of 'an eye for an eye' in the old Mosaic law, which did not discuss retaliation but the limitation of revenge. Saint Augustine, who already adhered to the principle 'do not repay evil with evil', saw a legitimate revenge in the old text of Moses and associated it with the *talio* of the Law of the Twelve Tables. This analysis was canonised in the Middle Ages. When Dirksen and Schöll drew up their Twelve Tables, they did not question this interpretation and failed to notice that reversing the order of texts 8.3 and 8.2 results in a much more realistic meaning: if one injures a comrade in arms, a compensation must be paid and the same will apply in case of injury of limbs, *talio esto*. The literature on the Twelve Tables contains other persistent interpretations. Until the first century BC the word *religio* meant 'funeral'. In the Twelve Tables the words appears several times in connection with patrician funeral matters. Many historians, however, begin to fantasise about religion when they see this term. The Law of the Twelve Tables also mentions 'capital punishments', which concern *capitis diminutio*, the loss of civil rights. For many readers, however, they are death penalties. Those who ridiculed officers could be thrown in the glasshouse and this was the revocation of a civil liberty. Interpreting this deprivation of liberty as a capital punishment results in the misrepresentation of life in the legions. In insolvency proceedings the praetor could *capite poenam dare* to a citizen, take away his civil rights, after which he was sold as a slave and the proceeds were divided among the creditors. According to some translators, however, the debtor was killed and cut into pieces, after which the creditors were each given a smaller or larger piece in accordance with their claim...

Bibliography. –The text of the Law of the Twelve Tables can be found in V. GIUFFRè, *Les lois des Romains*, Jovene, Naples 1977. Other editions can be discovered in *Fontes Iuris Romani Anteiustiniani* [FIRA], 3 vol., Florence 1941-1943 (republished 1964-1968) and in P.F. GIRARD, *Textes de droit Romain*. An English translation of the Twelve Tables can be found online: 'The Gutenberg Project EBook of the Twelve Tables', http://www.gutenberg.org/ebooks/14783. The Latin text and a large number of translations can be consulted online. On the issue of *talio* see L. WAELKENS, 'Talio herbekeken', in: *Ex iusta causa traditum, Essays in honour of Eric Pool*, Pretoria 2005, p. 404-410. Everything becomes clearer if one reverses the order of 8.2 and 8.3. The text concerning division can be found in 3.2.

§2. The heyday of the Republic (367 BC – 17 BC)

Around 400 the great ascendancy of Rome began. In 396 there was an important victory over the Etruscan city of Veii. In 367, power was consolidated. At the proposal of the tribunes C. Licinus Stolo and L. Sextius Lateranus, the *comitia centuriata* approved the *leges liciniae sextae*, which would determine the structure of the Republic for centuries. These agreements contained a gorgeous compromise between unity of governance towards the outside world and the internal flow of power and creativity. When treating the administration of the Republic, we will successively discuss the role of the Senate, the voting assemblies and the magistracy. In this context, note the balanced division of power and the legal pluralism, the multitude of enforceable sets of norms. Then, we will briefly consider the role of jurists in this military environment. In legal history, one always has to pay attention to the hierarchy of the norms and sources of law. This hierarchy expresses the balance between the rulers, the population and the jurists. In some societies, the centre of gravity is close to the commanders-in-chief, as in Pharaonic Egypt or eighteenth-century France. In others, it is closer to the population, for example in medieval Venice or the Batavian Republic, or closer to the courts, as in eighteenth-century England with its authoritative courts. Every day, jurists shift this centre of gravity slightly between these three poles. This small movement is the consequence of all of the conflicts which they resolved that day. For that reason, an examination of how the jurists functioned can be useful in any legal historical research.

1. The Senate

The Senate was not a representative body of the people, but, first and foremost, a forum for discussion. The Republic had a culture of open debate in the *curia hostilia* (the house of the Senate) and in the *forum*. Senators were appointed by the consuls until 312 BC and subsequently by the censors. During the elections of new magistrates, the Senate appointed *interreges*, interim leaders, for five days. The Senate could proclaim martial law, and this suspended all proceedings, including civil ones. Until 339 BC the Senate would have ratified the decisions of the *comitia*. In normal times, it had three competences: it administrated the federation, managed the budget and oversaw the non-civil administration of justice.

Whenever a new region was conquered, the Senate negotiated with the subjected people to conclude a *foedus*, a peace treaty. The Roman negotiators tried to obtain loyalty, taxes and soldiers. In return, they offered peace and civil rights. These civil rights, which did not cost the Roman Republic any money and had previously both bought unity in Rome and secured the motivation of soldiers, now also served to build the *foederatio*. Conquered peoples who joined with Rome were given aspects of *ciuitas*. For instance, when it was subdued by the Romans, Campania, which grew the corn that Rome lacked, was granted *commercium*, access to the free market in the entire Roman territory. In the late Republic, some provinces obtained *conubium*: if a subject of the province lived together with a Roman citizen, the couple's children were Roman citizens. Other regions obtained the recognition of their courts and case law. Around 200 BC Italy received *ciuitas sine suffragio*, the full civil statute without suffrage in Rome. When they were in Rome, people from regions with *ciuitas sine suffragio* were *peregrini* (pilgrims). The federation was governed by the Senate, which sent former magistrates to the provinces as proconsuls or propraetors so that they could supervise the execution of the treaty. Their most important tasks were to maintain public order, collect taxes and administer justice.

The revenues from the provinces filled the *aerarium*, the treasury of the Senate, which was used to pay the army and the administration. The Senate controlled politics through the budget and the allocation of public means. The magistrates were sovereign, but received their budget from the Senate.

The third competence of the Senate was the supervision of the non-civil administration of justice. The system of civil law was developed for the benefit of warriors in the army. For centuries, there must have been a second judicial system, which was replaced first by civil and then by imperial law. None of its sources have been handed down, but we do know of a name for it: *ius sacrum*. Jurists like Sulpicius Rufus, Trebatius Testa and Antistius Labeo wrote about *ius sacrum* until the first century BC.

We can presume – although such a presumption is not strictly necessary to understand current law and the reception of Roman law – that the *ius sacrum* applied to those who could not go to a civil court. The Senate appointed a *pontifex maximus* and *pontifices*; at the local level, there were *sacerdotes*. The Judaeo-Christian tradition adopted this terminology and used it to denote their priests who also served as judges. Once the Roman terminology was established in the Christian Middle Ages, it was projected back onto the Roman Republic; the Roman judges were turned into priests as well. For most historians, the world of the *ius sacrum* is that of Roman religion. There is no society without religion, the eighteenth century claimed. *Ius sacrum*, however, pertains to the administration of justice. *Sacrum* is an imperfect adjective of *sanciri*, to sanction; *sanctus* is its past participle and perfect adjective. In the Christian tradition a deceased person could be canonised by means of a trial (*sanctus*), but this has nothing to do with the Republic. Gaius clearly stated that the *populus romanus* decided what was *sacrum* (Gaius 2.5).

From the first century BC onwards the eastern religions spread in Rome. However, there are very few traces of religion in the Republic. Were the Lares and Lemures more religious in nature than fairies and werewolves? Were the Penates gods or mere references to the culture of a household, like mezuzahs or crucifixes? Maybe Jupiter was once a god on the Capitoline Hill, but in the Roman temples he welcomed the patricians. Ceres symbolised the plebeians and Juno the Samnites. The other gods were even more civil. Mars stood for the army, Mercury for free trade, Justitia for procedure, Fortuna for affluence. They were all *diuinus*, but that meant inviolable. *Deus* does not have a vocative, which leads us to suspect that it was the translation for Yahweh, the unassailable god who could not be addressed. The *arae* of the Republic were too tall to have been sacrificial altars. There is no proof that *sacrificia* were destroyed as in Israel, nor is there evidence that they did not fall to the judges. Confusingly, in the first century BC the Romans began to use the old word for funeral (*religio*) to indicate eastern transcendental religions that featured an afterlife. However, the example of Janus illustrates just how far interpretations can go. In times of war both doors (*ianuae*) of the *comitia centuriata* on the Forum were open. The soldier Janus looked through both at the same time. It was the historians who deified him. Afterwards, they looked for an explanation for Janus Clusius, Janus Geminus, Janus Junonius, Janus Quirinus... They thought these names referred to shrines and chapels in the streets of Rome. However, *ianus* was the common word for a doorjamb and passageway, a 'sottoporto' in the current language of the eternal city. What is so divine about a passageway by the Quirinal? And the *haruspices* who observed the flight of birds at the beginning of the session of the Senate in order to look for portents? During military campaigns no decisions could be taken before the bird-watchers had predicted the weather. Is it not beautiful that the Senate chose a ritual reminiscent of the army in the field rather than a stroke of the president's hammer to open its sessions?

In 300 BC, the office of *pontifex* was opened to plebeians. The first plebeian *pontifex maximus* was appointed in 254. The *ius sacrum* remained important until the end of the Republic. From Augustus' reign onwards, the emperors became *pontifex maximus*. In this manner they laid hands on the administration of justice in the provinces that were governed by the Senate. It is sometimes suggested that the emperors concerned themselves with theology and that this was in keeping with the Republican tradition of mixing law and religion. However, this story is mainly told because of the later blending of royal case law with ecclesiastical case law, which is erroneously connected with the *ius sacrum*.

Bibliography. – The best book about Roman religion, suitable for believers and non-believers, is K. LATTE, *Römische Religionsgeschichte*, [Handbuch der Altertumswissenschaft, V, 4], Munich 1960.

2. The voting assemblies and their *leges*

Just like the Forum, where politicians could occupy the *rostra* (orators' platform), the Senate was a place for discussion. Votes were not held in the *curia hostilia* itself, but in the room with the two *ianuae* in the building of the *comitia* across from the *curia*. Although these *comitia* are sometimes described as popular assemblies, they were actually voting assemblies which probably consisted exclusively of senators. We know of four voting assemblies, each of which had a different composition and dealt with other matters. In the case of a vote, the president proposed a text which could be approved or rejected. Discussion of the text was not permitted and there was no possibility of amendment. Those who were entitled to vote deposited a potshard on which they had inscribed VR (*uti rogas*, as requested) or A (*antiquo,* leave as it was) in an urn. If the vote concerned a death sentence, the options were C (*condemnito*) or A (*absoluito*). Sometimes, the presidents asked the assembly to approve a text (*leges rogatae*); at other times they asked to be granted the authority to write the text themselves (*leges datae*).

In the *comitia curiata* the initiative was taken by the *pontifex maximus*. Thirty people were entitled to vote: one from each of the ten *curiae* of the three centres that dated back to the Kingdom. They approved the *lex curiata de imperio* when new consuls and praetors took office and thus conferred sovereign power on them. The law faculties of the Middle Ages and the Early Modern Period often cited this *lex de imperio*. It was the text from which the jurists working at these faculties derived the principle that all power emanates from the people. Even when emperors or their delegates later passed on their power through the law of succession, medieval and early modern jurists considered this to have been the old power of the people which had been conferred by the *comitia curiata*. Until the third century AD the *comitia curiata* also approved *adrogationes* (fusions of *familiae*) and *testamenta comitiis calatis* in which an heir was adopted under the suspensive condition that he outlived the testator.

The *comitia centuriata* was the most important voting assembly. Votes were requested by the consuls and concerned military matters: the army, its financing or the organisation of the Republic. Both patricians and plebeians held seats. The population was classified into five tax brackets, a class of craftsmen, and proletarians. Monetary depreciation caused the first tax bracket, which consisted of those who had assets worth 100,000 asses, to become the most important group. It equipped eighty centuries of foot soldiers and eighteen centuries of cavalry. After some time this first tax bracket had an absolute majority in the *comitia centuriata* and consequently only the votes of this group were still counted. Consuls, praetors and censors were elected by this assembly.

The *comitia tributa* were presided over by the praetors. Votes were cast by the *tribus*, the districts of Rome and its immediate environs. After 241 BC there were thirty-one rural districts which represented citizens who held land and four urban districts which represented citizens without land. Apparently, ownership of land had a determining influence on this electoral college. Its voting members elected the quaestors, the *aediles curules*, a number of officers and the *uigintisexuiri*, who were a kind of magistrate. The *comitia tributa* must have been a voting assembly of patricians: appeals against the death sentence of a patrician were treated by this assembly.

In 287 BC the plebeians managed to have their *concilia plebis* admitted into the voting assemblies. These *concilia plebis* were convened and presided by their tribunes. Their plebiscites were not preceded by an opinion of the Senate. The *concilia plebis* elected the aediles and the tribunes of the people. Some plebiscites, such as the *lex aquilia* of 284 BC and the *lex falcidia* of 40 BC became important in civil law. Plebeian's appeals against their death sentences were treated by the *concilia plebis*.

A text that was adopted by the *comitia* was called a *lex*. Continental jurists must be wary of this word. It does not mean 'statute' and is certainly not a statute of the people. *Lex* was the old Latin word for anything that bound people. In English it can be translated as 'law', but Continentals have to understand it as 'tie'. In expressions like *lex aelia sentia* or *lex hortensia*, Romans first and foremost heard the adjectival name of the *lex* in question. They understood *lex aquilia* as aquilian liability. Contractual terms and even obligations arising from delict were *leges*. If *leges perfectae* existed, legal acts which were contrary to these *leges* were void. If there were *leges minus quam perfectae*, contrary legal acts were not null, but a fine was imposed. In case of *leges imperfectae* there was no predetermined sanction: the effects were worked out by the magistrates. The majority of the eight hundred fragments of the *leges* which have been handed down deal with the organisation of the Republic. Some thirty concern civil law.

Note. – The abovementioned predominance of an adjectival name over a noun is typical of Latin. A similar phenomenon can be observed in expressions with the word *rex* in the early Middle Ages. In *rex Allemanorum* or *rex Francorum*, the first word only gains its meaning from its combination with the name that follows. The changeover to the substantive use of the word *rex* as 'king' was a profound transformation. In the Germanic languages, we still use *rex* in compounds or as an adjective: examples include the adjective 'rich', the Dutch compounds *rijksdaalder* (rix-dollar) and *rijksmiddelen* (government resources) and the German compound *Reichskirche* (imperial church).

Bibliography. – The decisions of the *comitia* that were preserved have been published in P.F. Girard and F. Senn, *Textes de droit romain*, Paris 1967.

3. The magistracy and the edicts

Magistrates played the most active role in the daily administration of the Republic. They were appointed for one year and worked without hindrance during that period. The electoral procedure already contained guarantees for good government. There was a hierarchy of offices and candidates had to follow the *cursus honorum*. One could not become consul without having been lictor, quaestor, aedile and praetor. In addition, it was impossible to take the first step towards a career in the magistracy without having served in the army for ten years. All terms of office, except the censors', were limited to one year. Magistrates who stepped down could not be elected for one year. During that period, they had no immunity and could be called to account. Every magistrate had at least one colleague with the same authority who could blow the whistle on him. In addition, higher magistrates could intervene in lower magistrates' sphere of authority. At the end of a magistrate's career, the propraetoriate or the proconsulate beckoned. Former praetors and consuls could be appointed as provincial governor. As these governors received a commission on the revenues that their province sent to the Senate, this long-term prospect urged magistrates to govern in a way that would be appreciated. In the most affluent provinces governors only held their office for a few years, but this was long enough to enable them to live lives of luxury for generations.

Each magistrate could make binding decisions in his domain (*ius edicendi*). Before he could start working, he had to issue an edict. Only then did a consul or praetor receive the *imperium*, the sovereign power which included supreme military command as well as supreme authority and the competence to administer justice in cases of conflict. The voting assembly that transferred this power to a magistrate was never the assembly that had elected him. The magistrates' edicts were essential to the law of the Republic: it was by means of these edicts that all of the magistrates installed their own legal system, which they also enforced themselves. As a consequence, different legal systems coexisted in the Republic.

A. The consuls

The office of consul existed from the fifth century onwards. From 367 onwards, the term consul was reserved for the two most important magistrates. One of them could be a plebeian; the other was always a patrician. They had supreme authority and were the political and military leaders of the Republic. The years were named after them (eponymous office holders). They had the right of initiative in the *comitia centuriata*, where they requested their budgets. They exercised jurisdiction over the troops and over public goods, the goods and lands of the army, and could release prisoners of war. Within their jurisdiction, they were bound by their edict. In the Empire, their tasks were partially taken over by the emperor. Not a single edict of a republican consul has been preserved.

Every consul could appoint a *dictator* if he was of the opinion that Rome was endangered by a political deadlock. The dictator only exercised power and was not bound by an edict. His mandate ended irrevocably after six months. Then, both the dictator and his promoter could be called to account.

B. The praetors

In 367 a praetor was charged, as *collega minor* of the consul, with the private jurisdiction over *ciues*. Between 367 and 337 only patricians were eligible for the office of praetor – a compensation for the fact that they had lost one consul. Just as in the case of the consuls, this praetor was always a high-ranking military leader who was elected by the *comitia centuriata* and received the *imperium* from the *comitia curiata*. The praetor's decisions were subject to the right of veto of the consuls and the tribunes of the people. In the army, he concerned himself with private conflicts between soldiers, who were subject to civil law. Since veterans were also given civil rights, the praetor treated not only conflicts between soldiers, but also disputes between citizens who had left military service. He examined the extent to which civil law applied to these arguing citizens and provided them with instructions for the judge who had to settle their dispute. In 242 BC a second praetor was established, who would administer the civil rights of the *peregrini*. Because the federation grew, an increasing number of people with partial civil rights became involved in conflicts. The second praetor then examined the extent to which these *peregrini* could lay claim to these rights. He was called the *praetor peregrinorum*; his colleague was henceforth known as the *praetor urbanus*. In 168 BC compulsory military service was abolished and many people who had never fought were given civil rights. The office of praetor became less closely associated with the military, but remained intimately connected with the *comitia centuriata*. Civil law retained its military character. It was never based on universal principles or values. In addition, it still had the flavour of 'men's law' and served to resolve conflicts among companions and to restore comradeship.

The praetors did not pass judgement on the merits of cases. They only organised preliminary hearings. Quarreling parties who were of the opinion that they could lay claim to civil rights appeared before the praetor and requested a remedy listed in his edict. The praetors checked the parties' claims and, if appropriate, gave them a message for the judge who would make a decision on the merits of the case. This message stated that the case had to be dealt with according to civil law (see below). The legal system of the praetors was developed from one edict to the next. The *praetor urbanus* developed the normal civil law, while the *praetor peregrinorum* developed the *ius gentium*, which was adapted to the diverse civil statuses within the federation. Praetors usually adopted the greater part of their predecessor's edict, but corrections were made regularly. During the year existing remedies were adapted to unforeseen circumstances (*actio utilis*) or new remedies were introduced provisionally (*actio in factum concepta*). The *praetor peregrinorum* sometimes allowed parties to use a remedy of his colleague, in which case he inserted the formula *si ciuis esset* ('as if this man were a citizen').

In the second century AD the praetorian prefect Salvius Julianus codified the edict of the praetors in the *edictum perpetuum* (Perpetual Edict), which he introduced in the case law of the imperial courts. Shortly afterwards, Gaius analysed the problems which the introduction of the republican edict could cause in the imperial courts (see below). Because this *edictum perpetuum* was commented on often, the praetorian law is now the best-preserved branch of republican law. In 212 AD full civil status was granted to all free inhabitants of the Empire. The difference between praetorian law and *ius gentium* disappeared. Further on in this book, we will discuss how the praetors effectively acted within the framework of the civil law.

C. The censors

Although it was not the most important office, the censorship was at the very top of the hierarchy of positions. Only proconsuls were eligible. Censors were elected every five years by the *comitia centuriata*. The censors organised censuses and kept the census lists up to date. In these lists, citizens were assigned to classes and centuries which determined their military and fiscal obligations. The censors could reduce a cavalryman to the rank of a foot soldier or turn a slave into a citizen. Being put in a different category entailed risks even for veterans because it could have tax consequences. From 312 BC onwards (*lex ouinia*) the censors also appointed and discharged the senators.

It is sometimes suggested that the censors drew up their quinquennial lists without applying any criteria and that they practised their profession in an arbitrary manner. This does not tally with the logic of the Republic. Certain professions were exempted from taxes and entry in the *lustra* or census lists served as a title. It is hard to imagine that for centuries one man could influence the behaviour of hundreds of thousands of fellow citizens without there being any clear criteria. Not a single censor's edict has been preserved, but there are references, for example to an edict against the Latin orators, an edict against domestic courts ('Hausgerichte') and an edict of Cato the Censor that combatted the repudiation of spouses. The censors could take account of all circumstances: they could introduce norms which now come under family law, for example norms concerning guardianship or adoption, or could simply sanction morals or behaviour in the army. After 168 BC obligatory military service was abolished and civil rights were linked with birth within a *matrimonium*. There are no sources which connect this regulation to the censors, but because of their authority over matters of citizenship it can be assumed that they played a part in the interpretation of the notion of *matrimonium*. We do not know whether the censors were bound by their own edict. A veto against a censor's decision could be obtained from his fellow censor, but not from a tribune of the people.

The censors also managed the military buildings. Their own administration was accommodated in the *templum libertatis* on the Aventine Hill.

In the Imperial Period, the emperor would become censor for life. It seems that emperors mainly used their capacity as censor to control the composition of the army. The office of censor disappeared in 96 AD.

D. The aediles

In 367 BC two aediles of the temple of Ceres became magistrates. They were plebeians and had been elected by the *concilia plebis* since the fifth century. In 367 they were joined by two patrician 'curule' aediles. This board of four magistrates was charged with the urban administration (*cura urbis*) and composed an important edict to that end. It regulated the public order – which comprised the police and criminal law on the one hand, and on the other public trade. In the edict of the aediles notions such as *ciuitas* or slavery did not exist, because these were notions that did not pertain to the public order.

Offences against the public order were in principle brought before the aediles. In their edict they listed those deeds against which they would act and described the criminal procedure. The offences which they would punish were enumerated in their edict. *Actiones utiles* or *in factum conceptae* did not exist in the law of the aediles. They did not have the last word on death sentences of citizens. For plebeians, the possibility of appeal with the *concilia plebis* was preserved; patricians had recourse to the *comitia tributa*. Note that not every act which is currently considered to come under criminal law was brought before the aediles. Theft, damage to property, defamation or robbery could also be brought before the praetor as civil conflicts. Any fines fell to the claimants by way of retaliation. Desecrators of tombs could be brought before the praetor with an *actio popularis*. In such cases, the person who had reported the offence demanded a private fine. Other offences were prosecuted in *publica iudicia* – *publicus* refers to the consuls. From the second century BC onwards there were *quaestiones perpetuae* under the presidency of the praetors and with juries for serious offences. Some of these *quaestiones perpetuae* ended up before the Senate.

The aediles' supervision of public trade evolved from the regulation of street trade and the settling of commercial disputes in the city to the monitoring of the corn trade and the combatting of monopolisation in the entire realm. At the end of the Republic the supervision of the corn trade would develop into a responsibility within the system of the public distribution of corn (*cura annonae*).

During the Imperial Period, the responsibilities of the censors were absorbed by the emperor. Augustus and his successors were aediles by right. As a consequence, serious offences came before the imperial court. By the third century AD, these courts gained the monopoly on criminal law. At that moment, the criminal procedure became the imperial *cognitio extra ordinem*. The development of our criminal law is based on the reception of the criminal law of the Imperial Period. Through the emperor's absorption of the functions of the aediles, commercial law and the supply of corn also became imperial responsibilities.

One title from the Digest that concerns the edict of the aediles has been preserved: D. 21.1. It contains some aspects of commercial and criminal law that are of lesser importance. In addition, there is title C. 4.58 in the Code of Justinian, in which some problems concerning the continued effects of the actions of the curule aediles in the imperial procedure are discussed.

Bibliography. – L. GAROLFALO, *Il processo edilizio, Contributo allo studio dei iudicia populi*, Padua 1989.

E. The quaestors

The quaestors were another rung lower on the ladder. They were elected by the *comitia tributa*. They managed both the archives of the Capitol and, most importantly, the *aerarium* (treasury) for the Senate. In this manner, they played an important part in trade with the government. The Senate did not participate in legal transactions. Those who conducted trade with the government acquired debits and credits vis-à-vis the treasury, in the manner that was determined in the edict of the quaestors. The quaestors could pay a trader in cash from the treasury, but could also give him drawing rights vis-à-vis tax farmers and debtors. In addition, the quaestors kept the accounts of the Senate and opened credit lines for governors or the accountants of legions. They transferred the savings of soldiers who were serving in the legions to the bankers of their *familia* and prevented generals from exceeding their budget. In short, public finance and trade with the government were regulated in the quaestors' edicts. Sadly, we do not have any sources that offer a clear view of these matters. In fact, we can no longer even see where the boundary between the consuls' and the quaestors' financial management lay because this important body of law disappeared in the Imperial Period. Between the first century BC and the second century AD, the *aerarium* was gradually taken over by the *fiscus*. In the fiscal system, the emperor acted as a *ciuis* and trade with the government was treated under civil law. This would remain the case until the eighteenth century. There was, therefore, no reason to preserve old books about the edict of the quaestors.

F. The tribunes of the people

At the end of the Republic the plebeian tribunes (tribunes of the people) were also numbered among the magistrates. They were elected by the *concilia plebis*, had the right to convene and preside these assemblies and were given the right of initiative to hold votes on decisions (*plebiscita*). They could veto all decisions taken by magistrates (except dictators or censors), the Senate or the *comitia* if the decisions in question infringed the rights of the plebeians. It is not unlikely that they announced the manner in which they would exercise their right to veto in an edict.

G. The provincial governors

Before Sulla (138-78 BC), special praetors were elected for the administration of justice outside of Italy. In the first century BC the governors were granted jurisdiction in their province. They issued a provincial edict that determined how trade with the Roman government had to be conducted. The edicts of different provinces could diverge widely. In the first century BC there were attempts at unification. A *lex cornelia* asked the governors to meticulously respect their provincial edict and refrain from changing it without having a justified reason to do so. The supervision of the provincial administration of justice led to its becoming uniform. In the Early Principate an identical Provincial Edict would enter into force in all of the provinces that were governed by the Senate.

Conclusion

This effective legal pluralism with diverse edicts and magistrates who independently created their own body of law is a special characteristic of the Republic. Constitutional law, civil law, criminal law, commercial law or trade with the government were subject to different rules and procedures. They could differ per province because of the provinces' own edicts or their status within the federation, and could vary for citizens and peregrines. This system was not only operative at the level of Rome. Cities also had several urban magistrates who were authorised to issue edicts. Consequently, the rules also differed per city. Which law applied to whom and which court was competent to deal with certain conflicts? The magistrates dealt with these conflicts of jurisdiction and developed their own rules pertaining to conflict of laws in their edict. In case of a conflict of jurisdiction the magistrates declared themselves competent or incompetent. They did not refer cases to other courts. The harmonisation of the different edicts was politically sanctioned.

4. The jurists

At the beginning of this chapter, we advised the reader to keep an eye on the role of the jurists. It is, however, difficult to do this with regard to the Republican Period, not the least because it is hard to see who was professionally concerned with law and the resolution of conflicts. All magistrates were. Politicians were closely involved in legal life and the resolution of conflicts. It is striking that the republican jurists whose names we know were the descendants of *gentes* who had distinguished themselves in the army and the Senate. Licinius and Lateranus, the architects of the republican institutions, had prominent namesakes centuries later: a Licinius formed a triumvirate with Caesar and Pompey; a Lateranus was the most important opponent of Constantine in the fourth century AD. The jurists P. Mucius Scaevola (second century BC) and Q. Mucius Scaevola (consul in 95 BC, *pontifex maximus* in 87) were descendants of the Scaevolas who had distinguished themselves in the Etruscan wars of the sixth century BC. The jurist M. Iunius Brutus was a descendant of the Brutus who led the coup of 509 BC and an ancestor of the Brutus who was involved in the murder of Caesar. Servius Sulpicius Rufus (praetor in 65 BC, consul in 51) was both an excellent general in difficult times and the promoter of the *actio seruiana* in which lessors of farmland were granted a pledge and a 'droit de suite' on the harvest. He was the author of one hundred and eighty juridical publications and this shows that legal thought was still part of the basic logic of Roman civilisation at the end of the Republic. In order to develop the power of Rome, civil rights had been granted to warriors and inhabitants of the federation. In order to maintain the position of Rome politicians kept concerning themselves with the legal problems of soldiers and inhabitants.

The literature describes the tasks of the republican *iurisprudentes* as *respondere, cauere, agere. Respondere* means to provide advice, something which many legal scholars did in public. *Cauere* indicates the development of models and documents for legal practice. The German Romanists named the republican legal science 'Kautelarjurisprudenz' after these models. *Agere* was the provision of procedural assistance.

Few citations of republican jurists have been preserved. The oldest work concerning civil law of which the title has been handed down dates from the second century BC: Sextus Aelius Paetus' *Cunabula iuris*. The book itself has vanished. This is characteristic of the Roman Republic. For twenty centuries, Rome has been a fantasy world. In the Early Modern Era the Republic was overemphasised in the battle against royal absolutism. It is best to keep expectations low when trying to plumb the historical sources of the Republic and its law.

§3. The early Empire or Principate (17 BC – 284 AD)

In the first century BC the Republic was shaken by three civil wars. The republican institutions were no longer suitable for the administration of an immense realm with strong provinces. In 27 BC the third civil war was ended by Octavian, an excellent strategist who not only won battles, but must also be credited with one of the greatest achievements in legal history: the *pax romana*, the great peace. In 17 BC he declared the Republic restored. The Senate then gave him the title of Augustus, the elevated one. Many historians consider this moment as the end of the Republic and the beginning of the Empire. The real situation was more subtle. Augustus began his career as a general in the service of the Senate. In 30 BC he conquered Egypt, which he kept for himself. With Egyptian means he then took over Roman provinces and incorporated these into his own realm. As the Senate also retained provinces, the Empire and the Republic coexisted for a long time. The Empire gained more and more power, while the Republic became weaker. The latter, however, only disappeared in the second century AD when the emperor Hadrian had the *fiscus* absorb the *aerarium*. The *lex irnitana*, the municipal laws of Irni which were discovered in Andalusia in the eighties, date from the end of the first century AD and are a monument to the republican institutions.

Traditionally, the Imperial Period is subdivided into the Principate (17 BC – 284 AD) and the late Empire or Dominate, which lasted until 476 in Rome and until 1453 in Constantinople. This distinction will also be used in this book.

Since the Early Modern Era, the Empire has received a bad press because it was ruled by an autocrat. In the sixteenth century, Europe would be burnt to the ground by absolute monarchs who drew their inspiration from the Roman Empire. These monarchs were the terror of the enlightened minds of the eighteenth century, who considered the Republic to have been a democracy and deplored its decline. Even Mommsen (1817-1903) still thought of the rise of the Empire as an end point. Since then, Europe has become acquainted with the absolutism of popular sovereignty, which caused the disasters of the twentieth century. After seventy years of peace in Europe and one hundred and fifty in America, we have reached a better understanding of the progress that was made under Augustus. For the inhabitants of the Empire, the main characteristics of the Principate were peace and affluence.

The institutions underwent enormous changes during the Principate. Augustus split the realm into imperial and senatorial provinces. Under Hadrian (117-138) one single government for all of the provinces was established and the administration was organised in such a manner that the realm could survive without an emperor. The Empire reached its greatest extent under Trajan and remained peaceful and stable until the reign of Marcus Aurelius (†180) and Commodus (180-192), when the wars on the Rhine-Danube border and in Persia became too expensive. In 235 (the murder of Alexander Severus) a period of political instability dawned, which nineteenth-century Romanticism later labelled 'Reichskrise'. Under Postumus, Gaul temporarily seceded from the Empire; under Zenobia, Palmyra did the same thing. Even then, there was no anarchy. The institutions still functioned. In this century, Rome knew a Hellenistic period with, among others, Plotinus (204-270). Emperor Gallienus (260-268) was concerned about the central administration of justice. The power of Rome was once more demonstrated under Aurelianus (270-275) by the construction of the Muro Torto. The wars did cause political attention to shift to the East. In 284 a new regime was established under Diocletian which has been labelled as the late Empire or Dominate.

1. The institutions of the Principate

A. The imperial provinces

Augustus was the architect of the *pax romana*, the most difficult legal achievement, and one with which Rome had no experience.

Because of his battles in the service of the Senate, Octavian enjoyed the confidence of Rome. His opponent Antony, the loser of the third civil war, had fled to Egypt and married Cleopatra, the last pharaoh. Octavian challenged Antony, beat him and occupied Egypt. He kept the peaceful and affluent region outside of the Republic and considered it as his private 'family' property. He administred the country according to the local traditions. Two elements of his rule are striking. Firstly, in Egypt all immovable property belonged to the pharaoh; everyone who desired to exploit land had to pay the pharaoh. Land taxes were the pharaoh's most important source of income. Every year, these taxes were linked with the actual agricultural yield. This was very different from the Roman system in which the Senate's main source of income was a fixed annual sum, determined in the *foedera,* that was paid by the provinces. The Roman Empire had 'public' grounds which were leased and citizens held private land on which no taxes needed to be paid. Secondly, Egypt was governed through the administration of justice. No edicts were issued. Conflicts between its inhabitants were settled by local officials, who administered justice in the name of the pharaoh. If a litigant felt wronged by a decision, he could complain to the pharaoh that the official had not performed his task well. The case was then reviewed by appellate judges, who also worked in the name of the pharaoh. It was possible to lodge an appeal against their decision with the highest court in Alexandria, which looked for solutions which could be applied in the entire territory of Egypt and guaranteed that it would keep to its earlier judgements. In order to avoid appeals, the administration followed these 'precedents', which were experienced as legal rules. Officials and litigants always looked for solutions which dovetailed with the case law of the highest court. The advantages of governing through the administration of justice were a smaller need for political intervention, as well as good supervision of the administration and unity of law, and the fact that the people subject to the law felt respected.

Octavian's Egyptian revenues were enormous. He used them to develop the *annona* in Rome: a social security system that consisted of the distribution of Egyptian corn. In this manner, he earned the sympathy of the population. He also equipped an imperial army with which he could take action without having to ask the Senate for a budget. At the least sign of trouble in a province, Octavian took over the role of governor in that province and introduced the Egyptian regime, i.e. land taxes and government through the administration of justice. This became the regime of the 'imperial' provinces. Octavian's brutal interventions were tolerated in these troubled times. Peace was restored more quickly and taxes were not increased. The Senate had to accept this and was weakened whenever it lost a province to the emperor. During the third civil war, three hundred senators and two thousand people from the first tax bracket had been murdered. Many of the heads in which the institutions of the Republic had been stored, were gone, and the survivors were afraid. In addition, the peace and order in the imperial provinces outweighed the opposition of the Senate. In his new judicial system the emperor granted everyone the civil status with Roman liberties and gave every province the same rights. These equal rights and rules in all of the provinces resulted in a growing free market. There was an increase in prosperity that had a disarming effect. The *pax romana* was more profitable than the wars of the Republic and legitimised the new regime once and for all.

It is unthinkable that in a few years' time Augustus could develop a completely new legal system which could cure all of the late Republic's ailments. His rule was clearly inspired by his experiences in Egypt. He sought to translate these into legal notions which the Romans knew. He considered the imperial provinces as his private property, as *familia caesaris,* and applied the rules of Roman civil law to this territory. The emperor was a *paterfamilias* or – in the terminology of the *ius gentium* which was circulating in the imperial provinces – a *dominus.* In Roman law, slaves were family members. Augustus had thousands of slaves who were members of his *familia*. Tax money that was collected by one of his slaves was indisputably his. He used civil law mandates to delegate the administration of the provinces to legates, prefects and procurators who were free citizens, but when money was involved, the first emperors made use of slaves. In order to govern by means of the administration of law, Augustus established a central body in Rome. In this revolutionary period, the palace was protected by the praetorian guard. From the reign of Tiberius onwards it becomes clear that the head of the praetorian guard, the *praefectus praetorio*, had also become the chief of the administration and was running the jurisdictional government body.

A tremendous concern of the first emperors was the manner in which such a *dominium*, a dominion, could be passed on to a successor. Initially, the imperial provinces were passed on according to civil law as familial property. The first emperors emancipated their heirs and excluded them from inheriting the *dominium*. They then adopted their successor, who became the sole heir of the public domain. When the emperor died, the private mandates of the officials also ended. These had to be confirmed by the successor. In the course of the first century, the regime became more distinctive. If the public domain of the imperial provinces was transferred by means of the law of inheritance, it was by means of the law of inheritance used in the new imperial administration of justice. Therefore, the adjudication of the public domain was in the last instance a case for the praetorian prefecture. Apparently, the mandate of the prefect did not end when the emperor died. Because of this, many praetorian prefects were murdered. The system was already established when the first barracks emperors came to the throne in 68. In its capacity as an ultimate judicial body, the prefecture adjudicated the public domain to Galba. Once the public domain had been adjudicated, the new emperor once again held it privately as familial property.

In short, the emperors participated in legal transactions according to civil law. A trader who sold a good to the imperial army, sold it to the emperor. Anyone who dealt with an official in a remote station in Bithynia or Thebes was actually paying, speaking to, receiving something from or entering into an agreement with the emperor himself, albeit through a delegated official.

From the second century onwards, the Empire's regime was the one that would determine European public law until the seventeenth century. From the Palatine Hill, the *praefectus praetorio* led the administration in the name of the emperor. Many prefects were skilful administrators, for example Aelius Seianus or Afrianus Burrhus in the first century. The most famous Roman jurists, Salvius Julianus, Ulpian, Papinian, and Domitius Paulus were prefects. In all of the provincial capitals there were officials who supported smaller, more decentralised bureaus. The dispensation of justice mainly took place within the administration. Any administrative or judicial decisions of a local official could be appealed against and these appeals could eventually reach Rome, where a *consilium* presided by the *praefectus praetorio* functioned as the court of last resort. The prefecture guaranteed the equal treatment of equal cases. The decisions of the prefecture were published and lower officials took their cue from these precedents in order to prevent complaints. Tongeren kept a weather eye on Trier and Trier watched Rome. In this manner, the prefecture – and therefore also the emperor – ruled by means of the administration of justice. The fact that one court administered justice for the entire realm resulted in the development of an enormous zone which was subject to a unified law, a unique economic zone. Those who sent ships from Egypt to Pontus were familiar with the local law of transport. Someone in Hippo who had to receive a payment from Thessaloniki knew exactly what it was worth. People who know the law are better at assessing risks and become more enterprising.

Bibliography. – The hypothesis of the Egyptian inspiration of Augustus' regime is based on years of reading the *Chronique d'Egypte* of the Egyptological Foundation Queen Elisabeth (Brussels), the works of J. Pirenne, mostly in the *Recueils de la Société Jean Bodin*, and the Leuven scholars who studied the time of the Ptolomaeans.

B. The emperor and the republican institutions

Besides the imperial provinces, there were senatorial provinces with republican institutions. They would continue to exist for more than a century. Augustus tried to control these senatorial provinces as well and became a republican magistrate. Between 30 and 23, he served uninterruptedly as consul. In 23 BC he was elected as tribune of the people for life by the *concilia plebis* and consequently became immune. He gained the right to veto all decisions taken by other magistrates and the right to convene the Senate. Subsequently, he received the *imperium proconsulare*, and in 19 BC the *imperium proconsulare* for life, which meant that he also possessed the competences held by censors and consuls. As a consequence, he could act as a censor and appoint senators. He appointed senators from all of the provinces, including the imperial ones. The last censor was Domitian (emperor between 81 and 96). In 12 BC Augustus became *pontifex maximus*, head of the republican judiciary. With regard to the finances of the Republic, he replaced the elected quaestors by *praetores aerarii*. Under Nero, these were in their turn replaced by imperial prefects. The regular quaestors only retained the archives. The daily tasks which these republican magistracies entailed were executed by mandatories of the emperor, for whom bureaus of the emperor were established in both the emperor's and the senatorial provinces. Appeals against the officials who represented the emperor in those provinces could be lodged with his administration and could thus end up before the imperial appellate courts.

Just as before, the praetors continued to play a role in the civil procedure. They issued their edict every year. The emperor never became praetor, but in his capacity as consul and tribune he could always veto the decisions of the praetors. Nevertheless, even the emperor was confronted with praetorian law. Further on in this book we will see that that it was impossible to file an appeal against a republican civil procedure. If a procedure was instituted before the praetor, he asked the parties to which judge they wished to present their conflicts. From Augustus' reign onwards many parties in the senatorial provinces chose the emperor as their judge. The emperor did not administer justice himself; his local bureau represented him. If the local representative of the emperor pronounced a judgement, the party that was aggrieved by the decision could lodge an appeal. Aggrieved parties could invoke before the emperor the fact that his representative had not carried out his mandate properly. The judge of last instance for such complaints, irrespective of whether they originated from an imperial or senatorial province, was always the *praefectus praetorio*. His case law was known. Because of these possibilities for appeal, the local officials in the senatorial provinces also began to apply the new imperial law. In this manner, the law of the imperial provinces became applicable in the senatorial provinces as well, so that they could also enter the large free market that was characterised by equal rights.

From the beginning, the emperors based their administration of justice on the civil rights and liberties that had been developed in the Republic. The prefecture was familiar with this law, which had been compiled by the praetors in the Republic. In the years 133-138, under Hadrian, the decision was made to adopt the edict of the praetors in the imperial case law. Under the leadership of the prefect Salvius Julianus, the edict of the praetors was taken in hand. A new version of it was drawn up: the *edictum perpetuum* (Perpetual Edict), which would be applied by the prefecture. Through its adoption into the case law of the prefecture, the *edictum perpetuum* was imposed on the imperial provinces, at a moment that also the senatorial provinces were converted into imperial institutions. In Rome the praetors issued their edicts every year until the third century. The Perpetual Edict exerted a large influence on the imperial law and Roman jurists raised many questions concerning this document. Major commentaries, which would still be cited in the Roman sources centuries later, were written about this edict. On the basis of these citations Otto Lenel (1849-1935) tried to reconstruct the Perpetual Edict in 1883.

Bibliography. – O. Lenel, *Das Edictum perpetuum, Ein Versuch seiner Wiederherstellung*, Leipzig 1927 (reprint Aalen 1974).

There are traces of decisions of the Senate until the third century. In the first century AD we find decisions of the Senate that were not voted in as *leges* but were legally binding nonetheless, like the *senatusconsultum de aquaeductibus* (11 AD) which allowed the person who repaired an aqueduct to remove stones from adjoining plots; the *senatusconsultum macedonianum* (between 69 and 79), which made it impossible to claim back money that had been loaned to a *filiusfamilias*; the *senatusconsultum uelleianum* (middle of the first century), which made it impossible to summon women who stood surety; the *senatusconsultum trebellianum* that regulated debt issues in cases involving family fideicommissum; or the *senatus claudianum*, which determined that the *dominus* of a slave and the free mother of the slave's child could enter into a valid agreement that determined whether the child would enjoy the status of liberty or not. One would be inclined to think that the Senate was sitting in an appellate capacity, but this is not certain. Was there a kind of *prouocatio ad populum* in civil cases to avoid the emperor getting involved?

In Andalusia some remarkable texts from the first century AD surfaced. They help us to understand the law of the senatorial provinces better. In the nineteenth century five bronze tablets with excerpts from the municipal law of Malaga (*lex malacitana*) and one tablet with the municipal laws of Salpensa (*lex salpensana*) were found. In 1981 archaeologists discovered six bronze tablets with the municipal law of Irni (*lex irnitana*). These texts show how this organisation also functioned with magistrates at a local level. In addition, they include interesting rules concerning both the booking of municipal treasury transactions as well as the management of this treasury long before the invention of the artificial person.

C. The institutions of the capital

The city of Rome was neither part of an imperial nor of a senatorial province. In Rome the republican institutions were replaced by a metropolitan administration led by the *praefectus urbi*, the commander of the three urban cohorts. Two aediles remained active and were responsible for the street and market police, but they were placed under the authority of the *praefectus urbi*, who was also the judge of last instance. Because the *praefectus praetorio* worked within the same city walls, the urban administration was strongly influenced by the imperial administration. Nevertheless, it retained its own character. The republican civil procedure, for example, remained in use until the fourth century. The urban prefect used his own version of the praetorian edict.

The *annona*, the distribution of free corn, was unique to Rome. The third official in the hierarchy, second only to the *praefectus praetorio* and the *praefectus urbi*, was the *praefectus annonae*. He settled conflicts concerning the supply, transportation, storage and distribution of corn, and the fiscal exemptions that could be granted to suppliers. This food aid brought him political control of the city. Appeals against the *praefectus annonae* were lodged with the *praefectus praetorio*.

2. Classical Roman law

Gaining knowledge of the Roman law of the Principate is not easy. Of the three centuries of legal practice of fifty million inhabitants only a very small number of legal texts have been preserved. The Institutes of Gaius are the most important direct source. Some imperial decisions have been handed down because they were included in the Theodosian Code (438), were preserved on papyrus, or were included in the legal code of Justinian (sixth century). Some inscriptions, as well as some documents of legal practice, teach us something about the law. Apart from Gaius, the most important source is the Digest of Justinian (533), which was only drawn up three centuries later. This means that texts from the Principate were altered for centuries before they were recorded in the Digest. The lack of sources is not necessarily a bad thing. One does not have to know anything about material that cannot be examined. In the nineteenth century, however, the lack of sources led to great frustrations. Countless Romanists desired to reach the law of the Principate, which they gave the status of 'classical' Roman law. Some scholars dedicated their life to the reconstruction of legal texts from the Principate that they found in the Digest. They studied all of the later events which historians mentioned and scraped layers off the texts of the Digest on the basis of these external facts, just as Schliemann dug layer by layer towards ancient Troy. The Germans call this 'Textstufenforschung', research into the underlying textual layers of the Digest. This was a brilliant intellectual game, but it did not result in certainties with regard to the real content of 'classical' Roman law.

A. Famous jurists

Famous jurists of the early Principate were M. Antistius Labeo, a republican, and C. Ateius Capito, who was a supporter of the emperor. Labeo was a landowner who acted as a jurist in Rome outside of the agricultural season. He was not very well disposed towards the emperor and refused the office of consul. Nevertheless, Augustus granted him the *ius respondendi*, which meant that the emperor's judges were bound by Labeo's consults. Capito, who was won over to the new regime, did accept the consulship. Both of these jurists were still cited centuries later, for example concerning the *ius sacrum*.

Second-century names to remember are L. Javolenus Priscus, his pupil P. Salvius Julianus, Gaius and Pomponius. Pomponius was the only jurist to include some legal history in his works, namely in his *Enchiridium*. Salvius Julianus published two hundred scrolls concerning law. According to emperor Justinian (482-565), he was one of the two best jurists in Roman legal history. He was born in Africa, was consul in 148 and served as deputy of the emperor in different provinces. As the *praefectus praetorio* of Hadrian, he was paid twice the salary of his predecessor and led his emperor's administrative reform.

Gaius left us a special document. In 1816 B.G. Niebuhr discovered a palimpsest of his Institutes in Verona. The text, which dated from the fifth century, had been erased during the transliteration and had been overwritten with the letters of Jerome. Citations from Gaius were already known from the Digest, the *Collatio* (see below) and Boethius. A series of excerpts from Gaius was disseminated in the Middle Ages together with the *lex romana visigothorum*. It is on the basis of these excerpts that the Veronese text was identified as a manuscript of the Institutes. Circa 1820 a printed version was already circulating in the law faculties. Since then, two additional pieces have been discovered: one in 1927 in the papyri of Oxyrhynchus which are in Oxford and one in a papyrus that surfaced in 1933 in an antiquarian's shop in Cairo. The original text of the Institutes dates from the 50s of the second century. Gaius was a jurist from Asia Minor who seems, at first glance, to have written a commentary on the Perpetual Edict. He lists the problems caused by the introduction of the republican law in the imperial case law. His text follows the order of the Edict and repeatedly points out apparent contradictions in the Edict. Nevertheless, most scholars see his work as a textbook on Roman law. The correct interpretation of Gaius is hampered by three factors. First and foremost, sixth-century jurists used the work as a guide when drawing up the Institutes of Justinian, a work that is indeed a textbook. Gaius' Institutes however, are too unsystematic, too lacunal and too difficult to have been a textbook. A second problem is that Gaius was discovered in 1816, when the German jurists desired to draw up a civil code after the French model but did not have a single jurisdiction. Romantic Romanists came up with the idea of founding the new German civil law on the shared culture, just like the German dictionaries had been. Concretely, they considered this shared culture to consist of the old *ius commune*, Roman law. It was at that precise moment that this source of 'classical' Roman law surfaced. When ducklings hatch, they adopt the first adult duck that walks past as their mother and never reconsider this decision. Principles of nineteenth-century civil law were discovered in every institution in the Institutes and, just like ducklings, scholars never reconsidered this first interpretation. A third problem is that we have no frame of reference in which the vocabulary used in Gaius' day can be placed. Because of this, the Institutes remain a very difficult source. They do contain a treasure trove of information about the law of persons, the law of property and the law of procedure. The work dates from before the *constitutio antoniniana* (212), which abolished the separate *ius gentium*. Therefore, Gaius is the most important source of knowledge about the *ius gentium* which was different for peregrines than for full citizens. The Institutes of Gaius have been translated and republished often, but every new translation gives rise to new reasons for dissatisfaction.

Bibliography. – F. DE ZULUETA, *The Institutes of Gaius, with an English translation and commentary*, 2 vol., Oxford 1946 and W.M. GORDON and O.F. ROBINSON, *The Institutes of Gaius translated with an introduction*, London 1988. Editing and publishing Gaius was a complex process and the result is far from perfect. A chemical product was rubbed onto the original manuscript in order to make the effaced letters darker. As a consequence, the manuscript has become partly illegible. On a passage that was published incorrectly, see L. WAELKENS, 'Gaius IV,73: debet ou debetur?', *The Legal History Review 68* (2000), p. 347-356. Translations of the Institutes of Gaius are available in the main European languages.

There are three unforgettable third-century jurists who served as *praefectus praetorio* under the Severan dynasty (193-235). Citations from their works in collections of the fourth, fifth and sixth centuries ensured that they were remembered. Aemilius Papinianus (murdered in 212), who hailed from Syria or Africa, was Justinian's other favourite jurist. Some scholars claim to recognise his Latin, but it is possible that he mainly published case law. His pupils and successors Julius Ulpianus (murdered in 223) and Domitius Paulus summarised the law of the Principate in an impressive series of publications. Herennius Modestinus was a disciple of Ulpian. His works were still republished two centuries later.

Later references to their work show that the jurists of the Principate mainly published casuistry and case law. The possibility cannot be excluded that the works which circulated under the name of prefects had actually been drawn up by officials of the prefecture. The dissemination of this case law was essential to the smooth functioning of the legal systems. These authors also wrote commentaries on the Perpetual Edict. Some commented on the civil law in general. Pomponius' *Enchiridium* is said to have been a textbook. Maybe Ulpian's *Opiniones* and Paulus' *Sententiae* were textbooks as well. We hardly find any references to monographs. Paulus wrote one about military law.

B. The constitutions

When you want to fathom an ancient legal system, you have to examine the formal sources of law. These evolved considerably in the Principate. The legal pluralism characterised by the extensive role of edicts and magistrates was a thing of the past. The emperor and his administration had control over case law. The most important source of law was now the constitution, the decision of the emperor. Even in the senatorial provinces, the emperor was the successor of the consuls, censors, aediles and *pontifex maximus* and he adopted the edict of the praetors. In all of these functions, the emperor expressed himself in constitutions, of which there were four kinds: decrees, rescripts, edicts and mandates.

Decreta were the prefecture's judicial decisions on appeals against the judicial or administrative decisions of a lower official. Formally, these were imperial constitutions. The prefecture published them and guaranteed that it would apply these *decreta* in the same manner if an equal case arose in the future. Lower courts followed the precedents of higher courts. Officials followed the decisions of their superiors, who followed the governors, who in their turn tailored their decisions to those of the prefecture. Judges were not independent and could lose their position if they took self-willed actions. The prefecture – and thus also the emperor – ruled by altering or confirming the decisions of lower instances. If there were no conflicts, there was no need for law, but if there were conflicts, they were resolved in the same way throughout the entire Empire.

A second constitution was the rescript. If jurists were not certain of how the courts would respond to their constructions, they could request a ruling. Governors and judges also referred questions to the prefecture for a preliminary ruling. These questions were answered by letter. Pliny the Younger published rescripts which he had received when he was governor. Citizens had to consult the notice boards of their Forum, where their original letters were posted up with the answer written underneath. The *ualuae*, noticeboards of the prefecture, were in the *forum romanum* against the wall of the palace. Messengers passed these decisions on to correspondents and jurists published them. The administration was bound by its own rescripts. Those who were not convinced by a rescript from a lower administration could file an appeal against it. The final responsibility lay with the prefecture. Its rescripts were checked, compiled and published. They were just as authoritative as the decrees. If emperors conferred the *ius publice respondendi ex auctoritate principis* on private jurists, these jurists' opinions had the same value as rescripts. It remains unclear what the precedential value of private opinions was. Under Hadrian, the prefecture no longer complied with them.

The third form of constitution was the edict. In his capacity as a magistrate, the emperor could declare in advance how he would deal with certain cases if they were brought before him. It is said that administrative law and quite a large amount of commercial law were developed in this manner. Some scholars compare this competence to issue edicts with the early modern monarchs' competence to issue ordinances. They jump to the conclusion that the Romans also issued edicts concerning civil law. As a rule, however, nothing was decided in advance in private law. In the Early Modern Period it was also pointed out that edicts were necessary for Roman criminal law, because *nulla poena sine lege*. In Latin, however, *lex* is a normal word to indicate a legal precedent and in criminal law a lawsuit sufficed. Edicts could apparently survive the death of the emperor. It is possible that the *constitutio antoniniana* (212), by means of which Caracalla granted civil rights to all of the free inhabitants of the Empire, was an edict, but this was not necessarily the case. This constitution may also have been a decree. Despite the fact that it was clearly a decree, C.5.27.5 from the late Empire is traditionally described as an edict in which children were legitimised by their parents' marriage. Even the famous 'Edict' of Thessaloniki of 380 is obviously a decree.

A last category of constitutions were the imperial mandates which were valid within the administration. They expired when the emperor died or when the person to whom the mandate had been given left his position. Normally, they were confirmed by the new emperor in a way that was somewhat similar to the manner in which earlier magistrates adopted the edict of their predecessor. A similar confirmation of mandates is still pronounced whenever a new pope is installed in the Vatican. In the late classical legal sources we find references to mandate books which prove that in Roman law, mandates were also a source of law.

Bibliography. – On the classification of C. 5.27.5 see L. WAELKENS, 'La légitimité de C. 5,27', in B. ALTEROCHE, F. DEMOULIN-AUZARY, O. DESCAMPS, F. ROUMY (eds.), *Mélanges en l'honneur d'Anne Lefebvre-Teillard*, Paris 2009, p. 1031-1045. On the edict of Thessaloniki see L. WAELKENS, 'L'édit de Thessalonique, droit romain ancient ou ius commune?', in: S. GRODZISKI, D. MALEC, A. KARABOWICZ, M. STUS (eds.), *Vetera Novis Augere. Studia i prace dedykowane Profesorowi Wacławowi Uruszczakowi*, Cracow 2010, p. 1075-1088.

C. Classical law

In 1790 Gustav Hugo (1764-1844) called the law of the Principate classical Roman law. He considered Justinianic law to be a mere by-product thereof. Later in the nineteenth century, law dating from before the Principate was called pre-classical law, while the law of the late Empire was termed post-classical Roman law. Classical Roman law remained in vogue for a long time. It was idealised and was said to have declined during the late Empire, together with the great culture, the disappearance of which was described in Gibbon's 'Decline and Fall of the Roman Empire'. Gustav Hugo, however, did not have any sources of this classical law. Since then, we have discovered Gaius and a series of inscriptions from the classical period, like the *lex irnitana*. Many scholars, however, tested the sources of classical law against the ideals of their own legal system. The German Pandectists, who were involved with 'contemporary' Roman law, were masters of this art. Their concept of classical Roman law was perhaps useful for the liberal civil society of their time, but not really for legal history. And yet one should not underestimate the method of the Pandectists. By looking for legal historical arguments to improve society, they showed that they were good jurists. They followed the same method as Bartolus (†1357), Cujas (1522-1590) or M. Kaser (1906-1997), who started from the legal doctrine of their own time to explain Roman law and thereby improved legal thinking and legal education in a lasting way. Today, Romanists tend to opt for the historical approach towards Roman law.

In an old legal system, one does not merely look for the formal sources of the law, but also hopes to understand the substantive rules. Many nineteenth- and twentieth-century scholars tried to comprehend classical Roman law with modern legal notions and were bewildered by it. They did not come accross legislation and could not find a theoretical framework, definitions, legal logic, or Latin words for essential concepts such as competence, nullity or liability. It turned out that the Roman jurists were not interested in legal theory, legal philosophy, legal sociology or legal history. Mommsen (1817-1903) called classical Roman law an 'Unordnung'.

One does not need to look too far to find an explanation for this phenomenon. The law of the Principate was permeated with the Egyptian idea of ruling through the administration of justice. Why would the thought processes of Roman jurists correspond to our modern schemes of thought? There are so many different views on law to be discovered in legal history. Ancient Chinese law was aimed at survival in an inhospitable natural environment. In this context, the law did not pay attention to individuals, but focused on the regions' solidarity in case of natural disasters. The law served the anthill and not the individual ant. Is this an example of 'Unordnung' as well? Beware of looking for current Western standards in other times and societies.

In addition, the law of the Principate was functional. Wolfgang Kunkel (1902-1981) claimed that this was due to the fact that the Roman jurists shared the same social origins. Classical Roman law was an adjusted version of republican law. Augustus restored the civil rights and those who bring peace and affluence need little theoretical justification. However, we cannot claim that the dissemination of civil privileges and the unification of law in the great Empire were insignificant. These were original elements to which even the nineteenth century did not pay sufficient attention. And then there was the realisation of the *pax romana*, a peace that would be continually sought after in later times. Was that 'Unordnung' as well? Is peace not more orderly than the most beautiful military columns?

During the Principate, Roman law retained its focus on the resolution of conflicts. It only applied in cases of disputes and there was no law outside the courts. Unity was guaranteed by the appeal system and by the precedents of the prefecture. Judges and officials applied these. Their most important task was to deal with conflicts in such a manner that the resolution thereof could serve as a precedent. Their second duty was to issue rescripts that prevented conflicts.

D. 1.3.20-21. – Non omnium quae a maioribus constituta sunt, ratio reddi potest. Et ideo rationes eorum quae constituuntur, inquiri non oportet: alioquin multa ex his quae certa sunt subuertuntur.	Translation WATSON. – It is not possible to find an underlying reason for everything which was settled by our forebears. Accordingly, it is not right to go ferreting after the motives behind the things which are settled as law. To do otherwise is to subvert many present certainties.
D. 50.17.202. – Omnis definitio in iure ciuili periculosa est: parum est enim, ut non subuerti posset.	Translation WATSON. – Every definition in civil law is dangerous; for it is rare for the possibility not to exist of its being overthrown.

§4. The late Empire

Bibliography. – The most important reference work on the external history of post-classical Roman law is currently: F. WIEACKER, *Römische Reichsgeschichte*, II, *Die Jurisprudenz vom frühen Prinzipat bis zum Ausgang der Antike im weströmischen Reich und die oströmische Rechtswissenschaft bis zur justinianischen Gesetzgebung, Ein Fragment*, published posthumously by J.G. WOLF and others, Munich 2006. An excellent general historical sketch can be found in A. DEMANDT, *Die Spätantike Römische Geschichte von Diocletian bis Justinian, 284-565 n.C.*, Munich 1989. The *Cambridge Ancient History* makes use of a different periodisation: XII, *The Crisis of the Empire, AD 193-337*, Cambridge 2005; XIII, *The Late Empire, AD 337-425*, Cambridge 1997; XIV, *Late Antiquity: Empire and Successors, AD 425 600*, Cambridge 2001. In the pre-war edition of the *Cambridge Ancient History*, antiquity ended in 425, when the Middle Ages began. The military and political history of Justinian as described in E. STEIN, *Histoire du Bas-Empire*, II, *La disparition de l'Empire d'occident à la mort de Justinien (476-565)*, Paris-Brussels 1949 should cause the reader to lie awake for at least one night before the age of twenty-five.

The murder of Alexander Severus in 235 was the beginning of a period of political instability and military coups, although the administration guaranteed the continuity of daily government. Every now and then, agriculture, trade and industry were hampered by unsafe circumstances or armies that went on the rampage, but the Empire remained relatively prosperous. In 284 Diocletian was proclaimed emperor by his soldiers in Asia Minor. From Nicomedia, he managed to establish his power over the entire realm and to restore the Empire as a unity. Many historians call the period from 284 onwards the Dominate, because they believe that the emperor was as dominant as an eastern despot. In reality, however, he was still called *dominus* because the governmental machinery was his *dominium*.

The Romantics deplored the late Empire as a time of decline. However, life in the Empire was far from miserable. It became a favoured destination for migrants. The stone constructions of this period are extremely impressive and Latin literature reached new heights with authors such as Lactantius (ca. 250-325), Ammianus Marcellinus (ca. 330 - after 392), Ambrosius (340-395), Augustine (354-430), Cassiodorus (ca. 490-ca. 585) or Boethius (480-525).

Some Romanists mention the vulgarisation of Roman law in the late Empire. German scholars looked for the cause of this alleged decline in the law. They found it in the infertility of civilised men (Spengler), falling standards due to a lack of great personalities (Levy), provincialism and the popularisation of ideas (Wieacker), brutality and coarsening (Coing), vulgar emperors (Stühff)... Roman law was said to have been hard hit by the vulgar influence of Hellenism, Christianity and rural jurists. Although these authors would get into trouble today for such claims, some distinguished Romanists continue to express their views. The practical examples which they quote do not stand up to scrutiny. They claim that classical law was contaminated by ethical thinking and equity, even though these two notions only began to permeate Roman law in the seventeenth century, at which time no one took umbrage at their presence. They also allege that the distinctions between ownership and possession, and between ownership and *in rem* rights derived from ownership became blurred. Ownership, however, only originated from the thirteenth century onwards, while *in rem* rights that derive from it date from the seventeenth century. Let us just forget about this vulgar Roman law. It is a theory that was brought about by the romantic views of decline. In the nineteenth century notions of civil law were projected onto the 'classical' Roman law of the Republic and the early Empire. If it then turned out that these notions could not be found in the legal sources of late classical law, this had to be due to a decline. Perhaps a better conclusion is that nineteenth-century civil law did not exist in the 'classical period'. The late Empire may seem dreary to those who dream of an ideal Republic, but for the development of Roman law it was an extremely interesting period.

Below, we will stress four important elements of the Roman law of this period: Diocletian and the Tetrarchy, the fourth century and Christianity, the legal texts of the fourth and fifth centuries, and the Justinianic collection.

1. The era of Diocletian

A. The Tetrarchy

In 284 emperor Diocletian assumed power. He changed the institutions and split the Empire into two parts, each of which had its own administration, its own revenues, its own domestic and foreign policy and its own armies. The language of the Eastern Empire was Greek; that of the Western Empire was Latin. The Western economy, which was characterised by *latifundia* and a small number of cultural metropolises was very different from the Eastern urbanised world. Because the main hotbeds of unrest were in the East, Diocletian took up residence as emperor (*augustus*) in Nicomedia, a city by the Sea of Marmara that is currently known as Izmit. He appointed Maximian as his fellow emperor (*augustus iunior*) in Milan. Each emperor had one consul. In 293 Diocletian established the Tetrarchy. Each of the two parts of the Empire was again split administratively and two vice-emperors (*caesares*) were installed: one in Trier and one in Sirmium. The Tetrarchy had a hierarchical structure (*augustus senior, augustus iunior, caesar senior* and *caesar iunior*). When one of these disappeared, the others would rise to the next rank and co-opt a new *caesar iunior.* Every tetrarch had his own legions.

In his own reform Diocletian strove for a more speedy administration of justice. The distance between citizens and governors on the one hand and the imperial court on the other had to be reduced. He also desired that prefects be more attuned to legal life. Therefore, every tetrarch was given his own prefecture with a *praefectus praetorio.* The prefectures were divided into dioceses, which in their turn consisted of provinces. Having four prefectures did entail risks: their case law could begin to differ and the single market could disappear. For this reason, Diocletian built a chancellery in Nicomedia which supervised the unity of the case law of the supreme courts. The language of this chancellery was Latin. The chancellor (*magister officiorum*), whose council of state was the *consistorium,* became the most important official. A central treasurer was installed as well (*comes sacrarum largitionum*). Many historians portray Diocletian as a potentate, but he was first and foremost a military man. When restoring the institutions, he emphasised the importance of absolute respect for the Roman order. He opposed the Christians, because they put the majesty of their God above the majesty of the emperor. 'Lèse majesté' was punishable by death. This was not new, but history has not forgiven Diocletian for having been the last emperor who persecuted Christians.

After Diocletian's abdication in 305 the tetrarchs succeeded each other in a regular manner until 310, when the new *caesar iunior* Constantine seized power. Diocletian, who was still alive, thus witnessed the end of his Tetrarchy.

B. Roman law under Diocletian

Because the chancellery coordinated the administration of justice of the prefectures, many collections of case law were disseminated and kept in archives. This increased the chance of documents being preserved. There are only a few direct sources from this period, but the major collections of the fifth and sixth century were compiled on the basis of the judicial archives of Diocletian and his successors.

Numerous constitutions of Diocletian and Maximian concern judicial procedure and, in particular, appeals. The prefectures referred questions for preliminary ruling to the chancellery, which answered in rescripts. In addition, Diocletian gave persons seeking justice the possibility of requesting the review of a prefecture's decision by means of a supplication to the chancellery. These supplications are the precursors of our petitions for pardon. It cannot be excluded that this remedy was used to rectify the divergent case law of a prefecture.

Diocletian restored imperial control of the corn trade and adopted economic measures. He imposed a single currency and attempted to combat inflation, but his edict on prices was no more effective than the South-American edicts on prices of the twentieth century. Nevertheless, the Roman Empire seems to have been relatively affluent in the early fourth century.

A relatively large corpus of legal literature from this time has been preserved. Some Romanists point out that we do not know any great jurists from this period, while we do know the names of some of the older classical jurists. It is possible, however, that the third-century collections of precedents which were published under the name of Ulpian or Papinian were not written by these jurists. It is possible that they merely ordered their prefecture to draw up these collections. Because in the Tetrarchy there were four prefectures and a chancellor, it is more difficult to attach a name to the publications. Under Diocletian, two new collections of case law were compiled on the basis of the chancellery's archives. The Gregorian Code must have been published in 291. It consisted of fourteen books, each of which contained decisions in chronological order. The Hermogenian Code was probably published in 295 and then revised on several occasions. It contained constitutions of Diocletian and Maximian that were issued after 291. Both of these collections were lost, but were still known from other sources. Ulpian's commentary on the Perpetual Edict and on Sabinus were republished in this period, apparently with more recent authors' glosses and additions. A mutilated version of Papinian's *Responsa* was still being used in legal education. A constitution of Constantine, sent to the *praefectus urbi* in 321, states that courts could no longer use it because it was too unreliable. In Egypt, the *Responsa* would be in circulation for a long time. Around 300 an anonymous jurist also wrote an epitome of sentences attributed to Paulus. A fragment thereof is preserved in Leyden. These *Sententiae Pauli* were emended in the West until circa 450. They were used often in the administration of justice after the fall of the Western Empire in 476, and were copied and read until well into the Middle Ages.

Bibliography. – There is an English translation of the *Sententiae Pauli* by S.P. Scott, *The opinions of Paulus*, Cincinnati 1932 (reprint New York 1973).

2. The fourth century and Christianity

In 305 Constantius Chlorus (ca. 250-306) succeeded Diocletian. In 310 a war of succession broke out. Its victor was Constantius' son Constantine, who then became emperor from 312 until 337. His main fellow emperor was Licinius. In 325 Constantinople became the second capital of the Empire: it was equal to Rome and had its own *praefectus urbi* and *annona*. Under Constantine the Occident and the Levant grew further apart. Both realms would only be reunited for a short time under Theodosius I (379-395).

A. Constantine the Great

According to the Christian authors, Constantine furthered Christianity because he owed his victory by the Ponte Milvio to divine intervention. Together with his fellow emperor Licinius he decided in the Edict of Milan (313) that they would henceforth collaborate with the Christian bishops who had gradually built up considerable societal influence. It is an anachronism to write that Constantine acknowledged the Church, because the idea of a unified Church dates from the eleventh century. He did respond to the administration of justice of the bishops. In accordance with the Jewish tradition, Christians brought their conflicts before their spiritual leaders. In some regions the bishops' judicial activities had become more important than those of the imperial judges. Constantine could not ignore them, as the administration of justice was the primary way of ruling in this era. His acknowledgement of the bishops led to constitutions of 318 and 333 that concerned their jurisdiction. The decisions of the bishops were acknowledged, but their power to execute these judgements was not. If a summons or enforcement was necessary, the bishops had to ask the imperial administration for an exequatur, which would be executed by the imperial bailiffs (*exsecutores*). Injured parties could lodge an appeal against the exequatur of the imperial judges. As a consequence, the prefectures had to assess proceedings that had been instituted with the bishops. They could not reverse decisions, but they could judge the competence of the bishop involved. After all, there were many individuals who felt that it was incumbent on them to pronounce judgements which would be executed by the administration. The prefectures decided in a constitution whether a such an individual was a Christian bishop who came under the measure of Constantine or not. In addition, the prefectures checked whether the episcopal judgement that was invoked was incontestable. In order to determine this, they checked the procedure that the bishop had followed. These judgements concerning competence and procedure, which were expressed in imperial constitutions, lie at the basis of historians' belief that the emperors concerned themselves with theology.

It seems that, apart from acknowledging the episcopal administration of justice, Constantine also valued the social works of the Christians. He donated the expropriated Lateran domain to the *corpus christianorum*. It still accommodates the bishopric of Rome. In the Middle Ages the transfer of this domain in the 'Donation of Constantine' was associated with a transfer of legal power to the bishop of Rome.

After Constantine's rule many more imperial judgements concerning the ecclesiastical administration of justice would be pronounced. Some famous ones were the Edict of Thessaloniki (380) under Theodosius, the equalisation of rabbinical and Christian administration of justice under Arcadius and Honorius (C. 1.9.8 of 398), and Novella 35 (452) under Valentinian III (419-455). The latter text entailed a strict curtailment of the competence of the ecclesiastical courts, but in the Middle Ages its first paragraph would be taken to mean that Valentinian III made the episcopal audiences exclusively competent *ratione personae* with regard to cases involving the clergy and *ratione materiae* with regard to conflicts concerning religious matters.

B. Theodosius the Great

Theodosius I the Great (379-395, from Spanish Galicia) was one of the most renowned Roman emperors. He owes his reputation to the Milanese bishop Ambrose, who mentions in-depth discussions with Theodosius in his works. Under Theodosius the Empire was briefly reunited.

All school books state that in 380 Theodosius decided in the Edict of Thessaloniki that Christianity would be the official Roman religion. It is said that this decision can be found in C. 1.1.1, the first text of Justinian's *Corpus iuris*. Recent biographies of Theodosius, however, show that he was not a Christian. After 380 he still appointed the notoriously antichristian Tatianus as *praefectus praetorio* and the equally intolerant Symmachus as *praefectus urbi*. From the point of view of legal history, the matter is even more problematical: edicts could not impose beliefs. According to the Digest, no one had to tolerate that judgement was passed on his beliefs or opinions (D. 48.19.18). The main reason to doubt the postulate of an official Roman religion is that the traditional interpretation of the Edict of Thessaloniki can be read in all of the translations of C. 1.1.1, but not in the Latin text itself. The original text deals with the granting of an exequatur. The chancellery refused to grant an exequatur for the decisions of monophysite bishops. This tallied with the policy of attempting to reunite the East and the West (*cunctos populos*). All of the Western and many of the Eastern bishops were anti-monophysites. In its decision the chancellery determined how one could recognise orthodox bishops, who could be granted an exequatur: they believed in the Trinity and followed the apostle Peter. However, in the *Collectio tripartita graeca* the medieval jurists found an argument that the Code of Justinian used to begin with the text *Cunctis* (sic) which condemned heresy. They thought they found it in CTh. 16.1.2. For this reason, this text was inserted into the Code of Justinian in the twelfth century. This decision was never reconsidered. The interpretation that Theodosius the Great imposed Christianity on his realm dates back to the same century and was never revised either.

The text of the Edict of Thessaloniki can be found in the Theodosian Code 16.1.2 and in the Justinian Code 1.1.1. It is corrupt.

C. 1.1.2. – *Imppp. Gratianus, Valentinianus, Theodosius ad populum urbis Constantinopolae.* Cunctos populos, quos clementiae nostrae regit temperamentum, in tali uolumus religione uersari, quam diuinum Petrum apostulum tradidisse Romanis religio usque ad nunc ab ipso insinuata declarat quamque pontificem Damasum sequi claret et Petrum Alexandriae episcopum uirum apostolicae sanctitatis, hoc est ut secundum apostolicam disciplinam euangelicamque doctrinam Patris et Filii et Spiritus Sancti unam Deitatem sub pari maiestate et sub pia Trinitate credamus. Hanc legem sequentes christianorum catholicorum nomen iubemus amplecti, reliquos uero dementes uesanosque iudicantes haeretici dogmatis infamiam sustinere, diuina primum uindicta, post etiam motus nostri, quem ex caelesti arbitrio sumpserimus, ultione plectendos.

Traditional translation, taken from C. PHARR, *The Theodosian Code and Novels and the Sirmondian Constitutions, A translation with commentary, glossary and bibliography,* Princeton 1952 (reprint New York 1969), p. 440; cf. F.H. BLUME, *Annotated Justinian code,* 2nd ed. by T. KEARLY, published on the internet. – It is our will that all the peoples of our clemency shall practice that religion which the divine Peter the Apostle transmitted to the Romans, as the religion which he introduced makes clear even unto this day. It is evident that this is the religion that is followed by the pontiff Damasus and by Peter, Bishop of Alexandria, a man of apostolic sanctity; that is, according to the apostolic discipline and the evangelical doctrine, we shall believe in the single Deity of the Father, the Son and the Holy Spirit, under the concept of equal majesty and of the Holy Trinity. 1. We command that those persons who follow this rule shall embrace the name of Catholic Christians. The rest, however, whom we adjudge demented or insane, shall sustain the infamy of heretical dogmas, their meeting places shall not receive the name of churches and they shall be smitten first by divine vengeance and secondly by the retribution of our own initiative, which we shall assume in accordance with the divine judgment.

Our translation, however, is:

Cunctos populos, quos clementiae nostrae regit temperamentum, in tali uolumus religione uersari, quam diuinum Petrum apostulum tradidisse Romanis religio usque ad nunc ab ipso insinuata declarat quamque pontificem Damasum sequi claret et Petrum Alexandriae episcopum uirum apostolicae sanctitatis, hoc est ut secundum apostolicam disciplinam euangelicamque doctrinam Patris et Filii et Spiritus Sancti unam Deitatem sub pari maiestate et sub pia Trinitate credamus. Hanc legem sequentes christianorum catholicorum nomen iubemus amplecti, reliquos uero dementes uesanosque iudicantes haeretici dogmatis infamiam sustinere, diuina primum uindicta, post etiam motus nostri, quem ex caelesti arbitrio sumpserimus, ultione plectendos.

We desire that the joint peoples which this measure governs be versed in this religion concerning which [he] declares that the apostle Peter has transmitted it to the Romans [...] a religion preserved since the latter until the present [...] and of which he will render clear that the pontiff Damasus follows it as well as Peter of Alexandria, a man declared apostolic [...] this means so that we believe according to the apostolic discipline and the evangelical doctrine in the divine unity of the Father, the Son and the Holy Spirit under an equal majesty and under an inviolable trinity. We decree that those who follow this decision embrace the name of Catholic Christians, that all of the others, those who deny and the least healthy, when they pronounce sentences, tolerate the non-executability related to the heretical doctrine [that their forums do not receive the title of churches], that they must first submit themselves to our sovereign justice and then to the sanction of our sympathy, that we have found in this celestial arbitration.

See L. Waelkens, 'L'hérésie des premiers titres du Code de Justinien, Une hypothèse sur la rédaction tardive de C. 1,1-13', *The Legal History Review* 79 (2011), p. 253-296.

C. Roman law and Christianity

From the first century onwards, Roman culture was influenced by Christianity. Henceforth we find the mixture of *romanitas* and *christianitas* that would lead to the *latinitas* which we observe in the early Middle Ages, when both components could no longer be easily separated from one another. We know the works of the fourth-century Latin 'church fathers', Roman theologians who would prove to be of lasting importance to Christianity. Christians were no longer persecuted and their lifestyle was valued for its peaceable character. They projected religious elements onto Roman terms and symbols. In 382 emperor Gratian renounced his title of *pontifex maximus* because the Christians used that title for their pope. In addition, he had the altar of the *libertas* removed from the Senate. According to church historians, this was a token of tolerance towards the Christians, but it can also be interpreted as a sign that emperor Gratian preferred to see Christian symbols disappear from the governmental sphere. In either case, it is a sign of pressure from the *christianitas*.

Exactly how Christian Roman law was, or to what extent it was influenced by Christianity, is far less clear. In the fifth century the Romans relied on both the bishops and the imperial institutions to perpetuate their culture. After the fall of the Western

Empire in 476 the urban institutions of Rome were taken over by the bishop. Gregory the Great, who was elected pope in 590, had served as *praefectus urbi* in the past. One of his great concerns when he was pope was the administration of justice. When the Latin and orthodox bishops began to grow apart, one can also see how they were associated with Western and Eastern institutions, respectively.

There are studies about the influence of Christianity on Roman law, but it remains unclear which of the elements that went into the mix were originally Roman and originally Christian. Among the legal texts that were inspired by Christianity, scholars mention constitutions about the episcopal administration of justice and heresy; the bans on gladiatorial games and the branding of slaves; and case law that made it more difficult to conclude a second *matrimonium*, combated the exclusion of children or curbed prostitution... *Cum hoc ergo propter hoc*? Is it not possible that the Christians borrowed these elements from the Romans? We cannot measure the contributions of Christian jurists to case law. Some scholars claim that Papinian was a Christian, but this is known only unto God. It would take an enormous amount of research to first filter the Christian tradition that was adopted at that time in both the East and the West out of the Roman culture and then examine what is left. It was not only the fourth-century church fathers who mixed *romanitas* and *christianitas*. So did later theologians. It may even be impossible to split the Latin molecules into Roman and Christian atoms.

Bibliography. – We rate the following works among the most interesting studies of Christian Roman law: J. GAUDEMET, *L'Eglise dans l'Empire romain (IVe-Ve siècles)*, [Histoire du droit et des institutions de l'Eglise en Occident, 3,] Paris [1958]; B. BIONDI, *Il diritto romano cristiano*, 3 vol., Milan 1952-1954; A. BARZANO, *Il cristianesimo nelle leggi di Roma imperiale*, [Letture cristiane del primo millenio, 24,] Milan 1996; E. DOVERE, *Ius principale e catholica lex (V secolo)*, Naples 1999; P.R. COLEMAN-NORTON, *Roman state and Christian church, a collection of legal documents to AD 535*, 3 vol., London 1966.

Because of the larger number of sources, it is easier to determine the reverse influence, namely that of Roman law on Christianity. The first bishops proclaimed a strong message and were proselytes. However, they were not organised. It was Roman law which provided them with a model for their organisation. At the end of the fourth century the Christians had a territorial organisation with dioceses and vicariates, a decentralised administration of justice and a central organisation with prefects, a curia, and a consistory. It is striking to see that even today the Church is still so strongly marked by the Roman model. Consider, for example, canonical principles such as 'the law only applies in case of conflict' or 'any decision in the ecclesiastical administration emanates from the pope'. These principles are as old as the Roman statues in the museums of the Vatican. An admission card for the Vatican is called a *tessera*, just like the terracotta shards which people who entered the Roman Empire received at the border; the Vatican shop that sells food is called *annona*, like the imperial distribution of corn. This influence of Roman law not only concerned the organisation of the Church, but also the Christian doctrine. Law was the logic of Rome and also permeated the approach of the Latin bishops. Do not be surprised that Christian theology and moral philosophy sometimes have a slightly legal ring. This influence of Roman law can be seen clearly in the works of the Latin church fathers.

Tertullian (born circa 160), who does not perhaps happen to be the jurist Tertullian from the Digest, often uses legal terms with a non-legal meaning: *ius, persona, auctor, postestas, praescriptio, sacramentum...* Nevertheless, it is clear that he knew the law. He contrasts law and morality, for instance when he treats the separation of spouses, and attributes the prerogatives of the *pater familias* to God. The Christians were an association under Roman law, a *corpus* under the management of a *curia*. Tertullian was also the first person to compare the relation between a sinner and the Redeemer to that between a debtor and a creditor.

Cyprian (bishop of Carthage 248/9-258) discussed the divine *lex*, the *mandata* and *praecepta* of the Lord, the *traditio* of faith, the *crimen* and *delictum* of the sinner, the rich *possessor*... He compared the office of a bishop to that of a magistrate. Together, all of the bishops formed a *collegium* and were jointly liable for their actions.

Lactantius († after 326) was a courtier of Diocletian and Constantine. He modelled his *institutiones divinae* on the jurists' institutes. It was the first Latin handbook about Christian theology and morality. In this work, Lactantius used many legal terms and gave them new meanings, stating, for example, that God is *pater ac dominus* (father and *paterfamilias*). He also cited Ulpian and various constitutions concerning the rights of Christians. In his ethics, he emphasised *ius humanitatis, aequitas*, and wrote that people were *liberi* – children as well as equal and free people – vis-à-vis God.

Ambrose (Trier 339 – Milan 397), a jurist and son of a *praefectus praetorio*, was the governor of Liguria before he became the bishop of Milan. He worked in the imperial administration for a long time and later, as a bishop, thought about the development of Christianity in administrative terms. Councils concerning doctrinal points had to be conducted like trials with a precise complaint, interrogations, and, finally, a decision that had to be respected. He reasoned about theological problems in a legal manner. For example: "Can someone who broke off a first matrimonial relationship before his baptism remarry? – No, because baptism relieves someone of his sins, but not of a legal bond." His writings feature many legal terms, but it is pleasant to see how he has mastered them. According to him, we have obligations and debts towards God. He was attached to the *res publica romana* and was resolutely anti-barbarian, but God took precedence over both the Empire and the family. The emperor was not above Christian society; he was a member of it. The ancient *iustitia quae suum cuique tribuit* was an ideal for Christians as well.

The unknown author of the Ambrosiaster (Rome, between 366 and 384) was the first to use the term *ius ecclesiasticum*. He continually referred to institutions and civil law and tried to demonstrate the functioning of the community of Christians and their role in society by means of Roman law. For example: a bishop could ordain priests because his appointment entailed a delegation of the power to ordain. The author of the *Ambrosiaster* was the first to formulate the *priuilegium Paulinum*, the possibility for Christians to divorce a partner who refused to be baptised.

Jerome (Italy 345 – Bethlehem 419/420) was a jurist, but one who was so inspired by his faith that he wanted to be close to the sacred places and moved to Bethlehem. He is mainly known for his Latin translation of the Bible, the Vulgate. In his works, he used legal terminology. He cited technical legal terms, had a thorough knowledge of procedure and was interested in legal history. He tried to unearth the ethical dimension of law and stressed the evaluation of intention in criminal law. Furthermore, he distinguished between imperial and Christian norms. He applied an entire series of legal notions, like *auctoritas, debitum* or *Christi sponsae* to Christian life. The translation of the Bible which he made at the request of pope Damasus had a considerable impact on Latin Christianity. His legal thinking played a role in the translation process, for instance when he translated the Biblical judicial longsuffering (in Greek *epieikeia*) as the *aequitas* with which the prefecture at that time justified that equal cases had to receive equal treatment. In passages about relationships between two people he shows himself to have been a jurist who clearly distinguished the notions *coniugium* (cohabitation), *nuptiae* (wedding) and *matrimonium* (high-quality relationship), which would become synonyms in the Middle Ages. By applying these Roman notions to Biblical relationships, he influenced their meaning.

Augustine (Thagaste 354 – Hippo 430) was without a doubt the greatest Latin author. Reciting his work amidst Roman ruins, hearing the echoes of his message bounce off ancient walls and seeing the evening light change colour because of his message is the greatest experience on earth. For jurists, however, he can sound as harrowing as a screeching violin. Just like his master Ambrose, Augustine used legal terminology in his theological works. However, he did not respect their meaning. He expressed the relations between God and his people by means of legal notions: *chirographum*, pledge, promissory note, will and donation express this relationship, as do *pater, potestas*, domestic peace... On earth, people live as God's tenants, not as owners. People only have the use of things. Salaries, fees and rent money are surprising notions in theological treatises. *Bona fides*, equity, a supplication to God... Augustine continually transplanted such notions to his spiritual exercises. The *res publica* and *iustitia* would only be achieved in the kingdom of God... Augustine stressed the difference between Roman law and Christian morality, between the law of the court and that of heaven, but in doing so he actually transported Roman law into heaven.

The works of the Latin church fathers illustrate how the fusion of Roman law and Christianity progressed and how the Latin bishops were influenced by legal thought.

Bibliography. – J. GAUDEMET, *Le droit romain dans la literature chrétienne occidentale du IIIe au Ve siècle*, [Ius Romanum Medii Aevi I, 3, b], Milan 1978.

3. Legal texts from the fourth and fifth centuries

A. Old witnesses

Only a few manuscripts of Roman law from the fourth century have survived. The most important ones are the Vatican fragments. When the Institutes of Gaius were discovered in Verona, the Vatican's librarian, Angelo Mai, wanted to prove that his collections also held such treasures of Roman law. After a brief search he discovered three hundred and forty one excerpts from old constitutions and classical jurists in a palimpsest of Cassiodorus. They were published in 1821. Each fragment was accompanied by an *inscriptio* with a reference to an emperor or jurist. The excerpts were classified according to their subject: sale, usufruct, dowry, etc. The Vatican fragments were probably compiled between 318 and 324.

Another Vatican manuscript contained a *liber singularis regularum*, a relatively shoddy work from the 20s of the fourth century which was once attributed to Ulpian.

The *Collatio legum mosaicarum et romanarum*, a compilation which has been preserved in three manuscripts, also dates from the beginning of the fourth century. This work systematically compares extracts from the Septuagint that contain the norms of Moses with the decisions of five classical jurists, namely Gaius, Ulpian, Paulus, Papinian and Modestinus as well as with constitutions from the Gregorian and Hermogenian Codes and some constitutions of emperor Licinius (308-324). The latter are very rare, because Licinius was banished from collective memory in 324. The author of the *Collatio* must have been a Jewish jurist in Rome. In the West, the *Collatio* remained known.

The Vatican fragments and the *Collatio* are important sources of doublets. If we compare them to the Justinian *Corpus Iuris*, we often find that these two sources contain different versions of the same texts. By comparing these, we gain a clearer image of the history of the classical sources of law.

Another text that dates from around 400 concerns the *epitome Gai*. An *epitome* is an abridged version of a legal text or a complete work. In this case, it is an adaptation of fragments from the Institutes of Gaius. In the Middle Ages, we find this *epitome* as an appendix to the *lex romana wisigothorum*. It was widely diffused. Furthermore, a piece from a Gallic version of Gaius was found in a palimpsest in Autun. We also have a book featuring interpretations of the Sentences of Paulus and some scattered loose fragments containing citations from the classical compilations.

B. The Theodosian Code

The Theodosian Code, a work of enormous importance to Roman law, appeared in 438. Theodosius II (402-450, emperor of the East) wanted to republish all of the compilations that were being used in his courts because they were continuously confronted with unreliable precedents and because he found that the case law of the East and that of the West were diverging from one another. He not only wanted to republish the case law, but also the works of the classical jurists. A first initiative was the Law of Citations which was promulgated in the Eastern and the Western Empire in 426. Until further notice, courts would only be bound by the writings of Papinian, Ulpian, Paulus, Gaius and Modestinus. The other classical jurists lost their authority, unless they were cited by these five jurists. If these five contradicted each other, the judge had to follow the opinion of the majority; in a case where the votes were equal, Papinian was the jurist to be followed; if the latter remained silent on the matter, the judge was free. Some Romanists see this as an acknowledgement of the moral authority of these authors, but it is mainly an appreciation of the quality of the editions of their works in the 430s. All of the other jurists' works had to be republished. In 427 a commission started working on the project, but in 435 ambitions were scaled down drastically. The constitutions would be republished first. The re-publications of the compilations of precedents under the name of classical jurists would take longer than originally planned. Eventually, this project was only completed around 900 in Constantinople, in the Basilica. It may well be that the Law of Citations caused many works to be lost because they could no longer be invoked in the courts. Maybe these lost publications were the best juridical texts: the finest sources are often the ones that are adapted most frequently. The commission found out that even revising the constitutions was not a sinecure. In 435, it decided to limit itself to the constitutions since Constantine, which were preserved in the chancellery. Rescripts to private persons were no longer included. In 438 the Theodosian Code was published in the East. It was also sent to Valentinian III, the emperor of the West. It became binding in both empires on 1 January 439 and consisted of sixteen books, which were subdivided into titles. Each constitution mentioned the date and place of the decision and the emperor associated with it. In 447 Theodosius II sent a series of new constitutions to the West with a request to add them to the Code. Valentinian III added some new Western decisions to it. Both of these sets of additions were published together in 448 as the *novellae constitutiones*.

The Theodosian Code was an important document, which was disseminated in both of the empires. The Western Empire disintegrated thirty-eight years later. Until the eleventh century the Code remained the most important source of knowledge of Roman law in the West. Initially, it was actively used by the prefectures of the new kingdoms. Afterwards, the bishops cherished it because they found an enumeration of their rights in book 16. Texts of the Theodosian Code were often reproduced in the decrees of episcopal councils. The Code is cited in episcopal collections until the ninth century. From then on it lost its authority as the Justinianic Roman law permeated the West. In the East the Theodosian Code preserved its authority only until 529, when it was replaced by the Code of Justinian.

The compilation of the first edition of the Code was a complex process, but so was the production of modern editions of the text. In the East not a single copy was preserved. In the West only a few survived the transliteration. It was only in the sixteenth century that the search for manuscripts of the Theodosian Code began. In 1517 Pieter Gillis published a manuscript in Leuven that came from a Carolingian chancellery and which contained a series of constitutions and summaries of constitutions from books 9 to 16. In the same century there were editions by Sicard, Cujas and Pithou; the nineteenth century saw editions by Beck, Haenel and Mommsen. The main sources of these editions were the three hundred eighty-six constitutions of the Theodosian Code which had been adopted into the *lex romana wisigothorum* (see below) at the beginning of the sixth century, some sixth-century Vatican fragments and a Parisian manuscript that dated from the fifth or sixth century. In the seventeenth century Sirmond discovered a collection of constitutions by means of which he corrected the edition of the Theodosian Code. Additional fragments which had surfaced here and there in collections of manuscripts were included in nineteenth-century editions. Mommsen suspects that a fifth of the original code has been handed down.

Today the Theodosian Code is still an important source of the Roman law of Antiquity. The texts are longer than those in the Justinianic Code and the Theodosian Code contains more commercial law. Its study is a complex affair. Despite all of the work done by the publishers, there is not a single text in books 1 to 15 that can be read easily. Book 16 is different: most of its texts are comprehensible. One is inclined to think that the Code was copied for centuries solely for that final book about the rights of the bishops. But was this last book preserved better because of its contents or was it rewritten by episcopal chancelleries? A funny phenomenon concerning the study of this work is that all scholars find it difficult, but bravely hide their lack of understanding and accept mysterious interpretations. The translations of the Theodosian Code rely on the omertà of the reader who does not admit that he does not understand the texts. Many texts deal with tax law and social security, branches of law which were rather unpopular in the nineteenth century, and this is conducive to the construction of myths and dogmas which did not exist in the Roman law of the fifth century. Historians see a coercive economic system in the Theodosian Code, which is not reflected in any way in the sixth-century law of obligations which we know from the Justinianic collections.

Bibliography. – The Theodosian Code and the Novels of Theodosius and Valentinian III were most recently published by MOMMSEN, KRÜGER AND MEYER, *Codex Theodosianus*, I, *Theodosiani libri XVI cum constitutionibus Sirmondinis edidit adsumpto apparatu P. Kruegeri TH. Mommsen*; I, 1, *Prolegomena*; I, 2, *Textus cum apparatu*; II, *Leges novellae ad Theodosianum pertinentes edidit adiutore TH Mommseno Paulus M. Meyer*, Hildesheim 1990. An English translation was produced by C. PHARR, *The Theodosian Code and Novels and the Sirmondian Constitutions, A translation with commentary, glossary and bibliography*, Princeton 1952 (reprint New York 1969). Although often mysterious, this translation is impressive. Pharr respects the history of the text's interpretation and undertakes creative attempts at shedding light on hermetic passages. A French translation is currently being made under the leadership of S. Crogiez-Pétrequin and P. Jaillette. The best work about the external history of the Code is A.J.B SIRKS, *The Theodosian Code, A study*, Friedrichsdorf 2007.

Text. – An example of such an incomprehensible passage in CTh. 14.3.12 (370):

Secundum parentis nostri Constantini diuale praeceptum omnibus lustris pistores ex officio, quod ei corpori constat addictum, ad urbem sacratissimam destinentur. In quo illud conuenit praecaueri, ne quis hanc, quae personalis est, functionem pretio putet esse taxandam. Veniant suo tempore, quos causa constringit et ita ueniant, ut eos officium, quod tibi paret, pistorum patronis adque annonae prefectus apud publica monumenta consignet. Quod si quis iudicium statuto tempore personam, quae est destinanda, non miserit, ipse profecto remanebit obnoxius functioni, cui subtraxisse probatur obnoxium. In officium quoque poena competens exeretur, quod aut dissimulatione neglexerit aut fraude subtraxerit iudicem suum super ui legis et consuetudinis admonere.

Translation by Pharr. – According to the sacred Imperial regulations of Our ancestor, Constantine, breadmakers shall be dispatched every *lustrum* to the most sacred City, from the office which appears to be assigned to that guild. In the performance of this task precautions shall be taken that no person may consider that his compulsory service, which is one that is incumbent on persons, may be estimated at a price. As due reason constrains them, they shall come at their appointed time, and they shall so come as the office staff which serves you assigns them to the patrons of the breadmakers and the prefect of the *annona*. But if any judge at the statutory time should not dispatch the person who has been destined for that purpose, he shall immediately become and remain obligated to the compulsory public service from which he is proved to have withdrawn the person who was obligated. Also upon his office staff an adequate punishment shall be inflicted, because either by their connivance they neglected or by their fraud they omitted to admonish their judge about the force of the law and the custom.

According to the historians, Diocletianus decided that the sons of artisans had to continue the profession of their fathers. Bakers were especially sought after because allegedly there were too few of them for the *annona*. It is said that the above text contains an imperial decision about the recruitment of bakers. The prefect of Africa had to ship a bevy of bakers to Rome every five years. These would then be forced to work in the Roman bakeries. This is nonsense. In CTh. 14.3.1 we read that incompetent bakers lost their status. If this status was really that bad, it could not have been difficult for a baker to show that he was incompetent. In reality those who baked bread for the *annona* were exempt from certain taxes. The prefect of the *annona* issued the certificates of exemption but remained vigilant. In CTh. 14.3.12 one can (try to) read what happened to people who were registered in Africa in the tax lists (*lustra*) as exempted artisans before they emigrated to Rome but never turned up in the capital. See L. WAELKENS, 'La liberté économique dans le droit romain du Bas-Empire, Réflexions sur le statut des boulangeries conventionnées d'après le code de Théodosien', in: H. VAN GOETHEM, L. WAELKENS and K. BREUGELMANS (eds.), *Libertés, pluralisme et droit, Une approche historique*, Brussels 1995, p. 53-60.

4. Justinianic law

In 476 the Western Empire disintegrated. The Eastern Empire survived until 1453. The evolution of Roman law in the East does not fall within the scope of this book. Works that would never reach the West were already circulating in the Eastern Empire in the fifth century, for example the *Scholia sinaïtica,* a law book that was found in the monastery of Saint Catherine on the Sinai peninsula, or the Syrian-Roman law book of which a version was published in 1862 on the basis of Syrian, Armenian and Arabic manuscripts of the thirteenth century which all stemmed from a Greek model of 476-477. Nevertheless we will travel to the East to examine the law of Justinian because this law would become of paramount importance for Western Europe in the Middle Ages.

Bibliography. – The *Scholia sinaïtica* were translated into French by J. DE MALAFOSSE, in: P.F. GIRARD and F. SENN, *Textes de droit romain*, I, Paris 1967, p. 591-604.

Justinian was born in Illyria in 482 and died in Constantinople in 565. In the church of San Vitale in Ravenna a mosaic with his portrait has been preserved. He made a career for himself in the army under the protection of his uncle, who became the emperor Justin. In 527 he was called to Constantinople to become co-emperor. In the same year, he succeeded Justin. As emperor, Justinian wanted to restore the unified Empire around the Mediterranean. His means to attain this goal were weapons, law and unprecedented brutality. His generals Narses and Belisarius reconquered large parts of the Western Empire, but at a ridiculously high price. In North Africa, the largest part of the Latin civilisation was destroyed together with the Vandals. In Spain and Italy the war began in 535. When Justinian brought Italy into subjection in 554 with the help of the Lombards, ten per cent of the population had perished. After Justinian's death the country could no longer defend itself against the Lombards, who conquered it for themselves. Justinian also resolved theological issues with violence, and used force against, for example, the monophysites.

Justinian decided to bring Theodosian's failed project concerning law books to a favourable conclusion. He would compile a definitive version of both the constitutions and the authoritative texts of the classical jurists. The law schools of Cesarea and Alexandria, which deemed this project unrealistic, were closed. Subsequently, those of Beirut and Constantinople sent jurists to the chancellery. Under the leadership of chancellor Tribonian work started in 527 and was finished in 534. The results were not world-shattering. The Justinianic collection did not leave any traces in the legal life of the Levant. It was written in Justinian's mother tongue, Latin, a language that was not understood in the East. The compilation claimed to contain all of the law of a country with fifty million inhabitants, but was not even particularly voluminous. It was a very superficial, unsystematic and incomplete work. Important elements such as commercial law, tax law or the case law of the prefect of the *annona* were not even mentioned. The entire criminal law was contained in three scrolls. However, the work met the need which Tribonian's commission had deemed most important, namely to satisfy the dictator. He was so proud that he forbade the interpretation of his law codes. For the remainder of his life, the jurists let him believe that he was the greatest jurist of all time but after his death the work was consigned to the dustbin of history.

Five hundred years later, however, the Justinianic collection, which was then known as the *Corpus iuris*, became the catalyst of legal studies in the West. From the Middle Ages until the modern era it would play an extremely important part in the law faculties. Because of the *aleae* of history the whim of an obstinate dictator became the most important law book of all times. It is for this reason that Justinian's heritage should be cherished by all jurists, even by those who are only fascinated by the future. May they be moved by this heritage like COBRA painters by a Goya or like high-tech motor racers by an Indian V-Twin.

The Justinianic collection consisted of four works.

A. The Codex Iustinianus

In 528 Justinian formed the commission that had to recast all of the imperial constitutions that had the force of law into one code. The sources were the Gregorian Code, the Hermogenian Code, the Theodosian Code and all of the constitutions that had been issued since then, including rescripts to private persons. The commission could omit unimportant fragments from constitutions, smooth away contradictions and repetitions and add any necessary alterations at its own discretion. For each fragment, the Code mentioned in which year and by which instance the decision had been pronounced. In 529 the *Codex Iustinianus* was promulgated. The Code itself did not have force of law; its individual texts retained the force they had received at the time of their original promulgation. Other constitutions could no longer be invoked as precedents. The Law of Citations of 426 had also been included in the Code of 529. Commentaries on earlier constitutions could still be used insofar as they dovetailed with the new reading of the Code.

This first Code inspired a series of reforms, which were collected in the *quinquaginta decisiones* (the Fifty Decisions) in 530. While the Digest was being edited (530-533), it was found that other matters could also do with revision. Because of the many alterations, the Code was replaced by a new *codex repetitae praelectionis* in 534. The old Code was forbidden and was lost. The version of 534 has been preserved in its entirety. It consists of twelve books, which are subdivided into titles. Per title the constitutions, many of which stem from Diocletian, are ordered chronologically. The Code of 534 began with the current text C. 1.14.1. In the Middle Ages word had it that the old code started with thirteen titles *nomocanones,* texts that regulated the relations between bishops and emperor. It was thought that the *Collectio tripartita graeca* contained the key to reconstruct these thirteen titles – which were deemed lost – by means of other compilations of Roman case law. Some of these first thirteen titles were added to the Code in the twelfth century; others in the sixteenth. New texts were being interpolated into the Code until the nineteenth century.

Despite Justinian's much greater ambition, the entire *Codex Justinianus* is not more voluminous than the twenty percent of the Theodosian Code that was preserved. As a collection of case law, the Justinianic Code is not a wonder of the world. It does give us a good idea of the workings of the prefectures and the chancellery and of the principles of lawmaking in the late Empire. Reading it is not simple but instructive and therefore a pleasure for those who want to know the Justinianic law.

Bibliography. – On the genesis of the first thirteen titles of the Code, see our abovementioned article L. WAELKENS, 'L'hérésie des premiers titres du Code de Justinien, Une hypothèse sur la rédaction tardive de C. 1.1-13', *The Legal History Review* 79 (2011), p. 253-296.

B. The Digest

Just like Theodosius, Justinian also wanted to collect the *ius,* the classical legal science, in one work. In 530 the order to compile the Digest was given in the constitution *Deo auctore.* The title *Digesta* (in Greek: *Pandecta*) was taken from Salvius Julianus' most important compilation. The commission of Tribonian compiled the most important decisions of all of the jurists whom the emperors had given the assignment or permission to record or interpret the law. The limitations imposed by the Law of Citations no longer applied. The commission was allowed to interpolate the texts in order to remove superfluous, outdated or imperfect elements. Imagine the scope of such permission for jurists who were not legal historians. Poor classical jurists!

The works of some forty jurists were excerpted. A list of their names, which begins with Salvius Julianus and Papinian, can be found at the beginning of the Digest. Ulpian was cited most often. The five jurists of the Law of Citations account for four fifths of the entire Digest because their works were still circulating widely after 426. The contents of the Digest were spread over fifty scrolls (*libri*) which were subdivided into *titles,* each of which had a rubric (*ruber* = red, titles were written in red). Per title, there was a series of fragments of *leges,* which would be further split up into paragraphs in the Middle Ages. The first paragraph of a fragment was not numbered. It is cited as *principium.* Every fragment contained an *inscriptio* with the name of the author, the work and the scroll from which the fragment was taken. This all becomes clear when one takes a look at the Digest in a library. There are several hypotheses about the way in which the division into titles came about. Educational traditions seem to have had an influence here.

The work was finished after three years and was promulgated as applicable law in 533. The dictator was satisfied with his legal brilliance. In the introduction he declared that the entire body of law had now been written down. Judges were no longer allowed to listen to other advisers. After all of this beautiful work, interpretation of the law could certainly not be permitted anymore: this was punishable by deportation and the confiscation of assets. When flipping through the Digest, one quickly discovers that it is a superficial work. Like all good law books, it contains contradictions (compare, for example, D. 13.7.41 and D. 20.1.22; D. 35.1.24 and D. 50.17.161; D. 41.1.36 and D. 12.1.18) and duplications (for example D. 4.2.13 and D. 48.7.7 about Callistratus' mention of Marcus Aurelius' prohibition against private justice). Merely reading this book will not allow you to understand any of the Roman institutions. In addition, you cannot read a fragment without experiencing the irresistible urge to interpret it. The idea that the Digest will give you a clear picture of two thousand years of legal doctrine from a country that used societal thought as its logic, is a little exaggerated. Furthermore, it is strange that the Digest was written in Latin in a Greek world and that not a single manuscript of it was preserved in the East, where the regime survived until 1453.

The real life of the Digest started in the eleventh century, when a unique sixth-century manuscript was kept first in Monte Cassino and later in Pisa. Since 1406, the manuscript, which is known as the *littera florentina*, has been in Florence. In the eleventh century, it was used in legal education, a context in which the Digest was a hit. The fragments are short, simple and clear. One can read them with first-years, but they can just as easily be used as food for thought for seasoned jurists. The Digest is full of cases from which one can deduce rules and contains a lot of one-liners that can each fuel a debate that lasts an entire evening. Furthermore, the Digest is so general that it has the character of an 'opera aperta', which gains meaning in the same way as a modern work of art does: through the viewer's projections onto it. If one reads some texts of the Digest while keeping an image of legal education and casuistry at the back of one's mind, it becomes clear why this book became the most important work of legal doctrine in medieval Europe.

C. The Institutes

As the third part of his opus, Justinian had an elementary introductory work written, a textbook for students. Chancellor Tribonian and the *antecessores* Theophilus from Constantinople and Dorotheus from Beirut were commissioned to write it. It was published together with the Digest in 533 and was also given force of law. For its arrangement, the authors drew inspiration from the Institutes of Gaius. The work consisted of four books: principles of law, persons, assets and actions. The most important sources of the Institutes were: (1) old handbooks like the Institutes of Gaius, Ulpian and Paulus; (2) the Digest and (3) the Code of Justinian. The text is quite elementary, but retains its allure for students: it can be read from cover to cover in one day. A Greek adaptation was already circulating under Justinian: the Paraphrase of the Institutes, which was probably written by Theophilus. In 1534 Viglius of Aytta would be responsible for the first printed version of this Paraphrase.

D. The Novels

After 534 Justinian issued new constitutions, *novellae constitutiones*. We are familiar with these from three private collections. First and foremost there is the *Epitome Juliani*, a Latin summary of one hundred and twenty-four Greek novels from the years 535-555. This work was written in Constantinople. It was lost in the East, but in the West it would be a source of the law of the Novels for centuries. In medieval Bologna a different compilation was circulating: the *Authenticum*, which contained one hundred and thirty-four novels dating from between 535 and 556. In the *Authenticum* one can find the complete text of these constitutions, but in a literal translation *kata podas* (with the same word order) from the Greek. This clumsy Latin makes the *Authenticum* more difficult to read. The third source is the *Collectio graeca 168 nouellarum*, which contains constitutions of Justinian and his two successors. This collection became important in the East. Unlike the Digest or the Codex, it contains the complete text of many novels. In these, we can see how constitutions were drawn up in the prefecture or a chancellery. The Novels are not limited to judgments of the chancellery. They are our oldest source of elaborate legal texts that do not represent precedents, but are guidelines from the emperor to his judges. The Novels were known to many Western jurists from the ninth century onwards. They did not play a large part in the medieval legal education, but would serve as models for royal ordinances in the Renaissance.

Bibliography. – All of the parts of the *Corpus iuris* were known in the Middle Ages. The printed editions which most closely resemble the texts that were used in the Middle Ages are the fifteenth-century editions of De Tortis in Venice. The sixteenth century saw the appearance of critical editions of the *Corpus iuris*. For the Code, Haloander (1530) was important; the normative critical editions of the Digest were those of Blauwblomme (1523), Torelli (1553) and Denys Godefroy (1583). The latter edition was reworked by a jurist from Leuven, François de Maulde. The list of editions of the *Corpus iuris* that have appeared since the sixteenth century is impressive. The most recent edition is the *editio maior* of Mommsen and Krüger, which includes a long introduction and an important critical apparatus: [TH. MOMMSEN and P. KRÜGER,] *Digesta Iustiniani Augusti*, 2 vol., Berlin 1868-1870; [P. KRÜGER,] *Codex Iustinianus*, Berlin 1877. The edition that can currently be found in law libraries is the so-called *editio stereotypa*, which was reprinted innumerable times: [P. KRÜGER,] *Corpus iuris civilis*, Ia, *Iustiniani Institutiones*, Berlin 1872; [TH. MOMMSEN and P. KRÜGER,] *Corpus iuris civilis*, pars Ib, *Iustiniani Digesta*, Berlin 1882; [P. KRÜGER,] *Corpus iuris civilis*, II, *Codex Iustinianus*, Berlin 1877; [R. SCHÖLL and G. KROLL,] *Corpus iuris civilis*, III, *Novellae*, Berlin 1895. If you google *Corpus iuris civilis*, you can find these texts on the internet. There is a complete English translation of the *Corpus iuris*: S.P. SCOTT, *The civil law, including the Twelve Tables, the Institutes of Gaius, the rules of Ulpian, the Opinions of Paulus, the Enactment of Justinian and the constitutions of Leo*, 17 vol., Cincinnati 1932 (reprint New York 1973). For the Code, a better translation than Scott's is F.H. BLUME, *Annotated Justinian code*, 2nd ed. by T. KEARLY, published on the internet. For the Digest, a better translation is A. WATSON, *The Digest of Justinian*, 4 vol., Philadelphia 1985. The supreme publication for those who want to study the Florentine manuscript of the Digest is the photographic edition of A. CORBINO and B. SANTALUCIA, *Justiniani Augusti Pandectorum Codex Florentinus*, Florence 1988. The medieval *Authenticum* was published by G.E. Heimbach, *Authenticum novellarum constitutionum Iustiniani versio vulgata*, I-II, Leipzig 1846-1851 (reprint Aalen 1974).

How does one cite passages of the *Corpus iuris*? A reference to a text from the Code starts with a C, followed by the number of the book, the title, the fragment and, if necessary, the paragraph. The Edict of Thessaloniki, for example, can be found in C. 1.1.1. The system is the same for the Digest, with a D as initial letter, for example D. 26.7.37.2. The Institutes are abbreviated as 'Inst.', for example Inst. 1.2.9. In dogmatic texts, the Novels are referred to as 'Nov.' followed by the number of the Novel in the edition of Schöll and Kroll and the number of the paragraph, for instance Nov. 118.1. When referring to the opening paragraph of a text, we write D. 5.1.18*pr*. We italicise this *pr* and join it to the number of the fragment, according to the beautiful reference system of the *The Legal History Review*.

5. Back to the West

After Justinian reconquered Italy pope Vigilius asked the emperor to introduce his law in Italy. This happened in 554. The 'Pragmatic Sanction at the request of Vigilius' regulated the transition from the old case law and the Theodosian code to Justinianic law.

In 568 the Lombards who had fought for Narses and Belisarius took power in Italy. Their capital, Pavia, housed both the prefecture of Lombardy and a law school that considered Roman law as *ius commune* that applied to everyone. The Exarchate of Ravenna remained under Constantinople's control until 751 and is said to have applied the imperial law until that date. At the time of the iconoclastic fury of emperor Leo III, however, we see that Rome acted independently from Constantinople. A seed of Justinianic law lay dormant in the Italian soil, but it only started to germinate in the Middle Ages.

After Justinian we return to Western Europe. Roman law was, however, still evolving in Constantinople. In the Middle Ages this Roman law of the Levant was called Greek law. It had an influence on the commercial law and tax law of the countries which traded with Constantinople. From the fifteenth century onwards migrants from Constantinople exerted considerable influence on the West. During this period, many legal manuscripts that awakened the interest in Justinianic law were brought to Europe. An interesting compilation that arrived in the West at that time were the ninth-century *Basilica*. In these, jurists once again saw an attempt – in line with Theodosius' endeavour – to record all of the law that could be invoked in the courts.

§5. The tradition of Roman law in the Germanic kingdoms

1. The continuation of Roman law

Nineteenth-century Pan-Germanists claim that the Western Empire collapsed in 476 when the decadent Latins were confronted with the virtues and courage of blond Germans while the emperors occupied themselves with 'bread and circuses'. Apparently these historians were not yet acquainted with social security and the Olympic spirit. No one pays attention to the dynastic struggle in which these supposedly Germanic monarchs were involved in 476. Candidates for succession to the imperial throne always brandished inheritance rights to the public domain. In the first place, the emperor's sons were eligible for succession because the office of emperor was a military one. If there were no sons, the public domain passed via the emperor's daughters to one of their husbands. Many pretenders to the throne were married to imperial heirs and claimed the rights of their wife. The fact that they had armies at their disposal shows their involvement with power. The 'Hun' Attilla was Flavius Constantius' son-in-law and Valentinian III's brother-in-law. The 'Visigoth' Alaric was the brother-in-law of

Galla Placida, a daughter of Theodosius the Great. The 'Vandal' Huneric, whose father Genseric had seized Rome, was Valentinian III's son-in-law. Theodoric the 'Ostrogoth' was the son of emperor Zeno. Clovis was his brother-in-law. Clovis' wife Clotilde was the daughter of Chilperic, the nephew and heir of Ricimer. The latter was Western emperor Anthemius' son-in-law and had been entrusted with the care of the Western Empire by the Eastern emperor Leo. What makes everything even more complicated is that Clovis' sister was the grandmother of Matasuntha, who was married to Germanus, Justinian's cousin by marriage. In short, everything stayed within the family. After the death of Romulus Augustus in 476, the umpteenth dynastic struggle began, but it was the first that would remain unresolved.

The legions which the pretenders had at their disposal consisted for the most part of immigrants, but they were still Roman legions. For young foreign men the army was a means of getting into the Empire. At the border, they asked for a permit to travel to a Roman legion. As soon as they arrived there, they were given Roman civil rights, a salary and medical care. When they left military service, they definitively obtained these civil rights and had enough money to settle somewhere. By that time, however, they had been turned into seasoned Romans. In many of the legions immigrants from the same area were grouped together. In the Lombardic armies, for example, one could find many Low Saxon words. Around Grenoble, where veterans received land, one can find place names from the north, while the language of the Basque Country – another region where many veterans settled – is a mixture of Latin and Baltic words. There were certainly no 'Germanic' legions. The ethnogenesis of 'tribes' such as the Vandals, Goths, etcetera happened within the Empire itself, when its inhabitants gave all immigrants from the same region and period the same name.

The pretenders of 476 did not desire to defeat the Empire. They wanted to eliminate each other. In anticipation of their victory, they developed their own prefecture and administration and took care of the administration of justice in the territory that they controlled. At the end of the fifth century, a balance of power caused a deadlock. The Western Empire disintegrated into smaller domains which were ruled by kings who all thought they were Roman emperors. The Roman dream was never lost. The restoration of the Western Empire would be the ambition of many in the next millennium. The Merovingians, the Pippinids, the Carolingians, the German emperors... They all tried to reunite the West. In the Middle Ages the Roman dream also lived on at a more local level. Sovereign rulers like the king of France or the Count of Flanders claimed the role of emperor in their fief. In Germany an eroded version of the office of emperor survived. Those who held this office always considered themselves Roman emperors. In the Renaissance, the notion of a powerful Roman emperor became popular again as a consequence of the reception of ideas from Constantinople. Many kings managed to establish an absolutist regime after the Roman model with a centralised administration and a sovereign administration of justice. The wars between these different 'Roman' kings destabilised Europe. The Roman dream would only be abandoned during the pandemonium of the late sixteenth century.

Let us return to 476, which was an important year for the history of Roman law. The large single jurisdiction of the Empire, and with it the single market, disappeared. The division of the Empire had as a consequence that long-distance trade, distance payments and shipping became risky. Prosperity was undermined by the smaller markets and higher military expenditure. The prefectures continued to work, but their jurisdictions were smaller. The prefecture of the city of Rome came under papal control and continued to work within the 'Duchy' of Rome. The prefecture of Trier was occupied by the Burgundians. It was already relocated to Arles in the sixth century. From there, it moved to Marseille, where it functioned until the ninth century. The Ostrogoths established an administration with its own court in Pavia. The prefecture of the Visigoths first functioned in the region of Toulouse and was then moved, first to Tarragona and finally to Toledo, where it was still functioning in the eighth century. A study by Durliat about the evolution of public finance in the Merovingian and Carolingian kingdoms shows how these regimes continued to employ models that had been developed in Diocletian's time.

The inhabitants of the old Empire did not change their lifestyle overnight. Roman law was not a repealed law code. In principle, relations were continued in the same manner. The case law of the different zones only grew apart slowly; the jurists continued their activities and still had a close affinity with Roman law. We know the names of some twenty famous jurists who were active in Gaul between 476 and the ascendancy of Charlemagne. Libraries in France, Germany and Italy possess collections of Frankish models for legal practice which are full of Roman law. In the archives of old abbeys such as Farfa Sabina or Saint-Benoît-sur-Loire and in the south of France you can find contracts which were drawn up centuries after the fall of the Empire, but still refer to the Roman law of obligations. In Catalonia, Septimania, and Northern Italy the Roman law of wills and the dotal system of marital goods were still in effect in the high Middle Ages, at the time of the revival of Justinianic law. Throughout the former Empire the oldest records of customary law – which date from the twelfth century – share common provisions concerning inheritance law. The typically Roman family structure in which one citizen was liable for a group of people whom he gathered around him still surfaced in the Middle Ages, although the bishops promoted a different kind of family, which was based on the relationship between two people. A German scholar recently noted that many of the legal terms used in the early medieval law of persons are unclear and should be studied. As examples he mentioned *ciuis, homo, familia, dominium, potestas, auctoritas...* Is it not possible that these stem from Roman law? The most striking example of an aspect of Roman law which lived on in day to day practice was the system of civil rights and liberties, the privileges of warriors. In all of the Germanic kingdoms which developed out of the Western Empire, you can find that warriors had the Roman status of liberty with civil status and privileges. This status also features in the oldest English sources of law, like the law of Ine or Alfred. In the south of England the continuity of the Roman legal culture is striking. There are old sources in Latin and the status of liberty is a central element. In general, Roman culture was very resistant in this region where archaeologists make more Roman finds than anywhere else. The road from Lyon to Calais, which connected England to the Mediterranean, always remained open. Many English pilgrims visited Rome and Bobbio. Rome supported England in its conflicts with the Irish. Was England more Roman in character than Ireland at that time? English medieval law contains a large number of Roman elements which were not received via canon law. Consider, for example, the writ procedures under king Ethelred, the texts about cohabitation by king Cnut or the many civil elements which one can find in the English legal sources that Dorothy Whitelock compiled.

Bibliography. – A large amount of documentation can be found in the German *Zeitschrift der Savigny-Stiftung, Germanistische Abteilung*, both in articles and in the literature overview. Beware, however, of being too credulous. Before reading the *Germ. Abt.*, you should always say the following sentence out loud: "Institutions with a Latin name that already existed in Roman law are not necessarily of Germanic origin". The German scholar who complained about unclear terminology was: L. KUCHENBUCH, 'Abschied von der 'Grundherrschaft', Ein Prüfgang durch das ostfränkisch-deutsche Reich 950-1050', *Zeitschrift der Savigny-Stiftung, Germ. Abt.*, 120 (2004), p. 1-99. On the prefectures of the kingdoms, see: D. CLAUDE, 'Niedergang, Renaissance und Ende der Präfekturverwaltung im Westen des römischen Reichs (5.-8. Jh.)', *Zeitschrift der Savigny-Stiftung, Germ. Abt.* 114 (1997), p. 352-379. The forgotten Frankish books with models for legal practice were published by F. DE ROZIÈRE, *Recueil general des formulaires usités dans l'empire des Francs du Ve au Xe siècle*, Paris 1859-1871; cf. *Patrologia latina* 87, col. 693-902 and 151, col. 1429-1468. The abovementioned study of Durliat is J. DURLIAT, *Les finances publics de Dioclétien aux Carolingiens (284-889)*, [*Beiheifte der Francia*, 21,] Sigmaringen 1990. D. WHITELOCK, *English historical documents, c. 500-1042*, London 1996 (reprint 2007) provides excellent access to the old English texts. For Gaul: D. LIEBS, *Römische Jurisprudenz in Gallien (2. bis 8. Jahrhundert)*, Berlin 2002. The bibliography of O. Guillot is worth consulting as well.

2. The case law in the so-called Germanic kingdoms

The prefectures which were established by the pretenders to the throne continued the Roman tradition at the local level. They elaborated on the Theodosian Code, a compilation that was only thirty-eight years old in 476. The codes of Gregorius and Hermogenius were copied in Gaul as well. The new prefectures also published their own case law. Pieces of a *codex Euricianus* of 476 from Southern France, the *lex burgundionum* of king Gundobald (end of the fifth century, from the region of Trier), the *lex romana wisigothorum* or *Breviarium* of Alaric (506), the *lex romana burgundionum* (from the 510s), the *edictum Theodorici*, the *lex salica* (early sixth century) and the later *lex baiuvariorum* have been handed down. They are anything but ukases of wild warriors. If you read this case law, you will be amazed by its quality and sharpness. It features the results of discussions about procedural law and appeals, about the law of associations, the goods of the churches, fiscal matters and family law. In the *lex romana burgundionum*, for example, we read for the first time that a wedding resulted in the implied emancipation of the spouses. It also contains beautiful decisions concerning procedural law, like the decision that a judge could not revise a judgement that had already been pronounced and that he had to allow it to be checked by a higher official. In the Edict of Theodoric we read about associations that were led by a *curia*: if one of its members died, all of his rights returned to the *curia*. These collections of case law are not the only instances of royal administration of justice influenced by principles of Roman law. Examples can also be found in England. In the seventh century the Edict of Rotari (Pavia) testifies to knowledge of Roman law. A century later, this knowledge would still be present in the sentences of king Liutprand.

Bibliography. – The surviving compilations of case law of the 'Germanic' kings have been published in the *Monumenta Germaniae historica*. Studies about these texts can be found in *Ius Romanum Medii Aevi*, Milan, since 1961.

The importance of the Breviary of Alaric is confirmed by eight summaries of it which were made in Gaul in the eighth century. The most famous of these are the *Epitome Aegidii* and the *lex romana curiensis*. The fact that these works appeared in quick succession beautifully illustrates that notions of Roman law were still evolving in the eighth century.

The *lex romana curiensis* from the sixth century can be found at www.cesg.unifr.ch/ virt_bib/ manuscripts.htm, under Cod. Sang. 722. G. HAENEL, *Lex Romana Visigothorum*, Leipzig 1848 (reprint Aalen 1962) is an edition of the Breviary of Alaric in which each fragment is accompanied by its eighth-century interpretations. An example of a notion that can be seen to originate in this period is the concept of natural children. The Breviary includes a precedent of 371 concerning the will of a man who had both a relationship that was legally recognised and one that was not. The children born from both of these relationships are called *naturales*. If no heirs from the first relationship survived, all of the children born from the second relationship received a legal portion and the bequest that would result in some of the children receiving the entire inheritance was reduced. This can clearly be read in CTh. 4.6.4: *Placuit, manentibus ceteris quae de naturalibus liberis Constantinianis legibus cauta sunt, haec tantummodo temperare, ut is qui heredem heredesue filios ex legitimo matrimonio uel nepotes, qui filiorum loco habendi sunt, patrem quoque matremue dimittit, si ex consortio cuiuslibet mulieris naturales susceperit, unam tantum bonorum suorum et hereditatis unciam naturalibus uel mulieri donandi aut reliquendi habeat facultatem. Si quis uero nullo ex his quos excipimus, superstite morietur, atque ex muliere quam sibi adiunxerat naturalem pluresue demittet, usque ad tres tantum, si uolet, uncias tam in mulierem quam in naturales, quo maluerit iure, transscribat.* In the epitomes of the eighth century, however, the children from the second relationship are demoted. They are 'natural children' (as opposed to the 'legitimate children' from the first relationship) and their rights are curbed. For instance, in the Epitome Aegidii: *Si quis habuerit ex legitimo matrimonio filios uel nepotes aut patrem matremue habuerit, non amplius ad naturales filios uel matrem dari potest quam uncia una. Nam si defuerint personae superius nominatae, tres uncias eis dare potest.* According to the translation of C. PHARR, *The Theodosian Code and Novels and the Sirmondian Constitutions*, Princeton 1952, p. 86-87, natural children are already mentioned in the Theodosian Code: 'It is our pleasure that all the other provisions of the laws of Constantine with respect to natural children shall remain in effect, and only a part of the constitution shall be tempered, so that if a decedent should leave as heir or heirs children from a lawful marriage, or grandchildren that are to be regarded as taking the place of children, and a father or a mother also, and if from its cohabitation with a woman of any kind he should have begotten natural children, he shall have the right to give and leave only one twelfth of his estate and of his inheritance to the natural children or the woman [...].' This depreciation of 'extramarital' children was typical of the eighth century. On this subject, see L. WAELKENS, 'Dans quelles limites peut-on parler d'enfants naturels dans le droit romain de l'Antiquité?', *The Legal History Review* 80 (2012), p. 399-414.

There are hardly any traces that are unambiguous indications of an uninterrupted tradition of Roman law. Neither, however, is there any reason to assume that the early medieval kings did not found their case law on Roman bases. There was nothing to prevent a king from deriving his legitimacy from Rome and continuing to elaborate on familiar precedents. The case law of the different sovereign prefectures grew apart, but this did not change the fact that they had a shared origin. Further on in this book we will see that in some regions the early medieval administration of law was managed by bishops who were favourably disposed towards Roman law.

Charlemagne paid the same attention to case law. In the eighth century he conquered a large part of the Western Empire, as well as territories across the Rhine and the Main. He controlled the prefectures of Trier, Gaul and Pavia. The latter had been won by his father, Pepin the Short. Both father and son considered the prefecture of Pavia as the successor of the prefectures of Milan and Rome. Nevertheless, in 800 Charlemagne asked pope Leo III to anoint him and to crown him emperor. Later jurists found a basis for this papal authority to appoint the emperor in the Donation of Constantine of 325. In 800 the reasoning was simpler. The prefecture of the city of Rome had been taken over by the papal administration and Pepin the Short had acknowledged the pope's sovereign power over the region of Rome. In so doing, he had perhaps delegated the authority of the *praefectus praetorio* to the pope. This was a competence that was necessary to transfer the public domain to the emperor. In Constantinople, the coronation of Charlemagne was considered a histrionic affair. In their view, the one and only emperor was the Eastern one. Charlemagne defended himself against this Eastern opinion by claiming that the public domain had become his through acquisitive prescription – another argument from Roman law. The presence of the German emperors in Italy would be a sensitive issue. It was there that one received the crown of the West in the Middle Ages and that one was anointed emperor. As a consequence, Italy would occupy an important position in the development of the law.

In Charlemagne's day, a period of Roman law began that was very important for legal history, which is a theme of study for current Romanists. Charlemagne actively developed the Roman character of his office as emperor. Manuscripts testify to the revival of the old legal thought in the chancelleries of the ninth century, and we find Roman law in the capitularies. The Roman procedure was restored and applied by itinerant judges, the *missi dominici*. Charlemagne once more enforced old rules of social law, such as the guardianship of orphans or the responsibility of landowners for the sustenance of their tenants.

Roman law in the capitularies: F.L. GANSHOF, *Le droit romain dans les capitulaires*, [Ius romanum mediae aevi, 1,2,b,cc,1,] Milan 1969. On this period, see the other works of this author as well.

3. The influence of feudalism

The Carolingians had acquired the crown of the Western Empire, but had neither the military force nor the financial means to establish an administration after the Roman model. This led to the development of the feudal system. Parts of the public domain were enfeoffed to vassals in exchange for loyalty, military support and taxes – the three subjects of the negotiations between the Senate and the provinces in the Republican Era. The Middle Ages, however, were only familiar with one form of government: ruling through the administration of justice. In order to allow the vassals to govern their domains, sovereign jurisdiction and, by extension, the right to administer sovereign justice were delegated to them. In the feudal system, the king lent his sovereignty to his vassals. Those who received jurisdiction could outsource it further: imperial vassals appointed their own under-vassals, liegemen and lords who received the right to exploit part of a domain in exchange for loyalty, military service and taxes. Some liege lords transferred full sovereignty to their vassals as well, while others only granted their vassals limited jurisdiction and retained the other aspects of sovereignty. Some vassals were granted the competence to administer high justice; others could only administer middle or low justice. After some time, problems arose with the inheritance of feudal estates and succession, as well as with the transfer, leasing and pledging of domains by lords who could not fulfil their obligations. In some regions fiefs were divided among the heirs according to civil law in a case of intestate succession. This meant that the delegated imperial jurisdiction connected with the fief was subdivided as well. Rules regulating the transfer of jurisdiction were drawn up as well. Feudal lords had to settle these conflicts for their vassals. To this end, feudal courts were established which sought balanced solutions. After all, the lord who judged his vassals was, in his turn, a higher lord's vassal. The obligations which he imposed on his subjects could therefore be imposed on him as well by a higher authority. A refined feudal law was developed. In less than two centuries the privatisation of the administrative power resulted in a new order which would influence the public administration of some countries until the nineteenth century.

The feudal system, which had been established to restore the Roman order, undermined Roman law to a larger extent than any of the earlier revolutions. While Roman law needed a centralised justice system and a single market, the realm was split up into hundreds of domains with their own sovereign jurisdiction and a separate juridical system. In the twelfth century the first towns developed in Flanders and Italy. They also played a part in feudal law. Local communities entered into agreements with their feudal lords and purchased aspects of justice and sovereignty. As a consequence, urban courts were established. In all of these feudal and urban courts, imperial power was exercised, but the case law began to differ from region to region and from town to town. We have compilations of case law from different courts of the twelfth century. A comparison of those collections shows diverging case law that builds on the same Roman institutions. The feudal system was based on Roman law, but its development was clearly anti-Roman. Feudalism sabotaged the great restoration of Roman law that the Carolingian monarchs dreamed of. At the end of the Middle Ages a countermovement began to gain momentum. In this period, feudalism was curtailed in many regions by the introduction of the possibility of appeal against the ruling of a vassal (see below). These appeals, which were treated by the vassal's liege, then furthered the reception of Roman law.

Nevertheless, elements of Roman law continued to exist within the feudal system itself. Many powerful vassals claimed to be the emperor of their fief and took an interest in Roman law. Feudal judges who decided cases about donations, successions, or the pledging or transfer of loans invoked Roman law. In the County of Flanders familial interests began to supplant feudal interests from the eleventh century onwards. Feudal prerogatives became civil law. Around 1150 the Count of Flanders managed to acquire the imperial monopoly on violence in his county. The feudal case law of twelfth-century Flanders clearly contains Roman elements. In 1244 a network of feudal courts which heard appeals was established. Appeals against these courts could be lodged with the count's council. In England, feudalism would be demilitarised in the thirteenth century and civil law would begin to affect feudal relations.

In addition, we notice that principles of Roman law were applied in the administration of large domains. This is evident from, for example, letters from the chancellery of the counts of Canossa in the eleventh century and from the archives of large abbeys.

Feudalism eroded Roman law and changed its interpretation. A beautiful example thereof is the advent of individual ownership. Because of the excessive division of the public domain, the people at the bottom of the pyramid received feudal rights to a house, meadow or toll gate. Even such a small domain was delegated imperial *dominium*. Medieval *dominium* entailed the sovereign management of the goods in question and an exclusive right to them. In the history of property law one must always take into account the fact that in this domain Roman law was strongly influenced by feudal law.

Bibliography. – Many works have been written about feudalism. Feudal law has been the subject of far fewer publications. In order to gain an idea of the blending of Roman and feudal law the *Monumenta Germaniae historica* are an unsurpassed source. English feudalism, and especially its demilitarisation and its absorption into private law, are fascinating as well. Those who can read Dutch are privileged because they can access elaborate studies of the feudal law of the County of Flanders: D. HEIRBAUT, *Over heren en vazallen, Het persoonlijke leenrecht in Vlaanderen, ca. 1000-1305*, Brussels 1997. ID., *Over lenen en families (ca. 1000-1305), Een studie over de vroege geschiedenis van het zakelijk leenrecht in het graafschap Vlaanderen*, Brussels 2000; for the later period see R. OPSOMMER, *'Omme dat leengoed es thoochste dinc van der weerelt', Het leenrecht in Vlaanderen in de 14e e 15e eeuw*, Brussels 1995.

Feudal law also strongly influenced Roman law concerning the status of ecclesiastical goods. In Antiquity bishops received goods in trust in order to use them to realise the social goals of donators. From the third century onwards, abbeys also acquired assets to this end. After 476 the bishops took over the imperial *annona*, the poor relief system. In the sixth century both abbeys and bishops acquired the right to levy tithes on agriculture in order to finance their social works. Legally speaking, there was a large difference between the regime of the abbeys and that of the bishops. Abbeys were associations and could not die. The fiduciary rights to their goods were held by their *curiales* and when one of them died his rights reverted to the other *curiales*. In principle, abbeys did not hold immovable goods in *dominium* in the Middle Ages. They kept everything in possession and possessions were allodial. Interestingly, allodial goods fell outside of the scope of feudalism. In the bishoprics, however, the situation was different. The ecclesiastical goods of local bishops were assets that were property goods in trust, earmarked for specific purposes. Although the bishop in question could only use them for these purposes, they were part of his own assets. Bishops were usually elected, but after their election they still had to acquire the ecclesiastical goods. According to Roman law, the court that was competent to decide cases concerning the succession of a bishop was the imperial court. In the Middle Ages, this meant that the competent judge was a delegated feudal judge. Trust law was considered feudal law. It was before the feudal judges that candidate-bishops claimed ecclesiastical goods by means of a revindication. The court then checked whether their appointment was in order: if this was the case, they were entitled to the goods. If a sovereign lord wanted the ecclesiastical goods to fall to one of his allies, he had the ally compete with the bishop for the goods in court. The lord then adjudged the goods to his ally. If he wanted them for himself, he claimed that there was no successor so that he, in his capacity of *fiscus*, received the goods. In Roman law, a revindication required proof of *dominium* (see below). In many regions, the feudal judges deemed that such proof required a feudal claim. In other domains, they claimed that *dominium* was reserved for warriors, who had the *status liberatis* (see below). This led to the controversy concerning the *libertas ecclesiae*. Some rulers who had ecclesiastical goods fall to the *fiscus* subsequently put them at the disposal of the bishops as 'benefices'. In this manner, the ecclesiastical goods remained the ruler's, while the bishops received proceeds of the goods. In German this was called the 'Reichskirche'. This battle over the investiture of the bishops and the adjudication of ecclesiastical goods is a clear example of a conflict between Roman and feudal law. In this context, feudalism became a fine-meshed filter that impeded the reception of Roman law.

It is impossible to have a correct view of the medieval reception if one does not pay attention to the feudal law which overgrew the Roman visions on government, administration, case law or property law on more than one occasion.

Bibliography. – On the issue of bishops' goods, see L. WAELKENS, 'Libertas ecclesiae herbekeken', in: *Recht in geschiedenis, Een bundel bijdragen over de rechtsgeschiedenis van de middeleeuwen tot de hedendaagse tijd,* Leuven 2005, p. 491-499.

4. Legal education in the early Middle Ages

If we believe the historians, Roman law was still taught in schools in Rome, Autun, Aire-sur-Adour, Ravenna, etc. There are, however, no clear sources. On the other hand, *quaestiones ciuiles* were certainly studied in abbeys such as Farfa, Cluny, Saint-Benoît-sur-Loire, Sankt-Gallen and Fulda. It has been established that the chapter schools of for example Sevilla or Saragossa and the cathedral school of Aachen at the time of Eginhard shared this interest. In Pavia Roman law was taught as *ius generale omnium*.

It is practically impossible to find out where each manuscript of Roman law was kept in the early Middle Ages, let alone to discover whether they were preserved in schools, monasteries or chancelleries. The *Sententiae Pauli* are said to have been disseminated as a school book. In which circumstances, however, was Alaric's *Breviarium* studied in the eight century? In 604 Gregory the Great wanted to see the Digest used more often. How widely disseminated was it? Hincmar of Reims (845-882) is said to have had some knowledge of it, but there are no other mentions of it. A gloss on the Institutes was written in the abbey of Casamarí before the tenth century. Another one can be found in a manuscript from Cologne. The Code was circulating in Italy. Some alleged that only an epitome of it remained known, but it is unclear whether this was really the case. The Novels were known in the West through the *Epitome Juliani*. The Parisian *Capitula legis romanae* of the ninth century show that the bishops promoted Roman law. Studies concerning the *Collectio gaudenziana* (tenth century, South-Western Italy) show that laymen were interested in applying Roman law in legal practice.

In the twelfth century the compilers of the first books of the Code of Justinian used old compilations of Roman case law. These books were still known after all those centuries, but no one knows exactly how or where. This period is currently receiving a lot of attention. Let us hope that new studies about this manuscript tradition will appear.

Bibliography. – The best overview of the evolution from old Roman law to medieval law can be found in E. CORTESE, *Il diritto nella storia medievale*, I, *L'alto medioeve*, Rome 1995. Sceptics who want to be convinced have to delve into studies such as W. KAISER, *Die Epitome Iuliani, Beiträge zum römischen Recht im frühen Mittelalter und zum byzantinischen Rechtsunterricht,* [Studien zur Europäischen Rechtsgeschichte, Veröffentlichungen des Max-Planck-Instituts für europäische Rechtsgeschichte, 175,] Frankfurt/Main, 2004. On the *Corpus iuris*, see C.M. RADDING and A. CIARALLI, *The Corpus iuris civilis in the Middle Ages manuscripts and transmission from the sixth century to the juristic revival*, Leyden 2006. For the study of medieval texts on Roman law the most important research project is the Volterra Project of University College London.

§6. The reception of Roman law through the bishops and the Church

We have already discussed the osmosis of *romanitas* and *christianitas*. The Catholic bishops, however, did not limit themselves to incorporating notions of Roman law into their theology. They also developed their own canon law, which contributed greatly to the reception of Roman law in Western Europe.

It seems odd to talk about law in the context of the Church. Law is enforced, while you can evade every form of coercion by a church. All over the world every church – including the Catholic one, which has a status under international law – is subjected to local law. In some countries canon law concerning marriage still plays a part in the legal order, but generally speaking it has become rare for the Church to administer justice. This does not, however, mean that there is no more canon law. The Church still has a legal doctrine, a vision of law which concerns not only its internal organisation, but also national legal systems. The difference in comparison to classical legal doctrine is the theological nature of the input, the universal nature of the output and the fact that the final destination of man is taken into account in the process of society-building. Classic subjects are freedom of religion, marriage law, the safekeeping of creation and life, the law of peace, human rights, a humane criminal law without capital punishment, etcetera. Current canonists work through diplomacy and the pastoral activities of the bishoprics. The situation was very different in the past. From Antiquity until the Early Modern Era the bishops intervened in the resolution of societal conflicts and developed their own case law. It is this canonical law that is treated here.

1. The Roman origins of canon law

The first Christian societies appeared in the Jewish neigbourhoods. Just like the Jews, the Christians preferred to bring conflicts before their own religious leaders – bishops and priests – rather than before the imperial courts. Just like rabbis, these bishops and priests intervened in conflicts. Bishops who had many cases to settle organised hearings (*audientiae*). The old sources use the name 'episcopal audience' for ecclesiastical arbitrage. According to the *Didascalia apostolorum* (first half of the third century) this procedure became binding for Christians. If the parties did not become reconciled, the bishop could take a unilateral decision. The author of the *Didascalia* advised bishops to apply Roman law, but to adapt it to Christian principles. The execution of the judgements was left to the goodwill of the losing party and to societal pressure. If these two factors were not enough, the parties were referred to the imperial court.

As has been mentioned above, Constantine acknowledged episcopal decisions concerning private conflicts in 318 (CTh. 2.1.10) and again in 333 (Const. Sirm. 1; the authenticity of this text is controversial). From then on the winner of an audience could ask the imperial administration to execute the judgement. This caused a revolution. Imperial judges also heard the party that had lost the case before the bishop. It was possible to lodge an appeal against the exequatur of an imperial judge; the ultimate appeal lay with the prefecture in Rome. Those who had lost their case before the bishop, could easily defend themselves by claiming before the imperial judge that no episcopal judgement had been pronounced. The imperial judge then examined the procedure that had been followed by the bishop: had there been a decent summons, had a claim been formulated, had both sides been heard, were the facts proven, had there been a decision? In order to anticipate such questions the bishops adopted the imperial procedure and followed it during their audiences. Roman law thus influenced not only the bishops' decisions, but also the manner in which these were taken. This had consequences for the relations between bishops. In the fourth century imperial courts took into account the issue of whether the losing party had had the chance of lodging an appeal against the bishop. For this reason, the bishops gradually introduced the possibility of filing appeals with the bishop of Rome. In the third century, the latter had already been given a coordinating role in the theological discussions. Following the Council of Serdica (Sophia, 342/3) he could also deal with the judicial appeals. In this manner, the pope became *pontifex maximus*, the highest judge.

At the end of the fourth century the competence of the audiences in civil matters was once more limited to arbitrage. This did not, however, result in the bishops becoming less active in the judicial sphere. In 452 Valentinian III stressed that access to the audiences was always voluntary and that episcopal judges were only competent *ratione personae* if one of the parties was a member of the clergy and *ratione materiae* if the conflict concerned typically ecclesiastical matters (Nov. Val. 35). Criminal and commercial law did not fall within this competence. It is said that Majorian mitigated Valentinian's decision, but this constitution has not been handed down.

This development of judicial activity was at the origin of canon law. In order to make the audiences more efficient and avoid appeals, the bishops discussed legal matters in their local councils. We notice this for the first time in the canons of the councils of Elvira (305) and Arles (314). In the course of the fourth century several local councils formulated agreements with regard to the audiences. These 'canons' were disseminated widely and adopted by other bishoprics. Although they did not become directly enforceable, their application in the audiences and exequaturs of the imperial judges gave them legal status. Decretals dating from 384 onwards have been preserved. They are papal decisions modelled after the imperial constitutions. Just like those constitutions, decretals could be decrees as well as rescripts, edicts or mandates. The appellate decisions of the pope were published as decretals. In the fourth century 'canon law collections', compilations of law for the benefit of the audiences, were already being drawn up. Pope Leo (440-461) and pope Gelasius (492-496) were the first to decree excommunication for disciplinary matters, for example cases involving heresy and apostasy. In the West, canons and decretals always remained sovereign episcopal decisions. It is around these that Western canon law would be developed. In the East Justinian took control of the episcopal administration of justice. With his Nov. 123 (546) he introduced the possibility of filing an appeal against a patriarch's decision with the chancellery. Henceforth, the bishops had to take his policy into account. Between 554 (*sanctio pragmatica Vigilii*) and 728 (the donation of Sutri) this regime also applied to the bishop of Rome. The rare sources from this period do not allow us to measure the true influence of this regime on canon law. In 728 Rome became fully independent from Constantinople and the Empire. From then on the Greek *nomocanones* and the Latin *canones* were written in a different key. The Latin bishops began to think independently about law.

In the rest of this book we will only consider the Western tradition of canon law, which always had a close affinity with Roman law. From Antiquity onwards, canon law was a vector of the dissemination of this law. In the oldest canons you can already taste this mixture of law and salvation, spirituality and societal thought that is so typical of early medieval *latinitas*.

Bibliography. – The *Didascalia apostolorum* have been published by F.X. FUNK, Paderborn 1906. Const. Sirm. 1 can be found in the abovementioned edition of the Theodosian Code by Mommsen, I, p. 907 and following. This text was also included in the *Decretum* of Gratian (see below) in C. 11 q. 1 c. 35-36. Both versions have been published online. Nov. Val. 35 has been published in Mommsen's edition of the *Codex Theodosianus*, II, *Leges Novellae*. You can read about Majorian in the *interpretatio* that accompanies the text in Mommsens' edition. For canons, the source is K.J. HEFELE – H. LECLERCQ, *L'histoire des conciles d'après les documents originaux*, Paris 1907-1952.

2. The development of canon law in the early Middle Ages

In 476 the bishop of Rome took control of the administration and the jurisdiction of Rome and its environs. Justinian reconquered Rome in the sixth century. When the Lombards seized Italy, they left Rome in peace. Because it fell within the territory of the exarchate of Ravenna, the City remained part of the Empire. However, the pope seems to have exercised local jurisdiction. With the help of Pepin the Short he acquired full jurisdiction over the exarchate in 761. The prefecture moved from Ravenna to Rome, where it became the Apostolic Signatura in the high Middle Ages. In the meantime, the papal *audientia* had continued to function – it became the Roman Rota. The Signatura could grant an enforcement order; the Rota could not. The takeover of the prefecture by the pope resulted in an increased amount of attention being paid to Roman law. This double jurisdiction caused Christian Rome to consider the administration of law and legal thought as core responsibilities.

Other bishoprics also continued to organise audiences. This was clearly the case in Seville, Lyon, Milan and Toledo, where the local governments kept executing canonical decisions. Roman law still featured in the episcopal dispensation of justice. In 603, pope Gregory the Great (pope 590-604) asked the bishops to keep following the Roman *cognitio* procedure when they administered justice. Hincmar of Reims (born in 806, bishop 854-882) already wrote that Gregory's admonitions consisted of Roman law. The councils also continued to discuss legal issues. The Gallic councils of Orléans (533 and 549), Tours (567) and Mâcon (538) feature solutions based on Roman law. The works of bishop Isidore of Seville (560-636) are testimony to his sympathy for the Roman way of living and for Roman law. He organised the councils of Seville (619) and Toledo (633), where the bishops confirmed Roman legal rules. Both the canons and the case law of Rome were still compiled in canonical collections. After 476 more and more imperial constitutions began to crop up in these collections. In the *constitutiones sirmondianae* (Gaul, around 600), for example, one can find a series of old constitutions in favour of bishops.

In the Carolingian period the emperor and the bishops jointly organised the administration of justice by making use of itinerant *missi dominici*. They attempted to re-establish the old institutions, such as the guardianship of orphans. This close collaboration between imperial and episcopal judges illustrates that they both had the same view of the administration of justice. As in Antiquity, the royal judiciary supervised the adjudication of ecclesiastical goods to the bishops. In the feudal system many bishops only received these goods if they played a part in local legal life. Quite a few of these bishops knew the Roman culture better than the lords and their officials and were charged with the ordinary administration of justice. In other regions a separate canonical practice continued to exist. Collections from this period once again contain many elements of Roman law. Two collections from around 850, the abovementioned *Capitula legis romana* (called the *lex romana canonice compta* in earlier scientific works) and the *Excerpta bobbiensia*, were collections of Roman law for the use of the clergy. The *Collectio Anselmo dedicata* of the end of the ninth century contains two hundred and thirty-eight excerpts from Roman law, most of which originated from the Theodosian Code. The same source was used by Regino of Prüm (†915) for his *Libri de synodalibus causis*. In the letters of Hincmar of Reims we read about 'the law of the Christian emperor Justinian which the bishops approve and cherish'. It seems, then, that Hincmar was familiar with the Justinianic collection. Many excerpts from the writings of the Latin church fathers were also included in the collections of this period. In the canonical administration of justice these norms are often applied as canons.

In the ninth century a new kind of source surfaces, the *libri poenitentiales* or penitentials. These contained guidelines for confessors that answered the question: how does one respond, as a priest, to the specific behaviour of a confessant who asks for advice? These are interesting sources that offer information about daily life and also illustrate the spread of Christian morality. When they used texts from the penitentials, the compilers of canonical collections mixed moral and legal norms. This mixture would continue to influence canon law. Between the ninth and eleventh centuries the German bishops campaigned against the nobles who regrouped fiefs by means of familial alliances and inheritance law, a policy that had led to inbreeding and dynastic problems because planned heirs were not born or did not survive. In this context, the German bishops attempted to impose a mixture of moral rules and rules from Roman law concerning consanguinity and relationships. In this series of conflicts, which was further complicated by the Investiture Controversy, one can see the influence of this Roman-moral-canonical law grow. A famous case concerning divorce was that of Lothar II (emperor 855-869), who wanted to repudiate his childless wife Theutberga. The strict refusal of the canonical courts heralded the end of his realm.

In the tenth century feudal kings and bishops, who often pursued conflicting goals, had become too closely involved with one another. In the abbeys, a religious renewal began which was known in Western Europe as the Cluniac Reforms. Bishops had to become independent from the feudal order. The monk Hildebrand became pope Gregory VII. He made a stand for the new idea of a unified church, which had to realise its goals in an autonomous manner. Until the tenth century the word *ecclesia* signified a church building, a monastery or a bishopric. Gregory VII's unified church, however, was an association. This association's actions in the legal sphere seemed unjustifiable, so that the discussion with the imperial order soon began to focus on the rivalry between the emperor and the pope. During talks with the emperor Henry IV, Gregory VII and his entourage represented the situation as if the pope and the emperor were both successors of the Roman emperors, but in different domains. The emperor had delegated his domain to the feudal lords. The world of the bishops, however, was part of the domain of the pope, who had never divided his jurisdiction. If a bishop died or was transferred, his goods did fall to the fiscal authority, but with regard to ecclesiastical goods this fiscal authority was the pope. He was the one who decided to whom a vacant bishopric and all its goods would fall. This is, once again, the abovementioned Investiture Controversy. Historians describe this conflict as a brutal struggle for power over the investiture of bishops and access to judicial authority, but how could emperor Henry, who was full of good will and kneeled for the pope in 1070 in Canossa, understand the idea of the Church as a successor of the Empire? Charlemagne had been anointed by the pope, but the idea of the Church being an association that was comparable to the Empire was ridiculous. It was enough to make anyone lose his patience. The controversy also cropped up in the canonical collections. In the eleventh century, important compilations in which arguments for the single church were collected, were drawn up. Burchard of Worms (bishop 1000-1025) published his monumental *Decretum*, in which he incorporated Eastern Roman legal texts which seemed to indicate that 'the Church' had been acknowledged in the East since the sixth century. He never mentions, however, that the Eastern bishops had in the mean time been integrated into the imperial order. In the eleventh century this Justinianic law made its way into many collections. It was even invoked for the benefit of the Church's own judicial power. The *Collectio Brittanica* (Italy, around 1090) was one of the first collections of canon law that made ample use of the Institutes of Justinian and the Digest. In France bishop Ivo of Chartres (1040-1116) promoted Justinianic law. In his canonical collection (*Decretum*) he included more than two hundred excerpts from the Justinianic collections.

Bibliography. – P. FOURNIER and G. LE BRAS, *Histoire des collections canoniques en Occident, Depuis les Fausses Décretales jusqu'au Décret de Gratien*, 2 vol., Paris 1931-1932 (reprint Aalen 1972). Regino of Prüm has been published and translated by F.W.H. WASSERSCHLEBEN and W. HARTMANN, *Das Sendhandbuch von Regino von Prüm*, Darmstadt 2004. On the German ecclesiastical trials concerning incest see P. CORBET, *Autour de Burchard de Woms, L'Eglise allemande et les interdits de parenté (IXe-XIIe siècle)*, Frankfurt/Main 2004. Fournier-Le Bras' views on Ivo of Chartres are superseded. Instead see CH. ROLKER, *Canon law and the letters of Ivo of Chartres*, Cambridge 2010.

3. The establishment of the officialities and the adoption of Roman law

In the eleventh century, Petrus Crassus, a lay judge from Ravenna, wrote a defence of Henry IV in which he uses the expression *utraque lex*, both laws: the law of the emperor and that of the pope. The idea of a double fiscal authority with two domains and two laws became successful as a solution to a long-standing conflict in the West. The pope also became a fiscal authority; his 'Church' could be seen as a kind of realm. From this time onwards, we can speak of the Church and need no longer be so mindful of always writing 'the bishops'.

The Investiture Contoversy was resolved by emperor Henry V and pope Callixtus II in the Concordat of Worms of 1122. They both received jurisdiction, but their respective domains were not demarcated. In the second quarter of the twelfth century, there were feverish attempts to establish this demarcation. The four Lateran councils concerning the jurisdiction of the bishops were held in Rome between 1123 and 1215. Between 1125 and 1150 new texts with old Roman decisions about the relations between imperial and episcopal courts were continuously added to the Justinian Code. They became titles 1.1-13 of the Code. A second initiative was Gratian's *Decretum*. Sometime between 1122 and 1130 this monk from Camaldoli wrote a work in which he argued for the authority of ecclesiastical courts. His point of departure was Nov. Val. 35 (452), the last Western Roman decision about this conflict of jurisdiction. In the first paragraph of this novel one can read that the Church was exclusively competent *ratione personae* for conflicts to which clerics were party and *ratione materiae* for typically ecclesiastical matters. It is this statement that Gratian used as a platform for elaboration. In the first book of his *Decretum* he first explains the legal sources, and in particular the conflicts with the clergy. In this context he quotes centuries of case law and legal doctrine that illustrate how the Church had settled these matters since Antiquity. In the second book he sketched the matters which were, in his view, typically ecclesiastical. He invented thirty-six examples of conflicts (*causae*) and then argued and demonstrated how these had traditionally come under ecclesiastical jurisdiction. These were conflicts regarding simony and heresy, criminal law and criminal procedure, the organisation of the Church and ecclesiastical goods, wills of members of the clergy, ecclesiastical tithes and loans. A series of *causae* concerned the goods of monasteries. Then, Gratian treated the obligations of the ecclesiastical authorities, which included intervention in war and peace and excommunications. The last ten *causae* dealt with the family life of laypeople. Marriage was the central subject of these conflicts. Gratian also adopted the idea from Roman Antiquity that the Church could not execute judgements. Execution, being a form of violence, remained a military prerogative. The Church would appeal to the imperial order to have judgements executed. Let it be said here that despite Gratian's attempts the ecclesiastical courts neither acquired the competence to treat criminal cases, nor the supervision of war and peace. In the sources of the twelfth century, however, we do see that Gratian's *Decretum* was mostly adhered to.

The Church organised its administration of justice fairly quickly. In the twelfth century it began to employ itinerant judges, who were also called *iudices delegati*, just like the feudal lords to whom imperial jurisdiction had been delegated. However, there was still a large difference between feudal and ecclesiastical delegated judges. Feudal judges were invested with sovereign legal power. In the Church, however, the pope remained the sovereign supreme judge, the *pontifex maximus*. Just as in the earlier audiences, the ecclesiastical judges used the Roman procedure. Because the judges of the first instance were not sovereign judges, losing parties could file an appeal with the delegating bishop, against whom an appeal could be lodged in Rome. This increased people's confidence in the legal system.

At the end of the twelfth century all of the ecclesiastical judges were trained jurists. Their guarantees for a fair trial were far better than those of the feudal judges.

The latter had political motives, and fines and confiscations fell to them personally. After 1122 Western Europe immediately responded to the quality of the ecclesiastical administration of justice. Litigants and canonists used inventive methods to arrange for the ecclesiastical judges' competence over cases, as the following examples show. Since the eleventh century, celibacy had been imposed on the lower clergy as well. Consequently, the ecclesiastical courts introduced the law of wills for clergymen who did not have any descendants. Laymen soon began to ensure that ecclesiastical courts were competent *ratione personae* by including a legate to the local priest in their will. They then invoked the Roman law of wills. As this was imperial law, the feudal order had to execute these wills. In this manner, wills were reintroduced in northern and western Europe. The most fundamental change in the twelfth century concerned marriage. Christian doctrine discussed sexual relations. A plea was put forward that these relations therefore came under ecclesiastical jurisdiction *ratione materiae.* All sorts of conflicts were connected with marriage and thus brought before the ecclesiastical courts. The justification of this competence vis-à-vis the feudal judges is at the basis of both Western marriage law and the idea of access to law through marriage.

In the second half of the twelfth century the large bishoprics organised permanent courts to deal with appeals against the itinerant judges or to deal with cases directly. The first of these 'officialities' was established in Reims by bishop William Whitehands. A century later every bishopric had its own officiality. From the middle of the twelfth century onwards Rome also had to handle many appeals against episcopal decisions. The popes made use of these appeals to develop a thorough ecclesiastical law. There is a remarkable series of 'jurist popes' who all had a III in their name: Alexander III (1159-1181), Lucius III (1181-1185), Urban III (1185-1187), Clemens III (1187-1191), Celestine III (1191-1198), Innocent III (1198-1216) and Honorius III (1216-1227). These were followed in the thirteenth century by three more great jurist popes, namely Gregory IX (1227-1239), Innocent IV (1234-1254) and Boniface VIII (1294-1298).

If the ecclesiastical judges did not find any precedents in canon law, Gratian suggested that they use Roman law. This rule was confirmed by Lucius III (X. 5.32.1) and officially promulgated by Honorius III in the bull *Super specula* (1219, X. 5.33.28). Consequently, the Church applied Roman law – or at least medieval Roman law – to thousands of conflicts, even those of laymen.

Bibliography. – On the division of jurisdiction after 1122 see L. WAELKENS, 'L'hérésie des premiers titres du Code de Justinien, Une hypothèse sur la rédaction tardive de C. 1,1-13', *The Legal History Review* 79 (2011), p. 253-269. On the division of jurisdiction defended by Gratian: L. WAELKENS, 'Le décret de Gratien, Ouvrage scientifique ou plaidoirie d'un canoniste face à l'ordre impérial?', in J. HALLEBEEK, L. BERKVENS, G. MARTIN and P. NÈVE, *Recto ordine procedit magister, Liber amicorum E.C. Coppens*, Brussels 2013, p. 351-361.

The emergence of a second legal system revived long-distance trade in Western Europe and created the profession of notary. After 1122 the bishops agreed to develop the Church's headquarters in Rome. They decided to transfer part of their tithes to their principal seat. The transportation of coins over long distances, however, was a dangerous affair and an ingenious method of transferring money soon came into vogue. The *camera apostolica* outsourced the collection of tithes to Lombard bankers, who established agencies in the relevant regions. There, they lent the money they collected to traders, who used it to buy local goods. These were then sold in the south, where the traders' clients paid the Italian bankers. Artisanal products were harder to steal than money. On the way south, the products were exempted from tolls because tolls were feudal and could not be levied on ecclesiastical goods. Problems that occurred underway or at the final destination were brought before ecclesiastical courts, which all applied the same law, namely Roman law in cases of commercial conflicts. Certificates of origin had to show in a clear manner that the goods were ecclesiastical. Furthermore, the goods were accompanied by a letter of loan and a bill of exchange with four parties (agent of the bank, trader, client and parent bank) that functioned as a document of payment. In order to make sure that these documents had the same value everywhere, they were drawn up by *pronotarii apostolici*, ecclesiastical officials who were the precursors of our current notaries. The twelfth century also saw the appearance of annual fairs, where traders from all regions could enter into safe contracts because of *pronotarii* and could submit any conflicts to the local ecclesiastical courts. In medieval canonical texts you can read that the Church acted for distressed foreign traders. Nov. Val. 35 states that episcopal audiences were never competent in matters involving commercial law, not even when a case concerned trade conducted by a clergyman. The canonists, however, turned this into the rule that they were incompetent to hear cases about trade conducted by clergymen.

Bibliography. – On the origination of long-distance trade, see L. WAELKENS, 'The historical roots of Belgian commercial law'; *Krakowskie studia historii pánstwa i prawa* 6 (2013), p. 351-372.

4. Canon law at the universities

The flourishing of canon law coincided with the rise of the universities. As at so many other crucial moments, a confrontation with Constantinople was once more at the basis of this development. Roman law was already studied in Bologna in the eleventh century, but from the turn of the century onwards, thousands of Westerners saw the Mediterranean world, Constantinople and the East during the crusades. In Lincolnshire, the Beauce region or Meckelenburg, corn was the major source of affluence. How was it possible that life was better in the East, with its poor fields? Undoubtedly because this famous Roman law structured the society in a different manner! And what about the Eastern version of Christianity, Islam and Judaism? Were these religions as superior as the Eastern Roman law? In the mid-eleventh century Lanfranc of Pavia (1005/10-1081) studied the Digest with students in Bologna. He was at the cradle of the first law faculty. His student Anselmus of Aosta (1033-1109, later Saint Anselm of Canterbury) began a similar study of the Bible and the Latin church fathers in Paris and thus founded the first faculty of theology. Lanfranc and Anselms' method was the 'rational' approach, that of an accountant (*ratio* means account and *rationalis* accountant). The authority of the sources was not called into question. All of the old texts were authoritative (*auctoritates*). They had to be compared to one another and apparent contradictions had to be explained. As in accounting, the overall picture had to be perfect and if such perfection could not be attained, creative interpretations were a must – exactly as they are in the art of balancing account books.

In the 1140s Gratian worked in Bologna. He compiled a new version of his *Decretum*, in which he incorporated, among other things, Roman legal texts. In the meantime the ecclesiastical courts had begun to function. Many ecclesiastical judges sought support for their administration of justice and came to Bologna to study Gratian's work. They searched for documentation and considered the *Decretum* as the latest canonical collection. It was polished further according to the rational method and received a second name: the *Concordia discordantium canonum*. In Paris a second faculty was established before the mid-twelfth century: the *facultas Decreti*. The study of the *Decretum* led to the study of canon law. Some jurists from the south of England, from the circle of Lanfranc and Anselm, came to this faculty to study and teach and gave the study of canon law a strong impetus. An interaction between the administration of law and the faculties of ecclesiastical law began. These faculties studied both cases and dogmatic problems. Rome decided that future judges had to be trained in this milieu. This led to close ties between the faculties of ecclesiastical law and the ecclesiastical judges.

When it dawned on the canonists that ecclesiastical courts also had to apply Roman law, they started to study this Roman law at their faculties as well. A course on ecclesiastical law that was interspersed with Roman law at a very early stage was the *Summa super decreta* (1187) of Huguccio of Pisa, a professor in Bologna. In 1149 the Italian canonist Vacarius (ca. 1120-1200, counsellor of the archbishop of Canterbury for a long period) travelled to Oxford, where he introduced the study of Roman law.

Five supplements to the Decree of Gratian were written. These incorporated old canons which Gratian had neglected, but mainly inventoried new case law. In 1230 Gregory IX asked the Catalan Dominican and professor in Bologna Raymond of Penyafort to collect all of the new canon law since Gratian. Raymond arranged this material in five books: *iudex, iudicium, clerus, conubium, crimen*. This new compilation was promulgated as papal law in 1234 and became known as the Decretals of Gregory IX. The old *Decretum* of Gratian and the Decretals of Gregory together with some supplementary books constituted the *Corpus iuris canonici*, the corpus of canon law.

Bibliography. – The *Corpus iuris canonici* was reprinted often from the fifteenth century onwards. Currently, the critical edition is A. FRIEDBERG, *Corpus iuris canonici*, Leipzig 1879 (reprint Graz 1959). It has been published online by the Royal Library of Munich. Beautiful medieval manuscripts of the different parts of this corpus have been handed down. The first edition of the *Decretum* of Gratian can be found in six manuscripts. One of them, ms. Sankt-Gallen, Stifstbibliothek 673 (of 1132) can be consulted online at www.cesg.unifr.ch/virt_bib/handschriften.htm. Most of the manuscripts of the *Decretum* contain the version of 1140. One of the oldest thereof is ms. Antwerp, Plantijn-Moretus 55. Ms. Gent, UB 23 is a beautifully illuminated manuscript of the *Decretum* from the thirteenth century.

How is the *Corpus iuris canonici* cited? The *Decretum Gratiani* of 1140 consists of three parts. Part I contains one hundred *distinctiones*, which are subdivided into canons. The first twenty distinctions deal with the sources of law; the following ones with functions within the Church. The manner of citation is the following: Dist. 1.1. Part II is subdivided into thirty-six *causae* about legal acts and judgements, procedure, ecclesiastical goods, religious orders and marriage. The *causae* are divided into *quaestiones* and subdivided into canons. These are to be cited as follows: C. 11 q. 1 c. 35. In part II C. 33 q. 3 contains an important interpolation of texts from penitentials which is itself divided into five distinctions and subdivided into canons. Citations take the following form: *De paen.*, D. 1.1. The third part concerns ordinations. It is divided into five distinctions and subdivided into canons. Citations take the following form: *De consecr.*, D. 1.1. In the Middle Ages, canons were not identified by means of these numbers, but by means of their first words. Citation methods that are derived from this medieval method were used until the twentieth century. An example is Can. *Visis litteris*, C. 16 q. 4. The Decretals of Gregory are cited as X (*Extra*), are divided into five books and subdivided into titles and canons: X. 3.2.1. A complete *Corpus iuris canonici* contains in addition the *Liber Sextus* (*Sext.* 1.1), the *Clementina* (*Clem.* 3.5.1), the *Extravagantes* of John XXII (*Extr. Joan.* XXII) and the *Extravagantes communes* (*Extr. Comm.*).

During a preliminary period education in ecclesiastical law consisted of reading the main texts of the *Corpus iuris canonici*, while paying attention to internal connections. When reading the texts, the students wrote 'glosses' with references, explanations and short comments in the margins of their manuscripts. From 1230 onwards elaborate commentaries on the sources appeared. The best thirteenth-century commentary is that on the Decretals of Gregory IX by Hostiensis (Henricus de Segusio, professor at Paris, later bishop of Embrun, who died in 1271 as the cardinal of Ostia – hence the name Hostiensis). The *Speculum iudiciale* of Guillaume Durand (born in the Languedoc in 1230/1, professor in Bologna, later in the service of the Church in Rome, died in 1296 as bishop of Mende) is an unsurpassed treatment of procedure. He taught about this subject in the 1240s but composed his great publication in the 1270s. The greatest canonist of the fourteenth century was Johannes Andreae (1270-1348), whose daughter Novella was the first female professor of law. She wore a veil when she taught.

The medieval study of canon law was of great importance for the reception of Roman law. In the first place, the canonists studied Roman law for their own courses. They were responsible for the reception of Roman law into the five important bodies of law which have been mentioned above as the books of the Decretals of Gregory IX: *iudex* (principles of societal organisation and administrative law), *iudicium* (legal procedure), *clerus* (sounds as if it involves the status of the clergy, but it also deals with the law of wills), *conubium* (marriage, reception of Roman relationships between two people), *crimen* (principles of criminal law). A second influence was due to the canonists' familiarity with theology and moral philosophy. As Hostiensis put it: "The difference between a legist and a canonist is that canonists are also concerned about the final destination of those who are subject to the law." Consequently, the administration of justice in the officialities differed in tone from that of the legists. Canonists had a different view of reliability and liability. They were, for instance, of the opinion that Christian charity always had to play a part in private relationships and thus also in obligations, that everyone was liable for his promises, and that there could be no liability without guilt. In the twelfth century they developed marriage as a legal notion in order to establish the competence of the ecclesiastical judges. In the thirteenth century the theologians developed the ethical dimension of this notion and then handed it back to the canonists, who would from then on also see marriage as a beneficial way of life.

In the sixteenth century the ecclesiastical administration of justice would be absorbed into the royal sovereign administration of justice. In the seventeenth century, the royal courts would consider the ecclesiastical case law as an old Roman heritage.

Bibliography. – An excellent legal historical work that represents canon law as the original site of the reception of Roman law is the abovementioned E. CORTESE, *Il diritto nella storia medievale*, 2 vol., Rome 1995. The best introduction to the medieval sources is W. HARTMAN and K. PENNINGTON (eds.), *History of medieval canon law*, Washington, several volumes since 1999. A more concise overview is given by J. BRUNDAGE, *Medieval canon law, An introduction*, London-New York 1995. In Leuven we like to use Mgr. VAN HOVE's *Prolegomena*, Mechlin 1945, which has the peculiar feature that it is written in Latin. Good journals about medieval canon law are *Zeitschrift der Savigny-Stiftung für Rechtsgeschichte, Kanonistische Abteilung* and *Studia et documenta historiae et iuris. Studia Gratiana* (Rome) and *Bulletin of Medieval Canon Law* (Berkeley) have been discontinued but the old volumes still provide excellent hints. As an encyclopaedia, the *Dictionnaire de droit canonique* remains a series that is very hard to put down. A pleasant aspect of canon law is that many of its sources have been preserved in manuscripts throughout Europe. The works of the great canonists of the thirteenth and fourteenth centuries were republished by Bottega d'Erasmo in Turin in the sixties, for example JOHANNES ANDREAE, *In libros Decretalium novella commentaria*, reprint Turin 1966 and HOSTIENSIS, *Commentaria super Decretalibus*, reprint Turin 1965. They can also be found as old printed books in university libraries. Beware of Hostiensis: reading his work is addictive. Even the reprint (Aalen 1975) of GUILLELMUS DURANTI's *Speculum iudiciale* has become rare. Jurists must not pass by Santa Maria sopra Minerva in Rome without visiting the remains of Durand. A good key to the world of the medieval canonists (and legists) is offered by E.J.H. SCHRAGE, *Utriumque ius, eine Einleitung in das Studium des mittelalterlichen Rechts*, Berlin 1992.

§7. The reception of Justinianic law at the universities

In discussing the theologians and the canonists, we have already reached the medieval universities. The very first university, however, was the law faculty of Bologna, which was established in the eleventh century to study Justinianic law. After the crusades it made great strides.

1. The glossators of Bologna

The counts of Tuscany, especially Beatrice (1016-1076) and her daughter Matilda (1046-1115), launched legal education in Bologna. It was at their castle in Canossa that Henry IV became reconciled with pope Gregory VII in 1077. These counts owned domains in Tuscany, Lorraine, Swabia and Bavaria. Records from their chancellery show that they used the *ius commune* for the administration of their goods. In the eleventh century the Justinianic law came to the fore in the *ius commune*. In 1018 it was mentioned in the *Regesto di Farfa* and, shortly afterwards, in the canonical collection *Collectio brittanica*. For the Westerners of the eleventh century Justinian was not the tyrant he had been five centuries ago, but the noble builder of the Hagia Sophia and the Latin emperor who had brought Roman law and, as a consequence, affluence to Constantinople. His legal books were considered to contain the model for a durable society that offered room for both the emperor and the pope.

In the eleventh century the Digest surfaced: in a procedure between a Florentine and the abbey of Marturì in 1079 the judge of Canossa wrote that the decision had been taken *lege digestorum libris inserta considerata*. The man who rediscovered the Digest may well have been Lanfranc of Pavia (1005/10-1089), a counsellor of Beatrice of Canossa. He had studied law at Pavia and a chronicle mentions that he and his student Irnerius (ca. 1050-1125), who was considerably younger than his master, were at the basis of the legal education in Bologna. Lanfranc did leave seeds of the Digest in his wake. He left the service of the Canossa family to become a Benedictine. According to some, the famous manuscript of the Digest, which is currently known as the *littera florentina*, was then kept in the library of the abbey of Monte Cassino. Did Lanfranc find it there when he was a Benedictine? Maybe he discovered the manuscript in Pisa, where it was preserved for a long time before the Florentines took it away in 1406. In 1042 Lanfranc left for the abbey of Bec in Normandy where he became prior in 1045. "He introduced me to the Digest there," wrote Ivo of Chartres. In other words, Lanfranc had taken a copy of it with him. In Normandy, the Digest was copied again. Many of the oldest preserved manuscripts of the Digest come from Normandy. In 1063 Lanfranc became the abbot of Saint Stephen's in Caen; in 1070 he became the archbishop of Canterbury and the president of the *curia regis* of William the Conqueror. He used the Digest in England as well, as the decisions of king William show. Lanfranc was involved in the first study of the Digest in Italy, France and England. Why would we deny him the honour of having been the first to have introduced the Digest into legal education? All other hypotheses turn out to be dead ends. The authord of this book has long thought that Great Britain might have a separate Digest tradition because Edinburgh University Library owned an eleventh-century manuscript 'of British (?) provenience'. This, however, turned out to be a Norman manuscript from the late eleventh century. According to a current hypothesis, a different version of the Digest was circulating in Bologna: the *littera vulgata*, which differed from the *florentina* in many respects. The text of the *littera florentina*, however, is far from perfect. Even in the eleventh century, copyists will have added corrections. In short, there are enough reasons to assume that the *vulgata* also stems from the *florentina*, that single sixth-century manuscript that is now in the Biblioteca Medicea Laurenziana in Florence.

Bibliography. – Shortly before his death G. Santini wrote a beautiful article about the use of the Digest prior to 1079: G. SANTINI, 'Administration publique et droit romain dans la Normandie de Guillaume le Conquérant', *Revue historique de droit français et étranger*, 1995, p. 23-40. On the historical context, see H. CLOVER and M. GIBSON, *The letters of Lanfranc Archbishop of Canterbury*, Oxford 1979; E. and W. GOEZ, *Die Urkunden und Briefe der Markgräfin Mathilde von Tuszien*, [Monumenta Germaniae Historica, Diplomata, 5, Laienfürsten und Dynastenurkunded der Kaiserzeit,] Hannover 1998; and once again E. CORTESE, *Il diritto nella storia medievale*, II, *Il basso medioevo*, Rome 1995. In the proceedings of Marturì (1076) the use of the Digest does not seem to be new but well established: cf. CH. BIRR, 'Die Urkunde von Marturì (1076) und die Anwendung von D. 4.6.26.4', *The Legal History Review* 73 (2005), p. 279-300. For the comparison of the *florentina* and the *vulgata*, see H.E. TROJE, *Crisis digestorum, Studien zur historia pandectarum*, Frankfurt/Main 2011.

The Canossa family launched education in Roman law in Bologna. The oldest known jurist who taught there was a certain Pepo, a lawyer of Beatrice of Tuscany. The driving force behind the early period of the law school was Irnerius, who came from Lower Lorraine and had ended up in Italy via the chancellery of Canossa. Under his leadership the systematic teaching of Digest, Institutes and Code began. He was succeeded by the *quattuor doctores* Bulgarus de Bulgarinis, Martinus de Gosia, Jacobus and Hugo de Porta Ravennate. They were followed by Rogerius, Placentinus (who would later teach in Montpellier), Johannes Bassianus, Pillius and a whole series of others who established the reputation of Bologna.

They all used the Digest as their main textbook. This work is indeed fascinating. It contains thousands of short fragments which are written in Latin that is easy to read and which offer good material for discussion. A text that was once written in Constantinople as a caricature of a law book turned out to be the ideal book to use in legal education in the high Middle Ages. It retained this status for centuries. In Bologna the Digest consisted of three parts: the *Digestum vetus* (D. 1-24.2), the *Infortiatum* (D. 24.3-38) and the *Digestum novum* (D. 39-50). This tripartite structure was maintained until the Modern Era. Irnerius added the Institutes of Justinian to the curriculum. It would become the textbook for students beginning on their studies and professors embarking upon their careers. Apart from the Digest, the Code became the second important work – or at least books 1 to 9 did. Books 10 to 12 would begin to lead a separate life as the *Tres libri*. Further texts were added to the Code. In the twelfth century titles 1.1-13 were included, as has been mentioned above. The Emperor Frederick I had Bologna adopt his constitution *Habita* in the Code. This decision, taken at the Diet of Roncaglia (1158) granted jurisdiction to the university and safe-conduct to all of its students. It was interpolated after C. 4.13. The *Authenticum* along with the Novels of Justinian were known in twelfth-century Bologna. They were some years younger than the Code. If the *doctores* found a passage in the *Authenticum* that was inconsistent with the Code, they interpolated it after the relevant text of the Code because *lex posterior priori derogat* (a later law overrides the earlier law). This resulted in another series of new texts for the Code, known as the *authenticae*. A constitution of Frederick II, the *constitutio de statutis et consuetudinibus contra libertatem ecclesiae editis* (1220) was split up into different parts which were also interpolated as *authenticae*. Shortly afterwards, the constitution *Sacramenta puberum* was inserted after C. 2.27.1.

Bibliography. – These interpolations in the Code were published together with its main text until well into the nineteenth century, for the last time in the edition of the KRIEGEL brothers, where they are printed in italic type. In the MOMMSEN-KRÜGER edition they have been removed. In the English translation of Blume the *authenticae* are not translated; the translation of Scott does include them.

The *Authenticum* itself was also read in legal education in the twelfth century. After 1250 the *Libri feodorum* concerning feudal law were added. All of the Bolognese textbooks together were called the *Corpus iuris (civilis)*: *Digestum vetus, Infortiatum, Digestum novum, Codex* and *Volumen*. The latter contained the Institutes, the *Tres libri* and the *Libri feudorum*.

During the *lecturae* the students read the text of the *Corpus iuris*. They made notes, the so-called 'glosses', in between the lines or in the margins of their manuscripts. These glosses gave the first generations of Bolognese jurists the name 'glossators'. These glosses contain (1) explanations of words. They also feature (2) *allegationes*, references to other texts of the *Corpus iuris*. The glossators assumed that Justinianic law was unified. The texts were authoritative and were not called into question. If two texts seemed to be contradictory a solution was sought in (3) *distinctiones*, distinctions: "One text bears on this case and the other on that case." Simply making up these distinctions was not an option: arguments in favour of *distinctiones* had to be drawn from the *Corpus iuris* itself. Sometimes the glosses include (4) *notabilia*, short general rules that were distilled from the original text. In the thirteenth century the glosses began to feature more and more (5) *quaestiones*, legal questions of content that were raised on the occasion of the *lectura*. In the glosses you can find the typical logic of the legists: it was not the historical reality of Justinianic law that took the centre stage, but medieval rationalism, the logic of the accountant. Every fragment enjoyed *auctoritas*, was an authoritative source. The glossators tried to interpret all of these *auctoritates* in such a manner that they were reconciled like amounts in a balanced account. Those who were virtuosos with the internal logic of the *Corpus iuris*, enjoyed the best reputation. This was more than an academic game. In the twelfth century there already were judgements in the case law of Lucca and Pisa that were based on interpretations from the glosses.

In the first half of the thirteenth century Bologna saw its apogee. Hundreds of students were attending lectures. The students were accommodated according to their origin and stayed in *nationes*, nations. Just as *natura, natio* is derived from *nasci* (to be born), but it refers to a country of origin or a race. The nations collaborated to pay a *uniuersitas*, a pool of professors. The nations of the Italians had one *uniuersitas* in Bologna; the nations of the Ultramontanists had a second. Students from the German Netherlands were matriculated in the *natio teutonica*, the Flemish students ended up in the *natio picardica*. In the fourteenth century the name 'college' arrived from the north. When Charles V was anointed German emperor in 1530 in Bologna, he stayed in the Collegio di Spagna.

Important thirteenth-century glossators were Azo (†1215) and his student Accursius (†1260). Azo made a name for himself with his *Summa codicis*, a summary of the Code that was based on his glosses and circulated separately. It was already translated into French in the thirteenth century, when 'chi non ha Azzo non va all palazzo' was an aphorism. Accursius became famous because of the *glossa ordinaria*. He made a selection and synthesis of existing glosses on the *Corpus iuris* and wrote texts that connected them. Because of his position in municipal politics he acquired a monopoly on the sale of textbooks. For decades, every copy of the *Corpus iuris* that was sold included the Gloss of Accursius. Students took these copies home with them, to all the corners of the West. The *glossa ordinaria* would remain part of the *Corpus iuris* for centuries. The monopoly of Accursius slowed down the evolution of legal thought in Bologna, but also contributed to the interpretation of the glossators being disseminated throughout Europe as a completed doctrine.

Another student of Azo was Jacobus Balduini (†1235). His was an original mind. He trained famous professors. Only a small number of manuscripts of his lectures have been handed down, but if new views are expressed at the same time in Bologna by Odofredus de Denariis (†1265); in Paris by Sinibaldus Fliscus or Hostiensis; in Orléans by Guido de Cumis, Simon de Paris or Jean de Monchy; and in Naples by Andrea de Isernia, you can say that they derive from their mutual master Jacobus Balduini. Jacobus Balduini introduced a new method of teaching among the jurists, the *repetitio*. It was based on the *quaestiones de quolibet* of the theologians. Rather than reading the *Corpus iuris*, it involved two-hour long sessions during which a specific subject was explored in depth on the basis of an excerpt from the *Corpus iuris*. By having the students reason about the contents of the texts, Jacobus Balduini made a special contribution to the science of law.

Bibliography. – Editions of the *Corpus iuris civilis* with Accursius' Great Gloss can be found in most university libraries. A widely disseminated anastatic reprint of a Venetian incunabulum was published as *Corpus Glossatorum* 7-11, Turin 1968-1969. If you consult those, will notice two characteristics of incunabula: (1) the first printed letters were based on the letters that could be written with a goose quill and (2) the text is full of abbreviations. More readable types which could be printed in a smaller format so that there was no longer any need for abbreviations only began to be used in the sixteenth century. Also note that the excerpts of the *Corpus iuris* were not numbered. References to them consisted of the name of a title and the first words of the excerpt. D. 45.1.4, for example, is cited as *FF. de uerb. obl. l. Eadem dicemus.* FF is a medieval abbreviation for *Digesta* and l. stands for *lege*. With the lists of titles that can be found at the back of each volume and the lists of fragments at the beginning of each title, these references can be decoded. The glosses are marginal notes. In the main text, you will find letters which function as references to the glosses. Note the many *allegationes*. A gloss is still referenced with its first words, for example gl. *'Causa' ad* C. 1.4.2. Compare a gloss to the text of Jacobus Balduini cited below. Balduini's text breaks free from the text of the *Corpus iuris*, but is still written in the style of the *Corpus*. Balduini also uses a plethora of references. Modern editions include both the references in the old style and, between square brackets, those in the new style.

Text. – Jacopo BALDUINI, *Libellus instructionis aduocatorum*, ms. Vat.lat. 3980 (ed. N. SARTI, *Un giurista tra Azzone e Accursio, Iacopo di Balduino e il suo 'Libellus instructionis aduocatorum'*, Milan 1990, p. 156): [...] Sciendum est quia generaliter in qualibet actione prouidere debet aduocatus ut offeratur libellus in quo petitio proponatur. Hoc prouidere aduocatus actoris, hoc etiam debet prouidere debet aduocatus ut offeratur libellus in quo petitio proponatur. Hoc prouidere aduocatus actoris, hoc etiam debet prouidere aduocatus rei, nam si aliter fieret litis contestatio non ualeret, ut in auth. De exhibendis reis § Sancimus [Nov. 53.3.1], nam licet olim proponetur actio sine scriptis et sine libello, ut ff. de edendo, l. I § I [D. 2.13.1.1], et ff. de priuatis delictis l. finali [D. 47.1.3], nisi qualiter aliud inueniretur, quod inueniebatur alicubi dum conueniebantur uiri illustres, ut C. de dignitatibus l. Quotiens, lib. XIII [C. 12.1.17], uel dum conueniebantur principes agentium in rebus, ut C. de principibus agentium in rebus l. finali, lib. XII [C. 12.21.8], et idem in his qui seruiebant in consistorio principis domino imperatori, de quibus dicitur C. de consistorianis et ministerianis l. finali, lib. XII [C. 12.25.4], hodie tamen generaliter offertur libellus et in scriptis facienda est propositio actoris, et istud generaliter imminet aduocatis. Excipitur tamen in casibus in quibus libellus hodie non est necessarius. Unus casus est [...].

2. The commentators

In the course of the thirteenth century the civil war between Guelfs and Ghibellines was raging in northern Italy. In 1274 the law faculty of Bologna was closed on account of these troubles. Not long thereafter the city became a strategic centre of the Italian crusades. The students stayed away from the town. Many other towns began to recruit the unemployed *doctores* of Bologna. In this manner, 1274 became a turning point for the legal education. The professors, students, copyists and booksellers of Bologna dispersed and settled in Padua, Naples, Salamanca, Coimbra, Toulouse, Cahors, Lyon, Orléans... The *natio teutonica* moved from Bologna to Padua, which would remain an important law faculty for the German regions until the Modern Era. Those of Spanish nationality moved to Salamanca. The French could not migrate to the university of Paris because Roman law had been excluded from the Parisian programme by the bull *Super specula* (1219). They went to Orléans, where the teaching of law had begun in 1235. Renowned *doctores*, among whom were students of Jacobus Balduini, taught there. The legists of Orléans were closely connected with the *curia* of Louis IX, a monarch who was concerned with the improvement of the administration of justice. Between 1274 and the end of the century, the law faculty of Orléans reached its apogee in professors such as Jacques de Revigny (†1296) and Pierre de Belleperche (†1308). Until into the sixteenth century Orléans remained a training ground for jurists from the Low Counties. As in Bologna, the Dutch and people from Brabant stayed in the German nation, while the Flemish were accommodated in the Picard nation.

After a short time the law faculty of Bologna was re-started under the supervision of the papalist Guelfs. In the 1280s it remained a local faculty. At the end of the thirteenth century one of its students was Cynus of Pistoia (Guitoncino dei Sigisbuldi, 1270-1336). He would become a politician and would also teach in Siena, Naples, Perugia and Florence. He was an exceptional legal scholar, who saw that legal science had been disseminated across Europe and had taken root everywhere, and also realised the importance of the *repetitiones*. He collected the *repetitiones* from the new universities and incorporated them into voluminous commentaries on the Digest and the Code. Cynus was not a glossator, who wrote notes in the margins of his manuscripts, but a commentator who wrote entire volumes. For him, Roman law was *ius commune*, a law that was common to and for the Latin world. His works were hardly disseminated – they were too scientific to be spread far and wide.

One of Cinus' last students in Perugia, Bartolus de Saxoferrato (1314-1357) was responsible for a breakthrough in teaching. He became an assistant of Jacobus Butrigarius in Bologna and later taught in Perugia. He described Roman law as *ius commune* and contrasted it with *ius proprium*, the particular law of local courts. In Bartolus' descriptions, Roman law was not an elevated legal culture but a practical system for the administration of justice that could be mixed with local norms. Bartolus wrote consultations for advocates in which he made Roman law usable for all possible conflicts. His contemporaries took to this approach. Both his commentaries on the *Corpus iuris* and his consultations were disseminated widely. The concrete approach of Bartolus made it possible for feudal and urban judges to apply Roman law. Francesco Calasso, who furthered the study of medieval Roman law to a considerable extent in the twentieth century, considered Bartolus the greatest jurist of all time. He was followed by great jurists like Alberico di Rosciate (1290-1354), Oldradus da Ponte (†1335), Raniero di Forlivio (†1368), Luca da Penna (†1390) or Bartolomeo di Saliceto (†1412). Bartolus' student Baldus de Ubaldis (1327-1400) imposed even more innovations in his commentaries. He based his vision both on the tradition of the legists and the tradition of the canonists and was the first jurist who, in imitation of Thomism, took Greek logic and moral philosophy into account. Thus, he became a predecessor of the Renaissance.

In the fourteenth and fifteenth centuries several kings established new law faculties. The medieval *ius commune* could be used to reassemble fragmented feudal regions. If a liege lord could introduce appeals against the decisions of his vassals, he could revise all of their decisions and extend his sovereign power. The question, however, was which law he should apply in his sovereign court. The *ius commune* with its elaborate imperial regime and thorough procedures offered a good platform. In order to introduce the *ius commune*, however, the lord needed judges and officials who knew Roman law and hence the new monarchical law faculties. Academic law also proved beneficial to trade. These new law faculties of the fourteenth century sought professors who taught in the manner of Bartolus, because he personified modernisation. However, the fourteenth century took a turn for the worse and changed into a time of recession and misery, plague and cholera. The size of the population decreased and in history, such a situation always leads to conservatism. Preservation of what was left became the watchword. The Roman law of the commentators became one of the objects of this conservatism. Bartolism was cherished for a century. Scholars kept commentating the *Corpus iuris* as the Italian commentators of the fourteenth century had done. When the university of Leuven was established in 1425, professors who taught in the manner of Bartolus were still sought after. The last famous commentator was Jason de Mayno (1435-1519). In the sixteenth century this manner of teaching was called *mos italicus*.

These two conservative periods would be important for Western legal history. In the thirteenth century the Gloss of Accursius would captivate the West for fifty years. In the same manner a coagulated Bartolism left its mark on Europe between 1350 and 1450. Because of this, all of the European law faculties were on the same wavelength and the Latin world was provided with a common legal base, with parallel legal doctrine and case law. When the national legal systems became more diverse in the Renaissance, their laws remained based on common principles which had been developed in different countries during the previous two centuries.

Bibliography. – the best book about the law of the glossators and the commentators is once again E. CORTESE, *Il diritto nella storia medioevale*, Rome 1995. On the emergence of law faculties outside of Bologna, see L. WAELKENS, 'L'influence de l'Ecole de droit d'Orléans sur la doctrine bolonaise à la fin du XIIIe siècle', in F. STEVENS and D. VANDEN AUWEELE (eds.), *Houd voet bij stuk, Xenia iuris historiae G. Van Dievoet oblata*, Leuven 1990, p. 193-208. The canonists also kept a close eye on the evolution of Roman law. See for example L. WAELKENS, 'Raoul de Chennevières, Portrait d'un canoniste orléanais du XIIIe siècle d'après un manuscript de la Bibliothèque Nationale', in: *Etudes néerlandaises de droit et d'histoire présentées à l'université d'Orléans pour le 750e anniversaire des enseignements juridiques*, [Bulletin de la Société archéologique et historique de l'Orléanais, Nouvelle Série, t. XI, n° 68, mai 1985], p. 81-95. In the 1970s, works from the years 1270-1300 were republished in Bologna in the series *Opera iuridica rariora*. Among these were works of Jacques de Revigny and Pierre de Belleperche. CYNUS DE PISTOIA, *In codicem commentaria*, Frankfurt/Main 1578 was republished in Turin in 1965. Bartolus and Baldus can be found in university libraries. A complete Bartolus was published in Rome in 1996. The hypothesis of the congealment of Bartolism is elaborated in L. WAELKENS, 'Il Digesto all'epoca dei commentatori', in: D. MANTOVANI and A. PADOA SCHIOPPA (eds.), *Interpretare il Digesto, Storia e metodi*, Pavia 2014, p. 299-309.

3. The medieval scope of Roman law

The glossators and commentators collected an enormous amount of information about each fragment of the *Corpus iuris*. Their legal doctrine was far more extensive than the *Corpus iuris* itself. Legal doctrine was spun out around every text, with the original text only serving as a stepping stone. Was this *ius commune* still Roman? What the medieval jurists read in the old sources was new, as was the approach towards law. In Antiquity, procedure took the centre stage: there was no law outside of the court. Case law contained standard solutions for conflicts and points of departure for the settlement of new conflicts, but no grand principles. The prefecture sought practical solutions that were acceptable for the entire Empire. This approach could still be found in medieval England, where the *Curia regis* acted as the Roman prefecture had done and where the law was developed outside of the universities.

On the Continent, by contrast, Roman law was treated in the universities, which not only used Abelardus' method *per sic et non,* characterised by bookkeeper's logic: from the twelfth century onwards, legal thought was also embedded into Augustinian neoplatonism. Under the influence of the theologians and canonists, medieval Roman law became material in character. It represented notions and was supported by values. Claims became less important than what one could acquire through them. *Dominium* was no longer the status of *dominus* which one had to prove in order to receive a *reiuindicatio,* but a right to goods. Possession referred to having and keeping something rather than to the possessory action. An obligation was no longer something that one could acquire with an *actio in personam,* but a manner in which one was bound to someone else. An extensive doctrine of liability was spun around this. Marriage evolved from a manner of establishing the competence of ecclesiastical judges in the twelfth century to the moral status of cohabitation and a sacrament in the thirteenth century. The canonists examined the value of promises and agreements and deduced that these had to be binding. Roman criminal law was rethought in terms of guilt and punishment.

Despite all of this, the medieval academic law was Roman. The legists called it Roman and it was an important intermediate stage between the Roman law of the Middle Ages and that of the Early Modern and Modern Periods. It is there that the common European law was developed that would go down in history as Roman. The Roman dream still takes centre stage in this law, as does the reception of Roman legal sources. Romanists have to take medieval Roman law into account.

§8. The reception of Roman law in the Early Modern Era

In the fifteenth century the European population grew again. This brought economic growth, new insights and a new culture: the Early Modern Era. This period of history is visibly present in our historic towns and university buildings. In the kingdoms with central institutions libraries, archives and public universities were established. Many written sources were preserved there. The art of printing caused legal books to be disseminated on a large scale and one can almost always find a copy of the works published in this era. Monarchical and urban archives first and foremost preserved judicial archives. Everywhere in Europe, there are collections of judicial files from this era. Moreover, there are notes and courses of law students. What a change in comparison with the Middle Ages and its manuscripts, rare archives, short glosses and half-erased traces of ideas and legal notions. Nevertheless, the years 1450-1600 remain difficult to access. They are under a taboo. The Early Modern Period is a black page in the history of continental Europe. From 1450 onwards, Italy was submerged in war. Around 1530 the entire West was on fire and at the end of the century survival became a precarious matter. It is only in the seventeenth century that Europe became inhabitable again. The past miseries were repressed and erased from the collective memory. This repression makes it difficult to study the Early Modern Period.

One would expect that the study of Roman law ends here. The end of Roman law and the beginning of national legal systems, as some textbooks say. Roman law, however, remained prevalent. The monarchical sovereign councils which dominated the sixteenth century were built on the medieval *ius commune*. In the seventeenth century the *Corpus iuris* took the centre stage again; this time the common European legal culture was used to dismantle the nationalism of the monarchs. This was the *usus modernus pandectarum* or the *ius commune* of the Early Modern Period. There were so many changes in the interpretation of the Roman legal sources that even the view of the law of Antiquity and the Middle Ages was obscured. If one travels *amne adverso*, upstream, through the history of Roman law it is in the early modern period that one comes up against a wall of new interpretations of the *Corpus iuris* which are common to this very day. The meaningful study of Roman law is impossible without including this period.

Bibliography. – H. COING, *Europäisches Privatrecht, 1500 bis 1800*, I, Älteres Gemeines Recht, Munich 1985, p. 1-129 contains a beautiful overview of the reception of Roman and canon law in the sixteenth century. For legal works from the sixteenth and seventeenth centuries, the best library is that of the Max-Planck-Institut für Rechtsgeschichte in Frankfurt/Main. Large repositories of case law form that time are found throughout Europe. On the fact that the current interpretation of the Roman legal sources dates from the Early Modern Period, see L. WAELKENS 'Le droit romain antique, un produit de l'interpretation des Temps Modernes' in: *L'interprétation du droit, Actes des journées internationales d'histoire du droit, Besançon 30 mai–2 juin 2013*, Besançon [2015] (in print).

1. The advent and the repression of Greek culture

In the Early Modern Period Western Europe was strongly influenced by Greek culture. Do not associate this culture with Antiquity. The idea that Greek is connected with Antiquity is part of that wall of interpretations from the Modern Era. For centuries, *graecus* referred to the Levant and Constantinople. In the fourth century this city became the second capital of the Roman Empire; in the fifth century it became the only one. While the Western Roman Empire fell apart, the Greek Empire kept developing. Being the largest city of the Middle Ages and the most beautiful of all time, Constantinople – its palaces, domed churches, mosaics, purple skyline under the golden evening sun, its colours and scents in an inebriating microclimate – was etched in the memory of pilgrims, crusaders and traders. Constantinople controlled the trade routes with regard to corn, the trade in gold, copper, tin, iron from Anatolia, silk and cotton, alum and dyes, the trade in foodstuffs such as currants, chestnuts or pistachios, but also in weapons ranging from halberds to cannons. The Antikythera mechanism illustrated the technology of the city; the reliquary chapel of the palace and the grand orthodox services testified to its Christian status. The inhabitants of the Eastern Roman Empire called themselves *romaioi* and the Westerners *latinoi*. The Westerners in their turn called the Easterners *graeci* and, by the end of the sixteenth century, Byzantines.

During the Middle Ages, Western Europe was hardly influenced by the Greco-Roman culture. People who read Greek were few and far between; those who read Greek legal texts were downright exceptional. From Rome, almost no Greek had spread to the north. In the twelfth century, Greek was read in some centres of study like the abbey of Saint-Denis near Paris. The south of Italy and Sicily were under Constantinople's governance for a long time, but even there one finds but few Greek legal sources. The Western emperor Frederick II, who lived in Andria for a long time, did read and speak Greek fluently and had works translated into Latin. The Mediterranean trading cities, in particular Venice and Genoa, had close ties with Constantinople. In the twelfth century the Venetian quarter in Constantinople had twenty thousand inhabitants. Genoa built trading posts around the Aegean and the Black Sea. The archives of Venice and Genoa contain important testimonies to centuries of trade with the Greco-Roman world. In the late Middle Ages, the West was slightly less isolated. Most of its monarchs were familiar with Constantinople, its system of governance, trade and shipping, and manner of thought.

In the fifteenth century all of Western Europe was suddenly confronted with Greek culture, because of the influx of refugees. This immigration picked up speed around 1440 and became a tidal wave in 1453, the year in which the Turks captured Constantinople. Greeks kept arriving until well into the seventeenth century, when the Venetian islands were taken one by one by the Ottomans. The main destinations for the Greek immigrants were Venice with its islands, the Adriatic cities, Genoa, Florence, Rome, Naples, Lisbon and the Portuguese islands, Marseille, Barcelona, Seville and the Atlantic ports. From these places, many Greeks moved further into Italy, or on to Andalusia, Toledo, Lyon, Paris... Most of these immigrants were learned or rich. They had ships, imported artworks or tools, or arrived with phenomenal movable fortunes. Others brought shiploads of manuscripts. Their civilisation was overwhelming and their wealth caused an emphatic reception of their values. The impact of the Greeks on Western culture in the fifteenth century was the Renaissance. The study of Greek culture and philosophy began in the 1440s in Florence, which was surpassed by Venice in the 1480s. Moneyed Greeks settled in 'their' old capital, Rome, and built Renaissance palaces and domed churches with mosaics. In 1453, the plans for Saint Peter's – bigger than the Hagia Sophia, but with a Greek dome and mosaics – were presented in Rome. Bessarion, the former archbishop of Nicea was almost elected pope in the conclaves of 1455 and 1471. Greek shipowners searched for sea routes to restart their trade with Asia. Columbus descended from a Greek migrant family. When in Tordesillas the territorial superpower Spain bowed to the small country of Portugal, this was because Spain feared the former Greek marine ships that sailed from Lisbon and operated in the Atlantic Ocean. The French kings Charles VII and Louis XI had their own war fleets equipped and trained by Greek marines. New trade banks in Spain and Genoa created new trade flows. The silk industry was established in Lyon; embroidery and tapestry in the Low Countries, the weapons industry in Toledo and Austria. In Andalusia, on Corsica and the Portuguese islands there were attempts to grow Cyprian sugarcane, mastic trees from Chios, Egyptian cotton, etcetera. Behind all of these external changes lay a different tradition of thought. Attention was paid to mathematics and Greek logic became important for the natural sciences. At the universities, critical thought ousted medieval *auctoritas*. This led to the rationalism of the Early Modern Period. Even the attention to a healthy lifestyle which Justus Lipsius praised to the skies was Greek.

The Greek offer came at a time when the West was receptive to new ideas and was searching for new means. It sent a shockwave through Europe. The first consequence was new trade and economic development, which included phenomena like the golden age of Antwerp or the discovery of America. The political and religious changes would, however, destabilise the West. In politics, the Greeks promoted the absolutism which they had known in the Levant since Justinian. They did not care at all for the feudal system. At all of the courts, they sang the praises of absolutism and a centralised administration after the Roman models. They tried to tempt monarchs to organise a new crusade to free Constantinople. In order to wage a war within the feudal system, kings made use of the means of their vassals. A 'new' monarch, however, could loan money from the new bankers, buy weapons from the new traders and wage wars autonomously. If the king pledged feudal rights, he could loan without limitations. Many kings managed to introduce appeals against the decisions of their vassals and began to lead their country through a sovereign council. This was the basis of absolutism. The possibility of waging war autonomously, however, did not lead to a new crusade, but to wars between the different monarchs. In the fifteenth century the Italian wars started; during the sixteenth century, war was endemic throughout the West.

A second cause of destabilisation was religion. In New Castile tensions between Greek and Jewish immigrants on the one hand, and Muslims on the other, led relatively quickly to the imposition of Latin Christianity as the obligatory religion. This measure was not taken in the regions north of the Pyrenees. The Greeks professed a Christianity characterised by the absence of bishops and the old Greek resentment towards the pope. This Greek Christianity would be the germ of Protestantism. The first Reformist theologians were influenced by Greek thought concerning religion. The religious differences would lead to additional hostilities and religious wars. The kings would make use of these wars to subject the ecclesiastical courts to their sovereign councils.

Less than a century after the wave of immigration the tide had turned. The new culture did not have a strong enough foundation to deal with all of the side effects. The West was destabilised to an unprecedented extent. In the sixteenth century the Latin world was at the brink of extinction. The combination of the monarchical and religious wars led to the possibilities of survival becoming much lower than they had been for centuries. From 1510 onwards, the universities began to dike in Europe to protect it from the Greek wave. From 1560 onwards the jurists tried to revise the sources of the new law. They thought up scenarios which did not leave room for much sympathy for Greek culture. Once the economic advantage had been assimilated, we no longer needed those losers, who had not even managed to retain their own country with their grand ideas. Why would we import the Roman culture from the Levant if it had originated in our own cradle, Rome? In the second half of the sixteenth century the Greco-Roman culture was ousted and designated as 'Byzantine', a mocking name for this old colony of Rome. At the beginning of the sixteenth century Manucci in Venice alone published one book in Greek every month. Half a century later these contemporary Greek thinkers were reduced to the status of Byzantines. In order to decrease the Greek influence on religion, Greek culture was stamped as pre-Christian. The ties between the Greeks and the Reformation were cut. To this day, the Greek authors of the Early Modern Era are not read. The northern humanists applied themselves to the common Roman past, the Greek church fathers and the Greek Bible. They included Hebrew in this research and thus put Greek squarely in the sphere of Antiquity. The study of Greek became a study of a culture which we, Latins, had defeated in Antiquity. In order to undermine absolutism the Greek political culture was repressed and changed from an imperial and absolutist regime to a 'democratic' one. Constantinople disappeared from sight and was replaced by Pericles' Athens. He already defended a 'democratic' regime like that of Genoa and Venice, Geneva or the Republic of the United Netherlands against fanatical Habsburg picadors and the hoplites of Sparta, Philip II of Spain or the French Valois kings.

After the peace of Westphalia (1648), no one wanted to be reminded of the disasters of the sixteenth century. Greek culture had been repressed and buried. Only the teaching of Greek as a language remained. In this manner, Renaissance thought was only studied through linguistics, a neutral discipline. Science and mathematics were no longer experienced as being Greek. Even the jurists repressed the Greek model in the sixteenth century. A good illustration of this process can be found at the university of Bourges. Andrea Alciato (1492-1550) was attracted by King Francis I to teach Greek law there. From the very start, he pussyfooted around the subject. When Jacques Cujas (1522-1590) taught in Bourges, Greek law already consisted of the ancient sources of the *Corpus iuris*. François Hotman (1524-1590), who taught there a bit later, was fervently anti-Greek. In his *L'Antitribonien* he pleaded for national law.

The repression of Greco-Roman culture is demurely respected to this day. After the disaster of the Early Modern Era Pandora's box has remained closed. No one wants to raise the demons by writing about the Greek *romaioi* of Constantinople, Trebizond, Aleppo or Alexandria.

Bibliography. – L. WAELKENS, 'Réception ou refoulement? Pour une lecture grecque de l'histoire du droit de la Renaissance', in: B. COPPEIN, F. STEVENS and L. WAELKENS (eds.), *Modernisme, tradition et acculturation juridique. Actes des Journées internationales d'histoire du droit tenues à Louvain, 28 mai – 1 juin 2008*, Brussels 2011, p. 137-149; L. WAELKENS, 'Legal transplant of Greek caesaropapism in Early Modern times', in J. BALLOR, W. DECOCK, M. GERMANN and L. WAELKENS (eds.), *Law and religion, The legal teachings of the Protestant and Catholic Reformation*, Göttingen 2014, p. 213 230.

2. The sovereign monarchical lawcourts

In the sixteenth century many monarchs thought that they could fulfil the old Roman dream by becoming emperors in their country and by ruling through a central court after the model of the Roman prefecture.

The evolution towards larger principalities with a centralised administration of justice started in England in the eleventh century. In the twelfth century the Count of Flanders also considered himself to be *imperator in regno suo*. In France centralisation commenced in the thirteenth century, when the jurists who held a seat in the *curia regis* – the body that resolved conflicts pertaining to feudal law – also began to treat appeals against decisions of royal vassals. A vassal whose decisions could be reviewed by the *curia regis*, was subjected to the king. All of his decisions could be challenged. Louis IX established a Parliament with a permanent headquarters in Paris that was competent to hear these appeals. According to the legal doctrine of that time those subject to the law could lodge appeals with the king against all of the judges whose legal powers had been delegated by the king. However, there was considerable political resistance to the introduction of appeals. Everyone who was strong enough claimed to be the emperor of his land. In practice, higher appeals to the Parliament of Paris were introduced district by district on the occasion of the inheritance of fiefs or military interventions of the king. Appeals against Bourbonnais, Toulouse, Montpellier... were lodged with the king in the middle of the thirteenth century. The wars around 1300 between the count of Flanders and the king of France revolved around appeals against the Council of Flanders with the Parliament of Paris. The Count of Flanders had to bow to the king. The Hundred Years' War between England and France was about appeals to Paris or London.

Wherever the residents of a jurisdiction could file appeals with a royal council, the local court began to apply royal law in order to avoid appeals. As a consequence, the residence of the domain in question became inhabitants of the monarchy. The jurisdictions and, as a consequence, the possibilities for trade and exchange, became larger again. This resulted in affluence. Around 1450 the centre of France had become one single affluent country. In Spain the little medieval realms dating from before the 'Reconquista' grew into a kingdom with unified Cortes. The same evolution took place in Poland, Denmark, Sweden, Bavaria, Bohemia and Piedmont. In the Low Countries the great promotor of the royal councils was Philip the Good (1396-1467). He acquired a whole series of provinces and established a court of appeal in each of them. In 1425 he established the law faculty of Leuven in order to educate judges and officials who would impose the Roman law that he had seen in Constantinople. He established a *curia regis* as sovereign council that received appeals against the provincial courts of appeal. This instance evolved into the Great Council of Mechlin (Malines). The Burgundians recast the divided Netherlands into a strong nation in record time. Germany watched from the sidelines. In 1495 the imperial 'Reichskammergerichtshof' was established. It made extensive contributions towards the reintroduction of civil law, but did not manage to bring the principalities under the emperor's control. Separate nations such as Saxony, Bohemia, Bavaria or Austria originated there.

The royal sovereign councils became the axis of policy making. They played the role of the prefecture in Rome. Their judgements were royal decisions and they imposed their law on all of the lower courts. The monarchs managed to make their central courts apply the *ius commune*. This law worked; jurists had been trained in it at the universities; and it was the easiest way of eradicating particularism. In practice, this *ius commune* was Bartolism. In the course of the sixteenth century some monarchs went one step further in the reformation of the law. Rather than waiting until all conflicts were treated on appeal in their sovereign court, they asked for the case law of the lower courts and had it rewritten by their sovereign council. In this manner they decided beforehand which law they would pronounce if a case ever occurred. The royal chancelleries also drew up 'ordinances', guidelines for their officials. These would slowly evolve into guidelines for the population. In the seventeenth century the ordinances would become the basis of modern royal legislation and modern parliamentarianism which would replace the system of ruling through the administration of justice.

During the course of the sixteenth century, monarchs also began to subject the old ecclesiastical courts to their sovereign councils. The religious wars were a reason for this development. In Western Europe, we find four models that were used to neutralise the judicial authority of the Church. In the 1530s the kings of Denmark and Sweden assimilated the entire church into the royal government and the central government budget. The bishops became officials and all ecclesiastical decisions came under the supervision of the monarchical councils. During this process, even the charities of the bishops became part of the royal order. The central government thus acquired hospitals and schools and even the parochial pension funds that existed in Finland. In the nineteenth century these charities of the northern monarchs would serve as the model for the welfare state in Western Europe. A second regime can be found in the Reformed regions of Germany and the Northern Netherlands. The church and its social services became part of the communities. Conflicts in this sphere were treated by the civic aldermen's courts and, on appeal, in the royal councils. This model would be copied by the French revolutionaries in 1789. A third system can be found in the sixteenth century in countries with Catholic monarchs, such as France, Spain, Cologne, Austria, Bavaria or the Southern Netherlands, where the Church was eliminated in an indirect manner through the introduction of competing jurisdictions. The royal courts there allowed claims on the basis of canonical means and applied canon law to those cases. In this manner marriage, wills, descent or ecclesiastical goods were brought up in the royal case law. Because of this cheaper procedure, most of those who were subject to law diverted their conflicts that had an ecclesiastical slant to the monarchical courts. In these countries, Bartolism and the canonical administration began to merge in the sixteenth century. Canonical principles were adopted in general legal doctrine, for example the romano-canonical procedure, *pacta sunt seruanda*, good faith in all obligations, family and marriage as the basis of legitimacy, etcetera. England, finally, took a fourth path. In 1534 king Henry VIII introduced the regime of Constantinople. Against the highest ecclesiastical courts, those of York and Canterbury, appeals could only be lodged with the Privy Council in London. Appeals to Rome became impossible. As a consequence, the king could revise all ecclesiastical decisions, while the church continued to function autonomously. Because the highest instance for 'consistory courts' was not the same as that for the royal courts, the case law of both jurisdictions was never mixed. Consequently, no elements of canon law ended up in the ordinary royal case law; a development which is at the basis of many differences between English and Continental law.

Bibliography. – On the role of Roman law higher appeal in the formation of nations, see L. Waelkens, 'Le rôle de l'appel judiciaire romain dans la formation des Pays-Bas au seizième siècle', in: *Podział władzy i parlamentaryzm w przeszłości i współcześnie, prawo, doktryna, praktyka*, Warsaw 2007, p. 75-85. On the role of a law faculty in the formation of a nation, see L. Waelkens, 'L'influence de la fondation de la Faculté de droit de Louvain (1425) sur la formation des Pays-Bas', in: J. Krynen and M. Stolleis (eds.), *Science politique et droit public dans les facultés de droit européennes (XIIIe-XVIIe siècle)*', [Studien zur europäischen Rechtsgeschichte, 229,] Frankfurt/Main 2008, p. 251-261.

3. Changes at the law faculty of Leuven

A new era also began at the law faculties during this period. Through the printing press, some legal publications were disseminated throughout Europe. The legal scholars were mainly in the service of the national royal councils. At the universities we nevertheless find precursors of a new European legal doctrine, the *ius commune* of the Modern Era. In this legal doctrine, the striking elements are, in chronological order, Renaissance thought, the influence of the Reformation, humanism in law and the advent of natural law. These four phases of early modern legal thought each influenced the interpretation of the Roman legal sources in their own way. Legal scholars cannot of course be classified rigidly and this division must be taken with a pinch of salt. We will principally examine the evolution at the faculty of Leuven. There are too many early modern law faculties and too many printed legal works to survey in the scope of some pages. In the history of the law faculty of Leuven, however, the main lines of the evolution in Europe can be discerned. The same analysis can be made of other sixteenth-century law faculties, like the abovementioned school of Bourges. There, the French king Francis I had brought in the new approach with Andrea Alciato, who had been trained in Pavia and Bologna. In Bourges, Alciato taught great Renaissance minds like Guillaume Budé (1467-1535). He trained Reformist jurists like François Connan (1508-1551) and John Calvin (1509-1564). Hugues Doneau (Donellus, Chalon-sur-Saône 1527 – Altdorf 1591) became the prototype of the Reformed jurist in Bourges. With Cujas (1522-1590) and François le Douaren (Saint-Brieux 1500 – Bourges 1559) humanism took root in Bourges. Specific to Leuven, however, is the early advent of natural law.

Bibliography. – The best general overview of the legal history of this period is given by A. PADOA SCHIOPPA, *Storia del diritto in Europa dal medioevo all'epoca contemporanea*, Bologna 2007. H. COING (ed.), *Handbuch der Quellen und Literatur der Neueren europäischen Privatrechtsgeschichte*, II, *1500-1800*, Munich 1976-1977 offers an in-depth contextualisation and bibliography. For Leuven, we refer to L. WAELKENS, F. STEVENS and J. SNAET, *History of the Leuven faculty of law*, Bruges 2014.

A. The Renaissance in legal doctrine

Until the sixteenth century, Bartolism played a strong role in the administration of justice and legal education. In Pavia Jason de Mayno (1435-1519) still taught *more italico*, in the classical manner of the commentators. In Leuven this manner of working was thoroughly investigated by Nicolas Everaerts (Grijpskerke 1461 – Mechlin 1532). He was a professor between 1493 and 1505 and, at the same time, official to the bishop of Cambrai in Brussels. Then, he became a justice in the Great Council of Mechlin, president of the Court of Holland and president of the Great Council of Mechlin. His masterpiece, the *Topica seu loci legales* (1516, extended edition in 1533) was reprinted twenty-seven times in all of the great centres of legal juridical publishing in the sixteenth century alone. Everaerts set himself up as a typical Renaissance thinker: he surpassed the tradition of the commentators and analysed their methods in a critical manner. He did not, in the first place, consider law from the *Corpus iuris*, but from legal practice. He analysed how the jurists had built up their own logic since the Middle Ages and how they dealt with the Roman sources. His main conclusion was that the jurists employed 'micro reception': they continuously transplanted solutions from one area of the law to another, according to the current norms of the time. They applied Roman texts about wills to inheritance law, texts about ownership to feudal law, texts about land charges on ecclesiastical tithes, texts about sale to rental agreements, texts about marriage to spiritual relations... Everaerts had an eye for reality. For him, the point of departure was the study of case law. He was a great proponent of royal absolutism. What is surprising is that Everaerts did not see a difference between the legal thought of the legists and the canonists. He consciously mixed both. He also added a dash of moral philosophy to his recipe.

Everaerts' critical vision of Bartolism and his manner of dealing with the Roman sources profoundly influenced Reformed legal thinkers like Oldendorp, Catiuncula, Wezenbecius, Hotman... His practical approach to law, independent of the *Corpus iuris*, led to the *mos gallicus*. Charles Dumoulin (Molinaeus, 1500-1566) in France adopted his vision that in the first place one had to study the *ius commune* as it had been developed by the sovereign councils. Via Pieter Crockaert (1465-1514), Everaert inspired Francisco de Vitoria (1480/8-1555/60), who will be discussed below, and was the first non-jurist who wrote about justice and procedure, *de justitia et iure*.

In Leuven, the jurists who followed the approach of Everaerts broke free from the old tradition of mere commentary on the *Corpus iuris*. They introduced the new education in the form of *paratitla*, per title. In this new educational system, it was no longer the fragments of the *Corpus iuris* that were discussed, but the 'titles', the remedies at law that featured in these fragments. In the *Corpus iuris* the fragments were arranged per remedy. It was during this period that people started to consider the *Corpus iuris* per part and the term 'title' changed its meaning to 'heading of a subdivision'. In the middle of the century the first monographs were published, like Mudaeus' (see below) works about contracts of sale and real security, Pieter Peck's (Peckius, 1529-1589) works about maritime law or Elbrecht de Leeuw's (Leoninus, 1519/20-1598) about banking law. In this period we additionally find many consultations of professors which show the practical approach of law. Six hundred consultations of the Leuven professor Jean de Waimes (Wamesius, 1524-1590) which clearly elucidated the legal practice of this period were published.

B. The Reformist legal doctrine

The critical legal thought of Nicolas Everaerts exerted a large influence on the Reformed jurists. For reformers like Lucas of Leyden in Munster, Calvin in Geneva or Zwingli in Zurich, theology and law were closely related. Bypassing the dark Middle Ages, the Reformed theologians returned to the classical sources, the Bible and the church fathers. In the same manner they sought to align themselves with the real *Corpus iuris* without the glosses and commentaries of the Middle Ages and especially without the mess which the canonists had made of it. Their method was the exact opposite of Everaerts': Roman law had to be cleared of canon law. They looked at the old texts with visions from the new theology and with a sixteenth-century method of thought that had been influenced by Greek logic. In Leuven the first to take this path was Gabriël van der Muyden (Mudaeus, 1500-1560). He elaborated on the legacy of the medieval commentators, but advocated a *ius commune* without canon law. The *Corpus iuris* was the main source from which one could develop new law by using contemporary logic.

The main adherent of Mudaeus in Leuven was Matthias van Wesenbeke (Wesenbecius, 1531-1586). He became famous in Wittenberg, where he educated Bronkhorst (1554-1627), who would later become the frontman of the law faculty of Leyden. Just like Mudaeus, he tried to separate civil and canon law. In 1577 Philip II established four royal chairs in Leuven. In so doing, he aimed at the development of a romano-canonical law for the Netherlands. The faculty asked for two royal chairs for Roman law and two for canon law. This provided a better guarantee that the two branches of law would be separated. Leoninus himself held a royal chair of canon law for a long time in order to ensure that canon law remained a separate discipline.

In 1575 the University of Leyden was established as the second university in the Netherlands. It was clearly Calvinist in character. Under the influence of immigrants from the south, who were not very pleased with the local law, Leyden became a study centre for Roman law, in the sense of *ius commune* without canon law, and for humanism. The Huguenot Hugues Doneau (Donellus, Chalon-sur-Saône 1527 – Altdorf 1591) was attracted there from Bourges. It is here that the foundations were laid for the typical Dutch school of elegant jurisprudence, which was developed by jurists like Vinnius (1588-1657), Van Leeuwen (1625-1694), P. Voet (1619-1667), Ulric Huber (†1713) or Cornelis van Bynkershoek (1673-1743).

C. Humanism in law

Around 1450 the technique of movable type was developed. Publishers who worked for the European market were established relatively quickly afterwards. They devoted their attention to the common European culture and to works like the Bible, the church fathers, the Latin writers, the great classics from Constantinople, the *Corpus iuris* or the commentators on the *ius commune*. As part of their rivalry with other printers, they appealed to scholars to offer quality. It is from this group that the humanists originated. Being linguists specialised in textual criticism, they attempted to reconstruct the best editions of old texts from manuscripts. In the sixteenth century, they were given a second function. When Europe had become one large battlefield, they continued to converse across nations and arms. In their cultural world, they developed a neutral forum for discussion. This continued tradition of speaking about science and the common past became an important path to peace in the sixteenth century.

In the field of law, there were but few humanists. The first Fleming who became famous as a humanist in this field was Louis Blauwblomme from Ghent, who worked on an edition of the *Corpus iuris* for the publisher Claude Chevallon in Paris between 1522 and 1529. He was the first publisher who tested the text of the Digest against the *littera florentina*. Another famous edition of the *Corpus iuris* was produced by Haloander. It was published in Nuremberg in 1529-1530. In this edition, the Codex once more consisted of twelve books. In 1534 the jurist and politician Viglius of Aytta (1507-1577) published Theophilus' Greek paraphrase of the Institutes, as he had found it in a Venetian manuscript. In 1553, a critical edition of the Digest by Torelli appeared. Denys Godefroy (Dionisius Gothofredus, Paris 1549 – Strasbourg 1622) made an important critical edition of the entire *Corpus iuris* which first appeared in 1583. In later versions of this edition, corrections of François de Maulde (Modius, Bruges 1555-1597) were incorporated. Godefroy also published the Theodosian Code. A former student of the University of Leuven, Jacob Reyvaert from Lissewege (Raevardus, 1535-1586) published the Twelve Tables in Bruges in 1565.

D. The precursors of natural law

During the second half of the sixteenth century, jurists saw dramatic situations within society. The Roman law of the sovereign court had degenerated into a law of warlords who did not understand the *pax romana*. According to Roman law, the monarch guaranteed civil rights and a decent procedure through his administration. The monarchs, however, were not bound to precedents (*princeps legibus solutus*, D. 1.3.31) and could interpret the old civil rights in an arbitrary manner. In times of war, moreover, there were no more civil rights – the enemy armies were bound to no law. Since the Golden Bull (1356), however, in the Germanic Empire there had been rights which applied to everyone who was born in the Empire. The Habsburg monarchs had accepted these. According to the Fueros of Castile, to which the same monarchs were bound as kings of Spain, everyone who was born in the territory of the kingdom acquired civil rights as well. In Everaerts' work, we read relativising reflections about this. For Charles V and Philip II, the granting of these civil rights at the time of birth was also entrusted to the monarch, who did with this what he wanted. *Quod principi placet, legis habet vigorem* (D. 1.4.1). The only thing holding Philip II – as well as some other monarchs – back was his God-fearing nature. He only gave way to his Creator. Joachim Hopperus (Sneek 1523 – Escorial 1576) was the first professor of Leuven who taught that the system of governing merely through the administration of justice no longer applied. It was the Creator who had invested the individual with rights at birth. The courts were bound not only by precedents of higher courts, but also by such innate rights (*iura naturalia*).

In 1521 three thousand Castilian citizens travelled to Valladolid to defend their civil rights against emperor Charles. He unleashed a battalion, which massacred the column of demonstrators in Villalar. Francisco de Vitoria (1480/88-1555/60) reacted in Valladolid and later in Salamanca. He tried to provide the damaged intellectual life with a foundation in the medieval university tradition and began to test law against theology, canon law and Roman law. Through creation and baptism, people entered the divine order, which transcended the royal order. Roman and canon law were not only the law of the emperor and the pope. They were also valuable because they formed a part of the academic tradition. In Vitoria's masterpiece *De iustitia et iure*, justice and case law were confused. He adopted the scholastic method of Thomas Aquinas. Great minds like Martinus de Azpilcueta (1491-1568), Arias Pinel (✝1563) or Diego de Covarrubias (1512-1577) followed his lead. Followers of this new trend were called 'neoscholastics', 'Spanish scholastics' or 'second scholastics' by the legal historians of the twentieth century. Currently, they are referred to as the Spanish jusnaturalists. Outside of Salamanca, important followers of Vitoria were Francisco Suárez (1548-1617), who taught in Rome, and his student Luis Molina (1535-1600). Both their main works dealt with *de iustitia et iure* as well. Such a mixture of theology and medieval law could be found, for example, in their doctrine concerning sovereignty. Power had been delegated by the people to the monarchs, but the people could also revoke the delegation of the monarchs who were not performing their duties properly. Another example was their view on ownership. Ownership was not just based on what the monarch granted within feudal law, but also on divine rights which had been invested by God in those who made use of his creation. The Spanish *jusnaturalists* built on the medieval doctrine of unjust enrichment. If the balance was disturbed in the relationship between two persons without there being an ethically sound reason, this was a ground for recompense. They were no longer discussing the interpretation of the *Corpus iuris* and the *Corpus iuris canonici*, but law in general.

The works of Vitoria were forbidden in the Netherlands by Charles V, where the balance between Catholics and Protestants was precarious. In Leuven, the first scholar who stressed that theology played a role in law was Lenaert Leys (Leonardus Lessius, 1554-1623). Just like Molina, he had been a student of Suárez in Rome. In his *De iustitia et iure* (1605) he mixed the neoscholastic theory with the practical legal doctrine of Leuven. He did not integrate Catholic theology into his legal doctrine, but ethical thought which was acceptable to both Catholics and Reformists. His work no longer dealt with the administration of justice, but with law. Law had deeper roots than monarchy. Lessius' legal thought was also influenced by the economy. He continuously kept in mind the affluence that the free market had brought to Antwerp in the past and which contrasted sharply with the black misery at the turn of the century.

The sixteenth-century jurists of Leuven, and Lessius in particular, were an important source of inspiration for a prince of European letters, Hugo de Groot (Grotius, 1583-1645). He was a jurist, theologian and man of letters. In his general works about law, such as *De iure belli ac pacis* (1625) he proclaimed the new legal order which broke through at the beginning of the seventeenth century. He still cited Bartolus and Baldus and adopted many elements from Lessius, but with him, everything was bathed in the light of the innate rights, the *iura naturalia*. Civil rights were someone's rights. The subject was at the centre of law.

Bibliography. – On the relation between theology and law in Lessius an important work was written in Leuven by W. DECOCK, *Theologians and contract law, The moral transformation of the ius commune (ca. 1500-1650)*, Leyden-Boston 2012.

4. Subjective law

In Antiquity, the legal norm was, in principle, a right of action. In the Middle Ages, rights were imbued with a substantive aspect. In the Modern Era the meaning of the legal norm once again changed drastically because of the conviction that every right was a subjective right. "Every right is someone's right," Molina wrote. Grotius added that "A right is a moral quality of a person which he can use to legally have or hold something" (*De iure belli ac pacis* 1.4.4). This dovetailed with the Cartesian revolution. Descartes (1596-1650) was a jurist as well. He only met Grotius once, but lived in the same milieu: in the Northern Netherlands, in Paris and in the entourage of Christina of Sweden. For Descartes, the subject was the centre of the world as well. This was a cry of despair after decades of war and insecurity under the absolute monarchs. The Grotius of *De iure belli ac pacis* was a refugee, who had escaped the prison of Loevestein and had lost everything he had in the Netherlands. Every right is someone's right and the civil rights cannot remain the plaything of monarchs and armies. Can the losers of a war, the peaceful traders or housewives not lay claim to their civil rights? Freedom is our freedom, property our property, an action is something with which we ask *quod nobis debetur*... In this early seventeenth century we read how the civil acquisition of property served to make goods someone's goods. This was a far cry from the ancient view that law only dealt with conflict mediation and the administration of justice. The search for values in law was intensified. This search was not the exclusive task of the judge. The idea of an individual had been developed slowly in philosophy and case law since the fourteenth century. Around 1600 this individual suddenly came to the fore. All rights became subjective rights. From this new idea, Roman law would once again be read in a different manner.

§9. Roman law after 1600

In the seventeenth century the jurists attempted to curb absolutism. The fact that every monarch played the part of Roman emperor in his own territory, had given rise to a disastrous situation. What, however, could be done against the sovereign councils which checked the judgements of all aldermen's courts, lords and ecclesiastical judges and could revoke all of these decisions on appeal? In order to banish absolutism the jurists used means which had been developed in the sixteenth century. The most important means would be legal doctrine. The medieval legal doctrine had strengthened the administration of justice and had thus contributed to the development of the sovereign councils. During the sixteenth century the first independent legal doctrine was developed, in which jurists thought *de iustitia et iure*, about the functioning of law and procedure in general. This independent legal thought became a central element in the seventeenth century. The jurists would remove the creation of law from the sphere of influence of the sovereign councils and create new *fora*. The administration of justice lost its monopoly. Between 1600 and 1800 the number of cases introduced in the courts decreased drastically and the administration of justice was reduced to a quarter of its sixteenth-century size, while the population grew everywhere.

The foundations of the legal doctrine were laid in natural law and the *forum internum*. Subsequently, three new domains were developed within the doctrine: private law, public law and international law. The exertions of the jurists led to the *pax westfalica*. It is then that the intellectuals of Europe took over the torch from the jurists. Monarchical nationalism was repressed further during the Enlightenment, a cultural movement that attempted to be European. From the second half of the seventeenth century onwards, the power was shifted from the monarchs to 'the people'. At the end of the eighteenth century and during the nineteenth century the democratic regimes were developed; in the twentieth century these were followed by the socialist variants which were also based on the sovereignty of the people. These regimes, however, proved to be even more nationalistic than the nations of the sixteenth century. In the twentieth century, nationalism went off the rails again and Europe once again found itself involved in catastrophic wars. From 1945 onwards the jurists built the *pax europaea*. Dangerous notions such as nations or popular sovereignty were avoided in this search for a new law for Europe.

Roman law has proved itself useful in every great reform after 1600. For the development of legal doctrine, the *Corpus iuris* was an important source of law. The Roman 'civil' rights took centre stage in the development of civil societies. In the development of the *pax europaea*, the roots of European law are sought for via Roman law.

1. From natural law to the *forum internum*

Joachim Hopperus taught in Leuven in 1554 that people were invested with civil rights, the core of rights which had been received from Roman Antiquity (and will be discussed in chapter two), at birth. The same can be read in the Spanish jusnaturalists. In Brabant and Castile this doctrine was based on the Golden Bull (1356) and on the Fueros of Castile (around 1250) in which it could be read that in these areas people acquired rights by being born there. At the end of the sixteenth century it was stated that the Creator had invested the individual with these rights at his birth (*natura*). The absolutist monarchs did not yield to anyone, except their Creator. The jurists saw the Achilles' heel of absolutism. They pleaded for respect for natural rights. The sovereign councils ought to respect what God had invested people with. Because of this, the monarch lost his monopoly on law. For the development of innate rights, the jurists acknowledged the influence of theology on law. Theology was European and therefore not nationalistic. This theological component was strongly present in the Spanish jusnaturalists. Lessius shifted the focus from theology to ethics, which played a role in all legal norms. It was acceptable to both Catholics and Reformed people.

In the seventeenth century the 'innate rights' were the basis of the thought of the 'school of natural law', the Reformed counterpart of the Spanish jusnaturalism. It had a large influence on the Protestant countries. Grotius (1583-1645) was called the 'father of natural law'. He emphasised the subjectivity of all rights. In the Reformed countries it was harder to break down nationalism, because the churches were supported by the monarchs. In these countries the jurists stressed the freedom of conscience and the *forum internum* in which each subject could build up an internal resistance to the norms that were imposed by royal councils. The *forum internum* was not arbitrary. The Reformed theologians and the jurists developed policy lines which made the *forum internum* predictable as well. They too wanted to escape the sovereign councils. They also stressed the European dimension, and did so not only via Christianity, but also by the strict adherence to the Greek logic which had become established everywhere in the sixteenth century. Catholic legal thought with its centralised theological influence and the Reformed legal thought with its growing rationalism were never far apart. Both systems strove for law and justice outside of the court.

The new legal thought was accepted by the officials, including the judges – who were still officials at that time. This acceptance was first and foremost due to momentum. In 1600, Europe was exhausted because of the wars. Even the monarchs were at rock-bottom. Everything that could improve this situation was accepted. Secondly, the renewal originated with the law faculties. It was instilled into the young jurists. A third factor was the adoption of the case law of the canon law courts by the monarchical councils. On the European continent aldermen and justices were confronted with cases which had previously been dealt with before ecclesiastical courts. With regard to these matters, the aldermen and justices adopted the precedents of canon law. In this manner, many canonical principles were adopted into monarchical law. Examples include *pacta sunt servanda*, good faith in all obligations, marriage and legitimacy as admission ticket to the courts and civil rights, as well as ecclesiastical administrative law, which became important to the development of public law. The role of the canonical judge, who had legal power but was at the same time concerned about the final destiny of those subject to the law, can be found in the royal case law of the seventeenth century. In this context the Germans mention the 'Amtsgewissen' of the judge. This led to the internalisation of the law. When resolving conflicts, the Continental judges no longer merely thought of the reconciliation of interests: they also began to weigh values. These societal values were not derived from monarchs.

This inner search for law promoted the importance of legal doctrine. Within this doctrine three new matters were developed in the seventeenth century: private law, public law and international law.

Bibliography. – On the influence of theology on law, see W. DECOCK, *Theologians and contract law, The moral transformation of the ius commune (ca. 1500-1650)*, Leyden-Boston 2012; M. GERMANN, W. DECOCK et al. (eds.), *Das Gewissen in den Rechtslehren der protestantischen und katholischen Reformationen*, Wittenberg [2016] (in press).

2. Three new branches of law

A. From Roman civil rights to private law

During the sixteenth-century wars, the victors were free to deal with the losers as they pleased: the winner took it all. In natural law, however, civil rights transcended the competence of the monarchs. Grotius defended the new vision in his *De iure belli ac pacis* (1625). A war did not change civil rights at all, because these rights belonged to the subjects. The monarch and the justices who did not respect these rights would be called to account during the Last Judgement. The theological foundation of the civil rights offered a way out. For Descartes (1596-1650), whose rediscovered degree shows that he was a jurist, every subject remained a point of departure for rights even without the intervention of his Creator. In the legal world, this Cartesian revolution was expressed in private law. During the course of the seventeenth century, the civil rights, the most important heritage within Roman law, were increasingly considered as private rights of the individual which transcended national jurisdictions. In order to know their contents, the *Corpus iuris* was searched through. This European vision of private law promoted trade and cooperation across borders and contributed to the recovery of affluence.

The revival of the *Corpus iuris* and Roman law in the Modern Era was, therefore, ahistorical. People were not looking for old legal doctrine, but for new legal thought. With the *Corpus iuris*, they wanted to safeguard the private rights of the citizens. In this process, Justinianic law played the same part as humanism in the sixteenth century. It offered a platform to transcend particularism. In the *Corpus iuris*, the jurists no longer saw imperial case law which the sovereign courts could amend. In Leuven, Zoesius represented the *Corpus iuris* as a *lex generalis*, a law that was stronger than the monarchical case law. Most of the jurists considered it to be an unchanging text which one read like a Protestant Bible: immediately, without taking tradition into account, with current needs as the point of departure, with the convictions, Latin and logic of the moment. This approach is called the *usus modernus pandectarum*. The result was an 'Umwertung aller Werte'. Most of the Roman legal notions were given a new meaning. Below we will notice how notions such as *dominium* and *possessio, causa, tutela, legitimatio, matrimonium, obligatio naturalis, poena capitalis*, etcetera were given a new meaning which would be preserved until the twentieth century.

Bibliography. – For the degree of Descartes, see: J.-R. ARMOGATHE, C. CARRAUD and R. FEENSTRA, 'La licence en droit de Descartes, un placard inédit de 1616', *La nouvelle république des lettres* 2 (1988), p. 125-145. On the new meanings in Roman law: L. WAELKENS, 'Le droit romain antique, un produit de l'interprétation aux Temps Modernes', in B. BARNABÉ (ed.), *l'interprétation du droit, Actes des journées internationales d'histoire du droit, Besançon 30 mai – 2 juin 2012*, Besançon [2015] (in press).

B. The origin of public law

The relations between the monarch and the people were rethought. During the sixteenth century the monarchs had replaced the feudal lords in their administration with jurists in employment. In the seventeenth century, these jurists would reduce the power of their own monarch. In this context too, theology was appealed to and the *forum internum* played a part. The jurists began to ask themselves ethical questions about the relation between the monarch and his subjects. In this period the doctrine was developed that the monarch had received his power from God and would have to justify at the Last Judgement how he had used it. In that context, the theologians were also given the floor for a short while, but their part was gradually reduced and legal doctrine was developed. The fact that jurists had adopted principles of canon law played an important part in public law. Traditionally, the principalities in Europe were passed via private inheritance law to the eldest son. If there was no son, the realm was inherited via the eldest daughter, but her husband became the monarch because it was a military function. The seventeenth-century jurists, by contrast, received the Greek idea of a *politeia*, a 'state' of citizens who had their own interests and were opposed to the monarchs. Its interpretation was influenced by canon law. The Church was not a principality but a community which functioned according to the law of associations. Since Roman Antiquity, it had organised a jurisdiction that was not passed on through the law of inheritance. Territory and legal power, in other words, did not necessarily have to be inherited. In the legal doctrine concerning public law we read that the interests of the monarch and the 'state' diverged. In the second half of the seventeenth century, this idea developed into the view that a *politeia* could function well without a hereditary monarch and with elections and consensus.

At the beginning of the century, Gudelinus (1550-1619) taught a course in Leuven on feudal law in which the old system of monarchical power was explained. Antonio Perez (1587-1672) further developed it into the first course on *ius publicum*. He described the role of the monarch and the institutions that had developed from feudalism. The monarch was not bound by his case law, but he was bound by morality and natural law. Perez took principles of constitutional law from Tacitus, Cicero and Justinian to argue that authority had been curbed for a very long time. Perez exerted an extensive influence in northern Europe. One can see the same thoughts crop up in most of the law faculties and in legal practice. Famous examples can be found in Paris and London. When Louis XIV sent ordinances to his Parliament, he received remarks, remonstrances. His jurists' ideas about the 'state' clashed with his vision of 'the monarch'. Charles I of England had an even harder time of it. His jurists sentenced him to death because he did not respect the new ideas of public law.

Bibliography. – The manner in which the jurists employed by monarchs managed to bring absolutism under control can be read in the fluent works of Jacques Krynen from Toulouse. A powerful and easy-to-read work is J. KRYNEN, *L'état de justice*, I, *L'idéologie de la magistrature ancienne*, Paris 2009.

C. The origin of international law

As the third component of the legal doctrine, the law of peace was developed. In the sixteenth century Italian jurists like Andrea Alciato (1492-1550), Pierino Belli (1502-1575) and Alberico Gentili (1552-1608) were already writing about the laws of war. In the Low Countries, Balthasar de Ayala was on the same wavelength (1548-1584) with his *De iure belli*. At the beginning of the seventeenth century, the law of peace was developed as a reaction. Gudelinus was the first to consider the topic from the perspective of peace and not just from the viewpoint of the monarchs. After him, war and peace were often treated in public law. Nevertheless, international law became a legal branch with its own characteristics. There was, for example, no court that could judge these matters. The jurists were trained at the law faculty to prevent wars in an extrajudicial manner, to intuit conflicts between monarchs and to defuse them. At the law faculty, they became acquainted with the importance of the exchange of ambassadors, communication with the enemy and the shortening of conflicts if they became unavoidable.

3. The success of legal doctrine

By the middle of the century, the legal doctrine had been established everywhere. For the professor of Leuven Antonio Perez, a European law that transcended the different religious persuasions had grown around the *Corpus iuris*. For his colleague Diodorus Van Tulden (Tuldenus, ca. 1590-1645) the *Corpus iuris* contained the inviolable civil rights of the individual. The difference between private and public law was evident for Tuldenus, and he also treated the law of peace as an aspect of public law. The same approach can be seen in Germany in Samuel Pufendorf's (1632-1694) work. In 1661 he was given a chair of Roman law in Heidelberg. He would only accept it if it became a chair of natural law, and he was granted the first chair with that name. In the same year, his *Elementa jurisprudentiae universalis* appeared, in which he emphasised the universal dimension of private law. In 1667, this book was followed by his *De statu imperii germanici* with principles of public law and in 1672 by his *De iure naturae et gentium* in which international law was treated. The same tendency could be observed in France. Jean Domat (1625-1696) described Roman law as a pan-European legal system in *Les lois civiles dans leur ordre naturel* (1689). His *Droit public* was posthumously paired with this work. In England Thomas Hobbes (1588-1679) was a vehement proponent of law outside of the court and 'the state'.

The curbing of absolutism, the furtherance of law outside of the court, and the development of private, public and international law have led to the *pax westfalica*, the Peace of Westphalia (1648). Blue skies over Europe and the first structural peace since the *pax romana*. The joy about this peace would find its expression in baroque art. Non-jurists then furthered international cultural exchange and searched for a manner of thought which could transcend the national borders. This was the 'Enlightenment'. The shared patterns of thought were emphasised and the religious differences were minimalized and this led to rationalism. In this 'Aufklärung', the *Corpus iuris* was lauded as being part of the European heritage, while Roman law became an example of rationality. *Ratio* and Roman law both stemmed from the same idealistic Greco-Roman culture that had been developed in the Modern Era. What was 'rational' in law was therefore mainly determined by Roman law. For the jurists the *Corpus iuris* contained the *ratio scripta*. If jurists expressed 'reasonable' insights, they therefore sounded Roman. Christian Wolff (1679-1754) deduced a large amount of law from reason. It is striking how closely his reasonable law dovetailed with the *Corpus iuris* as this was interpreted by his contemporaries.

4. From royal sovereign councils to democratic rights

At the end of the seventeenth century it turned out that the dismantling of absolutism had been a success. There were wars after 1648, like the Wars of the Spanish and Austrian Succession in the Southern Netherlands, but they were not as destructive as the earlier wars. The public institutions and the private sector kept functioning. In all of the European courts, the number of cases decreased drastically in the course of the eighteenth century. Many courts found that the amount of cases fell to one fifth of the number that they dealt with around 1580. At the same time in the seventeenth century, a large rise in population began everywhere in Europe. If the number of people per square kilometre grows in a sustained manner, this is an indication of a structural curbing of conflicts and therefore of an improvement in the law. From the last quarter of the seventeenth century until around 1800 Europe also acquired a prosperity that it had not seen since the *pax romana*.

In the eighteenth century the interiorisation of law continued. The ball was still in the court of the law faculties. At the end of the century, this led to extreme opinions, such as the idealistic legal theory of Kant (1724-1804) and the 'Phenomenology of Spirit' of Hegel (1770-1831), in which law in its entirety was a theory. For the more practical jurists, the *forum internum* and legal doctrine broke the omnipotence of the sovereign councils, but law outside the court was not sufficiently enforceable. In the eighteenth century the demand for a societal consensus concerning extrajudicial norms grew. In private law there was the urge to codify; in public law there was an urge towards constitutionalisation. In this context, modern legislation had its origin. Several sovereign councils allowed their legal power to evolve into legislation. The monarchs promulgated ordinances that were addressed to the judges. In this manner, they ran ahead of the administration of justice. The Estates or States, which had approved taxes since the Middle Ages, attempted to gain a say in these new burdens that were imposed in advance. It is from this combination of legal power, anticipation of the administration of justice and actions of the States that parliamentary democracy originated. However, this leads us away from Roman law. The *Corpus iuris* remained present in the background. In eighteenth-century Leuven, all new law was taught as commentary on the *Corpus iuris*. In the works of the French jurist Robert Pothier (1699-1772), you can discover how the evolution from *ius commune* to civil private law already happened in the eighteenth century in the jurisdiction of the Parliament of Paris. Pothier, who was a practical character, still saw the Roman law of the Modern Era as authoritative law from which the royal case law could not deviate lightly.

At the end of the eighteenth century royal absolutism had joltingly come to a halt. Between 1790 and 1850, Europe was shaken. The power was rearranged in favour of the farmers and the bourgeoisie.

Bibliography. – An overview of the evolution of the *ius commune* in the Modern Era to the civil private law of the revolutionary period around 1800 can be found in the work of H. Coing that has already been praised above: *Europäisches Privatrecht*, I, *Älteres gemeines Recht 1500 bis 1800*, Munich 1985.

5. Nineteenth-century Roman law

Among the civil law codes that were promulgated around 1800, the Code civil of 1804 stands out. This legal code gained the force of law from Hamburg to the Netherlands, France and even the French departments in Italy. At the same time, the constitutions put the law at the top of the hierarchy of norms. The civil rights became civil law and Roman law had to provide this new civil law with a history. When they drew up the Parisian 'Code civil', the drafters based their text to a large extent on the *ius commune* of the Modern Era. The same tendency could already be observed in older codes like the General Law for the Prussian States (1794), the Code of Joseph II (1787), the Codex Bavaricus (1756) and the Codex Theresianus (1753). In the *ius commune* of the Modern Era, the monarchs had already been eliminated. Around 1800 the jurists and the bourgeoisie were not aiming at a revolution in civil law. They mainly desired that the *ius commune* be recast in the form of the new legal sources. Because of the influential French bourgeoisie in 1804 among other reasons, the Code civil gained the reputation of containing the most modern variant of the civil law.

In 1815 the map of Europe was redrawn at the Congress of Vienna. Shortly afterwards in Germany, there was a striving for a single civil law code for all of the German districts outside of Austria and the Netherlands. The German Romantic interest in legal history originated at the same time. At the end of the eighteenth century Edward Gibbon's 'Decline and Fall of the Roman Empire' (1764-1768) had heralded a return to Antiquity. In Göttingen, Gustav Hugo (1764-1844) started the search for ancient Roman law. It became an archaeological journey to an Antiquity that was buried underneath the modern interpretation of the *Corpus iuris* and tons of debris of legal history. He sought for the original meaning of the *Corpus iuris*, but was actually following the methods of the legal humanism of Donellus, the most wide-ranging author of the Reformation. Legal history, the Romantic view of Antiquity and the desire for a German civil law code would lead to a specific study of Roman law.

Carl F. Von Savigny (1779-1861), whom we have already met above, was anti-revolutionary. He appealed to legal history in his reaction against the civil revolution. He did not like the idea of capturing the rationalistic and idealistic interpretation of the *ius commune* in law codes. The *ius commune* had continuously evolved both in Antiquity and the Middle Ages as well as in the Early Modern Era. Why did it suddenly have to be ossified in laws? For a long time Germany remained divided concerning the controversy between Anton F.J. Thibaut (1774-1840) from Heidelberg, who was in favour of codification, and Savigny, who was against it. With his Historical School, Savigny aroused considerable interest in Roman law.

The most important objection to a German civil law code was that Germany had not been unified like France and contained more than twenty jurisdictions. There was a common culture, which allowed for the publication of dictionaries that could be shared by all of the districts. What was there to stop the development of a law code based on the common legal history? In the 1820s this common legal history was, for some, the 'German' law, but for the majority it was the *ius commune* and the common legal doctrine that had grown around the *Corpus iuris* in which one could find all of the legal notions that had been consecrated in the Code civil. They were therefore also part of the German legal world. Roman law provided a framework for legal doctrine. New elements, like civil marriage, private property or the liberal law of obligations were projected onto the Roman law of Antiquity. A new *usus pandectarum* was developed at the universities, which we now call 'Pandektistik'. Even the older Savigny played a part in this. He also began to see Roman law as an artificial game of legal rules, with its own 'Pandektenharmonistik'. In his 'System des heutigen römischen Rechts' (1840-1849) he provided an ahistorical systematisation of Roman law, which was useful for the legal doctrine of his time. The German jurists who elaborated on this Roman law that had been rendered topical were the Pandectists. The most famous ones were Georg Friedrich Puchta (1798-1846), Bernhard Windscheid (1917-1892) and Heinrich Dernburg (1829-1907). They wrote encompassing works about 'Roman law' in which all of the matters that were treated in the civil law codes were discussed. This kind of Roman law was represented in all of the law faculties. On German conferences about civil law, there were lectures about Roman law. The legal theoretician Rudolf von Jhering (1818-1892) called himself a Roman legal thinker. In his works, one can see how legal history and legal theory were mixed thoroughly. However, the jurists who focused on legal history never managed to compile a civil code. The 'Bürgerliches Gesetzbuch' only appeared when Germany became one country with one case law. It was compiled in the Reichstag in Berlin in 1895 and gained the force of law on 1 January 1900.

In the German nineteenth century some remarkable new editions of the *Corpus iuris* were made, such as the Kriegel edition of Leipzig 1840 (with the edition of the Novels of Osenbrüggen) and the abovementioned Berlin edition of Krüger and Mommsen. This nineteenth-century enthusiasm for Roman law also resulted in the publication of studies about Roman criminal law and Roman public law.

6 The Roman law of the twentieth century

In Germany Roman law and legal history were introduced in all law faculties. This study served as a model for the development of a thorough legal science which could compete with chemistry or the natural sciences. This German approach to Roman law can also be found in Great Britain, for example in Edinburgh with James Muirhead (1831-1889) or with John Austin (1790-1859) in London. The study of Roman law was introduced in France in the nineteenth century in order to provide a basis for the Code civil of 1804. When creating the Code civil, the French Romanists also fell back on the German 'Pandektenwissenschaft'. Around 1900 French civil law was well established and Pandektistik was no longer necessary there. In many universities, it continued to be practised for half a century, because of the strong reputation of the German study of Roman law.

From the moment that the German 'Bürgerliches Gezetzbuch' gained the force of law, Roman law served as an obligatory study to provide the new civil law with old patents of nobility. The Roman law that was taught was usually based on the legal doctrine of the Early Modern and Modern Era that formed the basis of the BGB. This remained the case until well into the 1970s. Once the civil principles had been restored after the world wars, this ahistorical approach towards Roman law was no longer necessary and it was excluded from the law faculties. The Spanish civil law code dates from 1889, but the country's civil society was shaken so violently in the twentieth century that the nineteenth-century Pandektistik was maintained until the 1980s. In Italy the new Codice civile was only introduced in 1942. Its establishment through Roman law is only coming to a close now. In Italy, Pandektistik and legal theory are strongly entwined, as they were with Jhering.

In many countries Roman law once again began to play its role of a legal historical course in the course of the twentieth century. Nevertheless, the German nineteenth-century tradition of Roman law persisted, even in countries that did not have to provide a foundation for a civil law code. It can be found in great celebrities like William Buckland (1859-1946) in Cambridge or Arthur Schiller (1902-1977) in New York. A series of world-famous Dutch Romanists have studied Roman law in a style that was related to German Pandektistik but had its own roots. Like the Reformed Germans, the Dutch scholars built up a tradition to read the *Corpus iuris* in, as it were, a presbyterian way, starting from their own world and legal training. This approach was strongly determined by legal theory but also by the 'open society' thought of the Dutch jurists.

The science of Roman law between 1900 and 1950 was summarised in a remarkably thorough manner by Max Kaser (1906-1997). He played as large a part in the history of Roman law as Accursius, Bartolus, Donellus or Pothier. Out of respect for the great masters of the nineteenth and twentieth century, many Romanists are still reasoning in the style that was immortalised by Kaser.

Bibliography. – For most of the questions of Roman law Kaser offers a good point of departure. See M. KASER, *Das römische Privatrecht*, 2 vol., Munich 1971-1975 and IDEM, *Das römische Zivilprozeßrecht*, 3d edition revised by K. HACKL, Munich 1996.

This pandectist approach no longer fits into the current law faculties. The popular sovereignty that was praised to the skies around 1800 has led to the democratic wars of the twentieth century, which were just as destructive as the monarchical wars of the sixteenth century. Both the civil regimes of the nineteenth century – France, England, Austria, Italy or Germany – as well as the socialist regimes of the twentieth century – like Spain, Germany, Russia or Italy – saw unseen societal conflicts. The common European culture of the Enlightenment seemed to have disappeared completely in the democratic and popular regimes. After 1945 the jurists were building up a new legal culture for Europe, which has already led to the EU and the *pax europaea*. Legal history and in particular the Roman *ius commune* are playing an important part in this new legal culture. In 1945 Helmut Coing (1912-2000, professor of Roman law in Frankfurt/Main) travelled to the most important American law faculties to talk about *ius commune* and promote the common legal culture. He established the 'Max-Planck-Institut für europäische Rechtsgeschichte' in Frankfurt. In 1945 Robert Feenstra (1920-2013, professor of Roman law in Leyden) also embarked on his *peregrinatio academica* through Europe. His Roman law was the admission ticket with which he could deliver lectures in each law faculty. His message, however, was the internationalisation of the law faculties. The same part was also played by the Romanist Jean Gaudemet (1908-2001, professor of Roman law in Paris), by Hans Thieme (1906-2000, initially a professor in Breslau, after the war in Freiburg) and by Fernand de Visscher (1885-1964, professor of Roman law in Leuven). In the fifties, they spun a network in Europe. As a common subject, Roman law became the platform to put jurists from different countries into contact with one another.

In the meantime the EU has reached cruising speed and the Romanists are put into service to deal with more content-related questions concerning European integration. As in the seventeenth century, the jurists are looking for a common private law for all EU member states. How did the differences between countries with a similar culture originate? Scientific study of the *Corpus iuris* and its history is required to provide an answer to this question. The financial crisis of 2008 was caused by a conflict between Anglo-American obligations and Continental obligations. Obligations are Roman, but how, when and why did both systems grow apart and what must jurists know in order to solve or prevent such crises? During the Greek crisis of 2010 it turned out that the EU States of the Levant's reasoning about government action was completely different from that of the Western members. This difference dates back to the Eastern Roman and Western Roman traditions. Is it not the Romanists who have to deliver the science to resolve such contradictions? Legal history has played a part in the drawing up of the Draft Common Frame of Reference. It also has a role in globalisation. Human rights build on Roman civil rights. Inhowfar can they be imposed on Asian or African societies? Here, the study of the origins of civil rights can help. When conducting trade with China, one sometimes wonders where European contract law comes from and whether there is any point in invoking it in this new context. Contract law is Roman law, so it is necessary to delve into legal history for a bit.

In Leuven Roman law is taught along the lines of the scientific renewal brought by R. Feenstra. He always read Roman texts together with the interpretation they were given in different periods. He looked at everything in a much more historical way than his predecessors. It is indeed true that we no longer create doctrine in order to undermine the case law of the absolute monarchs. We are not trying to anchor national civil law codes anymore. We are digging for the common roots of the law in the countries of the EU. We are digging... Studying Roman law does not involve looking back, but going deep. We are writing profound theories about the common character of Continental law, English law, Scandinavian law and Central European law. We are building a legal history that can fit into all of the European law faculties. Sounds beautiful, does it not?

Chapter II

Libertas and freedom, from civil law to human rights

The history of Roman law is first and foremost the history of civil law. In Antiquity, this was the law that regulated the private relations between soldiers and veterans. It was based on the privileges of the warriors. For centuries, people attempted to acquire these privileges without having to perform military service. In the Middle Ages, the canonists linked civil rights with procedural law, the right to good administration and a humane criminal law. In the Early Modern Era civil rights became subjective rights to which anyone could lay claim. In this chapter, we will attempt to survey the way in which the privileges of the Roman soldiers grew into fundamental rights for every man and woman.

1. The military *status libertatis*

The word *liber* only features in a few archaic texts. We will translate it into English as free, but in Antiquity, the word had a military connotation. Originally, it must have meant 'able-bodied man'. The *status libertatis* indicated the status of a soldier and the *templum libertatis* on the Aventine Hill accommodated the administration of the censors, where the conscription lists were kept.

The army and its campaigns took centre stage in the Roman Kingdom and the Republic, where men began to serve in the army at a very young age and everyone lived in a wartime economy. In the early Republic, military service lasted ten years, so that for an entire decade, young Romans faced death and joined forces in order to conquer their enemies. Life in the army camps was shaped by camaraderie, hope and dreams about Rome. Military ideology determined culture. For centuries, the Forum was a place for discussion about strategy, conquests and occupations. In short, the structure of Roman society was thought up by warriors.

The legionaries were given privileges as a motivation. The entirety of these privileges was called the *status libertatis*, the military status. In the last centuries of the Republic the word *libertas* was also used to indicate each of the separate privileges that made up the military status. Under the name *libertas* we find all of the original institutions of Roman law: wills (even after death, soldiers could freely dispose of their salary and spoils), consensual *nuptiae* (fighting and staying alive for one's beloved), *commercium* (access to the free market), the right to set up an enterprise (*familia*), the rights to adhere to a faith, to think freely, to exploit land without paying land taxes, and to lodge an appeal with the army against a death sentence (*prouocatio ad populum*). In addition, soldiers had political rights: they elected some officers and could run for the office of magistrate.

One of the privileges of the warriors was the *ius civile*. The word *ciuis* (which is now commonly translated as citizen) originally meant brother in arms. Cicero, for example, addressed old fellow legionaries as *ciuis mi*. Civil law was the procedure that was used to settle conflicts between warriors while taking all of their privileges into account. We will examine this procedure in more detail in the next chapter. The praetors were responsible for the civil law and determined during a first hearing how far the privileges of arguing soldiers played a part. If appropriate, these magistrates provided the parties with instructions which directed the judge who would decide on the merits of the case to treat the conflict according to civil law. In this civil procedure the praetors also supervised the execution of the judgement. Meritorious soldiers were granted civil status for life when they left military service, which meant that they could bring their conflicts with former comrades before the praetor even after they had left the army.

The *status libertatis*, access to civil rights, was conferred by the consuls and censors. The former could deploy foreign soldiers and grant them the *status libertatis* with immediate effect; the latter drew up the conscription lists. People who were not on these lists did not have to fight, but did not have access to civil privileges either. The praetors could withdraw civil rights when they settled conflicts between *ciues*. Those who did not have the civil status could join a warrior and enjoy his privileges, because the civil courts allowed *ciues* to act for third parties. In such a case, the *ciues* was liable for the third party, while the pledge of this liability was the pooled property of the citizen and the third party (community of goods). This arrangement is at the basis of the *familia*.

Whenever you consider an aspect of *libertas* in Roman law, you always find a text that denies this right to slaves (*serui*). *Serui* lived without the *status libertatis* and without civil rights. *Seruitus* was a concept that originated in the civil law. Here, we translate it as 'slavery', which is an early modern notion derived from the status of Constantinople's Slavic prisoners of war. 'Servantship' or 'serfdom' would have been better translations, but 'traduttore traditore' is a maxim that also applies in this context. The notion of slavery did not exist within the criminal law. Consequently, the 'manslaughter of a slave' did not exist either: manslaughter was not punished by civil law, but by criminal law, which only dealt with *hominem occidere*. Slaves did not have freedoms but did not fight either. They had a different status, which was not necessarily bad, seeing that Romans who were taken prisoners by an enemy also had this status. Deserters, those who refused to do military service and prisoners of war were also given the status of slaves. They were expected to support the war *in seruitudine*, by living in the service of a warrior. If a slave wanted to fight for Rome and was accepted by the military leaders, he was immediately given the *status libertatis*. This was the case for prisoners of war who defected to the Romans, but also for domestic slaves: Gaius 1.140 teaches us that domestic slaves could join the army against the will of their *paterfamilias* and could thus acquire civil rights.

2. The political *status libertatis*

The *status libertatis* and civil rights were strong motivating factors that were at the basis of the unprecedented strike power of the Roman legions. Moreover, these privileges did not cost any money. Pure legal thought was at the basis of the military power of Rome and would become a determining element in Roman logic.

Before long, Rome began to use these freedom rights to motivate conquered peoples. After each victory, Rome began peace negotiations. The Senate's negotiators had three aims: to ensure peace and the loyalty of the conquered people, to recruit new soldiers and to impose taxes (*tributum*). In return, they offered *libertates* and *ciuitas*, rights which did not cost anything but could bring considerable revenues. New soldiers were offered the full civil status. Roman soldiers earned good salaries, had a better chance of survival than conquered peoples because the army provided good healthcare, and they left the service as *ciues* for life. This was a tempting offer for young people whose district had been destroyed. Inhabitants who did not join the Roman military received fewer or more freedoms, depending on the interests at stake and the available room for manoeuvre. Through the peace treaty (*foedus*), a conquered region became a province of the federation, while its inhabitants more or less joined the Roman economic zone. The inhabitants of Campania, who grew the corn that Rome lacked, were granted *commercium*, full access to free trade in the federation. They could therefore earn their *tributum* by exporting corn. Other provinces' courts or procedures were acknowledged, while the inhabitants of still other regions were granted the possibility of entering into a civil relationship with a Roman citizen (*conubium*) or were allowed to till the land without paying land taxes, etcetera. In 381 BC the inhabitants of Tusculum received the full status of freedom. Around 200 BC all of the inhabitants of Italy received *ciuitas sine suffragio*, full citizenship without suffrage in Rome. From 242 BC onwards, a *praetor peregrinus* was elected to deal with cases involving *peregrini* (pilgrims, 'peregrines'), inhabitants who had such a partial status of freedom. By the end of the Republic the *praetor peregrinus* developed an edict which took account of the common denominator of all these partial statuses. His edict contained the *ius gentium*. These freedom rights of the peregrines were an important phase in the demilitarisation of the civil law.

A next step was taken in the second century BC. In 168 BC, after the Macedonian wars, there was such an influx of recruits that military service for Romans was abolished. How did the Romans then acquire their civil status? There are no republican texts about this, but in Gaius one discovers that the status of freedom was linked to *matrimonium*, the high-quality relationship of a couple who intended to stay together, take care of each other, have children and raise them. In such families, children received their father's civil status through birth and acknowledgement by the father. Inhabitants who did not grow up in such an entourage – the Romans called them proletarians – could still join the army to be 'civilised'. During their time in the military, the Roman ideology would be drummed into them. In Gaius and in later texts we read that Roman citizens could grant their slaves full civil rights by means of a *manumissio*, which did have to be presented to a magistrate.

In the late Republic a child acquired full civil rights through the father's acknowledgement. Mothers could ask the praetor to establish the child's status of freedom as a provisional measure. There must also have been a procedure for this in the edict of the censors, but all traces thereof have been lost. The status of freedom was an issue that cropped up often before the praetor. Those who were summoned to the praetor could allege that the plaintiff could not invoke civil law because he was not a citizen. The praetor then checked whether the plaintiff had been born in a *matrimonium* or not and decided in a *praeiudicium*, a prejudgement, whether the procedure could be carried on according to civil law. By means of the *uindicatio libertatis*, every Roman could seek certainty about his status with the praetor. Even a slave could make use of this claim. If he had not been able to bring a problem concerning his status before a judge, slavery would not have been a legal status. The dependency of civil status on *matrimonium* and acknowledgement by the father was abolished in the Empire. Under Hadrian (117-138 AD) the prefecture decided that children received the status of their mother at birth.

Until the second century BC the civil status was reserved for warriors and, as a consequence, for men. Once this status was acquired at birth and no longer required military service, there was no reason to withhold the civil status from women. In old texts freeborn women are called *ingenuae*. Did this mean that they were not *ciues*? In the Empire, women had civil rights. In D. 50.16.195.5 we read that a woman could be the head of her own *familia* and that she could therefore be a *paterfamilias* and was competent to act in court. According to D. 50.16.1, the first Roman rule of interpretation, the masculine expression *si qui* in legal texts always bore reference to both men and women. Was this already the case in the Republic? Until the 1980s Gaius (second century AD) was the oldest source. He mentions the *ciuis romana*, the Roman female citizen. In 1986 the *lex irnitana* of the first century AD was discovered, a text in which expressions like *is/ea, mutatus/ mutata...* put both sexes on a par in passages concerning civil and political rights. If we find civil rights for women in the oldest sources, there is no reason to assume that the jurists of the last century BC were of a different opinion. Nevertheless, civil rights remained connected with military aspects. In Caesar's day there was an instance of abuse of martial law when a politician was losing a lawsuit. The blue flag was raised above the Janiculus and the judges ended the case – all civil rights were suspended under martial law.

The consuls could grant citizenship to individuals and groups and made use of this power to enlarge their following during the three civil wars. Civil rights were also granted by the emperors. Augustus was accepted because he promised to restore the freedom rights. He himself granted freedom rights and civil rights to entire provinces and reformed the provincial edict to bring it into line with the civil law. In his new *cognitio* procedure he granted the same rights to all of the inhabitants of the imperial provinces. The establishment of appeals to the praetorian prefecture guaranteed equal treatment – and consequently an equal status – for millions of people. In the 130s the emperor Hadrian adopted the civil law of the praetors into the imperial case law by means of the Perpetual Edict. According to Gaius, who wrote slightly later in the second century, it was no longer important to be a *ciues* in his day. What mattered was that one had the status of freedom. In 212 the prefecture ruled in the *constitutio antoniniana* that all of the free inhabitants of the Empire had full *ciuitas*. Texts of the late Empire only mention the *status libertatis* that granted access to civil law.

3. Thinking about freedom

In his letters, the apostle Paul contrasted the Roman *libertas* with the Greek notion of *eleutheria*. He preferred Roman freedom to Greek libertinism. This famous Pauline freedom, which the theologians have analysed, was strongly Roman in flavour. According to the Latin Stoa, the meaning of life was to be found in the societal order. Roman intellectuals thought very highly of the model of civil society. The freedom which we find in the writings of the Latin church fathers is Roman as well. It concerned responsible participation in societal life. The old mentality of fighting together for a better world had survived. For Ambrose (340-397) true freedom was *iustitiae seruire*, to serve the law. Augustine (354-430) turned *libertas* into a postulate for a moral life. In his *Ciuitas Dei contra paganos* we read that God played a role in Roman society. If Christians could no longer realise this fraternity with God within the Roman Empire, they had to work towards the establishment of a free life in the heavenly Jerusalem. Boethius (480-525), who found the dismantling of the Western Empire hard to stomach, stressed *liberum arbitrium* in life. God created everyone free and in his own image. Ideal life became unattainable because of sin, but man could conquer sin and once again find the ideal society through *libertas*. And through Rome. A comparison of these contemplations about freedom with other social utopias strikingly shows the Christian writers to have been Roman patriots closely resembling the old comrades in arms who respected each other's civil rights and fought for a Rome with living space for free citizens.

4. From Roman to medieval freedom

Libertas still took the centre stage in the military ideology of the late Empire. In successive waves thousands of young men sought an income and a status in the Roman army, which was an attractive employer: legionaries earned five times the average income, received care and left the service with savings, civil rights and sometimes even a piece of land. If young men presented themselves at the border of the Empire (the *limes*), they were given a visa in the form of a *tessera* that was worn around the neck. This *tessera* gave them permission to travel to a specific legion, where they were indoctrinated with Roman ideology, the freedoms and the idea of a superior society that was worth fighting for. They were turned into invincible freedom fighters. Without much geographical knowledge, the Romans called these immigrants Goths, Vandals, Huns... according to the period in which they arrived in the Empire. The ethnogenesis of these so-called peoples was purely Roman. They only became Germanic centuries later.

In 476 the Western Empire was split up. All of its parts, the later kingdoms, had Roman legions and the doctrine of freedom was honoured everywhere. In Visigothic, Burgundian and Lombardic sources, among the Franks and the Bavarians, and in the Carolingian sources it turns out that words with the stem *fri* (free-, frei-, vriend...) always correspond to the terminology of the Latin *libertas*. C. Scott has described how Roman *libertas* was received. Just as in the late Empire, *ciuitas* did not play a role in the new kingdoms. *Libertas*, however was omnipresent. This status for warriors was even adopted beyond the boundaries of the former Empire, namely by the Norsemen. The words *ciuis* and *ciuitas* cropped up again in the Carolingian period, when *ciuitas* corresponded with the feudal divisions of the jurisdictions. When sovereignty was divided down to the level of fiefs in the high Middle Ages, *libertas* and *ciuitas* had also descended to that level. Able-bodied men were *ciuis* of a fief. *Libertas* was once again linked with the military status in the Middle Ages. Warriors received freedoms. Serfs did not, but they did not have to fight. They lived in *seruitute*, in the service of a warrior who granted them protection.

From the ninth century onwards, this exclusive granting of *libertas* to warriors caused problems for the bishops, who, being clergy, did not fight and consequently did not have the *status libertatis*. Without civil rights, however, they could not appear before a civil court. This caused the abovementioned problem of the *libertas ecclesiae*, the access of a bishop or a local church to the civil procedure. In some regions, the death or transfer of a bishop meant that the ecclesiastical goods that were in his name fell to the *fiscus*, who was the only heir. The bishop's successor could not claim them by law. In the ninth century, this problem was resolved in some regions by the introduction of a 'Reichskirche'. The local sovereign received the formerly ecclesiastical goods, but put the revenues at the disposal of the bishops as a benefice – at the disposal of those bishops who were favourably disposed towards the sovereign. In the twelfth century this issue was resolved by the introduction of the double *fiscus*: the pope would gradually become the *fiscus* with regard to ecclesiastical goods.

This continuity in the evolution from the Roman *status libertatis* to the medieval freedoms becomes clear in the charters of liberties of the cities. From the twelfth century onwards in Flanders and North-Italy and later throughout Europe, lords and communities entered into agreements in which the lords granted a list of freedoms to the communities' inhabitants. Traditionally, this development is depicted as countrymen extorting a *modus vivendi* from their lord and carrying off a series of rights. The charters of liberties contained freedoms such as a community's right to have its own jurisdiction, freedom of trade, the right to vote, freedom of organisation, the right to untaxed goods, the right to testate, freedom of contract, the right to free passage, etcetera. For the most part, they were freedoms that can also be found in Roman law. How could simple people have asked for these types of Roman institutions? No one asks for things he does not know. In reality, the charters of liberties were agreements between, on the one hand, kings and lords and, on the other, their free warriors. The former preferred receiving money to equip their own armies to having to appeal to these free warriors. The latter bought off their military service but managed to stipulate that they would keep their privileges in return for their money. These charters first cropped up in regions that were familiar with Roman law and where the *Corpus iuris* was known. In the towns that had freedoms the inhabitants once again tied in with the Roman *ciuitas*. In the word 'citizen' you can still discern a link with the status of a warrior, a man of a citadel, but in the charters of the towns the civil freedoms were demilitarised.

Consequently, the same civil rights appeared in the rural fiefs where the courts began to grant civil rights just as in the towns. Countrymen were citizens of their fief. In the Middle Ages, the possibility of appeal was introduced. The aldermen's courts of the fiefs against which an appeal could be lodged lost their sovereignty and became part of a larger jurisdiction. During this repression of feudalism, *ciuitas* evolved from *ciuitas* of a fief to *ciuitas* of a region and finally a kingdom. In England this can be seen to happen in the twelfth century. On the Continent, the possibility of appeal appeared from the thirteenth century onwards. In Flanders citizenship was a notion operating at the level of the castellanies in the thirteenth centuries. In the jurisdiction of the parliament of Paris it was still at the level of the fiefs in the thirteenth century, but already at the level of the kingdom around 1450. In the sixteenth century *ciuitas* had become a notion at the level of the royal councils throughout Europe.

Did foreigners have civil rights in the Middle Ages? The answer to this question depended on the degree to which the local law had been influenced by the academic *ius commune*.

Freedom and civil rights retained their military character until well into the seventeenth century. In times of war these were the rights of the victors. The defeated lost their civil status and were left without civil rights.

5. *Libertas* and *ciuitas* in medieval legal doctrine

In the courses of the medieval universities we do not find any grand theories about fundamental rights and freedoms. In the twelfth century the theologians studied Saint Paul's and the Latin church fathers' thoughts about freedom. *Ciuitas Dei* was at that time no longer read as God's citizenship on earth. *Ciuitas* was instead understood as a civic community. In the thirteenth century the Greek *eleutheria* was translated as *libertas* in the *Aristoteles latinus*. This corresponded with the notion of freedom that can be found in Inst. 1.3.1, an Eastern text of the sixth century. For Thomas Aquinas, the first philosopher who took Aristotelian philosophy into account, freedom became a person's right to do what he wanted, as long as he respected the freedom of others and the rules of the society.

The canonists hardly wrote about freedom. In his Decretum of 1140 Gratian did incorporate fragments of Augustine that dealt with *libertas*, but he did not go into the matter further. The canonists did develop the idea of 'innate rights' (*iura naturalia*). Gratian enumerated seven innate rights: life, self-defence, freedom, freedom of conscience, marriage, the right to use goods and the right to recovery of lent goods. Freedom was already innate. The canonists wrote about it when they treated *manumissio*. These texts show that they mainly associated freedom with non-slavery. In the writings of Hostiensis, who taught in Paris shortly before Thomas Aquinas, we find traces of the Greek *eleutheria*, the freedom to do what one wants. The main contribution of the canonists to the development of civil law was their development of the Roman civil institutions, for example the family, marriage, the will, and the idea of an obligation. As the second successor of the emperor, the Church also adopted Roman elements of administration. In their administrative law the canonists developed the Roman law on: sources of law, ruling through the administration of justice, dealings with people subject to the law, political rights, freedom of religion, the organisation of elections, judicial procedure and principles of criminal law. In addition, they constructed the framework into which the civil rights would be fitted in the Early Modern Era. They mentioned the differentiation between citizens and slaves that existed in Antiquity, but this difference did not have any importance in the canonists' administration of justice. When a case was brought before a canonical court, civil status was not mentioned. One was granted access *ratione personae* or *ratione materiae*, and mainly through marriage law. Once one had gained access, citizenship was no longer necessary and within the court, the same law applied to everyone.

In the *Corpus iuris* the legists encountered the word *libertas* twice: in D. 1.5.4 and in Inst. 1.3.1, which both describe freedom as a *facultas naturalis*. In Antiquity this term was clear: the status of freedom was innate (*natura* = birth, derived from *nasci*). In the Middle Ages creation came into the equation. Both texts defined freedom as living as one wishes as long as it is in a nonviolent and legal manner. In the first text, by Florentinus, the legists found the contrast between freedom and slavery. Slavery was considered an institution of the *ius gentium*. From these texts, they gleaned that freedom was natural and slavery was not. Did slaves have the status of freedom at birth? In the thirteenth century the prevailing opinion was that the status of freedom was reserved for citizens. In the fourteenth, the most widespread view was that all people were born free, but that they could lose their status as free men. An important influence was exerted by the theologians, according to whom all people were equal before God, who had created them in his image. Just as the canonists, the legists did not develop their own theory about freedom – their influence mainly consisted of furthering the Roman institutions. Roman law was *ius commune* and therefore law for everyone. *Ciuitas* and civil rights, however, were not universal. Citizenship was membership of a local community with sovereignty. In D. 1.2.2 the legists read that all law emanates from the people, but that the people had delegated judicial power to magistrates, who had in their turn delegated it further. The medieval feudal rulers were really exercising this delegated judicial power and their local case law dovetailed with Roman law. On the other hand, through their legal doctrine the legists did further the idea of universal rights. Foreigners could ask for the application of the *ius commune* in local courts. In case of conflicts of jurisdiction one also had to fall back on the Roman *ius commune* that was at the basis of the Western legal system. It as this universal order that had to be used as the starting point to decide such disputes.

The factual acknowledgement of the civil law was different in every court. It depended on the size of the jurisdiction. The courts of Pisa or Florence, the *curia regis* of the English king, the Parliament of the French king, the Cortes of the Spanish kings, the 'Hofrat' of Charles IV of Bohemia, the crown council of Cracow, the Signatura of the pope, etcetera, were at the head of growing jurisdictions in the Middle Ages. At an early stage, these courts were already led by jurists who had studied the *ius commune* and used it as royal law. They accepted the Roman law sooner than the courts where sovereign lords personally administered justice in person and were convinced that the best course of action was to start from the *ius commune* to amend the local case law. In the Late Middle Ages feudalism was curbed everywhere through the introduction of appeals against vassals, which were heard by the vassals' feudal lords. The Roman *ius commune* was also the foundation for this change. At the end of the Middle Ages we find the idea that the *ius commune* contains civil rights and that these are common to all people. These rights did still retain a military aspect: if a lord or king lost his power over the administration of justice, for example because of a war, his subjects lost their civil rights. Civil rights existed merely by the grace of the feudal, and later the royal courts.

6. Civil rights and absolutism

The sixteenth century, with its nations ruled by absolute monarchs, degenerated into a nightmare of war and misery. The West was in the grip of a combination of religious and royal wars and the jurists had to salvage the chances of survival in Europe.

In practice, the law was concentrated in the sovereign councils. Only they could grant – or refuse to grant – civil rights. As has been mentioned above, canonical case law was adopted by many sovereign councils across continental Europe. Consequently, canon law began to affect the *ius commune* of the royal councils. Civil rights which had been developed by the canonists ended up in the official case law. In the second half of the sixteenth century certain elements can be seen to appear, for example *pacta sunt seruanda*, good faith, marriage, equality between citizens, the idea of guilt, etcetera. For the canonists, there was a natural order in law which had been determined by God and which was known within the tradition of Christianity. This natural order which transcended the courts and the monarch cropped up in the general legal doctrine of the civilians in the mid-sixteenth century. Among the civilians of Leuven we find this transcendent natural law in Joachim Hopperus in 1554 and in Jan Tack (Joannes Ramus) in 1557. The jurists were supplied with a new category in the hierarchy of norms: law that transcends case law.

In the sixteenth century, Spain and the Netherlands shared a monarch. Castile had old ties with civil law. During the Reconquista the inhabitants of a 'regained' region were always granted civil rights. In 1245 Alfonso the Wise established the law faculty of Valladolid in order to recast the country into a nation where everyone enjoyed equal rights. In the Siete Partidas he guaranteed civil rights to everyone who was born in Castile. Emperor Charles, however, showed but little respect for these civil rights. In 1521 three thousand 'communeros' travelled to Valladolid to demonstrate for their civil rights. Charles had them slaughtered by a battalion of flamencos. Villalar would become a central notion for the jurists, among others for Francisco de Vitoria, who came to teach *de justitia et de iure* in Valladolid. In 1526 he moved on to Salamanca, where he would become a torchbearer for the political thinkers. Catalonia and Aragon were confronted with civil rights in very different manners. Traditionally, Aragon had had rights to Corsica. In 1453 Corsica suddenly fell to the Banco di San Giorgio, which held the island as a pledge for Genoese government debts. The bank wanted to turn it into a dependency from which it could recover the debt and suspended the civil rights on the island. The result was a complete shutdown of the Corsican society which still has consequences today. On Corsica, the chancellery of Aragon saw what a suspension of civil rights could lead to.

In 1492 Castile began to colonise America. The opinion of the conquistadors was that victors had control over all civil rights. The Spanish crown, however, wanted to avoid a Corsican impasse. In 1512 the Leyes de Burgos guaranteed freedom to the Indians. Accusations that colonists were violating the rights of the Indian population divided Spain. Did the colonists have to acknowledge the civil status of the Indians? In 1550-1551 Emperor Charles organised a hearing in Valladolid, where theologians and jurists would decide on the position to be taken. Charles promised to abide by the ruling. After a months-long discussion the verdict was that slavery had not existed since the Middle Ages and that the Indians had to be considered full citizens. In 1551, in other words, a government accepted that civil rights were everyone's rights and that even those who had lost a conflict retained these rights. Charles gave the American viceroys the assignment to protect the civil rights of the Indians.

This new attitude was reflected in the legal doctrine of Salamanca. The Spanish jusnaturalists were the first who comprehensively studied the judicial and political order. The absolutist polity with sovereign councils had developed out of medieval science, but had begun to grow rife. Francisco de Vitoria wanted to save Europe by once again tying in with the medieval academic tradition. He followed Nicolas Everaerts' vision that civil and canon law were two variants of the same legal thought and that moral philosophy was closely related to these. In *De iustitia et iure* he considered society from the viewpoints of the old faculties of theology, canon law and law. He attempted to adapt the old certainties to the political thought of the Early Modern Era. He was followed by a school of Spanish jusnaturalists, in whose works the first systematic analysis of fundamental rights can be found. From the legists they took the idea of popular sovereignty, the primacy of the law of the people and the justification for the deposition for a tyrant. They emphasised civil rights like due process, the acquisition of property, marriage, inheritance law or obligations. The sovereign courts had to guarantee these. Civil law was mixed with moral theology. The jusnaturalists also adopted the canonists' idea of a law that transcended the monarchs. In addition, they advocated the equal treatment of citizens. From the canonical legal doctrine of unjust enrichment they took the idea that any disturbance of the balance between citizens was cause for the payment of compensation. Because of the problems in Spain and America they developed a legal doctrine in which universal civil rights took the central stage. It was a theoretical doctrine, but it would nevertheless slowly but surely take hold in Europe. There is not a single line in the 'Déclaration des droits du citoyen et de l'homme' of 1789 which cannot be found elaborated in the works of these Spanish neo-scholastics.

Did the inhabitants of the Low Countries not have the same rights as the Indians? Under Philip II they were hard hit by repression. The jurists of Leuven found that the absolutist and merciless Habsburgs did fear their Divine Lord and considered themselves as bound by Christian duties. In Valladolid they had yielded to the theologians. The law faculty of Leuven could not immediately make the most of this situation. In the 1550s-1580s relations between the theologians from Leuven and Spain were strained, even during the Council of Trent. In Leuven, the theologians and jurists left one another alone, among other things because of the presence of Calvinist professors of law. At the end of the century, when survival in the Low Countries was precarious, Lessius (1554-1623) broke through the glass ceiling. He was influenced by the Spanish scholastics of Salamanca. He tied in with the mixture of law and canon law and with the new natural law of the civilians. He began to mix civil law with theology – or better: with Christian ethics, which were acceptable for both Catholics and Protestants, but were nevertheless Christian enough to influence the kings. The civil law that Lessius treated in his *De iustitia et iure* (1609) could hardly be ignored by the governments. Civil rights were everyone's rights. God had invested man with these rights at birth. They fell into this higher category which the canonists had rendered familiar. Kings and judges who did not respect them would have to justify themselves after their death. Grotius and Descartes would turn them into the civil rights 'of every subject'.

7. The individual rights of the seventeenth century

The seventeenth century was a long reaction to absolutism. As has been mentioned above, the major achievement of that century was its legal doctrine, the development of a generally accepted extrajudicial law. Civil rights became private law and began to transcend the competence of the sovereign councils. Grotius (1583-1646), who had fled from the Netherlands without any of his possessions, took over the torch from Lessius in his *De iure belli ac pacis* (1625). He wrote about the law that transcended the law of the kings. The civil rights were *ius commune* and as such, more fundamental than temporary local law. They were based on moral principles and would apply 'even if God did not exist or did not concern himself with human affairs'. Life, freedom, ownership, obligations, compensation... These are rights that cannot be questioned. In times of war the kings had to respect the fundamental civil rights of the defeated. This civil right that civilians, canonists and moral theologians had passed on, had to provide protection from the warlords. In the seventeenth century the old Roman privileges of warriors were, in other words, considered the privileges of peaceful citizens which the warriors had to uphold! Grotius' work was read in Reformed and Catholic countries and his cry of distress was repeated by most jurists. He was considered to be the father of the school of natural law, which stated that people obtained a corpus of rights at birth. In this manner, he became the forerunner of the development of universal rights for all people.

In public law, which was coming into vogue, observance of private law became a central theme. Consequently, civil rights began to savour of political rights. The jurists also emphasised immanent rights in public law. The peaceful European culture which was underscored during the Enlightenment began to inspire the jurists. In this ideal atmosphere even *ratio*, Greek logical thought, was adopted. At the same time, individualism around the Cartesian subject developed as well.

By the seventeenth century, the canonists had lost their jurisdiction. In some countries the Roman Catholic Church retained its jurisdiction in cases involving marriage and in several countries respect for ecclesiastical rules was commanded via the notion of sacrilege in criminal law. In principle, however, churches became moral authorities. Canon law, which savoured distinctly of Roman law, began to play a part in legal doctrine. Its output, however, did not consist of judicial decisions anymore, but of propositions for the *ius commune*. In the eighteenth century we find a large amount of canonical heritage in political theory. The prime examples thereof are the place of the subject within the state and eighteenth-century political theory concerning criminal law.

Conclusion

"Absolute monarchy cannot be reconciled with a civil society," Locke (1632-1704) wrote. This sentence takes the centre stage in the classical histories of civil rights and human rights, for instance the beautiful examples of S. Moyn, P.G. Lauren or L. Hunt. We will end our story here. In the eighteenth century the parliaments began to announce in advance how they would judge later conflicts. We have already described how legal doctrine began to ossify into law codes and constitutions.

The doctrine of the immanent rights which saved us from absolutism stayed in the jurists' memory. After the wars of the twentieth century, the civil rights of all people were recast and transformed into new sources, such as the Universal Declaration of Human Rights or the ECHR. These sources are part of the European survival instinct. They are now extolled as planetary human rights, in hopes that they will lead to world peace. Old privileges of Roman warriors... In the encyclical *Pacem in terris* of Saint John XXIII, which forms the basis of the current canonical law of peace, these 'universal' rights are represented as a means to further peace. Is the West allowed to simply thrust Roman law and Western *ius commune* on other regions via human rights? There is no objection to this: thoroughly tested medicines against war can always be recommended.

Bibliography. – We elaborated on the subject in L. Waelkens, 'De Romeinse oorsprong van de fundamentele rechten en vrijheden', *The Legal History Review* 71 (2003), p. 187-196. A more recent version is: L. Waelkens, 'L'origine romaine des droits et libertés fondamentaux', *Annales de la faculté de droit, sciences économiques et gestion de Nancy* 2 (2010), p. 187-210. E. Benveniste, *Le vocabulaire des institutions indo-européennes*, I, *Economie, parenté, société*, Paris 1969, p. 321-333 provides indications about the word *liber*. P. Grimal, *Les erreurs de la liberté*, Paris 1989 collected a large amount of citations about Roman freedom in a somewhat messy little book. C. Nicolet, *Le métier de citoyen dans la Rome républicaine*, Paris 1989 is suggestive about freedom and citizenship and invites the reader to reflect on these matters more deeply. On Roman law, Latin church fathers and medieval jurists, see E.J.H. SCHRAGE, *Libertas est facultas naturalis, Menselijke vrijheid in een tekst van de jurist Florentinus*, Leyden 1975. The study of F. SCHOTT, 'Freiheit und Libertas, Zur Genese eines Begriffs', *Zeitschrift der Savigny-Stiftung, Germanistische Abteilung* 104 (1987), p. 84-109 is especially profound. For more information on this subject, do not consult older works about Roman law, but recent literature about reception, such as C. FAÍREN-GUILLEN, 'Die rechtliche Mittel gegen Angriff und Eingriffe in die persönliche Freiheit von den römischen interdicta über die Lex Baiuwariorum bis zum Spanischen Recht des Mittelalters', *Zeitschrift der Savigny-Stiftung, Germanistische Abteilung* 109 (1992), p. 335-352. A comparative legal historical study can be found in *Gouvernants et gouvernés,* [Receuils de la Société Jean Bodin, 23,] Brussels 1986. In the works of the medieval canonists, look up *manumission.* A beautiful study about the medieval evolution of *ciuitas* is B. D'ALTEROCHE, *De l'étranger à la seigneurie à l'étranger au royaume, XIe-XVe siècle,* Paris 2002. On the Early Modern Era, see for example J. DUMONT, *La vraie controverse de Valladolid, Premier débat des droits de l'homme,* Paris 1995; L. WAELKENS, 'Villalar 1521, Une étape pénible vers les droits de l'homme', in: I. SZÁSZDI LEÓN-BORJA and M. GALENDE RUÍZ (eds.), *Imperio y tiranía, La dimension europea de las comunidades de Castilla,* Valladolid 2013, p. 277-295; J. PIEPKE, 'Die Frage der Menschenrechte im Amerika des 16 Jahrhunderts', *Theologie der Gegenwart* 33 (1990), p. 2-36; H.F. KÖCK, *Der Beitrag der Schule von Salamanca zur Entwicklung der Lehre von den Grundrechten* [Schriften zur Rechtsgeschichte, 39], Berlin 1987.

Chapter III
The law of civil procedure

Roman civil law mainly consisted of procedural law. It settled conflicts between *ciues*. The Romans only needed law in cases of conflicts, so the law did not exist outside the courts. The law of procedure only became a separate branch of law in the Middle Ages, when it was separated from the substantive law. This chapter about procedure is limited for the most part to civil law. The other procedures are largely undocumented. We have no information about the 'sacral' law, nor about the procedure before the consuls, censors or quaestors, but we do possess data about the procedure of the *aediles*.

Bibliography. – The standard work about civil procedure in the Roman law of Antiquity is: M. KASER, *Das römische Zivilprozeßrecht*, revised edition by K. HACKL, [Handbuch der Altertumswissenschaft, III, 4,] Munich 1997, XXXIV + 712 p. On the reception and the Romano-canonical procedure see R.C. VAN CAENEGEM, *History of European Civil procedure*, [International Encyclopedia of Comparative law, XVI, 2,] Tübingen-Paris-New York 1972, 114 p. The most important work of all time about the law of civil procedure is Guillaume DURAND, *Speculum iudiciale*, Basel 1574 (reprint Aalen 1975).

§1. The republican civil procedure

Most handbooks discuss the civil lawsuit *per legis actiones* as the oldest form. It existed until 17 BC and must have taken place before a court-martial until then. The most important source is Gaius 4.11-31, which states that this procedure stemmed from the Twelve Tables and later case law. Pomponius contradicted Gaius (D. 1.2.2.6) and most scholars now accept that the *legis actiones* are older than the Twelve Tables. However, the sources are too scanty to draw even this conclusion. Here, the first characteristic of the republican civil procedure can be recognised: the preliminary hearing and the substance of the case were treated by different instances. The first phase took place before the military hierarchy; the second before a judge. The preliminary hearing was held by a high-ranking military man – from 367 BC onwards the praetor – who checked to see whether the conflict was civil in character. If the parties wanted to continue, the praetor asked them to deposit a wager and referred the conflict to a senator or, from the second century BC onwards, to one of his colleagues in the army. During the second phase, the latter checked the facts and gave a decision. A second characteristic was that all sentences were monetary fines; judges could not impose performance in kind. If a compulsory execution was necessary, the parties returned to the praetor, who had their wagers at his disposal and could also take away civil rights from recalcitrant losers. Being an army commander, the praetor had an obvious interest in discipline.

The *legis actio* procedure was used until well into the Imperial Period for complaints on account of undutiful wills (*querelae inofficiosi testamenti*). The judges to whom the praetor referred cases were centurions, middle-ranking officers, over whose court he himself presided. In the Empire, a *praetor hastarius* presided over the court of centurions.

Example of a claim. – By means of the *legis actio sacramento in rem* a plaintiff could commence an action called *uindicatio*, which served to claim a person or object. While the plaintiff pronounced the *uindicatio*, he touched the person or object with a rod (*uindicta, festuca*); the opposite party did the same thing during the *contrauindicatio*. The praetor gave the order to let go. The plaintiff asked the defendant on which foundations he based his right to the person or good. He challenged the plaintiff to an oath and the deposit of a wager, after which the good claimed by both parties was temporarily awarded by the praetor.

A: *Hanc ego rem ex iure Quiritium meam esse aio secundum suam causam sicut dixi ecce tibi uindictam imposui.* – B: (*idem*). – Praetor: *Mittite ambo rem!* – A: *Postulo, anne dicas, qua ex causa uindicaueris?* – B: *Ius feci, sicut uindictam imposui.* – A: *Quando tu iniuria uindicasti, quigentibus assibus sacramento te prouoco.* – B: *Et ego te!*

§2. The formulary procedure

We are more familiar with a second republican procedure, the formulary procedure, which originated in the *ius gentium* after 242 BC. If a peregrine was involved in a conflict, the parties first appeared before the *praetor peregrinus*, who assessed which civil rights a peregrine could claim according to his province's peace treaty. He gave the parties instructions for the judge who would hear their case. This judge then took account of the civil rights of the peregrine in question. A *lex aebutia* of the second century BC made this type of lawsuit more widely applicable so that all cases between citizens could be treated according to this procedure. According to some scholars, the formulary procedure was originally meant only for proceedings that were instituted by means of *condictiones*, legal remedies used to claim a fixed sum of money. In the classical republican law, the formulary procedure was commonly used for all civil demands. This procedure was not only employed in Rome, but also by local instances. In the following text, the praetor takes the centre stage, but the role of the praetor was not reserved for the two praetors who sat in the *forum romanum*. According to D. 1.2.32, there was a praetor in every town and in every province. In the provinces and *municipia*, the role of praetor was played by the governors and the city magistrates, respectively.

According to some Romanists, a rescript of Constantius and Constans to the consuls (C. 2.57.1) abolished the formulary procedure. The Senate's provinces had already disappeared in the third century. Was the formulary procedure still in use in the capitals at that time? The text of the rescript does not offer unambiguous evidence of the continued use of the formulary procedure.

C. 2.57.1: Iuris formulae aucupatione syllabarum insidiantes cunctorum actibus radicitus amputentur.

Translation Blume. – Legal formulas, with the snares of their syllables laying a trap for the acts of all shall be completely abolished.

1 The preliminary hearing before the praetor

A. Summons and the institution of proceedings

The summons (*in ius uocatio*) was a private matter, in which the magistrates did not intervene. The best option for citizens was to invoke civil rights before the praetor in their capacity as old army comrades. If the defendant did not react, the plaintiff could pick him up at a suitable time and use some physical force if necessary. A defendant who did not want to appear could send a representative, in which case the representative had to stand surety and pay the fine if he lost the suit. In case of an adjournment, both parties were also asked to provide collaterals or to agree on penalty clauses by means of a *stipulatio*. If the defendant failed to turn up or his representative happened to be insolvent, the plaintiff could demand the immediate execution of the judgement.

During the preliminary hearing before the praetor, the plaintiff explained his claim and asked to be granted a legal remedy which the praetor had provided in his edict (*postulatio actionis*). The praetor checked to see whether this remedy was relevant. He verified whether the plaintiff could legitimately commence an action and whether the defendant could be sued by means of that action. Did both parties have civil rights? Could they take legal action in their own name? Were they *paterfamilias* or *dominus*, or was someone else liable for them?

The competence of the magistrate was checked as well. The defendant could argue that he had been summoned before the wrong instance. The Roman praetors were always competent, but in other *fora* the competent magistrate was the magistrate who had jurisdiction over the defendant's domicile (*actor sequitur forum rei*), the location of the immovable goods, the place where a contract had to be performed, or the place where the offence had been committed. We will return to the rules on conflict of laws that concern local competence later. In the Middle Ages, these rules would be at the basis of 'private international law'. It is unclear how a defendant could enforce compliance with these rules. If a local magistrate concluded that he was incompetent, he asked the parties to make a new appointment to bring the case before the correct instance (*uadimonium*).

According to a *lex* of 17 BC the praetors could take decisions that remained binding for eighteen months (*iudicium legitimum*) if they were pronounced within the *pomerium* around the Forum. Lower magistrates had *iudicium imperium continens*: they only had local competence and their decisions lost their legal effect when their duties ended.

B. Provisional measures

At the preliminary hearing, provisional measures could be taken. The interdicts were developed around these measures (*interdicere* = to pronounce interim judgements). The praetor's edict contained a limited list of interdicts which could be obtained from the praetor. We know them from Gaius and the sources of the Imperial Era, from D. 43. Examples include the interdicts on account of the use of violence, obstruction of a passage, denial of usufruct or a precarious legal relationship. The provisional measure was a decision about the parties' position during the suit. Which position was each of the parties allowed to take up? The pronouncement was a *possessio* (the right to remain seated, from *posse sedere*). The interdicts were 'possessory' measures.

The procedure was summary. Those who asked for an interdict had to prove some facts. When someone made use of the interdict *unde ui*, the praetor only checked to see whether violence had been used. If that was the case, he ordered the previous situation to be restored. Those who requested the interdict *uti possidetis*, had to prove that they had acquired an immovable good without violence and in a non-clandestine manner. He was then allowed to occupy the good provisionally. Sometimes the interdict served to end a disturbance (for instance the obstruction of a passage), to have an object returned provisionally, or to order a certain object to be produced. In order to confirm the interdict, the parties agreed on penalty clauses, which meant that they entered into a formal contractual agreement. During the phase before the judge, a party could demand, if necessary, that such a financial penalty be paid. The judge then decided whether the interdict had been granted justly or not. The judge's decision about restorative or exhibitory interdicts was merely a declaratory judgement and not a constitutive one. If this judgement was not executed, the aggrieved party returned to the praetor and asked for a *condictio* in order to claim the sum determined in the penalty clause.

The procedure that made use of interdicts was quick and cheap. The praetors attempted to resolve as many conflicts as possible in the first phase. If a person or a good was claimed, the praetor always pronounced a provisional allocation. For the beneficiary of the interdict, the case was settled at that moment. He could not institute a further *actio*. The party who was put at a disadvantage by the interdict, however, could. If he did not accept the provisional measure, he requested an action, a 'petitory' remedy (*petitio*, from *petere actionem*). A petitory remedy was the only means to react against a possessory measure.

A provisional measure could also concern the civil status of the plaintiff or the defendant. If one of them claimed that the other did not have civil rights, the praetor first cleared up this issue. He examined the situation and gave a preliminary ruling on the *possessio status*. The French term for this, 'possession d'état' is a reference to this old provisional measure.

Praetors' interdicts were military orders and applied *erga omnes*, towards all. Everyone had to respect them, even people who were not citizens – slaves, for example. If the suit was continued, interdicts remained in force until the judge's pronouncement. If the parties did not continue the suit and no one instituted third-party proceedings, the interdict continued to apply towards everyone. After some limitation period, the petitory remedy could no longer be used and the provisional measure became definitive. In the Early Modern Era, the fact that *possessio* applied towards everyone would be at the basis of its development into an *in rem* right.

The *interdictum uti possidetis* ran as follows:

Vti eum fundum (eas aedes) quo (quibus) de agitur nec ui nec clam nec precario alter ab altero possidetis, quominus ita possideatis uim fieri ueto.	So that you will not take this piece of land (that house) from each other with violence, in a clandestine manner or precariously, I forbid that violence be used to exercise authority over the piece of land (the house) in a way which is different from the current one.

C. *The* actio

At the end of the Republic, the edict of the praetor contained a list with over two hundred *actiones*, petitory remedies at law. At the preliminary hearing, the plaintiff requested an *actio* from that list. In principle, nothing could be claimed by means of the civil law if there was no specific action to claim it. A formless agreement (*pactum*) or a *fideicommissum*, for example, were not enforceable under praetorian law because the edict did not include a remedy for their enforcement. If a case was not fully covered by the edict, the plaintiff could suggest that the praetor adapt an existing action (*actio utilis*) or draw up an *actio* along the lines of the edict that was suitable to deal with the case under consideration (*actio in factum concepta*).

Apart from interdicts and *actiones*, the edict of the praetor also mentioned some situations in which the plaintiff could appeal to an *in integrum restitutio*, the restoration of the previous legal situation. For example, if a person who was under twenty-five discovered that he had been deceived by a contract and wanted his money back, the praetor provided the possibility of considering the contract as non-existent. The praetor did not terminate the contract, but rendered it transparent in case of a claim by a minor. The latter could then claim back his money by means of a *condictio indebiti* (recovery of undue payment). If the praetor had pronounced *in integrum restitutio*, the judge assessed this *condictio* without taking the contract into account. When two families merged (*adrogatio*) the debts of the family that was absorbed became non-enforceable because its *paterfamilias* had lost his status and could no longer be summoned before the court. In such a case, the praetors granted an *in integrum restitutio* to the *paterfamilias*' creditors, so that they could make claims as if the families had not merged. An *in integrum restitutio* could also be requested if acts had been committed under coercion.

Sometimes the parties asked for the appointment of an *arbiter*, a mediator. In such cases the parties' demands did not have to take a form provided by the edict.

D. The defence before the praetor

If the plaintiff had requested an action, the praetor asked for the standpoint of the defendant, who could react in different ways:

- defence on the merits: the defendant denied either the right of the plaintiff or the facts. The magistrate referred the case to a judge for treatment on the merits.
- defence by way of an exception: the defendant denied neither the right of the plaintiff nor the facts, but requested the magistrate to include an exception in the formula, a means of defence, something that was provided in the edict. If the defendant was challenged by means of a stipulation, for example, the judge would receive but little room for discretion. If the defendant could prove that the party demanding the stipulation was an untrustworthy man, the defendant had a right to an *exceptio doli*, which guaranteed that the judge would be granted considerable room for discretion. Exceptions were only granted according to conditions that were provided in the edict of the praetor.
- *confessio in iure*: the defendant could confess, admit that the plaintiffs were right or state that he would pay. If this happened, the conflict was resolved during the phase before the praetor. The plaintiff was not granted an action. If the defendant confessed, but did not agree with the sum to be paid, he could only be granted an *actio confessoria* to have the judge determine the precise sum on the merits. Later, confessions would be considered irrefutable proof.
- decisive oaths: if a case file looked scanty and the praetor doubted whether the judge would find a meaningful solution, he could propose a *iusiurandum in litem*

in cases in which a fixed sum of money was claimed. In the reception of the Roman law, this came to be called a decisive oath. The plaintiff requested the defendant to declare in court that he did not owe the sum. If the defendant swore this oath, he was in the clear. If he refused, he lost the case. He could tender the oath to the plaintiff and charge the latter to declare that he did not ask a cent too much. If the plaintiff complied with this request, the execution of the judgement could follow immediately. If new facts were discovered after a *iusiurandum in litem*, the case could be brought before the court again. Alternatively, a procedure concerning an insult towards the court could be instituted (a procedure that would later develop into the current 'contempt of court'). This oath before the court would later be considered a means of proof. False declarations would become perjury in the Middle Ages.
- if the defendant did not react, he lost his case.

E. The litiscontestatio

If the case was clear and the praetor agreed to grant an action, he asked the parties to which judge (*iudex*) they would go. Every fellow citizen could serve as a judge. In cases of doubt, names were proposed from a register with judges from the senatorial or knightly class (*album iudicum selectorum*). If no agreement was reached, the judge was chosen by lot.

Sometimes, specific judges were needed, for example *recuperatores*. These judges formed collegial courts. Originally, they were competent to deal with arbitration concerning the interpretation of peace treaties, i.e. in the field of the *ius gentium*. In the civil law, we read about their jurisdiction over some suits concerning freedom and cases concerning the public order. In some cases, the judge had to be a centurion or *decemuir*. In the late Republic we often find the emperor as the judge in a formulary suit. This procedure continued to exist in the senatorial provinces until the second century and in urban Rome until the third century, although imperial judges had been pronouncing verdicts in the imperial provinces for centuries. When choosing a judge, parties could opt for the emperor, in which case they knew that he would apply imperial law. Sometimes the parties asked for the appointment of an arbiter rather than a judge. This arbiter did not have to pronounce a verdict, but to bring about reconciliation. At the end of the Republic, the difference between judges and arbiters in the formulary procedure became blurred.

When the judge had been appointed, the formula was drawn up. The praetor granted the plaintiff the right to bring proceedings (*iudicium dare*). This was followed by the *litiscontestatio*, an essential phase in Roman procedure. The conflict was fixed before the court (*lis* = lawsuit, *contestatio* = conclusion). The *litiscontestatio* was an agreement between parties in which they accepted the legal remedies and the judges and committed themselves to accept the future decision. The *litiscontestatio* was a take-it-or-leave-it agreement. If the plaintiff did not accept it, he could not institute further legal proceedings; if the defendant refused, he lost the case. The right of action was consumed by the *litiscontestatio*. After this phase, it became impossible to apply to the praetor for the same action in the same case. There are opinions of jurists about what 'the same case' was. According to the *lex iulia iudiciorum priuatorum* of 17 BC the following conditions had to be met in order for the right of action to be consumed:

ius ciuile, actio in personam, iudicium legitimum. If one of the parties brought the case before a different instance afterwards, the local magistrate granted the defendant the *exceptio rei iudicatae uel in iudicium deductae* (objection regarding the case that has already been judged).

Except in cases in which the judge was appointed after the *litiscontestatio,* this was the end of the phase before the praetor. He wrote the *formula* on a strip of papyrus and handed it to the plaintiff.

F. Appeal against the praetor

It was possible to lodge a complaint about the decision of a praetor with another praetor or with a higher magistrate. In Rome, plebeians who were subject to the law could have the decision of a patrician praetor annulled by a tribune. If the role of praetor was played by a local magistrate, complaints were to be presented to the governors, the highest magistrates in the provinces. Appeals against the governors' decisions were possible as well. They were heard by the consuls.

2. The phase before the judge

The judge read the praetor's *formula,* which contained the judge's programme. The *formula* included the name of the judge and the parties or their legal representative, the facts to be checked, the manner of assessing them, the precise matter which the judge had to decide, and the manner in which the amount to be paid had to be determined. When the praetor decided to grant an *in integrum restitutio,* this was included in the formula as a fiction (*actio ficticia*). These *formulae* are wonderful examples of concise Latin sentences. They contain an *intentio* (what the plaintiff wanted to acquire and why) and a *condemnatio* (an order). The judge derived his competence from the *condemnatio,* which meant that he was bound by it. In actions for the division of goods an *adiudicatio* (adjudication) was requested. It authorised the judge to adjudicate goods definitively.

Examples of *formulae*

ACTIO CERTAE CREDITAE PECUNIAE: Si paret Numerium Negidium Aulo Agerio sestertium decem milia dare oportere, iudex Numerium Negidium Aulo Agerio sestertium decem milia condemnato, si non paret, absoluito.	If it turns out that N.N. has to give ten thousand sesterces to A.A., you, judge X., have to sentence N.N. to give ten thousand sesterces to A.A.; if this does not turn out to be the case, you must acquit him.
ACTIO EMPTI: Quod Aulus Agerius de Numerio Negidio hominem de quo agitur emit, quidquid ob eam rem Numerium Negidium Aulo Agerio dare facere oportet ex fide bona, eius iudex Numerium Negidium Aulo Agerio condemnato, si non paret absoluito.	Because A.A. has bought from N.N. the man concerning whom a claim is brought, you, judge, must sentence N.N. to the payment of the price of what he has to give to A.A. or what he has to do for him and what he owes by reason of 'good faith' on the grounds of this purchase; if this does not turn out to be the case, you must acquit him.

CONDITIO CERTAE REI: Si paret Nm. Nm. Ao. Ao. (tritici Africi optimi modius centum) dare oportere, quanti ea res est, tantam pecuniam iudex Nm. Nm. Ao. Ao. Condemnato, si non paret absolutio.	If it turns out that N.N. must give to A.A. (one hundred scoops of the best African wheat), you, judge, must sentence him to pay a sum of money amounting to the value of this matter; if this does not turn out to be the case, you must acquit him.

There is no *intentio certa* here, but a *condemnatio incerta*, because a judge could only sentence a party to the payment of a sum of money.

ACTIO EX STIPULATU: Quod As. As. de No. No. (incertum) stipulatus est, quidquid ob eam rem Nm. Nm. Ao. Ao. dare facere oportet, eius iudex Nm. Nm. Ao. Ao. c.s.n.p.q.	If A.A. was promised by N.N. in a stipulation... you, judge, must sentence N.N. to the price of what he has to give to A.A. or what he has to do for him; if this does not turn out to be the case, you must acquit him.
ACTIO PUBLICIANA: Si quem hominem As. As. emit et ei traditus est, anno possedisset, tum ei eum hominem, de quo agitur, eius ex iure Quiritium esse pareret neque is homo restitutetur, quenti ea res erit, tantam pecuniam iudex Nm. Nm. Ao. Ao. c.s.n.p.q.	If this man, whom the plaintiff has bought and who was delivered to him – provided that he had had the man for a year – would be the plaintiff's according to ius ciuile, and was not returned, you, judge, must sentence N.N. to pay to A.A. as much money as his interest in this case is worth; if this does not turn out to be the case, you must acquit him.
EXCEPTIO DOLI: ... si in ea re nihil dolo malo Ai. Ai. factum est neque fiat...	... if at least it turns out that in this case nothing came about through the plaintiff's guile...

The judge had a large discretionary competence with regard to accepting and rejecting a means of proof. The division of the burden of proof was left to him. The parties provided the evidence themselves; the judge could not force anyone. The most important means of proof were unilateral statements – confirmed on oath or not – confessions, testimonies, experts' reports...

The judgement (*sententia*) dovetailed with the formula and ran *condemno* (I condemn), *absoluo* (I acquit), or *adiudico* (I adjudge). If a party did not appear before noon, the judge could sentence him by default. If the judge was not equal to the case, he pronounced a *non liquet*. The judgement was absolute, by virtue of both parties' acceptance in the *litiscontestatio*. It was declarative between parties: it declared their rights, but did not create rights for third parties (*res inter alios acta aliis non praeiudicat*). There was one exception: divisions were constitutive and created a new legal situation for third parties as well.

Sentences always consisted of fines and never of a performance or the delivery of a good. The formula showed the value of the sentence. If the formula stated *quicquid dare facere oportet*, the judge determined the market value of the good and/or the performance. If he had to sentence a party to *id quod eius interest*, the parties' was at stake: both the loss of profit and the incurred damage were assessed (*lucrum cessans et damnum emergens*). If the formula contained the words *e bona fide*, he took account of all relations between the parties. The sum to which the losing party was sentenced could also be paid by a third party.

In the Republic, there was no possibility for appeal. Parties were bound by the *litiscontestatio* vis-à-vis one another; the losing party had to pay the winning party. If, however, the losing party was of the opinion that the judge had not dealt with the case well, he could enter into a conflict with the judge. For such cases, the praetor provided an *actio de iudice qui litem suam fecit* in his edict, the action against the judge who pronounced a bad judgement (D. 44.7.5.4). The losing party summoned the judge, both appeared before the praetor and a new case was begun according to the *formula* procedure. In the Empire, there was remedy against judgements *per formulas* if the parties had chosen the emperor as their judge. Seeing that the emperor delegated the assignment to pass judgement to a local representative, the losing party could lodge an appeal with the emperor in order to complain that the official had not fulfilled his mandate in an appropriate manner. He could request a new judgement from a court of appeal, or, after a second appeal, from the imperial prefecture. It is unclear in how far these appeals suspended execution or could counteract the *actio iudicati*.

3. The execution of the sentence and insolvency

The loser of a formulary trial had to pay the winner within thirty days. Failure to do so was considered a new conflict. The winner summoned the losing party before the praetor and requested an *actio iudicati*, an action on the judgement. The praetor heard the parties again. If he began to have doubts as to whether the first judgement had been passed in a regular manner, he referred this new case to a judge who had to assess the facts in a judgement. However, *infitiando lis crescit in duplum*. If it turned out that the loser's failure to pay was illegitimate, he was sentenced to the payment of double the original amount.

The defendant could claim insolvency and request personal measures or the liquidation of his assets. These remedies were based on the praetor's competence to pronounce *infamia* (measures to be taken within the *familia*) or to diminish civil rights (*capitis diminutio*). An example of a personal measure was *nexum*, which transferred the debtor to the family of the creditor, so that all of his earnings became part of the creditor's assets. When the debt had been paid off, a *nexi liberatio* followed. The praetor could also deprive the debtor of his civil status and place him in the family of the creditor as a slave. The creditor then had the possibility to sell the slave.

An old legal problem is the insolvency of a debtor: he wants to pay, but cannot. Usually, insolvent debtors do not have one single debt, but rather an entire series of debts. In cases of insolvency and conflict among creditors (*concursus creditorum*), all of the debtor's assets were seized (*missio in bona*). The creditors were granted seizure before judgement and announced this publicly during a thirty-day period, after which the praetor called all of the debtors together. They chose an auctioneer who sold the goods. Prospective buyers offered to pay a part of the debts; the auctioneer assigned the goods to the highest bidder. The buyer of the assets (*bonorum emptor*) became the bankrupt debtor's successor by universal title. Creditors could claim payment from him just as they had been able to claim payment from the insolvent debtor. With regard to normal debts, the part that had been agreed upon was paid off. There were preferential creditors whom the buyer had to pay in full. The main privileges in case of bankruptcies were: the costs incurred for the goods' storage, the *priuilegium dotis* (the wife's privilege with regard to the dowry), the *priuilegium pupilli* (the pupil's privilege in case of his guardian's bankruptcy), and the privilege of the account holder in case of his banker's bankruptcy. During the Principate, the privilege of the *fiscus* was added to this list. The costs incurred for the storage of the goods of a bankrupt person were protected by means of a pledge (*uersio in rem*).

If a debtor had become insolvent through no fault of his own, the praetor could allow him a favour: he could grant an assignment of the estate (*cessio bonorum*) on the basis of a text by Augustus. For the creditors, this had the same effect as a *missio in bona*, but there was no *capitis diminutio* (loss of civil rights). Special seizures, which involved the sale of certain goods in order to pay the debt, were highly exceptional.

§3. The aedilician procedure

The aediles were competent with regard to criminal, market and commercial law. In the Republic, they followed their own procedure, which was developed in their edict. In the Empire, the emperor took over the republican office of aedile. He introduced the *cognitio* procedure for matters of criminal, market and commercial law, so that the old aedilician procedure was lost. We still find some remains of the aediles' procedure in D. 21.1 and C. 4.53. These do not discuss criminal law, but they do allow us to see that a limited list of actions was also used for private suits pertaining to commercial law. The edict of the aediles has left traces in the current treatment of hidden defects in cases of purchase (see below).

It seems that claims in criminal law were lodged by the aediles. They were assessed by an elected jury. In a case of the death sentence, there was a possibility of appeal 'to the people'. This appeal ended up before the quaestors, who had to submit it to the *consilia plebis* if the condemned person was a plebeian and to the *comitia tributa* if he was a patrician.

Bibliography. – L. GAROFALO, *Il processo edilizio, Contributo alla storia dei 'iudicia populi'*, Padua 1989.

§4. The imperial *cognitio extra ordinem*

In his imperial provinces, the emperor Augustus introduced an entirely new procedure, the *cognitio extra ordinem* (extraordinary cognizance), which would be the most important Roman procedure for centuries. It was imported throughout Europe in the Middle Ages, and was based on the legal order that Augustus encountered in Egypt when he became pharaoh in 30 BC. When he introduced it in the Roman Empire, it was influenced by the republican procedure with which all of the jurists of the provinces were familiar.

The basic idea of the imperial legal system was that the emperor was presented with all conflicts, i.e. conflicts between people who were subject to the law, as well as conflicts between these people and officials. Within his administration, the emperor also organised judicial services. The *cognitio* procedure was the standard procedure for all of the cases that were treated by these services. Its main characteristic was that the decisions of an official could be appealed twice with the emperor, irrespective of whether the official in question had acted as a judge or had taken administrative decisions. These appeals were also treated within the administration, by a higher court of justice. The second appeal ended up before the praetorian prefecture. Augustus not only introduced judicial administration in the imperial provinces, but also had bureaus in the Senate's provinces, where he was competent as *pontifex maximus* in the *ius sacrum*, as consul and censor in the military sphere and as aedile in the criminal law and public trade. He did not administer justice himself in these provinces, but had officials perform juridical functions. Just as in the imperial provinces, appeals against these officials could be lodged with the emperor. It is therefore probable that these judges in the Senatorial provinces also followed the new procedure. In these provinces, the formulary procedure remained common for civil cases. The parties often chose the emperor as a judge; some governors always appointed the emperor as a judge in their formulary suits. These cases were entrusted to the emperor's local representatives, against whom appeals could be filed. The preliminary hearing was dealt with according to the praetorian procedure, while the judge's treatment on the merits followed the *cognitio* procedure.

Many of the texts about the *cognitio* procedure date from Diocletian's day. He reorganised the highest jurisdiction into four praetorian prefectures, two city prefectures and a chancellery. The *cognitio* procedure was the cornerstone of the imperial administration. Whenever a party to a suit was of the opinion that he was injured by the methods of a judge, he could lodge an appeal. This compelled judges of the lower courts to follow the case law of the higher judges. Many complaints concerned the actions of the judges themselves, so that the chancellery had to resolve many procedural issues. The answers of the prefecture and the chancellery developed into procedural law. We will return to the possibility of appeal below.

A. Jurisdiction

Texts about procedure from Augustus' day are rare. Augustus gave the consuls jurisdiction over conflicts concerning *fideicommissa*, which were not enforceable in the formulary procedure, and over the supervision of guardianship. Augustus himself was consul for life, so that this supervision became the task of the imperial administration. And what about the praetors? The precise evolution of the *praetorium* of the Senate's legions into the imperial *praetorium* is unclear. In D. 1.2.32 it can be read that there were eighteen praetors in the first century AD, but this text does not state the jurisdiction in which they worked. It has been said that Claudius charged two new praetors with the *fideicommissa*. Were they imperial officials, or did they work in the Senate's provinces? It does look as if the city prefect already had jurisdiction over the administration of justice in Rome, while the praetorian prefect had jurisdiction over the imperial provinces. Under Tiberius (14-37), the praetorian prefect was the head of the administration and administered justice in the emperor's name. He also treated final appeals. In the imperial provinces, the governors, who had received a mandate from the emperor, were competent to administer justice. They also organised the case-law of the lower officials.

In Diocletian's time, municipal authorities had jurisdiction over smaller conflicts, while the governors had jurisdiction over larger conflicts. Appeals against the municipal judges were filed with the governors and, if a second appeal followed, with one of the four prefectures. Appeals against the governors were treated at the level of the dioceses, a judicial division that was led by *uicarii*. Rome and Constantinople were outside the normal hierarchy and had their own city prefectures. The case law of the six highest courts was coordinated by the chancellery. If the case law of the prefectures was divergent, people subject to the law could use a request for pardon to ask the prefecture for a rectification.

B. Summons

In the imperial courts there were two ways for citizens to institute proceedings. The plaintiff could still summon the defendant privately to appear before the judge (*denuntiatio*). However, he could also address a request (*libellus*) to the judge and ask him to summon the other party. The judge who received a request took action *ex officio,* in his official capacity, but he did have to remain heedful of the complaints of citizens who thought that he did not perform his official duty well. If the judge decided to summon the other party, the summons was invested with governmental authority (*denuntiatio ex auctoritate*). Requests could also be used to commence an action concerning a conflict with a slave. A slave could not be summoned by means of the civil law, but did have to respond to a convocation or summons by the emperor or his representative. It was possible to ask for interdicts against slaves in a request. Provisional measures of the judge applied *erga omnes* and were also binding on slaves.

Text. – A *casus classicus* concerning the procedure against a slave is mentioned in C. 3.1.7 (a judgement of the chancellery subscribed in Sirmium in 294).

Cum debitoris tui seruum tibi pignoris iure obligatum bona domini sui quondam rebus humanis exempti tenere profitearis, aduersus eum dari tibi actiones contra ius postulas. Si quidem inter seruum et liberum consistere iudicium nullum possit. Ad possessionem itaque pignorum magis officio iudicis uenire te conuenit quam illicita postulare.

Translation F. H. Blume. – Since you say that the slave of your debtor who was pledged to you holds property from his former master, now taken away from human affairs, you unlawfully ask for a right of action against the slave, since no action between a slave and a freeman can be maintained. It behoves you, therefore, to ask for possession of the pledge at the hands of the judge, rather than for something that is not lawful.

A third possibility was the *euocatio*: the judge summoned a defendant or third party on his own initiative. If the emperor acted as criminal judge, the summons was an *euocatio.*

In the late Empire proceedings always began with a request. In civil cases, this request already had to contain the legal ground on the basis of which the other party could be summoned. If necessary, the court then had an *exsecutor*, a bailiff who was an imperial official, visit the defendant. If the defendant did not want to appear, he had to provide securities. The *exsecutor* could place the summoned person in pre-trial detention or seize some of his goods (seizure before judgement). If a defendant obstinately (*contumax*) stayed away without having made agreements, the lawsuit could take place in his absence and there could be a judgement by default. The judgement was an imperial pronouncement. It no longer had to be accepted in advance in the *litiscontestatio*.

C. The preliminary hearing

In the *cognitio* procedure the preliminary hearing and the treatment on the merits were conducted in the same court, even when they were treated by a different division or on a different date. During the preliminary hearing, the complaint was rendered more precise. Just as in the formulary procedure, the competence of the judges and the parties was checked. If their competence was questioned, a debate about this issue followed and the judge gave an intermediary judgement.

In the civil law, the plaintiff no longer had to rely on the remedies that could be found in the praetor's edict. He stated the basis of his claim (*petitio, persecutio*), but this basis could now also be a precedent of the prefecture. The emperor Augustus adopted the legal grounds of the Provincial Edict into his case law. The emperor Hadrian introduced the Eternal Edict. He asked the prefect Salvius Julianus to revise the republican praetorian edict and to introduce it into the case law of the prefecture as if it was a collection of precedents. In this manner, the republican civil law, and with it the *status libertatis* and the list of civil rights from the praetorian edict, was adopted into the *cognitio* procedure. The term *actio* became less precise and came to mean 'claim', but in the civil law these claims remained limited to those on the lists of the old praetors until the late Empire.

The term *praescriptio* cropped up as a synonym of the *exceptio*. In the late Empire, dilatory and peremptory exceptions were distinguished from one another. Exceptions that were made because the claim was not yet receivable, were dilatory: the debt was not yet due, there was no notice of default, the goods were not yet adjudicated, the defendant was too young, etcetera. Peremptory exceptions were based on factual grounds: the absence of a contract, non-delivery of goods, lies told by the other party... Peremptory exceptions which undermined the lawsuit itself were called declinatory exceptions in the Middle Ages: non-competence of the judge, lapsed claim, the fact that the opposing party happened to be a slave... Dilatory pleas had to be raised during the preliminary hearing, i.e. before the *litiscontestatio*; peremptory pleas could even be raised for the first time during an appellate hearing. The judges provided intermediary judgements about the admissibility of the remedies at law.

In criminal law, it was, according to some, possible to invoke the inadmissibility of the complaint if it was not based on an edict, because of the rule *nulla poena sine lege*. However, in Antiquity a *lex* was not a 'law'. *Leges* included case law. The principle *nulla poena sine lege* meant that there could not be any punishment without a lawsuit.

Provisional measures were adopted from the civil law of the Republic. Decisions to grant such measures were taken in intermediary judgements. What remained unchanged was that one could only react against a possessory measure by making use of a petitory remedy. In the late Empire, however, it was possible to lodge an appeal against a possessory measure (C. 7.69.1).

The preliminary hearing led to a *litiscontestatio*, which, however, no longer contained an agreement to accept the judgement and no longer consumed the right of action. From then on, these were consequences of the judgement. The *litiscontestatio* defined conflict in an exact manner, in Latin: defined the *causa*. The plaintiff could no longer change his claim. The *litiscontestatio* was included in an interim judgement.

D. Treatment on the merits

The treatment on the merits took place in the same court. In criminal cases, the judge examined the events that had taken place. He also had an obligation to investigate when he dealt with civil cases, but the scarce sources suggest that his examination was limited to a meticulous inspection of the case file and thorough interviews. He did not leave the court and did not perform any investigative acts. Henceforth, however, the judge did take the law of evidence into account. The prefecture received quite a number of complaints concerning the admission of evidence by judges and formulated precedents that later became rules of evidence. The law of evidence will be discussed further on in this book. The judge called up witnesses by means of a government order. A confession or *iuramentum* no longer ended a conflict. They became articles of evidence.

The procedure was accusatorial and less formalistic than the republican procedure. In a formulary trial, those who claimed more than was due (*plurispetitio*) ran the risk of not getting anything at all. In the *cognitio* procedure, the claim could be reduced. A claimant who intentionally asked more than was due committed a procedural offence and risked a fine. Defences by means of remedies and defences based on factual grounds were treated together. In addition, pleas no longer had to undermine the entire claim. They could lead to a reduction of the claim.

The conflict was settled by the judgement, which was not reasoned. It was written down and read out loud in the court. The judgement was a decision of the emperor and applied towards everyone. It was no longer limited to a pecuniary sentence or an acquittal. The judge could also force a party to perform a certain action and sentence one of the parties to pay the costs of the procedure. In the late Empire, judgements were registered. The losing party could appeal against the judgement. We will consider this appeal below, because the introduction of simple and cheap appeals against judgements fundamentally changed the law. After the judgement, appeals could be lodged against every aspect of the procedure. In addition, it was possible to file an appeal against judges who did not give a judgement within a reasonable period of time. Once the time limit for bringing an appeal had passed, it became impossible to lodge a new claim about the same case. The defendant who was summoned a second time concerning the same case received a *praescriptio rei iudicatae*.

E. The execution

Because judgements were imperial pronouncements, the administration was bound to execute them. The judicial administration had *exsecutores*, bailiffs who enforced executions, at its disposal. Criminal sanctions were executed by the military. In the civil law of the Principate, a sentence could still turn people into the personal status of *nexus* or slave of the winning party. In case of unwillingness to pay, the seizure of all of the party's goods (*uenditio bonorum*) could be replaced with the seizure of specific goods (*distractio bonorum*), the sale of which sufficed to pay the debt. In the late Empire bankruptcy only occurred in a case of conflicting rights of creditors and a lack of assets. A losing party who answered for his insolvency could relinquish his estate to his creditors in order to avoid losing familial or civil rights (*infamia, capitis diminutio*).

Conclusion

The *cognitio* procedure was clear and transparent. Because of the possibilities for appeal all aspects that led to dissatisfaction were dealt with by the imperial administration. Because appeals were not only used to deal with conflicts between citizens, but also with complaints against officials and grievances about government actions, this procedure was tremendously important for the emperor. He maintained contact with the people subject to his law. Because of the standardised treatment of the complaints and the clear precedents which the praetorian prefecture composed at the end of the procedure, the *cognitio extra ordinem* was the instrument par excellence that created the unified imperial law, which was at the basis of affluence and the *pax romana*. Just like the civil rights and liberties from the Republic, these are milestones of Roman culture. Once again, thorough legal thought generated large revenues at a low cost.

§5. The Romano-canonical procedure

Only a very small number of legal sources from the Middle Ages have been handed down. The sources that pertain to procedural law are even downright scarce. Nevertheless, they suggest that the manner of conducting a suit in the royal courts did not change drastically after the fall of the Western Empire in 476. The *leges romanae barbarorum* do not allow us to deduce that there was a break with earlier practices. The chroniclers of the Frankish and Carolingian era do not mention any great changes in this field either. Latin remained the legal language and this suggests that the lawsuits were probably still held in the Roman manner. The division of sovereignty in the kingdoms, and later in the feudal system, inevitably led to regional and local differences. On the other hand, the reception of the Roman procedural law can easily be followed in the canonistic tradition, where it had a considerable influence on all Western procedural law. If the *cognitio extra ordinem* was received in such a precise manner in the high Middle Ages, this was due to the reception of Roman law by the episcopal courts and the faculties of canon law. Canonical case law also influenced the reception of medieval law in the Early Modern Era, which explains why legal historians coined the name 'Romano-canonical'.

1. The *episcopalis audientia*

We have already mentioned that in Antiquity Christians had their own administration of justice, which was organised by bishops and *presbyteri* (elders or venerable clergy): the episcopal audiences. It was expected of Christians that they sought reconciliation in these audiences. If arbitration did not help, the bishop gave a unilateral judgement. *Didascalia* 2.45-53 states that it was best in such cases if the bishop applied Roman law, which he did have to enlighten with Christian principles. If the losing party could not reconcile himself with the result, the bishop or his judge convened a meeting with a view to reconciliation. In case of sustained unwillingness, the case was referred to the imperial court.

This episcopal administration of justice assumed considerable proportions in the fourth century. The church fathers mentioned these institutions. Saint Augustine, for example, wrote about his audience in Hippo, where he concerned himself with law and justice. This practice posed a threat for the emperor, seeing that the only source of law was governing through the administration of justice. If the bishops left their mark on this, this amounted to a seizure of power. On the other hand, their activities meant that the imperial administration did not have to bear the costs of this important local administration of justice. In 318/333, the emperor Constantine gave a ruling on the audiences. He acknowledged the competence of the bishops to judge civil cases. A constitution of 361 permitted the organisation of Christian audiences in every city or village (CTh. 16.2.16). Their judgements became enforceable if an imperial judge granted an exequatur. Christians could therefore ask an imperial judge for an exequatur of an episcopal judgement. Before the imperial judge granted an exequatur and referred the case to a bailiff, he checked the bishop's judgement. He heard both parties and assessed whether a decision had been taken. The imperial judges examined whether the bishop was a member of a recognised church (see chapter I) and whether there had been an unambiguous judgement. In order to do this, the imperial judges checked the procedure that was followed. Consequently, the bishops anticipated this assessment by adopting the *cognitio* procedure in their audiences. In C. 1.4.8 the term *cognitio episcopalis* is used. Both disciplinary and dogmatic conflicts were treated according to that procedure. Appeals could be lodged against the granting or refusal of an exequatur and many cases ended up before the prefectures. It did not take the prefectures long to notice that there were no possibilities of appeal against episcopal audiences. This raised the question of whether an episcopal judgement was a lawful decision. In 343/4 the bishops at the council of Sardica reacted by introducing the possibility of lodging appeals against the audiences. They would be treated by the bishop of Rome. The decisions of the council of Sardica have played a role in the establishment of his primacy.

In 398, under Arcadius, the prefecture ruled that the decision of an audience was only enforceable if the parties had voluntarily appeared before the bishop (C. 1.4.7). In the same circumstances, Arcadius and Honorius acknowledged the rabbinical administration of justice as well (CTh. 2.1.10, C. 1.9.8). The judges, in other words, considered the pronouncements of bishops and rabbis as arbitration. Valentinian III also determined the competence of the audiences in this manner in his Nov. 35 (452). Both parties had to agree to accept the judgement. As soon as one of the parties was forced to appear, the audience was deemed to be incompetent. Moreover, the bishops were only competent *ratione personae* to treat cases involving clergy and *ratione materiae* to treat cases involving typically ecclesiastical matters.

Under Constantine, the prefecture allowed appeals to be filed against exequaturs, but not against the contents of an episcopal judgement. This case law was confirmed in 408 (CTh. 1.27.2; C. 1.4.8) and led to the independence of the bishops in their domain. As long as there was no forced execution, the imperial order did not intervene. Justinian changed this state of affairs with his Nov. 123.21*pr.* of 546, which made appeals against episcopal judgements lodged with an imperial judge admissible. If the imperial judge confirmed the decision, the case was closed, but if he reviewed it, further appeal was possible. Appeals against the decisions and rulings of the patriarchs were possible as well – they were heard by the chancellery. In the East, the novel *Si quis litigantium* of 546 resulted in the submission of the Greek bishops to the imperial order. From then on, the patriarchs took the chancellery into consideration, because it could review the contents of all of their decisions if appeals were filed. At that moment, Justinian was losing his power over the West. His novel did not reach most of the Latin bishoprics. Rome itself remained an imperial region from the sixth to the eighth century – it was part of the exarchate of Ravenna. At the time, several papal decisions in the ecclesiastical sphere were reviewed by imperial judges. The popes Vigilius (in 555) and Martin I (in 655) died in the emperor's dungeons because they did not accept theological decisions. Pope Sergius escaped arrest in 695 when he refused to introduce the decisions of the council in Trullo in the West. Under the Franks and the Carolingians the popes would break loose from Constantinople. They would not be subjected to the Western emperor either. In the Middle Ages, *Si quis litigantium* was fished up by the glossators and added after C. 14.8 as an *authenticum* (see below the paragraph on appeals).

Bibliography. – See G. Vismara's excellent overview of the history of the episcopal audiences: G. Vismara, *La giurisdizione civile dei vescovi (secoli I-IX)*, Milan 1995. On Constantine's decision of 318/333: the text of 318 is in CTh. 2.1.10; that of 333 is *Constitutio Sirmondiana* 1, in the Mommsen edition of the Theodosian Code, I, p. 907 and in Gratian's Decretum C. 11 q. 1 c. 35-36. Its authenticity is disputed. Nov. Val. 35 is in the *Codex Theodosianus*, II: *Leges Novellae*. Aut. '*Si quis litigantium*' is included in the edition of the Code composed by E. Hermann, following C. 1.4.8.

2. The ecclesiastical jurisdiction in the early Middle Ages

In Gaul, episcopal audiences were active in the fifth century. This is evident from the *Constitutiones Sirmondianae*, canons and works by Sidonius Apollinaris. After 456, audiences in Burgundy, Visigothic Gaul, the Frankish regions under Clovis, Ireland and Lombardy are mentioned. The bishops of Milan, Lyon, Seville and Toledo still referred appellate cases to Rome. In 603 Gregory the Great reminded the bishops of the need to apply the Roman procedure when administering justice. This procedure was respected in Rome. There are Lombardic sources from the seventh and eighth centuries, a time of Christianisation. The bishops of Lombardy were given jurisdiction as royal judges. Under Liutprand they presided over the main courts. Dukes and bishops had the same kind of judicial powers at their disposal in this region. The situation remained the same under the Franks. Pepin the Short and Charlemagne found a mixture of royal and episcopal case law in Lombardy. Lombardic law does not mention exequaturs of ecclesiastical judgements. The *Summa Perusina* even contains Arcadius' and Honorius' texts about episcopal jurisdiction – although it leaves out the demand that the parties in disputes agreed with treatment according to ecclesiastical law.

When Charlemagne was anointed emperor of the West by the pope Leo III in 800, both he and the pope had the intention of restoring the Roman law. They jointly organised the itinerant administration of justice by the *missi dominici*, who followed the Roman procedure. In the Carolingian period this mixture of royal and ecclesiastical administration of justice remained in existence. In the feudal period the evolution of the system put the bishops at a disadvantage. The sovereign jurisdiction of the emperor had been delegated to local lords. The bishops could then be bound to the lords. When a bishop was elected, the ecclesiastical goods of his bishopric were put into his possession. If a conflict arose, it was brought before the imperial court in conformity with C. 1.2.14.10. In the ninth and tenth centuries the feudal lords of many regions refused to adjudicate ecclesiastical goods to bishops who did not please them (Investiture Controversy). In addition, they refused to grant exequaturs on substantive grounds. For this reason, many of the bishops played a part in the feudal order. Their case law fused with the imperial case law, something which is striking both in Anglo-Saxon case law and in Lothair's Empire. The imperial and episcopal case law were combined. The bishops had a longer tradition of contact with Rome than the feudal lords so that in many regions the Roman tradition of the bishops carried more weight than the more local tradition of the imperial judges. They were, however, placed under feudal supervision. In the ninth century Nov. 123.21 circulated in the West as *Epitome Juliani* 115.34. This contributed further to the mixture of the secular and episcopal orders. In the writings of Regino of Prüm (842-915) and in the decisions of the council of Meaux (848), it can be read that many bishops spent so much time working for the feudal order that they hardly got around to their core tasks. In current legal historical works, one can sometimes read that law originated in the religious sphere and that justice was administered by priests in prehistoric times. While this was indeed the case in ancient Palestine, there are no traces of priests serving as judges in Europe in primeval times. It is possible that this conviction stems from the mixture of episcopal and royal administration of justice in the Middle Ages.

There are no separate sources concerning the royal procedure of this period, which was still conducted in Latin. According to Regino of Prüm, Roman and canon law were quite similar to one another. We do find rules in the canonical collections. Both in civil and in criminal law cases were instituted by means of a complaint (accusatorial, by means of a Roman *libellus*). There was quite a stir about the admissibility of these complaints, which could be oral. Could laypeople charge clerics? According to Hincmar of Reims, they could. The procedure took place on a prearranged date and was oral and accusatorial. The suit could not be held without the accused party being present, unless the facts and his guilt were generally known. We will return to the law of evidence later. In the ninth century, the *in integrum restitutio* crops up. Its appearance attests to the continuous reception of ancient Roman law. A recurrent issue in the canon law collections are the legal costs charged to the losing party. In Antiquity, the administration of justice was an imperial matter and only exceptional expenses were charged to the parties. In the early Middle Ages, the salary of the judge was added to the costs.

Bibliography. – P. HINSCHIUS, *System des katholische Kirchenrechts mit besonderer Rücksicht auf Deutschland*, IV, Berlin 1888, passim; A. STEINWERTER, 'Der antike Rechtsgang und seine Quellen', *Zeitschrift der Savigny-Stiftung, Kanonistische Abteilung* 23 (1934), p. 1-116. Regino of Prüm's work was translated into German: W. HARTMANN, *Das Sendhandbuch des Regino von Prüm*, Darmstadt 2004.

3. The Romano-canonical procedure in the Middle Ages

A. *In the twelfth century*

The abovementioned Investiture Controversy was ended in 1122 with the Concordat of Worms, which gave both the German emperor and the pope jurisdiction. The practical organisation of the ecclesiastical administration of justice was treated in the Lateran Councils of 1123 (I), 1139 (II) and 1215 (IV). Just like the emperor, the pope delegated his jurisdiction to *iudices delegati,* but did so in a manner that differed from that of the medieval imperial feudal order. Like the emperors of Antiquity, the pope retained his sovereignty and the authority to act as judge of last instance. All of the bishops were given delegated jurisdiction. Most of them delegated it further to itinerant judges.

These itinerant judges initially applied the procedural rules that are contained in the canonical collections. Gratian collected data about them in his *Decretum.* In *Causae* 5 and 22 one can find the – rather rudimental – law of procedure. According to the *Decretum,* claims were made orally. At that point, the judge summoned the parties by means of a written document. Unwilling defendants were summoned three times. Both parties were interviewed. The procedure was inquisitorial; the judge attempted to find the truth behind the facts that the parties relied on. Gratian discussed some problems concerning oaths and testimonies. He included quite a few texts about the competence and the credibility of witnesses. The oaths that were used in courts were not Biblical oaths, because everyone had to speak the truth. However, oaths were necessary to put pressure on witnesses. Perjury was an offence punishable by death. The judge had to provide a judgement in writing. He was not allowed to let his own feelings influence his decision, nor to keep calling the facts into question, nor to give a suspended sentence. Each party could lodge an appeal with a higher judge within a ten-day period and had the possibility to file a second appeal with Rome if necessary. This possibility of appeal was Roman, but was at the same time of prime importance to the success of the ecclesiastical courts. The judgement acquired the force of *res iudicata* after the end of the period for appeal. Gratian extensively analysed the problems pertaining to unjust judgements, but still adhered to the Roman logic of legal certainty. Moral objections yielded to legal arguments. Gratian also stressed that ecclesiastical decisions were not immediately enforceable: the exequatur of the royal judge was necessary, just as it had been in Antiquity. In the twelfth century, this exequatur was requested from the local sovereign lord.

The publication of the *Decretum* led to the study of canon law in Bologna and Paris. The universities trained professional judges and followed the canonical administration of justice. When the science of canon law was developed, procedural law took centre stage. When they had to decide whether they would grant an exequatur, the feudal judges assessed whether the ecclesiastical judge had jurisdiction and whether he had followed the correct procedure. Therefore, the canonists studied the old Roman procedure, which was considered to be the norm. The Justinianic collections, however, did not treat the law of procedure separately and only mentioned it in between texts about substantive law. The twelfth century's considerable interest in the law of procedure called into life a new speciality: that of the processualists. They excerpted all of the texts that pertained to the procedure from the *Corpus iuris* and reconstructed the entire Roman procedure. The study of procedural law did not remain the exclusive domain of canon law. Jurists also applied themselves to this field. Early monographs concerning the law of procedure were Bulgarus' (1123-1141) *Summa de iudiciis* and Johannes Bassianus' *Summa quicumque uult* (around 1170).

B. In the thirteenth century

In the thirteenth century, the Romano-canonical procedure was treated extensively in the universities. Roffredus Beneventanus wrote his *De libellis et ordine iudiciorum* (1234) about imperial and canonical procedural law. Two Parisian students of Jacobus Balduini were adept at procedural law: Sinibaldus Fliscus (†1254 as Pope Innocent IV) and Henricus de Segusio (Hostiensis, †1271 as the cardinal of Ostia). The canonist Guillaume Durand (°1230/1231 in the environs of Narbonne – † Rome 1296) published his *Speculum iudiciale* in Bologna in 1279. Its second edition, which appeared in 1287, is an unsurpassed study within the field of European procedural law. It offers a systematic and crystal-clear analysis of the entire Roman procedural law, ranging from the summons and jurisdiction, the preliminary hearing with the *litiscontestatio*, the treatment on the merits and the law of evidence, to the judgement, appeals and *res judicata*. With regard to each of these subjects, Durand indicated the Roman sources and the canonists' and glossators' interpretations. Because of its clear arrangement, precision and all-encompassing character, many jurists have fallen back on the *Speculum iudiciale* when discussing procedural law. If one is not afraid of a little melodramaticism, one could state that the Romano-canonical procedure is the procedure which Guillaume Durand's book made famous.

The canonical procedure of the thirteenth century took place before a single sitting judge who had trained at a university. Apart from the procedure that commenced with a summons, the Roman procedure which began with a petition was accepted as well. The petition was delivered to the judge, who then summoned the defendant. Ecclesiastical judges needed the cooperation of the feudal order in case of a compulsory summons. Some processualists were of the opinion that petitions did not need to mention a legal basis, because the judge was expected to know the law (*iura nouit curia*). Most of the jurists followed D. 2.13.1, according to which the legal basis did have to be mentioned, so that both the judge and the opposing party would immediately know how and why legal proceedings were instituted. According to Roffredus, a summons contained the facts, the violated legal norm and the plaintiff's *actio*. Azo was less strict: the judge could declare the summons admissible as soon as it was somewhat understandable. For the students of Jacobus Balduini, a summons merely had to be clear and straightforward.

The summons was an invitation to the preliminary hearing. In most of the ecclesiastical courts, the judge who led the preliminary hearing was also the judge on the merits. He interviewed the parties just as a Roman judge would have and first and foremost sought to reach a precise understanding of the claim. The defendant formulated his dilatory and peremptory pleas. A new category of pleas was added: the declinatory pleas concerning inadmissibility. The invalidation of the Roman pleas represents a considerable part of the medieval literature on procedure. Contracts often contained *renuntiationes* in which parties renounced rights derived from Roman law.

A common stipulation consisted of the renouncement of a series of pleas. Were judges bound by this? Was the procedure not part of the public order? During this period, it was possible to employ a contract to depart from the law of procedure in some ways. This explains the considerable importance of pleas during the preliminary hearing. If the defendant and the plaintiff wanted to continue the lawsuit, a *litiscontestatio* followed, after which new declinatory pleas were inadmissible and peremptory pleas remained admissible.

Under Justinian, the judge could divide the case, deal with certain points in a definitive manner and allow appeals concerning these points to be filed before the entire lawsuit was concluded. The source for this was C. 7.45.15, a Greek text which the Western jurists did not read. The canonists derived from it that a case had to be divided into *positiones*, remedies at law, which had to be treated separately. *Confessio in iure* and evidence applied per remedy. Each remedy could lead to an interlocutory judgement and an interlocutory appeal. The civil lawyers, on the other hand, emphasised the Justinianic texts that limited interlocutory appeals and considered lawsuits as an indivisible unity. Only those who definitively lost a case, had an interest in lodging an appeal.

The judge could only accept facts if they had been thoroughly proved. The understanding of the facts became a search for *ueritas*, the medieval conception of the truth. Did the facts that were invoked in the court correspond to the truth? The means of evidence were testimonies, documents, suspicions, oaths and confessions (see below). The burden of proof was on the person who invoked a fact. If the evidence was insufficient, the judge continued his search for the full facts of the case. According to C. 3.1.9, he could not remain passive. In the civil lawyers' understanding, this text indicated that the judge acted in a proactive manner and actively interviewed people, but did not himself conduct an investigation outside of the court. The Fourth Lateran Council (1215) made a different decision, so that the canonists' obligation to investigate also applied outside of the court. This decision led to the introduction of examining magistrates.

Once the facts had been established and the debates were closed, the judge gave a ruling based on his own deep conviction (*conuictio intima*). This conviction did not have a bearing on the facts, but on the final judgement. There was always a possibility of appeal. The Church was the first institution to introduce centralisation and legal certainty via the Roman procedure of appeal.

C. The introduction of the Romano-canonical procedure

The Romano-canonical procedure was introduced into all of the ecclesiastical courts, which were placed hierarchically under Rome. Appeals could be lodged if the judge had not followed the procedure as it had been developed at the canon law faculties. The new procedure was experienced as reliable, mainly because of the supervision of the judges and the possibilities of appeal. This led to competition with the royal courts. This rivalry was beneficial to the people who were subject to the law.

In England, the separation of the papal legal order from the imperial legal order happened under King William I and the archbishop of Canterbury Lanfranc of Bec (Lanfranc of Pavia, archbishop 1067-1089). The consistory courts of the bishops would follow the Romano-canonical procedure in the twelfth century. They kept abreast of the evolutions in the new universities – initially those of Bologna and Paris. The canonists from Kent were closely involved in the study of procedural law at the 'Faculté du Décret' of Paris. Meanwhile, the king was developing royal courts which had their own procedure. Henry II paid a lot of attention to these. His point of departure was the procedure which the lords and bishops had shared earlier. The modernisations were inspired by the pure Roman procedure. The study of the *Corpus iuris* came to the fore at a favourable moment. However, this interest appeared in England before it was embedded in the context of the universities. As a consequence, the influence of Roman law on the royal procedure did not involve the universities. The English jurists were not influenced by the *artes* and were more independent from the canonists than their colleagues on the Continent. When the Romano-canonical procedure was being studied intensively on the Continent, England had already gone its own way. Some characteristics of the Romano-canonical procedure, like the role of examining magistrates, were introduced into England's ecclesiastical courts, but never into its royal courts. Another difference from the Romano-canonical procedure of the Continent was that the common law courts had more limited possibilities of appeal.

Pisa's court of appeal seems to have been the first Italian court that introduced the new academic procedure of Bologna in a city-state. It did so around 1160 and imposed this procedure on all of the city state's courts. The other Italian city states followed in the thirteenth century.

In the County of Flanders, the count established feudal courts and criminal courts, and authorised the first municipal courts. The latter drew inspiration from the canonists for their procedure. Countess Joan of Constantinople introduced modernisations in the royal procedure that were inspired by her counsellors' experiences in Constantinople, which had a centralised government and appeals that were heard within the administration. In the course of the thirteenth century, the Romano-canonical procedure was introduced. It is described in *ordines iudiciarii*. In the fourteenth century, appeals to the Parliament of Paris were enforced in Flanders. Sources of 1330 show that the procedure in the count's audiences was consequently adapted to the Parisian model. Sources of 1386 attest that the same thing happened in the Council of Flanders.

In France, Louis IX was undoubtedly the king who contributed the most to the introduction of the Romano-canonical procedure into his administration of justice. In the 1240s he introduced it in his *curia regis*, the forerunner of the Parliament of Paris. He realised the importance of this academic procedure for his administration. He attracted jurists from the law faculties to his parliament, which began to pay attention to all of the aspects of the Roman procedure. Separate chambers were even established for summons ('chambre des requêtes') and for the furnishing of proof ('chambre des enquêtes'). The judge's obligation to investigate was thoroughly developed by means of rogatory missions which were sent throughout the realm in case of complaints. Whenever Louis IX regained control over a region, he introduced the new procedure. He then allowed the population to file appeals against all of the decisions of the local lord with Paris. Among the first regions which were subjected to the Parliament in this manner were – besides the Île de France – Bourbonnais, Toulouse and Montpellier. Between the thirteenth and fifteenth centuries, the kingdom would once again be centralised and feudalism would be ousted. The Franco-Flemish wars of 1302-1305 centred on the possibility of lodging appeals against the Council of Flanders with the

Parliament of Paris. The lawsuits that had given rise to this conflict were not political: they were civil cases that were instituted by persons seeking justice. The consequence of these hostilities, however, did savour of politics: after 1305, the inhabitants of Flanders could lodge an appeal with the king against any decision of their count. Thus, the Flemish were given the same law as the inhabitants of Toulouse or Montpellier.

From the fourteenth century onwards ecclesiastical courts throughout the West were familiar with the Romano-canonical procedure. This procedure was then introduced in the royal councils. In the twelfth century, many people had elected to bring their conflicts before the ecclesiastical courts, because their procedure was transparent and reliable, and because the existence of appeals made the ecclesiastical case law superior to that of the royal courts. One hundred years later, this superiority also played a role for the royal courts which had adopted the 'new' procedure. In the meantime it had also become clear that appeals, the essential institution of the Romano-canonical procedure with which everything had started in Egypt, led to the nation-building that kings dreamt of. In the fourteenth and fifteenth centuries, many kings established a law faculty in order to introduce the Roman procedure in their country and oust feudalism by means of appeals against their vassals. Examples are Charles IV's Bohemia, Poland under Casimir the Great, Rudolf IV in Vienna, the Palatinate under Ruprecht I, Saxony under Frederick I, Aymon the Peaceful of Savoye, Piedmont under Louis of Savoye, Alfonso V in Aragon and Catalonia, Louis I in Hungary, Philip the Good in the Netherlands... They were strong kings who established a law faculty and courts in which the new procedure took centre stage. These monarchs knew that success would follow and pressed their chancellors to follow the Romano-canonical procedure as precisely of possible. The law was administered according to the book – Guillaume Durand's! Collections of case law from all of these regions have been handed down. They illustrate how the royal administration of justice was organised. In the Low Countries, the Romano-canonical procedure was furthered by the Burgundians and the Habsburgs. The law faculty of Leuven was established in 1425 as a study centre that would promote the Roman law and especially the Roman procedure in the royal councils of the Netherlands. Its goal was to unify the law in the Netherlands just as the Church, but especially Paris, London and Constantinople had unified their law. In 1526 the Treaty of Madrid between Charles V and Francis I determined that the County of Flanders would no longer lodge appeals with Paris but with Mechlin. For Flanders, this amounted to secession from France.

In Germany, the Romano-canonical procedure was introduced at the same time in all regions when the Reichskammergerichtshof was established in 1495. This Reichskammergerichtshof, however, did not manage to turn the German Empire into a nation in the Early Modern Period.

In the first half of the sixteenth century, the Romano-canonical procedure which had been developed in the Middle Ages was used and fine-tuned in the sovereign councils. *Stylus curiae* from this period, 'styles and manners of conducting legal proceedings', have been handed down throughout Europe. They show that the Roman procedure was an established and respected one. Because it was the procedure of the absolute monarchs and was enforced by the sovereign councils, it was applied in all of the lower courts, in the criminal law and even in the feudal courts in the regions were these still functioned.

§6. Appeals

The possibility of appeal was the most important institution of Roman law and the main pillar of the state under the rule of law. The emperor Augustus adopted it from Egyptian law and introduced it in the imperial provinces. In Egypt, all justice was administered by the pharaoh. Cases were brought before one of his local officials. Both his judicial and his administrative decisions could be contested with the nomarchs, the supreme judges of the forty-two jurisdictions. In case of complaints, they reviewed the decisions of lower officials. Appeals against the nomarchs could be lodged with the pharaoh's council in Alexandria. The foundation underlying these appeals was that both the nomarchs and the lower officials acted in the pharaoh's name. If they dishonoured him, people could point this out to the pharaoh and request a new decision. Augustus realised the simplicity and the power of that system: it allowed a ruler to have control over his administration and remain in touch with the day-to-day conflicts of the population. The nomarchs meticulously applied the solutions of Alexandria in their administration of justice. This led to the formation of one large jurisdiction where no one had to shy away from conducting trade because of legal uncertainty. The manner in which the Roman emperors introduced this system day by day can no longer be discovered. We do find the broad lines of appeals in D. 49.1-13 and C. 7.62. The subject will be treated in some depth to provide a better picture of the richness of Roman procedural law.

1. In the formulary procedure

In the Republic there were remedies at law that could be used against the actions of a magistrate, but they had little to do with the appeals that were lodged in the Empire. When a person was dissatisfied with a magistrate's decision in the Principate, he could complain to a higher magistrate, a colleague, or, in some cases, a tribune. Such a complaint was a *prouocatio* or *appellatio*; the intervention by the magistrate who was solicited was an *intercessio*. In republican civil lawsuits it was possible to react against the judgement of the praetor or a city magistrate. The result could be the quashing of the decision, but not its review. The case returned to the same instance. Those who had the *ius intercedendi*, however, could not quash a *litiscontestatio*, because a *litiscontestatio* was an agreement between the parties. After this agreement had been concluded, remedies at law were not admissible anymore. Appeals against the judicial decision itself were not possible. There are no clear sources about the practice, frequency and legal consequences of this procedure. If the party who lost a formulary suit thought that he had been treated unjustly by the judge on the merits, he had a conflict with the judge himself. He could commence a suit with the praetor by means of the *actio de iudice qui litem suam fecit* (damage caused by the judge, D. 44.7.5.4).

Augustus and his successors also introduced aspects of appeals in Rome and the Senate's provinces where the republican procedure continued to exist. Because the emperors also served as consul, censor and tribune of the people, they could quash the judgement of a praetor. On the basis of their power as proconsul, they could review the judgement of the governor of a province. From Augustus onwards, parties began to appoint the emperor as judge in the *litiscontestatio* of formulary lawsuits. The emperor then had this lawsuit conducted by his local representative, who, in principle, provided a decision according to the imperial law of the praetorian prefecture. Because the imperial official did not administer justice in his own name, but on the basis of a mandate from the emperor, it was possible to file an appeal against his judgements as well. The *ius intercedendi* of the emperor then did not pertain solely to the *in iure* phase, but also to the treatment on the merits. The intervention of the emperor was no longer limited to cassation: the emperor could also review the judgement. Subsequently, the emperors also began to review the first phase of the lawsuits on the grounds of their *imperium*. The quashing of republican *sententiae* by the emperor can be found under Claudius. The replacement of a judgement by a new one was based on the *cognitio* procedure and certainly occurred in the second century AD. Through the possibility to lodge appeals with the imperial administration, the formulary procedure developed into a *cognitio* procedure. This evolution contributed considerably to the unification of the law in the Senate's provinces and the imperial provinces and thus expedited the disappearance of the former.

2. In the *cognitio* procedure

When judges became officials delegated by the emperor, it became possible to file an appeal with the delegating authority on account of deficient fulfilment of their mandate. If a governor delegated his jurisdiction, the appeal had to be lodged with him (rescript of Antoninus Pius, D. 49.1.21) before an appeal could be filed with the emperor who had delegated his competence to the governors. Appeals against rescripts of the imperial administrations could be filed in the same manner. The emperor Nero delegated the right to pronounce appellate judgements concerning *cognitio* lawsuits to the Senate, where no further appeal was possible. Because of this, some legal institutions originated in *senatusconsulta* in the first century. From the second century onwards appeals from the city of Rome itself were treated by the *praefectus urbi*, while appeals from the provinces ended up before the *praefectus praetorio*. The emperor himself often pronounced second instance and sometimes even third instance judgments in appellate cases against the *praefectus praetorio* (this was typical of the Principate) or against the *praefectus urbi*.

Appeals were possible against all decisions, except those of the emperor and the Senate. Everyone who had an interest in a judgement, even a third party, could file an appeal. Those who took a decisive oath could not lodge an appeal concerning the object of the oath.

Appeals were lodged orally at the hearing, or in writing the next day (within two days if the appeal was filed by a third party). A new legal ground and new facts could be invoked at any stage. The appeal was served on the judge *a quo*, who either accepted or refused it. In the latter case, he had to justify his refusal in writing. A separate appeal against this refusal was possible. The judge against whom an appeal was filed, was obligated to state the grounds for his judgement in an administrative report for his hierarchical superiors (*litterae dimissoriae*). This was already an important element in the development of the protection of rights. Judges could lose their job if they were not adept at administering justice.

Appeals had a suspensory effect. From the introduction of the right of appeal onwards, rules were introduced to avoid the abuse of appeals to delay the execution of the judgement. Winning parties also had rights! If the claimant lost, he was sentenced to the legal costs. Professional judges could also decide that the lodging of an appeal was shameful and could impose a procedural fine on the losing party. This fine was added to the legal costs and could amount to a third of the value of the lawsuit.

3. In the late Empire

Appeals became an institution by means of which the emperors supervised not only the resolution of conflicts, but also the correct interpretation of the precedents that were contained in previous cases. We also find judgements about the admissibility of appeals themselves in the sources. The Theodosian Code features many such pronouncements. The compilation of these judgements brought new insights and Theodosius II adopted some important decisions concerning appeals in his novels. The subject also features in the Code, the Digest and the Novels of Justinian. Some Romanists wrote that the Roman law on this issue 'became increasingly complex', but the fact that jurists were given standard solutions which they could use without scruple did not really make legal life more complicated.

A. With whom were appeals filed?

In principle, appeals were filed with the delegating judicial instance and finally with the emperor. In practice, the appeal bodies were:

- the governors in case of appeals against municipal and delegated judges, and against decisions of the *rationales* (accountants, managers) of the imperial heritage.
- the *uicarii* or *praefecti praetorio* in case of appeals against the decisions of governors.
- the imperial chancellery (bypassing the *praefecti praetorio*) in case of appeals against the *uicarii*. The chancellery systematically delegated these cases to the prefectures, against which no further appeal had been possible since Constantine. In a novel of 439 the chancellery accepted a petition containing a 'supplication' to revise a decision of a *praefectus praetorio*. The imperial chancellery decided that it was free to treat or ignore requests like this one. A possible ground to revise such a judgement was, for example, that the administration of law in one prefecture differed from that of another. The supplication is at the basis of the petitions for pardon which still exist today. It can therefore be said that the *praefecti praetorio* and the *quaestor sacri palatii* of the chancellery exercised the highest ordinary judicial power in the provinces. Under Justinian, appeals against the highest judges (the *spectabiles*, which included the *uicarii* and the patriarchs) were no longer transferred to the prefectures. They were treated by the chancellery itself.
- the *praefectus urbi* in case of appeals from each capital.
- the chancellery in case of appeals against the *praefecti urbi*.
- the chancellery in fiscal matters.
- the chancellery in military matters.

In the late Empire, appeals were lodged by petitioning to the higher judge without the knowledge of the lower judge. This petition resulted in an *ex officio* examination. The judge *a quo* was asked to state the grounds of his judgement in writing and forward the file. The parties could absent themselves from the appellate proceedings, but were interviewed if they desired to be (as is the case with regard to our current notices of objection concerning fiscal matters). If points of law were unclear and there was a risk of divergent case law in one of the prefectures, the administration requested a rescript from the *consistorium,* the highest council of the administration. Against this rescript, an appeal could be filed with the chancellery. Justinian asked the parties to reappear and to engage in discussion once more.

B. When was it possible to file an appeal?

It was possible to appeal against all decisions, except decisions about debts that had been determined in an unambiguous manner (CTh. 11.36.19 = C. 7.65.4) and about cases that had been resolved by means of a decisive oath (C. 4.1.12). Constantine precluded appeals in criminal law in five cases: murder, adultery, poisoning, forgery and manifest violence, if there was a confession or if the facts were beyond doubt (CTh. 11.36.1; C. 9.12.6). Justinian preserved this rule (C. 7.65.2). This text was extremely important in the Middle Ages: it was the foundation for the inadmissibility of appeals in case of notoriety. The Gloss transplanted this principle from the law of criminal procedure to the procedure for civil cases.

A decision of Alexander Severus of 222, which would be very important to the reception, was included in C. 7.64.2. A judgement that went against manifest law was null. It was not necessary to appeal against it, since one could always rely on nullity, which was not subject to prescription. But what was manifest law?

C. 7.64.2 (222). – Si, cum inter te et auiam defuncti quaestio de successione esset, iudex datus a praeside prouinciae pronuntiauit potuisse defunctum et minorem quattuordecim annis testamentum facere ac per hoc auiam potiorem esse, sentiamus eius contra tam manifesti iuris formam datam nullas habere uires palam est et ideo in hac specie nec prouocationis auxilium necessarium fuit.	Translation F.H. Blume. – If, in a suit between you and the grandmother of the deceased about an inheritance, the referee, appointed by the president of the province, held that the decedent, though less than fourteen years of age, was capable of making a testament, through which the grandmother had the better right, such decision is so clearly contrary to the existing law that it can, manifestly, have no force, and no appeal was necessary in such case.
1. Quod si, cum de aetate quaereretur, implesse defunctum quartum decimum annum ac per hoc iure factum testamentum pronuntiauit, nec prouocasti aut post appellationem impletam causa destitisti, rem iudicatam retractare non debes.	1. But if the age was in question, and he held that the deceased had passed his fourteenth year and that the testament was valid by reason of that fact, and you did not appeal, or you abandoned the appeal after taking it, you can not reopen the matter once adjudicated.

C. Interlocutory appeals

Could one appeal against interim judgements, or did the parties have to await the definitive judgement and appeal against that? In principle, Constantine opposed interlocutory appeals (CTh. 11.30.2; CTh. 11.36.18; CTh. 11.30.50). Appeals led to the suspension of proceedings and thus caused delays. Perhaps the party aggrieved by the interim judgement would be put in the right by the final judgement, in which case he had no interest in contesting the interim judgement. Constantine did allow appeals when the judge declared peremptory pleas admissible in the interim judgement (CTh. 11.30.2), accepted prescriptions, committed procedural errors or granted possessory measures (CTh. 11.37.1). With regard to interlocutory appeals, the difference between peremptory and dilatory pleas subsequently became blurred. Justinian reaffirmed the principal inadmissibility of interlocutory appeals (C. 7.62.36), but in another judgement he accepted that a lawsuit could be divided, that decisions could be taken about separate points and that separate appeals could be lodged (C. 7.45.15). The contrast between these two texts would lead to the differing opinions of the canonists and the civil lawyers in the Middle Ages.

Appeals against the decision to proceed to torture (D. 49.5.2) and *praeiudicia* (preliminary judgements) about the personal status of the litigants (Inst. 4.6.13) were always possible. In the Middle Ages, there were considerable controversies about the acceptance of appeals against provisional possessory measures in the late Empire (repeated in C. 7.69.1).

D. The scope of appeals

Constantine punished unwarranted appeals with a fine. Justinian mitigated the fines and also imposed fines in case of the unjustified refusal of appeals by judges or the administration. Under Constantine, it was decided that the *causa* of a dispute could not be changed on appeal. In Antiquity, the *causa* was the conflict itself, the question of law. If the higher judge noticed that the appeal no longer centred on the original conflict, but on a new matter, he could reject it as an unjustified appeal. Until Theodosius II, appeals continued to develop in the same direction. They turned into an assessment of the first judgement. Constitutions that dated from after the judgement *a quo* could not be invoked in appellate cases. Justinian further expanded the procedure in his Novels. Suits were treated entirely anew on appeal, but appeals still monitored the legality of the suit rather than its equitability. Appeals dealt with the application of the law in the first judgement, and not with the consequences which the application of the law had for the parties.

4 From Justinian to the Middle Ages

After 467, the West lost its judicial unity. Appeals obviously continued to exist, because governing through the administration of justice remained the only form of government. The person who served as the judge of the last instance imposed his own rules on society. We do not only find mentions of the possibility of appeal in the *leges romanae barbarorum*, but also in Lombardic and Carolingian sources. The eighth-century epitomes of the

Breviary of Alaric clearly show that jurists were familiar with appeals. Remember that the old prefectures still functioned in Toledo and Marseille in the eighth century, and that the prefecture of Pavia remained active even longer. We have knowledge of Lombardic appeals against the *missi* of Charlemagne that were filed with the royal court. Appeals from the exarchate of Ravenna that were lodged with Constantinople are still mentioned in the *Summa perusina*. In the feudal period, the highest jurisdiction was increasingly split up and handed down to lower levels. In this manner, appeals disappeared in many regions as the high Middle Ages approached. In this period, when the highest jurisdiction had ended up in the hands of a local lord so that the first and the last judge were one and the same person, appeals disappeared in practice. There would, however, be a revival of appeals in feudal law as well. In Lombardic texts about feudal law, one can find appeals against vassals that were lodged with feudal lords. Such appeals are also mentioned explicitly in a text of the emperor Conrad II from 1037.

5. The rebirth of appeals

In 1122 the canonists acquired their own jurisdiction. In their new administration of justice, they organised their appeals just as they had found the institution in the Justinian law. In the middle of the century, the canonists' appeals were adopted by the civil lawyers. These appeals can be found in the Asburnham Law Book, the Tübingen Law Book and Pierre de Valence's *Exceptiones legum romanarum* (a synthesis of the Asburnam and Tübingen Law Books). These books include fragments from the Digest, the Code, the Institutes and the *Epitome Juliani*. The *Brachylogus iuris ciuilis* (France, 1160-1170) drew a clear regulation of appeals from the Justinian law. According to the *Brachylogus*, it was possible to appeal against all judgements. The civil lawyers had an eye for the quality of the canonists' case law which was due to Rome's supervision of the officialities and the officialities' supervision of the itinerant judges. In legal practice, however, the civil jurists ran up against the power of the feudal judges. Since appeals undermined the authority of these lords, those who exercised imperial jurisdiction in their village would not simply renounce their jurisdiction merely because of the civilian jurists' beautiful theory.

Nevertheless, courts of appeal cropped up here and there in the feudal order. In Pisa, a court where one could appeal against the lower city magistrate and the chamber of commerce was established in the twelfth century. The other Italian city states followed. If a faction could gain the upper hand during a local revolution in a city, it positioned itself as an appeal body that was hierarchically superior to the city judges. The highest juridical bodies were, after all, the hub of power in a medieval city. Appeals with the 'podestà' became possible in different Italian cities around 1200. Furthermore, strong feudal lords extended their power by establishing a new judicial organisation and imposing it upon their vassals. In the twelfth century Flanders, castellanies acquired jurisdiction over local conflicts pertaining to feudal law. Their decisions could be appealed against with the *curia comitis*, the count's council. In the thirteenth century the feudal judicial system would be developed further by means of feudal courts, appellate feudal courts and the count's court where appeals against the appellate feudal courts were heard.

The doctrine concerning appeals was mainly developed by the canonists, but the establishment of secular courts of appeal caused the civil jurists to adopt these appeals. Below, we will treat some elements of this subject as it was received by the processualists.

A. *The appellate judge*

Where did one find a *praefectus praetorio* in the Middle Ages? The canonists could find one in Rome, but what about the civilian jurists? They first projected the Roman texts onto the Italian institutions. For Azo, the 'podestà' in the cities of Northern Italy played the role of the *praefectus urbi*. According to him, one could, despite the jurisdiction that the university had received at the Diet of Roncaglia, lodge appeals against the judgements of the rector with the consuls of Bologna. Difficulties of interpretation arose concerning C. 7.62.32.3 (the appellate judge is the one who delegated his jurisdiction) and D. 49.3.1.1 (the appellate judge is the hierarchical superior of the judge who delegated the jurisdiction). For canonists, the problem was the following one: did appeals against delegated judges have to be lodged with their bishop or with that bishop's metropolitan? The canonists followed the latter text. Appeals against decisions of the itinerant judges of the bishop of Cambrai, for example, originated in Brabant but were sent straight to Reims. Azo resolved the contradiction by means of a distinction: the second text (D. 49.3.1.1) pertained to sub-delegation, which was possible with regard to specific matters, but not with regard to jurisdiction in general.

These texts were incorporated into the feudal legal system, in which the establishment of a fief went together with provisions concerning the exercise of jurisdiction. In Lombardic law and according to Conrad II, it was therefore possible to file appeals against vassals with their feudal lords. This principle was adopted in Bologna. By interpreting C. 7.62.32.3, Azo arrived at a hierarchy of appellate judges that was based on the delegation of jurisdiction within feudalism. Appeals against a vassal were always lodged with his feudal lord. The delegation of the highest jurisdiction, sovereignty, was the basic principle of feudal law and the general rule in most of the European regions. However, this delegation was not provided by the *Corpus iuris* and therefore not taken into account in the law faculties. It was not always possible to have a case treated by a higher instance in the feudal hierarchy: only two appeals were possible with regard to each specific point (interpretation of C. 7.70). The glossators' idea that the appellate judge was the feudal lord would lead to the curbing of feudalism. The vassals opposed this interpretation of the jurists, but the feudal lords took advantage of every possible intervention or local war to establish the possibility of appeal against their vassals.

Illustration. – Azo's distinction concerning the contradiction between D. 59.3.1.1 and C. 7.62.32.3.

D. 49.3.1.1. – Ab eo cui quis mandauit iurisdictionem, non ipse prouocabitur, nam generaliter is erit prouocandus ab eo cui mandata est iurisdictio, qui prouocaretur ab eo qui mandauit iurisdictionem.

Translation S.P. Scott. – An appeal is not taken to a person who has delegated his authority; for, generally speaking, it ought to be taken from him to whom the authority was delegated to him to whom the appeals would be taken from the official who delegated the authority.

C. 7.62.32.3. – Haec si appellatio fuerit oblata iudici qui non ex delegatione cognoscit. Eorum enim sententiis appellatione suspensis

Translation F. H. Blume. – These provisions apply when an appeal is taken from a judge who did not try the case pursuant to special qui ex delegatione cognoscunt, necesse est eos aestimare iuste nec ne fuerit appellatum qui causas delegauerint iudicandas.

assignment. For if decisions of judges who tried a case pursuant to special assignment are suspended by appeal, the judges who assigned the causes to be tried must decide upon review, whether the appeal is justly or unjustly taken.

The glossators wondered who these two different delegating authorities were. They searched the *Corpus iuris* for arguments in order to resolve this contradiction. The gloss of Accursius mentions most of those arguments: see gl. '*Ab eo*' *ad* D. 49.3.1.1, ed. Venice 1487 (reprint Turin 1968), f. 250 recto, at the bottom of the right-hand column. The principle of Roman law was that one appealed on the basis of the fact that the judge had not executed his assignment properly. The question was whether this appeal could be anything other than a complaint filed with the emperor who had charged the judge to provide a ruling. Azo discussed this problem in his *Summa Codicis* 3.13.12. He constructed a typically medieval distinction in order to resolve this contradiction. According to him, the text in the Code referred to the general rule, which pertained to the jurisdiction that the emperor or monarch entrusted fully to a certain instance. For Azo, the jurisdiction which was given to a vassal in feudal law fell into that category. One could, therefore, lodge appeals with a vassal's feudal lord. The text in the Digest, on the other hand, pertained to the cases in which judges entrusted a specific case that fell within their jurisdiction to other judges. This was the case, for example, when a judge charged a notary with the assignment to hear witnesses in his city. If a party appealed against this, the appeal did not end up before the sub-delegating judge, but before his hierarchical superior.

B. Actions of nullity

Alexander Severus' constitution C. 7.64.2 received a lot of attention. When the Roman law was received, jurists soon began to distinguish between appeals against unjust judgements (*contra ius litigatoris*) and appeals against judgements that were void because of Alexander Severus' constitution (*contra ius constitutionis*). Apart from the text from the Code, D. 49.8.1.2 also became a key passage. Actions of nullity were not restricted to a certain time period, while appeals were. For the first glossators, all judgements that were *contra ius*, i.e. against the Justinianic law, became null. This meant that feudal kings who did not apply Roman law pronounced invalid judgements and that their judgements were not enforceable. This view, however, proved to be untenable. Azo stated that only the judge's willing or explicit misapplication of the law resulted in nullity. If misapplications were unintended or tacit and in good faith, they did not amount to nullity. As the judge was under no obligation to justify his judgement, it was hard to assess nullity by means of Azo's criteria. After Azo's day, the criterion in legal doctrine became the following: appeals could be filed against unreasonable judgements, while actions of nullity could be employed against a manifest misapplication of the Justinianic law, for example a lack of respect for the Romano-canonical procedure.

The action of nullity later turned into the possibility of 'review' in the Romano-canonical procedure. For the sovereign monarchs, reviews were a new means that could be employed against the feudal judges. The monarchs allowed as many actions of nullity as possible. In the Parliament of Paris, the action of nullity was introduced in the thirteenth century. If lower courts did not follow the case law of the Parliament, the case could be reviewed on appeal. Judgements were reviewed either at the request of the parties, or at the request of the procurator of the monarch. Even if the judgement had acquired the force of *res iudicata*, review remained possible. Although the facts could not be revised anymore, the interpretation of the applicable law could. In the Early Modern Era we find the possibility of review in the case law of most of the sovereign councils. For centuries, these reviews served to assess the lawfulness of judgements. In the seventeenth century the Council of Brabant proclaimed its own sovereignty. The Great Council of Mechlin allowed this to happen, but regularly evoked cases 'for review'. Many of the professors of Leuven were involved in the Council's reviews as lawyers or consultants and they often imposed new legal doctrine on the judges in the process. In Germany, reviews of civil cases existed until the 'Zivilprozessnovellen' of 1905-1910. In many countries, reviews are still carried out today in case of miscarriages of justice that have acquired the force of *res iudicata*.

C. Interlocutory appeals

Justinian's principled prohibition of appeals against interim judgements can be read in C. 7.62.36. This text was written in Greek, a language that was not read in Bologna. The issue was also mentioned in passing in other texts. The Gloss summarised the discussion about interlocutory appeals and concluded that they were admissible according to the prevailing opinion (gl. '*Si clericus*' *ad* C. 1.4.2; gl. '*Sententia*' *ad* C. 7.62.6*pr.*). The main exception was still the decision to proceed to torture (several glosses on D. 49.5.2).

Canon law, by contrast, did acknowledge interlocutory appeals: lawsuits were divided into *positiones* and parties could appeal against any judgement concerning any remedy at law. The canonists had other interests than the civilian jurists. They tried to get to the bottom of the case before the parties went to a feudal judge to request an exequatur. Interim judgements often centred on matters of jurisdiction, and because this was a sensitive issue, the canonists had a preference for appeals against interim judgements. In the days of Odofredus and Accursius, this controversy between canonists and civilian jurists was expressed in the gl. '*Causa*' *ad* C. 1.4.2, the gl. '*Quaestionem*' *ad* D. 49.5.2 and the gl. '*Reddere*' *ad* D. 49.1.3.3. Because canon law influenced procedure throughout the West and because the legal practice of the officialities was more advanced than the royal administration of law, the canonical opinion began to outweigh the royal standpoint.

Civil jurists who were oriented towards legal practice, like Martinus de Fano (†1272), also defended the possibility of interlocutory appeals in civil cases. In this manner, these appeals made their way into the Early Modern Era. However, the counterargument – the delaying effect of interlocutory appeals – still carried weight as well. This explains the interpretation given in the legal doctrine and case law of the Early Modern Era: interlocutory appeals were admissible but if the interlocutory judgement did not pertain to investigative measures, the entire treatment of the merits fell to the appeal body as well so that no time was lost.

Interlocutory appeals concerning provisional possessory measures were always admissible according to the medieval lawyers. The interpretation of C. 7.69.1 caused controversies. If a provisional adjudication applied *erga omnes*, this adjudication could not be appealed against according to the canonists. Conflicts concerning possession had to be treated together with the (petitory) question of ownership. Restrictive interpretations of C. 7.69.1 only occurred in cases involving violent appropriation. Jacobus Balduini was of the opinion that the inadmissibility of appeals against possessory measures was unfair. The person who had a possessory title was the party who could address the judge first. The other party always had to have the possibility to oppose this before the suit on the merits began. In the *ius commune*, Balduini's opinion began to outweigh the Roman view.

D. Admissibility of appeals in criminal law

The five cases of C. 7.65.2 remained relevant. In criminal law, appeal became impossible after the confession of the facts. This rule did not apply to confessions that were made during judicial torture: gl. *'Aliquid dixerit' ad* C. 7.65.2. Azo generalised this rule within the criminal law; Accursius introduced it in civil cases. Appeals against notorious facts were never possible, because *ubi eadem ratio, ibi idem ius* ('if the substance of the issue is the same, justice must be identical'; Azo, *Lectura ad* C. 7.65.2). The administration of criminal justice resulted in large revenues for the feudal lords. They attempted to wrest confessions from the accused in every possible way in order to expedite cases and, in particular, to avoid an outcome where the accused filed an appeal. In cases of notorious facts – and confession – appeals were precluded. Actions of nullity remained admissible, but required a misapplication of the law.

E. Appeals against ecclesiastical courts

The two medieval legal orders stemmed from Antiquity. From Antiquity onwards, a royal exequatur was required if ecclesiastical judgements were not executed voluntarily. Was it possible to appeal against and question an ecclesiastical judgement before the royal court, for example on the occasion of exequatur proceedings? In C. 1.4.8 it can be read that appeals against ecclesiastical courts could not be filed with royal courts. This text would be at the basis of the Western tradition. The Novels of Justinian, however, contain a different view: according to Nov 123.21*pr.* of 546 (= *Auth. 'Si quis litigantium' post* C. 1.4.8) such appeals are possible. This would be the traditional view in the East. Placentinus (from Piacenza, a civil lawyer in Mantua and Montpellier around 1160, †1192) emphasised the argument of the novel, namely that an ecclesiastical judgement could be contested in a royal court. The novel was more recent than C. 1.4.8 and therefore replaced it. Azo resolved the contradiction between the Code and the Novels by means of a distinction, which can be found in Accursius' gloss (gl. *'Iudex' ad* Auth. *'Si quis litigantium' post* C. 1.4.8; gl. *'Contradicat' ad* Auth. 143.21*pr.*, Coll. IX, 15). Nov. 123.21*pr.* pertained to voluntary proceedings before a bishop, while C. 1.4.8 bore on matters which were normally the exclusive province of ecclesiastical courts.

In the sixteenth century the matter of appeals against an ecclesiastical court would become a central issue, not least because Constantinople was at the centre of attention. This city, which also had a judicial system with appeals, was ruled through the administration of justice. In all of the Protestant countries, Nov. 123 was interpreted as Placentinus had read it. Just as in Constantinople, the churches were placed under the emperor's control. He could review all ecclesiastical decisions. In the Catholic countries, Azo's distinction was retained. By dealing with cases which traditionally fell within the ecclesiastical jurisdiction, the royal courts began to compete with the ecclesiastical ones, but both systems retained their autonomy. Cases concerning marriage could be brought before either judicial system, but if one opted for an ecclesiastical court, its judgement had civil effect and it became impossible to lodge an appeal with the king. In the course of the seventeenth century the issue of exequaturs also began to have a bearing on ordinances. At the beginning of the century, ordinances were instructions which the king sent to his judges. They were part of the monarch's judicial power. Around 1650, however, these ordinances began to be considered as extrajudicial norms which were directly imposed on the population. Ecclesiastical instructions also changed into such norms. Many jurists were of the opinion that ecclesiastical instructions were not laws if they had not been confirmed by a royal *placet*. In Leuven, Zeger-Bernard van Espen (1646-1728) defended the opinion that a royal *placet* was required to make canonical principles enforceable, but such a *placet* also made them enforceable before the royal councils. For many people, this sounded overly Protestant. In France the 'appel comme d'abus' originated in the royal legal order. It could be employed against ecclesiastical courts that went beyond their jurisdiction. The royal legal order employed it to push the ecclesiastical courts to the sidelines. This illustrates how Nov. 123 continued to make itself felt in the background... In the eighteenth century it was still circulating in the legal doctrine of some Catholic countries which wanted to incorporate the remnants of the ecclesiastical administration of justice (Gallicanism in France, Josephism in Austria and the Netherlands).

Bibliography. – On the situation in the sixteenth century, see L. WAELKENS, 'Legal transplant of Greek caesaro-papism in Early Modern Times', in J. BALLOR, W. DECOCK, M. GERMANN and L. WAELKENS (eds.), *Law and religion, The legal teachings of the Protestant and Catholic reformations*, [Refo500 Academic Studies 20,] Göttingen 2014, p. 230-213.

F. Appeals against imperial rescripts

According to the Digest, appeals against the emperors were inadmissible, because the emperor was the person who was being appealed to (D. 49.2.2.1). Evidently, appeals could be filed against decisions that were made in the emperor's name. This principle was at the basis of the entire system of appeals. Rescripts were also issued by the administration and could be just as bad as judgements. Therefore, appeals against rescripts were possible in Antiquity. The medieval view, however, was different. C. 1.19.7, which stated that an imperial rescript that was contrary to the law had to be rejected by all judges, became the foundation on which an entire doctrine was built.

Gratian adopted this text into canon law. Rescripts in which Rome had made a mistake, did not have to be applied. If there were two different rescripts about the same point of law, only the first applied according to Alexander III. The second one had to be considered a mistake, unless it contained a reference to the first rescript. If the pope wanted to derogate from the law, he wrote *non obstante iure* – if he did not include this formula, the derogation was accidental. Ordinary judges could determine that such a mistake had been made. This led to judicial reviews of the lawfulness of papal rules. The glossators reasoned in the same manner and were therefore of the opinion that it had to be possible to appeal against imperial decisions which infringed the *ius commune*. Their reasoning was important to constitutional thought. Monarchs would be bound to the *ius commune*. The kings invoked other principles of Roman law to defend themselves: *princeps legibus solutus* (D. 1.3.31, the sovereign is above the law) and *quod principi placuit legis habet uigorem* (Inst. 1.2.6 and D. 1.4.1, what pleases the sovereign has the force of law).

In other words, the jurists distilled another possibility to test governmental decisions from C. 1.19.7. In the Early Modern Time, the result of this discussion would be the principle that one could react against a monarch's decision if it was not in line with the European *ius commune* of the era. This is a beautiful example of the manner in which the royal power was relativised through legal doctrine.

Bibliography. – On the canonists, see H. DONDORP, *Rechtmatigheidstoetsing, toetsing van pauselijke rescripten bij de decretisten en decretalisten*, Amsterdam 1988.

G. Objections

Could a party that had been sentenced *in absentia* file an appeal? In the old Roman law they could not because failure to appear in court was tantamount to having ignored the emperor's orders (D. 5.1.73.3, D. 3.1.13.4). In medieval practice, judgements *in absentia* were common because the summons issued in one jurisdiction did not apply in other jurisdictions and because of the limited publicity that was given to these summons. Irnerius already interpreted the Justinian texts concerning legitimate absence in a broad manner: C. 7.43.10 (absence out of necessity), D. 4.1.8 (absence *rei publicae causa*, for reasons of public duty), C. 3.19.2 (suit by the possessor in the absence of the owner). The Gloss distinguished between the real *contumax* (contumacious person) who did not turn up despite his knowledge of the proceedings, and the *ficte contumax* (notional contumacious person), concerning whom there was no proof that he was aware of the summons. By means of the texts of Justinian that aimed at the most equal possible treatment of parties during disputes, persons who remained absent were given more and more protection. A real *contumax* retained his rights until the *litiscontestatio*; a *ficte contumax* retained them even after the *litiscontestatio*. The latter *contumax* could also ask for the reopening of the debates by means of proceedings to have a judgement *in absentia* set aside. If a *ficte contumax* appealed against the judgement *in absentia*, his appeal was inadmissible: first, he had to institute new proceedings before the first judge.

H. The manner of appealing

In the Middle Ages appeals were lodged either orally at the hearing (restrictive interpretation of D. 49.1.5.4) or in writing within ten days (gl. *'Timore' ad* Nov. 23.1 = Coll. IV,2). The appeal was always lodged with the first judge, who wrote a report (*litterae dimissoriae*). If he did not write a report or stopped the appeal, parties could turn to a higher judge, who, in accordance with Roman law, imposed a fine on the first judge. The first judge had to hand over the entire file of the preliminary inquiry, but in Odofredus' comment (*ad* C. 7.62.15) it can be read that this happened only rarely in practice. The first judgement was deferred.

According to C. 7.62.24, the judge had to summon and inform the opposing party. According to the Gloss, the first judge could become the opposing party in the appellate case, following the system of the *actio de iudice qui litem suam fecit* (French 'prise à partie'). The glossators treated every *iudex a quo* (first judge) who wanted to sabotage appeals in a very strict manner. Feudal judges and judges within an administrative system considered appeals as a reprimand that undermined their position of power in a city or fief. In this context, the imposition of the Romano-canonical procedure meant a considerable step towards the development of a state under the rule of law.

The defendant did not necessarily have to attend the appellate proceedings. If he absented himself, he was sentenced to the costs even if he won the case (Nov. 49.1*pr.*). If both parties were absent, the appellant always lost (*ibidem*). The Gloss consequently advises defendants to stay away from the hearing in case of the appellant's absence, because the defendant would then immediately be put in the right (gl. *'Si uero neuter occurrit' ad* Nov. 49.1*pr.* = Auth. 58, Coll. V, 11).

According to the oldest glossators (Placentinus, Pillius), the burden of proof was on the appellant. The canonists also defended this position, because there was a refutable presumption that the first judgement had been lawful. Later, civil jurists (Johannes Bassanius and Azo, *ad* C. 7.62.7) defended the opinion that the burden of proof remained unchanged with regard to the elements of the case file pertaining to the first judgement. New elements were admissible (according to C. 762.62 and C. 7.63.4), but they had to be proved by the party who invoked them.

The judgement on appeal was a new judgement, even if it confirmed the first ruling. Periods only began to run from then on. A void first judgement could acquire the force of *res iudicata* on appeal. The fine which the Roman law imposed on a losing appellant was dropped if he seemed to have had a *iusta causa* to file an appeal. Justinian provided a procedural fine If he appeared obviously to have appealed wrongfully (C. 7.65.5.3).

6. The reintroduction of appeals in practice

Appeals were the central institution of the administration of Egypt and the Roman Empire. In the West, the division of sovereignty resulted in appeals becoming less important. The resurgence of appeals in the Middle Ages, however, was the ideal means of curbing feudalism and establishing centralised royal power. Appeals once again became a pivotal institution. Appeals were the basis on which the Italian city states and the centralised nations north of the Alps were built. In England, the possibility to lodge appeals against lower judges with the royal council existed from the eleventh century onwards. In Germany, appeals began to be heard in the Reichshofrat under Charles IV of Luxemburg and Bohemia (†1355). In the central territory of the king of France, it was possible to lodge appeals against local courts with the Parliament of Paris in the thirteenth century. In the fifteenth century, appeals were an institution that was used throughout the entire jurisdiction of the Parliament. The appeals from Flanders that were lodged with the Parliament of Paris between 1325 and 1526 have been studied. In Spain, central royal councils were established during the Reconquista against the Moors. At the end of the fifteenth century, appeals against local courts existed in each of the Spanish principalities. Under the Habsburgs, the merged

Cortes were the central appeal body for the entire territory of Spain. In Germany, appeals against the highest courts of the different principalities were organised in the Reichskammergerichtshof in Speyer in 1495. The aim was to turn the Holy Roman Empire into a single, unified nation and to subject the principalities to the emperor once again. The plan did not work. The situation in the German principalities differed widely. In some of these regions, the administration of law remained feudal until the nineteenth century. After the sixteenth century, the fight against absolutism was on every jurist's agenda. Nevertheless, the possibility of appeal was cherished because it had resulted in a major improvement of the quality of the administration of justice. In the eighteenth century appeals were depoliticised on the Continent when they were linked to the separation of powers. By the end of the century, the Continent's professional judges were independent judges, who used the new legal sources – doctrine and legislation – as the basis for their judgements. At that moment, appeals became so evident that no one saw their connection with the central institution of Roman law anymore.

Bibliography. – One of the most beautiful studies of Roman law was devoted to appeals: A. PADOA SCHIOPPA, *Ricerche sull'appello nel diritto intermedio,* 2 vol., Milan 1967-1970. This study offers a description of the institution from imperial times to the Middle Ages. It inspires its readers to rediscover the entire Roman law starting from this procedure which had mainly been studied from the viewpoint of dogmatics since the seventeenth century. With regard to the Early Modern Era, see M. FOURNIER, *Essai sur l'histoire du droit d'appel suivi d'une étude sur la réforme de l'appel,* Paris 1881; G. DU BREUIL, *Stilus curie Parlamenti,* Paris 1909; J. HALLEBEEK, 'Recursus ad principem, Zegers Bernard van Espen on the role of secular court in preventing the abuse of ecclesiastical jurisdiction', in: J. HALLEBEEK en B. WIRIX (eds.), *Met het oog op morgen, Ecclesiologische beschouwingen aangeboden aan Jan Visser,* Zoetermeer 1996, p. 64-71; A. WIJFFELS, 'Appelationen am Grossen Rat von Mechelen', *Beiträge zur Rechtsgeschichte Österreichs* 2013, p. 211-230; J. KOSTER-VAN DIJK and A. WIJFFELS, 'Les procedures en revision au Grand Conseil de Malines (1473-1580)', *Publication du Centre Européen d'études bourguignonnes (XIVe-XVIe s.)* 30 (1990), p. 67-97; C. SZIDZEK, *Das frühneuzeitliche Verbot der Appelation in Reichskammergerichts,* Cologne-Weimar-Vienna 2002.

§7. Evidence in Roman law

The structuring of observations has been an important theme of philosophy since the eighteenth century. By then, jurists had been concerning themselves with this issue for centuries. How does one resolve a conflict if everyone sees reality in their own way? When facts were invoked in a court and the opposing party challenged them, the judge assessed the *ueritas*, the reliability and the usefulness of the facts in adversarial proceedings. Although the Roman judges were traditionally confronted with evidence, the earliest texts that treat proof date from the Imperial Era. This is not only due to the scarcity of sources, but also to the introduction of appeals. It was only after their introduction that people could complain to the prefecture about the specific way in which facts had been accepted by a judge. The judgement of the prefecture then became a binding law of evidence. The precedents concerning the law of evidence led to judicial *ueritas*, the facts that were useful to the case. This *ueritas* was not a philosophical notion, because an agreement about the facts also led to *ueritas*. The Roman means of evidence were turned into a comprehensive system by the twelfth-century canonists. Their system was still a technique to make facts usable in a procedure, but the canonists' search for *ueritas* did inspire the theologians to search for the absolute truth. The old law of evidence also contained elements of intuition, trust and faith. In the Early Modern Era, judicial evidence would influence ideas about scientific evidence. In the scientific context, usability, persuasion, convictions and general acceptance took centre stage as well. The law of evidence is a beautiful example of a legal matter that was received by Western culture as a basic app for thought. If Kant tried to dig up the roots of observation and the basis for the acceptance of facts, he perhaps did so because he was a jurist and had a strong interest in the reception of legal thought.

1. In the oldest Roman law

According to some Romanists, there was no law of evidence before post-classical law. In the early Republic, we find texts about proceedings involving acts that were hard to prove. The Law of the Twelve Tables mentions the 'bewitching' of fruits of the field. How could the plaintiff substantiate the claim that the defendant had bewitched the fruits if the defendant asserted that the damage had been caused by a natural phenomenon? The person who proceeded against an alleged thief by means of the civil *actio furti* was not only asked to substantiate the facts, but also to prove the malicious intent of the perpetrator. Both of these examples show that there really were techniques to establish a vision of immaterial elements. Most Romanists, however, write that jurists did not occupy themselves with this issue. In Antiquity, Aquilius Gallus did not attach great importance to the means of evidence either: "Jurists are not interested in facts." Such a statement, however, is easily made. If a judge appeared to have erred in his assessment of the evidence during a formulary trial he could be challenged with the *actio de iudice qui litem suam fecit* (action for damage caused by the judge). The praetor then decided whether he allowed the claim. If necessary, a judge made an assessment to see whether the facts had actually been wrongly qualified. This is quite a juridical treatment of an evidentiary issue! The problem is that there are simply no textual sources that date from the Republic. All of the precedents concerning the law of evidence that have been preserved stem from the Imperial Period.

2. In the Classical Period

We find no comprehensive doctrine of evidence in the early Imperial Period either. A rescript of Hadrian mentions that there were no general rules concerning proof (D. 22.5.3.2). In the work of the Spanish rhetorician Quintilian (35-95) one can read a series of considerations concerning evidence. He did not write about the law, but about rhetoric and cited Aristotle's Rhetoric, Cicero, etcetera. As persuasive means, he mentions witnesses, documents, oaths, presumption, public opinion (*fama*) and judicial torture. This list already savours of a systematic treatment – in the first century! However, such systematic treatment cannot be found in the legal texts of the period. The classical texts feature individual considerations concerning *testes* (witnesses), *iusiurandum apud iudicem* (decisive oath during the phase before the judge), *tabulae* (clay tablets), *rumores* (rumours), *praeiudicia* (prejudgements), *signa* (external signs), *exempla* (examples), *argumenta* (invoked elements)... These terms are mentioned separately, but are never systematised.

In D. 22.3 concerning 'proof and presumptions' we find interesting texts by jurists from the early Principate. In principle, the person who invoked something also had to prove it, but if matters were difficult to prove, the judge was allowed to entertain a presumption. Judges were, for example, allowed to believe a mother when she talked about the birth of her child and there was no other proof of descent. *Veritas* is treated in this text from the Digest. In D. 22.3.13 we read that *causa cognita ueritatem excuti oportet.* In this context this can only mean that the judge had to extract a useful presentation of the facts. In a case in which the age of a party was a decisive factor, the judge had only taken a unilateral declaration into account. The prefecture was of the opinion that this was unjust: the judge should have based himself on all of the proof that had been provided in order to reach a presumption about the party's age. Legally speaking, this would have been more correct. Was the testimony of witnesses already a higher from of proof than documentary evidence at that time? A beautiful rescript is cited in D. 22.3.29*pr.* A judge had established that a couple's letters, which mentioned details about their children, were authentic. He considered these data more reliable than testimonies that contradicted them. "Rightly so!," Rome ruled. In D. 22.3.29.1, a text by Scaevola, *ueritas* crops up again. A mother who had been repudiated during her pregnancy later mentioned in documents that her son was *spurius* (autonomous at birth, not a relative of his father, see below). When she died without having written a will, the child's biological father accepted her estate for the benefit of the child. Her family, however, used the abovementioned documents to prove that the man had nothing to do with the child. The prefecture's reaction to this case is lovely: *respondit ueritati locum superfore* (reality takes precedence over *ueritas*). In this context *ueritas* therefore once more indicates a state of affairs which has been proved.

3. In the late Empire

A relatively large amount of late imperial judgements concerning the law of evidence have been handed down. Diocletian and Maximian dedicated constitutions to this subject, as did Constantine. In the *Codex Gregorianus*, the *Codex Hermogenianus* and the *Collatio*, the law of evidence is collected in a separate section. Theodosius II compiled the case law concerning evidence in CTh. 11.39, *de fide testium et instrumentorum.* Justinian devoted six titles to the issue: three in the Code and three in the Digest. The five items of evidence that appear time and again in these texts are: testimonies, writings, confessions, oaths and presumptions. Note that in the *cognitio* procedure confessions and decisive oaths had become irrefutable proofs, while in the formulary procedure they were means that ended the conflict.

Testimonies were the most important source of evidence. Constantine required at least two witnesses: *testis unus, testis nullus* (CTh. 11.39.3; C. 4.20.9.1). In D. 22.5 we read beautiful judgements concerning the definition of a reliable testimony. Witnesses who lived together were not considered separate witnesses. There was no obligation to give evidence against close family members or housemates. Children and parents not fit to testify against each other. Slaves only testified when there was no other evidence. Tax farmers could choose to remain silent. Adulterers were considered unreliable before the court as well. Magistrates were obliged to testify. If there was no other option but to have gladiators and other riff-raff testify, their statements only had evidentiary value after torture. We invite the readers to consult this title themselves. In his Nov. 90, Justinian returned to the risks associated with testimonies.

Written documents were considered less important. D. 22.4 *de fide instrumentorum* only contains six excerpts. The subscription of documents by witnesses began to be assessed (C. 8.18.11; C. 4.2.17 and 20; Nov. 73.1-2), so that these documents came to be considered equivalent to testimonies. All instruments could be contested in civil or criminal proceedings (*querela falsi*). According to C. 8.17.11, the socalled *lex Scripturas*, the chancellery of the emperor Leo decided in a case concerning multiple pledging that an instrument signed by known witnesses had more evidentiary value than an instrument signed by witnesses that were unknown or could not be found. At this time, registration by the administration already existed. Transfers of immovable property, for example, were registered from Constantine's reign onwards. The registration of documentary evidence became more important. In the context of the administration, *tabelliones* who drew up and registered documents were appointed. Their instruments had full evidentiary value in the *cognitio* procedure and took precedence over a testimony. If someone wanted to contest an instrument drawn up by a *tabellio*, he had to take proceedings on account of the forgery of documents.

Hint. – Titles D. 22.3-5 concerning proof are short and contain clear texts. They are beautiful material for those who want to become more closely acquainted with the Digest. The reader will notice that they do not testify to the existence of a comprehensive system of laws of evidence. Those readers who also get the chance on this occasion to peruse the texts from the Code that are cited above will experience the difference between the well-rounded texts from the Digest and the more thorny issues in the Code, which still savour of case law.

4. In the early Middle Ages

In the *leges romanae barbarorum* we find some beautiful judgements about evidence, but after these there is a media silence concerning the law of evidence.

Many historians write about the primitive Germanic means of evidence of the early Middle Ages: the trials by ordeal. They allege that under the influence of the Germanic peoples, the Roman law of evidence was replaced by Germanic 'unreasonable' evidence such as conspiracies, judicial duals and trials by ordeal. Let us remember the myths. Conspiracies involved the judge ruling in favour of the party who brought the most distinguished witnesses. In the case of a judicial duel, the judge gave the parties the order to resolve the dispute by means of a fight. Parties were allowed to let a champion take their place. The party who won the duel was right, because God gave strength to the righteous in battle. God played a similar role in ordeals of water and fire: he supported honest witnesses who put their hand into a fire or into boiling water and ensured that they did not get burnt. The funniest thing about the ordeals of fire is that historians believe in them. Critical historians claim that those who underwent a trial by ordeal did get burnt, but that the manner in which the burn healed allowed the judge to see what God made of the matter. If this really was the case, the question is whether it was God or the judge who really decided the case. There are even taller tales about ordeals of water. When women were accused, they were pushed under water. If they drowned, God did not help them; if they survived, they were witches and were burnt at the stake. Apparently, this was a good way of getting rid of a rival!

There are, however, scientific explanations of these procedures as well. The abovementioned means of evidence stem from the ninth and tenth centuries, a period during which feudal judges and bishops jointly administered justice in many regions. There are elements of both canon law and feudal law in these means of evidence. The judicial duels are consistent with feudalism, a military regime that was characterised by violence at all levels, even the lowest. One characteristic of these duels was that they were imposed by the feudal courts. Feudal judges were not averse to violence and sometimes avoided a private war by allowing duels between competing vassals. Conspiracies and trials by ordeal were related to *confessio in iure* and *iusiurandum in iure*, means which were also used in Antiquity when the facts could not be proved. After a confession or decisive oath, the judge could decide the case immediately. Both of these means also crop up in patristics and in the oldest canonical collections. The Romans could not deny something by means of an oath (C. 4.19.23), but the canonists did accept negative oaths (*denegatio*). They also attached great value to confessions, which had an absolving effect in the confessional box. Martyrdom was seen as the highest form of testimony (the Greek word *martyr* means witness). Denial by means of an oath and, if necessary, under torture led to absolution. Ordeals by water were denials by means of an oath which normally took place in a baptistery. Such ordeals led to absolution in the same manner as baptism did. Those who committed perjury while they were standing in holy water were acquitted, but were left to God's judgement. There was an element of torture in the trials by ordeal. Texts show that early medieval bishops were not averse to this. Ordeals by fire were denials by means of an oath that took place under torture. Finally, we point out that trials by ordeal were employed with regard to the five matters concerning which CTh. 11.36.1 states that appeal against the judgement was not possible and that the judgement immediately acquired the force of *res iudicata*. These allegedly unreasonable Germanic means of evidence, in other words, do fit into the history of the reception of the Roman procedure. In the most famous case of a trial by ordeal, the losing party was the emperor Lothair II, who wanted to divorce his childless wife Theutberga in order to produce an heir. Adultery was the only reason for divorce at the time, but Lothair could not prove that his wife had been unfaithful. Eventually, Theutberga stated that she had not committed any form of adultery during an ordeal by fire. Her statement not only meant the end of proceedings, but also that of the emperors of Middle Francia. It is unlikely that the emperor would have accepted this judgement if the imperial law had not been followed strictly.

A second means of evidence that cropped up in twelfth-century sources was the use of witnesses at episcopal synods. When bishops visited a parish, they or their delegated judges appointed synodal witnesses who provided testimonies under oath about the state of affairs in the parish. Synodal testimonies were a canonical means of evidence that was derived from the decisive oath. One witness sufficed for the provision of full evidence. In the synodal procedure, such oaths were used as evidence against third parties. Some bishops or delegated judges had synodal witnesses provide unilateral testimonies concerning the failings of certain worshippers, after which they imposed expiatory fines. The feudal lords had to collect these fines and deliver them to the bishops. In the twelfth century, the city of Bruges and the castellany of the Franc of Bruges opposed this means of evidence during proceedings against the bishop of Cambrai. Eventually, they won the case in Rome, where the final judgement was that bishops had to follow the Romano-canonical law of evidence. The unilateral evidence of the synodal procedure was abolished in 1215, at the Fourth Lateran Council.

Bibliography. – The classical work on trials by ordeal is H. NOTTARP, *Gottesurteilstudien*, Munich 1956. L. WAELKENS, 'Traces romano-canoniques dans les preuves germaniques', *The Legal History Review* 75 (2007), p. 321-331 contextualises the trials by ordeal in the history of Roman law. On the synodal procedure and the lawsuit of Bruges and the 'Franc of Bruges' against the bishop of Cambrai, see D. LAMBRECHT, *De parochiale synode in het oude bisdom Doornik gesitueerd in de Europese rechtsontwikkeling 11e eeuw-1559*, Brussels 1984.

5. The law of evidence of the Romano-canonical procedure

The Decretals of Gregory (1234) contain seven titles about the law of evidence. They show that there was a comprehensive doctrine concerning proof. This unification and systematisation of the law of evidence was the work of the canonists and processualists. Because of their legal practice, the canonists had ascendancy over the processualists. Important writers of the second half of the thirteenth century, like Guillaume Durand, attempted to show that the canonical law of evidence was based entirely on the Justinianic law. They collected all of the details in the *Corpus iuris* that pertained to the law of evidence and turned them into a single doctrine. In fact, the processualists of the twelfth and thirteenth centuries were the ones who created the Roman law of evidence. They also influenced all of the later interpretations of the Roman sources pertaining to the law of evidence.

The processualists assessed the evidentiary value of every means of evidence and arrived at a hierarchy of means of evidence. There were four degrees of evidentiary value: (1) general knowledge, (2) full proof (*probationes plenae*), (3) incomplete proof (*semiplenae*) and (4) additional proof. In criminal cases, there could not be a shadow of a doubt. Civil cases normally required full proof, but if there were no great interests at stake, incomplete proof often sufficed.

A. Notoriety

Notoriety, general knowledge, was the highest degree of evidence. Counterevidence and appeals against proofs were admissible: see C. 7.65. The word *notorium* only occurs in C. 9.2.7, but was the basis on which an entire theory was built. This theory was founded on Cor. 5.1.5, in which the Apostle Paul writes that he unjustly excommunicated someone without having carried out an investigation: in a case where the facts are manifest and unambiguous, the law allows for immediate action to be taken.

The processualists distinguished three kinds of notoriety: *notorium facti, notorium iuris* and *notorium praesumptionis*.

Notorium facti occurred when no one could question a fact in a meaningful manner. The canonists based this type of notoriety on Paulus' text. The prototype of *notorium facti* was *flagrante delicto.* Someone who ran away in public and was chased by someone who raised a hue and cry, was considered to have been caught *in flagrante delicto.* Further proof was not necessary. It was not necessary either with regard to offences that were committed during a hearing. In such cases, the judge could sentence the offender without conducting an investigation. Nevertheless, the medieval legists searched for a criterion for notoriety in the Roman sources. In D. 47.8.4.3, they read that a *rixa* (a fight on the street or in a bar) became a *turba* (disturbance of public order) if ten or more people came to blows. In other words: ten participants made the fight a public matter. The canonists inferred from this text that facts were notorious if one could find ten people who confirmed them. Azo defined notoriety in criminal law by means of this criterion; Accursius introduced this definition in private law. In the thirteenth century, the question was raised whether a rule of customary law was a fact or a law. The underlying question was whether customary law needed to be proved or not. The majority of jurists considered customary laws to be facts. If judges examined customary law, they asked onlookers or witnesses what the local customs were. The legal rules that were established in this manner could be revised on appeal. This was inconvenient, but also meant that the original interviewees had perhaps deceived the court. In 1270, under the influence of Symon Parisiensis, the 'Chambre des enquêtes' of the Parliament of Paris introduced the provision of notorious proof concerning rules of customary law by means of an 'enquête par turbe'. If the examining magistrate convened ten local specialists and listened to their collective conclusion, that conclusion was notorious. Consequently, the provision of counterevidence became impossible. In some countries, this form of evidence was adopted in the context of trials by jury. The judge involved ten people in the investigation of the facts and asked them questions. Their answers were notorious: neither appeals nor the provision of counterevidence was possible.

A second form of notoriety was *notorium iuris,* judicial notoriety. Public knowledge of the facts was not the only circumstance in which counterevidence and appeals were inadmissible. In Roman law, a confession (*confessio in iure*) had the same consequences. In the formulary procedure, a confession made at the preliminary hearing led to the conclusion that there was no conflict. In the *cognitio* procedure a judgement was still required after a confession was made, but this judgement could not be appealed. In the Romano-canonical procedure, confessions became notorious in character. This explains why such great importance was attached to confessions for centuries: if a judge could obtain a confession, he was protected against appeals and criticism from his superiors. The processualists made judgements which had acquired the force of *res iudicata* equivalent to confessions: *res iudicata pro ueritate accipitur* (from D. 50.17.207). If facts had been established in a judgement and appeals were no longer possible, these facts were *notorium iuris.*

A third from of notoriety was the irrefutable presumption (*notorium praesumptionis*) which can be found in legal commentaries from 1200 onwards. Facts that could not be rebutted were notorious. A classic example from Thomas Aquinas was that if a man and a woman under forty years of age lived under one roof for three months, they were also intimate with each other.

B. Full evidence

The processualists considered testimonies and written documents to be full evidence. These means could be used to provide conclusive evidence. Testimonies took precedence over written instruments ('témoins passent lettres', X. 2.12.10 by Innocent III). Much was written about testimonies at the time, and the medieval sources are a thousand times more comprehensive than the sources from Antiquity. They contain considerations about the selection of witnesses, summons, default of appearance, excusable absence, the manners of interviewing witnesses, the oath that witnesses were asked to take, the examination by the judge and the assessment of their answers, the evidentiary value of the testimonies and of the report on these testimonies, the consequences of a false testimony, etcetera. Whereas we only found some basic rules in Antiquity, like the need for two separate testimonies about each contested point, we now have an elaborate mass of data. What is striking is that the courts quickly began to follow the theory of the processualists and that the Romano-canonical procedure quickly spread to the aldermen's courts.

Written documents (*instrumenta*) could also lead to full proof. The official documents of a court had evidentiary value. Concerning private documents, importance was mainly attached to the witnesses that had signed the instrument (as in C. 8.17.11). Prima facie written evidence could be supplemented with testimonies. In his famous decretal *Scripta uero* (X. 2.22.2) Alexander III decided that an instrument signed by witnesses retained its evidentiary value after the witnesses' death if the text had been drawn up by a public notary who had also attached his seal to the document. The old tradition of officials who drew up official documents had been maintained in the former exarchate of Ravenna, the territory of which included Rome. The law faculty of Bologna developed the notarial profession on the basis of these officials' practice and Roman texts about the *tabelliones.* In twelfth-century Italy, public notaries were appointed by means of the authorisation of the pope or the imperial power. The instruments which they drew up, *instrumenta publica* or *instrumenta authentica*, had evidentiary value in itself in the jurisdiction of the pope or imperial power who had authorised the official. Nevertheless, these instruments were not notorious: it was possible to provide counterevidence or to file an appeal concerning the establishment of the facts. A *notarius apostolicus* had universal authority, but did not bind the feudal courts. Imperial notaries did not usually have universal authority. In the feudal system, the administration had been delegated to the local level, as had the notarial authority. Many courts considered notarial instruments to be prima facie evidence and therefore required additional testimonies besides the notarial deed. This explains the practice of having witnesses sign instruments in the presence of the notary – a practice that still exists today. In many regions, the evidentiary value of notarial deeds from other jurisdictions was accepted in the fourteenth century. Nevertheless, in the city of Bruges, commercial documents used when exporting goods to Italy were usually drawn up by Italian notaries who had settled in Bruges.

C. Imperfect and additional evidence

Incomplete evidence included ordinary prescriptions, rumours (*fama*), single testimonies, the party's own accounting records, the comparison of documents and the fact that the defendant had fled. All of these means had their own evidentiary value and characteristics, but in themselves they could not lead to the unambiguous establishment of facts. They played a role as additional evidence, for instance in a case of prima facie written evidence. For the canonists, oaths pertaining to the facts (*iuramentum*) were additional evidence. This downgrading of the Roman oath to a subsidiary means of evidence is striking. According to the canonists, one always had to be as good as one's word. Consequently, oaths made no difference.

In small cases, the judge could base his decision on incomplete evidence, for example when he was of the opinion that refusing to pronounce a judgement would cause more damage than any possible miscarriage of justice. This was impossible in criminal law, where there were no small cases.

D. The burden of proof

In principle, the burden of proof was on the party who invoked the facts. In the twelfth century the judge's obligation to investigate (*inquisitio*) was received. It could be found in C. 3.1.9, but its scope was not very clear: did this duty involve more than a careful examination of the case file and the thorough questioning of the parties during the hearing? According to the first legists, the judge was not even allowed to do more than this. The judge could charge others with investigative measures, for example by having the local notary question the witnesses, but when a judge did this, he could neither investigate anything that fell outside of the scope of his own assignment, nor ask questions himself. In 1215 the Fourth Lateran Council decided that the ecclesiastical judges' duty to investigate could lead them to leave the court for investigative purposes. They could make an official visit to the scene of the facts or send an investigating committee in their stead. This investigation method was received by the 'Chambre des enquêtes' of the Parliament of Paris. The itinerant judges which the Parliament sent to Flanders to investigate facts on the occasion of appeals against the Council of Flanders were at the basis of the Franco-Flemish conflict of 1302. The mastermind behind these missions to Flanders was the leading jurist Pierre de Belleperche. Many of the aldermen's courts adopted the practice of the *inquisitio* from the Parliament. In England, judges stayed in their courts. The investigation outside of the court had to be conducted by the person who invoked the facts (*accusatio*). In England, the investigative missions only existed in canon law, in the consistory courts.

E. The judge's own knowledge

Did the judge need proof if he knew the truth of the matter? Did his private knowledge of the facts play a role? D. 1.18.6.1 provided the basis for the discussion about this issue. From the mid-thirteenth century onwards, the prevailing opinion was that the judge could only rule *secundum allegata at probata*, meaning that he could only take account of the facts that were invoked and proved. He was only allowed to base himself on his private knowledge of the facts if they were notorious and appeals against the facts were inadmissible in any event.

Concerning d) and e). – The discussion as to whether a procedure needed to be conducted in an accusatory or inquisitorial manner dates back to C. 3.1.9, which we cite below. That the judge could only rule on the basis of the facts that had been proved and could not base his judgement on his own better knowledge is a conclusion which was connected with D. 1.18.6.1 (printed below) in the thirteenth century. On the judge's own knowledge, see F. MAFFEI, 'Il giudice testimone e una 'quaestio' di Jacques de Revigny (ms. Bon. Coll. Hisp. 82)', in *The Legal History Review* 35 (1965), p. 54-76. Both texts illustrate how Roman law functioned throughout history: scanty and unclear texts from Antiquity lead to commentary and become certainties in the *ius commune*. Also note the emendation in D. 1.18.6.1: the Florentine manuscript clearly says *gestarum*, but everyone corrects it to *gestorum* because the Romanists want to understand *ueritas rerum* as 'the truth of things'. Therefore, they consider *gestorum* as a genitive with *erroribus* even though it is better to read *rerum gestarum* as a genitive with *erroribus*.

C. 3.1.9 (321). – Iudices oportet imprimis rei qualitatem plena inquisitione discutere et tunc umtramque partem saepius interrogare, ne quid noui addere desiderent, cum hoc ipsum ad alterutram partem proficiat siue definienda causa per iudicem siue ad maiorem potestatem referenda sit.

Translation F.H BLUME. – Since it is to the advantage of both parties, judges should first of all clear up the nature of the question in dispute by careful inquiry and frequently ask both parties if they want to add anything new, whether the cause is to be decided by the judge himself or whether it is to be referred to a higher authority. Given at Sirmium, January 12 (321).

D. 1.18.6.1 – Veritas rerum erroribus gestarum non uitiatur: et ideo praeses prouinciae id sequatur quod conuenit eum ex fide eorum quae probabuntur.

Translation S.P. SCOTT. – The truth is not changed by error, and hence the Governor of a province must follow the course which is suitable by taking into consideration facts which have been proved.

Translation L. W. – Mistakes concerning the establishment of the state of affairs are not detrimental to the facts. Consequently, the governor of the province [*in casu* the appellate judge] will continue as it befits him on the basis of the facts which will have been proved.

6. The evolution in the Early Modern Era

The law of evidence beautifully illustrates the reception of Roman law. The Roman means of evidence that were introduced in Western Europe were those of the Romano-canonical procedure. The richness of this body of law did not stem from the few titles from the Roman sources, but from the legal doctrine which the processualists developed and from the universities' interaction with legal practice. In Guillaume Durand's work, one can read much more about the law of evidence than in the *Codex Theodosianus* and the *Corpus iuris*. In a brilliant study, Yves Mausen has shown how in the twelfth and thirteenth centuries the law of evidence of the law faculties was adopted in all of the regions that now constitute France. In the fourteenth century the law of evidence then shared the fate of Bartolism (see above): it was ingrained in practice in a conservative manner. Countless early modern *stylus curiae* or 'styles and manners of proceeding' of major courts – situated between Madrid and Cracow and between Stockholm and Naples – have been handed down. It is impressive to see how parallel these *stylus curiae* were. The law of evidence which we find in them hardly deviates from Guillaume Durand's *Speculum iudiciale*. The *ius commune* of the Early Modern Era was indeed European in character.

Here and there the hierarchy of the means of evidence was elaborated to include, for example, a hierarchy of presumptions and indications. A sum of incomplete proofs could then led to full proof. Matthias van Wesenbeke, Andrea Alciato, François Hotman and Hugues Doneau would oppose this practice in the sixteenth century. In these authors' works, we can observe a paradox of the reception of Roman law. They wanted to tear themselves loose from the canonists and align themselves more closely with legal practice. However, the Romano-canonical law of evidence had become so ingrained in practice that they contributed to the acceptance of canon law as *ius commune*.

Bibliography. – On the history of the law of evidence in general, see *La Preuve*, I-IV, [Recueils de la Société Jean Bodin pour l'histoire comparative des institutions, 16-19,] Brussels 1963-1965. These volumes contain a series of articles about the law of evidence of Roman Antiquity. They show how little we know about the Roman law of evidence, how much is nevertheless written about it and that the medieval development of the law of evidence plays a large role in readings of the Roman sources. On proof in the Middle ages, see J. Ph. Lévy, *La hiérarchie des preuves dans le droit savant du Moyen-Âge depuis la renaissance du droit romain jusqu'à la fin du XIVe siècle*, [Annales de l'Université de Lyon, II,5,] Paris 1939. A summary of this work can be found in the abovementioned *La Preuve*, III. On notoriety: L. Waelkens, 'L'origine de l'enquête par turbe', *The Legal History Review* 53 (1985), p. 337-346. The brilliant work about testimonies in the Romano-canonical procedure that we mentioned is Y. Mausen, *Veritas adiutor, La procedure du témoignage dans le droit savant et la pratique française (XIIe-XIVe siècles)*, Milan 2006.

§8. Conflicts of legal norms

In Belgium, private international law was codified in 2004. Until that time, the structure of its sources had largely been parallel to that of the *ius commune* of the Early Modern Era. Precedents and legal doctrine were used to construct arguments pertaining to this field of law. As regards contents, however, the private international law that was codified in 2004 still savours of Roman law and the *ius commune*.

Private international law offers points of departure when a conflict between citizens leads to a conflict between legal systems and the judge has to determine which law is applicable. In principle, each court compiles its own case law concerning such issues, but the matter was nationalised throughout Europe through the possibility of appeal in the Europe of Nations. Nevertheless, most countries' private international law is parallel to that of the other states. Judges demarcate their territory vis-à-vis their neighbours, but avoid creating new sources of conflict in the process. A certain form of common sense exists in this context. Traditionally, jurists traced the shared root of private international law back to the works of Bertand d'Argentré (Argentraeus, 1519-1590), Ulric Huber (1636-1694) and Johannes Voet (1647-1714). Belgian jurists tend to emphasise the role of Petrus Peckius (1529-1589) and Christinaeus (1553-1714).

In the early twentieth century the *communis opinio* was that private international law stemmed from Bartolus' 'theory of statutes', which described which law was applicable in case of conflict of city laws in Italy. E.M. Meijers (1880-1954), a professor of private international law in Leyden, continued to examine the writings of Bartolus, who often referred to 'Ja. de Ra.' and 'P. de Be.' Meijers wanted to fully understand these two authors (Jacques de Revigny and Pierre de Belleperche) as well and in the process he chanced on the university of Orléans, which would make him a celebrity among legal historians. According to Meijers, this university was at the basis of private international law. Today, medieval academic law has been studied more thoroughly. We also possess more sources. The same thirteenth-century rules pertaining to conflict of laws can be found in the works of civil jurists from Orléans like Jean de Monchy and Pietro Peregossi, in the writings of Parisian canonists like Hostiensis and Sinibaldus Fliscus, and in the output of Odofredus in Bologna and Andrea de Isernia in Naples. They were all students of Jacobus Balduini (†1235). Was he at the basis of private international law? Other traces lead to canonists like Huguccio of Pisa (†1210). If one investigates all of the medieval clues, on comes to the conclusion that jurists were mainly citing the *Corpus iuris* and that private international law stems from the Roman law of Antiquity. This is a beautiful example of a classical matter that was received from Roman law and then developed in the Romano-canonical procedure.

1. Classical rules pertaining to conflict of laws

A. In the Republic

One prevailing doctrine is that the Romans exclusively applied Roman law and were not familiar with conflicts of sets of norms. We have, however, already seen that the Republic was characterised by legal pluralism. Consequently, there was enough material for conflicts between bodies of law. The division among magistrates seemed simple: criminal law was the exclusive province of the aediles; trade with the Senate was exclusively treated by the quaestors. In civil law, however, we see that there was a need for rules pertaining to conflict of laws.

First and foremost, Roman citizens had conflicts with non-citizens. Each province had different rights according to its peace treaty. The *praetor peregrinorum* developed the *ius gentium* in order to deal with conflicts between parties who each had a different status. Peoples with which Rome had not concluded a treaty (*gentes exterae*) had the status of slaves according to Roman civil law. However, they could acquire temporary rights and travel within the Empire after they had obtained a visa at the *limes* (the outer border of the Empire). They received a *tessera fidei publicae*, a baked shard that mentioned an identification, the gate through which they had entered the realm and the validity of the visa. Many of these visas were issued to young immigrants who wanted to join a legion. Their visa granted them protection according to the common rules of the *ius gentium*.

A double problem arose with regard to private conflicts: (1) Which magistrate had jurisdiction? (2) Which legal system was applicable? The first rule which we find is that the answer to these questions depended on the magistrate who was consulted and his *lex fori.* The procedure to be followed was that of the magistrate who was called upon. This magistrate decided in his edict who he admitted and which law he would apply. If he came to the conclusion that he did not have jurisdiction, he did not refer the case but rejected it. Magistrates drew up their own rules for the referral of cases and their own rules as to which law they would apply. The praetor always applied civil law when he dealt with citizen's conflicts, but the *praetor peregrinorum* did not always apply the *ius gentium.* Sometimes, a conflict between two *peregrini* was referred to the judge for treatment under foreign law. This, however, was impossible when the praetor judged that the application of the foreign law was against the Roman *publica utilitas,* the Roman public order.

We have but little information about conflicts of Roman, provincial and local edicts. In the *lex irnitana* it can be read that local citizenship existed in Irni besides Roman citizenship and that everyone could address the local magistrates, who then checked (in their edict?) which law they would apply to the conflict.

B. In the Empire

Most of the texts about conflict of laws date from the Empire and are judgements pronounced by the prefectures and the chancellery. Each free Roman citizen had the same status. The jurisdiction of the imperial judges was limited by the kind of case (civil, military, fiscal...), the place, the domicile of the defendant and the plaintiff, and the amount of money involved. Conflicts with *honestiores* and cases about large amounts were brought before the governors immediately.

The first rule that was laid down was that the court where the case was initiated applied its own procedure and its own private international law (*lex fori*).

In cases of *actiones in personam* the competent court was either the court of the territory of which the defendant was a citizen or the court that had jurisdiction over his domicile (the choice between these two options was left to the plaintiff). In the Republic, one could not be a citizen of two cities. In the Empire, however, this was possible. In 212 the system of confederated cities was abolished and everyone became a citizen of the Empire (D. 50.1.33). One's domicile was the place where one resided and intended to stay. A funny detail from C. 10.40.2 is the following: students only became domiciled in the city where they studied when they had lived there for ten years. Defendants had to appear before the court, even if it was only to deny the jurisdiction of the magistrate or judge. In cases of *actiones in rem* the point of departure was also the defendant's location – more precisely the location of the holder of the asset that was mentioned in the *intentio.*

Parties could agree which judge they would go to (*forum prorogatum*). With regard to contracts, the plaintiff had the choice between the location where the contract had been concluded (*forum loci contractus*) or the place of the execution of the contract (*forum loci solutionis*). With regard to the assessment of the validity of the contract, the competent court was that of the place where the contract had been concluded. The place where the defendant was forced to execute his contract was usually that of his domicile.

Offences were assessed in the court that had jurisdiction over the scene of the offence (*forum delicti commissi*). If the defendant had fled to a different province, the governor of that province had to extradite him (D. 48.3.7). Exceptionally, the proceedings could take place in the *forum domicilii.*

With regard to wills, the competent court was the court of the location where the will had been drawn up. Wills were either drawn up orally in the *forum* or in writing before the judge and had to be dealt with there as well.

2. In the *ius commune*

In Antiquity, the differences between the practices of the various courts were small because the imperial chancellery strove for a unified law for the entire Empire. In the Middle Ages, however, Western Europe had become a patchwork of autonomous jurisdictions. Clear and uniform rules pertaining to conflict of laws were essential to the introduction of a *ius commune*. The civil jurists and canonists have applied themselves thoroughly to conflicts of customs (local case law), statutes (civic case law) and the academic Roman law. The most original jurist who treated private international law was Jacobus Balduini. His students spread his vision. The *sedes materiae* of private international law was a text from the Code, namely *Cunctos populus* (C. 1.1.1), i.e. the Edict of Thessaloniki. After all, in the first words of this edict the emperor mentioned 'all peoples that fell under his jurisdiction'.

A. Which custom was applicable?

Jacobus Balduini argued that the procedure, which included issues of proof and appeals, was always that of the local court.

The local court could try foreigners, but did the local law apply to them? According to the canonists, the local law always applied. Huguccio already defended this standpoint in the twelfth century. After all, *ciuitas* was not a criterion in the ecclesiastical courts. According to the civil legists, however, foreigners were not subject to local law. Jacques de Revigny derived from this view the conclusion that there could be no visa requirement because visas pertained to local law. There were exceptions: the local criminal law always applied, and foreigners had to respect the local law concerning goods, the conclusion of contracts and the form of legal acts (*locus regit actum*). These exceptions were discussed often. In the thirteenth century the Parliament of Paris treated some cases involving inhabitants of Flanders who claimed that they did not have to pay tolls in Péronne on the road to Paris. They were never put in the right. Another case pertained to the Parisian regulation that only members of the 'guilde des charretiers' could drive horses in the city. Some Flemish traders argued that this rule did not apply to foreigners, but the Parliament ruled against them. After this judgement, a Flemish driver had his official French colleague run alongside the team of horses. The court deemed that this was in accordance with regulations.

Concerning criminal law, Jacobus Balduini pointed out that foreigners were only subject to the *ius commune* and could not be punished for offences that did not exist within the *ius commune*. The canonists, however, defended that criminal law was strictly local and applied to everyone, on the basis of D. 2.1.20. Their opinion began to outweigh that of Balduini. Bartolus assumed that criminal law was a local matter, but that a lack of knowledge about provisions that were not *ius commune* was a ground for exemption. Could someone be prosecuted on account of offences which had been committed in a different jurisdiction? According to the canonists, this was not possible.

According to the civil jurists it was, but only if the offence was against the *ius commune*. Bartolus was of the opinion that in such cases the opinion of the criminal legislator had to be checked. Bartolus' opinion was followed by many jurists.

With regard to contracts, Jacobus Balduini still defended the rule that the law of the location where the contract had been concluded applied on the grounds of D. 21.2.6. Bartolus was the first to unearth the ancient Roman rule that the law of the place of the contract applied in cases involving the form and validity of the contract, while the law of the place of execution applied to obligations.

The local law always applied to goods, even if their possessor lived elsewhere. Both the canonists and the civil jurists agreed about this. Wills were to be dealt with according to the local law that applied where the goods were located. For Bartolus, however, this was not all that clear. According to him, one had to assess the intention of the local law, examine how the rules were formulated and then apply the distinction of the *ius commune*: with regard to norms that pertained to people (for example the rule that the eldest son had to inherit) the point of departure was personal law, but norms that concerned goods (for example the rule that goods had to fall to the eldest son) had to be considered from a territorial perspective. Once again, provisions that concerned people did not apply to foreigners. Here, one can observe another important principle of private international law: there is room for argument!

B. Does the ius commune take precedence over customary law?

In the Middle Ages, a second domain played a role in conflicts of norms. The aldermen's courts applied customary law; the urban rulers applied statutes. This was no different from the practice of the prefecture in Rome. These courts adhered to their ordinary case law. What, however, did the judge have to do if this local law conflicted with the *ius commune*? In D. 1.3.32 and the following texts the civilian jurists read that local law could replace Roman law, but in C. 8.52.2 they found that Roman law always took precedence over local customary law. One point which is typical of the civil jurists, is that they did not pay attention to the fact that the local judges had delegated royal jurisdiction. Customary law was popular law; the *Corpus iuris* was royal law. The monarch had received his power from the people (D. 1.2.2) and some jurists argued that the people could revoke this transfer of sovereignty. Was this perhaps the case here? The rule of the glossators and the commentators was that the *ius commune* took precedence over local case law. The delegation of jurisdiction could not be reversed in a snap. Imperial law took precedence over the customary law of the people. It was only in exceptional circumstances that a law could become obsolete and be replaced by the *consuetudo*. Examples were laws from which one could deviate by means of a contract or rules of *ius commune* which had become obsolete with the consent of the monarch. This problem disappeared in the Early Modern Period, because local law vanished in the national states and because the hierarchy of norms became part of public law.

3. In the Early Modern Era

In the Early Modern Era, there was a preference for territorial law: each nation state regulated everything within its own territory, while personal law became an exception.

The sovereign councils applied Roman law and considered themselves as exclusively competent to assess the *ius commune*. Foreigners had to request a privilege in order to function as citizens of a kingdom. In many nations the law of inheritance did not apply to them and 'le droit d'aubaine' continued to exist: the inheritance of a foreigner fell to the *fiscus*, the sovereign. This problem was solved by the introduction of letters of naturalisation, by means of which foreigners who were born outside of the nation's territory were granted the legal fiction of being born within the jurisdiction of the sovereign council. In Leuven, Nicolas Everaerts (1464-1532) and Petrus Peckius (1529-1589) defended Bartolus' old distinction between territorial law and personal law. The fact that the jurisdictions had grown did not mean that the principles of the *ius commune* had changed. They once again supported the principles mentioned by Bartolus. This medieval private international law would make its way through the seventeenth and eighteenth century with varying degrees of success. Because of the separation of public and private law and the abovementioned privatisation of the *ius commune*, the civil rights of private citizens became less dependent on the monarchs. In private relations, the jurists furthered the system that had been developed in the medieval *ius commune* – hence the term private international law. In the seventeenth and eighteenth centuries one can observe that in each nation there was a different kind of interaction between the pure territoriality supported by the royal councils and the system of the *ius commune* that was defended by the jurists. The legal doctrine of the seventeenth century held the *ius commune* in high esteem and the Enlightenment was a European movement in which nationalism was relativised. With regard to the rights of foreigners and the application of foreign law, the jurists who were active after the civil revolutions of the eighteenth century once again sought to align themselves with the sixteenth- and seventeenth-century jurists of private law and the authors of the *ius commune* whom we have mentioned at the beginning of this paragraph. These authors and jurists thus relayed Bartolus and the medieval private international law to the nineteenth century. This is why Bartolus' doctrine is so recognisable to specialists of private international law. It thus explains why they are inclined to trace their branch of law back to Bartolus and the sixteenth- and seventeenth-century advocates of the *ius commune*.

Bibliography. – On Antiquity, see J. PLESCIA, 'Conflicts of Laws in the Roman Empire', *Labeo* 38 (1992), p. 30-54; on the Middle Ages, see E.M. MEIJERS, *Études d'histoire du droit international privé*, published by P.-C. TIMBAL and J. METMAN, Paris 1967. The thirteenth-century case law of the Parliament of Paris can be found in A.-A. BEUGNOT, *Les Olim ou registres des arrêts rendus par la Cour du Roi sous les règnes de saint Louis, de Philippe le Hardi, de Philippe le Bel, de Louis le Hutin et de Philippe le Long (1254-1318)*, Paris 1844. On the Early Modern Era, see W. ONCLIN, 'La doctrine de Bartole sur les conflits de lois et son influence en Belgique', in: *Bartolo da Sassoferrato, Studi e documenti per il VI centenario*, II, Milan 1962, p. 373-398. On the conflict between customary law and *ius commune*, see L. WAELKENS, *La théorie de la coutume chez Jacques de Révigny. Edition et analyse de sa repetition sur la loi De Quibus (D.1.3.32)*, Leyden 1984, p. 310-324. On the status of foreigners in emerging nations, see B. D'ALTEROCHE, *De l'étranger à la seigneurie au royaume XIe-XVe siècle*, Paris 2002.

Chapter IV
The law of persons

Persona is the Latin word for mask. This basic meaning was then extended so that the word also came to mean actor and character. In Roman law, the word indicated an actor in the law of procedure. In Gratian's Decree (C. 4 q. 4 c. 1) we read that there were four types of *personae*, namely judges, defendants, plaintiffs and witnesses. Gaius writes in 2.1 that his first book is about *de iure personarum*, but it also discusses civil status, deals with slaves and children who did not act in the courts and involves couples' relationships. In other words, he also considered the supernumeraries to be *personae*. This is the notion of 'person' that can be found in the *Corpus iuris*: actors and supernumeraries in the courts.

This notion now sounds outdated. *Personae* have not been actors since the Early Modern Era. Instead, they have become subjects who are at the centre of the law: they are the point of departure of the subjective rights. The Civil code constructed a coherent sphere around the person which contains – besides the person – marriage and family. In the German nineteenth century the person became a carrier of rights and duties. In the twentieth century the person that was the key notion of personalism was put on centre stage in civil law. The Roman person and *familia* should never be considered from these more recent viewpoints. Here, we will discuss the persons and *familia* that Gaius mentioned, as well as the way in which these notions evolved in Antiquity and the Middle Ages. They are a far cry from the law of persons of the Early Modern Era.

Bibliography. – This handbook only offers a limited treatment of the law of persons. We mainly describe the law of persons of Antiquity, but also include signposts that point the reader towards the *ius commune*. The classic vision can be found in M. Kaser, *Das römische Privatrecht*, Munich 1971-1975. J. F. Gardner, *Family and familia in Roman Law and Life*, Oxford 1998 is a fascinating book about the *familia* in Antiquity, written by a Latin scholar who intuits the difference between the Roman *familia* and the modern family when she reads old texts. A broad classical analysis of the Roman law of persons and family law is provided by P. Bonfante, *Corso di diritto romano*, I, *Diritto di famiglia*, Milan 1963. With regard to the Middle Ages and the Early Modern Period, there are excellent works on the law of persons which are oriented towards one specific nation but also offer access to the *ius commune*. On the Southern Netherlands, see Ph. Godding, *Le droit privé dans les Pays-Bas méridionaux du 12e au 18e siècle*, Brussels 1987. With regard to France, A. Lefebvre-Teillard, *Introduction historique au droit des personnes et de la famille*, Paris [1996] sketches the history of personal status, marriage, descent and the protection of minors from Rome to 1804. Her book contains the best classic view of the history of the law of persons and family law and includes the interweaving of person, marriage and family. An instructive work on the medieval and early modern English law of persons is Sir J. Baker, *Baker and Milson's Sources of English legal history*, Oxford 2010.

§1. The *paterfamilias*, the main actor in the court

1. *Familia* and *paterfamilias*

In Latin, the word *pater* has three adjectives: *paternus, patricius* and *patrius*. The first refers to paternity, the second to the founders of Rome (*patres conscripti, patres maioresque*), and the third to houses and inheritances. The latter adjective was used in *patria potestas*, a Roman soldier's right to form a family.

Roman warriors had always attempted to invoke their civil privileges in the military courts for the benefit of their close circle. There was no reason why a *ciuis* would refrain from using his civil rights to act for his wife, son or servant. This custom of invoking civil rights for housemates and third parties was at the basis of the *familia*. It was already a common practice at the time of the Twelve Tables. The *familia* became a structure of liability for housemates (*famuli*). Each *ciuis* could act for others, in his capacity as *paterfamilias*. He acted as defendant and plaintiff for his *familia* in civil courts and could invoke civil rights for all of the members of his *familia*. He was, however, also liable towards other *ciues* for the actions of the members of his *familia*. Claims that he made for the benefit of his *familia* were treated as if they were his own claims; if he lost a lawsuit, he was personally liable. From the court's point of view, this liability involved a pledge not only of the *paterfamilias*' own property, but also of the property of his family members. The civil court saw the *familia* as a community of property. This explains how the *familia* became a community of both persons and property from the point of view of the court. Even if a *ciuis* had not taken any other people under his wing, he was still a *paterfamilias* – of a *familia* that consisted exclusively of his property.

Familia was a typical matter of civil law. In the *ius gentium* the term for a man who defended his interests in court was *dominus*. The term *dominium* was used instead of *familia*. In 212 AD the civil law was extended so that it applied to all free people. Henceforth, the terms *paterfamilias* and *dominus* were used interchangeably and *dominium* indicated the status of the *paterfamilias*.

In the classical law, the institution was developed fully. A person became a *paterfamilias* when he received civil rights. Those who were born within a *matrimonium* were born into a *familia* and could not act in the civil courts themselves; their *paterfamilias* acted for them. This *paterfamilias* was *sui iuris*, which meant that he acted independently for himself and his *familia*. Free persons who had a *paterfamilias* were *alieni iuris*: someone else was liable for them. There was no age limit that determined how long someone could remain within the *familia*. Members only left their *familia* when they were emancipated, when they died or when their *paterfamilias* died. From Hadrian's day onwards, children obtained the status of freedom at birth if their mother was not a slave. Free children who did not become members of a *familia* at birth became *sui iuris*, which meant that there were *patresfamilias* who were only a day old. Everyone who was *sui iuris* had a *familia* (Ulpian in D. 50.16.195).

The *paterfamilias* was liable for others and could therefore limit the freedom of action of his family members. This control that the *paterfamilias* had over his *familia* was called *patria potestas* in Latin. It can be translated as competence, but for centuries this term was read as 'paternal power', because the old notion of *patria potestas* was confused with the medieval feudal power that *domini* had over property and people.

The first rule of *patria potestas* was that the *paterfamilias* was free to put together his *familia*. He decided autonomously who was admitted into it and who was removed from it, and could also transfer people to other *familiae*.

When we discuss Antiquity, we write *familia* in Latin in order to avoid confusion with the medieval notion of family. The *familia* was a structure of liability and can therefore also be translated as 'undertaking'. It was not created by marriage and kinship, but based on assets and liability, and was characterised by a *paterfamilias* who served as the central figure and other people who joined and left the structure. In Latin, the word is also used to indicate a commercial undertaking. In the sources, we find *familia stationis, familia aquarum, familia gladiatoria, familia monetalis, familia thermensis, familia mansionis, familia publicanorum, familia uectigalis,* etcetera.

2. The *familia* of a woman

One would be hard put to find gender discrimination in the law of Antiquity. Egyptologists are struck by the fact that in Pharaonic Egypt men and women had equal rights in everyday life. In principle, this was also the case in Roman law. The status of a male slave was equal to that of a female slave. In D. 50.16.1 the first rule of interpretation states that in legal texts *si quis* also means *si qua* (cf. Gaius 1.72). In the old civil law, however, there was a large difference between men and women: civil rights were means to motivate warriors, and women did not fight.

Women were nevertheless granted access to the civil courts in an early stage. According to the oldest civil inheritance law, the death of a *ciuis* resulted in the devolution of the estate to his wife, sons and daughters if they were members of his *familia* at the time. Women could therefore inherit property within the civil law. One would expect that women had to go to a non-civil court, in the world of the *ius sacrum* for example, but when it came to inheritances they could lodge civil claims. According to the Twelve Tables, agnates acted for them in such cases. Women and children were not military personnel and were therefore given a *tutor*, a supervisor, in the civil courts. A *paterfamilias* could appoint such a *tutor* in his will, but if he did not, the praetor ensured that there was one. Men who served as the *tutor* of children in the civil court were liable. This *tutela* over children was the basis for the later development of guardianship (see below). Gaius wrote that women also had such a *tutor* in the civil court, but that this supervisor was never liable. He was merely a remnant of the old forms of proceeding. If a woman appeared without a *tutor*, the praetor appointed a bystander, but this was purely a formality. However, because this man was also known as a *tutor*, many Romanists insist that Roman women were 'under guardianship'. This is nonsense: she was invoking her own civil inheritance rights. It seems that in the late Republic women were not only civil heirs, but could also make use of all civil procedures to administer their property.

In the imperial law, the presence of women in civil courts was entirely unproblematic. Once civil law had been demilitarised, there was no longer any reason to reserve civil rights for men. A woman who was at the head of a *familia* was called a *domina*. The term *materfamilias* only rarely referred to the head of a *familia* (it is used in this sense in, for example, C. 1.48.1; C. 6.61.5*pr.*). In the second century AD most women had their own *familia* and were not members of the *familia* in which their husband lived. Relationships between men and women can be complex, but there is no need to construct far-fetched theories about the Romans, for whom *familia* had nothing to do with cohabitation or children, and everything with assets and liability. If a woman did live within her husband's *familia* and desired to be emancipated, she became the head of her own *familia* after the emancipation. Even a man and woman who enjoyed a harmonious relationship were usually part of a different *familia*. One rule pertaining to women was preserved: they were alone in their *familia*. Children normally ended up in their father's *familia* and not in their mother's. In the post-classical era, women did have slaves in their *familia*.

Bibliography. – This *tutela* for women in the republican law is mentioned in Gaius 1.150-154, 157 and 190-191. In the latter passage, Gaius writes that this was legal history. When consulting Gaius 1.190-191, the reader can experience how frustrating second-century Latin is. The lack of both context and a frame of reference make this Latin incredibly hard to understand. What was the *auctoritas* of a citizen who had formally taken over a woman's claim? Certainly not a male privilege, as many translators suggest. It is more likely to be a reference to the origin or point of departure of this civil claim. In Latin, *auctoritas* refers to origin and authorship. On *tutela* for women, see L. WAELKENS, 'Tutela mulierum herbekeken', in: M. DECALUWé, V. LAMBERT and D. HEIRBAUT (eds.), *Inter amicos, Liber amicorum Monique Van Melkebeek*. Brussels 2011, p. 295-304. The most important text that shows that women had their own *familia* in imperial law is D. 50.16.195.5: *Mulier autem familiae suae et caput et finis est.* Translation: 'A woman is both the head and end of her *familia*'. The possessive pronoun *suus* refers to the subject of the sentence, which means that this sentence is about the woman's own *familia*. J. F. GARDNER, *Family and familia in Roman Law and Life*, Oxford 1998 is surprised that jurists do not notice that most women were not part of their husband's *familia* in the Empire. Despite her brilliant insights, she is too modest to write that the Romanists are wrong in this respect.

3. Could a *paterfamilias* kill the members of his *familia*?

This question sounds absolutely insane. Nevertheless, it is mentioned in the scholarship of Roman law when the expression *potestas uitae necisque* is discussed. Some Romanists maintain that the Roman *paterfamilias* was almighty and administered sovereign justice over the members of his *familia*. 'He had the power of life and death over his housemates', 'If his wife had drunk wine, he could organise a court session (in German 'ein Hausgericht') with his kin and sentence her to death'. An Italian Romanist linked the latter idea with the Roman custom of greeting female relatives with a kiss and suggested that they did this to check whether they had been drinking. Another tall tale that crops up regularly is that the *paterfamilias* could freely have intercourse with his slave-girls. These, however, are the fantasies of anthropologists and Romanists who have spent too much time studying in their attics. The Digest explicitly states that a sexual relationship without *nuptiae* or *concubinatus* is punishable as *stuprum* (indecent assault, D. 25.7.5). The issue of the possibility to organise a 'Hausgericht' is somewhat more complicated.

The Decrees of the Kings mention the case of a man who found his wife while she was committing adultery and beat her to death, as well as a case of a man who beat his drunken wife to death. Both men were excused because of the circumstances in which they had killed their wife, but this does not mean that the killing of a family member

was permitted! Livy provides three examples of fathers who killed their sons and were praised by the people, but all three of these were exceptional cases that occurred in revolutionary times. No one saw them as a legal precedent. The nineteenth-century Romanists, however, were influenced by two additional elements, namely the fact that the words *potestas uitae necisque* cropped up in works of Gaius' and some classical authors, and the fact that 'Hausgericht' was not uncommon in nineteenth-century Germany.

Gaius wrote that slaves' lives had to be respected, but in 1.52 he mentioned the *potestas uitae necisque* which he thought existed in earlier times with regard to slaves. He added to this that all the earnings of slaves fell to the *familia* of their *paterfamilias*. The meaning of *uitae necisque* is probably connected to this. In Latin, the word *uita* is not an imperfect form like 'to live', but a perfect one that is derived from *uiuere*. It indicates the past and past experiences: everything that slaves had lived and experienced was the property of the *familia*. There is no doubt that the word *necis* refers to the dead, but it is not unlikely that *uitae necisque* was the product of folk etymology of *uitae nexique*. *Nexum* also pertains to the earning of a member of the *familia* (see below).

A *paterfamilias* could certainly not kill the members of his *familia*. *Familia* and the death penalty pertained to different bodies of law. The *familia* was a category of the civil law, in which the death penalty did not exist. Death penalties were the province of the aediles, whose law, in turn, did not contain the notion of the *paterfamilias*. In criminal law, free people could file an appeal against their death sentence with the Senate (*prouocatio ad populum*). The *lex poetilia* of 326 BC protected Romans from private violence. In 1.53 Gaius wrote that the person who used violence against his own slaves was prosecuted. Constantine punished all excessive disciplinary measures against slaves (CTh. 4.8.6*pr.*; C. 8.16.10). The same thing can be read in *Collatio* 3.3 and D. 1.6.2. Whoever killed a slave was prosecuted for murder (CTh. 9.12.1; C. 9.14.1).

Where, then, does this myth come from? Mommsen wrote about the *ius uitae necisque*. Around 1830 there were still thousands of lords in Saxony who had acquired the highest jurisdiction (which included legal power of life and death) through the inheritance of feudal rights. During the revolution of 1830, one of the demands was the abolition of these feudal rights. The parliament of Dresden decided to expropriate these feudal laws, but this was a slow and expensive process. At the time of the revolution of 1848 there were still more than one thousand private fiefs with jurisdiction. This situation was denounced by the law faculty of Leipzig, where the young liberal Theodor Mommsen, who had just been appointed, was shocked by the continued existence of private justice which he – unjustly – described as a remnant of Roman law. However, what the young Mommsen from Leipzig wrote was later read with the same reverence as the pieces that were written by the old, wise Mommsen from Berlin...

Myths and dreams. – And what about the famous stories about the ill-treatment of slaves, such as the story about Vedius Pollio who threw his slaves to the morays? Such stories are more successful than the Roman law, but must be taken with a pinch of salt. In SENECA, *De ira* 3.40 we read: *Cum cenaret diuus Augustus apud Vedium Pollionem, fregerat unus ex seruis eius crystallinum. Rapi eum Vedius iussit ne uulgari quidem more periturum, murenis obici iubebatur quas ingentes in piscine continebat. Quis non hoc illum putaret luxuriae causa facere? Saeuitia erat. Euasit e manibus puer et confugit ad Caesaris pedes nihil aliud petiturus quam ut aliter periret, ne esca fieret. Motus est nouitate crudelitatis Caesar et illum quidem mitti, crystallina*

autem omnia coram se frangi iussit complerique piscinam. During a banquet in Augustus' honour that was held at Vedius Pollio's house, a young slave broke a crystal platter. Vedius Pollio gave the order to throw the boy into the pond as prey for the morays. The boy sought protection with Augustus, who had Vedius Pollio's tableware broken and the pond filled. The same story can also be found in DIO CASSIUS 42.23, who adds that the emperor asked whether he would now also be fed to the morays. In SENECA, *De clementia* 1.18.2 the story is generalised, as if Vedius Pollio punished every slave who did not behave according to his liking in this manner: *Quis non Vedium Pollionem peius oderat quam serui sui, quod murenas sanguine humano saginabat et eos qui se aliquid offenderant, in uiuarium (quid aliud quam serpentium) abici iubebat.* This version was then adopted again, for instance in PLINY THE ELDER, *Historia naturalis* 9.39. As it is a more spectacular story than the first one, it seduces more people.

Bibliography. – For hypotheses and texts about *uitae necisue potestas*, see R. YARON, 'Vitae necisque potestas', *The Legal History Review* 30 (1962), p. 243-251.

4. Losing *patria potestas*

A *paterfamilias* could lose his status. If a Roman citizen lost his *status libertatis* because he had been taken prisoner of war, because of a criminal conviction to forced labour or because a civil court had sentenced him to slavery on account of insolvency, he underwent a *capitis diminutio maxima* and lost all of his civil rights. He could no longer appear before the civil judge and his *familia* devolved as if he had died. If he regained his status as a free man later, he enjoyed the *ius postliminii*, a complete re-establishment of his rights to the extent possible. His *familia* was also reassembled to the extent possible.

A *paterfamilias* also lost his status when two *familia* merged (*adrogatio*). One family was absorbed by another and the *paterfamilias* of the disappearing *familia* lost his *patria potestas*, but without losing his status of freedom. He became a member of the new *familia* and had inheritance rights. This was a *capitis diminutio minima.*

A third formula, the *capitis diminutio media,* was an intermediate form. The praetor could also revoke someone's rights partially when he executed his judgement. This happened in case of *infamia* or if a debtor was placed within the family of his creditor as a *nexus* (see below). The *nexus* retained his status of freedom, but could no longer act in court himself and was forced to temporarily become a member of a different *familia.* The difference with the minimal *capitis diminutio* was that *infamia* was a judgement and that the judge could revoke more or less civil rights. In the imperial law, this judgement was invested with government authority. The judge could already pronounce the punishment of *infamia* in his first judgement and did not have to wait until the execution.

5. The medieval family

This Roman *familia,* the community of persons and property that was led by a *dominus* who could use the shared property and was solely liable, also existed in the Middle Ages. In the early Middle Ages, people who did not want to fight became serfs: they put themselves in the service of a free warrior and contributed their property, which was pooled with that of the warrior. The warrior defended his serfs as a Roman *paterfamilias.* Families after the Roman example which could be put together at will could still be found in Austria, Switzerland, France, Italy, Hannover, Bremen... in the eleventh and twelfth centuries. In Southern France, there were 'confrèrements' in which several households merged into a *familia* after the Roman model, with one liable *paterfamilias* and a community of people and property.

Bibliography. – Examples of families after the model of Roman law in France: F. POUDRET, 'Vie communautaire et separation, Confrontation de la pratique médiévale et du droit savant', *Revue historique de droit français et étranger* 74 (1996), p. 199-220. For Germany, see L. KUCHENBUCH, 'Abschied von der Grundherrschaft, Ein Prüfgang durch das ostfränkisch-deutsche Reich', *Zeitschrift der Savigny-Stiftung, Germanistische Abteilung* 121 (2004), p. 1-99 (and our remarks on this study in *Revue historique de droit français et étranger* 84 (2006), p. 135).

The clearest cases of the continued existence of the *familia* according to Roman law can be found in canon law. Until the Modern Era, the pope and his bishops each lived in a *familia* according to Roman law, the *familia papalis* and the *familia episcopalis*, respectively. The pope or bishop and his immediate entourage – the curia in case of the pope and the canons in case of a bishop – lived together within a structure characterised by shared property for which only the pope or bishop were liable. All of the ecclesiastical property of the bishopric was part of the *familia*; the expenses and revenues of the members of the *familia* became part of the papal or episcopal property. This *familia* according to canon law was acknowledged by the monarchs on the grounds of the division of jurisdiction after the Concordat of Worms.

In the civil law of the Middle Ages, religious brotherhoods were also *familiae* according to Roman law, with community of property and an elected *paterfamilias*. In the course of the thirteenth century these confraternities were given the status of colleges (see below), so that they could survive the death of their *paterfamilias*.

Apart from these special cases of the continued use of the Roman *familia*, an entirely new family was developed for private people in canon law from the fifth century onwards. The church fathers and bishops read in the Bible that if a man and woman moved in together, they had to leave their respective parental homes and establish a new household. The Bible described the traditional 'kidushin'. In the Latin world, this house was associated with the *familia*. Couples who lived together had to remove themselves from their *familiae* and establish a new one. The innovation, in other words, was a double one: (1) the couple's cohabitation resulted in their tacit emancipation from their *familiae* and (2) from then on they shared a new *familia*. The Roman formula of a couple with two *familiae* became impossible in this context. The oldest case-law in which one can find this formula is the *lex romana burgundionum* of the end of the fifth century. The new family was established without the intervention of the *patresfamilias*; the emancipation was tacit. This new type of family then slowly began to conquer Europe. In the south it becomes common in the sixth century, but it can only be found in Bremen in the tenth century, more precisely under archbishop Adaldag, whose administration of justice exerted a large influence on the Christianisation of Denmark. It seems that the new family was well-established by the twelfth century. Throughout Europe, the collections of case-law of that period mention families that were led by a man and a woman whose property was joint. One half of this property fell to the shared children of the couple when one partner died; the other half remained with the surviving partner. Here, we see the canonical notion of family in which both partners are independent, have equal rights and joint property. This community of property was the canonical version of Roman family law. It was not a *paterfamilias* who lived in a community of property with his family members, but a couple and their children. The major difference was that the familial community was established by operation of law.

The old Roman texts about *familia* were read in the medieval universities. Both the canonists and the civil lawyers thought of the new family according to canon law when they read the word *familia*. In the meantime, civil law had once again become men's law, characterised by privileges for warriors. None of the civil lawyers and canonists remembered the Roman *familia* that belonged to a woman. D. 50.16.195.5 cannot be found in any of the medieval handbooks.

In the twelfth century, the notion of marriage was developed in canon law (see below) and the new family became linked with this marriage rather than with cohabitation. When the canonists and civil lawyers then connected *patria potestas* with marriage law in the twelfth and thirteenth centuries, the husband was given the role of *paterfamilias*. He was the one who adminstered the property. Hostiensis, for example, wrote that the husband received the wife's dowry. This meant that the dowry was no longer administered by the *paterfamilias* of the husband's *familia*. A husband represented his wife in court without a mandate and in some regions he could even be prosecuted for his wife's actions. The competences that Roman *patresfamilias* could use to avoid liability suddenly became means of exercising authority in a personal relationship.

The notion of family developed in medieval Roman law did not dovetail with the tradition of most of the Western aldermen's courts. These were used to working with the canonical family that was established through cohabitation. In the thirteenth century, the community of property with similar rights of administration for men and women came into conflict with the academic interpretation of the Justinianic texts. In the fourteenth century the universities began to gain the upper hand. Married women lost their legal capacity and could only bind the family with regard to her 'household mandate' – which meant that they could make all daily purchases for their family. This is a far cry from the Roman *familia*. In the work of Jean Masuer, a fourteenth-century jurist from Riom, we read for the first time that the family is the natural cell of society. It was formed by marriage and nature, and the *paterfamilias* could not change anything about this. For this reason, Masuer refused to accept adoption. In his work we already encounter the notion of family that would be used by most of the sovereign councils of the sixteenth century.

Bibliography. – J. JORDA FERNANDEZ, 'Pàtria potestat i emancipació per caus de matrimoni, Del dret romà a la seva concreció als Costums de Tortosa I als Furs de València', *Rivista de dret historic català* 1 (2001), p. 93-124; W. BARKHAUSEN, 'Erzbischof Adaldag und König Harald Gormsson, Über das bremische eheliche Güter- und Erbrecht und seine Beziehungen zu den dänischen Landschaftsrechten', *Zeitschrift der Savigny-Stiftung, Germanistische Abteilung* 111 (1994), p. 363-401. The abovementioned book of JEAN MASUER is *La pratique judiciaire tant civile que criminelle, recue et observée par tout le Royaume de France*. Since the sixteenth century, several printed editions of this text have been published. For the twelfth-century collections of case-law, consult the series of E.M. MEIJERS, *Le droit ligurien de succession en Europe occidentale*, Haarlem 1928-1967.

§2. Family members

The Roman *familia* was a community of persons and property. The *paterfamilias* was free to compose his *familia* and to transfer property and people to another *familia*. This freedom was part of his *libertas*. This paragraphs deals with persons; property will be treated further on in this book.

Because the *familia* was a structure of liability, it was important that people – and certainly creditors – knew to which *familia* a person belonged. The transfer of a person from one *familia* to another was therefore a public event. On market days there was an official scaleholder on the *forum*, before whom one could execute a *mancipatio*. In the presence of five witnesses, a *paterfamilias* claimed that a specific person belonged to his family. If the old *paterfamilias* of that person was present and did not react, the person was transferred. The transfer was settled by tapping a coin against the scales. We will treat different kinds of 'mancipatory acts' below. No one could be admitted into another *familia* without a public transfer. A *paterfamilias* who kicked someone out of his family in an informal way still had to cover this person's debts.

The *familia* was the point of departure for liability, for paid and outstanding debts, and for assets and liabilities. Data pertaining to these issues have been registered for centuries. Consequently, the history of accountancy can help us here. By means of old accounting documents, one can discover who credited and debited which accounts, when they did so and in which manner this happened. An analysis of these documents can teach us much about the history of the law of obligations, but also about the Roman *familia*. In Roman account books, one can see the interaction between the members of a *familia* as well as the position given to assets and liabilities. A Roman *paterfamilias* used double-entry bookkeeping: he kept a diary (*codex expensi et accepti*) in which he wrote down all of the family's credits and debits vis-à-vis the outside world, and an account book (*codex rationum*) in which each family member had an account. In Roman accounting, the *paterfamilias* is the subject of the verbs *debet* and *credit*. He was the only person who was entitled, as well as the only person who was liable. He debited and credited for all of the members of the *familia*. What he received from the outside world according to the diary (*credit*) was owed to a family member in the account book (*debet*). What he paid to the outside world (*debet*) was withdrawn from the account of a family member (*credit*) in the account book. This does not mean that every Roman was an accountant. Most Romans had a banker who was responsible for their accounts. Those who did not keep accounts could not enjoy limited liability (see below) and faced more difficulties in case of liquidation and division.

We have no private account books from the early Middle Ages. In this period, such account books were not necessary, since a medieval *familia* consisted of one household.

Bibliography. – On Roman accounting, see L. WAELKENS, 'Gaius IV,73: debet ou debetur?', *The Legal History Review* 68 (2000), p. 347-356, with bibliography. A typical characteristic of Roman accounting is that obligations are also registered as cash entries. This seems unlikely to Latinists, but was highly convenient for cashiers, who could immediately see the debits and could easily calculate the balance of an account. Double-entry bookkeeping is often – and persistently – believed to be an Italian invention introduced by LUCA PACIOLI (1445-1517), *Summa de arithmetica, geometria, proportioni et proportionalita*, Florence 1494. Double-entry bookkeeping can, however, also be found in some of the twelfth- and thirteenth-century account books in the archives of Genoa and Venice. These are the books of firms which did business with Constantinople and used double-entry bookkeeping so that they could invoke the limited liability of their agents in the East. In 1494, Pacioli provided an overview of the arithmetic of Constantinople which covered algebra, Euclidian geometry, probability calculus and, at the end of the book, bookkeeping. It is a typical Renaissance work that summarises knowledge from Constantinople.

1. The *paterfamilias*

The Roman *paterfamilias* had his own account in the account book and was himself a family member. A *familia* without a *paterfamilias* was possible if the *familia* was not liquidated after his death and the members kept the *familia* undivided (*ercto non cito*). Earnings and expenditures fictitiously fell to the deceased until the liquidation and division took place. This was a very unstable situation. The Twelve Tables already determined that every heir could demand the division and liquidation of the *familia* by means of the *actio familiae erciscundae*. The creditors of an undivided estate could address any member of the *familia* and ask payment. If the person who was addressed could not recover the costs from another member, he had to request the liquidation of the *familia*. New creditors of an undivided *familia* addressed the person with whom they had done business. The latter could then recover the costs from the members of his *familia*. If this was to no avail, he could ask the division of the *familia* by means of the *actio familia erciscundae* – or by means of the *actio communi diuidundo* if there were no more traces of the old *familia* and it was mainly accessions of the community that had to be divided. In the Middle Ages, this regulation continued to apply to *familiae* after the Roman model. Papal and episcopal *familiae*, however, could not be divided. The successor had the right to revindicate the *familia*. In the new family developed in canon law, undividedness was an extended community of property between spouses; division was a matter of marital property law.

2. Wives

A steady relationship with a *paterfamilias* or male family member did not necessarily mean that a woman became a member of her partner's *familia*. There were three possibilities: she could have her own *familia*, stay in her old *familia* or transfer to that of her husband. When the woman transferred to her husband's family on the occasion of the wedding (*nuptiae*), the necessary mancipatory act was the *coemptio*. This act made her a family member, but not necessarily an heir. She was only given the status of an heir (*filiafamilias*) if her husband was the *paterfamilias*. If she entered the family by means of a simple *mancipatio*, her status was *in mancipio*: even if her husband became *paterfamilias*, she would never acquire the status of *filiafamilias*. If she was independent and was transferred to her husband's family, an *adrogatio* was required, a fusion of her own *familia* and that of her husband. She immediately acquired the status of heir of the *paterfamilias* of her husband's *familia*. In the Republic, patricians could make use of the old and rare procedure of the *confarreatio*, which took place before the *pontifex maximus* and ten witnesses in the temple of the Capitoline Hill. It took the form of a short play during which spelt bread was offered. In case of a *confarreatio*, the wife always transferred to the *familia* of her husband. Her children became eligible for magistrate's offices that could only be held by patricians. In case of lack of clarity, a woman could become part of her husband's *familia* through prescription. If a couple lived hand in hand for a year (*in manu*) the *paterfamilias* of her husband's *familia* was presumed to cover her debts. An absence of three nights sufficed to prevent prescription and to maintain the presumption that the woman did not depend on her husband's *familia* with regard to financial matters (*ius trinoctium abesse*).

A wife could leave the *familia* in different ways. This did not have anything to do with marital problems, but with money and liability. The woman's original *paterfamilias* could call her back to his *familia* by means of a *remancipatio* that was symmetrical with the first *mancipatio*. A *confarreatio* could be undone by means of a *diffareatio*. An *emancipatio* was needed if the woman desired to become independent: an intermediary person admitted her into his *familia* as a free person *in mancipatio* and then immediately broke that bond by means of a *manumissio* (see below). An emancipated woman had her own *familia*. If a woman moved out because she had entered into a new relationship, she did not leave the *familia*. The same person continued to cover her debts. As far as third parties were concerned, only a mancipatory act removed a person from his or her *familia*.

Some scholars are shocked by the fact that a wife became a *filiafamilias* in Roman law. They think that this meant that she acquired the status of a daughter of her husband... This, however, is incorrect: if she was a *filiafamilias*, she was not her husband's daughter but a *filiafamilias* of her *paterfamilias* – even if this *paterfamilias* was her husband. *Filiafamilias* did not mean daughter, but heiress. Dutch-language handbooks often mentioned that in Rome women came under the 'marital power' of their husbands, but it is not clear what this means.

In the Christian family of the early Middle Ages, the wife was not a family member. Both spouses were titularies of a shared family. This meant that if one of them died, the surviving spouse was not an heir. If the community of property was liquidated, other rules concerning the property of cohabiting people played a role. In the twelfth-century universities both the civilian jurists and the canonists projected the situation of the old Roman *familia* onto the Christian family. For these jurists, the husband was a *paterfamilias*, while his wife was a family member. In many regions, this view came into conflict with the customary case-law concerning nuptial agreements. In the sixteenth century the vision of the law faculties was generalised in the royal councils on the Continent. The canonical marriage and the Christian family were incorporated into the royal order when it adopted the jurisdiction of the ecclesiastical courts. The combination of the canonical notion of family, the medieval vision of the Roman family and Roman inheritance law resulted in a strange mixture. In private law, as well as in the civil law codes and civil society, the woman was emancipated from her old family by means of her marriage. She became a family member of her husband, but not his heir.

3. Descendants

'Descent' was not a category of Roman family law, because descent was not a central element of the *familia*. There was no word for 'children' to indicate what the English still call kin. In Gaius and in classical literature we find the term *liberi* to denote children vis-à-vis their parents, but this does not express a position within the *familia*. The word mainly emphasised that these children had the status of freedom. This can be seen in Gaius 1.82 and 86. *Liberi naturales* were a person's own, biological children. The sources also mention *liberi* who were not family members. In D. 50.16.220 further descendants are also called *liberi*. The Latin word *pueri* is never used in a legal context. The *lex romana burgundionum*, 37, uses the word *naturales* for a person's own children. The Twelve Tables and Gaius mention agnates, people who were related through birth. Agnates were a kind of patriarchal relatives (Gaius 1.156-157), but outside of the *familia*. Agnatic relations played a role in inheritance law and guardianship, but not in family law. *Filius* is not a position within the *familia* either: see for example Gaius 1.66 and following, although we can read about the *iustus filius* in 1.77. This word derives from **feuere* and it means 'born unto'. *Filius* was not a familial status; *filiusfamilias* was. The latter status was that of (1) the children of the *paterfamilias* who were members of the *familia* and (2) his wife if she was a member of his *familia*. These persons became independent when the *paterfamilias* died. According to this criterion the children of a predeceased son could also be *filiifamilias*. D. 50.16.220.3 states that *filii* can be grandchildren, but this text is not about *filiusfamilias*. The children of *filiaefamilias* (daughters) were members of the *familia* of their father or were independent.

One could, in other words, become a member of a *familia* through birth. This was the only way of entering a family without a formal legal act. Children ended up in the *familia* of their father, not in that of their mother. However, not all children became members of a *familia*. In order to be admitted into a *familia* at birth, they had to be (1) *liber naturalis*, a freeborn child. From 168 BC onwards, the status of the children was determined by that of the father; from Hadrian onwards their status depended on that of the mother. Freeborn also meant 'born alive': a Roman child had rights from the moment it was conceived, but only acquired them through birth. A stillborn child did not have a status in the *familia*. (2) The mother had to be joined to the father by means of *nuptiae*, the wedding which made a relation public. *Filiifamilias* were conceived after *nuptiae*: they were born no earlier than seven months after *nuptiae* and no later than ten months after the dissolution of the relationship. (3) According to D. 25.3 the child had to be recognised by the father (and not by the *paterfamilias*). If the father refused to recognise the child or was absent, the mother could have the statute of the child established in a prejudgement pronounced by the praetor or the *cognitio* judge. This prejudgement granted *possessio status*, a provisional measure that applied *erga omnes*. A father who was not given the chance to recognise his child could have his paternity established in a prejudgement and appoint a *curator ad uentrem*, who defended the familial interests of the child. Children who did not have the status of *filiusfamilias* were *spurii* or *uulgo quaesiti*. They were independent. If they became *ciuis* at birth they became *paterfamilias* or *domina* from the first day of their life onwards and had inheritance rights to their mother's property. They were blood relatives of their mother, but not of their father. If they were *nothus* – unacknowledged children of a known father – these children were not blood relatives of their father according to the law of inheritance, but their factual situation did lead to impedements to cohabitation with their father's relatives.

The notion that *liberi naturales* only had limited rights because they were extramarital 'biological' children dates from the eighth century. The earliest instance of this notion can be found in epitomes on Alaric's *Breviarium*.

The status of *filiusfamilias* was lost when a person was mancipated to a different *familia*, in which the mancipated person was *in mancipio*. A person also lost his status as *filiusfamilias* when he was emancipated. Just as emancipated wives, an emancipated man became independent. Women were transferred to an intermediary by the *paterfamilias*. The intermediary then released her through a *manumissio uindicta* before the praetor. Men were mancipated to the supernumerary three times and mancipated back to their original *familia* twice, where they were *in mancipio*. If a *paterfamilias* mancipated a man three times, this man became independent by operation of law (Twelve Tables 4.3). This meant that the intermediary did not have to release the man when he was transferred to him a third time. Thus, they avoided establishing the legal relation of *patronus*, which had legal consequences for men. The procedure for the mancipation of men was a bit longer, because men could take other people with them to the new *familia*, something which also had to happen in public. From Trajan onwards, an emancipation could be enforced by means of *cognitio* proceedings (D. 37.12.5). The emperor Anastasius allowed the *paterfamilias* to demand such a legal emancipation (C. 8.48.5). Justinian required the agreement of the emancipated person before a public official (C. 8.48.6). This imperial form of emancipation continued to be used in the Middle Ages. When imperial jurisdiction had been delegated to local judges, emancipation became a voluntary procedure in most regions. It took place before the aldermen, who established that both the father and the son agreed to the emancipation. In the Early Modern Era, which was characterised by royal administration, the procedural requirements of C. 8.48.5-6 were reintroduced: emancipations took place before a public official who represented the monarch.

Could a child be transferred to a different family in return for payment? This was a controversial issue. Diocletian forbade the sale of children (C. 4.43.1). Under Constantine, we find a case in which such a sale was tolerated because of poverty, but the *paterfamilias* could always ask for the child to be returned and everyone had the right to buy off or replace the child with a person *in mancipio* (c. 4.43.2). Theodosius I and Valentinian III opposed the sale of children. Justinian adopted Constantine's judgement in the Code. Giving new-borns away without receiving payment or abandoning them was never forbidden, but this resulted in the *paterfamilias* losing his connection with the foundling or the child that was given away (CTh. 5.9.1). The new *paterfamilias* chose to admit the child into his *familia* as either a free person or slave. From Justinian onwards, foundlings were always free (C. 1.4.24). The transfer of children in return for money was opposed by bishops, abandoning them was not.

Bibliography. – On the status of *filiifamilias* and *filii naturales* and the limiting of the rights of 'natural children', see L. WAELKENS, 'Dans quelles limites peut-on parler d'enfants naturels dans le droit romain de l'Antiquité?', *The Legal History Review* 80 (2012), p. 399-414.

4. *Legitimi*

The word *legitimus* means 'by operation of law'. In the Roman law of Antiquity, *legitimi* were not 'legitimate children', but 'heirs by operation of law'. In the Middle Ages, they would become legitimate children, who were always heirs.

In the Greek church fathers' works one finds descendants who are *nothus*. In Inst. 3.6.97 Quintilian writes: *nothum qui non sit legitimus Graeci uocant, latinum rei nomen non habemus*. A bad translation of this sentence is: 'The Greeks call those who are not legitimate bastards, but there is no word for this in Latin'. Note the eternal clash between cultures that always plays a role in translations: Quintilian calls these children *non legitimus* even though the notion of bastard was not used in Roman law.

In short, it was through birth that one became a *filiusfamilias* and acquired inheritance rights. In C. 5.27 the word *legitimi* was used for free biological children (*liberi naturales*) who became heirs by operation of law, according to new case-law of the prefecture. Consequently, the freeborn children of a woman were her *legitimi*, her heirs or successors by operation of law – this was the case even when she had never celebrated *nuptiae* or did not live within a marriage. If she celebrated *nuptiae* or lived within a marriage later, these children also became *legitimi* of her husband, but they were second in line after his *filiifamilias* and retained this status after the dissolution of the marriage. If the woman later had other children outside of *nuptiae* or marriage, they were once again her *legitimi* and no one else's. Under Justinian, the prefecture decided that a son who received a donation from his natural father with the additional assignment to become a *decurio* had to be considered an heir by operation of law. Nov. 74 contains another case: if a free mother could not live in *nuptiae* or *matrimonium* with her partner because of a legal rule, the judge could consider her child to be the father's heir by operation of law. If a person did not have any free descendants who were legal heirs, other descendants who lived in the same *familia* could be considered to be heirs by operation of law (C. 5.27.6).

In other words, the *legitimus* of 5.27 referred to the law of inheritance and the liquidation of the *familia*: the judge could make a *legitimus* an heir and successor. For centuries, however, this title was considered as a text that treated the 'legitimisation' of 'illegitimate' children. This interpretation dates back to twelfth-century canon law. It is at this time that the *legitimi* of C. 5.27 were promoted to the rank of family member. In the twelfth century, the ecclesiastical courts became competent if a case fell within the scope of marriage law. The ecclesiastical judges tried to interpret this jurisdiction as broadly as possible. According to their case-law, married people were not the only parties who could raise a matter with the ecclesiastical courts: their family members could also access the ecclesiastical courts. By operation of law, the children of a canonical marriage were admitted as well. They were therefore *legitimi*. In the twelfth century, being a *legitimus* did not lead to inheritance rights, but to access to the ecclesiastical court. In title C. 5.27 an entire series of people became *legitimi* through the circumstances in which they lived. This was called the *legitimatio*, which can be translated as 'legitimisation'. In canon law, legitimacy both meant legal membership of the family and access to the court.

Sometimes, it was hard to prove a couple's married state. What if there was proof that a child had been born prior to their marriage? Was such a child a *legitimus* as well? From C. 5.27, fragments 3, 5 and 10, the canonists distilled the rule that children born prior to marriage were legitimised by the subsequent marriage of their parents. X. 4.17.6 says: *Tanta est uis matrimonii ut qui antea sunt geniti, post contractum matrimonium legitimi habeantur*. Translation: 'The power of marriage is so strong that (children) who were born prior to it are also considered legitimate after the conclusion of the marriage.' Then, a controversy arose regarding interpretation: the canonists claimed that legitimation was only possible if the child had been conceived within a concubinage, while the civil lawyers adhered to a stricter interpretation of the Code and also accepted the legitimisation of a child born from an adulterous relationship. In the latter case, the canonists denied the possibility of legitimisation, but they did grant the child a claim to maintenance, with an *actio de partu agnoscendo* that was based on D. 25.3 but never existed in Antiquity.

In the sixteenth century the idea of legitimacy was adopted by the royal courts of law. In the seventeenth century, this idea dovetailed with the private law that became independent from the monarchs. In the *ius commune* of the Modern Era it was through birth within a marriage that one received the legitimacy that provided access to all civil rights. The situation of children who were born out of wedlock and the legitimation of children born from an adulterous relationship became important subjects of discussion in the legal doctrine. With regard to the legitimisation of children from an adulterous relationship, the parents' married state at the time of birth became the factor that decided the status of the child. In 1804, however, the compilers of the Code civil once again opted for the parent's married state at the time of conception as criterion: see art. 331.

In the nineteenth century legitimacy then underwent an evolution: legitimacy as private access to citizenship turned into legitimacy as access to the legal systems of the civil nations. In these nations, civil status was recorded meticulously, because it was this status that was the key to... legitimacy.

Bibliography. – L. WAELKENS, 'La légitimation de C. 5.27.5' in: B. D'ALTEROCHE, F. DEMOULIN-AUZARY, O. DESCAMPS and F. ROUMY (eds.), *Mélanges en l'honneur d'Anne Lefebvre-Teillard*, Paris 2009, p. 1031-1045. The text C. 5.27.5 is published supra, in the introductory chapter of this book.

5. Adoption

In the Roman law of Antiquity, adoption was a common procedure. People who did not descend from a *paterfamilias* received all the rights of a *filiusfamilias* when they were adopted. The legal act necessary for an adoption could be compared with an emancipation, as it also involved the transfer of the adoptee to an intermediary. However, the *manumissio* was replaced by an *in iure cessio* before the praetor or the judge: the adopting *paterfamilias* claimed the person and his old *paterfamilias* yielded. The transfer was a radical one: the bond with the old *familia* was gone and the adoptee was given the status of *filiusfamilias*. In Latin: *adoptio imitatur naturam*, 'adoption imitates birth'. Even if there was no blood relationship, the adopted person had to abide by the prohibitions pertaining to incest.

During the late Empire, the case-law changed. An overview can be found in C. 8.47.10 and Inst. 1.11.2. Complete adoption was only possible if the adopter was an ascendant of the adoptee. If this was not the case, the adoptee would always have ties with his old *familia* – he would also inherit from his old *familia*. Adoption proceedings took place before an official, who simultaneously took the consensus of the adopted person into account. Medieval jurists called the two kinds of adoption that existed in the late Empire 'complete' and 'less complete adoption'.

Adoption was a problematic issue in the Middle Ages. There is, for example, a large amount of Lombardic case-law about what was called *thinx* in that region, while in

Franconia, the equivalent notion of *affatomia* was a much-disputed matter in case-law. Christians considered their admission into God's family through baptism to be a kind of adoption. As early as the sixth century, the relation between a godfather and his godchild was compared to an adoption. It led to a 'spiritual blood relation'. Many collections of canon law contain Roman texts about adoption. Gratian collected these in his *Decretum*. The canonists considered adoption to be a solution for the problems of many children. The admission of abandoned children was seen as adoption after the example of CTh. 5.9.1.

In the universities, adoption became a complex subject. The Roman *familia* had been replaced by the canonical family. Disrupting this family simply on the basis of the will of the *paterfamilias* was considered abnormal. And yet the canonists and civil lawyers attempted to integrate the Justinian legal concept of adoption into their family law. The identification of natural and adoptive descent led to the differentiation of consanguinity, legitimate and spiritual kinship. Legitimate kinship was nevertheless second-rate, just as 'natural' children were considered to be inferior to legitimate children. This depreciation was expressed in Latin as follows: *adoptio imitatur naturam*, 'adoptive descent imitates natural descent'. An adopted person received the adopter's status of freedom as well as inheritance rights, but retained his original civil status if that was better than that of the adopter. In the thirteenth century, we find the academic legal doctrine concerning adoption in the Italian cities, the fueros of Spain, and the case-law in the expanse from England to Poland. In addition, we find models for adoption in the thirteenth- and fourteenth-century formularies for notaries in Italy and Southern France, which shows that it was a common practice.

In several countries, a movement against adoption originated within feudal law. Adopted sons were excluded from feudal law. Lords could not organise their succession by means of adoption. In many regions, immovable property fell under feudal law, which meant that an adoptive child could not inherit any immovable property either. When feudalism was privatised, this mistrust of adoption continued to exist with regard to immovable property. The family was the fundamental building block of society and this block could not be formed by means of adoption. In the late Middle Ages and the Early Modern Era, adoption was limited. It came under the competence of 'higher justice'. Most of the sovereign courts deemed that a couple could no longer adopt if they had natural children. In many regions, adoption disappeared entirely. In the *ius commune* of the Modern Period Roman adoption continued to exist, but it only offered a solution for married couples who did not have children or whose children had predeceased them. Adoption then afforded them some security for their old age and the possibility of succession. The situation of adopted children was still compared to that of natural children, who only received complete inheritance rights if there were no other children. The jurists of the *ius commune* of the Early Modern Period still expressed the latter opinion with... *adoptio imitatur naturam*. In Western Europe adoption re-emerged in eighteenth-century private law. In civil society, the idea of citizens having the possibility to make decisions about the composition of their family surfaced again. In the Netherlands, adoption only made a reappearance in 1974.

Bibliography. – F. ROUMY, *L'adoption dans le droit savant du XIIe au XVIe siècle*, [Bibliothèque de droit privé 29,] Paris 1998.

6. *Adrogatio*

If it was not a family member but a *paterfamilias* who was adopted, the legal concept involved was *adrogatio*, by means of which both the *paterfamilias* and his entire *familia* were transferred to the adopter's *familia*. This means that *adrogatio* involved the merger of property. This was supervised by the administration. In the Republic, a vote in the *comitia curiata* was required. The Senate examined whether the *adrogatio* was in the interests of both parties. On this subject, see Aulus Gellius, *Noctes Atticae* 5.19. Scholars sometimes write that supervision was necessary because the disappearing *familia* had to renounce its household gods in a *detestatio sacrorum*, but these academics err. *Sacra* are not divine matters: the Roman people and the Senate decided what was *sacrum* (Gaius 2.5). The biggest problem with an *adrogatio* was that the debts of the absorbed family were no longer due. This is the reason why republican praetors already gave an *in integrum restitutio* to all of the debtors: they could bring proceedings as if the *adrogatio* had not taken place. Only men could be adrogated in the Republic. Diocletian changed the procedure. *Adrogatio* was requested from the administration and was granted by means of a rescript. Henceforth, women and freed people were adrogated as well (see C. 8.47.2.1 and 6-8). Thus an emancipated woman could reintegrate the *familia* of their husband. *Adrogatio* became pointless in medieval Roman law because of the changed conception of the family.

7. *Nexum*

Nexum was a mancipation in republican law by means of which a free person was placed in a *familia* in order to work there. The reason for a *nexum* could be a person's debts: if an insolvent debtor became a *nexus*, all of his earnings belonged to his new *familia*. When his debts had been paid, he changed families again through a *nexi liberatio*. The main characteristic of *nexum* was the special liability of the *paterfamilias* for obligations that were concluded by the *nexum*. If a debtor made claims pertaining to such an obligation, they had to take the form of an *actio noxalis*. The formula for the judge then read as follows: 'Sentence the *paterfamilias* of the *nexus*, unless he renounces the *nexus*'. The *paterfamilias* was then free to either pay or transfer the *nexus* to the debtor's *familia*. This option limited the liability of the *paterfamilias*. A *paterfamilias* who admitted an insolvent debtor as a *nexus* in debt bondage did this as a last resort to get his money back and thus enjoyed a relative certainty that he would not incur more costs because of the *nexus*. If the worst came to the worst, he could ask the praetor to convert the *nexum* into slavery.

However, *nexum* could also be a voluntary agreement, which was entered into in order to establish a business with limited liability. A person entered the *familia* in order to perform a task. A salary was paid to his original *familia*, or it was agreed that the *nexus* could leave the family after a specific period and would then receive a share of the profits. Debtors knew that they were dealing with a *nexus* and that the *paterfamilias* would renounce him if the project failed. Consequently, everyone became very careful. This is a characteristic consequence of limited liability, which was always favoured by jurists. Limited liability leads to an increase in the number of economic initiatives and careful cooperation during which everyone considers the risks that they run. *Nexum* is the oldest form of conducting business with limited liability that we know.

Bibliography. – L. WAELKENS, 'Nexum, de oudste vennootschap met beperkte aansprakelijkheid?', in: *Collatio Iuris Romani, Études dédiées à Hans Ankum à l'occasion de son 65e anniversaire*, published by R. FEENSTRA, A.S. HARTKAMP, J.E. SPRUIT, P.J. SIJPESTEIJN and L.C. WINKEL, Amsterdam 1995, p. 603-606; L. WAELKENS, 'Nexum et noxalité', in: H. JONES (ed.), *Le monde antique et les droits de l'homme, Actes de la 50e session de la Société internationale Fernand de Visscher pour l'Histoire des droits de l'Antiquité, Bruxelles 16-19 septembre 1996*, Brussels 1998, p. 89-94.

8. People *in mancipio*

A. Mancipium

In Antiquity, all of the other family members were *in mancipio*. They entered the *familia* through a simple *mancipatio* and could be mancipated to another *familia* or become independent through a *manumissio*. This category of people included foster-children (*alumni*), apprentices, clients for whom the *paterfamilias* acted in court and slaves. The *paterfamilias* was exclusively liable for them and their earnings belonged to the familial community of property. If another *familia* called them back before the court, they were claimed by means of a revindication. Any person *in mancipio* could be called back in such a manner; it is not true that only slaves were revindicated. Nevertheless, there is the myth that slaves were considered objects because they were revindicated and *res* = object. But what is a human object? The similarities between slaves and people *in mancipio* are significant, the only difference being that slaves did not have any rights to freedom. In short, *manumissio* did not indicate the freeing of slaves in Antiquity, but the emancipation of those who were *in mancipio*.

In Antiquity, peregrines did not have a *familia*. They could, however, have slaves. There must therefore have been a status equivalent to *in mancipio*. *Duplex dominium* in Gaius 1.54 is a reference to this status, but sadly enough the lack of context once again means that we cannot understand Gaius properly.

Were *coloni* family members *in mancipio*? Someone will have to work this out. They seem to have been free lessees who contracted with a *paterfamilias* to till his land. Many examples show that he paid their *tributum* (land charges) and *capitatio* (head taxes) or was liable for them. These elements suggest that they were family members. However, the status of *colonus* was often connected with the growing of corn for the *annona* and land owners had to concede advantages to them in order to profit from exemptions of taxation assigned by the prefecture of the *annona*. This is another matter that has not yet been fully researched.

B. Slavery

When interpreting texts about slavery, one should not be influenced by 'Uncle Tom's Cabin' – a book from nineteenth-century America. The Latin word *seruitus* is translated both as servility and servitude. In the Middle Ages, these two meanings began to diverge. Roman slavery cannot have been all that bad, because it was the civil status that was awarded to Romans who were taken prisoners of war. If a Roman decided not to perform his military service or left the army prematurely with the permission of the commanders, he was given the status of slave in the Republic. According to Gaius 1.140, a slave who entered the army won his freedom. Slaves could be powerful people. An imperial slave who was a tax collector could make honest artisans' or shopkeepers' lives a misery, but they had no choice but to put up with this. The fact that the bishops accepted slavery suggests that it was not a scandalous status. Moreover, slavery was a category of the civil law that did not exist in the criminal law. Criminal law did not protect citizens; it protected people. See for example the case-law mentioned in CTh. 4.8.6*pr.*; C. 8.46.10; CTh. 9.12.1; C. 9.14.1. There were slave rebellions at the end of the Republic, a time of general crisis. These indicated a social problem, not a problem pertaining to status. Too many prisoners of war had been brought to Italy and the hostility towards this surplus of costly slaves led to major disturbances, but did not cause legal problems.

Slaves did not have the *status libertatis*. They did not possess any civil rights, but did not have to fight either. If one draws up a list of all the differences between a slave and a free person, the result is an inventory of civil rights. However, slaves were not without rights. They were protected by the criminal law, in which civil categories did not play a role. They could also file complaints with the civil courts and ask to be transferred to a different *familia*. Finally, they could go to the army and acquire civil rights there. In the civil courts they could only bring one claim, the *uindicatio in libertatem* (claim to 'freedom'). When they did so, their civil status was assessed. In the Republic, this was probably a military *legisactio* procedure. It still existed in the Empire (see D. 40.12). During the proceedings, the slave was granted provisional freedom (D. 40.12.24*pr.*). The freedom of a slave could also be claimed by a third party, who was then an *assertor in libertatem*. Had it not been possible to assess a person's status as a slave in a court, slavery would not have been a legal status. A slave who lost such a vindication procedure was a real slave who had brought real civil proceedings. The reverse was possible as well: a *paterfamilias* could claim someone's servility by means of a *uindicatio in seruitutem*. Those who worked with slaves could not bring any other civil claims against them, but could have them appear in court. One could not summon them, but had to send a request to the court and ask for provisional measures. This can be read clearly in C. 3.1.6-7, as already mentioned above. Provisional measures applied *erga omnes*, i.e. also for slaves, who could only negate them by means of the *uindicatio in libertatem*.

C. 3.1.6. – Seruus in iudicio interesse non potest nec, si condemnatio aliqua in personam eius facta est, quod statutum est subsistit. – 7. – Cum debitoris tui seruum, tibi pignoris iure obligatum bona domini sui quondam rebus humanis exempti tenere profitearis, aduersus eum dari tibi actiones contra ius postulas, si quidem inter seruum et liberum consistere iudicium nullum possit. Ad possessionem itaque pignorum magis officio iudicis uenire te conuenit quam illicita postulare.	Translation Blume. – A slave cannot be a party to an action; nor if a judgment has been rendered against him can the decision stand. 7. Since you say that the slave of your debtor who was pledged to you holds the property of his former master, now taken away from human affairs, you unlawfully ask for a right of action against the slave, since no action between a slave and a freeman can be maintained. It behooves you, therefore, to ask possession of the pledge at the hands of the judge, rather than for something that is not lawful.

A person could become a slave when he was taken as a prisoner of war, because of a judgement, or through birth. If an enemy captured a Roman, the latter lost all of his civil rights. If he escaped, they revived (*ius postliminii*). If he died as a prisoner, his will was nevertheless executed (D. 28.1.12, the *fictio legis corneliae* from around 80 BC). Deserters and those who prematurely left the army became slaves. Prisoners of war who joined the Roman army became free citizens immediately. Subject peoples became slaves, but were given civil rights in their peace treaty or by the consuls. For that reason, slavery was considered to be an institution of the *ius gentium* (D. 1.5.4). A person could also become a slave because of a judgement. The higher magistrates in the Republic and the emperors could take away a person's civil rights. A person who was imprisoned provisionally or who was sentenced to service in the mines (*ad metalla*) temporarily became a slave. A death sentence included slavery. A free woman who had relations with a slave without the permission of the latter's *paterfamilias* was sentenced to slavery by Claudius (*senatusconsultum Claudianum* of 54 AD, case-law later repealed by Justinian, Inst. 3.12.1). A free woman who had relations with her own slaves was sentenced to death by Constantine; her children became imperial slaves (CTh. 9.9.1*pr.*; C. 9.11.11). When executing private judgements, the praetor could decide to sell a debtor *trans Tiberim*. This expression once meant 'as a prisoner of war of the Etruscans', but by the classical period it had come to mean 'as a slave'. The most common way of becoming a slave was through birth. Children received the status of their mother (*partus ancillae*). If the mother had been free during the pregnancy for as much as a moment, the child was freeborn (*fauor libertatis*, D. 1.5.5.3, *Pauli Sententiae* 2.24.1-3, to be claimed by means of the *uindicatio in libertatem*). How did women become prisoners of war if they did not fight? Were they taken as war booty? It cannot be excluded that in the oldest times life *in seruitute* (in servility) was the normal civil status of all those who did not fight, even when they were born on Roman soil. There are mentions of slaves who had rights in the *ius sacrum*.

Slaves could earn and spend money in the civil law and had the same status as the *filiifamilias* when they did so. If necessary, they had an account in the register of their *familia* and could enter into agreements with their *paterfamilias*. They could, for example agree that they would buy their freedom by means of that account. Slaves could also enforce this agreement by means of the *uindicatio in libertatem*.

Buy their freedom... Here, we encounter a large difference with other family members: slaves had a price. Consuls who carried away thousands of slaves as war booty attempted to receive the highest possible price for them. Soldiers who had received prisoners of war could transfer them to another *familia* in return for money. In the late Republic, peregrines also acquired slaves. They did so through *emptio uenditio*, private contracts of sale. The scruples that Roman case-law expresses concerning the sale and purchase of children cannot be found with regard to the sale and purchase of slaves. Nevertheless slave traders (*mangones*) received a bad press in daily life, just as the current negotiators in football circles.

C. Manumissio

Conquered peoples were given the status of prisoners of war, but could be freed by the commanders of the army. The consuls, the Senate and the emperors granted a full or partial status of freedom to the conquered. In daily life a *paterfamilias* could give his slaves the status of freedom through a *manumissio*. This was a legal act by means of which he removed members who were *in mancipio* from the *familia*. For slaves, a *manumissio* conferred civil status. *Manumissio* was supervised by the magistrates in the Republic and by the imperial administration in the Empire.

A first form of *manumissio* was the *manumissio uindicta*, which initially took place before the praetor, and later before the imperial judges. An outsider claimed this for the benefit of someone who was *in mancipio*. If the *paterfamilias* agreed, the praetor or judge registered the *manumissio*. If the beneficiary had previously been a *filiusfamilias* of another *familia*, he returned to this *familia*. The *manumissio* of a slave resulted in his receiving the status of freedom. For slaves, this amounted to a kind of emancipation. A second form was the *manumissio censu* by means of registration in the conscription lists and tax lists by the censor. According to Gaius 1.140 the agreement of the *paterfamilias* was not required. As this *manumissio* was a decision of the censor, it can be suspected that his edict mentioned the circumstances in which such a *manumissio* was possible. In the Empire, it was the emperor who decided in these cases. The third form of *manumissio* was by means of a will. Wills were dealt with by the courts. There was, consequently, always some form of government supervision over the freeing of slaves. According to Gaius 2.152, a release by means of a will could even be executed against the wishes of the slave himself. Constantine introduced a fourth form of *manumissio*, namely the *manumissio in sacrosanctis ecclesiis* before a bishop. He accepted that an episcopal audience could decide about the freeing of a slave, but imperial supervision was maintained by means of exequaturs.

Apart from these formal forms of *manumissio*, there was also the praetorian liberation, which came about in an informal manner. In the Republic it could be claimed before the praetor; in the Empire it could be claimed before a court. A *paterfamilias* who had declared a slave free in an informal manner in a letter or in the presence of witnesses was bound by this decision. Case-law acknowledged that a *paterfamilias* who lived in a high-quality relationship (*in matrimonio*) with a female slave informally freed her. Their children were free as well. In this manner, the slave did not acquire civil rights and remained *in mancipio* so that nothing changed for debtors and third parties. The slave could, however, make use of a *uindicatio in libertatem* on the grounds of an informal liberation. Justinian immediately gave civil rights to slaves who had been freed in an informal manner (C. 7.6.1).

Under Diocletian, the prefecture ruled that a *manumissio* could also be acquired through prescription (C. 7.22).

In the *lex fufia caninia* (2 BC), Augustus decided that the unlimited freeing of slaves was no longer possible: those who had less than ten slaves could only free half of them, those who had between ten and thirty could free a third, those who had between thirty and one hundred were limited to a fourth, those who had between one and five hundred were restricted to a fifth and those who had more than five hundred slaves could only free one hundred. In the *lex aelia sentia* (4 AD) Augustus added that a *paterfamilias* who liberated a slave had to be at least twenty years old, that the slave had to be at least thirty years old, and that liberations that aggrieved debtors were void. American historians write that Augustus was engaging in social engineering in order to maintain his slave state. However, he was mainly trying to preserve his new system of social security (the *annona*). Freed slaves arrived 'en masse' to live at his expense rather than at the expense of their *paterfamilias*.

Those beneficiaries of a *manumissio* who did not return to their own *familia* but became independent were given the status of *libertus*, freedman. They retained a bond with their former *paterfamilias*, who remained their *patronus*. If they did not have any heirs and had not drawn up a will, he could claim their inheritance. He also became their children's guardian. On the occasion of a liberation, agreements were often made about the execution of odd jobs. The performance of these agreements could be enforced by means of the *actio operarum*. In the case of informal manumissions through cohabitation, the man was the *patronus* of his partner, but in this context agreements about odd jobs were impossible (D. 38.1.46). According to a decision of the prefecture of Constantinople, the *paterfamilias* could cancel a liberation in a case of severe ingratitude (C. 6.7.2*pr.*). If a woman who was free because of cohabitation with a man left him for another man, her liberation was cancelled by operation of law. The emperor could grant liberation from patronage (*natalium restitutio*).

D. Medieval slavery

The slavery of Antiquity lies buried underneath the story that historians have spun about it. With regard to the Middle Ages, slavery is still a subject where observation is falsified by repression and indignation. It is said that private slavery and domestic slaves no longer existed in the Christian period. There are, however, many medieval phenomena that cannot be understood without the Roman *seruitus*. How can one understand the statuses of *serui, homines, manentes, libellarii, angariales, massarii...* without thinking of the old slavery? Early medieval serfs had a status that can be compared with that of the Roman slaves: no military service, no civil rights, working for a warrior and being part of his house. The idea that this had nothing to do with slavery dates back to the thirteenth century, when civil lawyers compared serfs to the *coloni* of C. 11.38 rather than to Roman slaves. Serfs were not sold, could get married, could have personal property, and could appear before the court. The civil lawyers did not realise that their vision of antique slavery was influenced by contemporary notions like the canonical family or the Christian marriage. The *contubernium* of Roman slaves was put on a par with marriage in the Middle Ages (see below).

In Bologna, Jean de Blanot taught in his course of 1256 that the private slaves of the Romans were *homines alterius*, people who belonged to others. How was that possible? Medieval families only had room for a man, a wife and children. Slaves therefore must have belonged to others as objects. After all, they were claimed by means of a *re*vindication. However, this did not really matter anymore because slavery had disappeared. Jacques de Revigny found it unlikely that the Romans 'had' people, but Bartolus repeated that they had *actiones in rem* about slaves and that this meant that they 'had' and 'possessed' these slaves. As is the case with many dogmas, one must take his interpretation into account today, even if it is only to understand the historians.

Some medieval people were nevertheless familiar with the real status of the slaves of Antiquity. In the twelfth and thirteenth centuries, Jewish communities acquired charters of freedom just like other communities. These charters exempted them from military service and sometimes also gave them their own tax regime. The money for crusades and the destruction of Jerusalem was a thorn in the flesh of the Jews. Many of these charters can be found in the Rhineland. Frederick Barbarossa did not desire to give the Jews in his Italian districts their own charters, but he did grant them a separate status. According to Saint Augustine, Titus reduced all of the Jews to imperial slaves in 70. Since Frederick was Titus' successor, he was of the opinion that the Jews were still members of his *familia*. This meant that they did not have to fight, were exempt from taxes and were under his personal protection. Frederick II took the same attitude in 1236-1238. Louis IX of France adopted this position as well, but used it against the Jewish communities. If they were imperial slaves, he could freely dispose of their property and treat them like Roman slaves. The same theory cropped up again in Bracton's work, in the 'fueros' of Aragon and in thirteenth-century Portuguese sources. It is only at the end of the thirteenth century that this doctrine was replaced by another one, namely by Rudolf of Habsburg who wrote that Jews were not Roman slaves but free medieval serfs. This discussion shows that in academic contexts, people were still familiar with the real status of slaves in the *familia caesaris*.

Bibliography. – On *homines alterius*: C. TAVILLA, *Homo alterius, I rapporti di dipendenza personale nella dottrina del Duocento, Il trattato de hominiciis de Martino de Fano,* Naples 1993; E. CONTE, *Servi medievali, Dinamiche del diritto comune,* Viella 1996. On the position of medieval Jews: A. PATCHOVSKY, 'Das Rechtsverhältnis der Juden zum deutschen König (9.-14. Jahrhundert), Ein europäischer Vergleich', *Zeitschrift der Savigny-Stiftung für Rechtsgeschichte, Germanistische Abteilung* 110 (1993), p. 331-371.

E. Slavery in the Early Modern Era

In Constantinople the slavery of Ancient Rome (*douleia*) disappeared in the tenth century, but the serfdom of prisoners of war (*aichmalosia*) had continued to exist. Many Slavonic prisoners of war from Eastern Europe were traded there – hence the name 'slaves' rather than 'servants'. Around the Mediterranean, this Roman status of slavery for prisoners of war was still a familiar concept as well. Many prisoners of war worked as slaves in the Eastern Empire while redeeming their freedom. The Saracens and later the North African Arabs sold prisoners they took during raids and crews of privateered Western ships as slaves. After the fall of Constantinople the Ottomans also offered prisoners of war and captured inhabitants for sale. Christian movements permanently collected money to buy the freedom of these slaves. In 1453 Eastern slave traders settled in the West. In that year, slave markets were held in Genoa, Barcelona and Seville, where the local population rebelled against them. There were also attempts to introduce an oppressive regime in Corsica which caused an enormous commotion. Lisbon had fewer problems with this.

In the fifteenth century, Greek ship-owners sought a new route from Lisbon to India. Together with Portuguese traders, they established trading posts on the African West Coast, where missionaries began to buy the freedom of prisoners of the internal wars. This became a lucrative business for the Africans, who forced the charitable organisations to make extreme efforts by killing the prisoners whose freedom was not bought. The Greek traders were familiar with this situation and offered these Africans the possibility of buying their own freedom by working as agricultural labourers on the plantations of Madeira and later Brazil. The Greeks had moved their plantations of sugarcane from Cyprus to the Atlantic islands and attempted to plant cotton since they no longer controlled the cotton trade from Egypt and India. Their plantations were short of workers. The African prisoners were given the status of Roman private slaves as this was defined by the medieval law faculties: they were property and were owned by their masters. In this manner, the interpretation of the legists suddenly became important. The combination of a growing supply of slaves in Africa, a growing need for agricultural workers in the colonies and the theory that slaves could be sold as private property was the beginning of an enormous early modern social drama. English, French and Dutch traders, who were most closely aligned with the Greek culture of the sixteenth century, conducted slave trade between Africa and the plantations until well into the eighteenth century.

Western jurists did not have any problems with the slavery of Antiquity, but did struggle with colonial slavery. In 1551 the Spanish king granted civil rights to all of the inhabitants of his colonies so that native slavery became impossible there. The English Admiralty pronounced judgements in which it accepted slavery aboard English ships, but those who escaped a slave ship in an English port could not be reclaimed by the captain or shipper because slavery did not exist in England. In Pennsylvania the first riots against slavery broke out during the Germantown Protest (1688). Louis XIV of France introduced the 'Code Noir' for his colonies in order to protect the slaves. However, because it acknowledged slavery, it kept this status in existence for two centuries. France, England and the United States tolerated slavery until the nineteenth century. For centuries, the proponents of slavery took their arguments from Roman law and the *ius commune*. Since the nineteenth century, they have fulminated against the Roman law. Let us not give these people more authority than necessary and refrain from explaining the slavery of Antiquity from the viewpoint of colonial slavery.

In our day and age slavery is said to have been abolished through all kinds of interventions, but what about the Geneva Conventions about prisoners of war and compulsory labour? And what about the sale of football players? Do they really have nothing to do with the old notion of slavery?

Bibliography. – On the origin of colonial slavery, see L. WAELKENS, 'La personne et le travail en servitude dans le droit romain antique et medieval', in: F. LARONZE et J.-M. TUFFERY-ANDRIEU (eds.), *Les normes du travail, Une affaire de personnes?*, [Brussels 2015] (in press).

§3. Limited liability for family members

In Antiquity the *paterfamilias* was the only member of the *familia* who acted in the civil courts. The members of his *familia* enjoyed his civil rights and he was fully liable for the debts of the *familia*. The property which all the family members had pooled in a community of property served as security. Because of his liability, the *paterfamilias* could prevent the family members from running up debts. Acting under property law was his exclusive task (*patrimonium*). Free people who lived under *patria potestas* had rights of freedom and were criminally liable, but they did not have any proprietary rights. If family members entered into obligations themselves, they were not enforceable. They had the character of natural obligations: the creditors were not given a remedy at law, but the payment of the debt was not an undue payment. The question can be asked whether excluding family members from legal life in this manner was perhaps a counterproductive measure that led to an economy of old gentlemen. Did this limitation amount to a failure to recognise *commercium*, each person's free access to trade? This question is the subject of this paragraph. When the *familia* was developed in the republican law, remedies at law were created that not only gave family members access to the market, but also allowed the *paterfamilias* to control his liability. These were the *actiones adiecticiae qualitatis* ('actions with an additional modality'): actions pertaining to the debts of family members that were initiated against the *paterfamilias*. An additional modality which limited the liability of the *paterfamilias* was added to the formula of these actions. It is through these remedies at law that business with limited liability, a strong incentive for trade, was developed in Roman law.

1. The *actio de peculio*

One aspect of the *status libertatis* was that soldiers could freely dispose of their salary (*peculium*) and their spoils. How was this possible when they were still members of a *familia*? After all, membership of a *familia* normally meant that all earnings became part of the familial community of property. The cash that soldiers kept for themselves could be spent freely without their payments being undue. Soldiers could save money by depositing it in the account of their legion, but they could also transfer money home. The military quaestors sent the soldier's pay to his *paterfamilias* as *peculium*. The latter then credited the amount in the familial community of property, but debited it into the soldier's account. Soldiers who were members of a *familia* could enter into any obligation that did not exceed the sum in their account. The creditors requested payment from the *paterfamilias*, who paid with the *peculium* and credited the amount from the account of the family member. Creditors could also inspect the account beforehand. If a conflict arose and they went to the praetor on account of the debts of a person who had a *peculium*, they initiated proceedings against the *paterfamilias* but indicated to the praetor that the case was about *peculium*. The additional modality that the action was an *actio de peculio* was added to the formula. In this manner, an *actio uenditi* became an *actio uenditi de peculio*; an *actio conducti* became an *actio conducti de peculio*... Such a remedy was a claim 'with an additional modality' (*actio adiecticiae qualitatis*). For an action concerning *peculium* the *paterfamilias* was only bound for the amount of *peculium* that the family member had in his account. If the account was empty, the *paterfamilias* was absolved. In other words: his liability was limited to the *peculium* that his account books mentioned (D. 15.5.44). If he could not provide account books, he lost this advantage (D. 2.13.4.3). A warrior could also dispose of his *peculium* in a will. When the will was executed, the assets which he disposed were claimed from the *paterfamilias*, who once again used the *peculium* to pay out the dispositions. In the classical law, a military *peculium* was called a *peculium castrense* (D. 49.17). Justinian also acknowledged the use of this system for the earnings of some officials (*peculium quasi castrense*, C. 3.28.37).

The *peculium* was already used for trade with limited liability in the Republic. The *paterfamilias* could voluntarily grant a *peculium* to slaves and *filiifamilias*. These accounts were kept on a separate sheet. The *paterfamilias* then covered the legal actions of the holder of the *peculium* to the extent of a pre-agreed amount. The family member then used this amount to conduct trade for which the *paterfamilias* only had a limited liability. All revenue and expenditure was registered in this special ledger account. If the business was successful, the amount in the account increased, as did the credit for those to whom the family member owed money. If the business operated at a loss, the amount in the account decreased. The liability of the *paterfamilias* ended when the account was empty. If that was the case, the creditors did not get anything. A *peculium* could be granted to all family members, including slaves who thus also became economic operators. It is with such accounts that slaves bought their own freedom. It was common practice for a slave and his *paterfamilias* to agree on conditions for release as a reward for what the slave earned for his *paterfamilias*. If a slave had collected the price of his release in the account and was not freed in a peaceable manner, he could go to the praetor or the *cognitio* judge with a *uindicatio libertatis*. During the proceedings that followed, the accounts were checked and witnesses were heard to examine whether the conditions for release had been fulfilled.

In short, the *peculium* offered many possibilities to have family members act independently. In addition, it provided the benefit of trade with limited liability, which is extremely important to a sound economy. Traders take more initiatives if they cannot ruin their family. Suppliers become more careful and continuously weigh their risks. Those who are making a profit can take more risks; those who make losses have to restrain themselves.

If an *actio de peculio* was not accepted because of the insolvency of a business with a *peculium*, the praetors or *cognitio* judges checked to see whether the case involved a *concursus creditorum* (concurrence of creditors). They could order the liquidation of the business and the division of the remaining property in the account among the creditors according to the abovementioned insolvency rules. In such cases, it was as if only one account went bankrupt instead of the entire *familia*. In this context, the jurists had to make a consideration: limited liability furthered trade and was beneficial to society, but creditors were harmed when a business failed. Where was the balance between the pros and the cons? Other remedies at law were developed around the liquidation. If it turned out, for example, that the *paterfamilias* had aggrieved one creditor more than the others, the latter received an *actio tributoria* with which he could force the *paterfamilias* to pay the deficit.

If the *paterfamilias* transferred money from the *peculium* to his own account (profit-taking or reservation), the *peculium* and his liability decreased by the same amount (D. 15.1.16 and D. 34.4.11.3). The creditors (or, normally, their bankers) kept an eye on such transfers. If the *paterfamilias* transferred money from the slave's account to his own account, the *peculium* of the slave decreased, but the transferred amount was deducted from the sum that the slave had to collect to buy his freedom (D. 4.1.6). If a *paterfamilias* closed a *peculium* unexpectedly and without reasons he remained fully liable.

2. The *actio de peculio et de in rem uerso*

Some obligations that were entered into by a family member could be enforced even if the family member did not have a *peculium*. A classic example is the purchase of basic provisions for the *familia*. In the legal history of many countries, this example was received as the 'implicit household mandate'. Creditors could use an action with the additional modality of *actio de in rem uerso* (action concerning enrichment) to force the *paterfamilias* to pay them. The *paterfamilias* could not invoke the argument that this family member could not run up debts which the *paterfamilias* had to cover. The *paterfamilias* was, however, only liable for the growth of the family's property through the family member's dealings (Gaius 4.72a) – i.e. the *paterfamilias* was only liable for the enrichment. In large cases, he could return the property that had been bought and enlarged the familial property. Alternatively, he could limit the payment thereof to the true enrichment which they had caused for the *familia*. A classic case was that of the slave who had borrowed money to pay the debts of the *paterfamilias*. The latter later alleged that he did not have to pay this loan because the money had been borrowed by a slave. However, the *familia* had been enriched by the payment of the debts and the court decided that the *paterfamilias* was liable *de rem in uerso*.

In the classical era there was one common formula that was used to deal with both *peculium* and enrichment, namely the *actio de peculio seu de in rem uerso*. This formula could also be employed to handle situations in which both *peculium* and enrichment played a role. If a *paterfamilias* noticed that a family member's business was going downhill, he could transfer the money that was still in the family member's account to his own account. If the creditors or the judge discovered this during the proceedings, the amount of that transfer could be included in the liability as *de in rem uerso*, as retained earnings.

C. 4.26.7.3 mentions a beautiful judgement about the *actio de rem in uerso*. Someone had entered into a contract with a *liber agens*. On the grounds of this contract, he received the *actio de in rem uerso* against a *paterfamilias* who had been enriched at his expense. This *liber agens* could be a child or a free person *in mancipio*. In the Early Modern Era, however, this text from the Code was read as if the *liber agens* was not a family member. Some jurists then decided that the *actio de in rem uerso* was not only used to deal with familial settlements, but was also a general action to demand the restitution of 'unjustified' enrichment. This was a typical reasoning of the *ius commune* of the Early Modern Period which deviated from the meaning which the text of the Code had in Antiquity.

3. The *actio noxalis*

With regard to *nexi*, the liability of the *paterfamilias* was limited to the renouncement of the *nexus*. The debts of *nexi* were claimed before the court by means of an action with the additional modality of *actio noxalis*. In the republican formula or the imperial *litiscontestatio*, an amount was demanded 'unless the defendant prefers to hand over the *nexus*' (*noxae deditio*). In a case of such an action, the *paterfamilias* was given the choice between paying or handing the *nexus* over to the creditor. His liability was, in other words, limited to his attachment to the *nexus*. This noxal action also existed in the law of obligations which arose from delicts (see below). In cases involving an offence committed by a family member – theft, for example, or a wrongful act – the *paterfamilias* was sued with noxal actions. He was given the choice between paying the retribution or compensation, or handing the offender over to the creditor.

Text. – Formula of an *actio noxalis* in the case of a slave who stole a golden dish. The theft was reacted against by means of the *actio furti* (action on account of theft) in which the additional modality of *actio noxalis* was incorporated:

Si paret Ao.Ao. a Sticho seruo Ni.Ni. paterae aureae furtum factum esse, qua de re Nm. Nm. Aut pro fure damnum decidere aut Stichum noxae dedere oportet, quanti ea res fuit, cum furtum factum est, tantae pecuniae duplum aut noxae dedere iudex Nm.Nm. Ao.Ao.c.s.n.p.a.	If it turns out that a golden dish was stolen to the detriment of A.A. by Stichus, the slave of N.N., and N.N. must pay the compensation on account of theft or must hand over Stichus, you must sentence N.N. to pay twice the value which the object had at the time of the theft or to hand over of the slave. If it turns out that this is not the case, you must acquit him.

4. Extension to people who are not members of the *familia*

Gaius 4.71 mentions two actions with an additional modality that transcended the *familia*.

The first is the *actio exercitoria*. A family member who captained a vessel of his *paterfamilias* could incur normal debts in order to keep the ship operative. He did not need the permission of the *paterfamilias*. If they were not paid, the creditors filed claims against the ship-owner and included the *actio exercitoria* in their action. However, the liability of the *paterfamilias* was limited, namely to the costs that were necessary for the exploitation of the ship, such as the costs for provisions, maintenance, or repairs. Case-law extended this action to include independent captains. It became possible to use the *actio exercitoria* against a ship-owner whose captain was *sui iuris*. This development continued in the classical period: if a captain was sentenced to pay costs that could have fallen within the scope of the *actio exercitoria* according to case-law, the ship-owner and the captain were always jointly liable for payment. In this manner, the use of limited liability began to transcend the familial context.

The second example was the *actio institoria*. The *paterfamilias*' possibility of establishing a *peculium* for a family member was extended so that he could also open such an account for someone who was not a member of his *familia*. If a *paterfamilias* appointed such a person as manager, he agreed in an *institutio* that this manager would receive a credit as if he were the holder of a *peculium*. In his business, the manager posted up a notice stating his capacity as an *institor*, the principal whom he worked for, and the circumstances under which he was covered. The creditors of the *institor* could then lodge claims directly against his principal, but their actions included the additional modality of *actio institoria*. The liability of the principal was limited to the balance of the *institor*'s account – just as it was limited to the balance of a family member's *peculium*. The function of the *actio institoria* is comparable to the *actio de peculio*. The principal could not refuse to pay, unless the total debt of the *institor* was higher than the credit that he had been awarded. In this manner, a *paterfamilias* appointed an extrafamilial manager with regard to whom his liability was limited.

In Gaius 4.71 we can read about the *actio de institoria*. D. 14.3 compiles case-law pertaining to this matter. Sadly, these texts do not provide a clear image of how items were credited and debited to this third-party account. We do mention the following elements. The *institor* could either be an independent person or a member of a different *familia*. He could therefore receive a salary from the principal. According to Gaius 4.71, the *institor* and the principal were jointly liable. A supplier who demanded payment could therefore choose between suing the *institor* by means of the action of the seller, or suing the principal with the action of the seller formulated as *actio institoria*. It would seem, then, that the *institor*'s liability for the debts was not limited, while the principal's liability was. However, if the creditor should have known that he was dealing with an *institor*, the latter was covered with regard to all agreements concerning which he could invoke *bona fides* (because if he could invoke this, all of the relations between the two contractors were taken into consideration). The sums that the manager had paid himself could be claimed back from the principal on the grounds of their agreement. According to D.14.3.1, this agreement could be a procuration or a *negotiorum gestio*. In both cases, the *institor* acquired property or services for the principal. He could reclaim all the costs which he had incurred for him. Assets therefore ended up as part of the property of the principal. Originally, the *paterfamilias* did not have any direct claims against the creditors of his *institor*. In the third century, there was a controversy about this issue. It seems that direct actions against these creditors appeared at this time. At least according to Marcellus, the principal received direct claims against the parties that contracted with his *institor* (D. 14.2.1-2). According to Salvius Julianus, the agreement between the principal and the *institor* could also be a *societas* contract (D. 14.3.13). In a Roman *societas*, assets were 'co-owned' and debts were to be paid by the *socius* who had incurred them. Liquidation and division happened according to the agreements in the *societas* contract and took into account all of the legal relationships between the *socii*. If the relationship between the principal and the manager was not clear, the court could fall back on *negotiorum gestio* so that the case was treated as if the manager had acted for the principal solely out of goodwill. In case of *negotiorum gestio*, the principal acquired direct actions, but his *institor* was only liable for serious faults.

In D. 14.3 we discover how ever more people who acted for third parties were presumed to be *institores*: stewards, salesmen, bankers... Papinian mentions an *actio ad exemplum institoriae actionis* (see mainly D. 14.3.19*pr.*). He clearly states that independent people could act for third parties and could acquire both assets and liabilities for them. In an intermediary passage (in D. 45.1.126.2) Justinian repeated the principle that no one could acquire rights of action via a third party. The contradiction between these two texts raised doubts among the Romanists for centuries. However, D. 45.1.126.2 applied to strict obligations that were entered into by means of stipulations, while Papinian probably dealt with obligations *e bona fide* (the difference will be discussed below).

5. In the Middle Ages and Early Modern Era

The *actio quasi institoria* of Papinian was received well in the Middle Ages. In the small medieval families the idea of the *dominus* acting for his family members had been relegated to the background. Almost any act for others became a matter of representation. Bartolus claimed that anyone who received an authorisation from someone else acted for the latter as a *quasi institor* and therefore established both

liability and rights of action for this other person. In the *ius commune*, agency and authorisations would be developed further along these lines on the basis of D. 14.3.9*pr.*

In the Middle Ages, *peculium* and the limited liability of family members were of no importance because trade was conducted by independent persons and jointly liable spouses. *Vniversitates* acted in long-distance trade (see below). They did not enjoy limited liability. After 1453 the *institutio* once again gained importance. It hailed from Constantinople, where it was called *pekoulion* at the time. On their ships, the Greek traders employed purchasers who acted independently for third persons and enjoyed limited liability. In Greek such a manager was called a *faktionarios*; this became a *feitor* in Portuguese. In 1453 some traditional German textile traders of the Fondacco dei Tedeschi, among whom were the Fuggers, Welsers and Vöhlins, became factors of the Greek traders, ship-owners and bankers. They successfully introduced the Greek staple trade with limited liability in the West.

Text. – A *consilium* of Bartolus. A lawyer consulted Bartolus about the claim of a farmer who had delivered a pig to someone he thought to be an employee of a butcher. He did not receive his money because the buyer alleged that he had to claim payment from the butcher, who in his turn stated that he had not bought anything. Bartolus resolved this conflict by means of Roman law, in fourteenth-century central Italy... Note that the word *factor* occurs twice in the text, in explanations of what an *institor* is. These are additions of the Greek publisher. This edition of 1506 was published by Thomas Diplovatatzes (Corfu 1468 – Pesaro 1541).

BARTOLUS, Consilium 79, ed. Venice 1506, f. 25r. – Quidam uendidit uni institori carnificis seu factori unum porcum nec fuit sibi de precio satisfactum: qui porcus fuit macellatus ad apothecam ipsius domini, ipso presente. Cum uendenti non sit de precio satisfactum, queritur qualiter et quando et aduersus quem sibi consulatur? Dico, quod consulitur domino per actionem institoriam quae quondam est introducta in fauorem illorum qui contrahunt cum institore seu factoribus, ne contrahentes decipiantur, ut l. 1. de instit. Secundo dico quod ibi consuletur duplici uia, scilicet aduersus institorem et dominum, ut probatur in l. Si quis mancipiis § Seruus, ff. De instit., et ne equiuocemus in institore, dico quod institor est ex eo quod ad negotia gerenda instat uel taberne sit prepositus uel alii negotiationi, ut l. Institor, eod. tit. et l. Institoria, eodem titulo. Preterea institor est ille qui comparandi uel emendi gratia in merces est positus. Exponit gl. in agnos vel pisces, et omnia ista. Talis qui uero emit istum porcum huiusmodi est, ergo et recte contra illum et formare petitionem etc. Bar.

Someone had sold a pig to the *institor* or factor of a butcher and the price was not paid to him. The pig was slaughtered in the workshop of this *dominus*, and in his presence. When the price was not paid to the seller, the question arose how, when and against whom he could take legal action. I say that judgement should be passed against the *dominus* (the butcher) by means of the *actio institoria*, which was once introduced for the benefit of those who contract with an *institor* or with factors so that the contractors would not be deceived, according to D. 14.3.1. Secondly, I say that judgement can be passed in a double way, namely against the *institor* and against the *dominus*, as D. 14.3.17.1 shows. In order to avoid making ambiguous statements about the *institor*, I say that someone becomes an *institor* by guaranteeing commercial actions or because he is an employee who has been employed by a shop or another commercial undertaking, as D. 14.3.3 and 18 state. Moreover, whoever is appointed

appelatur institor. Et dominus tenetur etiam si institor in fraudem faceret et contraheret, quia imputet sibi quod talem preposuit, ut ff. De exer. l. 1. § Vt enim, et ff. de instit., l. Sed etsi pupillus § Prescribere, neque potest allegari per dominum 'ergo non preposueram eum ad emendum uel contrahendum', quia eo ipso quod quamuis est [sic] prepositus taberne uel stationi, uidetur uelle dominus quod cum eo contrahatur et tenetur. Casus est Insti., Quod cum eo qui in ali. po. § Exercitoria et § Institoria, cum sequentibus, nisi expresse prohibeat, ut ibi. Preterea multum facit presentia domini qui uidetur ratificare factum per institorem ut ipsemet illud fecisset, ff. De insti. l. 1. § Magistrum, et poterat prohibere si uolebat, sibi ergo imputet, arg. l. Si eo, de remis. pig., et quod non in l. Si rem alienam, De contrahen. emp., et l. Si autem, ff. Ad Mace. Preterea illa ratione tenetur, quia ille publice tabernam administrabat pro domino et prepositus publice credebatur; tunc dico aut iste est interrogatus a iudice qui debet interrogari: ut l. 1. De interro. ac. et l. Vbi: 'Aut praeposuisti eum, aut non?', si dicit 'sic, habeo praepositum', quod tenebitur per iura praeallegata; si dicit non et tunc presumptio et error communis facit contra, quia publice credebatur istum esse talem prepositum ad questum, idest ad lucrum faciendum et iste communis error facit ius, ut l. 1. C. de test. et l. Barbarius Philippus, de offic. preto., facit optime l. Si quis, Ad Mace.: dicit enim ibi textus sic agebat, sicut contrahebat, sic publicis muneribus fungebatur, et C. e. tit. l. Nec Zenodorus. Consideratis rationibus crederem, saluo semper consilio saniori, quod ille dominus teneatur in solidum ad precium et ad interesse. Potest ergo agere

to purchase property is an *institor*. This is stated in the gloss ['*Ad merces comparandas*' *ad* D. 14.3.5.7] with regard to lambs or fish and these kinds of things. The person who bought this pig is of this kind, so he is correctly called an *institor*. And his *dominus* is liable even when the *institor* acted in a deceitful manner and contracted, because he is responsible for having appointed such a person, as D. 14.1.1.20 and D. 14.3.11.3 state, and the *dominus* cannot invoke 'I have not appointed him to purchase or enter into contracts', since the mere fact that someone was appointed as an employee of a shop or trading post causes the *dominus* to be considered to desire that his employee be contracted with and causes [the *dominus*] to be liable. This matter is also treated in Inst. 4.7.2 'unless he explicitly forbids it', like there. In addition, the presence of the *dominus* plays a large role, because it seems to validate the act by his *insistor* as if he had done it himself, according to D. 14.1.1.5; he could have stopped the act if he had wanted to and is therefore liable for it, according to the argument C. 8.25.6 and if he had not been able to stop it, according to D. 18.1.28 and D. 14.6.3.3. Moreover, the *dominus* is liable for the reason that the other publicly managed the shop for him and was generally considered to be his appointed employee; then I say, or the *dominus* is questioned by the judge, who must question as D. 11.1.1 and 22 say: 'Have you appointed him or not?' If he answers: 'yes, I appointed him', then he is bound by the abovementioned legal texts. If he says he did not appoint him, there is nevertheless a prescription and he has the common error against him, since it was generally thought that he was such an employee in the business who had to make a profit. A general error leads to law, as in C. 6.23.1 and D. 1.14.3; and as D. 14.6.3 expresses beautifully: 'he acted, he contracted, he exercised public authority'; and in C. 4.28.2. After consideration of these reasons, I believe, save a better judgement, that this *dominus* is bound to pay the full price and interests. The seller can therefore take legal action against him, bring proceedings, etcetera.

§4. Man and woman

In Roman law, marriage and cohabitation had little to do with the *familia*, which was a structure of liability in which sexual relations did not play a role. The canonical family was very different: it was established through cohabitation. Marriage existed within canon law in the twelfth century; in the thirteenth century it was developed by the theologians. After the nationalisation of canon law in the sixteenth century, marriage took centre stage in the civil law. Because it became an institution of civil law at that time, we discuss the relationships between men and women here, in the context of family law.

Bibliography. – There is a large amount of literature about the history of Western marriage, which is traditionally considered from the viewpoint of the civil marriage of the nineteenth and twentieth centuries. A good overview ranging from Rome to the present day can be found in J. GAUDEMET, *Le marriage en occident, Les moeurs et le droit*, Paris 1987. An accessible historical introduction to the marriage law within our current civil law is also provided by A. LEFEBVRE-TEILLARD, *Introduction historique au droit des personnes et de la famille*, Paris 1996, p. 103-229. We will diverge from this traditional view when we discuss the Roman law of Antiquity and the Middle Ages. See L. WAELKENS, 'Medieval family and marriage law, From actions of status to legal doctrine', in J. CAIRNS and P. DU PLESSIS (eds.), *From casus to regula, The creation of the ius commune*, Edinburgh 2010, p. 100-122. There are some impressive medieval commentaries about marriage law. Everyone should have read Hostiensis' commentary *De matrimonio* before they go out into the world.

1. Relationships between men and women in Roman law

In Roman case-law, various terms referred to the relationship between a man and a woman: *coniugium, coniunctio, nuptiae, matrimonium, contubernium, uir et uxor, consortium, concubinatus*... Each of these legal terms indicated another aspect of the man-woman relationship. It is a common mistake to consider *coniugium, matrimonium* and *nuptiae* to be words that refer to the same institution. This view is reminiscent of Claude Lévy-Strauss, *Les structures élémentaires de la parenté*, in which all man-woman relationships, ranging from the relationships in the South-American selva, the Ottoman harems, Stalinist family law and African matriarchal regimes to those in Insulindia, are called 'mariage'. The introduction of *Amne adverso* cited C. 5.27.5, a text that is special because it uses all of the terminology pertaining to man-woman relationships. In this introduction, we have included both the traditional translation of this fragment, in which the 'civil' marriage takes centre stage, and our own translation in which the specific legal terms have the meaning which we will explain below.

A. Coniugium *and* coniunctio

In texts from Antiquity, the imperfective form *coniugium* and the perfective form *coniunctio* both refer to a long-lasting sexual relationship between two people of the opposite sex. The difference between both was that a *coniunctio* was over, while a *coniugium* was not. The relationship between a male and a female slave, which was called a *contubernium*, was a *coniugium* (D. 23.3.39.1). An incestuous relationship was a *coniugium,* although it could not be a *nuptiae* (Gaius 1.59). A concubinage was a *coniugium* as well (Council of Toledo, canon 17; cf. Ovid's Metamorphoses 14.298 and 10.295). A *matrimonium* was not necessary a *coniugium*: in case of captivity, the *coniugium* was over, but the *matrimonium* could continue to exist (see for example C. 5.16.24.2; C. 5.17.1). A *coniugium* that continued to exist after the death of a partner was unthinkable. If the blood relationship between a man and a woman who lived in *coniugium* was too close, the couple was separated (D. 48.5.39.4).

Relationships between direct descendants were forbidden. In addition, there were prohibitions of incest pertaining to collateral relatives: up to and including the sixth degree in the Republic, up to and including the third degree in the classical period, up to and including the fourth degree under Theodosian and once again up to and including the third degree under Justinian (Inst. 1.10.4). These prohibitions were extended to include direct non-consanguineous relatives because... *adoptio imitatur naturam.* The prohibition of marriages between blood relatives was originally related to eugenics and therefore applied to all relationships (see for example D. 23.2.8).

Saint Augustine wrote about sexual intercourse in works like *de bono coniugali* and *de coniugiis adulterinis.* These do not deal with what we call marriage, but with an enduring cohabitation. The latter work contains his famous view that adultery and bigamy were issues related to *coniugium.*

B. Vir et uxor

This seems to have been the normal expression for spouses. It can be compared with the French 'mari et femme', the German 'Gatte und Gattin, Gemahl und Gemahlin', the English 'husband and wife' and the Polish mąnż i żona'. *Vxorem ducere, maritum habere* indicated the state of being joined. This is what one said about a couple that lived together if it was not important to know the exact status of their relationship. This term could refer to citizens, peregrines and people whose status was unknown. Whether there were civil consequences attached to this, depended on the familial position of both partners and of their *conubium.* The latter was a privilege that was granted in the peace treaties. The descendants of spouses with *conubium* were given civil rights. In the early Middle Ages this cohabitation was called *maritagium.* It is from this word that the English 'marriage' and the French 'mariage' derive.

In the sources we read that an *uxor* did not necessarily have to be *in matrimonio* (see for example D. 49.15.12.4 and D. 48.5.7). Those who celebrated *nuptiae* as children only became spouses when they reached adulthood (D. 23.2.4). People who lived in an incestuous relationship would never become wife and husband (D. 48,5,14,4). *Vir et uxor* was the criterion for the *actio rerum amotarum* of D. 25.2: spouses could not steal from each other, but there was a specific action that could be used if they had taken things away from their partner.

C. Concubinatus

This difficult notion can be found in D. 25.7. There could be a concubinage if *nuptiae* or *matrimonium* were impossible. *Concubinatus* was only possible if the relationship was not indecent. Monogamy and *pubertas* were required. The judge derived the existence of a concubinage from the intentional bond between both partners (*ex sola animi destinatione*, D. 25.7.4). He assessed whether the case involved *affectio uxoris* or *affectio concubinae* (D. 24.1.3.1 *in fine*). A concubinage with a child was impossible (D. 25.7.1.4). If *nuptiae* could be presumed, the relationship was not a concubinage (D. 23.2.24). At the Council of Toledo (400), the bishops accepted that men who were not joined in matrimony but had a *concubina* instead of a wife would not be excluded from the communion as long as they limited themselves to one woman. Since conjugal relations were also informal, the difference must have been the intention. Was a concubinage perhaps a life without major plans? We encounter concubinage as an accepted man-woman relationship until the twelfth century, for example in Dist. 34 c. 4.

D. Nuptiae

Nuptiae means 'wedding' or 'to get married' and refers to vows and the start of an official cohabitation: in French 'noces'; in German 'Trauung', 'Heirat', 'Vermählung' or 'Hochzeit'; in Polish 'ślub'. In Roman law, it is clear that this is not the same thing as *matrimonium*. Case-law about this matter was incorporated in D. 23.2. The verb *nubere* was only used with regard to women; the equivalent for men was *uxorem ducere*. The plural *nuptiae* indicates the commitment of both the man and the woman. *Nuptiae* includes aspects of a sexual nature (*coniunctio*) and aspects pertaining to property law (*consortium*) (D. 23.2.1). It required the consensus of the spouses: *nuptias enum non concubitus, sed consensus facit* (D. 50.17.30 and D. 35.1.15). Because of the consequences concerning property, the consensus of the spouses' *patresfamilias* – if they had one – was required as well. His consensus could be obtained before the court (D. 23.2.2). In the post-classical era, it was the agreement of the fathers that was asked instead of that of the *patresfamilias*. Justinian also demanded the consensus of parents who did not exercise authority if the spouses were younger than twenty-five. The *libri mandatorum* mention impediments for officials and soldiers, who could not enter into *nuptiae* in their province.

Nuptiae could be proved by all possible means, including presumptions. A couple's promise that they would produce descendants could serve as proof of their wedding (Aulus Gellius 4.3.2). In the classical period, it was common to draw up a wedding certificate (*tabulae nuptiales*). When proving *nuptiae*, the central element was the beginning of cohabitation in the conjugal home (D. 23.2.5, *deductio in domum mariti*, the husband carries the wife over the treshhold). The consummation of the relationship was not essential (D. 23.2.7), but *nuptiae* normally led to a *coniugium*, so that close blood relatives could not conclude *nuptiae*. Other prohibitions were inspired by conflicts of interest: weddings between a guardian and a pupil (D. 23.2.59), and in the post-classical era weddings between a curator and his ward were forbidden. *Confarreatio* was a form of wedding.

The main legal consequences pertained to family law. After *nuptiae*, descendants could become members of the *familia* of the father. It was only after *nuptiae* that a dowry could be established. The establishment of a dowry was proof of *nuptiae*. A woman who proved that there had been a wedding could claim a dowry after the relationship ended. Weddings also entailed consequences pertaining to criminal law. The offence of *adulterium* (adultery), for example, was a matter that involved *nuptiae* (D. 48.5.35).

An engagement (*sponsalia*) was a promise to celebrate a wedding, not the promise of a marriage. In the Republic, this promise was made by means of *stipulatio* (D. 23.1.2). It could include a penalty clause. In the Imperial Period, we find informal engagements (D. 23.1.1). Fiancés were not obliged to marry, but they did have to contribute to the costs of a cancelled wedding. There is fourth-century case-law about a bride who had to return double the value of an engagement gift (*arra sponsalica*) because she had broken her promise without having a reason to do so. In another case, the decision was that an engagement was broken if *nuptiae* had not been concluded three years after the *sponsalia* (C. 5.17.2).

In order to avoid confusion as to the parentage of her children, a widow could not remarry for ten months. *Nuptiae* concluded during this period remained valid but were punished with *infamia*, a reduction of civil rights. In the late Empire, this period was extended to one year. It also applied in case of divorce. According to Justinian, the husband could not remarry for one year after an unwarranted divorce either.

E. Matrimonium

In Roman Antiquity, *matrimonium* indicated a high-quality relationship between a man and a woman. We translate it into marriage (in French 'matrimoine', but since the thirteenth century the word 'mariage' has been used for this notion; in English 'matrimony', but since the Middle Ages the word 'marriage' has also indicated this concept; in German 'Ehe'; in Polish 'małżestwo'). *Matrimonium* is often confused with *nuptiae* in legal historical research, despite the fact that the Roman sources clearly distinguish between both. There could be a *matrimonium* without a consensus about *nuptiae* (D. 23.2.22). Adultery was related to *nuptiae*, but not to *matrimonium* (D. 48.5.35). A *matrimonium* could continue after the devolution of the *familia* (C. 5.16.24.2). The Code contains a judgement about a conflict in which someone claimed that a *matrimonium* was also possible after the demise of a partner. The prefecture did discuss the matter (C. 5.15.2), but this does suggest that there was a difference from *nuptiae*. A female slave could live in *matrimonium* with her *dominus* but could not conclude *nuptiae* with him. The term *contrahere matrimonium*, which is employed by Gaius, in the Digest and in the Institutes, is a source of confusion. Most Romanists understand the term from the medieval viewpoint that a marriage was a contract. However, in this context, *contrahere* meant 'to attract', 'to drag along' or 'to acquire'.

Matrimonium cropped up in Roman law in cases involving (1) the children's status of freedom, (2) the return of dotal property, (3) the return of gifts after a relationship had ended and (4) the establishment of the fact that a couple had separated. Only the judge could decide whether the couple lived in *matrimonium* or not. He took account of the *affectio maritalis*, as well as of the couple's intention to stay together for life in a monogamous relationship (even if this was an illusion), take care of one another, have children and raise them together. In other words, it was the internal resilience of the relationship that was considered in order to assess whether it was a *matrimonium* or not. It was nevertheless a sexual relationship, because eunuchs could not invoke *matrimonium* (D. 23.3.39.1). The judge could decide that a *matrimonium* continued to exist during a temporary separation. This *affectio maritalis* was a legal notion and not merely a poetical one: see for example D. 24.1.32.13; D. 24.1.3.1; D. 39.5.31*pr.*; D. 48.5.14.4; C.

5.17.1. In addition, *matrimonium* was a notion of the civil law. When combining all of these elements, one gets the impression that *matrimonium* indicated an intense and civilised cohabitation between a man and a woman.

Gaius linked the status of freedom to *matrimonium*. If *ciues* lived in a caring relationship, so that one could expect that they would raise their children thoroughly, their offspring received the status of freedom at birth. When a female slave lived in *matrimonium* with a *dominus*, her children also received the status of freedom at birth. The slave herself was freed (informal manumission). In conflicts about this informal manumission, the criterion was once again the *affectio maritalis*, the quality of the relationship.

In the other three cases, the judge mainly assessed whether the *matrimonium* was over or not. In D. 23.3-5 we read about the recuperation of dotal property. If a woman claimed her dowry back by means of the *actio rei uxoratae* or, later with the *actio dotis*, the judge examined whether (1) it could be proved that there had been *nuptiae* which gave rise to the establishment of a dowry and (2) whether the *matrimonium* had really ended. If there was still a *matrimonium*, the dowry was not returned. It appears that it was not returned either when there had been no *affectio maritalis*. Such discussions also occurred after the death of one or both spouses, for example when the heirs of the woman demanded that the heirs of the husband returned dotal property. The Code even mentions a case involving defendants who refused to return a dowry to the heirs of a woman because after death there was still *affectio maritalis* between the two spouses. The prefecture, however, decided that there was no *affectio maritalis* anymore: the *matrimonium* ended when one of the spouses died (see the abovementioned fragment C. 5.15.2).

The next issue in which *matrimonium* was important can be found in title D. 24.1, which treats gifts during a relationship. When a relationship was broken off, gifts only could be claimed back if there had been a *matrimonium*. When a *matrimonium* was ended, the accounts which were based on the *affectio maritalis* were settled. When a simple relationship was ended, everyone kept what they had received from their partner.

Finally, we find that *matrimonium* was also an issue in a case of divorce (see below). When a judge had to decide whether *nuptiae* had been ended, he also examined the *affectio maritalis* and the status of *matrimonium*.

Many Roman spouses never knew whether they lived *in matrimonio* or not, but this was of no importance as long as there was no conflict about an issue with regard to which *matrimonium* was a criterion in the case-law. This baffled the nineteenth-century civil lawyers: how was it possible that there were marriages without formal requirements or government supervision over the conclusion of the marriage? Did this perhaps mean that *matrimonium* was not a legal matter? Some scholars claimed that a Roman marriage was a social fact with legal consequences, a 'verwirklichte Lebensgemeinschaft'. This conception dovetailed better with the 'Zeitgeist' of the Pandectists than with ours. It is a beautiful example of their interpretation of the Roman law.

F. Diuortium

The Latin word *diuertere* means 'to divert'; *diuortium* means 'diversion'. In the sixteenth-century it became the Latin word for divorce.

In the Roman law of Antiquity, the termination of a relationship was a factual matter that could be brought up before the court. Romans did not file for divorce; the termination of a relationship was only examined in court on the occasion of another conflict. A party could, for example, ask the judge to grant an *actio dotis* (action for the payment of the dowry). If someone used the *actio rerum amotarum* to reclaim property that was taken away by his or her partner, the judge could examine whether the two were still in a relationship. The *actio rerum amotarum* played a role in conflicts between spouses, but was inadmissible when it was proved that the two were no longer a couple (D. 25.2.3). In non-marital cases, the judge sometimes had to decide whether two people had been married or not at the time of a certain event. Had a party to the proceedings acquired civil rights at birth? Could a mother refuse to continue to pay for the education of the children? Even when *nuptiae* were proved, the judge could establish that there was no longer a *matrimonium*. Divorce by mutual consent was easy to establish until Justinian's day. Nuptial agreements that excluded the possibility of separating were void, as were penalty provisions that determined a compensation for the commission of acts which could cause a judge to decide that they were no longer a couple (C. 8.38.2).

The judge faced a more complex problem when he decided that a separation involved *dissensus*. This meant that one of the partners claimed that the relationship was terminated, while the other still believed in its existence. According to Aulus Gellius, the unilateral termination of a marriage was accepted by the old law in two cases. (1) If the woman had remained a member of her original *familia*, her *paterfamilias* could claim her back with a *uindicatio* or interdict. Antoninus Pius declared these interdicts inadmissible if the daughter was happy in her relationship (D. 43.30.1.5). (2) A spouse could be cast off on account of facts (*repudium*). This possibility was already included in the Twelve Tables. In the Republic, such a rejection could happen in an informal manner. Often, a messenger was sent (*nuntium remittere*). He could then later give evidence.

The case-law of Constantine accepted a much larger number of *diuortia*, i.e. divergent actions, as grounds for a unilateral divorce. Either spouse could cast off the other if he or she was captured or banished. The woman could cast off her husband because he had committed a murder or had desecrated a grave, but not because he drank, gambled or womanised. The husband could repudiate his wife if she committed adultery. If one spouse cast off the other, remarriage was rendered more difficult. This means that the case-law became more restrictive when it came to giving a new relationship the character of a marriage after the dissolution of a previous marriage had been established.

In 439, at the request of the prefect Hormisdas, the chancellery of Theodosius II provided an overview of the imperial case-law about the grounds for unilateral divorce. It is cited below. The adultery of either spouse could lead to him or her being cast off. A wife could cast off her husband because he had hit her or because he had let a women enter their house without her permission. A husband could cast off his wife if she was involved in human trafficking, etcetera. If one reads all of these precedents, one comes to the conclusion that a spouse never had to put up with violence or fear for his or her physical integrity.

C. 5,17,8. – *Impp. Theodosius et Valentinianus AA. Hormisdae pp.* Consensu licita matrimonia posse contrahi, contracta non nisi misso repudio solui praecipimus. So-	Translation Blume. – We direct that a lawful marriage may be entered into by consent, but cannot be dissolved without sending a bill of divorce. For regard for the

lutionem etenim matrimonii difficiliorem debere esse fauor imperat liberorum. 1. Causas autem repudii hac saluberrima lege apertius designamus. Sicut enim sine iusta causa dissolui matrimonia iusto limite prohibemus, ita aduersa necessitate pressum vel pressam, quamuis infausto, attamen necessario auxilio cupimus liberari. 2. Si qua igitur maritum suum adulterum aut homicidam uel ueneficum uel certe contra nostrum imperium aliquid molientem uel falsitatis crimine condemnatum inuenerit, si sepulchrorum dissolutorem, si sacris aedibus aliquid subtrahentem, si latronem uel latronum susceptorem uel abactorem aut plagiarium uel ad contemptum sui domi suae ipsa inspiciente cum impudicis mulieribus (quod maxime etiam castas exasperat) coetum ineuntem, si suae uitae ueneno aut gladio uel alio simili modo insidiantem, si se uerberibus, quae ab ingenuis aliena sunt, adficientem probauerit, tunc repudii auxilio uti necessariam ei permittimus libertatem et causas discidii legibus comprobare. 3. Vir quoque pari fine claudetur nec licebit ei sine causis apertius designatis propriam repudiare iugalem, nec ullo modo expellat nisi adulteram, nisi ueneficam aut homicidam aut plagiariam aut sepulchrorum dissolutricem aut ex sacris aedibus aliquid subtrahentem aut latronum fautricem aut extraneorum uirorum se ignorante vel nolente conuiuia appetentem aut ipso inuito sine iusta et probabili causa foris scilicet pernoctantem, nisi circensibus uel theatralibus ludis uel harenarum spectaculis in ipsis locis, in quibus haec adsolent celebrari, se prohibente gaudentem, nisi sui ueneno vel gladio aut alio simili modo insidiatricem, uel contra nostrum imperium aliquid machinantibus consciam, seu falsitatis se crimini immiscentem inuenerit, aut manus audaces sibi probauerit ingerentem: tunc enim necessariam ei discedendi permittimus facultatem et causas discidii legibus comprobare. 4-8 [...]. D. u id. Ian. Protogene et Asterio conss. [449].

children demands that a dissolution of the marriage should be more difficult. 1. We, moreover, designate with clearness by this most salutary law the causes of a divorce. For as we justly forbid the dissolution of marriages without just cause, so we want a married party, who is pressed by adverse circumstances, to be freed by our, though unfortunate, still necessary assistance. 2. If any woman, therefore, finds that her husband is an adulterer, murder, poisoner, conspirator, against our regime, or is condemned for forgery, or is a violator of sepulchers, a robber of sacred edifices, a highwayman, a harborer of highwaymen, a cattle thief, a kidnapper, or that he, in contempt of his home, associates with lewd women while she herself is looking on, which especially exasperates chaste women, or if she proves that he laid snares for her life by poison, sword, or in any other sinister manner; or that he inflicted lashes on her, which is an insult to free-born people – then we give her permission, necessary in such case, to avail herself of the help of divorce and legally prove the causes thereof. 3. The husband shall be restrained in like manner, and shall not be permitted to repudiate his marriage-yoke without clearly designated causes, nor shall he expel his wife from his home in any manner, unless she is an adulteress, poisoner, murderer, kidnapper, violator of sepulchers, robber of sacred edifices, accomplice [of] highwaymen, or seeks the society of other men without his knowledge or consent, or spends the night away from home against his will and without just cause, or seeks, without his consent, enjoyment at the circus, theatre, or amphitheater in the places in which these are usually given, or lays snares for him by poison, sword, or in any other sinister manner, or is accomplice of persons conspiring against our regime, or participates in a crime of forgery, or lays audacious hands on him; for in that case we give him the necessary right of divorce and to legally prove the causes of action.

According to C. 5.17, Justinian was relatively liberal. He included the impotence of the husband, abortion and immoral behaviour as grounds for divorce. In Nov. 22 (536) he adopted the grounds of Theodosius and the Code. In Nov. 117 (542) he enumerated another series of pronouncements, in which one can find faults on account of which a spouse could be cast off (adultery, conspiracy, immoral behaviour) as well as grounds which did not constitute faults (impotence of the husband, war or entrance into a convent or monastery). Here, we also find the case of a husband who kept a concubine close to his conjugal home. He was sentenced to the division of his property. On the basis of the combination of this Novel and C. 5.17.8.2, the French authors at the end of the eighteenth century decided – to the shame of their German and Spanish colleagues – that the husband could only be cast off according to the *ius commune* on account of his keeping a concubine in a house that was the joint property of himself and his wife (community of goods).

According to many authors, Augustus obliged divorcees to remarry, because women had to be married between the ages of twenty and fifty and men between the ages of twenty-five and sixty, unless they had three or four children – depending on whether they were free or freed. If they did not comply with this rule, they lost part of their inheritance rights. It is not, however, so certain that this was an attempt at 'social engineering' aimed at the repopulation of the country, as some authors claim. Augustus decided that women who had three children were exempted from inheritance taxes. In 320, Augustus' rule was revoked; henceforth remarriage led to a reduction of the woman's inheritance rights. This new regulation, however, mainly aimed at the protection of the children of the first relationship. Valentinian I required the agreement of the family when a young widow wanted to remarry (C.Th. 3.7.1). In his Nov. 134 Justinian forbade remarriage. Once again it is hard to infer whether he opposed new relationships or was of the opinion that only one relationship could have the status of a marriage.

G. Manus

This last issue pertaining to the relationships between men and women is connected with the *familia* rather than with the man-woman relationship itself. A woman never entered the *familia* of her partner by entering into a relationship with him. Admittance into the *familia* required a *confarreatio* or *coemptio*, an act of mancipation in which either her *paterfamilias* or, if she was independent, a legal representative played a role. The writings of Gaius and the *lex irnitana* state that if the *paterfamilias* of her husband was liable for her, a woman was not *in mancipio* in this *familia*. She became an *uxor in manu*. If the situation was unclear and two spouses had lived hand in hand for a year (*in manu*), the creditors could presume that a transfer to the new *familia* had taken place. They could address her new *paterfamilias* about her debts. Law 4.4 of the Twelve Tables already stated that if the wife did not stay in the marital house for three nights a year (*trinoctio abesse*), this transfer was not presumed. Her absence for three nights was enough to prove her financial independence or to demonstrate that she had remained a member of her original *familia*. When discussing this law, many books state that a Roman woman's marriage meant that she fell under the marital power – that of her husband, not that of her husband's *paterfamilias*. The scope of this idea escapes the present writer. Transfers to the *familia* of the husband did not occur in the *ius gentium*. In the classical period, marriages with a transfer to the *familia* of the husband became an exception.

2. The reception of man-woman relationships

A. The early Middle Ages

In Antiquity, the bishops already defended the man-woman relationship that was inspired by the Jewish 'kidushin'. The first Christians married 'under the *huppa*', as was the Jewish practice. Did this dovetail with Roman law? In the Vulgate, Saint Jerome – who was a jurist – clearly uses *coniugium* to indicate cohabitation and *nuptiae* to refer to a wedding or 'kidushin'. The word *matrimonium* only occurs six times in the Vulgate (Ruth 13, 2 Chr 9.14, Prv 30.23, Eccl 23.22, 1 Cor 7.10 and 38) and it always refers to a high-quality relationship. This notion was not central to Christian doctrine. In the writings of Saint Augustine, the word *matrimonium* does not occur. He wrote about the durability of *coniugium* and the definitive character of *nuptiae*. The bishops mainly hammered at the unbreakable nature of a long-term relationship (*coniugium*). In line with the Jewish tradition, the bishops also opposed the interference of parents or *patresfamilias* in man-woman relationships. They objected to the permission of the *patresfamilias* for *nuptiae*. The *patresfamilias* had to emancipate the children who were getting married (if they were not independent yet). In addition, the bishops furthered the practice of drawing up *tabulae nuptiales* on the occasion of the wedding. These *tabulae* contained promises for life, despite the fact that such promises were invalid according to the Roman case-law. The bishops defended that *nuptiae* led to the automatic emancipation of the man and woman and to the establishment of a new family. Their idea became successful in the sixth century.

After the disappearance of the Western Empire, man-woman relationships continued to appear in the royal case-law. The *lex romana burgundionum* was the first to acknowledge tacit emancipation through *nuptiae*. We already find texts about man-woman relationships in the fifth-century Code of Euric and still encounter them in the eleventh-century case-law of Knut II of England.

The bishops and priests were aiming at the establishment of sexual morality. In the eighth century the Augustinian ideal of a durable and unbreakable man-woman relationship became popular. This can be noticed in the *libri penitentiales*, penitentials which were drawn up as a guide for confessors, as well as in moral literature (Paulinus of Aquileia, Alcuin, Jonas of Orléans, Autpertus...). From then on the legal aspects of man-woman relationships also crop up in collections of canon law. The Council of Paris (829), for example, decided that a man-woman relationship could not be terminated. The Council of Chalon (813) acknowledged *contubernium* as a full relationship. In collections of canon law, one can find Augustinian excerpts about *coniugium* that are linked with marriage. The term *matrimonium* is extremely rare in collections of canon law.

In the Carolingian era the bishops were involved in the royal administration of justice. They imposed rules of marriage law, such as the rules that forbade relationships in a case of overly close consanguinity. Many German feudal lords were summoned before the courts because they entered into relationships with blood relatives. Their marriage politics were aimed at the reunion of fiefs which had been split up through inheritance. This practice gave rise to inbreeding – planned heirs were not born or died too early – and led to divorce if a marriage remained childless. In this context, the episcopal judges began to impose the Roman rules about forbidden relationships and tried to maximise their scope. Some courts interpreted the Roman degrees of consanguinity in terms of *parentelae*. The consequence was that the forbidden fourth degree of consanguinity no longer indicated relationships between cousins, but descent from a common ancestor four generations back. Some courts stated that the texts of Roman law that pertained to consanguinity always mentioned forbidden degrees and that the rule was therefore that cohabitation was forbidden as soon as any consanguinity was discovered. In these lawsuits, the freedom of cohabitation was limited by canonical judgements concerning the establishment of a man-woman relationship and a family.

Bibliography. – Those who want to read about man-woman relationships in the *penitentiaria* without ploughing through Latin patrology, can consult Regino of Prüm: G.W.H. WASSERSCHLEBEN and W. HARTMANN, *Das Sendhandbuch des Regino von Prüm* [Ausgewählte Quellen zur deutschen Geschichte des Mittelalters, 42], Darmstadt 2004. On the development of the man-woman relationship by the Carolingian moralists, see *Il matrimonio nella società altomedievale*, [Settimane di studio del Centro italiano di studi sull'alto medioevo, 24,] 2 vol., Spoleto 1977. On the lawsuits concerning man-woman relationships involving overly close consanguinity, see P. CORBET, *Autour de Burchard de Worms, L'église allemande et les interdits de parenté (IXe-XIIe siècle)*, [Ius commune, Sonderhefte, 142,] Frankfurt/Main 2001. Beware: as is usually the case, these works do not distinguish between the different Roman terms concerning man-woman relationships and take *matrimonium, coniugium* and *nuptiae* to refer to 'marriage'.

B. The development of marriage in the twelfth century

In 1122 ecclesiastical jurisdiction was acknowledged in the Concordat of Worms. However, this Concordat did not provide a division of jurisdiction between the worldly and the ecclesiastical instances. In the first edition of his Decree, Gratian already invoked the Church's jurisdiction *ratione personae* over conflicts involving clergymen, and its jurisdiction *ratione materiae* over conflicts pertaining to typically ecclesiastical matters (see among other texts C. 11 q. 1). Gratian's text was linked with the last judgement of the Roman prefecture concerning the legal competence of the bishops, Nov. 35 by Valentinian III (452), with which the Carolingian prefectures were familiar. The ecclesiastical judges also accepted the old rule of Constantine (CTh. 2.1.10 and C. 11 q. 1 c. 35-36) which stated that they could not execute judgements without an imperial exequatur. In the Middle Ages, this exequatur was granted by delegated feudal judges.

The people who were subject to the law were sympathetic towards the new ecclesiastical administration of justice: it allowed appeals, the judges' financial interests in the cases were smaller, and the judgement was assessed by an executive body. One manner of ensuring that the ecclesiastical court had jurisdiction, was to claim that the conflict was the consequence of a man-woman relationship and therefore part of the ecclesiastical sphere *ratione materiae*. When he drew up his novel, Valentinian III had had theological disputes, liturgical matters, etc. in mind. In the twelfth century, however, people were inclined to include man-woman relationships in the ecclesiastical sphere because the Church concerned itself with morality. Gratian devoted a lot of attention to this issue in his *Decretum*. Some regions were quicker to accept *coniugia* as ecclesiastical matters than others. This view gained momentum around 1150. Problems pertaining to rent, discussions about maintenance costs, inheritances and descent... were suddenly connected with man-woman relationships and could therefore be brought before the ecclesiastical courts. Many lawsuits in these courts began with a discussion about jurisdiction *ratione materiae*. This discussion was settled in a *praeiudicium* (prejudgement), which could include a *possessio status* in which it was decided that one or both parties had the status of a cohabiting person. This status then led to the court having jurisdiction over the case. All sort of aspects and details of the man-woman relationship were dealt with in these prejudgements. According to Roman law, it was not possible to lodge an appeal against such a prejudgement. The losing party could, however, raise the matter of jurisdiction with the feudal judge who had to grant the exequatur. It is for this reason that the canonists began to accept appeals against prejudgements: in this manner, the matter of jurisdiction was first clarified within the canonical administration of justice. Under Alexander III, the Roman Rota pronounced many judgements about man-woman relationships and the ecclesiastical jurisdiction over this issue. Because the feudal judges were bound by Roman law, the canonists departed from Roman law as much as possible in order to ensure that the exequaturs would be granted. Since the ecclesiastical judges only had one aim, namely to obtain jurisdiction, it was no longer important to distinguish between *coniugium, nuptiae, matrimonium, uir et uxor*, etcetera. These notions had all become golf clubs that were used to hit the same ball.

C. The development of marriage in the thirteenth century

Disputes about jurisdiction were at the basis of the development of marriage law, which was characterised by an elaborate case-law and doctrine. It became a separate branch of canon law. *Matrimonium* became the central notion because it was the most noble one. All of the Roman rules were tossed into one big pot and the positive requirements for a marriage were skimmed from the surface: monogamy, for example, or *pubertas*, consensus and the permission of the parents. The beginning of cohabitation became the consummation of the marriage. The *ciuitas* of the man and the woman was replaced by membership of the Church. In addition, impediments to marriage were distilled from Roman law: examples include consanguinity, relatedness through marriage and spiritual relatedness. Marriages were based on consensus, as *nuptiae* used to be, because *consensus facit matrimonium nec concubitus*. A large amount of case-law was developed around this consensus. Because of the Roman words *contrahere matrimonium*, the canonists considered marriage to be a 'contract'. It was established both through *uerba de futuro* (the promise to marriage or the engagement), which could only be revoked by both partners or by the bishop if he had a good reason to do so, and through *uerba de presenti* which expressed the consensus. But what about a cohabitation concerning which a consensus had never been pronounced? Was such a cohabitation a clandestine marriage? Not necessarily: the consensus could be informal. The interpretation of the existence or non-existence of consensus was the most important issue in medieval marriage law.

Marriage savoured of Roman law throughout the Middle Ages. Even the difficult issue of dissolvability was justified by means of Roman arguments. In late Roman case-law it was sometimes decided that a new relationship after a *matrimonium* could not receive the status of a *matrimonium*. In the early Middle Ages, confessors were still of the opinion that a man-woman relationship could be terminated because of the unfaithfulness of a partner, but in the thirteenth century the Church acknowledged neither repudiation nor divorce by consent. It made use of Roman grounds to develop the separation from bed and board. The legal situation of people who were separated from bed and board according to ecclesiastical law was similar to that of divorcees in the late Empire.

At the end of the twelfth century the theologians took over the torch and further developed the abovementioned manner of cohabiting. They linked the vision of the church fathers with the new institution of the canonists. The *coniugium* of the canonists became the *coniugium* of Saint Augustine. In the works of Thomas Aquinas, it grew into Christian marriage. In the thirteenth century the word *matrimonium* was omnipresent. Marriage became a sacrament. Concubinage, which still appeared in Gratian's Decree, disappeared. A typical characteristic of the canonical commentaries of the thirteenth century is the mixture of theology and marriage law. "A canonist also thinks about salvation," Hostiensis wrote. In the thirteenth century the Church promoted a procedure which consisted of the declaration of the promise of marriage in church and public vows that were pronounced outside and in the presence of witnesses, after which there was a solemnisation in the church.

The canonists always emphasised that marriages were concluded between two people and not between two families. When two people married, a new family originated. Marital fidelity and the duty to maintain one's partner were identical for both the husband and the wife in canon law. The rules of family law were linked to the new status of marriage in the twelfth century. Matrimonial property law became a matter between spouses. In the thirteenth century the canonists and civilian lawyers gave the *maritus* the prerogatives of the *paterfamilias*. According to Hostiensis, for example, husbands owned the dowry, could represent their wife without a mandate or could be criminally liable for her actions.

That marriage was a new concept in the thirteenth century is illustrated by an enormous bug in the system that cannot leave a jurist indifferent. It was through marriage that the canonical court became competent and that a couple's children were granted legal protection as *legitimi*. However, if a defendant disputed the jurisdiction of the court during the initial hearing and could show that there was no marriage, there was no *familia* either. Those who wanted to end a relationship could find something in the plethora of rules about *coniugium, matrimonium, nuptiae* and *consensus*. The most common ground of nullity was consanguinity. In Roman law, a divorce did not impact the *familia*, but in canon law the children of a marriage which was void slipped through the net. In the thirteenth century the canonists tried to resolve this problem by deriving an un-Roman maintenance obligation from D. 25.3.5.1. Even if a marriage was declared to be a nullity, the parents had to provide for the children. The existence of this makeshift solution, however, shows that marriage law was a novelty that was not yet fine-tuned.

D. The nationalisation of marriage in the Early Modern Era

In the sixteenth century marriage law became an issue of the *ius commune*. The functions of the ecclesiastical courts were taken over by civic and royal jurisdictions.

Around 1500 many sovereign courts took canon law into account and by the middle of the century canon law had been incorporated into the royal case-law in many regions. In this manner, marriage was nationalised as well. In the Early Modern Era, marriage law would become part of civil law throughout the West.

As the importance of marriage in the civil law grew, the consequences of a void marriage became worse. In the Greek church, divorce and remarriage were possible. In 1516 Erasmus called the indissolubility of marriage into question by calling its sacramental aspect medieval. Luther agreed with him. The advantage of a divorce was that the legitimacy of the children was not questioned after the termination of the marriage. This Greek divorce was also found in the Roman sources and was therefore also considered to be a Western institution. The word *diuortium*, which originally indicated divergent behaviour and grounds for divorce, was promoted and came to denote a legal institution to dissolve *matrimonium*. Protestant jurists pleaded for the 'reintroduction' of Roman divorce, as if divorce was not a Greek institution but one that hailed from Rome. In reality, the sixteenth-century possibility of divorce was a combination of the Greek possibility of remarriage on the one hand and, on the other, an extension of the legal consequences of the medieval separation from bed and board.

Between 1545 and 1563 the reunion of Catholicism and Protestantism was discussed at the Council of Trent. However, divorce was not accepted by the Catholics and the indissolubility of marriage was confirmed. In order to combat the problem of illegitimate children, the ecclesiastical marriage law was reformed in the decree *Tametsi* (1563). Private or clandestine marriages were made impossible. A valid marriage had to be concluded in a church after an assessment of the requirements and *impedimenta*. The marriage was recorded in ecclesiastical marriage registers. In this manner, marriage lost its consensual character and became a formal legal act. In addition, extramarital relationships were denounced on moral grounds in order to avoid the conception of children out of wedlock. In many monarchies, the marriage law of Trent was introduced as royal law. National states wanted to laicise ecclesiastical marriage by taking over the position of the Church in marriage law. Within their national law, they created a solemn marriage that was concluded by the monarch or his administration and registered. When public and private law became two separate branches, marriage became a matter of private law. The institution that had once originated as a gateway to the ecclesiastical courts thus became a means of access to civil law.

Conclusion

In the nineteenth century, Tridentine marriage was an important institution of the civil law in most Western countries. This was new. In Grotius' work, marriage was not mentioned as an essential element of our civil rights, but in the civil codes of law it was. The Protestant possibility of divorce was incorporated in many civil systems. The idea that marriage led to the establishment of a family and that the family was the foundation of the state caused this civil marriage to be blown out of proportion. This also explains its decline today. Now that nationalism is disappearing, state interference in the conclusion of marriages is no longer desirable. It is typical of our Latin Western world that secularisation leads to a new search for a private marriage after the Roman model. Currently the status of *de facto* cohabitants is being developed in several Western countries. In this context, the partners' will to stay together and build a future leads to legal consequences which are different from the consequences of accidental or provisional cohabitation. In fact, the story already came full circle in 1970, when jurists wrote that the assessment of cohabitation had to take account of the couple's intentions, their *affectio maritalis*.

§5. Marital property law

In legal history, marital property law is an important matter because families have been established through marriage since the Middle Ages. Marriage therefore had a determinating influence on property. The ending of a marriage also involved liquidation and division. This was not the case in Antiquity, when people were free to pool property in any way they wanted. Nevertheless, man-woman relationships entailed consequences that pertained to property law. Roman couples used property for their cohabitation, committed themselves to their relationship and had accounts to settle when they separated. If a relationship was over, the (*paterfamilias* of the) man could revindicate property, while the (*paterfamilias* of the) woman could ask for the accounts to be settled by making use of the *actio rei uxoriae* – and later the *actio dotis*. The subject of the Roman system is not liquidation and division, but case-law around one remedy.

As soon as the *nuptiae* were concluded, the woman was given a *dos* (dowry) in her husband's *familia*, even when she was an independent woman or a member of a different *familia*. A dowry was earmarked property, which was intended for the couple and their children or for the woman after the dissolution of the cohabitation. The *paterfamilias* was liable for the maintenance and growth of the property. He could not encumber the dowry with usufruct or pledges. The simplest means of establishing a dowry was to introduce new property because of *nuptiae*. These assets could be donated by everyone, but it had to be clear that they were meant for the dowry. A dowry that was donated by a person from whom the woman would normally inherit was called a *dos profectitia*. If the dowry came from someone else, it was a *dos aduenticia*. A dowry that was only established for the maintenance of the woman was a *dos recepticia*. It could be reclaimed by the donor after the dissolution of the *matrimonium*.

The *paterfamilias* kept dotal accounts in which both property and obligations were registered. The *actio rei uxoriae*, and later the *actio dotis*, served to claim the balance of this account. If the *familia* devolved, the dowry fell to the new *familia* of the woman. If the marriage was dissolved, the woman received the dowry. The judge could only allow this action when the *nuptiae* had been terminated with the consent of both parties, when the woman could prove repudiation or if she demonstrated clearly that the *matrimonium* was over. The amount that was adjudicated to the woman was not necessarily the balance of the dotal account: it could be the amount that should have been in this account. The judge who settled a dispute about a dowry was bound by a series of precedents. If the dowry consisted of capital property or investment media that had remained intact, the normal growth could be claimed. On the other hand, the judge could also determine that nothing had to be returned, for example because the entire dowry had been used during the cohabitation for abnormal benefits for the woman. In a classical case, a woman had used the means of her husband's *familia* to enrich another man, for whom she then left her husband. The judge subtracted these expenses from her dowry. If a woman manifestly lived beyond the means of her family, the judge could take this into account when calculating the dowry that had to be given to her.

If the dowry was established by the spouses themselves, the calculation became a little more complex. In principle, gifts between spouses were invalid. Gifts on account of the wedding (*ante* and *propter nuptias*), however, were permitted both before and after the wedding. In this manner, the man could establish a dowry for his wife, or add some property to her dotal account. These specific gifts were added to the capital that the woman took with her after a divorce or the demise of her partner. If there was no dowry, if the dowry was too small in view of the circumstances, or if the *paterfamilias* did not keep thorough accounts, the judge could presume that there had been gifts on account of the wedding. This was certainly the case if the couple's holdings had increased substantially during the marriage. A woman who had conducted trade could lay claim to the balance of her *peculium* account by means of the *actio dotis*. The judge decided whether he would add that money to the dowry or not.

A woman always had a dotal account in her husband's *familia*, even when she had her own *familia*. The contributions which she made to her husband's *familia*, for example in order to help bear the costs of the household, were added to her dotal account (D. 23.3.56.1: *ibi dos esse debet, ubi onera matrimonii sunt*). Expenses that were paid from that account were deducted from it.

During the relationship, the *paterfamilias* had a natural obligation towards the woman. If the *actio dotis* was brought, this became an absolute obligation. Hence the first sentence of D. 23.3.75: *Quamuis in bonis mariti dos sit, mulieris tamen est.* Translation: even when the dowry is part of the capital of her husband, it still belongs to the woman. Beware: in casu, this *maritus* was the *paterfamilias*. In case of a bankruptcy, a Roman woman had a privilege on the dowry. In the post-classical era, a right of pledge was added to this privilege by operation of law, so that the woman had a stronger right than the *paterfamilias*.

The personal effects of the woman (*parapherna*) did not belong to the *familia* of her husband, but the *paterfamilias* of that *familia* did bring the actions concerning this property.

The dotal system remained important in the Mediterranean. From Constantinople, it was also exported to the Arab world and Eastern Africa. In the Latin world, the Christian family became significant. This marriage involved men and women being emancipated from their original *familiae* and jointly managing property. In this system, the termination of a man-woman relationship also meant the end of the community of property. This, in turn, entailed liquidation and division. The separate action for the dowry did not exist anymore. The old Roman case-law concerning the *dos* nevertheless continued to play a role in these liquidations for a long time. In the south of France, for example, many courts were confronted with the question of whether the *dos profecticia* should be deducted from the share of the donor's estate which the woman would receive ('l'exclusion de la fille dotée'). In the north, the dowry was also treated in the *ius commune* on account of liquidations and divisions. The allocation and advance acquisition of specific property became the central issue in this context. Consider, for example, art. 757 Code civil about the right of reversion or anomalous inheritance.

Until the twentieth century the dotal system of the *ius commune* appeared in many civil codes of law. In the twenty-first century it has become a rarity.

Bibliography. – On the abovementioned natural obligation, see L. WAELKENS, 'Dos naturaliter mulieris est dans D. 23.3.75', in: H. DONDORP, J. HALLEBEEK, T. WALLINGA and L. WINKEL (eds.), *Ius romanum – ius commune – ius hodiernum, Studies in honour of Eltjo J.H. Schrage on occasion of his 65th birthday*, Amsterdam-Aalen 2010, p. 399-410.

§6. The protection of liable minors

The actors in court also included guardians and curators, who acted for people who had become independent too soon. A distinction was made between the 'guardianship' of minors and the 'curatorship' of people who were younger than twenty-five. This distinction does not exist in current law, where those who are not adults are always minors.

1. Guardianship

Women and children who acted in a civil court, for example on account of the inheritance of their *paterfamilias*, were given a legal representative or *tutor* (guardsman, guardian; *tueri* means 'to look around' and *tutela* was the term for a sentinel's shift in the army). This guardian acted for his 'pupil'.

As has been mentioned above, this legal representation remained very superficial for adult women. Their *tutor* was not liable. A *paterfamilias* could nominate a guardian for his wife or daughters in his will, or a *tutor* could be appointed by operation of law. If a woman appeared before the praetor without a representative, the latter could appoint any *ciuis* as *tutor*. In the imperial law, this guardianship of women no longer existed because the woman acted *iure liberorum*, i.e. according to the procedure for free people.

The *tutor* who acted as a legal representative for children had a more difficult task. The praetors introduced remedies by means of which a pupil could call his *tutor* to account. It is out of the case-law surrounding these remedies that the notion of guardianship developed. The guardianship of young people is dealt with extensively by Gaius in D. 26-27 and in his Inst. 5.28-75. The large number of titles in the *Corpus iuris* indicates the significance of guardianship in Antiquity. In a society that was continuously confronted with death, such an institution was indeed very important. Children were constantly being helped through such difficult periods. Guardianship allowed their property to be spared to a certain extent. Creditors were protected by this institution as well. In a world in which life was uncertain, guardianship allowed people to construct devices that would outlive them.

Orphans had a guardian until adulthood. According to the legal school of the Sabinians, boys were *impuberes* until they were clad in the *toga uirilis*; according to the Proculians, they became adults at the age of fifteen. Girls always reached adulthood at the age of twelve. A distinction was made between *impuberes infantes* (children who could not speak) and *impuberes infantia maiores* who could express themselves when they performed legal acts. *Impuberes* should not be confused with minors.

2. Types of guardians

A guardian was appointed in a will, by operation of law or by the administration.

Testamentary guardianship (*tutela testamentaria*) must have been the oldest form of guardianship. It can be found in the Twelve Tables. Wills were a civil right 'par excellence'. Citizens were given the right to decide what would happen with their property after their death at a very early stage (see below). When they appointed a guardian in their will, they could arrange access to the civil court for their heirs. The testamentary appointment of a guardian was a common practice in the Republic. The *testator* could select a guardian for his surviving relatives from a wide range of people, who were, however, allowed to refuse this duty. With regard to some guardians, such as slaves who were released in the same will, a confirmation (*confirmatio*) by the praetor was required. A guardianship began when the will was executed or at the time of the *confirmatio*. A testamentary guardian could not refer his task to someone else. From Claudius' reign onwards (41-51), a person could not refuse testamentary guardianship according to the imperial law if there was no ground for exemption.

The Twelve Tables already mention the statutory guardian (*tutor legitimus*) as well. The *tutor legitimus* was the person who became a guardian by operation of law when there was no testamentary guardian. In general, the statutory guardianship was assumed either by the closest male adult agnate or by several male adult agnates who were of the same degree of kinship to the pupil (Twelve Tables 5.6). The guardian of a freedman or freedwoman was the *patronus*. If there was no *patronus*, one or more agnatic relatives served as guardians. The guardian of an emancipated person who had not yet reached adulthood was the *manumissor*. In the late Empire, blood relatives took the agnates' place. It was impossible to refuse statutory guardianship. When children under statutory guardianship reached adulthood, their guardian was liable for the administration of their property even though he had never accepted the guardianship! In the Republic, the statutory guardian could transfer his assignment to another person. This happened by means of *in iure cessio*, i.e. before the praetor, who supervised such transfers. In the post-classical era, the grounds for exemption that applied with regard to magisterial guardianship (see below) also applied with regard to statutory guardianship.

Those who did not have any close agnates were not given a statutory guardian. From the *lex atilia* (210 BC) onwards, the *praetor urbanus* or governor of the province appointed a magisterial guardian (*tutor datiuus*) in such cases. After Claudius, the consuls could appoint guardians; from the reign of Marcus Aurelius onwards, the special *praetor tutelarius* could appoint them; and in the post-classical era the *praefectus urbi* could do so as well. The appointment of a magisterial guardian had to be requested by the close relatives of the pupil. This meant that the mother was obliged to file this request: D. 26.6.2.2. A magisterial guardianship was a *munus*, an assignment from the government. The magistrate appointed someone whom he thought would be a suitable guardian. Objections to this appointment could be lodged with the magistrate himself, and, in the Imperial Period, with the administration. The treatment of these objections resulted in the development of grounds for exemption that could be invoked before the magistrate. There was quite a lot of case-law about this subject, and many opinions were given about it. Among the grounds for exemption that were accepted were old age, illness, the fact that the pupil lived too far away, the fact that the guardian who was appointed had already had to accept other pupils, the fact that he had many children himself, the fact that he had already been appointed to execute other government assignments, or that he was in active military service... In the Empire, one could suggest a more suitable candidate, but Justinian abolished this possibility again. From 390 onwards, the mother could become her children's guardian, but if she did so, she was required to refrain from marrying during her guardianship (C. 5.35.2). According to Justinian, the mother took precedence over collateral relatives (Nov. 118.5, in the Middle Ages this text was inserted into the Code *post* C. 5.32.2 as Aut. '*Matri et auiae*').

These three types of guardianship cropped up in the medieval towns and fiefs. According to the civilian jurists and canonists, the existence of magisterial guardianship indicated that the appointment and supervision of guardians was an important task of the monarchs and delegated judges. In the Early Modern Era, it was stated that the monarch and the government were the ultimate guardians ('Obervormundschaft') and that they delegated their assignment to the daily guardians who actually managed the pupils' affairs.

Text. – In Antiquity and later periods parental authority was exercised by the *paterfamilias* and the father, respectively. In C 5.32.2 we read that the mother could ask to be appointed as the guardian after the demise of the father. In Justinian's Nov. 118.5, mothers and grandmothers who wanted to assume guardianship took precedence over everyone except the guardian whom the deceased *paterfamilias* had appointed in his will. The Code was not ratified by Justinian. The individual texts that were included in the Code had received the force of law when they were first promulgated. C. 5.32.2 dated from 390; the Novel from 537. *Lex posterior priori derogat* (the younger text takes precedence over the older one). For the legists of the twelfth century, this Novel seemed to be correcting the text from the Code. In such cases, they inserted a citation from the novel after the relevant text from the Code. Until the nineteenth century these *authenticae* (which were named after the *Authenticum*, the source from which they were cited) were printed in the Code. In the Mommsen-Krüger edition of the Code, these *authenticae* were no longer included after the fragments of the Code, but listed at the end. The mother's guardianship is a beautiful example of an important matter that was received through such medieval *authentica*. It is for this reason that we include the citation below.

C. 5,35,2. – *Imppp. Valentianus, Theodosius et Arcadius AAA. Tutiano pp.* Matres, quae amissis uiris tutelam administrandorum negotiorum in liberos postulant, priusquam confirmatio officii talis in eas iure ueniat, fateantur actis sacramento praestito ad alias se nuptias non uenire. 1. Sane in optione huiuscemodi nulla cogitur, sed libera in condiciones quas praestituimus uoluntate descendat: nam si malunt alia optare matrimonia, tutelas filiorum administrare non debent. 2. Sed ne sit facilis in eas post tutelam iure susceptam inruptio, bona eius primitus, qui tutelam gerentis adfectauerit

Translation BLUME. – Mothers who have lost their husbands and ask to be appointed to manage the affairs of their children must, before they can be legally appointed to perform such duty, make a statement under oath, made of record, that they will not remarry. 1. Of course, no woman shall be forced to make such choice but must voluntarily agree to the conditions we have laid down. For if women prefer to enter into a second marriage, they cannot have the guardianship of their children. 2. And in order that a woman who has lawfully undertaken a guardianship may not easily violate said condition, nuptias, in obligationem uenire et teneri abnoxia rationibus paruulorum praecipimus, ne quid incuria, ne quid fraude depereat. 3. His illud adiungimus, ut mulier, si aetate maior est, tunc demum petendae tutelae ius habeat, cum tutor testamentarius uel legitimus defuerit uel priuilegio a tutela excusetur uel suspecti genere submoueatur uel ne suis quidem per animi aut corporis ualetudinem administrandis facultatibus idoneus inueniatur. 4. Quod si feminae tutelas refugerint et praeoptauerint nuptias, tunc demum uir illustris praefectus urbis adscito praetore, qui impertiendis tutoribus praesidet, siue iudices, qui in prouinciis iura restituunt, de alio ordine per inquisitionem dari minoribus defensores iubebunt. *Dat. XII Kal. Febr. Mediolani, Valentiniano A. IIII et Neoterio conss.* [390].

we direct that the property of a man who wants to marry such woman who carries on the guardianship shall be pledged and held responsible for the proper management of the property of the children, lest anything be done carelessly or be lost through fraud. 3. We also add that a woman who is of age shall have the right to ask for the guardianship only when there is no testamentary or statutory guardian, or when any such person is excused by reason of his privilege, or when he is excluded on account of being suspected, or when he is unable to manage his own property on account of mental or bodily ill health. 4. But if women abstain from guardianship and prefer marriage, then only the illustrious prefect of the city, together with the praetor, who attends to the appointment of guardians, or the judges who administer the laws in the provinces, will, after investigation, direct guardians of another kind to be appointed for minors. Given at Milan January 21 (390).

Authent. De heredibus ab intest. § Ex his [Nov. 118,5]. – Matri et auiae secundum ordinem tutelam etiam ante agnatos subire permittimus, si inter gesta nuptiis aliis et Senatusconsulti Velleiani auxilio renuntiauerit, solis testamentis tutoribus eas praecedentibus, legitimis et datiuis postpositis. Defuncti namque uoluntatem praeponi uolumus. Praeter has autem aliis mulieribus interdicimus officium tutelae subire.

Translation Scott. – We forbid women to undertake the burden of guardianship, except in the case of a mother or grandmother. We permit them only to undertake a guardianship, in the order of their inheritance, and that only after they have renounced, by an entry on the public records, a second marriage and the benefit of the Velleian senate decree. If they do this, they have preference as to guardianship over all collateral relatives, and only testamentary guardians shall have a preference over them, for we want the will and the choice of the deceased to govern.

3. The remedies of the pupil

As soon as he reached adulthood, the pupil was granted remedies against his guardian. Against a magisterial guardian, he could use an *actio de rationibus distrahendis* (action for the unravelling of the accounts). This remedy was already mentioned in the Twelve Tables and it possessed a penal character. If it turned out that the guardian had stolen property, the pupil could use this action to demand twice the value of the stolen items: once by means of compensation and once by means of retribution (D. 26.7.55.1; D. 27.3.1.24; compensation and retribution will be treated in the chapter on the law of obligations). A pupil who wanted to take action sooner or who was represented by a third party could file a request with the court. The *accusatio suspecti tutoris* (accusation of a suspect guardian) was a complaint that was lodged in a *cognitio* procedure because of an offence committed by a testamentary guardian. If this guardian was guilty of deceit or serious neglect of duty, he could lose civil rights such as the right to assume guardianship (as an aspect of *infamia*). Sometimes a guardian was asked to conclude a *satisdatio rem pupilli saluam fore* (a stipulation with a guarantee to safeguard the property of the pupil).

By the end of the Republic, the *actio tutelae* appeared. This was an action by means of which a complete settlement of the administration of the guardian was enforced. A considerable amount of case-law about this *actio tutelae* has been preserved. It involved *bona fides*: if this action was brought, all of the relations between the guardian and the pupil were taken into account in the assessment. However, the action had a high tolerance threshold. The guardian was only liable if he was guilty of deceit, gross negligence or manifest maladministration. A guardian who was sentenced because of maladministration could, once again, lose his civil rights (*infamia*). Justinian demanded that guardians administered their pupils' property as carefully as they administered their own goods. He thereby increased the guardians' liability. In his turn, however, the guardian could use the *contraria actio tutelae* after the end of the guardianship in order to reclaim the costs which he had incurred for his pupil and which he had paid out of his own pocket.

From Constantine's reign onwards, pupils were automatically given a hypothec over their guardian's property (CTh. 3.30.1 = C. 5.37.20).

It is around the interpretation of these diverse remedies at law that the institution of guardianship, which would stand the test of time, developed. Here, we only will discuss some aspects of this case-law. The legal acts of an *impubes infans* (a child that could not express itself) were performed by the guardian. An *impubes infantia maior* could perform legal acts himself. If the pupil acted independently, he could only improve his situation. Legal acts that entailed risks or liabilities needed to be confirmed by the guardian (*auctoritas tutoris*). If there was no such confirmation, the other party could not claim anything. A pupil could not transfer ownership and his unilateral obligations were void. Mutual agreements only created rights for the pupil: he or she could not incur duties (*negotium claudicans*). The other party to the agreement could, however, use the *exceptio doli* against the claims of a pupil. The defendant could use this exception in order to have the judge consider the entire situation between the pupil, the guardian and the defendant if the latter was of the opinion that the pupil was abusing his status. From Antoninus Pius' reign onwards, a guardian could lodge a *condictio* on account of unjustified enrichment against his pupil.

In his capacity as a legal representative, the guardian was granted all of the remedies that were necessary to administer the property of the pupil. He could request *possessio* and could bring an action to revindicate the property of his pupil. He also took legal acts to alienate some of his pupil's property. This is a beautiful illustration of Roman legal logic. The Roman law of Antiquity was a law that only bore on conflicts and only existed in the courts, where it was the guardian who acted. Therefore it seemed as if all the rights were his, until the pupil became an adult and the accounts were settled. To the jurists of the Middle Ages and the Early Modern Era, who were sensitive to the substantive rights underlying the claims, it sounded as though the guardian owned and possessed the pupil's property. The guardian indeed acted vis-à-vis third parties as if the property were his. In his account books, however, he had to keep his own accounts separate from those of his pupils. By means of the *actio de rationibus distrahendis* the pupil could reclaim twice the value of the items that the guardian had credited or debited wrongly or which he had not credited or debited at all. If there was no amicable final settlement, the case was brought before the court by means of the *actio tutelae*. The Roman jurists have left us a considerable number of opinions about the guardian's liability for problems concerning investments, the safeguarding of immovable property, the purchase of speculative assets, the recovery of claims, etcetera. See for example the titles D. 26.7 and 27.9. From the reign of Marcus Aurelius (161-180) onwards the *praetor tutelarius* supervised guardians. In 195, Septimius Severus forbade a guardian from selling rural immovable property (D. 27.9.1.2). After 235 the value of all assets began to fluctuate more and the regulations concerning careful administration became stricter. Constantine extended the prohibition pertaining to sale so that it included the sale of all immovable property and valuable objects.

In the *ius commune*, guardianship was inspired by the Digest to a large extent. The stories about the *missi dominici* and knights who made a stand for widows and orphans are tales about the reception of guardianship. Magistratorial guardianship was already common in the early Middle Ages and delegated feudal judges were involved in issues of guardianship. In thirteenth-century texts, one can find mentions of governmental supervision of guardians.

Bibliography. – An illustration of guardianship in the Middle Ages and the Early Modern Era can be found in Ph. GODDING, *Le droit privé dans les Pays-Bas méridionaux du 12e au 18e siècle*, Brussels 1987, p. 132-138.

4. Curatorship of people under the age of twenty-five

The other institution that was important with regard to the protection of independent young people was the curatorship of those who were younger than twenty-five. The Twelve Tables already provided curators for the spendthrift and the insane. Normally, the curator was the closest agnate. If there was no suitable agnate, the praetor appointed a curator himself (D. 27.10.13). Under Justinian, the curator was always appointed by the government. His assignment was determined on a case-by-case basis.

The curatorship of minors originated later. Around 192 BC the *lex laetoria* introduced a special protection for those who were younger than twenty-five. A person who had seen that such a youngster was deceived, could bring a penal action against the deceiver. This was an *actio popularis*, which led to a private fine. If the action was successful, the deceiver was sentenced to pay a private fine to the plaintiff. The young person himself did not receive any part of this fine. During the next stage, the praetor granted the victim of an excessive obligation the *exceptio legis laetoria*. With this action, the victim could defend himself against the claims of a deceiver. Finally, there was the *in integrum restitutio*. Minors who had been deceived could demand a return to the *status quo ante*. Mitigating circumstances were developed in the case-law. If the minor had been accompanied by a *paterfamilias* who was of age, the creditor could claim that this *paterfamilias* had acted in the same manner as the curator of an insane or spendthrift person. The case-law acknowledged that the rights which minors derived from the *lex laetoria* indeed ceased to apply if they did not act alone. This case-law could cause a conflict between the minor and his companion: 'It is because of your actions that I lost my rights as a minor'. Such a conflict was treated as an issue of *negotiorum gestio*, which was sanctioned by means of the *actio negotiorum gestorum*. Those who acted for others without being asked to do so could be held liable for errors or gross negligence. Someone who was of age and accompanied a minor had the same liability as a guardian with regard to this *negotiorum gestio*. The Roman texts which have been preserved do not allow us to infer whether every accidental companion of a minor could be charged as a curator, or whether a curator was someone with whom the minor had a long-term curatorial relationship. The *actio negotiorum gestorum* seems to indicate a coincidental relationship, but this action also seems to have been used for the curatorship of spendthrift and insane persons, who apparently had a long-term curator. The idea that a curator of minors was also appointed by the praetor is taken from Gaius 1.197, but the manuscript from Verona is illegible here and the text has been emendated with the Institutes of Justinian. In C. 2.37 and Inst. 1.23, there are quite a few texts that allow us to infer that curatorship for minors was organised according to fixed rules in the late Empire and served as a continuation of guardianship. At least Justinian's commission seems to have understood curatorship in this manner.

In the Middle Ages, Inst. 1.23 was interpreted as if the curatorship that concerned the actions of minors was of the same nature as the curatorship of insane or spendthrift people. It was said that Roman minors could file a request with the imperial court in which they asked for the appointment of a curator. According to the medieval legists, every Roman minor had his own curator. In line with this interpretation of the Institutes, jurists no longer drew the distinction between guardianship and curatorship in the West. All guardians were appointed by the authorities. This interlacing of the two institutes in its turn influenced the interpretation of the old texts. In nineteenth-century literature, one can even read that a Roman curator was often the ex-guardian, who administered the property of his minor.

This interlacing of guardianship and curatorship complicated the reception of the concept of minority. The Roman *familia* was replaced with the family in the Middle Ages. A person who married was automatically emancipated and automatically became independent. Later, priesthood also led to tacit emancipation. In many regions it was usual to emancipate all children who were of normal intelligence, which meant that they could lay claims in the court themselves. Sadly, there is no medieval case-law about the status of 'minors' who acted independently after they had been emancipated by their parents. In the sixteenth century, the Roman status of minority was dredged up again, but as a general means to protect young people. Minority was linked with legal capacity and no longer bore exclusively on independent youngsters. The rules about minority also applied to children under parental authority and independent children under guardianship. In addition, the rules of Roman guardianship, for example the rule about their capacity to express themselves, were applied to all children. Texts that limited the liability of independent youngsters were used as the basis for substantive rules that established the incapacity of all young persons.

§7. Associations and legal persons

In our current law, associations engage in legal transactions. Sometimes separate assets also have an interest and act as an 'association' in the court. Were these associations persons in Roman law as well? In the nineteenth century Savigny coined the term 'legal persons' ('juristische Personen'). They functioned as a person and acted through legal fictions. In the overview below, the origin of the legal person is treated as well.

1. Trade with the government in the Roman law of Antiquity

A. Trade with the government in the Republic

Today, the state and bodies governed by public law are associations 'par excellence'. They have legal personality and institute legal proceedings as persons.

In the Republic, there was a *populus romanus*, but one could not conduct trade with it. The army and the central organisation were paid with the Senate's money, which was symbolised by the *aerarium* (the treasury). It was administered by the quaestors, who executed the decisions of the Senate. Consuls and governors of provinces who were given a budget, contacted the quaestors. The latter also had legal relationships with private people. These relationships concerned the management of domains that belonged to the Senate, the collection of taxes, the execution of public works, the renting of buildings, etcetera. Legal acts relating to the quaestors did not fall under civil law, but were regulated in the quaestors' own edict. If there was a conflict, they followed their own procedures and granted specific remedies at law. No one thought of trade 'with the community' or 'with the state'. Magistrates and citizens conducted trade with the quaestors.

Gaius 2.11 states that in the Republic, there was a category of property called *res publicae*. They were military domains, which could be granted in concession. This property was not part of anyone's private property, Gaius wrote, it belonged to the *uniuersitas*. Who was that? The public at large, the army or simply no one – the sky and the clouds? This is once again an example of the enigmatic nature of Gaius' work. Later, *uniuersitas* would become the Latin word that indicated what we call an association (see D. 1.8.1).

B. Trade with the government in the Empire

In the imperial provinces, the Egyptian model, in which all land belonged to the pharaoh, was rapidly introduced by the emperor Augustus. Because of this quick introduction, quite a large number of new sitations were indicated with terms that already existed in the civil law, like *familia caesaris*. The administration worked in the emperor's name and on his authority. It was the emperor who acquired and spent assets. The property, income and revenue of 'the government' constituted the public domain. During his office, this public domain was the personal property of the emperor (*dominium caesaris, familia caesaris*; its nickname is *fiscus*, the begging basket of the emperor). The emperor himself took legal actions as a person, namely as a citizen in cases pertaining to civil law and as a member of the military in the context of the maintenance of law and order. The public domain of the first emperors was not separate from their personal property. They organised their succession by adopting a candidate and excluding other heirs from their inheritance. In the course of the first century the system was finetuned. The *fiscus* became part of the emperor's office and was no longer his private property. Unlike in the case of his patrimony, the *fiscus* did not fall to his heirs, but to the person who succeeded him as emperor. When the emperor died, any candidate who wanted to succeed him could revindicate the public domain before the imperial courts. However, there was only one judge whose mandate had not ended when the emperor died: the *praefectus praetorio*, the highest judge and the general of the praetorian guard. In a judgement he adjudicated the public domain to the person with the best entitlements. It is not surprising that many prefects were murdered.

Under emperor Hadrian (117-138) the *aerarium* was taken over by the *fiscus* and the Republic disappeared. All of the provinces were henceforth part of the imperial public domain. Trade with the government was always trade with the emperor. There was no need for legal fictions like the legal person or associations. Nor was there any need for the idea that the public domain was a foundation: it was the property of the emperor. During an interregnum, the public domain had the status of property under sequestration. Revenues were credited and expenses were debited, but nothing could be claimed. Settlements could only be handled by the new emperor when he had taken office.

This concept of adjudicating property to a person who held a certain position was also used for other public offices. D. 33.1.20.10 mentions a specific legacy for a judge and a temple guard. Such legacies had not been bequeathed to those who held the office. They could be claimed by their successors. The same was true of ecclesiastical property: it was the personal property of a bishop as long as he was in office. If he died or was transferred and a conflict arose, his successor could revindicate the property before the court. The court assessed the appointment of the successor and adjudicated the property to the person with the best entitlements (see C. 1.2.14.10). This formula remained in existence in the Middle Ages and can still be found in current English law. The property of the Cinque Ports belongs to the Warden of the Cinque Ports during his office. The Royal Mail belongs to the Postmaster General, and if there is a problem, claims must be lodged against him personally. After his retirement, the institution passes to his successor.

Municipia (municipalities) held public property in the manner that Gaius described. In the third century, Ulpian (D. 3.4.2) wrote that they were a *uniuersitas*. In his work, this notion from the *edictum perpetuum* already refers to an association. Associations had their own property consisting of assets and debts. However, municipalities did not appear before the court. The municipal council made decisions by majority vote; the aldermen collected and disposed of assets according these decisions. The treasurer debited and credited items. Aldermen who entered into agreements that were not covered by the municipal council had to pay themselves. If a municipality wanted to bring proceedings, the physical people who were members of the municipal council appointed a physical person as their representative. He was appointed *ad hoc* (D. 3.4.6.1) and acted as a *persona* in the court. However, we can already see that important principles of the law of associations were beginning to appear: the legal representative did not act for the members of the municipal council, but for the *uniuersitas*. Assets which he obtained became *res publicae* that belonged to the municipality. If he lost the case, the members of the municipal council could not be sued for payment. The only possibility was the seizure of the public property of the municipality. If the legal representative incurred costs and these were not reimbursed, he claimed them from the municipality (D. 3.4.7), but even then the municipality did not become a person. If the municipality did not authorise the treasurer to pay after the judgement had been passed, a complaint was filed with the governor of the province, who could dispose of the municipal property. In other words, the *municipia* functioned as current legal persons do: they were governed by bodies who appointed legal representatives and had their own property. However, they were never party to legal proceedings and were therefore not persons. When the system failed, the governor intervened in the emperor's name.

2. Trade with civil associations in Antiquity

In Antiquity, a de facto association was a *corpus*. We understand this word to mean 'collection' in expressions like *corpus christianorum* and *corpus iuris*. When the Lateran domain was donated to the *corpus christianorum*, however, the word did not denote an association: it was, after all, the bishop of Rome who received it. In the Theodosian Code we encounter *corpora nauicularia* (shipping companies) and *corpora pistorum* (bakeries) involved in large-scale production and shipping for the prefecture of the *annona*, for the public social works. They were trade unions of shipowners and bakers who collaborated so that they were large enough to make deals with the *annona*. There is case-law about these cartels, but it was hardly ever studied. It seems that *corpora* did not act as independent entities. In the Middle Ages, the term was used by professional associations who formed cartels in order to make price agreements. In D. 3.4.1, Gaius' commentary on the provincial edict teaches us that there were *corpora* that had a legal form and conducted trade just as the Republic did: one person performed legal acts, but the treasury and the property were joint property, *res communes*. Marcianus wrote at the end of the second century that the property belonged to an *uniuersitas* (D. 1.7.2). Below, we will treat various legal forms that were used in this context.

A. Familia

The manner in which an association could be structured as a *familia* has already been discussed. The Latin word for an undertaking was *familia*. Within a *familia*, trade with limited liability could be organised. The *paterfamilias* acted for all of the family members. As an association, the *familia* could not survive the death of the *paterfamilias*. The association could be maintained in a *consortium*, but this was an unstable situation: the continued existence of a *consortium* could not be enforced, while its dissolution could be. As has been mentioned above, the Roman *familia* continued to exist in the Middle Ages and the Early Modern Era as the legal form of association used by organised brotherhoods.

B. Fiducia

An important concept of Roman law was the *fiducia*, the trust. It can be compared with the abovementioned system of entrusting the public domain to the emperor. A *paterfamilias* could administer the property of a third party *in fiducia*. The property was transferred to his *familia*, where it became 'earmarked' property – in Latin *more dotis* (comparable to a dowry). The purpose for which this property was to be used was recorded in a *pactum fiduciae* (fiduciary agreement). If this *pactum* was not respected, the person who had transferred the property was granted the *actio fiduciae*. This was an *actio e bone fide* by means of which the entire situation could be assessed and all agreements concerning the fiduciary transfer could be enforced.

Associations often made use of this concept. Members transferred their contribution to the account of the *dominus* who led the association. He could only use this money for the designated purpose. If he used it for anything else, the members of the association could use the *actio fiduciae* against him. In order to protect himself, he entered all revenue and expenditure in a separate *fiducia* account. If a new director was chosen for the association, the old one transferred all of the association's property to his successor. A majority vote was considered to be the expression of everyone's opinion (see D. 50.1.19), so everyone agreed to his *pactum fiduciae* being transferred to the new director. The members of an association usually made agreements about what would happen with the fiduciary property if the owner died unexpectedly. One possibility was that the property would be transferred by his heirs. Such an agreement could be enforced by means of the *actio fiduciae*. If no agreements had been made, the rule was that the *actio fiduciae* could be used against every heir who had received fiduciary property during the division. This method was used by associations until the Early Modern Era. Legal personality was not necessary because the director of the association acted in the court.

This concept was also used to establish investment funds. An average citizen could not invest in residential buildings, storehouses or aqueducts, but a *fiducia* made this possible. The investor transferred the money to a private person, who would hold it in trust. There was a *pactum fiduciae* that detailed the type of investment, the administration fee, the risk profile, the securities (for example a plege on the property that was bought), arrangements concerning the transfer of the fiduciary property after death, etcetera. The *actio fiduciae* could be used against any person who held the fiduciary property. It is possible that the person who entrusted his property to a fiduciary received a pledge by operation of law (allusion in C. 5.13.1b).

The abovementioned ecclesiastical property that was adjudicated to bishops was also held in trust. The bishops received donations that were earmarked for poor relief, care of the sick, the organisation of memorial masses or education. The bishops had a fiduciary obligation towards the donors and their heirs. In the literature, it is sometimes stated that the *piae causae* (earmarked donations; the Latin term is traditionally translated as 'donations with a charitable purpose' or simply as 'charities') were at the basis of both foundations and the law of associations, but normally these *piae causae* were fiduciary transfers to bishops or *curiae* (see below).

Fiducia does not occur in the *Corpus iuris*, but does feature in the Theodosian Code (see for example CTh. 5.1.3 and CTh. 15.14.9). It was also described by Boethius (*Ad Ciceronis topica* 4.10.41).

C. Societas

Societas (partnership) was one of the four kinds of consensual contracts in Roman law.

Consensual contracts were versatile and flexible. An agreement that one Roman would buy some vegetables for another Roman on the market was a *societas*. So was the collaboration between the directors of the firm of Ateius, which was the market leader in oil lamps for half a century and employed thousands of workers. A partnership was a common venture, which involved people entering into agreements about a goal that was to be realised, the contribution of property and the division of revenue. It should not be confused with the current concept of association, because it did not enter into agreements with the outside world. The *socii* only had an agreement with one another. A commercial cooperation could involve several simultaneous *societates*. If traders had established a partnership, each of them could establish a new partnership with an *institor* who acted for him. Each commercial act that these *institores* performed could in its turn be part of another partnership. Conflicts were brought before the court with the *actio pro socio*, an *actio e bona fide* where the judge assessed the entire situation between the partners with regard to the contract in question. Property that had been contributed to a partnership could be revindicated by every *socius* and was therefore part of the *familia* of each partner. An outsider who conducted business with a member of the partnership only had a bond with this one partner. This meant that the liability of each *socius* was different: he was liable to the extent of his own property, of which the joint assets were part.

Familiae collaborated in a *societas*. It could not survive the death of a partner and it was always dissolved when an associate died. The contract of partnership could arrange for a new partnership to begin between the surviving associates, but even then the first *societas* had to be ended and the property had to be divided – and this made the new *societas* weaker.

D. Curia

In the late Empire we find the word *curia* for a collective government. This old word for the thirty *curiae* became a metonym for the Senate, the *curia hostilia* or *curia pompeiana*, and later for any government. In the late Empire, associations were led by a *curia*. The bishopric of Roma had a *curia*, and so did abbeys and hospitals. In his Dialogues 2.11 and 4.37, Gregory the Great uses the word *curialis* to indicate someone who acts for others. An important text is *Ed. Theod.* 27 (511-515): 'if a *curialis* has died without a statutory successor and without a will, his place falls to his *curia*, to the exclusion of the *fiscus*'. Apparently, a *curia* was an association of fellow owners. An authorised member could act as though all of the abbey's property was his. When he died, however, all of his rights returned to the chapter. The property belonged to the *uniuersitas* of the abbey. It did not matter who that was. A debt to a *uniuersitas*, was not a debt to its individual members, nor were the debts of the *uniuersitas* the debts of its members (D. 3.4.7.1). It did not matter that the members were always changing (D. 3.4.7.2). As far as the court was concerned, only the *curia* mattered. In Nov. 7 Justinian forbade abbeys, convents, hospitals, orphanages, etcetera from alienating immovable property. The prohibition was aimed at the directors of these institutions.

According to *Ed. Theod.* 27, this *curia* could survive the death of its members. Here, we encounter a private and 'immortal' association with property that fell within a *uniuersitas* according to the words of D. 3.4. The property that had been donated to an abbey for a good cause (*pia causa*) were technically the fiduciary property of the *curiales*. Property that they bought separately was owned or possessed by them. The *uniuersitas* did 'have' these *res communes*, but it had no rights to them. *Res communes* were located 'in the cloud', they only became legally relevant when the *curiales* did something with them.

In the Middle Ages, the word *curia* would crop up as a word for management, while *uniuersitas* would begin to be used as the Latin word for association or union. Both the latter word and the Dutch word 'vereniging' (een = one) are literal translations of *uniuersitas*. In Hungarian, a university is an 'egyetem' (egy = one).

3. Trade with associations in the Middle Ages

A. Abbeys and bishoprics

In the early Middle Ages, all of the abovementioned elements cropped up. Abbeys, hospitals, churches and bishops had an association's property at their disposal.

In the Carolingian era, Louis the Pious promulgated Nov. 7.1-2 for the West. It prohibited those who managed abbeys or institutions from alienating immovable property. This clearly shows that abbeys and institutions had and managed property without problems. The immortal character of a *curia* turned out to be important during the feudal era. As long as there was a *curia*, the association's property was allodial (*allodium*) and fell outside of the scope of feudal law. Problems concerning *dominium*, by contrast, were brought before the feudal courts. The property of a *curia*, however, never devolved and could not therefore be adjudicated to the *fiscus*. When they got involved in proceedings concerning immovable property the abbeys appealed to the protection of ownership to avoid the politicised feudal courts (see below). This ensured that the abbeys did not get involved in politics and made cultural revolutions like the Cluniac Reforms possible.

Fiduciary ownership of immovable property, however, underwent fundamental changes in the feudal era, when this type of ownership became an aspect of feudal law. All provincial property belonged to the emperor. Feudalism was based on the transfer of earmarked property, and this included fiduciary property. The feudal courts were first and foremost geared to the administration of the land and to war. Feudal lords granted land in return for military support. Private fiduciary ownership of agricultural land disappeared. It would crop up again in England when feudalism was privatised in the twelfth century and in some urban courts, but on the Continent this privatisation would only take place in the sixteenth century, when exclusive ownership became a popular concept. For bishops, the situation was different. From the ninth century onwards, bishops who held their ecclesiastical goods in fiduciary ownership were confronted with the problems concerning *libertas ecclesiae*, which we have treated in an earlier chapter. When one bishop was succeeded by another, vacant goods could be claimed before the feudal judges. In many regions these judges refused to adjudicate the goods to bishops who were not favourably disposed towards them and did not make contributions to the war chest. Many ecclesiastical goods became part of the public domain. Many bishops then received 'benefices' (the revenue of specific property) in order to organise poor relief.

The matter of the episcopal goods was resolved after the Concordat of Worms in 1122. The bishops defended the idea that there were two *fisci*: if ecclesiastical goods fell to the *fiscus*, that *fiscus* was the pope. However, the bishops did not manage to convince the worldly authorities of their view. *Dominia* continued to come under the jurisdiction of the feudal courts. An important evolution, however, was that vacant benefices were adjudicated by the pope.

B. Colleges and universities

In 1158 the emperor granted autonomous jurisdiction to the law faculty of Bologna. The consequence was that the faculty could organise itself according to its own insights. The professors combined their interests by establishing a *societas*. Each year, every professor also entered into a separate *societas* with his group of students. He negotiated his fees in this agreement.

In the twelfth century, student housing was provided by foreign lords who sent people from their region to the law faculty. These student houses received benefices and property in order to provide for the students and give them scholarships. In Bologna, these houses were called *nationes* (nations). They were led by *curiales*, who were the fiduciary owners of the property of the nations. This was possible because they came under the exclusive jurisdiction of the rector, who had an interest in the continued existence of these funds. At the end of the twelfth century, the nations established two *uniuersitates scolarium*: one for the Italian students and one for the *ultramontani*. From then on, these associations of students paid the professors, under the supervision of the nations. In the thirteenth century the two universities merged and the one remaining *uniuersitas* acquired the right to elect the rector. This meant that they also had the jurisdiction. The rector determined the fees, collected the money from the nations and used it to pay the professors. The *uniuersitas* bought buildings. These buildings were then owned by the *uniuersitas*, according to its own law.

Some other old universities, such as those of Paris or Cambridge, did not have jurisdictions, but came under the jurisdiction of the local bishop. These schools were *uniuersitates magistrorum et scolarium*, associations of students and professors, which were acknowledged by the officiality and also had their own property – this was possible on the basis of canonical case-law. It was in Paris that student houses were first called 'colleges'. The word *collegium* can be found in D. 47.22. In Antiquity, it meant meeting or assembly. In the Roman army and in the provinces, a close eye was kept on such gatherings. *Collegia tenuiorum*, assemblies of ordinary people were not subject to this supervision. In Paris, the term was adopted to indicate student houses (Collège de Sorbon, Collège d'Harcourt...). These houses were also led by *curiales*, trustees, and the competent court had a strong interest in their continued existence.

The associations also cropped up in the courses that were taught at the universities. An association could have property. If the association only had one member left, it stopped being an association; the last member became the holder of the property (D. 3.4.7). But what happened when this last member died as well? Did the property of an abbey fall to the *fiscus* when there were no more *curiales*? The answer to this question can be found in the gloss '*Nomen uniuersitatis' ad* D. 3.4.7.2. Moses of Ravenna (professor before 1144) taught that there was no objection to property belonging to the immaterial aspect of a church, namely that which lived between the walls and made the church more than a simple building. According to Joannes Bassianus, however, the situation could be compared to the devolution of an undivided estate. Expenditure and revenue are collected and paid by the estate. If there is a successor, the entire estate devolves to him from the moment of his predecessor's death onwards. The revenue of vacant prebends and benefices did not fall to the *fiscus* either, but to the successor. [A prebend is a fixed allowance paid at the expense of a property; a benefice is the full revenue from a property.] At the next stage, an association whose members had all died was compared to a deceased person. As long as his inheritance had not been divided, the deceased continued to receive revenue and incur expenses. In the thirteenth century, the problem did not only concern abbeys, but colleges as well. In Sinibaldus Fliscus' (†1254) commentary on X. 2.20.57 the fictitious person crops up: *cum collegium in causa uniuersitatis fingatur una persona* (since a college is considered to act as a person in proceedings that concern an association). In short, the goods did not belong to the deceased director, but to the person of the college. Jacques de Revigny (†1296) used the term *persona representata* in this context. The patrimony of an association 'represented' the association, just as an estate represented the person of the deceased. Because it was a *persona representata*, a college remained the owner of its property even when it had no members. In D. 46.1.22, Revigny read that an estate could play the role of a person, just as a college or a municipality could. This fiction that was used in case-law was incorporated in the articles of some colleges: the goods were *res communes* of the college and even when there were no more trustees, the goods continued to belong to the college itself. There could be no legal proceedings concerning these goods until there was a new board of directors. In this manner, the founders of colleges were offered the best guarantee that their donations would always remain earmarked for scholarships and could not fall to the *fiscus*. The academic jurisdictions enforced this theory and ensured its integration in legal practice. In the case of prebends and benefices, which did not consist of property but of revenue, this *persona representata* ensured continuity. A benefice that had been granted to a chair did not devolve when the holder of the chair died. The chair kept the benefice until a new professor was appointed. Bartolus called this the doctrine of the *persona ficta*, the fictitious person created at law. Because of his work, this fictitious person who could have rights and duties became an important concept in the *ius commune*.

The legal concept of the medieval *collegium* continued to exist on the Continent until the French Revolution. Essentially, the *fiducia* was partly recuperated. The directors of a college could only use the goods for the purpose for which they were intended. If they used them for other purposes, they could be sued by the donors. A college was a trust that escaped feudal law because the trustee became immortal and because the colleges were removed from the jurisdiction of the feudal courts in the Middle Ages.

4. The fictitious person in the Early Modern Era

A. Incorporation

Up to the eighteenth century, small associations made use of the concept of fiduciary ownership. Fiduciary ownership of movable goods had continued to exist because these goods did not come under the jurisdiction of the feudal courts. In many towns, which had also become independent from the feudal courts, fiduciary ownership was once again extended to include immovable rights. As in Antiquity, the director was the fiduciary owner of the goods. He passed them on to his successor.

In the fifteenth century, the English monarchs introduced the status of *corpus* or college as a privilege for the shipping trade. In England, some matters like shipping came under one single royal jurisdiction. Until 1453, this jurisdiction included Western France. The privileges that the monarch granted were therefore acknowledged by a large amount of courts. In these courts, 'incorporated' shipping companies acted as fictitious persons. The judge consulted the articles of the association to find out who was allowed to act in court and followed the decisions of the *curia*. Later, other firms were incorporated after the example of the incorporated shipping companies: milling houses, and in the sixteenth century trading firms. On the Continent, incorporation only appeared in the sixteenth century because it required larger nations in which royal privileges were acknowledged in a large jurisdiction. In the Low Countries, the first incorporations cropped up in the seventeenth century. The institution existed until the nineteenth century. Only colleges, business houses and industrial firms with a royal privilege could act as fictitious persons in the courts. All other associations appeared 'in person'.

B. In public law

In the Act of Abjuration (1581) eight jurisdictions in the Northern Netherlands deposed their King Philip II as highest judge. The possibility to dethrone a king was already discussed in the fourtheenth-century *ius commune*. According to D. 1.2.2, popular sovereignty took precedence over royal sovereignty. In his *Contra tyrannos*, Bartolus described the legal composition of a country without a monarch. The councils of the seceded Dutch provinces appointed a stadtholder, a substitute for the king, and transferred their sovereignty to him. The consequence was that the stadtholder also received the public domain of Philip II as property that was linked to his function. At the beginning of the seventeenth century, Grotius was still thinking along the same lines. In the course of the seventeenth century, there would be a major reaction against absolutism: extra-judicial law appeared, as did legal doctrine and the division between public and private law. The position of the monarch was weakened. The notion of *politeia* had been received from Constantinople, where the word indicated a sovereign people that lived in a country, the 'state'. Was this 'state' perhaps an association of interested citizens? In 1655 the Parliament of Paris refused to adopt decisions of Louis XIV because they went against the interests of 'the state'. In London, the sovereign people came into conflict with the king in 1649. The judges of the Parliament, whom the king had appointed to enforce respect for the law, ordered the monarch to be decapitated because he did not respect the state. Thomas Hobbes (1588-1679) wrote that a people was a *persona naturalis* and that the state was a *persona ficta* (later a *persona artificialis*) that was geometrically composed of the interests of individuals. This fictitious person acted through the organs that it had been given by natural persons. The German author Samuel Pufendorf (1632-1694) was the first person who mentioned the state as a *persona moralis*. Christian Wolff (1679-1754) handed the idea down to the eighteenth century. Apart from physical persons, there were also moral creatures with moral attributes like power, law, obligations, etcetera. A moral person could be an individual or a group that became the bearer of these attributes. The state was a complex moral person, whose will was the will of all. By the French Revolution, nations were considered to be legal persons who who acted through the procedures that had been agreed on by the members of the association.

C. In the private law of the eighteenth and nineteenth centuries

From the eighteenth century onwards, jurists inquired as to why an incorporation required a privilege. Was it not the case that the real authority that granted the privilege of incorporation was a moral person? How real was such a moral person? Why did the creation of persons with legal rights require the intervention of the state? The seventeenth-century legal doctrine and the *forum internum* led to the idealisation of the law. For the idealists, it was evident that legal persons were created freely, even in private law. In Kant's phenomenal world, legal persons had the same possibilities as living people. A legal person was only an idea, but was working with this idea so different from working with the perception which one had of an actual person? This perception had, after all, been converted into an idea in the human consciousness. Such German idealist conceptions exerted a considerable influence on the jurists of the first half of the nineteenth century.

The Code civil of 1804 was rather reluctant concerning persons that took up a position between the individual and the state. Concessions were still required for the establishment of legal persons. The private limited company mentioned in the Code civil did not have legal personality. This negative attitude towards legal personality was prevalent until Savigny's time. Savigny (1779-1861) reacted against idealism. According to him, only actual people could have legal rights. However, he did acknowledge the practical use of legal persons. Allowing associations and property to act autonomously in the courts created a range of possibilities. The incorporation of the trading firms that sailed to America, China and India had been very lucrative. The capitals that had been raised had allowed for the execution of large-scale projects. These incorporated firms enjoyed limited liability and allowed for a more active risk management. Perhaps the industrial revolution could benefit from this legal concept. Maybe the introduction of 'juristische Personen' (legal persons, the word was coined by Savigny) would result in new possibilities. Savigny came to the conclusion that everyone should be able to create legal persons, as long as these had a specific goal. They had to be limited to the realisation of a corporate purpose. Savigny did not think government supervision was necessary. The situation had to be clear for trade partners and courts. The principle of the *persona ficta* was also accepted in the individualistic 'heutigen römischen Recht' of the nineteenth century. Jhering attempted to bridge the gap with the Roman law by considering legal persons to be the separate property of the members, but this view had only a limited influence. Under the influence of Savigny, the Prussian law gave citizens the possibility to freely establish legal persons who were temporary and efficient. In the space of just a few decades, this legislation was adopted throughout the Continent.

In nineteenth-century Germany the discussion about legal personality gained momentum because of the will of Johann Friedrich Städel (1728-1816). He bequeathed his art collection and his fortune to a foundation that still had to be established. This foundation would run a museum and an artschool. In his will, Städel appointed some friends as the directors of the foundation and as executors of the will. They requested the incorporation of the foundation in Frankfurt and accepted the estate in the name of the foundation that they would establish. The first museum was opened in Städel's house on the Rossmarkt – revenue and expenditure were paid and collected by the undivided estate. The king of Bavaria, who visited the museum, was interested in the collection of five hundred paintings. He argued that Städel had bequested the art to an uncertain person, and that the bequest was therefore void. He found two distant relatives in Strasbourg who would inherit the fortune if the will was declared void and made these heirs an offer. The executors and the heirs would be involved in legal proceedings until 1828. Both parties requested dozens of opinions from law faculties as well as from individual professors. These opinions show how the idea of the legal personality of a foundation originated and grew. They document an evolution in legal doctrine: the initial uncertainty about this testamentary disposition gradually developed into the certainty that the will created a legal person and that this legal person could claim the paintings. In 1833 the Städel'sches Kunstinstitut was inaugurated in the Neue Mainzer Strasse.

In nineteenth-century England there were two possibilities for those who wanted to make a large investment: an incorporated (Inc.) or a trust with fiduciary property. Because of the introduction of trade in the shares of associations and the private limited company (Ltd., 1851), the legal doctrine and the case-law no longer dovetailed with reality. Who appointed the directors and what whas the exact relationship between the trustee and the shareholders if a trust consisted of shares that could be bought and sold anonymously? Under the influence of Austin and Lindsey, who had studied in Bonn, the English case-law introduced the concept of the legal person. The board of directors was accountable to the legal person of the trust. England introduced the legal person for practical reasons and took it to extremes. In 1914 an English car producer refused to pay the bills of a German supplier of tyres. In Continental v. Daimler (1915-1916) it was decided that the English subsidiary company of the German firm Continental was an English person and therefore maintained all of its rights during the war. In Anglo-American economic practice, the legal person was banalised until it became a mere means of avoiding costs. When you want to clear goods in an English port, you can buy a dormant company with an unpaid capital of £ 1 and legal persons as partners and director. Everyone accepts that the legal person who clears the goods is a genuine Englishman. This means that he does not have to pay his VAT at the border, but can settle it at the end of the quarter. What an evolution since the medieval colleges!

Bibliography. – R. HELMHOLZ and R. ZIMMERMANN (eds.), *Itinera Fudiciae, Trust and Treuhand in historical perspective*, [Comparative studies in Continental and Anglo-American legal history, 19,] Berlin 1998 and R. MEHR, *Societas und universitas, Römischrechtliche Institute im Unternehmensgesellschaftsrecht vor 1800*, Cologne-Weimar-Vienna 2008 contain extensive bibliographies about this subject.

Chapter V
The law of inheritance

In our legal system, the law of inheritance does not affect one's situation like social security law or tax law do. Inheritances no longer determine feudal positions; it has become easier to acquire wealth; most people only inherit goods at a relatively advanced age; and tax law reduces inheritances. The Civil code opted for a reserve portion (a minimum guaranteed share of the estate) and equal rights for all children, so that immovable property is continuously repartitioned. In legal history, however, inheritance law is the main branch of civil law. During times when survival was not evident, the continuity of property played a larger part. Good inheritance law made long-term investments, loans and depreciations possible. A society in which assets and liabilities could continue to exist after a person's demise, was stronger than a society in which everything ended at death.

Despite the lesser degree of importance that inheritance law has today, this branch of law and its history remain fascinating. They express the fundamental balances in a society. If someone died intestate, goods fell vacant – who could take them up without causing a conflict? We can learn more about a society by examining how it dealt with inheritances than by studying political theory and political history. The law of inheritance is an excellent means to get acquainted with a foreign culture.

The Roman civil law of inheritance not only played a role when a *ciuis* died, but also when he lost his civil rights. If this happened, there were vacant goods, as well as remaining family members and unpaid liabilities. The *familia*, which was a community of people and goods, devolved. Roman case-law protected creditors and linked the liabilities to the assets. Debts could be claimed despite death or deprivation of liberty. In this manner, Roman law made long-term loans and large investments possible. It became a system that allowed Romans to safely create something that would outlive them. In addition, Roman law featured the unique concept of a will, which *ciues* could use to take legal action even after their death.

In the Institutes of Gaius and Justinian, inheritance law is treated as an appendix to property law, because inheriting is a manner of acquiring property. From the fourteenth century onwards, you can find the consequent conviction that heirs have an *in rem* right to the inheritance. Originally, however, inheritance law was part of family law, since it dealt with the end of a *familia*.

§1. Hereditary succession

This paragraph is dedicated to the civil law of intestate succession, the settling of the *familia* of a person who had not drawn up a will (*ab intestate*).

1. The composition of the estate

A *familia* was liquidated when a *paterfamilias* died or lost his civil rights (*capitis diminutio maxima* and *media*). Initially, a *familia* without a *paterfamilias* was a *consortium*, an undivided community. All of the assets remained together and the creditors could claim payment from any of the virtual heirs. The identity of these heirs will be discussed below. Every interested party could request the liquidation of the *familia* and could, if necessary, enforce this liquidation before the court by means of the *actio familiae erciscundae*. Heirs could claim their part of the assets with the *petitio hereditatis*. The latter action was aimed at the acquisition of goods (D. 5.3.25; D. 6.1.27.3), but according to the case-law it was an *actio e bona fide*, which meant that it involved the assessment of the entire situation. This action also led to the settlement of the *familia*. This settlement required an arrangement with regard to the family members, the goods of the *familia* (assets) and the debts of the *paterfamilias* (liabilities).

When the *familia* devolved, the heirs became independent and received their own *familia*. They took the position in law of the deceased (*succedere in locum defuncti*). With this phrase, the classical jurists expressed that the substance of their rights was the same as the substance of the rights of the deceased *paterfamilias*. It is only in the post-classical period that one can read about 'succession to the rights' (*succedere in iura defuncti*). Family members who did not become independent were given a place in one of the new *familiae*. A wife who lived hand in hand with an heir (*in manu*) and was therefore a family member of her husband's *paterfamilias*, became a family member of her husband's new *familia*. Children followed their father. People who were *in mancipio* and were not re-vindicated were divided among the new families, but slave couples could not be split up.

Before the goods were divided, the estate was inventoried and, if necessary, wound up. An important rule was that creditors were involved in the process of inheritance. This is neither an evident nor a universal rule. Before the Twelve Tables, Roman case-law already linked the division of the goods to the assumption of liability. The creditors were interested parties in a case of succession. All of the goods that belonged to the familial community were included in the estate. In addition, all receivables in the journal of the *paterfamilias* were reconciled. Not all assets were inheritable. Some rights, like usufruct or use, simply disappeared. The debts from the journal of the *paterfamilias* were reconciled as well and became part of the estate. Account was taken of natural debts that became due because of the death, such as a dowry. Some debts expired: claims *intuitu personae* (because of the person of the deceased), which included, for example, the contractual obligation to act as an expert or artist. Mandates ended at death, because they were always *intuitu personae*. If there were claims arising from delict, a distinction was made: claims for retaliation expired, but claims for compensation did not. The securities that the *paterfamilias* had provided were inventoried as well: goods that had been pledged (when the estate was divided, these goods were linked to the debt for which they served as a security) and obligations to stand security (in Roman law, these were limited to two years and divided equally among all heirs).

An estate had a negative value if there were more debts than assets. In their edict, the praetors included means to protect heirs from liability. Heirs who cohabited with the *paterfamilias* were given the right to distance themselves from the estate (*beneficium abstinendi*). Other heirs could renounce the inheritance (*repudiare*). They did not receive anything, but would not be liable for the debts either. If no one accepted the estate, the estate creditors filed a petition for bankruptcy with the praetor. The creditors also faced other problems. If an heir was insolvent, they ran the risk that the assets of the estate would serve to pay other debts. In that case they demanded securities from the heir. Even when the latter did not provide securities, the praetor could pronounce the bankruptcy of the estate (D. 42.5.31*pr.* and 3). Sometimes creditors requested the separation of the estate (*separatio bonorum*) so that the amounts owed to them were recovered first (D. 42.6.1*pr.* and 2). If the praetor or *cognitio* judge allowed this, the estate was wound up without the heirs' involvement. If there was a surplus, this could qualify for division.

A person's exact indebtedness is rarely clear. Justinian gave each heir the possibility to accept the inheritance under the benefit of inventory (C. 6.30.22). The heir then had sixty days to draw up an inventory and decide whether he would accept the estate or not. In this manner, every heir could avoid inheriting more debts than assets.

When an estate was inventoried, debts were not necessarily settled. They could also be passed on to certain heirs when the estate was divided. Examples are investment loans that were linked with investments or trade liabilities that were passed on together with a commercial undertaking.

2. The division

A. Towards civil law in the Republic and the early Empire

Gaius teaches us that when a *familia* was dissolved, the 'agnates' of the *familia* became independent. For the *paterfamilias*, the agnates of the closest degree were his wife *in manu*, his children that had remained within the *familia*, and the people he had adopted and adrogated. They were his direct heirs (*sui heredes*). The estate devolved in as many equal parts as there were agnates who became independent. The wife *in manu* received a share in the estate that was equal to the share of the other heirs. Heirs inherited *per stirpes* and their *sui heredes* had a right of substitution. This means that if one of the heirs had predeceased the *paterfamilias* or had lost his civil rights, his heirs who were still in the *familia* received his share of the estate. They inherited individually, but together they only had a right to one share, which was divided among them. In the Republic, children who had been emancipated did not inherit, but if their children had remained members of the original *familia*, they substituted for their parents and each acquired an equal part of their parent's share. In the republican civil law, an inheritance was the liquidation of a *familia*. Those who were no longer members of the *familia* were not involved. Emancipated children or children who had been transferred to a different *familia* did not inherit anything.

If a *paterfamilias* had no *sui heredes*, the closest agnate from the previous generation, with whom the *paterfamilias* had once lived in a *familia*, became an heir. Adrogation, adoption and *conuentio in manu* were considered to be equal to birth when the closest degree of relationship was computed. If there were several *adgnati proximi* of the same degree, they inherited *per capita*.

B. Adjustments in the praetor's edict

According to Gaius 3.25 and following, the edict of the praetor made a series of adjustments to the civil law. These changes were not necessarily republican: it is possible that they were introduced by Salvius Julianus, who drew up the *edictum perpetuum* that Gaius discussed.

The praetor himself called on people who could receive *bonorum possessio intestati* (provisional assignment of the goods of a person who had died intestate) to accept the estate. He provided the *interdictum quorum bonorum* in his edict for this purpose. The assignment of movable goods became definitive if no one lodged a *petitio hereditatis* within the next four years. The time period with regard to immovable goods was ten or twenty years, depending on whether the domicile of the person who filed the *petitio hereditatis* was located in the same province or not. This provisional assignment could first and foremost be requested by the children of the deceased who had left the *familia* and were no longer *sui heredes*. If there were no such children, people who had once been agnatic relatives but had left the *familia* or had lost their civil rights could claim the estate. They claimed in their capacity as blood relatives. Finally, blood relatives who were related to the deceased through daughters were eligible to inherit. Consanguinity thus became an important new criterion. There were three ranks that were eligible for inheritance, and each of these excluded the next: (1) the children, (2) the other agnatic relatives and (3) the blood relatives. In the case-law under Hadrian, the latter category also included children as heirs of their mother and the mother as heir of her children.

C. Post-classical heirs

Many constitutions about the law of inheritance from the period between Constantine and Justinian have been preserved. In that period the law followed the line set out by the praetor. Agnation was ousted by consanguinity (cognation). It is said that the difference between *hereditas* and *bonorum possessio* disappeared at this time, but the sources do not offer clear proof of this. Relatedness through women was put on a par with relatedness through men. Emancipated people were put on a par with heirs who had remained in the *familia*.

There were four categories of heirs, who could claim the inheritance if the previous category had not done so within the last one hundred days. These categories were named after rubrics from the *edictum perpetuum*:

- *unde liberi*: freeborn children within the *familia*, including adopted and emancipated children, but excluding children who had been adopted by another *familia*. A *curator uentris* was appointed to defend the interests of unborn children.
- *unde legitimi* (heirs by operation of law): for men, these were the children of the women to whom they were wedded or with whom they lived *in matrimonio*, as well as the children that their wife had had earlier if these children were not another man's heirs by operation of law; the *unde legitimi* of a woman were all of her freeborn children.
- *unde cognati*: blood relatives up to and including the sixth degree. Each degree excluded the next.
- *unde uir et uxor*: the surviving spouse.

If no one turned up, the praetor sold the estate for the benefit of the creditors. In the Republic, a vacant estate fell to the *aerarium*; in the Empire it fell to the *fiscus*.

D. Novel 118

Justinian abolished the difference between *heres* and *bonorum possessor* and did not take agnation into account. In his Novel 118 of 543 (complemented by Novel 127 of 548) he introduced four categories of heirs who were eligible in the following order and excluded each other.

- the descendants, *per stirpes* and with endless substitution.
- the ascendants, brothers and sisters: in the ascending line, the degree of consanguinity mattered. One parent excluded all grandparents. If there were several ascendants of the same degree but from different sides of the family (the father's and mothers' side), there was an equal division: one half of the estate went to the paternal relatives and the other went to the maternal relatives. Each half was then divided *per capita*. Full brothers and sisters were put on a par with parents or grandparents. The children of brothers and sisters had the right of substitution, but their children did not. If there were only children of brothers and sisters, it was not clear whether they inherited *per capita* (Azo) or *per stirpes* (Accursius). This controversy lasted throughout the Middle Ages. The Reichstag of Spiers of 1529 opted for Azo's interpretation.
- half-brothers and half-sisters, and their children by substitution. In other words, in stepfamilies the criterion of consanguinity played a role.
- further relatives in the collateral line. The closest relative excluded all others. In case of several relatives of the same degree, the estate was divided *per capita*.

In the Justinian system, the surviving spouse did not get anything. According to the older Novel 53 of 537, a 'poor' surviving spouse or a woman who had received neither a dowry nor gifts on account of the wedding received a quarter of her husband's goods after her repudiation or her husband's death. It is very likely that this rule continued to apply.

E. *The complaint on account of an undutiful will (*querela inofficiosi testamenti*)*

The application of the law of intestate succession was guaranteed to a certain extent by the case-law. With regard to some heirs, it was impossible to fully diverge from this law by means of a will. A portion of the estate was reserved for these heirs. This concept of the reserve portion originated in the case-law concerning the *querela inofficiosi testamenti* (complaint on account of an undutiful will).

From the late Republic onwards, everyone who thought that he had improperly (*contra officium pietatis*) not been remembered sufficiently in a will could lodge an objection 'on account of an undutiful will'. In the Republic this was a special procedure which involved officers serving as judges (*centumuiri*). In the provinces and the Empire such cases were treated in the *cognitio extra ordinem*. The judges had a large discretionary power and the pleading could be passionate. Gradually, settled case-law about the *querela inofficiosi testamenti* developed. Everyone could institute it (D. 5.2.6.1), but only for the benefit of the children, parents, brothers and sisters of the deceased (D. 5.2.1). For a long time, the undutiful exclusion of an heir resulted in the will being declared void. The estate was then divided according to the law of intestate inheritance.

Justinian laid down norms concerning the disinheriting of these privileged heirs in Novel 115 (542). Children, parents, brothers and sisters who were eligible according to normal inheritance law could be fully disinherited in a will if they had misbehaved towards the deceased or had acted against public morals (unworthiness). Without these grounds of exclusion, these two classes of heir always received a legal portion (*portio legitima*) before the estate was divided. The will was not void, but it was limited. The reserved part which could not be bequeathed by means of a will was at least a quarter of the property (inspired by the *quarta faldicia*), a third if there were between one and four children, and half if there were more. The medieval jurists elaborated on this rule and developed the doctrine that no conditions could be attached to the legal portion. For them, the legal portion always took precedence over the will.

If a freedperson had no children or had disinherited them, half of his estate fell to his *patronus* as a due portion (Gaius 3.41, *debita portio*). In the post-classical era, this portion was reduced to a third. The *patronus* could file a request for *bonorum possessio* with the praetor to obtain that portion and could in this manner claim it back from a third-party acquirer if necessary.

When it came to protected heirs, the inheritance law took precedence over the will. When a will was declared void because of irregularities, people also fell back on the ordinary law of inheritance.

F. *Obtaining the inheritance*

If judicial intervention was necessary, the means to claim a share in the inheritance in the civil law were the *hereditatis petitio* and the *interdictum quorum bonorum*. However, heirs who lived with the deceased did not have to lodge a claim with the praetor. They became heirs automatically. If they did not want the inheritance, they had to renounce it explicitly. They were then released by the praetor or the judge if they had not got involved with the estate in any way. Heirs who did not live with the deceased (*extranei heredes*) had to accept the estate tacitly or explicitly. If they did not want the inheritance, renouncement was not necessary – although it was preferred that they renounce the estate. In the Roman law that was received in the Middle Ages and the Early Modern Era, heirs who lived with the deceased also had to accept the estate.

If acceptance was necessary, the estate remained undivided until it was accepted (*hereditas iacens*). Diverse legal constructions were developed for the assignment of revenue and debts during this period:

- the early classical jurists assumed that acceptance had a retroactive effect until the time of death (D. 45.3.28.4).
- later, the fiction was developed that the *hereditas iacens* was a continuation of the person of the deceased until the moment of acceptance (D. 41.1.33.2; D. 41.1.34; D. 3.5.20.1; D. 41.1.61*pr.*). This was important for the medieval doctrine of legal personality.

G. *The reception of Roman inheritance law*

The reception of the Roman law of inheritance is a delicate subject to study. Half of the legal historical sources pertain to the law of inheritance, which was always a hot topic.

One cannot therefore expect to find undiluted Roman law in the case-law of the Middle Ages or the Early Modern Era. Many legal historians who determined the differences between the Roman law as it was described in the nineteenth century and the case-law of the Early Modern Era concluded that our inheritance law was 'native', i.e. of Germanic origin. Ideas such as equal division of an estate between the maternal and paternal side of the family of the deceased, substitution or degrees of consanguinity had perhaps been received from Roman law, but the grand principles of the division of inheritances were not Roman in origin. Is this true? Or does the 'Germanic law' perhaps stem from the dreams of the Early Modern Era? Did the seedy 'Germanic' immigrants who joined the Roman Empire even have an inheritance law? The ethnogenesis of these 'peoples' happened only when they came into contact with the Latin world. They became distinct 'peoples' because the Romans labelled them as such.

After 476 the Roman law of inheritance still had political importance, because the public domain was passed on through inheritance. This topic was discussed regularly. The Middle Ages saw several dynastic crises that were caused by the childlessness of German emperors. Time after time, contenders to the throne made use of the Roman law of inheritance in order to attempt to substantiate that they were the heirs of the deceased emperor. German sources were not used in this context. Of course the law of inheritance evolved: in the feudal system with its many sovereign courts, interpretations began to differ. And yet many Roman elements from the imperial era survived. A gorgeous illustration can be found in the abovementioned 'Ligurian law of inheritance' by E.M. Meijers (1880-1954).

The oldest collections of private case-law concerning the law of inheritance date from the twelfth century. Meijers studied them and discovered considerable similarities in the twelfth-century law of inheritance of an area from Liguria, via Raetia, Austria and Switzerland to Auvergne and Burgundy; from Tours to Angers and Saintes; via Lorraine and Northern France to the Netherlands. The shared provisions which he found did not correspond with the Roman law which he knew from the works of the German Pandectists. Did this mean that the law of inheritance was of Germanic origin? No, because he did not find the Germanic inheritance law that the German legal historians described either. How, then, was it possible that there were so many similar elements in such a large area? He presumed that a third system, a pre-Celtic law of inheritance, had had a determinative influence on European legal history. He called this the Ligurian law of inheritance, after finds concerning the La Tène culture had been made in Liguria.

The following elements were similar in the twelfth-century law of inheritance in the areas that Meijers researched:

- all goods belonged to the *familia*. The *paterfamilias* could emancipate children, and if he did so, they lost their inheritance rights. 'Unlike in Roman law', all children were treated equally in case of intestate succession. They received half of the estate; the surviving spouse retained the other half. According to Meijers, this was the case because these peoples were familiar neither with the dotal system nor with the distinction between ownership and usufruct.
- the debts were divided *pro rata* among the heirs, *a rato* the assets they received.
- If there were no descendants and the goods went to ascendants, the estate was divided between the paternal and maternal lines. Sometime this division did not happen according to the Roman rules (50-50), but according to the origins of the

goods: *paterna paternis, materna maternis.*
- housemates did not have to accept the inheritance, other heirs did.
- the right of substitution existed: the estate was inherited *per stirpes*, not *per capita.*
- for collateral relatives, the degree of consanguinity was determinative.

What is immediately striking about this list is that there are Roman antecedents. The linking of debts to assets was Roman, as were equal rights for all children and the substitution by children's children. Emancipated children lost their share in the estate of the family, as Gaius described. The division of the estate into shares for the paternal and maternal relatives had been newly introduced by Novel 118, with which jurists had become familiar during the Middle Ages. The requirement of acceptance was Roman as well. Also note the presence of the Roman inheritance rights of blood relatives in the collateral line, which are after all very specific. Even the vague distinction between ownership and rights of use is not un-Roman. Further on, we will see that the exclusive ownership which the Pandectists found in Roman law is actually an invention of the Early Modern Era. It resulted from the privatisation of feudalism. The most striking element, however, is that the Ligurian law of inheritance only cropped up within the borders of the old Empire: it existed in the Netherlands, but not beyond the Rhine; and can only be found south of the Danube.

What Meijers – and many other legal historians with him – did not see, is that the Roman law of inheritance concerned the winding up of a *familia* and that the *familia* of Antiquity was different from that of the twelfth century. The old Roman community of goods had evolved into a marital community of goods that was administered by two people. When one holder died, only half of the estate devolved. The surviving spouse kept his or her half and the children received the other. The surviving spouse and the children were jointly liable for the debts. That Meijers did not find any 'Germanic' law in his texts can also be explained easily. What was called 'Germanic law' in the nineteenth century was actually the customary law of the sixteenth century, the law that could be found in the sovereign courts and manors of that era. Ultimately, this customary law also derived from Roman law, but it had evolved to such an extent between the twelfth and sixteenth centuries that many could neither see the old Roman principles in it, nor the common principles that could be found across Europe in the twelfth century. Even the reception of Novel 118 which we find in the twelfth century, had been forgotten by the sixteenth (see the text below). Everyone acknowledges that the twelfth century was a century of *ius commune.* We should therefore not be surprised when we find it in the sources.

Bibliography. – The Ligurian inheritance law is described in the abovementioned series of publications by E.M. MEIJERS, *Le droit ligurien de succession en Europe occidentale*, Haarlem 1928-1967. That the 'Germanic law' was a myth is now also proved by the study of F.L. SCHÄFER, *Juristische Germanistik, Eine Geschichte der Wissenschaft vom einheimischen Privatrecht*, Frankfurt/Main 2008.

About a small book with large consequences and Novel 118. – Jacques Cujas (1522-1590) was not openly involved in the politics of his time. He merely sought time for his study, especially his study of legal texts from Antiquity. In 1567 he found Bourges unsafe and sought a more quiet place to work. He wanted to return to Valence, where he had taught in 1556-1559, and exchanged chairs with François Hotman, who taught in Valence and was willing to put up with a bit of tumult in order to acquire a chair in Bourges. In his second period in Valence, Cujas applied himself to the study of the Novels of Justinian. Starting from the Greek collection, he subjected the novels to a critical study and published a small book about it: *Novellarum constitutionum imperatoris Iustiniani explicatio,* Valence 1569. This little book is at the basis of all later studies of the Novels and is considered to be a 'great' work in the world of Roman law. However, it was not only a work read by scholars. In 1567-1569 Jacques-Auguste de Thou (1553-1617), who would later be known as Thuanus, studied law in Valence. He was a strong admirer of Cujas. Jacques-Auguste was the son of Christophe de Thou (✝1582), who had been the president of the Parliament of Paris since 1555 and thought highly of the humanists and Cujas. He followed everything that Cujas wrote. Christophe de Thou was charged with the ratification of the customary law of the jurisdiction of the Parliament of Paris and was busily engaged with this project since 1555. He revised most of the customs before 1567. From then on, he was engaged in the development of a new custom of Paris. It appeared in 1580 and its major innovation could be found in the law of inheritance. All of the rules of inheritance law had been streamlined according to the principles that were contained in... Novel 118 of Justinian as described by Cujas. The newly ratified custom of Paris unexpectedly emphasised that all sons and daughters had equal rights according to the law of inheritance, that the parents and grandparents of the deceased had inheritance rights when there were no children, and that the inheritance fell to the closest blood relatives if there were no ascendants either. The right to deviate from this order by means of a will was limited to a considerable extent if there were children. If de Thou did not draw on Cujas' book or on his son's course notes when drawing up the custom of Paris, then the reader can find us guilty of a *cum hoc ergo propter hoc*! The story does not end with the custom of Paris of 1580. This custom was considered authoritative and many courts held it up as an example of good case-law. The idea of completely equal rights for all children continued to gain ground. Originally a typically urban principle, it began to be adopted by the case-law from rural areas. It meant that property was continuously repartitioned and that the composition of assets was different every generation. When a Code civil for the French territory was drawn up in 1804, it was also meant for the Netherlands. Jurists from this region were involved in the development of this code of law. With regard to the law of inheritance, the compilers of the Code civil fell back on the system detailed in the custom of Paris, which turned out to be quite generally established by 1804. In addition, this system could be used to weaken the strong position of landowners and large farmers. This Code civil of 1804 is still applicable in Belgium today. This explains why Belgium also has a law of inheritance with equal rights for all children, in accordance with the grand principle that Cujas had defended in his little book. Of course, this book was only the seed of this entire societal evolution, but it was a mustard seed. [Translated from L. Waelkens, 'Jacques Cujas (1522 1590)', in: C Coppens, J. De Landsheer en D. Sacré (eds.), *Justus Lipsius (1547-1606), Een geleerde en zijn Europees netwerk,* Leuven 2006, p. 446-454).]

§2. Wills

Wills are a typically Roman legal concept. The idea that the desires of a person who is no longer there can have legal consequences is by no means an evident one. Warriors were granted the privilege of determining what would happen to their pay and booty even after their death. Wills originated in the army and evolved into the most important civil right. They are typically Roman. Research conducted by the 'Société Jean Bodin' has shown that throughout the world the law of wills always derives from the reception of Roman law.

Roman soldiers were free to decide who would receive their pay and booty after their death. If the *rationalis* (accountant) of a legion or a *decemuir* knew what the desires of a fallen soldier were, they saw to the execution of these wishes. This motivated the deceased's fellow soldiers. There were hardly any formal requirements for the wills of frontline soldiers. The *Corpus iuris* features the examples of a dying soldier who wrote in the sand and another who wrote on his shield with blood. Their last wills were enforceable (see C. 6.21.15). At the time when the concept of the *familia* was being developed and the income of non-independent soldiers ended up in their *familia*, these soldiers retained the right to write a will in order to determine what would happen to their *peculium castrense*. Veterans retained the right to draw up a will for the rest of their life. For the Romans, the will became the most solemn legal act in social life. It was acknowledged in the *ius gentium* at a relatively early stage and was a liberty that was coveted by the conquered peoples that negotiated a peace treaty with Rome.

Bibliography. – *Actes à cause de mort – Acts of Last Will*, 4 vol., edited by L. WAELKENS, Brussels 1992-1994 [Recueils de la Société Jean Bodin, 59-62].

1. Form

A. *The mancipatory will*

Soldiers' wills were relatively informal, but outside of the army there were some formal requirements. An old type of will that crops up in the sources is the *testamentum calatis comitiis* that was made before the *comitia curiata* and by means of which a person without heirs could appoint inheritors. The most important type of will under the civil law, however, was the mancipatory will. In the presence of the testator, a *familiae emptor* (a buyer of familial property) claimed that the familial and private property of the testator would fall to him after the testator's death. The *familiae emptor* then read the assignment (*nuncupatio*) which detailed to whom he would deliver the property of the testator. The *familiae emptor* soon became a mere supernumerary. He was not an executor. Despite the *mancipatio*, the goods did not become part of his property. After the death of the testator, only the appointed heirs took action.

At the end of the Republic, wills were written down on wax tablets (*tabulae*), which were shown while the *familiae emptor* pronounced the formula for a *mancipatio*. The tablets were sealed by witnesses. Although the contents were no longer made public, this will was still called an 'oral will'. After the testator's death, his goods were divided as the *nuncupatio* or wax tablets detailed. If a discussion ensued, the heirs appointed by the will claimed their rights by means of the same *petitio hereditatis* which was also used in the law of intestate succession.

B. *The praetorian will (*bonorum possessio secundum tabulas*)*

A second type of will was the praetorian will, which consisted entirely of a written document. It was written on sealed wax tablets by the testator and presented to the praetor or imperial judge, without a *mancipatio* having taken place. The existence of the will was registered by the court registry, where the will could also be deposited. The beneficiaries of this will could ask to be put in possession of the goods that had been left to them. They then received *bonorum possessio secundum tabulas*, i.e. a preliminary adjudication which granted possession. Heirs appointed by a mancipatory will took precedence over heirs appointed by a praetorian will. They could demand the surrender of the goods with the *hereditatis petitio*. This was a strict claim that pertained to strict obligations (see below). Under Antoninus Pius (138-161) the prefecture granted the beneficiaries of a praetorian will an *exceptio doli* against this *petitio hereditatis*. Consequently, the judge had to examine the entire situation, assess which will was the most recent and which aspects of the older will were revoked by the newest. The criterion became the most recent statement of intent, because a will could always be revoked by the testator without formalities. Mancipatory and praetorian wills thus became of equal value.

C. The post-classical evolution

In the post-classical era, the oral will with five witnesses was still distinguished from the written testament with seven witnesses that led to *bonorum possessio*. Theodosius II required seven witnesses for both types of wills (Nov.Th. 16). Within the space of a single day, the will had to be signed by both the testator and the witnesses and sealed. The witnesses did not necessarily know the contents of the act. This form was adopted by Justinian (C. 6.23.21).

Under Valentinian III a third type of will appeared: the handwritten or holographic will. In 446, the prefecture accepted the legal effect of a will without witnesses that was dated and signed by the testator. If such a will was presented to the court and its authenticity could not be doubted, it had the same value as a will with seven witnesses. The handwritten will of Nov. Val. 21 cannot be found in the Justinianic compilation. The consequence was that this type of will was not developed further by the medieval legists. Mediterranean legal practice, however, was still familiar with this type of will in the early thirteenth century. It does not occur anymore in the Mediterranean customary law after 1270, because it was not a Justinianic concept. However, the southern practice gradually found its way to the north. In the archives of notaries, you can witness the rise of the holographic will, which was gradually acknowledged by the local case-law. This reception was supported by C. 6.23.19, which states that a public will of unknown origin that had been deposited with a court or with the local authorities did have legal effect. In the Middle Ages, this rule developed into the practice of depositing a will with a notary or aldermen's court. In C. 6.23.19 the prefecture also decided that an informal will that had been attached to a request could not be questioned anymore on second appeal. The case discussed in the Code concerned dilatory and peremptory exceptions, but according to the medieval jurists this text also acknowledged handwritten wills that were deposited with the court in an informal manner after the testator's death. From the fifteenth century onwards, the handwritten will began to be used in the Parisian region. Through the custom of Paris it then ended up in the Civil code. The prevalent theory that the holographic will of the Civil code did not stem from the Roman law, but from the customary law of Paris is therefore incorrect.

2. Contents

Originally, soldiers' wills served to pass on goods. Once the will had found its place within the civil law, it also began to play a role in the winding up of the *familia*. A *paterfamilias* could arrange this winding up himself by means of a will. He could appoint guardians and even release slaves. The most important provision of the will was the testamentary disposition. In addition, the will contained legacies and *fideicommissa*.

A. The testamentary disposition

In the testamentary disposition (*heredis institution*, institution of the heir), one or several universal legatees were appointed. They were not assigned specific goods, but an entire estate or a fraction thereof. They replaced the heirs. Without a testamentary disposition the will was void, because it was the disposition that linked the assets and the liabilities: the universal legatees took over the debts.

According to Gaius 2.117, a testamentary disposition required specific phrases. Under Constantine, all phrases were valid. A testamentary disposition could be subject to suspensory conditions, but neither to a suspensory period (D. 28.5.34), nor to resolutive conditions or a resolutive period (Gaius 2.184). Once one became an heir, one always remained an heir (in medieval Roman law: *semel heres semper heres*). A period, a resolutive condition or a condition that went against public morals, were considered not to have been written. The goal was to consider as many wills as possible valid in order to respect the will of the testator as much as possible. However, the situation of the creditors also played a role and claims on account of a will were *stricti iuris*. They had to be explained just as stipulations were, without any account being taken of the external elements (which will be treated in the chapter about obligations).

If a *paterfamilias* wanted to replace his sons with a universal legatee, he had to disinherit each of his sons in the will. Otherwise, the will was void. His wife and daughters could be dealt with in one breath because their situation was less complex. After the division, they always ended up in a one-person family. If the testator had forgotten someone, even a *postumus* (unborn child) the will became void. In the *ius gentium*, the situation was similar. Disinherited wives and children did keep the legitimate portion which they could claim by means of the *querela inofficiosi testamenti*. Thus, their independent status was guaranteed as well.

C. 28.6 is dedicated entirely to substitution. If the universal legatee had died before the testator or renounced the estate, a second legatee could be appointed (*substitutio uulgaris*) (Gaius 2.174-178). Pupillary substitution (*substitutio pupillaris*) was a special case. If the heir who was appointed first became *sui iuris* when the testator died but was not an adult yet, he could not yet draw up a will himself. One needed to be an adult (men reached adulthood at fifteen; women at twelve) in order to be able to draw up a will. If his heir was not an adult, the testator could appoint a subsidiary heir who would receive the estate if the primary heir died before he reached adulthood. Testators who wanted to deviate from the normal order could thus prevent that their estate fell to the regular heirs in case the universal legatee died too soon (Gaius 2.179-183). Later, quasi-pupillary substitution was developed. If a father appointed an adult child who was mentally ill, he could also appoint the child's heir (C. 6.26.9 of Justinian, see D. 28.6.43*pr.*).

The *causa curiana* about a subsidiary general legatee. – In 93 BC a trial concerning the will of M. Coponius was held in the Forum. He had appointed his unborn child as his universal legatee and a certain Curius as the child's substitute. After Coponius' death, it turned out that there was no child. The intestate heirs, who were defended by Q. Mucius Scaevola (whom Cicero considered to be the best rhetorician among the jurists), claimed that the will was void and that the substitution was therefore void as well. Curius, who was defended by L. Licinius Crassus (the best jurist among the rhetoricians according to Cicero), claimed that Coponius apparently desired to exclude his intestate heirs. The court followed Crassus: their respect for the desires of the testator was greater than their respect for a strict reasoning about voidness. [After CICERO, *De oratore* 1.180.]

B. Special legacy

A will could also contain disposals (of people or assets) under particular title. Roman law used legates (*legata*) and *fideicommissa* for this purpose. Their beneficiaries were legatees under particular title. The word legacy probably derives from *lex* – in the sense of a special condition that was included in a *mancipatio*. Legacies were mentioned in the Twelve Tables and it is sometimes claimed that they served to arrange the fate of the disinherited. There are many precedents from the classical period concerning this matter (mainly in books D. 30-32).

A legacy could only be made in a valid will. When the will was invalid, the legacies were invalid as well. If a special legacy was invalid, the rest of the will remained valid. The legacy had to be valid when it was made, not when the estate devolved (*regula catoniana*). The testator could revoke a legacy either formally (see D. 34.4.3.8) or tacitly (for example by selling the bequeathed object). The two main forms were the legacy *per uindicationem* and the legacy *per damnationem*.

By means of a legacy *per uindicationem* the testator arranged the fate of a person or good of which he was the *paterfamilias*. The text of the legacy had to contain *do lego* (I give and bequeath), for example: *Titio hominem Stichum do lego* (to Titius I leave my slave Stichus). This person or good then immediately fell to the *familia* of the legatee when the testator died. If there were problems, the legatee could claim the legacy by means of a *reiuindicatio*. A usufruct or servitude could be established by means of a legacy *per uindicationem* as well and could also be claimed with the *reiuindicatio* after the testator's death. A legacy *per uindicationem* gave the legatee a right *in rem*: the legatee could claim the legacy from anyone who had the good. There are many opinions of jurists about the correct formulation of legacies *per uindicationem*. In addition, there are texts about the transfer of goods by means of a legacy *per uindicationem*. According to the Proculians, the good did not belong to anyone until it was claimed. According to the Sabinians, the legatee became the owner immediately after the testator's death, but his ownership came to an end when he renounced the legacy (Gaius 2.195). Later, jurists adopted a middle course between both interpretations: ownership was uncertain until the legatee had claimed the good; when the legatee claimed the good he was presumed to have been its owner since the death of the testator (see D. 30.86.2).

The phrasing of a legacy *per damnationem* contained the words *damnas esto* (you are due), for example: *heres meus Titio hominem Stichum dare damnas esto* (my heir shall be bound to give my slave Stichus to Titius). This legacy resulted in a right *in personam*:

it established a personal obligation towards the appointed heir. Each service that could be the object of a *stipulatio*, could also be the object of a legacy *per uindicationem*. Common legacies *per uindicationem* were the establishment of a *peculium*, a dowry (usually under the suspensory condition of marriage), maintenance, annuities... By means of a legacy *per damnationem*, a testator could even bequeath goods that were not his. The execution of such legacies was left to the general legatee. A legacy *per damnationem* could be claimed from the general legatee by means of the *actio ex testamento* (action on account of a will). This was an *actio stricti iuris*, which meant that the judge did not consider the entire settlement of the will. Just as was the case with a *stipulatio*, the legatee could claim his interests by means of this action (*quanti ea res interest*) if the object of the legacy was a *certum*. If the good was an *incertum*, the legatee could claim its market value (*quidquid dare facere oportet*). If a legacy had been tacitly revoked according to the general legatee and the legatee did commence the strict *actio ex testamento*, the general legatee received an *exceptio doli*. The *actio ex testamento* then lost its strict character and the judge could examine the entire case (Gaius 2.198).

In the imperial law, the difference between legacies *per damnationem* and *per uindicationem* disappeared. In the *senatusconsultum neronianum* (between 54 and 68) a judge decided that a legacy *per uindicationem* that was invalid according to the civil law (for instance the bequeathing of a good that was not part of the *familia*) was turned into a legacy *per damnationem* in so far as the contents of the legacy allowed this. On this subject, see *Epitome Vlpiani* 24.11 (translated by J. MUIRHEAD, *The Rules of Gaius and Rules of Ulpian*, Edinburgh 1880, p. 416). Constantine allowed every phrasing for both types of legacies, as long as the intent of the testator was clear (C. 6.3.15, presumably of 320). Finally, Justinian (C. 6.43.1.1 of 529) determined that all legacies were of the same nature and that the legatee could use an *actio in rem* or an *actio in personam* (personal claim against the appointed heirs). Moreover, the legatee received an *actio hypothecaria* against the person who held the bequeathed good. After all, there was a legal hypothec on this good (see the section on pledges).

There were limits to the amount of property that could be bequeathed by means of legacies. The *lex furia testamentaria* (between 204 and 169 BC) forbade those who were not blood relatives of the testator from accepting legacies that were worth more than one thousand asses. The universal legatee could immediately claim four times the amount above one thousand from any person who had accepted an excessive legacy. The remedy which the universal legatee used to claim this sum was the *manus iniectio*. The *lex uoconia* (169 BC) determined that no one in the first tax bracket could receive a legacy that was more valuable than the goods inherited by all of the other heirs together. According to the *lex falcidia* of 40 BC, the testator could bequeath at most three quarters of his property by means of legacies. If the appointed heir ran the risk of receiving less than a quarter (*quarta falcidia*), he could have the legacies reduced. The *lex falcidia* was also in the interest of the special legatee: if the appointed legatee refused because he did not get anything anyway, the will became void and the special legatee did not receive anything either.

An important criterion for the validity of a legacy was that it had to be granted to a person. The beneficiary could not be an *incerta persona* who could not claim it. There is beautiful Roman case-law about this. What the universal legatee did not have to pay out, he could keep himself. In other words, he had a good reason to be difficult. Who would claim a legacy 'to the poor' or a legacy to a good cause? C. 6.48 and Nov. 131.9-11 contain examples. A legacy to Christ fell to the local church of the testator's domicile. A legate to a saint could be claimed by the president of a charitable organisation that was dedicated to the saint and located in the town of the testator. If such an organisation did not exist, the local church could claim the legacy. A legacy to the poor or the prisoners that did not contain further specifications could be claimed by the local bishop for the specified purpose, even when the testator had forbidden the bishop from interfering. After all, the bishops organised social services and their general ledger made it possible to trace whether they used the legacy according to the testator's will.

C. Fideicommissa

Fideicommissa were requests which the testator made to someone who would receive a benefit from the testator's estate. *Fidei committere* meant to appeal to someone's goodwill. In current language, they are known as dispositions in trust. In the republican civil law, *fideicommissa* could not be enforced. From Augustus' reign onwards, they became enforceable in the imperial procedure (Inst. 2.22.1 and 2.15*pr.*). Unlike a legacy, a *fideicommissum* could fall to a non-citizen (until Hadrian forbade this). *Fideicommissa* were used to bypass the *lex furia* and the *lex uoconia*. A *fideicommissum* could be imposed on anyone who had an interest in an inheritance, even on other fideicommissaries (for example in the case of fideicommissary succession, see below), on creditors (see D. 30.77) or on the *fiscus* who obtained a vacant estate (D. 30.114.2).

Fideicommissa could be established in every possible way: usually, there was a codicil, but they could also be established orally or by means of gestures. Justinian required the presence of five witnesses. In order to grant a *fideicommissum*, the testator had to be capable of making valid bequests. The fideicommissary received a claim on an *incertum*.

In principle, a *fideicommissum* was an encumbrance on a legacy. In wills it was often difficult to distinguish whether a legacy was subject to a condition or a *fideicommissum*. Especially when it was the general legatee who was encumbered, there could be discussions about whether a legacy was subject to a condition or a *fideicommissum*. The distinction was important: legacies led to strict obligations, while the obligations linked with *fideicommissa* were gradually explained *e bona fide* – which meant that all circumstances were taken into account. Gaius 2.268-283 still lists a series of differences between a legacy and a *fideicommissum*. With regard to some points, these two institutions were put on a par. The *quarta falcidia*, for example, began to be applied to *fideicommissa* (*senatusconsultum pegasianum*), but the freedom to establish *fideicommissa* for anyone's benefit was limited. Justinian laid down that the rules for *fideicommissa* could also be applied to legacies and that the rules for *fideicommissa* began to apply for legacies (C. 6.43.2 of 531; D. 30.1, interpolation of a text by Ulpian that was taken entirely out of context). When there were doubts about the qualification of a provision, it had to be seen as a *fideicommissum* because *fideicommissa* allowed for less restrictive interpretations (C. 6.46.2.2).

Unlike legacies, *fideicommissa* could encompass the entire estate. This made fideicommissary succession possible, something which implied diverging from the old principle 'once inherited, always inherited' (*semel heres, semper heres*). The testator appointed an heir on whom he imposed the *fideicommissum* to pass part of or the entire estate to a certain person. The universal legatee could then use stipulations (*stipulationes emptae et uenditae hereditatis*) to make certain arrangements with the fideicommisary, for example concerning the debts. If the universal legatee did not do this, all of the debts remained his responsibility. The *fideicommissum* to transfer goods to an appointed person could also be imposed on a fideicommisary. Under Hadrian, the prefecture decided that legacies and *fideicommissa* to *incertae personae* (uncertain persons) were not possible. A fideicommisary who had not been conceived yet was an uncertain person. Justinian abolished this rule, but determined that fideicommissary succession could not extend beyond the fourth generation (Nov. 108.1 of 541). In the Middle Ages, this was called *substitutio fideicommissaria*, an institution that allowed people to keep goods in their *familia* – hence the name *fideicommissa familiae relicta* (family *fideicommissum*, see D. 31.69.3 and D. 31.32.6). In the Middle Ages, this fideicommissary succession was used as a means of circumventing the received Roman law of inheritance and of maintaining, for example, a right of primogeniture (entailed estates).

A *fideicomissum* was somewhat similar to the *fiducia*, which could be used to transfer goods from one living person to another with conditions attached to this transfer in a *pactum fiduciae*. With a *fideicommissum*, it was possible to transfer property under conditions after death. Gradually, more and more goods were bequeathed with fideicommissary dispositions by means of which trust arrangements were established. Bankers received legacies with instructions that detailed how they had to invest the money and spend the revenue. The danger was that the typically Roman link between the assets and liabilities of an estate would be broken. If the general legatee had to pass on a large amount of assets while the general liability for debts remained his, the old Roman principle of linking liabilities and assets was infringed. The *senatusconsultum trebellianum* regulated the relationship with the general legatees and the creditors shortly after the introduction of the enforceability of *fideicommissa*. The *fideicommissor* who was granted an entire estate received a *petitio hereditatis*, an *actio familiae erciscundae utilis* against his fellow-*fideicommissarii* or fellow-heirs; the heir received the *exceptio doli* against the testator's creditors, while the creditors received direct *actiones utiles* against the fideicommissary.

Fideicommissa were received in all countries of the *ius commune*. They can already be found, for example, in the twelfth century, in the court of the university of Bologna and the canonical courts that had jurisdiction over the universities. A legacy to a college in a university town was usually a legacy to the administrators of the college, accompanied by a *fideicommissum* that detailed that the donation could only be used to pay studies. Bartolus and Baldus fused *fiducia* and *fideicommissum* and turned them into a single subject in the medieval *ius commune*.

In the Early Modern Era, fideicommissary trust law largely lost its relevance because of the specific development of *in rem* rights. When feudalism was privatised, private ownership became a central notion. Feudal law received a bad reputation as a relic of absolutism. Eternal rights to someone else's goods were a form of feudal law and were therefore combatted. In the seventeenth and eighteenth centuries the doctrine and the case-law interpreted them in a restrictive manner. In France and the Low Countries, fiduciary ownership was abolished during the French Revolution. The civil code only retained family *fideicommissum* with regard to goods that were bequeathed to incapable people. In some countries, the entailing of estates was accepted in early modern private law. This was the abovementioned fideicommissary succession by means of which large domains could be preserved. In France and Belgium, this was forbidden by article 896 of the Civil code, because it was contrary to the continuous repartitioning of property which the bourgeoisie had opted for during the French Revolution. In the nineteenth century, entailing was still a common practice in Spain and some German regions such as the Kingdom of Saxony. During the interbellum it played an even larger part in Transylvania, where it was commonly used to keep the large corn farms in the hands of one person. In England, feudalism was already privatised in the Middle Ages and *in rem* rights were not reformed there during the fight against absolutism. In the legal systems that were heavily influenced by England, trusts among the living and the establishment of trusts by means of wills remained in existence and these institutions evolved further without problems. The trust law of the Norman Islands contains a considerable number of provisions that dovetail more closely with the medieval Continental *ius commune* than with the English law.

D. The codicil

A codicil (*codicilli*) was a written document, usually a letter, in which the testator asked someone to execute a *fideicommissum*. It did not contain a testamentary disposition. From Augustus' reign onwards, codicils became legally effective (see Inst. 2.25*pr.*). Until Justinian's day, no witnesses were required; later five witnesses were necessary. The codicil could either be confirmed in the will or not. If it was confirmed, it was presumed to be part of the will (but it could not change the testamentary disposition). If it was not confirmed, it could only contain a *fideicommissum*. The Justinianic codicil with five witnesses was received in Western Europe during the Middle Ages.

3. The reception of the will in a nutshell

In the Mediterranean, the Roman will continued to be used after the collapse of the Western Empire. The Lombards confirmed it (Liutprand, Rotari), as did the Visigoths (Chindasuinth, Recceswinth, Erwig, Breviary of Alaric). In Catalonia, Septimania and Lombardy, wills always continued to exist. The twelfth-century case-law of the Italian cities dovetailed with their continued existence. In more northern regions, the Roman will disappeared between the sixth and eighth centuries, depending on the region. The archives of the abbeys testify to this disappearance.

During the twelfth and thirteenth centuries, the will crops up again in town charters. One sometimes reads that a new kind of will originated at this time, namely the customary will. It is said that this will was not Roman and that it derived from donations to the Church. It is also said that confessors extorted donations from dying people in return for their salvation. This is nonsense. Charging money for sacraments was simony, an offence that was punished with the priests' excommunication throughout the entire history of the Church. The reception of the will happened via different channels. The Church was indeed involved in this reception. In the Carolingian era the pope and the emperor agreed on a forced Christianisation of the Empire. One of the elements of this Christianisation was the elimination of the heathen practice of burying the dead with their weaponry and in their best attire. The best way of stamping out this practice was to seize these goods when a person died. In the feudal system, this royal right ended up in the hands of the lords. It was the basis for the feudal lord's right to inherit the best movable good (*ius optimi catalli*). In many regions, one could circumvent this right by donating the good in question to a church. This explains why medieval churches sometimes possess large collections of weapons. In diplomatic acts, one can also find transfers of immovable goods and feudal rights to abbeys which historians interpret as donations in return for salvation. In this context as well, a more nuanced view is necessary. The abbeys were the financial backers of lords who went to war. They accepted feudal goods as collateral. Often, it was agreed that the collateral would fall to the abbey if the lord died intestate. This transfer certainly had nothing to do with salvation!

The reception of the will in the West got into its stride in the twelfth century. In the Concordat of Worms (1122) the Church received its own jurisdiction. Relatively soon afterwards, it was accepted that suits in which clergy were involved were treated before ecclesiastical courts. From the eleventh century onwards, celibacy was gradually introduced for the lower clergy and the desire to bequeath property arose. Consequently, the ecclesiastical courts introduced the law of wills for clergy. *Ecclesia uiuit lege romana*, so the law that was introduced was the Roman law of wills. The ecclesiastical judges also applied the Roman law in order to acquire exequaturs without problems – theoretically, Roman law was the law of the feudal judges. Once the law of wills existed for the clergy, laymen quickly discovered a means to enjoy this ecclesiastical law of wills as well: they included a legacy to their priest, to an abbey or a cult in their will. When these legatees claimed the legacy, the clergy became involved in the will and the ecclesiastical court was competent. It made sure that the exequatur would be granted and thus enabled laymen to draw up a valid will. This also explains the considerable interest in legacies to the Church. Under Alexander III (1159-1181) there was an intensive development of canonical case-law about wills. In many countries, the law of wills became a canonical matter. In England, the Roman freedom to bequeath was introduced by the Norman prelates in the *consilia regis*. The law of wills remained the competence of the consistory courts until the Wills Act of 1837.

In the thirteenth century the Parliament of Paris became the competent appellate court of Toulouse and Montpellier, where wills had never disappeared. The Parliament took decisions about the law of wills and the northern regions of the jurisdiction of the Parliament thus became reacquainted with the will. In the County of Flanders, the will appeared in the thirteenth century and became common in the fourteenth, when Paris had unmistakably become the appellate court for cases from the Council of Flanders.

In the German principalities of the Low Countries, use was sometimes made of executors (*exsecutores*). The testator appointed an executor and gave him the assignment to divide his goods. The executor immediately received the goods, but not their use. When the testator died, the executor became his successor. This institution is said to have been un-Roman because there was no testamentary disposition in the will. The appointment of the testator was the most important element. He received the estate with a resolutive time limit. The executor could wind up the estate, establish pious foundations and execute the division. Do not become too fixated on the lack of a testamentary disposition. The law of wills had evolved because of the practice of the officialities. Canonical case-law accepted wills without an *institutio heredis* (testamentary disposition, appointment of a general legatee). The intestate heirs then became the general legatee and were liable for the debts. The canonists were of the opinion that all unambiguous wills could be considered to be nuncupative wills, mancipatory wills. The canonical courts no longer required seven witnesses. Instead, they required proof according to the Romano-canonical procedure. Several medieval legists wrote about the *exsecutor*. Romano-canonical principles were engrafted into it. Some considered the task of the executor to be a guardianship (*tutela*); others saw it as a public obligation (*munus*) with legal consequences concerning refusal, liability, settlement, etcetera. Nevertheless, it is clear that Roman law was also applied to devolution and division. The Glossators reintroduced the doctrine of substitution, as well as the legal reserve and disinheritance. No matter how many variants or modalities one finds, it is clear that they were all based on the Roman will, with the freedom to bequeath, unilaterality and revocability. Bartolus and his student Baldus de Ubaldis summarised the attainments of the civilian and canonical lawyers and these were disseminated to all universities and sovereign courts of the Modern Era through Bartolism.

In the German kingdoms the case-law of the Reichskammergerichtshof would generalise the will. In 1512 the will with seven witnesses of the *Corpus iuris* and the oral testament before a judge or notary that was recorded in writing (*tabulae*) were introduced in the Empire-wide ordinance concerning the notarial profession.

The law of wills that was received was of course not the Roman law of Antiquity. It was permeated with other elements. An example: the freedom to bequeath immovable property was not only limited by the reserve in the Middle Ages, but also by feudal elements like the 'retour lignager', which served to keep feudal goods within one family. Do not, however, focus too much on these exceptions. If wills were received from Roman law throughout the world – as the abovementioned research by the 'Société Jean Bodin' has shown – the legal history of Western Europe will also be imbued with it.

Chapter VI
The law of property

Introduction: real rights

Real rights are a typical development of the seventeenth century and must be considered in the context of the division between public and private law. Absolutism was based on the fact that the monarch was the *dominus* of his territory, which meant that he had authority over people and goods. In the seventeenth-century legal doctrine, authority over people was redefined in public law, while authority over property was revised in private law. In this manner, a new theory about the private holding of goods appeared in the early modern *ius commune*. This theory eventually resulted in the development of real rights. In the seventeenth century, Heinrich Hahn (1605-1668, a professor in Helmstedt) analysed the *actiones in rem* of the *ius commune*. He came to the conclusion that there were five real rights: ownership (which, according to him, included emphyteusis and superficies), possession, servitudes (real servitudes such as easements and personal servitudes such as usufruct), pledge and inheritance.

From then on, these real rights were projected onto the Roman law. It was said that the *actiones in rem* were real actions. The Roman law made use of *actiones in rem* and *actiones in personam*, besides other actions like the *actiones praeiudiciales*. The difference between *actiones in rem* and *actiones in personam* was emphasised in the Early Modern Era. The former were commenced against a single person, who was mentioned in the action; the latter were commenced against everyone who held the person or good that was mentioned in the claim. A legacy *per uindicationem*, for example, established an *actio in rem* that could be commenced against everyone (the *reiuindicatio*), while a legacy *per damnationem* established an *actio in personam* (the *actio ex testamento*) by means of which only the general legatee could be sued. A 'droit de suite' was attached to the actions *in rem*: the good in question could be followed. In Roman Antiquity, however, there was neither a limited system of real rights nor a hierarchy of real rights. 'Derived' real rights or real rights *in re aliena* (to another person's goods) did not exist. *Ius in rem, ius in re, ius reale*... were discussed in the Middle Ages, but it was Grotius who put ownership at the top of the hierarchy and placed the 'limited real rights' beneath it. Here, we once again arrive at the private ownership of the seventeenth century.

Since in the seventeenth century real rights were rights to goods, a theory about goods was developed as well. Its basis was D. 1.8, which originally centred mainly on the jurisdiction over property. Not all goods played a role in the civil law. Some goods could not be brought on the market (*extra commercium*) and could not be claimed within the civil jurisdiction. Citizens could not dispose of *res diuini iuris* (goods under inviolable law). The ground in which someone was buried (*res religiosa*) was no one's property. *Res sacrae* were earmarked by the military authorities and if other people disposed of them, they were judged according to the criminal law. *Res uniuersales* belonged to a community or association and were traded via people who had been appointed. *Res communes omnium* (common goods), like coasts or the ocean, fell under the jurisdiction of the consuls. If rights at sea or the right to free navigation were threatened, one lodged a complaint with the consuls. If there were problems concerning *res publicae* (the military domain) and public goods (*usus publicus*) like watercourses, public roads, streets and squares, one turned to the consuls or quaestors or, in the cities, to the aediles. These goods could not be claimed. If there was a conflict between citizens about the rights to use *res publicae*, the praetors made use of interdicts.

Because of their importance in the current civil law, we will discuss the real rights according to the 'classical' categories of the Early Modern Era.

§1. Possession

Hahn classified possession as a real right even though there was no *actio in rem* for possession in the *Corpus iuris*. In the seventeenth century, a differentiation was made between possession, ownership and tenancy of a good. This differentiation also appears in the current civil codes of France and Belgium. According to article 544, ownership is the right to have the enjoyment and disposal of a good in the most absolute way possible, as long as the owner does not act in breach of the law. Ownership is said to be an absolute right, a unique right and the principal real right on which all of the other real rights depend. Possession is said to imply a more factual relationship with the good, as well as the factual possibility of alienating it (art. 2228 Civil code and Belg. Cass. 16 May 1885). A tenant had the rented good in his factual power, but did not have the prerogatives of the possessor. He did not have a real right. According to the Pandectists, ownership, possession and tenancy stemmed from the terms *dominium, possessio* and *detentio* in the *Corpus iuris*. In Antiquity, these three words indicated legal concepts that were a far cry from our current categories. *Detinere* simply meant that a person kept a good, i.e. had it with him. Tenants, those who had goods on loan, and depositories held goods without enjoying legal protection against third parties. *Dominium* was the status of a *dominus* or *paterfamilias*. The disposal of familial goods was an aspect thereof. *Possessio* was the status of a person to whom the judge had granted a provisional measure. In other words, the history of possession does not begin with real rights, but with preliminary measures.

1. Possession and interdict

D. 43 sums up the interdicts. These were standard solutions that the praetor or *cognitio* judge pronounced in cases of nuisance that ranged from the obstruction of a road or passage (D. 43.13 and 19) to hindrances caused by herds on common land or by sewage works (D. 42.23). The praetor or judge resolved these conflicts by means of preliminary measures. After proof had been furnished and some summary facts had been checked during the preliminary hearing, an interim judgement was pronounced (*interdicere*). Such an interdict always entailed a *possessio*. One of the claimants was allowed to remain in possession.

In the Republic, these interdicts were listed in the praetor's edict, just like the actions were. They were introduced in the imperial case-law by the *edictum perpetuum*. The most famous one was the interdict *unde ui* (D. 43.16), which could be requested by everyone who was a victim either of violence or of a person who had taken the law into his own hands. If the violence was proved, the victim was granted *possessio*. The previous situation was restored and the injured person was provisionally allowed to retain *possessio*, even when he had no arguments that would lead to the judge finding in his favour in a later lawsuit (see for example D. 41.3.25).

Such a *possessio* did not have anything to do with real rights, because *possessio* did not only pertain to goods. A preliminary decision about the status of a party to the trial also resulted in *possessio*, namely *possessio status* (possession of status). An interdict applied *erga omnes* (towards everyone). In Antiquity, prior to Justinian, appeals against *possessio status* were not possible. If one wanted to react, one had to commence proceedings on the merits. When it was received by later jurists, *possessio* was mainly used to allow a person to retain goods. Because it applied *erga omnes*, possession was listed among the real rights. In the current law, a judgement about a person's possession of status, civil status or nationality still applies *erga omnes*, although no one thinks of real rights in this context.

2. Protection of the possession of goods in Antiquity

Some interdicts, in other words, pertained to the protection of rights to goods. They are at the basis of the current notion of possession. Three important interdicts in this context are *uti possidetis*, *utrubi* and *unde ui*.

A. The functions of the possession of goods

In the Republic, the army gave military property (*ager publicus populi romani*) in concession to private parties, either in return for payment (the *agri uectigales*) or for free (the *agri occupatorii*). Vis-à-vis the army this particular private party was in a *precarium* (precarious legal relationship, *preces* = petition, prayer). The army could revoke this concession *ad nutum*, without ceremony. Did the private party enjoy legal protection? Perhaps he had legal protection according to the edict of the consul or quaestor, but these edicts have not been handed down. However, if the precarious possessor's enjoyment was disturbed by another citizen, the conflict was a civil one. The precarious possessor could summon the other party before the praetor or preliminary judge. If he simply proved that he was a precarious possessor, he received the *interdictum uti possidetis* (interdict for immovable goods) at the introductory hearing. He could use it to remove the other party from the land involved. The legal status which the interdict had created for the beneficiary was *possessio*. In this context, possession received a policing function: it protected a party against the actions of a third party.

The procedure that made use of interdicts was more simple and cheaper than the procedure that employed actions. This more efficient procedure also began to be used by the praetors for the protection of the use of private land. Those whose ownership was disturbed could request a revendication. In addition, they received an *interdictum uti possidetis* (interdict for immovable goods). In the third century BC, the *interdictum utrubi* began to be applied to movable goods. Both of these interdicts concerning private goods would give rise to a considerable amount of case-law: see D. 41.2. The interdict *quem fundum* was added to the list of interdicts that could be used in cases involving immovable goods. A claimant could ask to be granted this interdict when the defendant did not turn up. In such cases, the claimant did not even have to prove that he had a title. In other words, one could choose between an action and an interdict if one wanted to commence legal proceedings about a good.

Because of the greater simplicity and cheapness of the procedure that used interdicts, the praetors at one point decided to refuse to admit repersecutory actions unless the parties had first tried to solve the problem by means of interdicts. For example, one could only file a proprietary claim (*reiuindicatio*) if one had first lost one's case in a procedure by means of interdicts. In this context, possession was given a procedural function: revendications were inadmissible if they were not preceded by a judgement concerning possession. Those who translate *possessio* into possession and *dominium* into ownership, like the Pandectists did, would have to conclude that one could only become an owner if one did not have possession...

B. Conditions for the protection of the possession of goods in the classical Roman law

Protection of possession among private parties only existed for goods that could be brought on the market (*in commercio*). The possessor had to have a physical (*corpore*) and intentional (*animo*) connection with the good in question. In addition, he had to prove that the good had been acquired through an acknowledged legal act (*iusta causa*).

The criterion of physical control led to colourful case-law. It was accepted, for example, that one had factual power over goods if one had taken a hold of them, if they were in a warehouse to which one had the keys, if one paid a guard to watch over them, etcetera. There was a physical connection with land if one had walked around it, but also if it had been pointed out from a tower (D. 41.2.18.2). However, an acquisition that had taken place only by means of a written document did not suffice. In such circumstances, the other party could claim that the first party had indeed had the good, but had physically left it since then.

The second element was the intention (*animus*) to keep the good. There was a lot of case-law about this matter as well. Interdicts were not granted to people who were no longer interested in the good. Sometimes, a person was granted protection of possession with regard to goods that he only had in an intentional manner (*animo solo*). In such cases, it had to be certain that the party would materially recuperate the goods. The classical example was a mountain pasture: such pastures were abandoned during the winter, but this did not mean that someone else could take them (D. 41.2.3.11). A slave who had run away could only be claimed back with an interdict if it was almost certain that he would be found (Gaius 4.153).

The third condition, title (*causa*), referred to the legal act by means of which the good had been acquired. Consequently, the following people enjoyed protection of possession:

- the person who had received land in precarious possession: such people were protected against third parties, but not against the owner of the land or the army. If a citizen granted precarious possession of land to a fellow citizen and got in trouble about it, he could also receive an interdict against the precarious possessor, namely the *interdictum de precario* (D. 43.26*pr.*).
- the emphyteuticary. Emphyteusis was a long-term, inheritable and alienable right of use. According to the Emperor Zeno it was neither a lease nor a purchase, but a contract *sui generis*.

- the usufructuary and the superficiary enjoyed protection against the owner and third parties.
- the pledgee. A person who had received a good in pledge could claim it with an interdict if the debt which the pledge covered was not paid.
- the sequestrator with whom a good was deposited during a lawsuit.

These holders did not obtain the goods for themselves, but nevertheless received possession. If the precarious legal relationship was revoked – if emphytheusis, pledge or sequestration ended – the protection of possession ended as well.

Furthermore, in the case of the private acquisition of property, a series of legal acts were considered to be *iusta causa possessionis* (legal acts that gave rise to protection of possession). This type of protection of possession was called civil possession (*possessio ciuilis*) in the classical period. Examples of titles were acquisition through purchase (*pro emptore*), through the execution of a legacy *per uindicationem* (*pro legato*), through a stipulation or a legacy *per damnationem* (*pro soluto*), through a gift on account of a dowry (*pro dote*), by taking an abandoned good (*pro derelicto*), etcetera.

A possessor had to have possession *animo et corpore* and a possessory title from the outset. This title could not be changed afterwards. A person who had borrowed something could not claim after some time that it had been given to him. This rule (*nemo sibi ipse causam possessionem mutare potest*) appears in thirteen texts from the Digest (for example Papinian in D. 5.4.10) and in two constitutions of Diocletian (C. 4.65.23 and C. 7.32.5).

Tenants, who had actual control over a good, had no claim to protection by means of an interdict, because a tenancy agreement was not a possessory title. They were the mere holders of a good (*detentor*, *detinere* = to have with one). However, they did not need protection of possession. In a case of disturbance, they litigated by means of a personal action against their lessor, who had to remove the disturbance. The lessor therefore had to be given means like the interdict in order to be able to evict third parties. It is for this reason that tenants were not granted protection of possession in legal history.

An important rule of procedure was that interdicts were only available for a period of one year. Those who did not react to a disturbance within one year, were no longer granted protection of possession.

C. Extinctive prescription

A party could react against a possessory remedy by making use of a petitory remedy. This could be a revendication or another *actio*. Examples are the *uindicatio seruitutis*, which could be brought against the person who had received protection of possession on account of usufruct, or the abovementioned *petitio hereditatis*, which could be instituted against the *bonorum possessor intestati*. In a case of *possessio ciuilis* – in other words, in a case involving legal acts which led to the acquisition of goods – this claim had to be brought within a certain time period. Concretely, the possessor received the defence of the long term, the *praescriptio longi temporis*, against the claim. If the possessor could invalidate the claim by means of this defence, his possession of the good became definitive.

Case-law concerning the granting of this *praescriptio* was developed. In order to invalidate the claim with a means of defence, the defendant had to have possessed the good for a prolonged period of time. For movable goods, this time period was four years; for immovable goods it was ten years if the claimant and the defendant lived in the same province (under Justinian: in the same town) and twenty years if they lived in different provinces. In the classical law, this time period began anew whenever the good was transferred. It is only from the post-classical period onwards that the prescription period continued if a new acquirer obtained the good under particular title (Inst. 2.6.12-13).

The *praescriptio* caused the claim and the defence to be assessed *e bona fide*. If these words occurred in the formula of an action, the judge was expected to consider all relations between the parties. In the case of a strict action, such as the *stipulatio* or the *actio e testamento*, by contrast, the judge was not allowed to do this. In some circumstances, the defendant received an *exceptio doli* (defence on account of deceit) during the preliminary hearing. In such cases, the judge considered the entire situation even though the actions involved were strict ones. In the case-law, this effect of the *exceptio doli* also applied to the *praescriptio longi temporis*. In the Digest, one can read that the judge could take all of the circumstances into account in order to decide whether the defence of the long term was legitimate or not. If someone had obtained a good from a pupil without the permission of the pupil's guardian and had not known that he was dealing with a pupil, he could invalidate the revendication of the good many years later by means of the *praescriptio* (D. 41.4.2.15-16). It appears that the pupil should have reacted sooner. In another case, a person had acquired goods that were encumbered by a pledge. The goods were claimed by the pledgee years later. In response, the defendant invoked the *praescriptio longi temporis*. According to the claimant, the defendant did so wrongfully, because the claimant's pledge also enjoyed protection of possession. However, there had been no indication at the time of transfer or afterwards that the goods were encumbered with a pledge. The judges deemed that this was not a correct way for citizens to treat one another. The defendant was therefore granted the prescription that invalidated this late revendication of the goods. Beware of jumping to the conclusion that *bona fides* meant that the possessor had to act in 'moral' good faith. In D. 41.3.13.2, we find the case of someone who had bought a piece of land by order of a third party. The piece of land was transferred to the buyer, who never transferred it to the third party. Ten years later, the third party claimed his land. The mandatory invalidated the claim by means of the *praescriptio longi temporis*. Apparently, it was not normal among citizens to wait for such a long time before claiming back a good.

In the context of prescription, this *bona fides* causes quite a lot of confusion, because *bona* and *mala fides* also crop up in the context of the establishment of purchase and sale agreements, where good relations between both parties are essential, and in the context of *ususcapio*, which was a means of obtaining ownership. However, Paul points out in D. 41.4.2.1 that possession and *usucapio* are not to be confused with one another.

The *praescriptio longi temporis* could be used to make possession definitive. Definitive possession was not ownership. In Antiquity, definitive possession meant *uti frui habere possidere*: the possessor had the use of the good (*usus*) and its proceeds (*fructus*); the possession was part of his goods (*habere*); and he was granted protection of possession (*possidere*).

In the late Classical period, the defence of the very long term, the *praescriptio longissimi temporis*, was developed. It involved a time period of thirty years and could be used to invalidate any claim. The person who could invoke the exception of the very long term with regard to immovable goods had the highest right to these goods that one could acquire in the provinces. With regard to immovable goods, the payment of land taxes (*tributum*) was considered to be proof of custody. In the Eastern Empire, this remained the case until 1453. This opinion was adopted by the Ottomans, according to whom the party who was entitled to land was always the party that paid the land tax.

3. The medieval reception of possession

A. Possession of immovable goods

In the Empire, all land was crown land, i.e. it was – to use a bad translation – in imperial ownership. One could not exploit land without paying *tributum* (land tax) to the monarch. In the Republic, citizens did have land in *dominium*, which meant that this land was exempt from taxes. When all of the provinces became part of the imperial territory, the right to own land was only retained in Italy. Justinian revoked this rule and made private *dominium* possible in all of the provinces, but his measure came too late for the West, where rights to goods were already being guaranteed by means of protection of possession. This, at least, is the impression that one gets when one reads the Theodosian Code and the *leges romanae barbarorum*. In the feudal system of the Carolingian era, the *dominium* of the emperor was split up. It was delegated to those who received a fief that consisted of land and jurisdiction. Consequently, *dominium* fell under the feudal law and within the competence of the feudal courts. A study by Jean Durliat has demonstrated how abbeys and private proprietors remained outside the scope of the feudal law by making use of *possessio*. If a *uniuersitas* had *possessio*, its land never devolved and could, consequently, never fall to the *fiscus*. Here lie the origins of allodial goods, which remained outside of the scope of the feudal law. This notion was important for the canonists. Hostiensis, for example, wrote extensively about *praescriptio* and *possessio*, but rarely mentioned *dominium*.

In the canonical case-law we discover the importance of the extrajudicial acquisition of possession by means of *praescriptio*. In this context, we also find the time period of one year and one day that was the typical period within which one could request an interdict. Because of the changed importance of the interdict, however, its position within the procedure had also shifted. One obtained *possessio* after one year and a day, at the moment when no one could make use of an interdict anymore. Prior to that moment, one kept the good in custody (according to the commentaries on X. 1.31.11). X. 2.26.20 states that this extrajudicial *custodia* could not have been established in a *mala fide* way. The *bona/mala fides* that appears here is that of the canonists: it refers to the reliable and Christian treatment of one's fellow man. The church fathers translated the Greek word *pistis* (faith) as *fides*. When the canonists encountered the terms *bona fide* and *mala fide* in the *Corpus iuris*, they consequently took them to mean, respectively, 'in keeping with charity' and 'sinful'. This is why they maintained that one had to act 'in good faith' during the entire period of prescription (Conc. Lat IV, adopted in X. 2.26.20). The civil lawyers, however, interpreted the *Corpus iuris* in a different manner: for them, the *bona fides* that was mentioned in connection with possession was the same as the *bona fides* that was required at the time of a purchase or *usucapio*. This *bona fide* was only necessary at the outset of possession: *mala fides superueniens non nocet* (subsequent bad faith does not do harm).

B. Possession and ownership

Because of its new function in the retention of allodial goods, a separate petitory claim for *possessio* was developed in the Middle Ages. It was based on C. 7.39.8*pr.* In the gloss *'Etiam actionem' ad* C. 7.39.8*pr.*, we read that this action did not automatically lead to *dominium*. After so many centuries, possession had become a right: for the glossators, it was no longer a factual situation that gave rise to an interdict. *Dominium* and *possessio* became sacrosanct because they and their corresponding actions had coexisted as means of retaining goods for a very long time. The consequence was that the abolition of one of these notions became unthinkable in later legal history. From the twelfth century onwards, the cities bought their freedom from feudal obligations. In civic case-law, there was room for non-feudal, freehold *dominium* as it was described in D. 41.1. In this context, the difference between feudal *dominium* and allodial *possessio* was no longer important. What, then, was the difference between *possessio* and *dominium*? Was there room for both systems? Placentinus was the first who tried to subordinate *possessio* to *dominium*. This evolution towards the primacy of *dominium* is also clear in the abovementioned gl. *'Etiam actionem' ad* C. 7.39.8*pr.*

As the glossators and commentators considered possession to be a right to goods that was enforced by means of a (petitory) possessory claim, their analysis of D. 41.2 no longer linked *possessio* with the procedure by means of interdicts. What they found in the Digest were the material conditions for their notion of *possessio*. Azo defined possession as the material and intentional detention of a corporal object that was acknowledged by the law (*possessio est corporalis rei detentio corporis et animi, iuris adminiculo concurrente*). According to Bartolus, possession was the right to stand on a certain good and to receive legal protection with regard to that good. The medieval jurists' reasoning was less procedural than that of the Romans and had been influenced by the conceptual mode of thought. When discussing *possessio,* they stressed 'to sit on it', i.e. the fact that someone had an object with him. *Dominium,* by contrast, was defined as the right to fully dispose of a physical object in so far as this was not forbidden by the law.

C. The reception of the case-law concerning possession

The Roman remedy at law pertaining to possession which was invoked most often in the courts and universities was the interdict *unde ui* (D. 43.16), the general interdict against the use of violence. If something had been violently taken from someone, the victim could recover his goods by making use of this remedy. The case had to involve both violence and robbery. The latter notion was gradually interpreted as meaning any unlawful removal of goods, i.e. any removal that was not accompanied by the establishment of new possession. This establishment of possession was found in the Digest. Those who were entitled to an interdict in Antiquity became 'possessors' in the Middle Ages. Under the influence of the canonists, this remedy's scope was enlarged to include not only the removal of goods, but also that of rights, for example the right to usufruct, emphyteusis or *census*. The procedure *unde ui* was already applied in the officialities at a very early stage, so that this procedure exerted a larger influence than the procedure *uti possidetis*.

The Roman texts concerning the *interdictum uti possidetis* were also reshaped in the legal doctrine of the medieval legists. The procedure by means of interdicts was no longer concluded at the introductory hearing. Instead, it was initiated as a procedure by means of actions. The *interdictum uti possidetis* became the procedure that was used when possession was contested but the object had not been taken away. In the case of a conflict between two possessors, it was presumed that the oldest possession took precedence.

The third remedy at law which involved possession was the *redintegranda*. This remedy originated with the canonists and was influenced by the customary procedures to claim goods. The local law of the Middle Ages also relied chiefly on possession to organise protection of goods. If one reads about medieval notions such as seisin, the old *uti frui habere possidere* is never far away. In case of a *redintegranda*, the person with the best entitlement received the good. Violence did not need to be proved. The person with the best entitlement was he who could prove that he had *possessio* under Roman law. This procedure was purely canonical (see C. 3 q. 1 c. 3-4) and was applied in the officialities but nevertheless sanctioned the definition of possession that the civil lawyers had distilled from the Justinianic texts. If a person could prove his right to possession but did not have the good, his rights were restored. This rule did not only apply to the possession of goods, but also to the possession of rights (*quasi-possessio*). The *redintegranda* could be brought against anyone – even against a defendant of good faith – except the owner. Towards the end of the Middle Ages, the *redintegranda* disappeared. Even in the officialities, it was replaced by the possessory procedure *unde ui*. In the meantime, however, the *redintegranda* had exerted a considerable influence on the latter procedure: the element of violence was relegated to the background, while the qualification of possession was brought to the fore.

In these three procedures, the material conditions for protection of possession were adopted from the Roman law. Consequently, the notion of *possessio* became important throughout the West. In canonical courts and aldermen's courts of lower jurisdiction the discussion concerning ownership and revendication was avoided for a long time so as to prevent competition with the feudal courts. In the Roman law, possessory claims expired after one year. A disruption that had taken place more than a year ago could no longer give rise to an interdict. This explains why many customs mention acquisitive prescription after one year and one day.

Bibliography. – The abovementioned work by Durliat is: J. DURLIAT, *Les finances publiques de Dioclétien aux Carolingiens (284-889)*, Sigmaringen 1991; on the glossators and commentators, see L. MASMEJEAN, *La protection possessoire en droit romano-canonique médiéval (XIIIe-XVe siècles)*, Montpellier 1990.

4. Possession in the Early Modern Era

The rise of sovereign justice in the Early Modern Period brought with it both a curbing of feudalism and the unification of the law. The fear to invoke ownership disappeared together with the competition between aldermen's and ecclesiastical courts on the one hand, and feudal courts on the other. In the Early Modern Era, we encounter the protection of possession based on Roman law. Examples include 'maintenue' and 'complainte' in the law of France and the Low Countries. In general, however, possession was made subservient to ownership.

In England, feudalism was privatised from the twelfth century onwards and *dominium* became a right to the revenues from immovable goods. For the daily exploitation of the goods, *possessio* continued to be used. On the Continent, the process of de-feudalisation was different. The introduction of the possibility of appeal deprived the vassals of their sovereign jurisdiction, while they retained the exploitation of their domains. In the terminology of the Early Modern Era: they retained *dominium*. In the seventeenth century, at the time of the rise of private law, this right was categorised under private law. Grotius and his contemporaries translated it as 'ownership'. One could claim this ownership by means of a revendication. It was a former imperial right, i.e. the highest possible private right. Possession was inferior to it. If the possessor could invalidate the revendication by means of a *praescriptio*, he had apparently acquired the highest right, which meant that he was the owner. In the countries that made use of the *ius commune*, one sees that the old extinctive prescription of the possessor was recast into the acquisitive prescription of the possessor. In the legal doctrine, *usucapio* (acquisition of ownership through use) and the *praescriptio longi temporis* (definitive acquisition of possession) were put on a par. In the meantime the canonical case-law was adopted by the civil administration of justice. As a consequence, the *bona fides* of the canonists – the Christian concern and reliability that was a condition for acquisitive prescription – was also introduced. In article 2269 of the Civil code, the civil lawyers' interpretation carries the most weight: subsequent bad faith is not harmful. The contrary vision, *mala fides nocet* in the case of acquisitive prescription, is one of the few rules from their rich past that the current canonists still know. It no longer has any practical importance, but still figures prominently in can. 1512 CIC 1917 and can. 198 Codex 1983.

Because of its rich tradition, Hahn still included possession in his pentarchy, but the notion had played its part. It became an aspect of ownership and jurists sought to define it. The old case-law concerning the factual acquisition of a good with the intention of keeping it gained the upper hand. All of the old Latin texts about *possessio* were henceforth read as if they dealt with the factual dimension of possession. In the law codes of the nineteenth century, the notion was ossified and definitively came to indicate the factual authority over a good. The Pandectists, finally, read the Roman word *possessio* as if it indicated possession as it was defined in art. 2228 of the Code civil. Consequently, we cannot expect the notion to make historical sense. Today, no one really knows what to do with the concept of possession. It falls prey to jurists who need 'des notions à contenu variable' in the law of property in order to develop new formulas.

§2. Ownership

Since the seventeenth century, ownership has been a mythical notion of private law. 'No law without ownership', was a nineteenth-century adage, as was 'free ownership is the most useful legacy that Rome has left us'. According to the Pandectists, the Roman notion of *dominium* indicated this ownership. In Antiquity, however, this word meant 'the status of *paterfamilias*', i.e. mastership. Gaius discussed it as part of the law of persons. It is only in the medieval legal doctrine that *dominium* became a substantive right to goods. In sixteenth-century legal practice, the notion appeared only rarely. In the seventeenth century, ownership became a subjective right. In the eighteenth, *dominium* came to be interpreted as civil ownership. However, the concept that was called ownership in article 544 of the Code civil mainly derives from the old rights of emphyteuticaries and vassals.

1. Ownership and *reiuindicatio* in Antiquity

A. Reiuindicatio

The revendication was an action by means of which the *paterfamilias*, who was known as the *dominus* in the imperial law, could claim a person or good. He could request this claim if proceedings by means of interdicts had resulted in him losing the case. When he requested a revendication, the praetor or the *cognitio* judge asked him to prove his *dominium*, i.e. the fact that he was the *paterfamilias* or *dominus* of the good in question. In D. 41.2, we find case-law concerning this proof of *dominium*. This text clearly shows that *dominium* was not a right, but a state of affairs that had to be proved. Let the reader be warned: we translate the word *dominium* as 'ownership', but it actually referred to a state of affairs. *Dominium* would only become a right in the Middle Ages, just like *possessio*. In Antiquity, the principal proof of *dominium* was the manner in which the person or good had become part of the *familia*. This explains the supreme importance of the acquisition of ownership, which we will discuss below and which originated from the case-law concerning the awarding of the revendication. When the Roman law was received, the manner in which a good or person had ended up in a *familia* became the manner of acquiring ownership rights over this person or good. Sometimes, it was simply impossible to prove acquisition. In those cases, the Roman case-law made use of a second criterion, *proprietas*. This word indicates 'close involvement' as well as 'individuality' or 'a person's own good' (for example in D. 7.1.14.6). Case-law on the scope of *proprietas* also appeared. Just as, concerning *possessio*, jurists described the situation in which a person was granted the protection of interdicts, they described, with regard to *dominium* and *proprietas*, the circumstances in which someone had to find himself in order to be granted a revendication. In D. 41.1 the awarding of the revendication is discussed. *Dominium* and *proprietas* became equivalent notions in Gaius and the Digests. The civil lawyers considered them to be synonyms.

The oldest form of the revendication only served to resolve a conflict. In the *legis actio in rem* both parties claimed that a good or person belonged to their *familia*. The judge then decided who was most entitled to it. In another conflict about the same good or person, the same judge could come up with an entirely different adjudication. In the first place, he took into account the manner in which the good or person had ended up in the *familia*. If this had happened by means of a *mancipatio*, the individual from whom the person or good had been acquired (the *auctor*) could be summoned in order to safeguard the rightful acquirer. If the judge decided against the claimant, the latter was granted an *actio auctoritatis* (claim on account of eviction) against the *auctor*. By means of this action the claimant could claim twice the value that he lost. There was, therefore, neither an absolute right nor a subjective or highest real right.

In the *formula* procedure, a revendication resulted in a pronouncement as to who was the *paterfamilias* rather than in a decision about which of the parties had the best entitlement to the good or person. Proving that a good or person had belonged to the *familia* of all one's predecessors in title was a thorny issue. In the classical period, revendications were only allowed if the conflict had already been assessed during a procedure by means of interdicts. In such procedures, it sufficed to prove that the good or the person had not been obtained *ui, clam aut precario* (with violence, surreptitiously or precariously). If the conflict was resolved by means of an interdict, the revendication was postponed. The person who had obtained the person or good enjoyed protection of possession. The revendication could not be brought against the mere *detentor* (holder) of the good in question. Holders could only be sued by means of an interdict. Justinian also allowed actions to be brought against a fictive possessor who did not have possession either because he had disposed of the property in a deceitful manner (*dolo malo desinit possidere*) or because he feigned possession in order to allow a third party to acquire the good through prescription. The person against whom an *actio in rem* was brought was not obliged to defend himself. If he refused the *litiscontestatio*, the there was no judgement on the revendication. If the good involved in the case was an immovable, the praetor then granted possession to the claimant (*interdictum quem fundum*).

With regard to movable goods, the judge of the preliminary hearing granted an *actio in personam* if necessary, namely the *actio ad exhibendum* (action to display, see D. 40.4.1 and following). If the defendant did not react to this, he became *indefensus* and could be declared bankrupt. If he reacted but lost the case, he had to pay just as much as in the case of a revendication, but there was no judgement on the question of ownership.

The *formula* of the revendication ran as follows: *Si paret rem qua de agitur ex iure Quiritum Ai. Ai. esse neque ea res restituetur, quanti ea res erit, tantam pecuniam iudex Nm. Nm. Ao. Ao. c., s. n. p. a.* ('If it turns out that the object concerning which legal proceedings were instituted belongs to the claimant according to the civil law, and the object is not returned, you, judge, must sentence the defendant to pay as much money as the good is worth; if this does not turn out to be the case, you must acquit him'). In other words, the surrendering of the good was not obligatory in a case of revendication either. The fact that in the Republic and the early Principate a party could only be sentenced to pay a sum of money meant that ownership was of relative importance. At the preliminary hearing, one could demand sureties, just in case one won but did not obtain the surrender of the good. There were, however, ways of obtaining surrender. It was possible to include a restitution clause in the formula. If the defendant did not want to surrender the good, the winning party could determine the value of the good under oath (*litis aestimatio*) and received this amount.

The right to bring a revendication was a civil right, i.e. a right that had at one point been granted to warriors and veterans. It always concerned goods to which the army of the emperor did not have any rights and which were therefore free from taxation. One could not revendicate a good that lay outside of Italy, because all non-Italian land was subject to *tributum*. This tax-free character (freehold) was typical of goods that could be revendicated.

B. Remedies with equivalent consequences

Gaius explains how one could gain just as much control of goods without having *dominium*. Traditionally, the Romans differed between *res mancipi* and *res nec mancipi*. If *res mancipi* (slaves, land, beasts of burden and agricultural tools) had not been transferred by means of a mancipation, the person who had obtained them had them *in bonis* (as part of his goods), but could not immediately revendicate them. These goods were then considered to be his own after a certain time period – one year for movable goods, and two years for immovable goods. Until then, the original *paterfamilias* retained the right to revendicate the goods. However, if he used the revendication against the man to whom he had delivered the goods, the praetor granted the latter the *exceptio rei uenditae et traditae* (exception of the good that was sold and delivered) or the *exceptio doli* (exception on account of fraud). The person who had obtained the good could employ these exceptions to invalidate the revendication and thus, Gaius writes, the acquirer had a stronger right than the *paterfamilias.* The Pandectists called this stronger right 'bonitarian ownership' because they reasoned that such a right must be a kind of ownership. Justinian abolished the difference between *res mancipi* and *res nec mancipi,* so that this bonitarian ownership does not occur in the *Corpus iuris* and was of no importance to the *ius commune.*

The *actio publiciana* did feature in the *Corpus iuris.* In the first century BC, the urban praetor Publicius introduced it for people who had obtained *res mancipi* without a mancipation and were in the process of becoming owners through acquisitive prescription. If such people lost these goods, they did not have the right to revendicate them. However, they could receive the *actio publiciana,* by means of which they could litigate against every person who had control of the good. The type of control over a good that could be enforced by means of this action was called 'praetorian ownership' by the Pandectists. The *actio publiciana* was an action that served to determine who had the better right to the good rather than to decide who had an indisputable right to the good. The proof of civil transfer by one's predecessors in title was no longer valid. The claimant had to substantiate that he had obtained the alienated object by legal title (*iusta causa possessionis*), i.e. not deceitfully, and that he had lost the good during the acquisitive prescription period. The fiction that the limitation period had ended was included in the formula of the action (it featured an *irrealis*; see our treatment of the *formula* in the paragraph about the *formula* procedure); the claimant received exactly what he would have received if he had been able to bring a revendication. The defendant could only invalidate the *actio publiciana* by means of the *exceptio iusti dominii* (exception of lawful ownership). Against this exception, the claimant of the *actio publiciana* could use the reply of the sold and delivered good or person (*replicatio rei uenditae et traditae*) if he had received the good or person from the other party in a correct manner. The judge, in other words, had to assess three claims on the occasion of a single action. The ownership of the predecessors in title was no longer proved. Justinian adopted the *actio publiciana* in D. 6.2. In the Middle Ages, this action did not have any feudal aspects and it was used to obtain custody. In this context, Bartolus spoke of *quasi-dominium.* Quite a few civil lawyers began to think about the content of the concept of custody and saw it as a foundation of possession.

C. The scope of the notion of ownership in Antiquity

The scope of *dominium* was relatively limited. Roman ownership was not available to everyone: it only became important after a procedure by means of interdicts. The interdicts, bonitarian ownership, the procedure by means of a *legis actio in rem,* the *actio publiciana* or the *praescriptio longi temporis* all resulted in a similar right. *Dominium* of a good did not mean a right to the good or person itself – a revendication led to a financial sentence, not to the surrender of the good. In addition, *dominium* did not mean that one could freely dispose of the good. The designated use of some goods had to be respected, for example in the case of a dowry or fiduciary goods. In addition, the right of disposal of the goods was limited by the censors, who controlled, for example, construction and demolition permits. Government decisions interfered with familial assets: those who repaired aqueducts, for example, could extract building materials from surrounding plots without having to provide compensation. The right of ownership was also limited territorially. Immovable goods outside of Italy could not be revendicated (see Gaius 2.7 and C. 7.31.1).

Prior to Grotius, ownership was not the highest real right from which the other real rights were derived. There was no hierarchy of *actiones in rem*. In the courts of law, parties requested the remedy that they thought most suitable to resolve a conflict, just as golfers choose the best club from an entire caddy in order to hit a good drive. The *uindicatio seruitutis* (vindication of a servitude) or the *uindicatio ususfructus* (vindication of a usufruct) were analogous to the revendication. The revendication of a slave was on a par with the *uindicatio libertatis*. Although usufruct was limited in time, it was actually a stronger right than *dominium*: if a good was encumbered by a usufruct, one could not obtain it by means of a revendication. The revendication also gave way to the *actio publiciana*, despite the fact that the latter only established 'the best right' of one of the parties. Throughout Antiquity, *dominium* remained the status of the *paterfamilias*. The word did not refer to a unique notion of ownership.

2. Evolution in the Middle Ages

The medieval interpretation of ownership was influenced to a considerable extent by feudal law. The moral philosophers imbued the concept with values. The civil lawyers also interpreted *dominium* and *proprietas* as a substantive right. Ownership no longer exclusively concerned revendications. The circumstances in which one was granted a revendication turned into the right itself. In 1066, the introduction of the Roman law in England went hand in hand with the Conqueror 'subleasing' his rights to his subjects, a practice which resulted in a mixture of Roman and feudal law. The Continent would follow suit.

A. The feudal law

Charlemagne wanted to restore the Western Empire, but did not have the necessary means. He considered his territory to be the old *familia caesaris* and the provinces were part of his *dominium*. Vis-à-vis the emperor of the East, he defended his rights to the West by stating that he had at least acquired *dominium* through a prescription of thirty years. His successors leased pieces of this public domain to 'vassals' in return for loyalty, military support and taxes. These vassals then subleased their domain to sub-vassals, who in their turn divided the domain even further. The abovementioned feudal law, with in some districts separate feudal courts, was developed around conflicts concerning adjudications, successions, transmission and the scope of the abovementioned leasing of the public domain. In these jurisdiction, liege lords judged their vassals. They nevertheless drew up nuanced laws: each liege lord was someone's vassal and could also be called to account. Over the next centuries, the public domain was divided further and further. Eventually, a fief could consist of one house, a local right to levy tolls, or the monopoly to operate a local mill. The feudal law remained military in character for a long time: those who received a fief owed military service to their lord. In England and Flanders, the feudal law lost its military character in the twelfth century. Feudal rights were henceforth experienced as patrimonial rights. Even then, these rights were still associated with the idea that a part of the highest authority had been bestowed on the vassal. Some population groups privatised fiefs by buying their freedom from feudal obligations and thus established towns.

In the medieval law faculties, scholars searched the *Corpus iuris* for information about the status of the feudal law. The monarch lent his domain to others – did this mean that he lost it? What did a vassal receive when he had acquired sovereign rights to a domain – did he perhaps receive *dominium*? And which right to his territory did this vassal retain when he leased it to subvassals? Both the lord and the vassals had rights to the domain, but they had different claims to the same goods. Could this be *dominium*? The glossators found the key to a solution in C. 11.62.12.1, which describes a case in which imperial domain was given in emphyteusis. In this passage, they read that the emphyteuticary was a *dominus*. C. 4.66.1-2, however, mentioned that the person who had granted emphyteusis had *dominium*. According to D. 13.6.5.15, two persons could not have the same right to a good. Consequently, there had to be several kinds of ownership. In twelfth-century Bologna, Pillius and Jacobus Colombani introduced the difference between *dominium directum* (direct ownership) and *dominium utile* (useful ownership). These notions were derived from the difference between *actio directa* and *actio utilis*. The person who granted emphyteusis retained *dominium directum*, while the emphyteuticary received *dominium utile*. This 'divided ownership' would be disseminated in Western Europe via the gloss.

Subjunctive or indicative? – The relevant passage from the Code contains a penstroke with great consequences.

C. 11.62.12 (434). Possessores uel emphyteuticarii patrimoniales qui fundos minime nunc usque compararunt, eodem largitatis modo nequaquam ad eorum comparationem urgueantur, sed tamquam pretiis depensis, sic eis nostri numinis beneficio potiantur, ut, quod iuris alter inferendo pretium consecutus est, hoc nostra liberalitate praedictus emphyteuticarius habeat. 1. Illud quoque ius, in quibus coluit praediis, quod aut ex successione aut ex comparatione priuata aut nostri numinis liberalitate aut quocumque modo possedit, sciat inlibatum intemeratumque seruari: licentia eis concedenda etiam libertates mancipiis ex fundis patrimonialibus atque emphyteuticariis, cum fundorum sunt domini, praestare.

Translation Blume. – Possessors or emphyteuticaries of patrimonial land, who have not heretofore purchased it, shall through our liberality, not at all be compelled to purchase it, but may hold it by favor of our majesty as though they had paid the purchase price, so that the right which another acquired by payment of the price, the aforesaid emphyteuticary shall have through our liberality. 1. The right, too, in the land which he has cultivated, which he has by right of possession by private purchase, by favor of our majesty, or in any other manner, shall be preserved undiminished and undisturbed. He shall also have permission to emancipate slaves on the patrimonial and emphyteutic land, since he is the proprietor of the land.

> The last lines play a decisive role: emphyteuticaries are said to be owners. The edition of Mommsen and Krüger (on the left hand) reads *cum fundorum sunt domini*, a *cum instrumentale* followed by an indicative, which is to be translated into 'as if they were the owners of the land'. Blume translates this phrase into 'since he is the proprietor of the land', as if the Latin text contained *cum* + a subjunctive. This confusion dates back to the Middle Ages. Many manuscripts and most of the editions of the humanists read *cum fundorum sint domini*: *cum* + a subjunctive, a construction which is to be read as a *cum causale*. In a manuscript in which all of the letters consist of strokes, it is easy to mistake *sunt* for *sint*. *Cum* + a subjunctive is a current pattern, while *cum* + an indicative is a rare combination. One cannot blame the professional copyists who copied these texts for such a small mistake. All the same, this single missing stroke is the foundation of the entire theory of divided ownership, which had a determinative influence on the law of ownership for centuries. This penstroke is the legal historical equivalent of Cleopatra's nose, a detail that changed Western history. In the words of Blaise Pascal: 'Le nez de Cléopâtre, s'il eût été plus court, toute la face de la terre aurait changé'.

Ownership was, in other words, linked with emphyteusis. What was emphyteusis? Long-term concessions, by means of which the government allowed people to exploit grounds, existed in the Republic. These people's relationship with the government was precarious, but vis-à-vis third parties, they were owners who were protected by interdicts. The right to exploitation was heritable and could be pledged. A *uectigal* was paid to the government every year. In the third century AD, this right to exploitation became a *ius perpetuum* (perpetual right), a right to land for which *tributum* (land tax) was paid. In addition, people were familiar with the Greek legal concept by means of which one could receive a heritable right of enjoyment to land in return for the payment of a canon and fulfilment of the obligations to improve (*melioratio*) and plant the ground (*emphuein*). Ulpian called this concept the *ius emphyteuticon* (D. 27.9.3.4). In the Justinianic texts, the notions *uectigal* and emphyteusis have merged: *ager uectigalis* is a synonym of *ager emphyteuticarius* (D. 6.3.11). The jurists of the late Empire were divided about the qualification of emphyteusis. Was it an *emptio uenditio* (purchase-sale), or rather a *locatio conductio* (rent-lease)? The Emperor Zeno (476-484) turned emphyteusis into a new right, something mid-way between *emptio uenditio* and *locatio conductio*. See C. 4.66.1: emphyteusis was characterised by protection of possession, the payment of a canon, the emphyteuticary being allowed alienate the good and the owner having the right of first refusal. It became a *ius in re*. Justinian developed the matter further in C. 4.66.2-4 (529-534). He granted an *actio in rem* by means of which the emphyteuticary could claim his rights from third parties, and, if municipal land was involved, from the members of the municipal councils. Emphyteusis of ecclesiastical land was limited to three generations (Nov. 7 and Nov. 120).

In the medieval legal doctrine, the term emphyteusis first cropped up among the glossators. Salatiele and Rolandino dei Passagieri, two thirteenth-century professors from Bologna who wrote extensively about the notarial profession, discussed the notion of emphyteusis thoroughly. It became more important than it had ever been in Antiquity. It was linked with the feudal legal concept of investiture. Liege lords had *dominium directum* and vassals had *dominium utile*. This differentiation was then applied to other legal notions. Rogerius already compared the situation of the emphyteuticary with that of the superficiary (see below). This superficiary also received *dominium utile,* while the owner of the land had *dominium directum.* In the medieval view, a lease of more than ten years was opposable to third parties in the case of sale. A long-term lease, in other words, also had to comply with the rules of emphyteusis. The notion of divided ownership was also projected onto these long-term leases. Some civil lawyers were of the opinion that usufruct should be added to this list, since, according to them, the usufructuary had *dominium utile.* In France, emphyteusis first cropped up in the thirteenth century. A fourtheenth-century practioner called emphytheusis the feudal law of the third estate. In the sixteenth century, Nicolas Everaerts was of the opinion that the leap from emphyteuticary to vassal was a beautiful example of the reception that characterised legal logic.

The old practice of the feudal courts, which took decisions about problems concerning the public domain, was consequently recuperated by the glossators and linked to the *dominium* of D. 41.1. It remained a theoretical construction. Were there ten *domini directi* and one *dominus utilis* if a piece of land was leased and sub-leased ten times? Did the ten direct owners have the same right to the good? Such questions are early modern ones that depart from the notion of absolute ownership. In each medieval case file, there was only one *dominus directus* and one *dominus utilis,* irrespective of what their role was in a different case.

B. The influence of the moral theologians

Just like the jurists, the medieval theologians studied the Roman society of Antiquity. Concerning the notion of ownership, they set much store by the convictions of Augustine, who was a Roman and therefore an authority. For Augustine, God the Father was *paterfamilias* and *dominus.* We still pray '*Domine Deus*', but for medieval man this phrase meant that the ultimate ownership of the world was God's and that man only had ownership for a specific purpose, namely in order to complete his assignments on earth. Human ownership was based on divine ownership and on the donation of the earth during the Creation. Some people compared God's power over the earth to the *dominium* that was bestowed on the occasion of feudal investiture. It implied a permanent duty of justification towards the highest liege lord. There was no ownership without reference to God; all dominion over objects had to be justified to Him. Thomas Aquinas and the later Thomists also asserted that ownership was part of the natural order desired by God.

In the Middle Ages, the moral theologians laid the foundation of the social doctrine of the Church, which has since then been under constant development. The abovementioned divine dimension of ownership has always played a part in doctrine. No one has unencumbered ownership. Everyone who has goods at his disposal, carries responsibility as a consequence. The moral theologians incorporated ownership and possession into their reflections on dominion over things, on the exercise and the distribution of that authority, and on poverty and wealth. From the thirteenth century onwards, the theologians' reasoning about legal notions was strongly conceptual in nature. They started from a different *facultas,* a different logic, when they approached these notions. According to Thomas Aquinas, possession was an application of ownership. He did not clearly differentiate between ownership and possession, but it is obvious that he was not thinking of revendications and interdicts. This reflection

about the divine and ethical dimension of ownership furthered the conceptualisation of ownership to a large extent. No other legal notion was deified to the same extent. In the late Middle Ages, philosophers like Johannes Gerson and William of Ockham began to laicise ownership. They no longer traced it back to God's will, but rather looked at its meaning in legal transactions. However, they still continuously assessed whether *dominium* over objects could be reconciled with God's will.

There were issues on which the theologians never reflected, such as the transfer of claims, the ranking of debts according to their priority in the case of bankruptcy, and the transformation of collateral loans into stock. However, they did think about various forms of society, retribution and compensation, collaboration and the rendering of services... and ownership. The early modern evolution of ownership into the highest right was partly due to the theologians.

C. Bartolus' notion of ownership

It is in Bartolus' work that we find the first definition of *dominium* in which we can discern the modern notion of ownership. Bartolus linked ownership to the disposal of goods. Ownership was the right to fully dispose of a physical object within the limits of what the law allowed. This formula contains the Greek notion of liberty (*eleutheria*). This idea of being allowed to do everything that is not forbidden had entered the medieval body of thought through the *Aristoteles latinus* (the Latin translation by Willem van Moerzeke).

BARTOLUS ad. D. 41.2.17.1. – Quaero quid sit dominium. Et potest appellari largissime pro omni iure in re incorporali, ut habeo dominium obligationis et ususfructus. Et uide glossam in § Nihil commune, supra, eodem [D. 44.2.12.1], et de hoc uidetur textus in l. Qui usumfructum, in fine, supra, si ususfructus petatur [D. 7.6.3] et hoc uidetur dicere glosa in fine magnae glosae [gl. 'Pars dominii' ad D. 7.6.4]; et isto modo non assumo hic, sed prout dominium cadit in rebus corporalibus et hoc mode loquitur titutlus de acquirendo rerum dominio [D. 41.1]. et Inst. primo ponit de rerum diuisione, postea ponit de seruitutibus et usufructu et de usu et habitatione, ut ostendat, quod aliud sit dominium in rebus corporalibus quam in incorporalibus. Quid ergo est dominium? Responde: est ius in re corporali perfecte disponendi, nisi lege prohibeatur. Ius: hoc dico ad differentiam ipsius rei corporalis, quae est facti; et ideo dicitur 'de acquirendo rerum dominio' in rubrica quod aliud sit dominium quam res. Et hoc probatur per legem Et an eadem § Actiones, infra,

I ask what *'dominium'* is. It can be used in the widest sense to indicate any right to an incorporal object, for example: I have *dominium* of an obligation and of a usufruct. See the gloss, above, at D. 41.2.12.1 and also see the text in D. 7.6.3; and this is what the gloss seems to say at *lex* 4, above in the title 'Concerning Usufruct', at the beginning of the great gloss [D. 7.1.14]. I do not interpret it in this manner here, but rather as *dominium* is found in the case of corporal objects and it is in this manner that the title 'Concerning the acquisition of the ownership of objects' [D. 41.1] speaks of it. Justinian [in his Institutes 2.1; 2.3-5] first speaks about the division of property, and then about servitudes and usufruct and about use and residence, in order to show that *dominium* of corporal objects differs from *dominium* of incorporeal objects. What, therefore, is *dominium*? The answer must be: it is the right to fully dispose of a corporeal object in so far as this is not forbidden by the law. I speak of a 'right' in order to differentiate it from the corporeal object

de exceptione rei iudicatae [D. 44.2.14.2]. Et de re corporali dixi ad differentiam incorporalium in quibus non cadit dominium proprie, ut dicta lege Qui usumfructum [*corr.* D. 7.6.4] et quod ibi notatur supra, de usufructu. Quare dico 'perfecte disponendi'? Per legem In re mandata, Codice, mandati [C. 4.35.21], et quoad differentiam possessionis, quae est ius insistendi rei, ut dixi supra, eodem, lege 1 [D. 41.2.1]. Quare dico 'nisi lege prohibeatur'? Propter rem pupilli et propter ea quae ponuntur in lege 2, supra, de his qui sunt sui uel alieni iuris [D. 1.6.2].

itself, which has a factual character; and it is for this reason that the rubric says 'Concerning the acquisition of the ownership of objects', because ownership is not the same thing as an object. This is also proved by the *lex* 'And of the same' § Actions, below in the title 'Concerning the exceptions of *res iudicata*' [D.44.2.14.2]. I have said 'of a corporeal object' for the purpose of distinction from incorporeal objects, with regard to which *dominium* in the strict sense does not occur, as in the abovementioned *lex* 4 and what the gloss says there, above in the title 'Concerning Usufruct' [D. 7.1.4, gloss *Pars dominii*]. Why do I say 'to fully dispose'? Because of the *lex* 'On mandate' [C. 4.35.21] and for the purpose of distinction from *possessio,* which is the right to hold an object, as I have said above in the same title, in the first *lex* [D. 41.21]. Why do I say 'in so far as it is not forbidden by the law'? Because of the assets of the pupil and because of that which is stated in *lex* 2, above, in the title 'Concerning those who are *sui iuris* or *alieni iuris*' [D. 1.6.2].

Nevertheless, Bartolus' notion of ownership was still a far cry from the current concept. He classified different types of *dominium* as ownership:

- *quasi-dominium* acquired by means of the *actio publiciana.* In the Middle Ages, some scholars considered this to be a form of ownership. This kind of ownership featured in the legal doctrine until well into the nineteenth century, but it had little practical importance.
- *dominium directum*: a liege lord's ownership. Bartolus limited this kind of ownership to corporeal objects. This continued to be the case after his lifetime, so that incorporeal objects (like copyright) could not be the object of ownership in Continental law, unlike in English law. Direct owners could use the revendication. Jacques de Revigny (†1296) mentioned, without attaching great importance to it, that on the grounds of C. 7.31.1 only Italians could be *domini directi* and that all other peoples only had *dominium utile.*
- *dominium utile*: the form of ownership of the emphyteuticary, the vassal, the superficiary. These owners received the *reiundicatio utilis*, an adapted action that was introduced in imitation of the *actiones utiles* used in the Roman law. Jacques de Revigny was already of the opinion that the vassal's was the most important form of ownership. This is also an important conclusion of Baldus (†1400).

In Bartolus' definition, *dominium* no longer referred to the status of the *paterfamilias*, but to the disposal of goods. This change could also be ascribed to the structure of medieval families, which differed widely from that of the Roman *familia.* Revendications of people no longer existed. Feudal ownership was increasingly considered as a system to manage immovable goods.

This notion of ownership was disseminated through Bartolism. It came to be a central notion of the *ius commune*. The idea of a highest real right did not exist yet in the Middle Ages. This idea only appeared in the Early Modern Era.

3. The development towards the single and individual notion of ownership of the Early Modern Era

In the Early Modern Era, the power of the feudal lords was curbed. Many lost their sovereignty because of the introduction of appeals. Feudalism continued to exist as a tax system. Those who had a piece of land in fief, paid an annual sum of money to their lord, who in his turn paid his own liege lord, etcetera, until a part of the money eventually ended up in the royal coffers. Each successive lord could pocket some of the money. Rights to leased land were bought as investments. Emphyteusis had largely turned into a system of interests as well. The direct owners' rights to the annual canon had been divided further and further for generations, until these direct owners could no longer practise their right of first refusal. The heirs of the emphyteuticaries paid the heirs of the lessors an annual canon as if it were a land tax. Direct ownership was experienced as 'a right to interests', a hereditary income. The sixteenth century saw the parallel emergence of *census*, which involved debenture loans which did not have to be paid back, were freely marketable and gave a right to a perpetual interest. In every day life, *census* and emphyteusis were analogous institutions.

Freehold ownership existed in the towns. In the Netherlands it was decreed in 1527 that the transfer of immovable goods had to be registered under penalty of nullity. This was a step in the direction of a general system of freehold ownership. Once it had been established who owned which plot of land, the land taxes could be re-organised. Henceforth, the monarch no longer had to rely on the heirs of the old feudal lords.

In the Renaissance, legal doctrine and moral philosophy converged. The Thomistic tendency to consider ownership as an element of the natural order became important. The Spanish jusnaturalists emphasised the divine ownership, from which worldly ownership had been derived by way of a concession to mankind. Both the collective ownership of the first people and the individual ownership which originated from it later were forms of this single kind of ownership. The idea that ownership was part of the natural order played an especially important part. It was one of the innate civil rights. Because of its divine and imperial aspects, many considered it to be the highest innate right. Gradually, the influence of the idea of the divine origin of ownership waned, while the idea of the human foundations of the notion gained importance. This was part of the subjectivisation of the civil rights. Sometimes, philosophy plays the same part as poetry: it expresses the hidden currents in a society. Great philosophers intuit imminent changes sooner than others. They sensed the advent of the single notion of ownership. In the sixteenth century, commentaries appeared which called the division of ownership unreal. Only one of these different forms could be true ownership. The Greek immigrants, who were not at all impressed by feudalism and all the different types of owners, also had an influence on this issue. These Greeks had experienced the 'real' ownership of ancient Rome, the tax-free ownership of land. In addition, they were familiar with the supreme ownership of the emperor, which led to him having the power to disown everyone. Some jurists also mention this right to disown in the West: the *dominium eminens* of the monarch. This right was no longer associated with *dominium directum*. It can be found until the eighteenth century.

From the sixteenth century onwards, Bartolus' opinion carried the most weight in the legal doctrine. In the Early Modern Era, François Hotman (1524-1590) adopted Bartolus' definition. His right to dispose of a corporeal object corresponded to the notion of ownership used in the urban case-law, as well as to the single ownership of the philosophers and the 'true' ownership of the Greeks. In the system of the divided ownership of immovable goods, Bartolus' notion of ownership was associated with *dominium utile*. In the sixteenth century, more and more people defended the opinion that the only true ownership was *dominium utile*. We can find this view, for example, in the writings of the influential Charles Dumoulin (1500-1566). In the Italian case-law, the real right of the *dominus utilis* disappeared relatively soon, so that the practice of securing the financing of immovable investments by real-estate leasing also disappeared. This security functioned as follows: a banker financed an investment, retained the *dominium directum* of this investment and gave *dominium utile* to the purchaser who would use the immovable good. This user paid installments to the banker. When the price was paid, the leasehold property became freehold. In the Early Modern Era the Italian case-law was adopted throughout the Continent and real-estate financing by leasing disappeared because bankers lost their security.

In 1569, in the most miserable period of religious and political wars which Continental Western Europe ever experienced, the Pope Pius V's bull *Cum Onus* condemned *census* and emphyteusis because they were inequitable. In the case of emphyteusis, there was no solidarity between the emphyteuticary and the lessor. If one held a house in emphyteusis and it was damaged during the war, one was still responsible for the damage; if one had land in emphyteusis and could not exploit it during times of war, one still had to pay the annual canon. The Rota also attacked *census*. Rights to *census* could never be established in the case of a loan that served to buy consumables. Capital goods had to come with the guarantee that they would yield the *census*. Only the *dominus directus* of the goods could establish rights of *census* to them. These rights of use contrasted sharply with the *locatio conductio*, the personal rental contracts of Roman law in which *remissio mercedis* played an important role. Rents were reduced when the renter could not use the good or if the yields were too small because of circumstances outside of his control. According to the canonists, pledges and hypothecs were more just securities in the context of financing than the *in rem* agreements of *census* and emphyteusis, because the holders of pledges and hypothecs shared in the depreciation of the goods. The bankers of England, Geneva, Zurich and Frankfurt did not take the case-law of the Rota into account. In Catholic countries like Spain, Italy, France, Cologne or Bavaria, however, this case-law was well-received. Financing by means of *census* and emphyteusis was questioned. The royal courts of law which had adopted the canon law also began to question the real right of the direct owner. This was another step in the evolution from different kinds of ownership to one single kind of ownership.

The seventeenth century saw the privatisation of the civil law in the Continental legal doctrine. Jurists reacted against everything that had gone wrong during the last twenty-five years of the sixteenth century. In this new private law with its subjective rights, there was no room left for feudal rights. According to Grotius, ownership as a private subjective right was absolutely necessary for the legal system. Other real rights were merely offshoots of this right. Just like Donellus, Grotius no longer considered emphyteusis to be a real right. When Hahn drew up his *numerus clausus* of the real rights, he did not include feudal rights and rights to *census* in the list. For the eighteenth-century Pothier (1699-1722), double ownership and the real right of the *dominus directus* were a thing of the past in France. He adopted Hotman's definition solely with regard to *dominium utile*.

In France and the Netherlands, it would take until the French Revolution before the notion of ownership was unified. In 1789, feudalism was abolished in France; the Southern Netherlands followed suit in 1795. Interests, *census* and divided ownership disappeared together with feudalism. In the Code civil of 1804, there was only one kind of ownership left. The definition of ownership in art. 544 had been derived from Pothier: this single kind of ownership was not *dominium directum*, but *dominium utile*, i.e. the emphyteuticary's *dominium*. The ownership described in article 544 of the Civil code is, in other words, the old emphyteusis!

Germany only left the feudal era in the nineteenth century and adopted the Code civil's absolute and individualistic notion of ownership. In Germany as well, real ownership was 'useful ownership', i.e. the old *dominium utile*, which prevailed over all other real rights. And emphyteusis? In the General State Laws for the Prussian States (1794) the emphyteuticary still received *dominium utile*. Savigny was the first German jurist who wrote that emphyteusis was a right to someone else's good. In 1850 all feudal rights were abolished in Prussia. 'Obereigentümler' and those who had rights to *census* lost their rights without being compensated. The *domini utiles* received full ownership, even though in Germany their rights had always been compared to those of emphyteuticaries. In other principalities, like Saxony, feudalism was never abolished. Feudal rights were expropriated instead.

In the Netherlands, emphyteusis was reintroduced as 'un droit de jouissance sur la chose d'autrui' by a law of 1824. It was comparable to usufruct and could be established for at most ninety-nine years. This reintroduction happened under the influence of the Northern Netherlands, where heritable long-term emphyteusis was considered necessary with a view to impoldering land or preparing it for development.

Bibliography. – Most authors project the nineteenth-century notion of ownership onto Antiquity. Current literature, however, opens a new avenue. See, for example, G.C.J.J. VAN DEN BERGH, *Eigendom, Grepen uit de geschiedenis van een omstreden begrip*, Deventer 1979 (2nd edition 1988), which features an extensive bibliography and excerpts from the works of old authors. A thorough reading of D. 41.1 can also be a good starting point for a contemplation of ownership, but many jurists have already lost their way in this text. The reader can consult Nicolas Everaerts' *Topica* in order to discover which legal capers jurists can cut when they interpret texts. A good summary about feudal rights, *census*, interests and different real rights in the Southern Netherlands in the Middle Ages and the Early Modern Era can be found in Ph. GODDING, *Le droit privé dans les Pays-Bas méridionaux du 12e au 18e siècle*, Brussels 1987, p. 153-190. The late R. Feenstra has written extensively about ownership and the role of emphyteusis in the development of our notion of ownership: R. FEENSTRA, 'L'emphythéose et le problème des droits réels', in: *La formazione storica del diritto moderno in Europa, Atti del terzo Congresso internazionale della Società italiana di storia del diritto,* Florence 1977, p. 1295-1320; reprints of articles about this subject can be consulted in R. FEENSTRA, *Legal scholarship and doctrines of private law,* [Variorum Collected Studies, 356,] Ashgate 1996, III and XIII and in R. FEENSTRA, *Histoire du droit savant (13th-18th century), Doctrines et vulgarisation par incunables,* [Variorum Collected Studies, 842,] Ashgate 2005, I-V. An important study about the feudal aspects of *dominium* is G. LEYTE, *Domaine et domanialité publique dans la France médiévale (XIIe-XVe siècle),* Paris 1996. A more recent work is T. RÜFNER, 'The Roman concept of ownership and the medieval doctrine of dominium utile', in: J.W. CAIRNS and P.J. DU PLESSIS (eds.), *The creation of the ius commune, From casus to regula,* [Edinburgh studies in law, 7,] Edinburgh 2010, p. 127-142. On the influence of theology on the development of the notion of ownership, see M.-F. RENOUX-ZAGAMÉ, *Origines théologiques du concept moderne de propriété,* Geneva-Paris 1987. On the role of Spanish scholastics in the development towards a single notion of ownership, see among others W. DECOCK, *Theologians and contract law, The moral transformation of the ius commune (ca. 1500-1650),* Leyden-Boston 2013, p. 352-374. On the problem of divided ownership, also see L. WAELKENS, 'Enkele grondslagen van de leasing in het ius commune', in: B. TILLEMAN and A. VERBEKE (eds.), *Leasing,* Bruges 2007, p. 1-16. Finally, on the notion of ownership in the context of the drafting of the Civil code, see H. SIEGRIST and D. SUGARMAN (eds.), *Eigentum in internationalem Vergleich 18.-19. Jahrhundert,* [Kritische Studien zur Geschichtswissenschaft, 130,] Göttingen 2000.

§3. The acquisition of ownership

'Claimant, you request a revendication in order to get your property back, but how did this person or this good end up in your *familia*?' This was the classic question that the judge asked during the preliminary hearing. The amount of case-law that was developed concerning the judge's granting or refusing this revendication was considerable. In the reception, this case-law was converted into the doctrine of the acquisition of ownership, which cannot be viewed in isolation from the development of the notion of ownership. Classic answers to the question of how a good had been obtained were: 'It was acquired from another person in an honest way', 'I have had it for years', 'I was the honest finder of this good' – in more juridical terms: it was obtained by means of transfer, acquisitive prescription or an authentic manner of acquiring ownership.

1. Transfer

A. Acquisition from another familia

The first possible answer was: 'It was transferred to me from another *familia*'. Such a transfer resulted in the predecessor in title losing his right to revendicate and the new *paterfamilias* receiving this right. In the classical period, we find the term *dominium transferre,* which means 'to pass on the dominion over a good'. From the Middle Ages onwards, the term was taken to indicate transfer of ownership, as if it was not the good that was transferred, but the ownership thereof. If a party invoked transfer, the judge paid attention to four issues:

- the status of the alienator: was he an independent citizen (*sui iuris*) and an adult?

- the position of the alienator: he had to be the *dominus* of the good or the person. In the Middle Ages, this condition was turned into the requirement that the alienator had to be the owner. In this context, a sentence from the *Corpus iuris* was cited, namely that no one could transfer more rights than he had himself (Ulpian, D. 50.17.54). This rule originally referred to inheritances, but had been adopted into the *Corpus iuris* as an isolated sentence. The same Ulpian also mentions in D. 41.1.20*pr.* that no one should transfer more rights than he himself has to a person or object. When Roman law was received, this rule led to considerable concerns when a pledge was enforced. A person who bought pledged property from a pledgee became the *dominus* of the good – apparently, the seller could transfer a right that he did not have. This problem, which caused much ink to be spilled, goes back to the medieval view that ownership was no longer a factual situation that had to be proved, but rather a substantive right that was transferred as such.
- a title: this is the legal action on the basis of which the transfer was made.
- delivery: according to the civil lawyers, Roman ownership was transferred at the time of delivery. The acts by means of which a good was delivered were therefore legal acts.

B. Acknowledged means of transfer

The Roman case-law accepted that some common means of transfer resulted in the acquirer having *dominium* of the transferred person or good. These means were:
- *mancipatio*: this legal act took place on the market, where someone declared in the presence of the official scale-holder and five witnesses that a person or good belonged to his *familia*. The acquirer then tapped a coin (*nummo uno*) against the scales. If the previous *paterfamilias* was present and did not react, he lost his *dominium*. The new *paterfamilias* then had a stronger claim to the person or good. Some Romanists were of the opinion that the *mancipatio* had originally been a kind of contract of sale. It was, however, clearly an act of delivery, which granted *usus* (right of use) and *auctoritas* (guarantee against eviction). The *auctor* was the predecessor in title and could be drawn into the lawsuit concerning the revendication of the good or person. In a case of eviction, this *auctor* risked an *actio ex auctoritate*, by means of which he could be forced to pay twice the value of the person or good. According to some, the *actio ex auctoritate* lost its importance when the *mancipatio* became a mere transfer action, because its value as a mere act of delivery was limited to twice the copper coin. In the Twelve Tables, there was a two-year guarantee against eviction if the property involved was an immovable good and a one-year guarantee if the property was a movable good. These are the time periods for acquisitive prescription, which we will treat below when we discuss *usucapio*. Proving that a *mancipatio* had taken place was a very good way of substantiating that a good or person belonged to a certain *familia*. The claimant who could provide evidence of a *mancipatio* was entitled to a revendication; the defendant who could prove that there had been another *mancipatio*, could invalidate the claim. Until well into the classical era, the *mancipatio* was the most common transfer act for *res mancipi* (slaves, cattle, agricultural tools, land in Italy). It was used for sale and purchase, gifts, *fiducia*, etcetera. In the Theodosian Code, the term *manceps* is still

used to indicate an owner. In the late Empire, deeds of *mancipatio* were drawn up which mentioned – justly or not – that goods had been transferred by means of a *mancipatio*. In this era the *mancipatio* also remained a formal legal act; the reason for the acquisition was not considered. Justinian had the *mancipatio* removed from the legal texts.

- *in iure cessio*: cession before the judge. This was an instance of voluntary jurisdiction: a judicial decision about a matter concerning which both parties were in agreement. The alienator and the acquirer appeared before the praetor or the *cognitio* judge. The latter party claimed the good or person and the other party immediately agreed. This amounted to a confession in the first phase of the lawsuit, the consequences of which have already been discussed. After this confession, the judge of the *cognitio* procedure wrote a judgement. The alienator's cession of the person or good had the force of *res iudicata* and was registered by the court. Like the *mancipatio*, it was a formal transfer: the reason or manner of the transfer were not taken into account. It is not clear whether a third party could still revendicate the good. What is certain, however, is that there was no guarantee against eviction by means of the *actio ex auctoritate*, a term that, like *mancipatio*, cannot be found in the texts of the *Corpus iuris*. Nevertheless, the *in iure cessio* was commonly used in the Middle Ages. When immovable goods were transferred, it was common practice throughout Europe to make use of voluntary jurisdiction before the aldermen's court, so that the transfer was public and was registered.
- *traditio*: informal transfer. In the *Corpus iuris*, this became the only possibility because of the abovementioned removal of *mancipatio* and *in iure cessio*. *Traditio* became the most common manner of transfer. We have devoted a separate section to it.

Traditionally, legacies *per uindicationem* and the *adiudicatio* are also considered to be means of transfer. The legatee of a legacy *per uindicationem* indeed received the right to revendicate when the estate devolved. The will was sufficient; delivery was not necessary. However, this was not really a transfer, because the predecessor in title no longer existed. The same was true of the *adiudicatio*, which was an adjudication by the court in the case of division and distribution. Those who were adjudicated a good, could henceforth revendicate it, even though there had been no act of delivery. In the case of *adiudicatio*, there was no predecessor in title either, so that it can hardly be described as a transfer.

2. Informal transfer, i.e. *traditio*

Informal transfer was common in Antiquity, and tradition was the act of delivery 'par excellence' of the *Corpus iuris*. A good or person was moved from one *familia* to another in an informal manner. One did not necessarily have to be a *ciuis* in order to transfer a person or good in this manner. From the *actio publiciana* onwards, this method was also used to definitively transfer *res mancipi*. An informal delivery could give rise to discussion about the status of the people or goods after the transfer to the acquirer, or about whether the acquirer had become their *dominus*. In this context, the medieval civil lawyers paid attention to two aspects: how had the delivery happened and which legal act (*causa*) had conditioned it?

A. The actual transfer

Which kinds of acts of delivery allowed the acquirer to revendicate the person or good? The civil lawyers differentiated between several types of informal acts in the *Corpus iuris*:

- *traditio simplex* (simple delivery): the object had been handed over.
- *traditio longa manu* (delivery with the long hand), also known as *traditio symbolica* in the Middle Ages. The name 'with the long hand' derives from D. 46.3.79: having someone count out money and watching the process amounted to accepting the money with a long hand. In another lawsuit, it was accepted that immovable property that had been indicated from the top of a tower had actually been transferred. Transfers that took the form of handing over keys (D. 41.2.1.21) or appointing a guard to watch a supply of timber also fell within this category.
- *traditio breui manu* (delivery with the short hand). This term was invented in the Middle Ages as the counterpart of the above-mentioned long hand. In the case of delivery with the short hand, a person acquired a good that he already had. Examples include the lessee who bought the property he rented, or the usufructuary who bought a good that he already possessed. In an important constitution, Diocletian emphasised that delivery was necessary for transfer of ownership (C. 2.3.20). If the acquirer already had the good, however, such a transfer was no longer possible, so the transfer that had happened in the past was reclassified.
- *constitutum possessorium* (stipulated transfer of possession). This term was derived from D. 41.2.17.1 in the sixteenth century. A *constitutum possessorium* occurred when someone transferred the ownership of a good, but either retained possession of this good by means of usufruct, or retained the good by renting it. This can be compared to the modern 'sale and lease back': someone sells his business premises or machines in order to acquire money, and then immediately leases them back so as to be able to continue his business activities. The transfer involved in such cases – there always had to be a transfer – consisted exclusively of the changing of the title on the grounds of which the good was held. D. 41.2.17.1 was interpreted by means of a text by Celsus (D. 41.2.18*pr.*). This text described how one could change a possessory title and begin to possess for another. From this text, jurists derived the point that it was possible to transfer a good by merely declaring that one would henceforth possess the good for another, even when there was no mention of the establishment of a usufruct or a lease.

B. Delivery pursuant to a valid title

Actual delivery did not suffice to transfer ownership. A student who is silently handed a pen by a classmate becomes its owner if the pen was a gift, but not if it was merely lent to him. This second aspect of transfer of ownership can also be found in the *ius commune*, where the *causa traditionis* played a role. There is confusion among the Romanists about this notion, because from the Early Modern Era onwards *causa* has meant 'cause'. Originally, however, the word indicated the conflict or the contested legal act. In the Romanists' works, one often reads that in the oldest Roman law, transfer of ownership happened by means of the legal act that preceded delivery. In addition, these Romanists state that it was only the classical development of *traditio* that caused ownership to be transferred at the time of *traditio*. Finally, they claim that a causal system of transferring ownership was developed in order to avoid breaking the link with the previous legal act. According to D. 41,1,31*pr.* and other texts, *traditio* could only give rise to a transfer of ownership if there was a lawful reason for this transfer (*iusta causa* or *iustus titulus*). Valid titles were, for example, a purchase contract, a donation, the establishment of a dowry, or a loan. If there was no such legal title, the *traditio* only transferred custody and was not a legal act. In the nineteenth century, jurists even began to wonder if there was a consensual transfer of ownership in the Justinianic law. After all, Justinian abolished the abstract mancipation and the *in iure cessio*. Moreover, Inst. 2.1.40 seems to contain a point of departure for a consensual transfer of ownership where the consensus brought about the transfer of ownership, and where no previous legal act was necessary anymore if the consensus was followed by a transfer.

This, however, is far-fetched. A *causa* was not a cause and one should not look for a 'transfer of ownership' in these texts, but for an actual transfer that led to a revendication. In Antiquity, the *causa traditionis* was the legal character of the transfer itself. In a case of sale, donation, legacy *per damnationem*, *fiducia*, establishment of a dowry, etcetera the transfer was the reason why one could bring a revendication. In a case of rent, loan for use or tenancy, however, one never received the right to revendicate. The idea that a formless agreement (*pactum*) preceded the transfer and that this agreement then 'caused' the transfer or non-transfer of ownership at the time of *traditio* is an example of a typical sixteenth-century reasoning. It was at that time that formless agreements became binding (see below).

Bibliography. – On the meaning of *causa* in Roman law, see L. Waelkens, 'La cause de D. 4.44.2.3', *The Legal History Review* 75 (2007), p. 199-212. In Antiquity, *causa* meant 'conflict', 'lawsuit' or 'legal act' – the latter meaning derived from the former. In Antiquity, the Greek word *aitia* had the same meaning: see for example E. Dickey, 'New legal texts from the Hermeneumata pseudodositheana', *The Legal History Review* 52 (2014), p. 30-44. On the *traditio*, see J.H. Dondorp and E.J.H Schrage, *Levering krachtens geldige titel, Enige grepen uit de geschiedenis van de vereisten voor eigendomsoverdracht*, Amsterdam 1991.

C. Possession serves as a title

In the early Middle Ages, a person could not revendicate his goods that lay outside Italy. This rule is confirmed by the sixth-century *lex salica* and the seventh-century *lex ripuaria*. Instead, people made use of protection of possession. The revendication was reserved for feudal goods. Movable goods, in other words, were only eligible for possession, namely by means of the abovementioned establishment of possession after a year and a day. This was still the case in the twelfth century. The academic legal scholars, however, were confronted with the fact that in the *Corpus iuris*, *dominium* bore on all goods and not just on the immovable goods of the monarch. These jurists were inclined to put ownership and possession on a par. Strikingly, the conditions for possession (actual control of the good, intent and title) were comparable to those for transfer of ownership by means of *traditio*. The examples of corporeal possession that were mentioned with regard to possession cropped up again in the context of *traditio*. A person who had possession had, in other words, already made it through a first selection: apparently, he had already received *traditio*. If he also had the right title, he actually had *dominium*. According to gl. '*Vacuam' ad* C. 4.19.12, Placentinus already taught in the twelfth century that the possessor of a good was presumed to be its owner. This tied in with the notion of ownership that usufructuaries enjoyed because of their *dominium utile*, or that beneficiaries of the *actio publiciana* enjoyed because of their *quasi-dominium*. Moreover, according to the *Corpus iuris*, the revendication could only be brought after a possessory procedure. Here, the civil lawyers found an argument for both notions being similar, but not of equal value: ownership was superior. It was, as it were, possession that was granted on appeal.

In the Modern Period, the feudal law disappeared and *dominium utile* became the most important private right. The emphyteuticary, the usufructuary and the superficiary had enjoyed protection of possession since Antiquity. In the Modern Era they received ownership through their *dominium utile*. From then on, the possessor was presumed to be the owner. However, possession was still inferior to ownership: it was a rebuttable presumption. The person who disturbed someone's possession could prove that he was the owner, in which case he was acquitted. This became a rule of the *ius commune*. We can find it in the seventeenth-century oeuvre of Jean Domat (1625-1696) as well as in the eighteenth-century works of Christian Wolff (1679-1754). This relation between ownership and possession, which only caused more confusion about possession, was expressed in article 2279 of the Civil code: as regards movable goods, possession is considered to be a title. Note that the Civil code does not say 'a title of ownership'. Those who had possession did not have to demonstrate a valid title; those who claimed ownership did. Article 2279 only pertains to movable goods: from the sixteenth century onwards, the ownership of immovable goods was only transferred at the time of registration (in the Low Countries this has been the case since 1527). The early medieval tradition that movable goods were only eligible for possession still played a role in the background in 1804.

D. The development towards a consensual transfer of ownership

Art. 1583 of the Code civil states that there is an immediate transfer of ownership in the case of a purchase-sale, without a transfer action having taken place. What is the context of this rule?

The idea that ownership could not be transferred without a valid title was derived from the medieval doctrine of *traditio*. According to Bartolus, there had to be a consensus about the *causa*, the nature of the legal act that played a part in the transfer. If one party thought that the good was being sold while the other thought that it was being donated, there was no transfer of ownership. This reasoning was a first step towards transfer of ownership through consensus.

The glossators pointed out that transfer actions were unnecessary in the case of *constitutum possessorium*, where ownership was transferred through the seller's declaration that he would henceforth possess in the name of the buyer. In the fourteenth century, this formula became common in French notarial practice. All deeds of sale stated that the seller immediately continued his possession in the name of the buyer. In this context, acts of transfer were no longer necessary to establish a transfer of ownership either. This was a second step towards consensual transfer of ownership.

Under the influence of the theologians, the parties' intention became the constitutive element in contracts on the early modern Continent (see below). For Francisco de Vitoria, ownership could be transferred through mere consensus, for example through a donation and the acceptance thereof. He considered the actual transfer to be non-determinant. Hugo Grotius also defended this possibility of transferring ownership by means of an explicit consensus. The consensus in a case of purchase-sale then led to both the transfer of ownership and the obligation to deliver the good. Many authors of the Enlightenment adopted these ideas. Under the influence of this legal doctrine, the Parliament of Paris extended the notarial practice of the *constitutum possessorium* in the Modern Era. The clause was presumed to be included in contracts which did not feature it literally. In 1804, this case-law was adopted in article 1583 of the Civil code.

The evolution was different in Germany, where transfer of ownership without delivery was impossible until well into the nineteenth century. Savigny was nevertheless of the opinion that transfer of ownership was also connected with consensus, and not merely with the *causa* or the title of the transfer. In Inst. 2.1.40 he read that the intention of the person who wanted to transfer ownership at the time of delivery carried more weight than the *iusta causa*. He switched from a 'causal' to an 'abstract' transfer of ownership. The *traditio* was necessary, but there was a kind of agreement, 'ein dinglicher Vertrag'. Ownership was transferred through consensus at the time of delivery. There was no need for a reason or a reference to a previous legal act. This view ended up in the Bürgerliches Gesetzbuch, according to which a transfer action is necessary to bring about the transfer of ownership, but this can no longer be checked against a valid title.

Inst. 2.1.40. – Per traditionem quoque iure naturali res nobis adquiruntur: nihil enim tam conueniens est naturali aequitati, quam uoluntatem domini. Volentis rem suam in alium transferre, ratam haberi. Et ideo cuiuscumque generis sit corporalis res, tradi potest et a domino traditia alienatur. Itaque stipendiaria quoque et tributaria praedia eodem mode alienantur. Vocantur autem stipendiaria et tributaria praedia, quae in provinciis sunt, inter quae nec non Italica praedia ex nostra constitutione nulla differentia est.

Translation Moyle. – Delivery again is a mode in which we acquire things by natural law; for it is most agreeable to natural equity that where a man wishes to transfer his property to another person his wish should be confirmed. Consequently corporeal things, whatever be their nature, admit of delivery, and delivery by their owner makes them the property of the alienee; this, for instance, is the mode of alienating stipendiary and tributary estates, that is to say, estates lying in provincial soil; between which, however, and estates in Italy there now exists, according to our constitution, no difference.

E. Retention of title

A last important issue in the context of *traditio* is the possibility of not transferring ownership until the price of the good has been paid: the owner delivered the good, but retained the right of ownership. Retention of title originated in the Italian commercial law of the Middle Ages, but was based on Roman law.

Before the classical era, a purchaser could only receive a revendication from the praetor if the price of a bought good had been paid or if this payment had been formalised in a stipulation (according to Varro, *De re rustica* 2.1.5; see the Twelve Tables 7.11). This corresponded to the practice in the case of a *mancipatio*: if a price had been agreed upon, it was promised at the moment of transfer. In D. 18.1, which concerns purchase-sale, retention of title is limited by a series of texts. For Pomponius, a sold good only became the buyer's when the price had been paid, when another satisfaction had been given or when the buyer had received credit from the seller (D. 18.1.19). This credit could be interpreted broadly: if the seller did not demand cash payment or cash on delivery, he granted supplier credit. According to 18.1.6.1 and D. 18.3.4*pr.*, a seller who had not been paid could withdraw from the contract. His claim for recovery of the good, however, had a personal character, which meant that he claimed the good back as a seller, not as an owner. This was repeated in C. 4.54.3, a judgement of 222. The case-law in other words accepted the stipulation of retention of title, but interpreted it restrictively. This can also be seen in D. 43.26.20 and C. 4.54.3, which detail cases in which the good sold was transferred in precarious possession.

In the Middle Ages, C. 4.54.3 was the main basis for the development of retention of title by the civil lawyers. They did not emphasise its limitations, but the possibility of stipulating it. In this manner, the Italian commercial law practice of title retention was given a foundation in Roman law. It was then adopted by the French and Italian notarial practice. Italian traders commonly included this clause in their sale agreements. In the thirteenth century, the *in rem* character of the revendication was no longer questioned. In Italian trade, this *in rem* character also applied in the case of the buyer's bankruptcy and towards third-party acquirers. In the medieval cities of the Low Countries, France and Germany, purchase in instalments took the form of an emphyteusis with a transfer of ownership after the last payment. This resulted in an *in rem* character and payability even after bankruptcy. In the Early Modern Era, this formula became impossible because the emphyteuticary became the real owner and the lessor lost his right to bring an *in rem* claim. In the *ius commune* of the Modern Era we find yet another form of retention. In the eighteenth century, retention of title was formulated as a *pactum adiectum* (accessory agreement) to the sale agreement. This accessory agreement, which could be enforced by means of the seller's principal action, determined that non-payment gave rise to the nullity of the contract of sale. The good could then be reclaimed on account of undue delivery.

Bibliography. – On retention of title: R. FEENSTRA, *Reclame en revindicatie, Onderzoekingen omtrent de rol in de ontwikkelingsgeschiedenis van het recht van reclame gespeeld door den Romeinsrechtelijken regel omtrent eigendomsovergang en prijsbetaling, bij koop (In. 2.1.41)*, Haarlem 1949; M.J. MAASS, *Die Geschichte des Eigentumsvorbehalts, insbesondere im 18. Und 19. Jahrhundert* [Rechtshistorische Reihe, 224], Frankfurt/Main 2000.

3 Acquisitive prescription (*usucapio*)

In handbooks of Roman Law, both *usucapio* and *praescriptio longi temporis* are traditionally discussed under the heading 'acquisitive prescription'. *Vsucapio*, however, was actually a manner of proving *dominium*, while *praescriptio* was a defence that served to perpetuate possession. The confusion between these two notions arose because D. 41.3 deals with the procedure regarding prescription. This title of the Digest bears on prescription in cases involving possession as well as in cases pertaining to ownership. In the Middle Ages and the Early Modern Era, however, this title was not read as a tenet concerning procedure, but as a method of acquiring goods. The consequence was that *usucapio* and remedies at law were blended with the medieval reasoning about the retention of goods and early modern concerns about placing control over goods in private hands.

Gaius 2.42-50 treated *usucapio* separately, but the legists were not familiar with this text. It was said that this institution stemmed from the Twelve Tables. If a transferee used a movable good for one year or an immovable good for two years, he received the revendication even when the good was a *res mancipi* that had been transferred without a *mancipatio*. The person who had transferred the good to the acquirer was then released from his duty to guarantee (*auctoritas*). He could no longer revendicate the good himself.

A good could only be obtained through *ususcapio* if it was on the market, *habilis* ('haveable'). Goods that had been stolen or misappropriated were not *habilis* (*lex atinia*, second century BC). The person who was entitled to misappropriated goods had thirty years to reclaim them, irrespective of how often they had been transferred. The Code civil imposed a different rule: the goods had to be reclaimed within three years' time (art. 2279, the time period was inspired by C. 7.31.1.2). *Usucapio* could not be invoked against a woman who had lost goods because she had pledged them free of charge for the benefit of a third person and the pledge had been enforced. According to the *senatusconsultum uelleianum* she had thirty years to revendicate these goods.

D. 41.3.22-24 required that the usucapient had the goods *bona fide*. Account was, in other words, not only taken of the actual situation, but also of the rights of others. It is pointed out, for example, that *usucapio* was precluded by the *possessio* of third parties, for example by an inderdict *unde ui*.

In C. 7.31.1.2, Justinian extended the time frame for *usucapio* to three years for movable goods.

When the Roman law was received, *usucapio* was associated with the *praescriptio longi temporis*. Both measures together led to one method of becoming a good's owner through prescription. During the period of prescription, one needed to have possession of the good.

4. Natural ways of acquiring ownership

Goods could also end up in a *familia* without a transfer, namely through the establishment of an 'original' *dominium*. In the process of reception, this came to mean: through natural ways of acquiring ownership. This issue treated extensively in both the Digest and the reception. It is a picturesque matter that was much-discussed in the agrarian societies of Antiquity and the Middle Ages.

A. Occupation

Ownerless property (*resnullius*) ended up in a *familia* through occupation. Examples were fish and game, which became the property of the fisher or hunter, irrespective of where they had been caught. Hunting and fishing were incorporated into art. 715 of the Code civil as ways of acquiring ownership. This legal rule was inspired by the

French Revolution. Hunting rights were old feudal rights which were regarded with envy, so the law code of 1804 clearly repeated that everyone was free to hunt and fish. The Roman *occupatio* of game served as an old foundation for this new right. *Occupatio* also included plunder during times of war and the occupation of unattended goods (*res derelictae*). In the latter case, *usucapio* was necessary if the good involved was a *res mancipi* (with *pro derelicto* as title), but if the good was a *res nec manicipi*, one immediately received the revendication. A treasure fell to the owner of the land, until Hadrian divided it equally between its finder and the owner of the land (cf. Justinian in Inst. 2.1.39, D. 41.1.63. Also see art. 716 Civil code).

B. Perception of fruits

'As you sow, so you shall reap': according to the Digest, the person who had put energy into the cultivation of crops became the owner of the yield (D 22.1.45). Fruits that did not require labour became the property of the owner of the land when they were separated from the plant (*separatio*), see for example D. 22.1.25.1. A tenant had to harvest (*perceptio*) in order to become the owner of the yield (D. 7.4.13). Before the harvest, the fruits of the earth were part of the *dominium* of the landowner. This benefited the tenant: if a third party alienated the fruits, the tenant brought an action against his lessor, who could make use of the revendication and the possessory actions that were necessary to pursue the stolen fruits. Tenants needed neither ownership nor possession.

C. Accession

If different goods were confused or attached to one another, the new good ended up in the *familia* to which the most important part belonged. *Accessorium sequitur principale.* This was the principle of accession: the main thing attracted the accessory one; the *dominus* of the most important thing also received everything that had been added to this thing. Consider, for example, plants that became the property of the landowner (D. 41.1.7.13). The Digest and Gaius 2.70-74 treat accession extensively. They describe issues concerning alluvion and avulsion of land, watercourses that doubled as borders and whose courses were suddenly changed, the formation of new islands, etcetera. In the Middle Ages, there was a great interest in these problems as well. In the fourteenth century, for example, there was a lawsuit between the viscount of the Franc of Bruges and the abbot of Ter Duinen. The suit revolved around the ownership of an island that had begun to form in the sea while land was being impoldered near Coxyde. The viscount claimed the island because it lay outside of the zone that had been given in concession to the abbey for the purpose of impoldering. The abbot, however, maintained that this was a case of *alluuio*, that the new land therefore acceded to the abbey, and that this new land was not an island because a laden vessel could not sail around it. Neither party, however, contested that the solution would come from the Digest.

In the case of confusion of movable goods, the new owner was the person whose good had contributed most to the value of the new good. If it was a composite good and the parts could still be separated, every previous owner could revendicate his part. In the case of specification (when someone created a new good by processing material that belonged to someone else), the Sabinians were of the opinion that the owner of the base material became the owner of the processed good. The Proculians, however, held the view that the processor became the owner if his labour was more valuable than the raw material. According to Justinian, the owner of the raw material became the owner of the new good if this raw material could still be recovered; otherwise, the processor became the owner. See for example Inst. 2.1.15; D. 41.1.7.7. But what if one made a precious painting on someone else's cheap panel? On that issue, see Gaius 2.78. In the case of accession, the revendication was not the ultimate remedy at law. The rights of the person who had become a good's owner through accession were counterbalanced by the rights of those who were aggrieved by this accession. Examples were the right of superficies and the right of retention.

The right of superficies concerned constructions that were built on another person's land. In Roman law, the building and the land below it always became part the *familia* of the landowner through accession. One could not become the owner of one floor of a building without owning the land. The ownership of the building always gave way to the ownership of the land (*superficies solo cedit*) and could not be revendicated. The superficiary did receive protection of possession by means of the interdict *de superficiebus* (D. 43.18.1*pr.*), which he could use to keep both the owner of the land and third parties out of his building. Justinian granted the owner of the building an *actio in rem* (D. 43.8.1.3). This meant that the building's owner could institute proceedings on the merit in order to enforce his right. The medieval civil lawyers considered this *actio in rem* as similar to the right of the emhyteuticary, i.e. as *dominium utile*. They regarded the *actio in rem* of the superficiary as a proprietary claim by means of which the *dominium* of the building could be claimed. In the Early Modern Era *superficies* continued to exist as a form of ownership on another person's land. The superficiary paid an annual fee to the heirs of the original landowner. *Superficies*, in other words, also played a part in the system of annual 'interests'. During the French Revolution, *superficies* was abolished together with emphyteusis. It was reintroduced in the United Kingdom of the Netherlands by the law of 10 January 1824.

By means of the right of retention, a person could withhold goods when they were revendicated on account of accession. A tailor, for example, had made an item of clothing out of a client's expensive raw materials. The new piece of clothing became the property of the client through accession. The customer, however, did not pay and revendicated his good. The tailor received an *exceptio doli* in the formula of the revendication. By means of this exception, he could invalidate the revendication until he was paid for his work. Until that time, he had 'retention'. The right of retention was not only mentioned in the context of accession. It was a right of every contractor, of everyone who refined or repaired an object as a contractor (with a *locatio conductio*). Contractors could also withhold goods until they were paid. We have received the right of retention from the Roman law, but find it difficult to classify it as a real right. It is because of this that the possibility to claim this right is often discussed in bankruptcy cases. The right of retention has to be formulated precisely in order to be opposable to the owner. In Roman law, the situation was simpler: the invalidation of the revendication meant that there was no judgement on the ownership of the good.

Confusion remains of topical interest. – A painting by Jan STEEN, *The Wedding of Tobias and Sarah*, was cut in two pieces. One part became the property of the town of The Hague in a roundabout way. The other part was in a Russian palace until 1917. In the 1930s an antique dealer from Amsterdam, J. Goudstikker, bought it at an auction in Berlin. During the war, Goudstikker's collection was appropriated by Goering. After the war, it was restituted to the Dutch State. In 1998 the original painting was restored and exhibited in the Bredius museum in The Hague. The Russian part represented three quarters of the value of the restored painting; the Dutch part one quarter. In 2005 Goudstikker's heirs revendicated the artwork, claiming to be the owners of the entire painting. All of the old Roman remedies at law concerning accession were brought up. The Hague, however, withheld the painting on the grounds of the equally Roman right of retention until the value of its piece of the painting and its share in the costs for the restoration would be paid. Eventually, a settlement was reached in 2008.

§4. Usufruct and servitudes

Hahn included servitudes (*seruitutes*) in his list of real rights. He classified both the so-called personal servitudes (*ususfructus*) as well as praedial servitudes (*iura praediorum*) as *seruitutes*. These two rights were yoked together on the basis of D. 8.1.1.1 and Inst. 2.3.3. Today, personal and real servitudes are still mentioned together in the German, Austrian and Swiss civil law, but not in the Code civil. In Antiquity, one of the meanings of the Latin term *seruitus* was slavery, which also implied a form of servitude. Hahn, however, based himself on the actions, more specifically the *uindicatio seruitutis* and the *uindicatio ususfructus*. The former could not be used to set a slave to work.

When treating the actions, we will not discuss the *actio negatoria* and the *actio confessoria* of the Romanists, which were derived from D. 8.5.2. A *de cuius* had bequeathed a piece of land to one man and the usufruct of the hindmost part of this land to another. Afterwards, both legatees had a conflict about the right of way with regard to the front part of the land. The usufructuary could not claim this right in a petitory manner, because the *actio confessoria* [i.e. the *uindicatio seruitutis*] could only be brought by the *dominus*. However, the court granted the right of way by means of an interdict. The *actio negatoria* that could be used to counteract the granting of this right was of course the revendication. In the gl. '*Qui negat*' *ad* D. 8.5.2, one can see how the glossators turned this *actio negatoria* into a specific action to deny that there was a praedial servitude. Henceforth, the actions that were used to claim usufruct and praedial servitudes were called *actiones confessoriae* by the civil lawyers; while the actions to counteract them [namely the revendication of the possessory claim] were called *actiones negatoriae*. We do not follow the civil lawyer's terminology.

1. Praedial servitudes (*iura praediorum*)

A. Definition and types

Praedial servitudes originated because the exploitation of an immovable good required arrangements with neighbours. These arrangements could be made in a contract. Praedial servitudes, however, were inseparable from the land. The exploiter of the servient land tolerated a limited use of his good by the exploiter of the dominant tenement, irrespective of the latter exploiter's identity. The Roman law distinguished between rural praedial servitudes (*iura praediorum rusticorum*) and urban praedial servitudes (*iura praediorum urbanorum*).

The four oldest rural praedial servitudes were the right of way, of driving cattle, of driving carts and of channelling water (*iter, actus, uia, aquaeductus*). These were *res mancipi*. Later, other types of servitudes were added to this list, for example the right to water cattle (*seruitus pecoris ad aquam appelandi*).

Urban praedial servitudes were, for instance, the right to let rainwater drip onto someone else's property (*seruitus stillicidii*), the right to discharge water collected in a gutter onto someone else's property (*seruitus fluminis*), the right to use a neighbour's wall to support beams (*seruitus tigni immittendi*), or the right to claim a view (*seruitus altius non tollendi*). Some of these behaviours among neighbours were sanctioned by the censors in the Republican Era and only became part of the civil law during the Principate.

B. The establishment of praedial servitudes

Praedial servitudes were claimed by means of the *uindicatio seruitutis*. Just as in the case of a revendication, one could obtain the inclusion of a restitution clause. The action was normally aimed at the owner of the servient land (D. 8.5.6.3), but could also be brought against the possessor if necessary (D. 8.5.10.1).
When granting a praedial servitude, the judge took account of the following elements:

- the servitude had to be beneficial to the dominant tenement (*utilitas fundi*): D. 8.1.8*pr.*;
- proximity (*uicinitas*): D. 8.3.7.1;
- the perpetual nature of the legal act (*perpetua causa*): praedial servitudes that consisted of a right to collect water were only granted if the subservient tenement had a constant source of running water (D. 8.2.38);
- tolerance; nevertheless, there were praedial servitudes which required actions (*seruitus operis ferendi*), such as the maintenance of a retaining wall (D. 8.5.6.2);
- the servient and the dominant tenement could not belong to the same owner (*nulli res sua seruit*: D. 8.2.26).

In Italy, the old rural praedial servitudes were established by a *mancipatio*, while all others were established by means of *in iure cessio*. If one transferred an immovable good, one had the possibility of retaining a servitude. In the provinces, praedial servitudes were established through agreements and stipulations: Gaius 2.31; D. 45.1.2.5. By abolishing the notion *res mancipi*, Justinian enlarged the scope of the latter method of establishment to include all praedial servitudes. In this manner, the establishment of a praedial servitude through retention in the case of the alienation of an immovable good also became possible in the case of a *traditio*.

In the Republic, one could obtain a praedial servitude through use (*usucapio*). A *lex scribonia* of the first century BC abolished this possibility, except in cases where servitudes had existed from time immemorial: see D. 8.5.1*pr.* and D. 39.3.1.23. Justinian granted the *praescriptio longi temporis* to the owner of the dominant tenement. With this *praescriptio*, he could invalidate the revendication of the owner of the subservient tenement if the latter questioned the praedial servitude. In the Middle Ages, the civil lawyers' reasoning was that *praescriptio* required proof of possession, i.e. proof of possession of a right (*possessio iuris*). D. 8.5.10*pr.* contains the term *quasipossessio*, which was associated with this possession of a right.

The civil lawyers distinguished between perpetual praedial servitudes which could be acquired through prescription and non-perpetual praedial servitudes which could not be obtained in this manner. The Code civil of 1804 featured yet another distinction: see articles 650-651.

C. The termination of praedial servitudes

In the classical era, servitudes were ended by an *in iure cessio* before the court. Under Justinian, the cession of a praedial servitude could simply be served. A praedial servitude ended by operation of law when the subservient and the dominant tenement were confused within the same *familia* (*confusio*, see D. 8.1.18 and D. 8.4.9). If the two tenements were separated later, the praedial servitude did not revive. Those who sold the foremost part of a plot and kept the hindmost part had to beware: right of way did not originate by operation of law if the owner of the dominant tenement had caused the tenement to be enclosed. A praedial servitude could also end because of non-use or because of use contrary to the original praedial servitude for a period of two years (*usucapio libertatis*). Note the terminology: just like slavery, a praedial servitude was *seruitus*; liberation from it was also *libertas*. Justinian also introduced the use of the *longi temporis praescriptio* against the person who claimed a praedial servitude.

If the possessor of the dominant tenement unjustly exercised an alleged servitude, the owner of the subservient tenement had to claim the denial of the praedial servitude. This happened by means of an *actio in rem* against anyone who did not respect the rights of the owner, in other words: by means of the revendication.

D. The reception of praedial servitudes

The Roman system of real praedial servitudes was simple and reliable. There are no data about the reception in the early Middle Ages, but the glossators and the commentators propagated these servitudes. In the Modern Era, they remained a core element of the *ius commune*.

2. Usufruct

According to D. 7.4.1, usufruct is often *pars dominii*, i.e. it is part of the rights of the *paterfamilias* or *dominus*. Medieval jurists considered *dominium* as the substantive right to ownership and used this text as the basis for their point that usufruct was an aspect of ownership.

A. Definition

Usufruct is one of the two legal notions that are defined in the Roman law: it is the right to use the goods of another person and to reap the fruits of this good without affecting its substance (D. 7.1.1, see also art. 578 of the Civil code). It was a personal servitude that ended, in principle, when the beneficiary died. The right originated as a means of supporting surviving relatives without definitively leaving them the goods (*legatum ususfructus*). One heir received the bare ownership of the good, another was given the usufruct.

All goods, movable and immovable alike, could be subject to usufruct. In the Roman law, it was possible to create a usufruct of money (D. 7.5.2.1: *quasi ususfructus*). The usufructuary then obtained full ownership, because he could not do anything with the money without affecting the substance thereof. Money was a commodity according to Roman law. The usufructuary promised by means of a stipulation (the *cautio usufructuaria*) that he would return a sum equal to that which he had originally received. What he really received was the value of the interest on the money (D. 7.5.3).

The usufructuary could lease the good to another person (D. 19.2.9.1). He could also pledge (D. 20.1.11.2) or sell (D. 18.6.8.23) it. In the case of a pledge, it was not the good itself that was pledged, but the usufruct. Similarly, in the case of a sale it was only the right of usufruct that was sold. After all, it was essential that in those cases the usufruct also ended when the usufructuary died. In order to calculate how much a usufruct was still worth, the life expectancy of the usufructuary was taken into account. The table of life expectancy that was used by the prefecture can be found in C. 35.2.68. It is known as Ulpian's life table; see it below, VIII, §4, 3, c.

B. Remedies at law

A usufruct was created just as a praedial servitude was, but not through a *mancipatio*. In the classical period, *usucapio* of a usufruct was probably impossible. The usufructuary could make use of the *uindicatio ususfructus*, which the Romanists also call *actio confessoria*. By means of a revendication or a petition for an interdict, the owner could try to deny that there was a usufruct. Some Romanists were surprised to find that in the fourth and fifth centuries the *uindicatio seruitutis* was described as a claim that was equal in value to the revendication. Basing themselves on the modern notion of ownership, they concluded that the ancient Romans considered usufruct to be a kind of ownership that was limited in time. This was not true: each claim required the correct *actio* and claimants selected one remedy from an entire arsenal of available remedies without thinking of a hierarchy of real rights. Justinian defended this classical view. The usufructuary also had an interdict at his disposal to protect his right. Since Justinian, the *praescriptio longi temporis* has played a role in the acknowledgement and denial of a usufruct.

A usufruct ended through cession of the right of usufruct (originally by means of *in iure cessio*, consensually under Justinian), through the consolidation of ownership and usufruct in the same hand (*consolidatio*), through prescription because of non-use (non-use for a period of two years in the classical period, non-use for the time period of the *praescriptio longi temporis* under Justinian), through the demise of the usufructuary and through the perishing of the good with regard to which the usufruct had been established. If a usufruct perished, the owner of the good received back the right to the fruits and the right to use the good (Inst. 2.4.4).

C. The reception of usufruct

In the Middle Ages, the rights of vassals were not only based on the old case-law about emphyteusis, but also on Roman texts about usufruct. At this time, usufruct was already considered to be an aspect of ownership (interpretation of D. 7.1.4). The rights of the usufructuary and the owner were compared to one another. Late Scholastic moral theology paid considerable attention to usufruct. Once more, usufruct was compared to the rights of the vassal and the emphyteuticary, as well as to the single kind of ownership. The view that the use of a good and the enjoyment of its revenues were aspects of full ownership has contributed to the development of the early modern notion of private ownership.

Some other real rights. – Apart from usufruct, there were some other limited personal servitudes, such as the right to inhabit a house (*habitatio*), *usus* (the use of a good and its revenues for one's own use, see D. 7.8.8.1, D. 7.8.12.1 and D. 7.8.13). In a legacy, one could bequeath a right to the work of animals or slaves (*legatum operarum seruorum uel animarum*). The donation of the labour of serfs, which can be found in medieval records, derives from this.

§5. Real securities

Securities are accessory contracts that serve to protect a main agreement. In Roman law, there were both personal securities (sureties) and real securities (pledges). A pledge agreement was an accessory agreement to a contract: it was agreed that the creditor could recover the costs from certain a good if the principal debt was not paid. In the *ius commune*, a pledge led to an *actio in rem* with a 'droit de suite'. Hahn classified it as one of the real rights.

Securities are a necessary evil. Rights are enforceable, except in the case of insolvency. Securities serve to attempt to heighten enforceability in the context of insolvency. They are also useful because creditors tend to minimise the importance of their debts and to undermine long-term debts. In addition, securities were used to create new commercial possibilities. Roman traders cooperated with bankers and gave them securities. The result was that the traders needed less capital. Consider the classical formula of merchant bankers: when a trader purchases goods, he receives a loan for half of the value of his purchase if he pledges his stock; when he sells goods, half of the value of the invoice is lent to him if he pledges the invoice. Securities are high-tech means: they can create wealth when used adeptly, but ignorance leads to a credit crunch. Since the great credit crunch of the sixteenth century, the Greco-Roman banking techniques have been banished from the Continent. Henceforth, capital companies, which had collected money beforehand, were required in trade and industry even though such companies have too much money in good times and too little in bad times. This results in increased costs. Involving financiers in trade and giving them securities with every transaction results in a more finely honed business acumen.

1. Legal acts in the law of pledge

In the case of a security, there is a principal debt and an accessory agreement of pledge. The principal debtor is the pledger; the principal creditor is the pledgee or pledge creditor. The pledged property could be transferred to the pledge creditor or not; the ownership of the good could be transferred to the pledge creditor or not. Real securities were based on agreements about the revendication and the interdict. If the principal debt had not been paid and the pledged property had not been transferred, the pledgee could use a possessory interdict to claim the good wherever it was – even if it was with the pledger. If the good had been transferred, the pledger could use the revendication to claim it back after payment of the principal debt. The praetor or *cognitio* judge granted the pledge creditor protection by means of interdicts. The pledgee could then claim the pledged property by means of an interdict. If the owner revendicated it, the pledge creditor received an *exceptio doli* against this claim, by means of which he could exercise his right of retention (C. 8.26.1.2). To summarise, the main rights in the law of pledge were, in modern terms, ownership and possession.

There are wild stories about the origins of pledges. According to some, the Roman pledge originated in pawnshops. We are familiar with medieval pawnshops such as the 'monti di pietà' and with early modern ones such as the Wenceslas Coeberger's Mount of Piety in Antwerp, but there are no ancient examples. In Dutch we read about 'fist pledge' if the pledged property was kept 'in the fist' (*pignus depositum*), but the Latin word for fist is *pugnus*, not *pignus*. According to some Romanists, *pignus* was originally a *pactum*, an formless contract that only became enforceable as an accessory clause of a principal agreement. This, however, is impossible: additional clauses were only enforceable together with main agreements in the case of obligations *e bona fide* (see below) and pledges also occurred in the context of strict obligations.

The classical term *pignus* applied to pledges on movable and immovable goods. A pledge with transfer of the good was a *pignus datum*; a pledge without transfer was a *pignus obligatum* – or in later Greek terminology, a *hypotheca*. According to Marcianus, there was no difference between *pignus* and *hypotheca* (D. 20.1.5.1). Romanists claim that the Justinianic compilers took Marcianus' text out of context by removing the words 'as concerns the *actio seruiana*'. For Ulpian, *pignus* implied the transfer of the good, while *hypotheca* did not (D. 13.7.9.2). The terminology used in art. 2072 of the Code civil was pledge ('gage') for movable goods and antichresis ('antichrèse') for immovable goods. In Belgium, antichresis on an immovable good was called 'hypothec' in the Mortgages Act of 16 December 1851.

With regard to the law of pledge, the Roman law mentions *dominium* and *possessio*, as well as the *actio fiduciae*, the *actio seruiana*, the *actio hypothecaria*, the *actio pigneratica in rem* and the *actio quasi seruiana*.

2. The *actio fiduciae*

A first kind of pledge was established by means of the fiduciary transfer of ownership. A good was transferred in ownership. There was an agreement, formulated in the *pactum fiduciae*, that a pledge would be established. The pledge creditor received the revendication to claim the good; the pledger received the *actio fiduciae* by means of which he could enforce the agreements that were included in the *pactum*. Gaius calls this *fiducia cum creditore contracta* (fiduciary transfer to a creditor).

The *actio fiduciae* was an action *e bona fide*. If it was brought, the judge took account of all the relations between the parties. A *fiducia* that served as a security was connected with a principal agreement and was therefore considered by the judge when the *actio fiduciae* was brought. The debtor of a principal agreement transferred a good to the creditor by means of a mancipation or *in iure cessio*, with the accessory clause (*pactum fiduciae*) that the good would be returned by means of a mancipation or *in iure cessio* when the principal debt was paid. These acts of delivery ensured that the agreement between creditor and debtor was public. The creditor of this principal claim could bring a revendication. The trustor could therefore keep the good with him. He continued to enjoy its use; the creditor did not have to maintain the good. In the Digest, we find a pledger who rented the good from its fiduciary owner. In the terms of the *ius commune*, he had transferred the ownership by means of a *constitutum possessorium* and had tenancy of the good in his capacity as renter. If he did not rent it, he had the good precariously (*de precario*), so he received protection of possession against third parties. The trustor could not acquire *dominium* by keeping the good with him, because that would have entailed a change of title. If the debt was paid, the good did not necessarily have to be transferred back by means of a mancipation of *in iure cessio*. The pledge creditor lost his revindication and there was a transfer by operation of law. Or, to say it like the medieval legists did: there was a transfer of ownership by means of *traditio breui manu*. If there was neither a mancipation nor an *in iure cessio*, *res nec mancipi* changed ownership immediately; *res mancipi* changed ownership after acquisitive prescription.

The fiduciary owner could also keep the good with him. The trustor who took it back before the end of the agreement, could invalidate the revendication of the pledgee by means of a special title (*usureptio e fiducia*) after one year. This was not theft (Gaius 3.201).

According to some Romanists, the *fiducia* originally fell under the edict of the censors until the civil *actio fiduciae* was introduced in the third century BC. They claim that by means of this action, the trustor who had paid his debt could demand either the return of the good or a compensation if the fiduciary owner had transferred the good further. In reality, however, he could only get the value of the good back. He did not have a revendication with a restitution clause. He could not pursue the good itself without a revendication. He could also receive a compensation if the fiduciary owner had not taken good care of the good. If the fiduciary owner had incurred costs to preserve the good, he could reclaim them by means of the *actio fiduciae contraria*.

Gaius 4.182 mentions that a fiduciary owner who had betrayed someone's confidence could lose civil rights (*infamia*). This *infamia* implied the temporary loss of some civil rights and was probably the civil law variant of sanctions that featured in the law of the censors.

In the Empire, the *fiducia* fell into disuse. It required a mancipation or *in iure cessio*. The latter became the more convenient option because of the case-law concerning the *actio seruiana*. In the *Corpus iuris*, *fiducia* is not mentioned anymore. In the Theodosian Code and legal practice, however, it did continue to play a role, but because the civil lawyers did not adopt it, there was no mention of fiduciary securities in the *ius commune*. They were rediscovered in the nineteenth century, when the Institutes of Gaius were found. In Germany, where the registration of pledges was impossible in most principalities, this type of real security boomed in the nineteenth century. As a consequence, the German legislator did not think it necessary to include obligatory registration of pledges in the Bürgerliches Gesetzbuch.

3. The *actio pigneraticia*

It is said that in the fourth century BC the praetor introduced an *actio pigneraticia* (action on account of a pledge). A *pignus* was organised around this. The person who transferred pledged property to a principal creditor, could claim it back by means of this *actio pigneraticia* after the end of the principal agreement. This *actio pigneraticia* was a personal action against the pledgee. Damage to the pledged property was also recovered by means of this action. In the classical period, *pignus* was a real contract (*contractus re*) which was brought into being by the delivery of the pledged property. The pledgee received protection of possession. He could claim the good by means of an interdict. In principle, the *pignus* was therefore assessed during the preliminary hearing. The *actio pigneraticia* was a petitory claim which the pledger could bring against the pledgee if the judge had ruled in the latter's favour at the preliminary hearing.

Even when the principal debt was not paid, the pledge creditor could not keep the good just like that: the pledger demanded by means of his *actio pigneraticia* that the good would be sold and that he would receive the *superfluum*, the amount of the selling price that remained after settlement of the principal debt. Direct execution on the pledge – by retaining it in its entirety after non-payment – was always frowned upon in legal history. Expiration clauses in which parties agreed that the good would fall to the pledge creditor in the case of non-payment of the principal debt were void according to classical case-law. At the end of the Republic, a clause stipulating sale (*lex commissoria*) was incorporated into pledge agreements. This clause detailed that the pledgee had to sell the good in the case of non-payment of the debt. In the late classical era this clause was always presumed to have been written into the contract. Justinian excluded the possibility of different clauses. If the pledger did not manage to sell the property in good circumstances, he could ask the judge to grant him ownership (*impetratio dominii*). Simply keeping the good was not allowed. Under Constantine, the prefecture was confronted with an agreement of pledge containing a clause which stated the following: the pledge would be considered to have been sold to the pledgee for the price that was owed, or to have been given as payment. The case-law forbade this clause. Justinian preserved this prohibition (CTh. 3.2.1 = C. 8.34.3), which still exists in the current civil law (art. 2088 of the Civil code).

Under the emperor Gordian (238-244 AD) the prefecture established another precedent that would always remain famous. A banker had given credit and had accepted goods of the client as a pledge. The loan was paid back and shortly afterwards the client took out a new loan. He could not pay this second loan back and the banker proceeded to enforce the pledge. The client brought an *actio pigneraticia* and demanded the entire value of the pledged property: the pledge agreement pertained to the first loan, not to the second. The judge of the preliminary hearing granted the pledgee an *exceptio doli* against the *actio pigneraticia*, so that the judge on the merits of the case could take the entire relationship between both parties into account. The pledger brought the case before the prefecture, which confirmed the granting of the *exceptio doli* (C. 8.26.1). The pledge creditor, in other words, had the right to retain the pledged property. The civil lawyers called this the 'Gordian right of retention'. It enabled the use of current accounts that only required the establishment of one single pledge. The Gordian right of retention still exists in the current civil law (art. 2082 Code civil, second subsection, which, however, does not apply between merchants anymore in Belgium: Cass. 9 November 1894, *Pas.* 1894, I, 27).

By means of the *actio pigneraticia*, the pledger could claim the proceeds of the sale of a pledged property, or at least demand that these proceeds would be deducted from his principal debt. Sometimes, the agreement of pledge included a clause of *antichresis.*

This meant that the revenues of the pledged property fell to the pledge creditor. The most important text about *antichresis* is D. 20.1.11.1. In the Middle Ages, *antichresis* was called 'vifgage': the pledged property 'lived' for the pledge creditor. Vassals who suddenly needed money – usually to fulfil their military obligations – commonly borrowed money from an abbey and pledged their fief in return. The abbey could exploit the fief and use its revenues to pay off or 'amortise' the debt (in German: 'Totsatzung'). As an extra security, the abbey often requested a testamentary donation of the fief, which the pledgor could revoke when he returned from battle. Hence the many donations of fiefs to abbeys. The pope Alexander III forbade the stipulation of *antichresis* if it served to obtain excessive interests and to circumvent the ecclesiastical prohibition of usury. In the Middle Ages, the general rule remained that a pledge in the civil law was a 'mortgage', i.e. that the pledged property was 'dead' to the pledge creditor.

Pignus was the predecessor of both the classical pledge and the mortgage on immovable property that was bought on installments.

An example from a cartulary of Cahors, found on the internet. – '28 mars 1230. L'évêque Guillaume de Cahors, en son nom et au nom du chapitre, reconnaît qu'il a reçu des consuls et des citoyens de Cahors une somme de 200 marcs d'argent qu'ils lui ont prêtée pour les intérêts de son Église et spécialement pour payer les Lombards Juvénal et compagnie. En gage, il donne, avec le consentement de son Chapitre, tout son droit seigneurial de monnaie et les revenus qu'il en tire, ses moulins et ses droits sur les moulins, les eaux et les chaussées depuis la Roque jusqu'au port Bullier [...]. Quand l'évêque aura remboursé sa dette aux consuls, les gages seront rendus par les consuls.'

4. The *actio seruiana*

The *actio seruiana* originated in the context of agriculture. In regions with only one harvest per year, some farmers only have a lot of money once a year. For the lessor, the consequence was that collecting the rent became a more delicate matter. In the Republic, contracts of farmland tenancy (*locatio conductio*) were often accompanied by a pledge on the items of equipment that the farmer brought to the land (*inuecta, illata, importata*) and on the yield. This pledge also became common in the context of other rental agreements (see Labeo in D. 20.6.14 and Africanus in D. 47.2.68.8). At the end of the Republic, it was presumed that this pledge agreement had been concluded implicitly in all contracts of lease and rent. The lessor claimed his right to the pledge by means of the normal claim on account of lease (the *actio ex conducto*). This was an *actio e bona fide*; the implicit pledging was an aspect of the entire rental relationship. Of course, it remained a pledge without transfer. In the first century BC the lessor received the *interdictum saluianum*, an interdict to claim the yield and the goods that the tenant kept on the land. By means of this interdict, the lessor could claim these goods wherever they were and block them until he received payment. This, however, diminished the marketability of the harvest. In order to restore this marketability while safeguarding the rights of the lessor, praetor Servius introduced the *actio seruiana*. This was an *actio in rem* which could be brought against anyone who kept the goods with him. The formula included a restitution clause. This meant that the lessor could recover the debt from everyone who had acquired the harvest, or the *inuecta et illata*. Traders in agricultural produce could buy and sell freely, but henceforth had to keep an eye on whether the farmer had paid his rent.

Under the prefect Salvius Julianus, an appeal case involved a pledge that had been established with a 'droit de suite', as in the case of an *actio seruiana*. The prefecture's acceptance of this pledge probably resulted in the *actio quasi-seruiana* which is mentioned in some texts. This case-law was developed further and Ulpian mentions that the *actio seruiana* could be invoked by all of the pledgees if the pledger had pledged a good which he owned or with regard to which he could at least have brought the *actio publiciana* (D. 20.1.18). Consequently, all of the pledgees received a real action by means of which they could claim the pledged property, irrespective of where it was. It is hard to differentiate between different actions in the *Corpus iuris*, but Ulpian seems to have confirmed in D. 20.1.17 that in general pledges were protected by a real action: *pignoris persecutio in rem parit actionem creditori* (the claiming of the pledged property generates a real action for the pledge creditor, D. 20.1.17). This is the text that Hahn based himself on when he called *pignus* a real right.

5. Consequences of the *in rem* character of the claim on account of pledge

Because of the *in rem* character of the action on account of pledge, it was no longer necessary to transfer the pledged property. The pledgee could, after all, collect it from anyone who had it. This presents us with a series of uncertainties, which the *Corpus iuris* does not remove. How, for example, could the pledge still be a real contract which was only established at the time of the transfer of the goods in question? However, we mainly see a series of new possibilities which are the consequence of the *in rem* character. Because transfer was no longer necessary, it became possible to pledge incorporeal goods, like a claim on a debtor, as well: D. 13.7.18*pr.*; D. 20.1.20; C. 8.16.4. This was interesting for traders. If a trader had sold on credit, he could pledge the invoice to his banker and borrow an advance on the payment.

If one could pledge goods and claims without surrendering them, it also became possible to establish mortgages on capital. These were 'general mortgages' – see for example D. 20.1.6. A trader could, in other words, pledge his production resources or aspects of his trade in order to borrow money to run his business. For the banker, these were valuable securities, and the trader would not need these goods anymore if his business folded. A trader could, for example pledge his stock and all of his claims and receive credit amounting to half of their value. These items changed continuously and the credit fluctuated according to the value that was pledged. This is what the English call floating charges.

A classic case of a general mortgage discussed in the Digest is the pledged business (D. 20.1.34*pr.*). The trader pledged all of the assets which he used in his trade and which were saleable: for example his stock, his right to a good spot on the market, his brand, a favourable rental agreement that had been concluded with emphyteusis and was therefore transferable, etcetera. Such a general mortgage sometimes gave rise to the following question: to which assets did the real right of the pledge creditor apply? It has been derived from some texts that the pledge creditor had a 'droit de suite' to all assets which the debtor had alienated from his own capital during the period of the legal general mortgage: for example D. 49.14.47*pr.*; C. 7.63.6. Did this mean that the pledge creditor of a business had a 'droit de suite' to all of the goods that had been bought by customers? The general rule was the following: the list of assets which fell under the general mortgage was only drawn up after the death of the trader or at the time of execution, see for example D. 20.1.34. It was therefore impossible to reclaim goods from clients. The 'droit de suite' did apply to goods that had disappeared because of an impending execution. The beneficiary of a general mortgage first and foremost had an *in rem* privilege in the case of the trader's death or bankruptcy. It was only then that it was determined on which goods his real right bore.

The fact that the pledge no longer had to be surrendered also had negative consequences. There was, for example, the risk of multiple pledging. A person could pledge the same good, which he kept with him, several times (D. 44.2.19). In the classical era, it was presumed that there was a tacit agreement that the second pledge would only take effect when the first debt was paid. In the post-classical era, both pledges were valid simultaneously, but the first pledgee had a right of priority vis-a-vis the second (D. 20.4.12*pr.*; C. 8.17.3). The first pledge creditor was the only one who had the right to sell the good, but the second pledge creditor could buy him out (*ius offerendae et succedendi*, D. 20.4.11.4 and D. 20.5.5*pr.*) and was subrogated to the rights of the first pledge creditor. Otherwise, he only had a right to the *superfluum* of the sale of the good. The late Empire saw the creation of a series of precedents concerning the ranking of pledge creditors in the case of multiple pledging (C. 8.17). In 472 the prefecture of the emperor Leo pronounced the so-called *lex Scripturas* (C. 8.17.11): in order to find out which pledge had been establish first, the judge took account of the quality of the witnesses mentioned on the deed of pledge. A pledge with known witnesses who could be summoned if necessary took precedence over a pledge with obscure witnesses who could no longer be traced. *Scripturas* had a considerable influence in the Middle Ages. It was best to establish a pledge before a notary or through voluntary jurisdiction before an aldermen's court. In the Early Modern Era, this practice was replaced with registration by the monarchical administration. The problem was that notarial registration or deeds drawn up by the administration only made sense in large jurisdictions. A registration made in a sovereign town or domain was not valid in neighbouring jurisdictions. The success of the registration of pledges grew when jurisdictions were unified and the Europe of Nations was formed in the Early Modern Era. In small jurisdictions, registration was always of little use. This is the reason why there was hardly any reception of the *lex Scripturas* in the German regions. Germany has consequently always had a problem with the publicity of pledges, which was still not provided for in the BGB. Different projects to introduce registered pledges remained a dead letter. In the nineteenth century, however, Gaius was rediscovered and jurists fell back on *fiducia* for real securities. This is still the classic means of establishing real securities in Germany.

6. Pledges by operation of law

In Roman law, pledges were not only established by agreements. The case-law also accepted cases in which the pledge was established by operation of law. The first that was established in this manner was the pledge on *inuecta et illata*. Another pledge by operation of law was established in the context of a building loan: the lender automatically received a mortgage on the new building (D. 20.2.1). A wife received dotal goods in pledge by operation of law. A pupil received a legal right of pledge to the goods that his guardian bought with his money (D. 27.9.3*pr.*). The latter two examples once again illustrate the power and the use of real securities with a 'droit de suite'. The revendication and the means to protect possession were awarded to the *paterfamilias* who kept the wife's goods with him and to the guardian who managed the funds of his pupil, because these people needed these remedies for management purposes. At the time of settlement, when it became useful for them, the wives and pupils had a pledge with 'droit de suite' at their disposal. Why would they have needed ownership, like the early modern Romanists thought? The pledge on a capital by operation of law was another step forward. In the Principate, the *fiscus* required a pledge from the debtors of overdue tax payments. Gradually, this developed into the *fiscus* receiving a tacit general mortgage on the assets of the tax debtor. After the classical era, the special legatee also received a mortgage on the general legatee's share in the inheritance by operation of law. This resulted in the special legatee having a real right.

7. A selection from the reception of the Roman law of pledge

Traces of the Roman regulation concerning pledges can be found throughout Europe. The pledging of fiefs by means of an *antichresis* was a widespread practice. In the County of Flanders it can be found in the feudal law of the eleventh century. In the thirteenth century, one can find many contractual pledges on immovable property, usually with the establishment of a 'vifgage'. Contracts with stipulated general mortgages on variable capitals cropped up almost at the same time. It is said that in the old French law, which underpins the Code civil, only pledges with transfer existed before the thirteenth century. The agreement of the liege lord was necessary to pledge immovable goods. This was only possible in the form of a 'vifgage'. We find a trace of this in the Code civil: in art. 2072, a pledge on immovable property is still called 'antichrèse', even though such pledges had not been limited to 'vifgage' for a long time. In medieval trade, credit accompanied by a pledge was rare. The principal security that was disseminated, from Italy, was retention of title. Except for deferred payments covered by bills of exchange, there were few other means of financing long-distance trade.

In the fifteenth century, trade was reoriented by the Greek commercial banks which established themselves in the West. Their ways of using real securities in financing trade have not been studied yet, but we are familiar with the Greek loans (*contractus trini*) to monarchs in return for pledges on *regalia* and feudal rights. From 1473 onwards, the Fuggers borrowed money to the Habsburgs in return for a pledge on their copper mines. Under Maximilian I, the Fuggers obtained the mines when the pledge was enforced. When Genoa could not repay its loans to the Banco San Giorgio, the bank received the entire island of Corsica as the result of the enforcement of a pledge. After the credit crunch of the sixteenth century, the Continent did not have much sympathy for real securities. Securities that were based on divided ownership or went together with the establishment of rights to *census* disappeared. All efforts were directed at the acquisition of ownership and capital. This era saw the development of the classical mortgage on the occasion of the purchase of immovable property in full ownership, which is still common today. This mortgage was established before the local courts with respect for the *lex Scripturas*. In addition, the simple loan in return for a possessory pledge became popular in the Mounts of Piety and between private persons. Pledges that resulted in the pledgee receiving ownership of the good after non-payment were combatted everywhere. The enforcement of possessory pledges was monitored by the aldermen's courts. Mortgages by operation of law were more common in Flanders than in Brabant. The general mortgage by operation of law for the benefit of the *fiscus* was introduced throughout the Netherlands.

General mortgages were received by the *ius commune*. In sixteenth-century notarial practice, a general mortgage was stipulated on the occasion of every written agreement. Eventually, it became a stipulation that was presumed to be present in all agreements. The consequence was the erosion of the general mortgage. The 'droit de suite' connected with the action on account of pledge no longer applied to general mortgages in the eighteenth century. It only applied to special mortgages, as was later expressed in art. 7 of the Belgian Mortgages Act. In France, the generalisation of the general mortgage led to the consular judges' practice of treating divisions in the case of bankruptcy as multiple pledges. The person who had the oldest claim, could recover debts from the assets first. The French parliaments did not follow this practice and applied the regulation of the *ius commune*, i.e. the pro rata division of the assets among the creditors.

The biggest problem with regard to pledges concerned publicity. In some regions, the *lex Scripturas* was not introduced, if only because the administration or the notarial practice did not get into their stride in these parts. Non-possessory pledges to movable property led to difficulties in those regions where possession served as a title of ownership. Some sovereign councils denied opposability towards third parties in the case of such a pledge. Legal and general mortgages nevertheless needed publicity. They were gradually subordinated to the special mortgages because of the precedence given to written pledges. In the Early Modern Era, pledges with transfer and mortgages without transfer were differentiated more clearly. Mortgages on movable property were suppressed almost everywhere. This explains why the term mortgage was limited to immovable property in recent history. In the Code civil, the registration of the deed of pledge became obligatory. In Belgium, the pledging of immovable property was regulated by the Mortgages Act of 1851, in which registration is obligatory as well. The rights of priority were incorporated in the same act.

The easy pledging of trade goods and trade receivables, which was typical of merchant banking, disappeared everywhere on the Continent except in Amsterdam and Hamburg.

Bibliography. – Concerning the Southern Netherlands, see Ph. GODDING, *Le droit privé dans les Pays-Bas méridionaux du 12e au 18e siècle*, Brussels 1987, p. 215-226 on immovable goods and p. 256-257 on movable goods.

Chapter VII
The law of obligations

Bibliography. – Book 3 of Justinian's Institutes contains an overview of the principles of the late imperial law of obligations. The standard work on the history of Roman obligations is R. ZIMMERMANN, *The Law of Obligations, Roman foundations of the civilian tradition*, Cape Town-Wetton-Johannesburg [1990]. The vision of Roman private law that was developed in the nineteenth and twentieth century was described magistrally by M. KASER, *Das römische Privatrecht*, 2 parts, Munich 1971-1975. Kaser's textbook, which is a précis of his handbook, has been translated by R. Dannenbring: M. KASER and R. DANNENBRING, *Roman private law, A translation*, Durban 1968. P. BIRKS, *The Roman law of obligations*, edited by E. DESCHEEMAEKER, Oxford 2014, is based on the courses of Birks in Edinburgh. H. COING, *Europäisches privatrecht 1500 bis 1800*, I: *Älteres Gemeines Recht*, Munich 1985, p. 391 and following contains a beautiful summary of the reception of the Roman law of obligations in national legislations. R. Feenstra wrote elucidating introductions about contracts and torts. For these scientific gems, see R. FEENSTRA and M. AHSMANN, *Contract, Aspecten van de begrippen contract en contractsvrijheid in historisch perspectief*, [Rechtshistorische Cahiers 2,] 2nd edition, Deventer 1988; R. FEENSTRA, *Vergelding en vergoeding, Enkele grepen uit de geschiedenis van de onrechtmatige daad*, [Rechtshistorische Cahiers, 6,] adapted by L.C. WINKEL, Deventer 2002. On the medieval and early modern reception in the Southern Netherlands, see Ph. GODDING, *Le droit privé dans les Pays-Bas méridionaux du 12e au 18e siècle*, Brussels 1987, p. 415-524, the most beautiful study of legal history that was ever published in Belgium. A good handbook in Dutch is J. HALLEBEEK, *Fons et origo iuris, Een historische inleiding tot het vermogensrecht*, Amsterdam 2006. The same author compiled a casebook on liability law: J. HALLEBEEK, *Lijf ende goedt, De juridische bescherming van de menselijke persoon en diens vermogen, Een schets van de westerse rechtsgeschiedenis*, Amsterdam 2014.

It has often been said that 'the law of obligations is the most important legacy of the Roman law'. When they consider Roman law, jurists are attracted for the most part to obligations. This is so because our law of obligations was developed in the early modern *ius commune* and is therefore steeped in the way of thinking of the *modernitas*. For this reason, the texts of the *Corpus iuris* dovetail more closely with current legal doctrine. The overview of the law of obligations that will be presented below will attempt to include earlier periods of legal history as well. The first paragraph deals with obligations in general and already touches on the sixteenth-century fusion between civil law and canon law. This first paragraph begins with a discussion of some special agreements from the law of contract are discussed. Then, we will divide the matter according to the distinction which became the most important when the Roman law was received: the distinction between strict and *bona fide* obligations. The second paragraph deals with stipulations, which had a considerable shaping influence on the English law of contract. The third paragraph focuses on *bona fide* obligations, which have shaped the Continental law of contract. The fourth paragraph treats obligations arising from delicts. Finally, some special contracts are considered.

§ 1. Obligations in general

1. Obligations and liability

In classical Roman law, an obligation (*obligatio*) was a situation that led to an *actio in personam*. The creditor (*creditor*) was granted an *actio*; the debtor (*debitor*) was the defendant; the amount due was the debt (*debitum*). The *ius commune* explained the term *obligatio* by associating it with *ligare* (to bind). A debtor was bound by his obligation just as an ox with a rope tied around its horns. Gaius wrote that obligations were debited and credited in account books, which means that they did not only come into being when a claim was brought. This view was handed down to the Middle Ages via Justinian: it is the bond of the law which binds us in a mandatory way to perform a certain prestation according to the legal rules (Inst. 3.14*pr.*). Old account books, in which we can see how obligations were valued, are therefore an important source for the history of obligations. In Roman Antiquity, obligations were nevertheless defined by procedure: there were only as many types of obligations as there were *actiones in personam*. Each of these actions could only be used to sue one person. The bond between the debtor and the creditor was an individual one.

Judges were more tolerant of some dealings that led to actions than of others. In the case-law, a level of tolerance was developed for each action: the 'liability'. Above a certain threshold, the obligation was enforceable; below this threshold, it was not. This different liability per *actio* did not appeal to medieval tastes. The moral theologians had already developed the notion of responsibility, and the jurists scoured the *Corpus iuris* for a similar system of 'liability'. This was developed in the *ius commune*. French law used a single word for both notions: 'responsabilité'. In the *ius commune* of the Modern Era, the doctrine of liability became 'Schuldrecht' – the 'pièce de résistance' of German private law. On the Continent, one cannot speak of obligations without mentioning liability.

Although this liability will be discussed thoroughly below, we will already mention one element of it here, namely the notice of default (*interpellatio*). An obligation only became due if the creditor gave the debtor an ultimatum. If he brought the debtor before the judge without having done this, the debtor could raise the defence of inadmissibility. He was not liable. See D. 45.1.23-24. A debtor only became in default (*in mora*) and liable after he had received a notice of default. From then on, he could be held liable for every default, even in the absence of fault (*mora debitoris perpetuat obligationem*), and the interest on his debt began to run. In the Digest, we find some cases in which there was no need for a notice of default, for example when the term of delivery turned out to be an essential element of the obligation. The glossators called this *mora ex re* (default arising from the matter itself). With regard to this essential term of delivery, the glossators formulated the rule *dies interpellat pro homine* (the term of delivery gives the notice of default instead of the creditor). In the *ius commune* of the Modern Era, some jurists concluded that whenever an obligation featured a due date or term, it was not necessary to issue a notice of default. According to them, notices of default were only necessary if no term had been fixed. Among the German jurists, this interpretation carried the most weight; the French tradition adhered to the Roman regulation. The old Dutch law featured the principle *dies interpellat pro homine*, but the nineteenth-century Dutch Civil code followed the French tradition (art. 1274 of the Dutch Civil code). In the new Dutch Civil code, the rule of *dies interpellat pro homine* was reinstated (art. 6.1.8.8). Delivering a day late is therefore a dangerous business in Germany and the Netherlands.

If a debtor did not accept the prestation, the case was one of *mora creditoris* (default of the creditor) (D. 30.84.3). The liability of the debtor was reduced to liability for deceit. In the case of monetary debts, the debtor could be relieved by means of a consignation of the payment, see articles 1257-1264 of the Civil code.

2. The law of obligations and canon law

In the field of obligations, liability took the centre stage for the civil lawyers. In the *ius commune* of the Early Modern Era, the views of the canonists also played a considerable role. Because obligations concerned the individual relations between people, the moralists and canonists developed an interpretation that was based on Christian charity. In the sixteenth century, the canonical courts were subjected to the monarchical system of justice and many principles of ecclesiastical law ended up in the general legal doctrine (see chapter I). From the end of the sixteenth century onwards, jurists attempted to replace the laws made by the courts with extrajudicial law. At the end of the sixteenth century, theology influenced the law and in the seventeenth century the *forum internum* and the legal doctrine were developed. At that time, the Reformed jurists were also contributing towards the internalisation of the law. They transplanted formerly canonical principles onto the monarchical law. In England the consistory courts continued to function separately, so that their precedents did not influence the monarchical courts. A series of canonical notions therefore became part of the Continental law of obligations but not of the English law of obligations.

A first example is *culpa*. In Antiquity, this word indicated disorderly conduct, a blow dealt to society (*culpare* = to hit). The moralists and the canonists equated *culpa* with an ethical mistake, a sin. They were of the opinion that there was no liability without sin. The civil lawyers did not go that far, but did remember that there was no liability without fault. No-fault liability did not exist in the *ius commune*.

For the canonists, *bona fides* was central to all obligations. In Antiquity, the phrase *bona fides* indicated that the judge had to consider all relations between two parties. Such cases required adversarial proceedings. *Fides*, however, became the Latin word for the Christian faith. The canonists took the step from procedural *bona fides* to 'acting in good faith', i.e. treating each other with *charitas* and Christian reliability. Traders were allowed to be artful and shrewd, but not to act without charity. This *bona fides* could not be renounced, which meant that it always played a role in the law of obligations. One had to interpret, judge, act and execute in a *bona fide* manner.

The canonists also stressed equity. According to Domitius Paulus, those who had been purposefully wronged *contra naturalem aequitatem* (contrary to the innate equality) could invoke the *exceptio doli* (D. 44.4.1.1). Papinian also reminded his readers of the fact that under the civil law they could never impose an *iniqua condicio* on anyone else (D. 50.17.74). Under the Roman law of Antiquity, one could not treat fellow men as one pleased, because of the *aequitas*. The medieval legists did not write much about *aequitas*. In the twelfth century, Martinus de Gosia was of the opinion that *aequitas* was God himself, the source of all law. Nevertheless, he reminded his readers that the Roman *aequitas* meant the equal treatment of equal cases. Among the civil lawyers, in other words, the notion of *aequitas* continued to play a role, although its meaning had changed into 'equality'. The situation was different among the canonists. The Latin church fathers, including Jerome in the Vulgate, used *aequitas* as the translation of the judge's benevolence, the charitable justice in which love of one's fellow man played a role. For Augustine, justice was not perfect unless every party was considered a brother in Christ. In the thirteenth-century *Aristoteles latinus*, *aequitas* became the translation of *epieikeia*, wise judgement. According to Aristotle, *epieikeia* implied that departing from the settled case-law was possible in concrete cases. Thomas Aquinas concluded from this that if the commonwealth or the equal treatment of those subject to the law were jeopardised, *aequitas* took precedence over the settled case-law. His contemporary, Henricus de Segusio, dug up an old definition by Cyprian: *aequitas* is justice that is practiced in a long-suffering way. He drew attention to the care of souls that was of prime importance for the canonists. Baldus, who was Bartolus' most important student and who taught both civil lawyers and canonists, took this Greek *aequitas* into account. He called the settled case-law *aequitas scripta*. Under the influence of canon law, which was suffused with the dream of ethical justice, the Spanish jusnaturalists, finally, developed the new meaning that *aequitas* would receive in the civil law: equity. When the canon law was tossed into the melting pot of the Continental sovereign courts, Reformed jurists like Donellus still tried to bar this equity. For Donellus, *aequitas* was not a grand principle of moral justice, but the Roman technique of applying precedents 'in an equal manner' to cases about which the law remained silent.

An example of how *epieikeia* began to affect the legal doctrine is *inaequalitas*, unjustified inbalance. For the medieval canonists, the balance between two citizens could not be disturbed if there was no ethical reason for this disturbance. Every enrichment of one person at the cost of another that was 'without cause' had to be compensated. Such an unjustified enrichment led to an obligation: the enriched person had a debt with the impoverished person. In the sixteenth century we find *aequalitas* in the *ius commune*.

It is, in short, impossible to understand the 'Roman' law of obligations without taking the canonists into account. The English law of obligations was never subjected to this canonical influence. The English universities began to study the Roman legacy much later than the Continental universities. The consequence was that the English law was less conceptual and did not incoporate the canonical doctrine of liability. One should nevertheless avoid exaggerating the differences. In the seventeenth and eighteenth century English law was dogmatised as well, among other things by the education provided by the inns of court.

3. Sources of obligations

In Roman Antiquity, every obligation was different. Nevertheless, some Roman jurists tried to distinguish different types.

According to Gaius 3.88, there was a *summa diuisio* between obligations that arose from a contract and obligations that arose from a delict. In D. 44.7.1*pr.*, the compilers of the *Corpus iuris* incorporated a text from the *Res cottidianae siue aureae* which they attributed to Gaius. This text mentions three sources of obligation: contracts, unlawful acts and other legal acts that could give rise to a obligations according to a judgement. According to Justinian (Inst. 3.13.2), there were four types of obligations:

a) obligations arising from contracts (*ex contractu*): i.e. obligations that arose from agreements which could be enforced by means of civil actions and from *pacta* (formless agreements) for which the law provided an action.
b) obligations arising from quasi-contracts (*quasi ex contractu*): these obligations did not arise from agreements, but from circumstances. However, they were comparable to obligations arising from contract. Examples are *locatio conductio*, custody, legacy, undue payment. The glossators called these obligations arising from quasi-contracts (*ex quasi contractu*). This term was adopted in article 1371 of the Civil Code (quasi-contrats).
c) Obligations arising from unlawful acts (*ex delicto*): these obligations arose from civil delicts, for which the law provided an action, not from acts that fell under the criminal law. Those who were guilty of theft (*furtum*), insults (*iniuria*), damage to property (*lex aquilia*) or a robbery brought a civil obligation on themselves. The victim was the creditor; the perpetrator was the debtor.
d) Obligations arising from quasi-unlawful acts (*quasi ex delicto*): according to Justinian, this category consisted of a number of cases in which wrongful damage had been caused but no delict had been established. One example was the *actio de deiectis et effusis*: if something that had been thrown or poured from out of a window had ended up on someone's head, he could go to the civil court and bring this action against all the occupants of the floor from which the object or liquid had been thrown, even against those residents who had nothing to do with the matter. Other examples were the *actio de iudice qui litem suam fecit* (damage caused by the judge) and, according to some, the *actio de pauperie* (action on account of damage done by domesticated animals, see below). The glossators called these quasi-delicts, a term that was adopted in article 1370 of the Civil code.

In article 1370, we also find a category that does not stem from Justinian: obligations arising from the law. This term goes back to the early modern *ius commune*. For some jurists, quasi-contracts and quasi-delicts simply led to obligations 'arising from the law', by which they meant 'arising from the *Corpus iuris*' (interpretation of D. 44.7.52). In his *Traité des obligations*, Pothier wrote that obligations arising from the law sprang from 'la loi naturelle' (from innate rights). The classic example was the maintenance obligation in family law. Maintenance could be enforced as an obligation. The canonists had derived this rule from the *Corpus iuris* – which in fact contains no such rule. Via Pothier, the canonists' provision ended up in article 1370 of the Civil code. This article should therefore not be taken to mean that every law is a source of obligations.

Notabilia. – Article 1134 of the Civil Code also contains such a strange use of the word 'law': all agreements serve as laws for the parties. This 'law' is based on D. 50.17.23. Contracting parties who wanted to depart from the normal rules of liability were bound by their stipulation that detailed this departure, because *legem enim contractus dedit*, i.e. the contract gave it a binding character. Domat (1625-1696) wrote about this passage in French and translated *lex* as 'loy'. This expression stood the test of time and ended up in the Code civil.

4. Sources of obligations arising from contracts

Gaius and Justinian further subdivided the obligations arising from contracts. A Roman contract was a kind of obligation, because it was unilateral. Bilateral contracts date back to the sixteenth century (see below, in the section about causality). According to Pedius, a contract required a *conuentio* (meeting). According to Ulpian in D. 2.14.1.3, this *conuentio* always included a *consensus*. Not all contracts, however, were established through consensus. Nor was it possible to conclude a consensual contract about everything. There was no freedom of contract in Antiquity, because the number of actions and obligations was limited. If one made an agreement that did not take a form protected by the law, it was a *pactum*, an agreement for which the law did not provide an action. As regards content, it was possible to contract about everything (1) by making use of stipulations, which could be used to promise everything, or (2) by concluding a *pactum* and executing one's own part of the agreement: this execution caused the prestation promised by the other party to become an obligation (doctrine of innominate contracts, see below).

Gaius 3.89 classified the obligations arising from contracts on the basis of the manner in which they had been concluded. This resulted in the following categories: *contractus re, contractus uerbis, contractus litteris* and *contractus consensu*. Justinian adopted this classification (Inst. 3.13.2). It can also be found in D. 44.7.1, the first text of the important Digest's title on obligations and actions.

*A. Obligations arising from the transfer of a good (*contractus re*)*

In real contracts, the obligation arose because a good was transferred or pointed out. Real contracts were crucial to Egyptian and Greek law, but were of lesser importance in the Roman system.

An example provided by Gaius was the *datio mutui*, the loan for consumption, where the transfer of the goods gave rise to the obligation to return goods of the same kind. In D. 44.7.1.2-6 we read that the contractual obligation also arose from the transfer of the good in the case of loan for use (*commodatum*), deposit (*depositum*) and pledge (*pignus*). By this pledge, Gaius meant the pledge with transfer of the good. When this text was adopted into the *Corpus iuris*, the transfer of the pledged property had not been necessary since a very long time. In the context of *contractus re* we should, in other words, not take the statement that the obligations arose from the *traditio* too literally.

In the case of *commodatum* (free loan for use), a good was transferred on loan for use. The person who lent out the good could make use of the *actio commodati* (action on account of loan of use) in order to get the good back or to claim damages. If he was the owner, he could also make use of the revendication. The person who received the loan could bring the *actio commodati contraria*, which he could use to recover costs or to ask a compensation for a defective good. There is case-law about both actions in D. 13.6.

In the case of a deposit (*depositum*), the depository was not allowed to use the good. It could be claimed back by means of a revendication or an interdict. If the good had been damaged, the depositor could bring the *actio depositi* (action of deposit) against the depository to claim damages. The obligation to take care of the good arose at the time of transfer. The threshold for liability on the part of the depository was much lower in the case of a deposit in return for payment than in the case of a deposit without remuneration. In the latter case, only deceit (*dolus*) or gross negligence (*culpa lata*) resulted in liability. Liability with regard to loans for use and deposits was determined, in part, by utility: the greater the benefits, the greater the liability (D. 13.6.5.2-3 and D. 44.7.1.5).

*B. Obligations arising from words (*contractus uerbis*)*

These obligations centre around the *stipulatio,* a formal legal act in which an obligation arose through the pronunciation of specific phrases. They will be discussed below.

*C. Obligations arising from writing (*contractus litteris*)*

Gaius 3.128-134 explains how obligations arose from registration in account books. Did this occur when two people had debt claims against one another and then set these off against each other? No, because Gaius writes about *compensatio* elsewhere, and we also have texts about setoffs in D. 16.2. A setoff did not lead to a new obligation. Gaius was probably discussing phenomena such as clearance between bankers. Bankers kept their clients' accounts and transferred money to each other for their clients. For that purpose, these bankers had accounts with each other. If banker X transferred money to banker Z for client Y, he put the money directly into the account of Z in his own ledger. Within this internal account, there were of course setoffs (Gaius 4.64). Every day or week, bankers calculated the amounts that they owed to one another. They cleared these by noting them down in their financial diary. These obligations between bankers did not arise from consensus, nor from words or on the occasion of the transfer of a good, but merely from the registration of the debt. For Gaius, this meant that these obligations arose from writing. As a reminder, we mention that Gaius did not write a handbook, but rather listed the problems which he thought would be caused by the adoption of the Perpetual Edict into the imperial case-law.

Justinian adopted the written contract in Inst. 3.21, but phrased it differently. The example he gave was that of a loan below par. A person borrowed one hundred from a banker, but promised in a stipulation to pay back one hundered and ten the next year. According to the classical law, the borrower had an *exceptio non numeratae pecuniae* (exception that the sum had not been counted out) to defend himself against the banker's claim. Under Justin (Justinian's predecessor), the prefecture decided the following: if a written deed (*cautio*) with a stipulation had been drawn up that mentioned the full facts of the loan below par, the lender no longer had to prove that a flawless relation underlay his claim (C. 4.30.13). The *exceptio non numeratae pecuniae* was consequently inadmissible. The obligation was, in other words, saved by the written document, although it was based on a stipulation, an oral obligation. Under Justinian, the prefecture enlarged the scope of the protection granted to the lender. If the other party had promised he would pay back a certain amount and had confirmed this promise in writing, he lost the right to invoke the *exceptio non numeratae pecuniae* after two years, even though the full facts were not described in this written confirmation (C. 4.30.14). The author of Inst. 3.21 was of the opinion that in such cases, an obligation arose from writing: after two years the promiser was no longer bound by the stipulation, but by his written promise.

The medieval Romanists dedicated lengthy comments which focused on the unilateral written contract to this passage from the Institutes. Jacobus Balduini was the first to clearly state that an obligation that has the force of a stipulation can arise from writing. Jacques de Revigny developed this doctrine further in an important *repetitio* about Inst. 3.21. According to him, written obligations could also arise from letters. They were valid even if they did not mention a *causa*. This doctrine about written obligations was not adopted by the Italian commentators, but it can be found in the English deeds and in the 'Anerkennung' treated in articles 780-781 of the Bürgerliches Gesetzbuch.

*D. Obligations arising from consensus (*contractus consensu*)*

Both Gaius and Justinian mentioned four agreements in which the obligation arose from consensus: *emptio-uenditio* (purchase-sale), *locatio-conductio* (rent or lease, contracting, contract of employment), *societas* (partnership) and *mandatum* (mandate). The obligations that arose from these agreements were connected with actions of good faith (*actiones ex bona fide*). Beware: purchase-sale and *locatio-conductio* were unilateral contracts as well. The obligation of the buyer and that of the seller – the *locator* and the *conductor*, respectively – were both unilateral. If one of these parties brought a claim, the judge did take the entire relationship between the parties into account, because the formula of these actions included the words *e bona fide*.

Obligations arising from consensus seem to have been a Roman innovation. In Hellenistic law, sale remained a real contract. In some medieval Western legal systems, rent and sale also retained aspects of real contracts: they were established when an advance was paid (earnest penny, God's penny). According to some, obligations arising from consensus stem from the *ius gentium*. The peregrine praetor attempted to make some of the common contracts in his edict more flexible, so that they would be more usable for people with different civil statuses. The four obligations that arose from consensus already became popular during Antiquity because they were so flexible and allowed parties to freely stipulate.

5. Specific and generic obligations

In the *ius commune*, we find other distinctions, such as the distinction between specific and generic obligations. In the case of a specific obligation, the delivery of one irreplaceable good or service became due, for example the delivery of a specific horse. If this delivery became impossible, the debtor was relieved of liability. In the case of a generic obligation, only the type of object that had to be delivered was specified, for example 'a' horse. According to Javolenus, one could then deliver the worst specimen of the species (D. 17.1.52), but according to Ulpian it had to be of average quality (Ulpian in D. 30.37*pr.*). Justinian confirmed the latter opinion. If a person owed someone else the delivery of a type of object and consequently had a generic obligation, delivery could be demanded as long as objects of the intended type still existed: *genus non perit* (a type does not perish). If the debtor could not lay hands on the goods, he either went bankrupt, or was excluded from the market. After all, thoughtless traders do not belong on the market. In the Middle Ages, a distinction was made between *impossibilitas* (objective impossibility, caused by circumstances) to perform an obligation and *difficultas* (subjective impossibility, i.e. the performance of the obligation was impossible for this specific debtor). In the case of objective impossibility, the debtor was relieved, because 'nul n'est tenu à l'impossible' (*impossibilium nulla obligatio est*). Under Justinian, this rule from the Digest (D. 50.17.185) applied to performances that had been impossible from the very start. The moral theologian Thomas Aquinas enlarged the scope of this rule so that it included cases of arising impossibility. Subsequently, this principle was applied in the ecclesiastical case-law. The debtor remained liable, but was not in default (*mora debitoris*). It was impossible to exact payment of accumulating interests or damages from him. For the civil lawyers, generic obligations could only give rise to *difficultas*, but not to *impossibilitas*. This was still an issue in the modern *ius commune*. The German jusnaturalists treated this problem extensively. A new distinction cropped up in the legal doctrine: the liability of a debtor who had himself rendered the performance of an obligation more difficult or impossible ('positive Forderverletzung') was not assessed in the same manner as the liability of a debtor who was confronted with an impossibility that he had not caused himself.

6. Alternative obligations

In the case of an alternative obligation, two or more prestations were indicated as debt, but the creditor was only entitled to one of these. See, for example, D. 45.1.138.1 and D. 18.1.34.6. In principle, the debtor chose which prestation he would perform, unless otherwise agreed. If the performance of one prestation became impossible, the debtor was not relieved: he was obliged to perform the other prestation (D. 25.1.128).

D. 18.1.34.6. – *Paulus libro trigesimo terio ad edictum.* Si emptio ita facta fuerit: 'est mihi emptus Stichus aut Pamphilus', in potestate est uenditoris, quem uelit dare, sicut in stipulationibus, sed uno mortuo qui superest dandus est: et ideo prioris periculum ad uenditorem, posterioris ad emptorem respicit. Sed et si pariter decesserunt, pretium debebitur: unus enim utique periculo emptoris uixit. Idem dicendum est etiam, si emptoris fuit arbitrium quem uellet habere, si modo hoc solum arbitrio eius commissum sit, ut quem uoluisset emptum haberet, non et illud, an emptum haberet.

Translation SCOTT. – If a purchase is made in the following terms: 'Either Stichus or Pamphilus is purchased by me', the vendor has the right to deliver whichever one he pleases, as is the case in stipulations; but if one of them should die, the survivor must be delivered, and hence the risk of the first slave attaches to the vendor, and that of the second to the purchaser. But if both of them should die, the price will still be due, for the one who survives the other is always at the risk of the purchaser. The same must be said if the purchaser had the right to select which one he wished to have; provided it was only left to him which one he would purchase, and not whether he would make any purchase at all.

7. Natural obligations

Salvius Julianus used the term *naturalis obligatio* (natural obligation). It can be found a couple of times in the *Corpus iuris*, where the term is used in connection with a wide variety of acts. It is never defined, and it is not clear what these obligations had to to with *natura* (birth). Maybe the term should be translated as 'engendered' obligations.

Or perhaps the term was derived from the obligations of children (*naturales*). They were certainly not moral obligations that arose from morals or propriety. These *obligationes naturales* had the following characteristics. They could not be enforced. If these obligations were performed, the *paterfamilias* could not make use of the *condictio indebiti* (claim on account of undue payment, D. 12.6.13*pr.*). Performance was not a donation. When a slave had paid a natural obligation in cash, the payment was definitive as well. These obligations could be secured by means of a *fideiussio* or a pledge (D. 46.1.16.3, Gaius 3.119a). If an obligation was secured in such a way, the guarantor or pledgor could not invoke that the principal debt was not enforceable. If the debtors of natural obligations became independent, their obligations became due.

The Pandectists were most troubled by D. 46.1.16.4, from which one can derive that some natural obligations were, in fact, enforceable: *naturales obligationes aestimantur* [...] *si actio aliqua eorum nomine competit*. According to many Romanists, this is a corrupt passage. This is the easiest solution if you do not understand a Roman text: blame a careless copyist. However, this text becomes far less complicated when one reads it with the Roman *familia* in mind. Family members had obligations towards one another and obligations towards non-family members. All were registered in the account books and were therefore real obligations. The performance of some obligations could be obtained from the *paterfamilias* by means of actions with an additional modality; others were purely internal, but could suddenly become due. It was common for a *paterfamilias* to agree with his slave on the circumstances in which the slave could buy his freedom. The slave's earnings fell to the *paterfamilias*, but were debited from his account in the *familia*. If the *paterfamilias* did not honour the agreements or did not debit correctly, the slave could bring the matter before the judge by means of the *uindicatio libertatis*. The judge then took account of the internal agreements and accounts, which had until then been natural obligations. Another example of internal obligations that became enforceable, can be found in D. 35.1.40.3. A *paterfamilias* liberated a slave in his will and left him the five gold coins which he owed him according to his account books. The universal legatee claimed that this debt was not due and payable and that he did not owe the slave anything. The judge, however, decided that the legacy had to be executed. Gaius 4.73 mentions a case in which a creditor had internal obligations play a role in the calculation of liability in the context of an *actio de peculio*. In C. 5.12.30.1, we read that dowries also consisted of natural obligations. They were registered and taken seriously, although they could not be revendicated. When *nuptiae* ended, these natural obligations became due. In the classical period, the jurists' interpretation was that obligations which a pupil had entered into without the assistance of his guardian were natural obligations as well. There were no moral obligations involved.

Where did the idea of 'moral' obligations come from? In the *ius commune*, no one kept the Roman *familia* in mind, and this is why natural obligations became such a complex matter. "A source of desperation," Cujas wrote. In the gl. *'Obligauerint' ad* D. 5.3.25.11, we read that a natural obligation arose merely from goodwill, *ex instinctu naturae*. The civil lawyers explained D. 46.1.16.4, which concerns natural obligations that become enforceable, by comparing these obligations to consensual agreements (*pacta*, see below) and to the promise of a dowry – which also became enforceable when they were executed. Bartolus compared natural obligations to *pacta* as well. Both became enforceable 'if there was an obvious reason'. The canonists taught the same thing. They gave the example of the *antidora*.

If someone received a prebend or a fief, it was self-evident that the income of the first year fell to the granter of the prebend or fief: *naturaliter est debitor ad antidora obligatus.* In the conceptual thought of the Middle Ages, paying the *antidora* became a 'natural' obligation, i.e. an 'evident' obligation. The Spanish jusnaturalists, however, associated natural obligations with natural law: they were obligations of a higher order that could perhaps not be enforced in a court, but could certainly be enforced within the divine order. In Lessius' work, natural obligations became moral obligations. Nevertheless, the association between obligations and *pacta* continued to play a role. In the sixteenth century, the civil lawyers adopted the canonists' theory that *pacta* were always enforceable (*pacta sunt seruanda*, see below). Was the same true of natural obligations? Donellus opposed every adoption of 'papistical' law. For him, *pacta* were only enforceable if there was a *causa*, for example an economic reason (see below for a treatment of the causality of obligations). According to him, the same was true of *antidora* as well: like *pacta*, they were only enforceable when they had a *causa*. Similarly, natural obligations became enforceable when this was reasonable and equitable. Grotius accepted both tendencies: according to some, natural obligations had to be executed because this was proper according to the higher natural law, but sometimes natural obligations became enforceable under the civil law because of a clear reason – *pacta*, for example. In the seventeenth century, both Protestants and Catholics incorporated the natural obligations in the framework of the *forum internum*. Honour and conscience became just as normative as the court. In the *ius commune* of the Modern Era, the main emphasis was on the moral aspect. For Pothier, the reversal of natural obligations that had already been performed was impossible because the reason for this performance was a moral debt. One paid this debt in order to appease one's conscience and that was a sufficient reason to say that it was not an undue payment. This would remain an important element in the nineteenth century: natural obligations were moral obligations that were not enforceable, but if one performed them it was impossible to reverse them.

Bibliography. – L. Waelkens, 'L'origine romaine des obligations naturelles', *Revue historique de droit français et étranger*, 90 (2012), p. 311-327; Idem, 'Dos naturaliter mulieris est dans 23,3,75', in: H. Dondorp, J. Hallebeek, T. Wallinga and L. Winkel (eds.), *Ius romanum – ius commune – ius hodiernum, Studies in honour of Eltjo J.H. Schrage on the occasion of his 65th birthday*, Amsterdam-Aalen 2010, p. 399-410. On the example of Gaius 4.73, see L. Waelkens, 'Gaius IV,73: debet ou debetur?', *The Legal History Review* 68 (2000), p. 347-356. *Naturalis obligatio* is mentioned in D. 44.7.14; D. 46.1.16.4; D. 12.6.13*pr.* (*naturaliter seruus obligatur*); and Gaius 3.119a. The idea that someone was bound *natura* can be found in D. 50.17.84 (*is natura debet*) and in D. 16.2.6 (*quod natura debetur*). D. 46.3.5.2 says that a *pactum* was binding *naturaliter*. The *obligatio naturalis* was contrasted with the *obligatio ciuilis* in D. 46.1.16.3 and D. 46.2.1-2.

§ 2. Strict obligations

An important distinction is that between strict and *bona fide* obligations. Liability for *bona fide* obligations depended on a large number of circumstances, unlike liability for strict obligations. Proof of the existence of a strict obligation sufficed to make it enforceable. The Pandectists considered strict obligations to be a formalistic remnant of an early phase of the development of the Roman law. This is nonsense. Twenty-first century public law is full of formalistic elements, but that does not mean that it is underdeveloped. Strict obligations had one major advantage: they could be used to conduct trade. Traders put strict obligations on the market. They were used to conclude supply contracts for staple goods. The smooth functioning of the market for basic goods allowed for better budgeting, created more opportunities and resulted in cheaper selling prices. Roman society benefited from all of this. *Bona fide* obligations, by contrast, were better geared to the sensitivities of daily life and of consumers, but could not be used to establish a stock market.

The most important legal act that resulted in strict obligations was the *stipulatio* of D. 45.1 – the title which would become the most important text from the Digest about the theory of obligations in general. A stipulation could be used to establish any agreement to deliver a good or service, or to perform or refrain from performing an act. Other strict obligations were those that arose from a legacy *per damnationem*, in which case the special legatee was the creditor and the general legatee was the debtor. In case-law, the obligation of the general legatee of a legacy *per damnationem* was almost always compared to an obligation arising from a stipulation.

Stipulationes e bona fide? – The Pandectists claimed that stipulations lost their strict character in the classical period and became 'causal'. They state that a stipulation became unenforceable when the reason for which it was made no longer existed. However, this theory, which was based on the interpretation of D. 44.4.2.3 and the gl. *'Causa' ad* D. 44.4.2.3 in the early modern *ius commune*, is far-fetched. A precedent that had such a wide scope would definitely have been incorporated in D. 45.1 and Inst. 3.15-20. Stipulations with a strict character can still be found in the Middle Ages and the Early Modern Era, for example in deeds that remained enforceable if the reason for which the stipulation was made had disappeared. In Antiquity, D. 44.4.2.3 treated a case in which the *exceptio doli* was admissible with regard to an *actio e stipulatu* brought by a claimant who had committed deceit. We will return to this issue in §1, 1, b and in §3, 3, f.

1. Stipulations (*stipulatio*)

*A. A verbal contract (*contractus uerbis*)*

In Antiquity, a stipulation was a formal, verbal interrogation that was followed by an acceptance: 'Do you promise to pay me one thousand sesterces? – Yes, I promise you this'. The question and the answer followed one another and the main verb was repeated. Originally, this was the verb *spondere*: *Spondesne...?* – *Spondeo*. In later instances, we also find *fidepromittere*: *Fidepromittis...?* – *Fidepromito*. In the classical period, all verbs were used, including Greek ones: *Dabis...?* – *Dabo*; *Homologeis...?* – *Homologeo*. Witnesses were not necessary and stipulations offered limitless possibilities.

The debt had to be clear, or clearly determinable. Case-law accepted that it was determined by the creditor, the debtor or an outsider. See Gaius 3.140-143, D. 17.2.76 and following, and D. 17.2.6. It had to be possible to express the debt in terms of money. In a previous chapter, we have already mentioned formulas for actions in which the debt was determined immediately, and others in which the debt was determined by the judge. In the case of a stipulation, the debtor was bound to pay either a *certum* (a definite debt) or an *incertum* (an indefinite debt).

Obligations to pay a *certum* concerned either a definite sum of money (*certa pecunia*), or the delivery of a certain good or an amount of a certain kind of good. If such an obligation was not performed, one could bring a *condictio* (action for a definite debt). If the debt was not a sum of money, the judgement mentioned the market value of the goods involved. If the stipulation had been to deliver X measures of grain for price Y on day Z, the seller could not deliver and the market price was twenty percent higher on day Y, the creditor did have a right to the surplus value of the grain. If the impossibility to deliver a good involved *culpa* on the part of the debtor, the formula of the *condictio (certa rei)* included the fiction that the good still existed, so that the obligation could be enforced (*perpetuatio obligationis*) and the market value of the good could be determined. In Antiquity, *culpa* did not refer to a fault or culpability. In the ablative, it meant 'in a disruptive manner', i.e. through negligence or carelessness for example.

In the case of other obligations arising from stipulations, the debtor was bound to deliver something with an uncertain but determinable value: an *incertum*. In such cases, the creditor had the right to bring the *actio ex stipulatu*. According to the formula of this action, the judge sentenced the debtor to the value of the prestation or good he was bound to perform or deliver (*quidquid dare facere oportet*). This value concerned not only the market value, but also a compensation for incurred damages and lost profits (*lucrum cessans et damnum ermergens*). Justinian was of the opinion that the liability that applied to disruptive non-delivery was the same as that which applied in the case of a *condictio certae rei* (see D. 9.2.52.3). If the debtor did not deliver and thus caused a disruption, there was no need for a fiction. The judge had enough means at his disposal to sentence the debtor to the payment of a monetary compensation.

Stipulations could be made to depend on another legal act, for example: 'Do you promise to give me *ex causa donationis* (because of a donation)', or '*quod ex empto mihi debes* (what you owe me because of a purchase)'. If this other legal act (*causa*) did not take place, the promiser was relieved of his obligation. Note that the word *causa* referred to another legal act, rather than to the causal nature of our current obligations, which will be discussed below. A link with another legal act did not make an obligation any less strict, as is demonstrated by the frequent inclusion of penalty clauses in stipulations: 'and if you do not do this, do you promise to pay me X?'

B. Written stipulations?

The *Corpus iuris* contains two texts about written documents that contained a stipulation clause: D. 2.14.7.12 and C. 8.37.1. The medieval jurists were familiar with a third text about written stipulations, namely *Pauli Sententiae* 5.7.2. It is not unlikely that these three texts are different versions of the same precedent dating from 200 AD.

C. 8.37.1 (200) – Licet epistulae, quam libello inseruisti, additum non sit stipulatum esse eum cui cauebatur, tamen si res inter praesentes gesta est, credendum est praecedente stipulatione uocem respondentis secutam.

Translation BLUME. – Although it was not added to the letter, which you inclosed in your petition, that a stipulation was exacted by the promisee, nevertheless, if the transaction took place in the presence of the parties, it is to be considered that the answer of the promisor followed a preceding interrogation (*stipulatione*).

If a deed included the words 'thus it was stipulated' and evidence that there had never been a stipulation was lacking (as for example in C. 8.37.14), the presence of a stipulation was presumed. The precise wording became irrelevant. It seems that the Eastern emperor Leo's prefecture accepted in 472 that any written obligation, irrespective of its wording, had the legal consequences of a *stipulatio* (C. 8.37.10). This was an important issue in the *ius commune*. The civil lawyers distinguished between formal stipulations and written deeds, but also linked letters of stipulation to the *contractus litteris*. For them, it was not possible to create strict obligations by means of letters detailing question and answer. Obligations could, however be created by means of written documents that were drawn up in the presence of the parties. Several of the written stipulations from this era still exist in commercial law: examples are bills of exchange, notes of hand and promissory notes.

2. Transfer and *nouatio*

A. *The relativity of strict obligations*

A stipulation led to a unilateral obligation of a *promittor* (promitor) towards a *stipulator*. The *promittor* was a debtor; the *stipulator* was his creditor. The stipulation remained a legal act between two people that could not favour a third party: *alteri stipulari nemo potest*. A stipulation could not create a debt that consisted of a benefit for a third party. The *ius commune* adhered to this rule as well. If the *stipulator* did want to create a benefit for a third party, he could include a penalty clause: '... and do you promise to pay me X if you do not do this?' On this issue, see the important text D. 45.1.38.17.

Notabilia about obligations that benefited third parties in Antiquity. – D. 45.1.38.17 only applied to stipulations that were strict legal acts. In legal history, this became the *sedes materiae* for third-party stipulations in general. In Antiquity, there were other means of having oneself bound by a third party. If a *paterfamilias* gave a member of his *familia* a *iussum* (authorisation), the *actio quod iussu* resulted in the unlimited liability of the *paterfamilias* for any obligation into which his family member had entered and which fell within the scope of his authorisation. The *paterfamilias* could also be sued if he had confirmed the obligation of a member of his *familia* (*ratihabitio*). A *procurator* who had a mandate could act for his principal with a certain decorum, for example as a lawyer. An *institor* (manager) acted on behalf of his principal. A captain could bind a shipowner so that the latter was liable for any actions of the captain that concerned the regular exploitation of the ship (*actio exercitoria*). If members of a *familia* used their *peculium* to conduct business, their *paterfamilias* was bound at most for the amount in the *peculium*. An *institor* made his principal liable towards third parties if he presented his *institutio* agreement. Creditors could then bring the *actio institoria* against the principal. Papinian granted an *actio quasi institoria* against the *paterfamilias* if the latter had had someone act as a kind of procurator. In the Middle Ages, Bartolus developed the power of attorney on the basis of this *actio quasi institoria*. A mandate was performed free of charge or led to a debt of honour (*honorarium*), but a power of attorney could be executed against remuneration. The holder of a power of attorney had to impart the name of his principal and could only contract within the scope of his power of attorney. In all those cases, the person who was bound agreed with the actions of the holder. In 1348, under Alfonso the Wise, the Corte of Castile judged that obligations that benefited third parties were possible and that such a third party could be granted a claim on the basis of someone else's actions. The third party's agreement was not mentioned in the decision, but it can be presumed that the third party would not bring a claim if he did not agree. In the sixteenth century, consensual agreements became enforceable (*pacta sunt servanda*, see below). In this context, it became possible for third parties to claim the performance of certain obligations. The canonists supported this view. In the law of Antwerp this led, for example, to the establishment of life insurances with regard to which third parties could bring a claim. The Reformed jurists, for whom the rule of *pacta sunt servanda* was overly papistical, reacted against this tendency. They dragged up D. 45.1.38.17 and presented it as a general principle of the law of obligations. Around 1600, the life insurances were deleted from the case-law of Antwerp and the relativity of obligations was under discussion. Grotius resumed this discussion: in his opinion, a stipulation for the benefit of a third party was possible if the third party agreed to it. On third-party clauses, see E.J.H. SCHRAGE and D. IBBETSON, *Ius quaesitum tertio*, [Comparative studies in Continental and Anglo-American legal history, 26,] Berlin 2008. In this volume, also see the following contribution about Grotius: L. WAELKENS, 'Ius quaesitum tertio, Dutch influences on Grotius', *ibidem*, p. 175-189.

B. Nouatio

Because a stipulation only bound the two people involved, it could not be transferred. The major benefit of a stipulation, the fact that the obligation that resulted from it could be sold, was realised by means of *nouatio*, i.e. the substitution of one debt for another (D. 46.2.1*pr.*-1). An existing obligation – which did not necessarily have to be detailed in a stipulation – was replaced with a new stipulation. Usually, the prestation that was mentioned was 'that which was due because of the existing obligation' (for example *quod mihi Seius debet* or *quod ex testamento mihi dari spondesne?*, D. 45.1.75.6). The old obligation was cancelled by the novation. One of the following elements of the new stipulation had to be new: the debtor, the creditor, a time period or a condition (D. 46.2.28). Aquilius Gallus (first century BC) introduced the *stipulatio aquiliana*, which allowed for the novation of an entire series of debts at once (Inst. 3.29.2 and D. 46.4.18.1, *quidquid te mihi ex quacumque causa dare facere oportet opertebit praesens in diemue*).

According to the glossators, debt substitution by means of a stipulation was not the only instance of novation: *litiscontestatio* and judgements were novations as well. Stipulations were voluntary, while the other two forms of novation were compulsory. In the thirteenth century, novation could also take place tacitly, as long as the intent to novate was proved. In such cases, the old obligation tacitly lost its value according to Revigny and Belleperche. Bartolus specified that even a tacit novation required a new contract. This new contract did not necessarily have to be a stipulation, but a formless agreement (*pactum*) did not have a novatory effect.

According to the civil lawyers, novation also occurred when proceedings were conducted by a *procurator in rem*. He was a third party to the conflict, for example a lawyer, who was prepared to conduct the proceedings and to pay if he lost. The *litiscontestatio* that was concluded by such a procurator had a novatory effect. Consequently, it was deduced that the extrajudicial renunciation of a claim to a *procurator in rem suam* had a novatory effect. This was another means of transferring a claim. The transfer of a debt to a procurator, however, did not have a novatory effect.

3. Strict securities

In order to further enhance the value of stipulations, one could add securities to them by means of an *adstipulatio*. In classical Roman law, personal securities were considered to be safer and more practical than real securities. In the early Middle Ages, people were somewhat reluctant to use these Roman techniques, but all of the modern systems of security stem from the Justinianic *fideiussio*. In the *ius commune*, the problem of accessoriness took the centre stage. After all, the security had to be cancelled together with the principal debt.

A. Sponsio, fidepromissio, fideiussio *in Antiquity*

Sponsio is mentioned in the Twelve Tables. It probably consisted of a stipulation in which a *sponsor* promised the payment of a sum of money that was owed by another person. Although *sponsio* has become a synonym for *stipulatio*, a *sponsor* always remained a surety. In the Republic, a *sponsio* became a stipulation in which an ancillary debtor bound himself to the same prestation as the principal debtor who had detailed a debt in a stipulation. The classical question was: *Idem dari spondesne?* ('Do you promise that the same thing will be given?'), to which the answer was *Spondeo* ('I promise'). If the principal obligation was not contained in a stipulation, it was first converted into a stipulation through a novation. *Sponsio* could not be inherited passively: heirs were not bound by it. If the *sponsor* paid, he originally received the right to levy an execution on the principal debtor (*manus iniectio*). Later, he received the right to bring an *actio depensi* against the principal debtor. The accessority of the obligation of the *sponsor* vis-à-vis the principal obligation was limited. A surety, for example, remained liable for the (invalid) obligation of a non-adult who had acted without his guardian (Gaius 3.119). Be careful with 'accessoriness' in Antiquity. The term *accessorius* dates back to the glossators, and the modern doctrine of 'accessoriness' to the Pandectists.

The formula to be pronounced was different in the case of a *fidepromissio*. Some Romanists suppose that the *fidepromissio* originated in the law of the *ius gentium*. Others consider the term *fides* to be a reference to civil law. Just like *sponsio*, *fidepromissio* could not be inherited passively. The *actio depensi* was not applicable to it (*lex publilia*, presumably fourth century BC).

Four republican laws concerned both *sponsio* and *fidepromissio*. The *lex apuleia* determined that if there were several sureties and one of them had paid more than his share, he received a right of recourse against his fellow sureties. The *lex furia* determined that the liability of the sureties lasted at most two years and that in the case of plurality, each surety was only liable for part of the debt. The *lex cicereia* obliged creditors to clearly state their claim and the number of sureties. According to the *lex cornelia* of 81 BC, finally, people could only stand surety for a certain amount per year. This provision was only abolished by Justinian.

The first century BC saw the origination of a third type of stipulated security, namely the *fideiussio*, which was formulated as follows: *Id fide tua esse iubes? – Iubeo* ('Do you cover it? – I cover it'). The *fideiussio* could be inherited passively and none of the old case-law (except the *lex cornelia*) applied to it. This stipulated security could be used by *peregrini*. The term *iubere* (to order) probably referred to the *iussum* (authorisation), i.e.

the *iussum* of the *actio quod iussu*. The surety, as it were, authorised the principal debtor to enter into his obligation.

In the context of the *fideiussio*, accessoriness was limited as well. Just as in the case of a *sponsio* or *fidepromissio*, payment was required if the principal debt was cancelled because the debtor was not an adult or a minor. What was new was that the *fideiussio* remained valid if the principal debtor was a slave or *filiusfamilias* and the obligation was therefore a natural one. In principle, the surety could not bind himself for a larger amount than the principal debtor (Gaius 3.126, also see art. 2013 of the Civil code). He could invoke most of the exceptions of the principal debtor (Ulpian in D. 46.1.32, see also art. 2012 of the Civil code).

If several sureties acted together, they received the benefit of division (*beneficium diuisionis*). Hadrian decided this in a rescript (the *epistula Hadriani*, mentioned in C. 3.121, see also art. 2026 of the Civil code). If all of the sureties were solvent, the creditor had to claim an equal share from each of them, instead of the entire sum from one of them. If one of the surities was insolvent, the share of the others increased. According to the Romanists, immediately claiming the money from the most solvent surety was considered improper in the Republic. They also state that this surety was given the right to lodge the *actio iniuriarium* (action on account of insult) in the Principate. Finally, they are of the opinion that the principal debtor could only bring his claim against the surety or principal creditor once, because of the extinctive character of the *litiscontestatio*. This situation remained the same, according to the Romanists, until Justinian abolished the extinctive effect of the *litiscontestatio*, so that both the principal debtor and the sureties were only relieved if the debt had been paid in full (C. 8.40.28*pr.* of 531). In 535 Justinian granted sureties the benefit of excussion (*beneficium excussionis*). They received the right to use this defence if the creditor had not instituted proceedings against the principal debtor first (Nov. 4). It was only then that the security became accessory.

There was no *actio depensi* in the case of *fideiussio*. In order to get money back from the principal debtor, the surety made use of two other remedies at law:

- *actio mandati contraria* (contrary action of mandate): seeing *fideiussio* as a mandate and the principal debtor as a mandator allowed the surety to claim his costs back by means of this claim.
- the benefit of cession of actions (*beneficium cedendarum actionum*): when the creditor was paid, the surety could claim the creditor's right of action against the principal debtor (see D. 46.1.17). Justinian generalised this: the surety was always granted cession of the action against the principal debtor. This was the basis for the doctrine of subrogation, see art. 2029 of the Civil code.

B. Reception

The medieval civil lawyers claimed that the *fideiussio* had become a written deed under Justinian, even though *fideiussio* is not mentioned among the written obligations. For the civil lawyers, a surety required a written contract and the words *fideiubere* or *promittere*. Even after the notion of consensus became common in the sixteenth century (see below), a *fideiussio* remained a written document. Its prototype was the guarantee for a bill of exchange (in Belgium currently art. 30-32 Bill of Exchange). This is a relict that indicates that strict written obligations like English debt also existed on the Continent.

In the case of such an obligation, the security was not accessary to the main debt in Middle Ages. There were attempts to counteract the reception the Justinianic rule by having the surety contractually waive the benefit of excussion. Another means was to have the surety promise to bind himself as principal debtor (*debitor principalis*) or as surety and principal debtor (*fideiussor et debitor principalis*). The glossators did not recognise this clause, but among the Bartolists it was a commonplace. At the end of the Middle Ages, this clause was interpreted as a waiver not only of the benefit of excussion (*beneficium excussionis*), but also of the benefit of division (*beneficium diuisionis*). This interpretation was adopted into the early modern *ius commune* and is at the basis of article 2021 of the Code civil: the surety can waive the benefit of excussion or can undertake to be jointly liable, together with the debtor. In English law, the medieval aversion to *beneficium excussionis* and *beneficium diuisionis* became deep-seated. This remained the case in the Early Modern Era.

Securities are an example of how strict obligations still played a role on the Continent in the Early Modern Era.

*C. Solidary liability (*in solidum*)*

Solidary liability originated when several debtors bound themselves fully for the same debt. If one of them paid, all of the debtors were relieved of their liability. Roman case-law introduced solidary liability by operation of law in the case of plurality of debtors and an indivisible debt. Justinian acknowledged this, for instance, in the case of plurality of guardians. Stipulations also resulted in solidary liability if several debtors bound themselves to pay the same debt. This happened when several people acted together as sureties.

In the case of solidary liability, several elements were to the advantage of all of the debtors, for example the payment, the fact that the performance of the prestation became impossible, etcetera. Some elements were only to the advantage of one debtor, such as confusion of debts (*confusio*, D. 46.1.71*pr.*), or the *capitis diminutio* of a debtor (D. 45.2.19). In the classical period, lodging a claim against one debtor led to the consumption of the action that had until then been aimed at all of the debtors. There was a concurrence of claims until one *litiscontestatio* made them all disappear (see D. 45.2.2, Scaevola in D. 13.1.18). The Pandectists called this 'Konsumptionskonkurrenz'. Under Justinian, the extinctive effect of the *litiscontestatio* was undone, so that the different claims coexisted until the definitive payment of the debt (C. 8.40.28.2). For the Pandectists, this became 'Solutionskonkurrenz'. This distinction caused a major dogmatic debate, in which it was posited that the former formula led to one 'Korrealobligation', while Justinian's system led to 'Solidarobligationen' with several solidary obligations.

The debtor who had paid received an action of recourse against the other debtors, on diverse grounds. In the case of indivision, for example in the context of a partnership or inheritance, he had the right to bring the *actio communi diuidundo* (claim to separate and divide). If there was proof of a mandate, he could make use of the *actio mandati contraria*. In all other instances, he could say that it was a case of *actio negotiorum gestorum* and lodge the *actio negotiorum gestorum*. Papinian gave the debtor who had paid the right to claim the creditor's right of action, so that he could lodge the same action against his fellow debtors (forced cession, D. 26.7.38.2). Justinian introduced an independent right of recourse against fellow debtors (D. 9.3.2, C. 8.39.1.1 of 531). Voet and Perez were of the opinion that this passage indicated that a debtor who had paid could claim the entire sum minus his own share from each of his fellow debtors. According to Pothier, he could only claim each of his fellow debtors' share of the entire debt. The German BGB followed Pothier.

In D. 45.2.11 one can find a *mutua fideiussio*, a mutual security, by means of which a principal debtor and a third party stood surety for one another. This strongly resembles a solidary obligation.

Notabilia: other personal obligations. – In Antiquity, it was common for the surety to give a moneylender the assignment to lend money to someone (*mandatum pecuniae credendae,* mandate to lend money). If the money was not paid back in time, the money lender brought the *actio mandati contraria* against the mandator to receive compensation for the damage which he had incurred while executing the mandate. See D. 46.1.13. A mandate was a consensual agreement that did not require a stipulation. Everything could be arranged by means of letters and from a distance. It was easy to use one's right of recourse, and there was no need to fear that the *litis contestatio* would have an extinctive effect: the action on account of a loan of money and the *actio mandati contraria* were entirely separate from one another. The creditor could litigate against the surety first. The latter could then ask for cession of the claim. The benefit of division did not exist. Surety by means of a mandate also had disadvantages. It could not be linked with a novation and serve to cover old debts. Under Justinian, most of the rules pertaining to *fideiussio* – such as the benefit of division – began to apply to securities established by means of a mandate.

4. *Mutuum*

We have already mentioned *datio mutui*, the loan for consumption. *Mutuum* was a combination of mutual stipulations by means of which trade was financed. A trader asked a banker to buy corn at price X in order to sell it back to him at price Y six months later. The banker promised the trader to keep the grain available on demand and the trader promised to purchase it. They could both receive a *condictio* before the court. In Roman Antiquity minted specie was also a commodity. If the banker promised to deliver sum X on day X and the trader promised to pay sum Y in six months, they contracted a loan of money by means of *mutuum*. We do not have enough data about this method. Hopefully, new information will surface during the preparation of an edition of the clay and wax accounting tablets of two families of bankers, the Sulpicii from Puteoli and the Jucundi from Pompei.

5. From the stipulation to English contracts

In the Middle Ages, the stipulation was considered to be the principal contractual obligation. Contracts were unilateral. The glossators and commentators had no problems interpreting the texts and in the Early Modern Era, one finds that the word contract meant the same thing as in Latin. This basis of strict obligations can be found on both sides of the Channel. In the English Middle Ages, covenants and debts had begun to differ slightly from Roman Law because of the multitude of jurisdictions, but they had retained their strict character. In the sixteenth century, the contractual obligations (and the obligations arising from delict, see below) suddenly began to change radically on the Contintent. Throughout Europe, canonical law began to pervade the monarchical courts. The monarchical judges, who suddenly began to treat cases that would formerly have come before a canonical court, also adopted many principles of the canonical law of obligations. All contractual obligations now became *bona fide* obligations, formless agreements became enforceable, etcetera. In England, the consistory courts continued to function independently and coexisted with the other courts. Their highest authority was the Privy Council, while the highest authority of the other courts was the Parliament of Westminster. Because of this, the canonical law of obligations did not influence its monarchical counterpart. Henry VIII tried to acquaint the universities of Oxford and Cambridge with the heavily altered law of the Continent by financing royal chairs for Continental *ius commune*. The inns of court and the case-law, however, did not accept the fusion of civil and canon law. Obligations arising from consensual agreements, which became the rule on the early modern Continent, were not recognised by English case-law. The jurists had contracts correspond more closely to the Roman stipulation. Since that time, the general view has been that 'contract is promise'. Verbal contracts remained important in England. The medieval doctrine of the stipulation letter and written contracts was central to the development of the strict written contracts. The rules pertaining to strict verbal obligations were applied to written obligations. The problem of stipulations that benefited third parties, i.e. the problem of the relativity of obligations arising from stipulations ('privity of contract') was typical of the stipulation. However, it remained a crucial problem of the English law of obligation until circa 1650. The case-law used D. 45.1 to state that the basis of a stipulation was the promise of a benefit. Such a stipulation could only lead to a claim if the claimant had an interest in the stipulation. This rule was at the origin of the notion of consideration. Consideration was exported from the context of obligations to that of bilateral contracts because consideration was interpreted as *do ut des*, where the interest in a counterperformance was the consideration. The consequence was that two obligations were linked with one another. In the case of breach of contract, the pleas before the court treated both the substance of the promise and as well as consideration.

The fact that English contract law focused on the stipulation also had as a consequence that novation and strict suretyship remained common. English law dovetailed more closely with Greco-Roman law and England could introduce merchant banking more easily. In addition, it was easier to buy and sell contractual obligations in England. Because they used strict obligations, the English managed to conduct trade with less capital. If England acquired a unique position in the trade in both staple goods and supply contracts, this is mainly due to their preference for strict obligations. The English law of obligations was much more Roman than the Continental law of obligations, which would allow *charitas* to pervade all types of obligation.

Bibliography. – Writing about English law, and in particular comparing it to Roman law, is a delicate matter. The British Empire was more important than the Roman Empire and English jurists cannot believe that their law underwent Roman influences. Therefore, the reader should discover these influences for himself. A good introduction to the history of English private law is J.H. BAKER, *An introduction to English legal history*, London 2002.

§3. Obligations *e bona fide* (in good faith)

In the Republic the praetors introduced actions with regard to which the formula included the words *e bona fide*. They were adopted into the imperial law, among other things via the Perpetual Edict. Almost every action on account of a contract was an action *e bona fide*. In this book, obligations that were claimed *e bona fide* will be called obligations in good faith or bona fide obligations. While the English law of obligations was mainly based on Roman strict obligations, the early modern Continental law of contract was developed within the context of *bona fide* obligations.

1. Bona fide obligations in Antiquity

A. Actiones e bona fide

If a Roman judge was confronted with bona fide obligations, he first and foremost took account of the circumstances in which the obligation had arisen. Had it perhaps arisen out of deceit (*dolus malus*) or under duress (*metus*)?

Actions *e bona fide* did not only serve to bring a claim pertaining to the principal debt, but also to enforce connected committments. These were often not contained in the contract. Some general accessory obligations pertained to all obligations in good faith, such as interest in the case of late payment or compensation at the expense of the person who had executed his obligation badly (D. 19.1.1.1; D. 19.1.13.14). These aspects were part of every bona fide obligation. In the case of actions of strict law, one did not automatically have a right to interest and compensation. In the case of a *condictio*, only the market value was taken into account. Any compensation was pursued separately by means of the *actio de dolo*.

Apart from these general accessory obligations, the case-law also developed special additional obligations for each specific action. The guarantees against eviction and against hidden defects, for example, were developed in the case-law concerning a specific bona fide action, namely the *actio empti* of the buyer.

Formless ancillary agreements (*pacta adiecta*) were enforced by means of the principal action. They were presumed to be part of the principal obligation if they had been made at the same time as this principal obligation (Ulpian in D. 3.14.7.5, Papinian in D. 18.1.72*pr.*). With the *actio fiduciae*, for example, a truster could claim everything that was included in the *pactum fiduciae*. The fiduciary owner had the obligation to do everything that was mentioned in the *pactum*. The case-law enlarged the scope of the obligation so that it also included later formless ancillary agreements. Consequently, a deferment of delivery, stipulated in a consensual manner long after the principal agreement, became part of the principal obligation of the seller. A beautiful example can be found in D. 12.1.40.

According to classical case-law, the judge actually considered the entire situation between the claimant and the defendant. He also took account of other obligations be-

tween the same parties. In the case of bona fide contracts, reciprocal obligations were linked. In the context of a purchase-sale, for example, the obligation of the buyer and the obligation of the seller were different contracts, each of which was enforced with a different bona fide claim. If one of these claims was lodged, the position of the other party was also considered.

B. The exceptio doli

In the case of an *actio e bona fide*, it was possible in every stage of the lawsuit to invoke that there had been deceit. No special remedy at law was required. In the case of strict obligations, however, this was not equally evident. If a defendant wanted to invoke deceit, he had to indicate this at the preliminary hearing, where he requested the insertion of an *exceptio doli* in the *condictio* or in the *actio e stipulatu.* Once the *exceptio doli* had been granted, the judge on the merits based his judgement of stipulations and legacies *per damnationem* on the standards which he used in the case of an *actio e bona fide.* In other words: the obligation lost its strict character and was judged *e bona fide.*

The case-law about the granting of the *exceptio doli* is found in D. 44.4. D. 44.4.2 contains the case in which the exception was inserted into an *actio e stipulatu.* In the early modern *ius commune* this text was misinterpreted as indicating that the stipulation ceased to exist when the reason for stipulating no longer existed. The sentence *Si quis sine causa ab aliquo fuerit stipulatus* [...] *exceptio* [...] *doli* [...] *nocebit* was read as 'if someone had stipulated with someone else for no reason, the *exceptio doli* could be inserted' [and the stipulation was assessed *e bona fide,* so that the claim was invalidated]. *Sine causa,* however, means 'without conflict'; *ab aliquo* means 'with a third party'. Our interpretation of how this sentence was understood in Antiquity is the following. The person who requested the *exceptio doli* had not necessarily been the victim of the deceit that was invoked. This person could also request the exception when the claimant had deceived someone else, even if this victim had never brought this deceit before a court. The legal reasoning underlying this text was that deceivers and cheats should not use strict obligations. The judge examined their activities exhaustively. If the result was that they were barred from large-scale trade, it was their own fault. On this subject, see: L. WAELKENS, 'La cause de D. 44,4,2,3', in *The Legal History Review* 75 (2007), p. 199-212.

D. 44.4.2, edition by L.W. on the basis of the photographic edition of the *littera florentina.* – Palam est autem hanc exceptionem ex eadem causa propositam, ex qua proposita est de dolo malo actio. Sequitur ut uideamus in quibus causis locum habeat exceptio et quibus personis obiciatur et quidem illud adnotandum est quod specialiter exprimendum est de cuius dolo quis quiratur. Non in rem, si in ea re nihil dolo malo factum est, sed sic, si in ea re nihil dolo malo actoris factum est. Docere igitur debet is qui obicit exceptionem dolo malo

Translation L.W. – It is clear that the basis for the exception is the same type of conflict as that for which the action for deceit is granted. Subsequently, we see in which conflicts and against which parties to the proceedings the exception could be invoked. Note that the person whose deceit gives rise to the request for an exception should be mentioned explicitly. Deceit cannot be relied on against everyone (*in rem*) 'if something deceitful happened in this case', but only 'if the claimant committed deceit in this case'. The person who

actoris factum, nec sufficiet ei ostendere in re esse dolum, aut si alterius dicat dolo factum, eorum personas specialiter debebit enumerare. Dummodo hae sint quarum dolus noceat, plane ex persona eius qui exceptionem obicit in rem opponitur exceptio, neque enim quaeritur aduersus quem commissus sit dolus, sed an in ea re dolo malo factum sit a parte actoris. Circa primam speciem quibus ex causis exceptio haec locum habeat, haec sunt quae tractari possunt. Si quis sine causa ab aliquo fuerit stipulatus, deinde ex ea stipulatione experiatur exceptio utique doli mali, ei nocebit, licet enim eo tempore quo stipulabatur nihil dolo malo admiserit, tamen dicendum est eum, cum litem contestatur, dolo facere qui perseueret ex ea stipulatione petere, etsiue cum interponeretur iustam causam habuit, tamen nunc nullam idoneam causam habere uidetur, proinde et si crediturus pecuniam stipulatus est nec credidit, et si certa fuit causa stipulationis, quae tamen aut non est secuta aut finita est, dicendum erit nocere exceptionem.

raises the exception must substantiate that something happened which involved deceit on the part of the claimant. It will not suffice for him to show that deceit was involved, or if he says that something happened which involved deceit on the part of the other person, he will have to list the people who were involved one by one. As soon as it turns out that they belong to the category of people whose deceit causes damage, it is evident that the person who invokes the exception can rely on this exception in the case at hand. It is not even necessary to find out who was deceived, but only to determine whether the claimant has committed deceit in the case at hand. Regarding a first example of those conflicts in which this exception is applied, the following elements can be mentioned. If someone has stipulated with a third party without a conflict ensuing and an *exceptio doli* was then requested on account of that stipulation, it will prejudice him. Even if he had not admitted to anything deceitful at the moment of the stipulation, it will be necessary at the moment of the *litiscontestatio* to pronounce whether he who continues to claim on the basis of that stipulation does not do so in a deceitful manner. Even if his case was in order at the time when the exception was raised, he now seems to have no certainties in his case, just as if he had stipulated that he would receive money and did not receive anything and when there was certainly a conflict concerning this stipulation that was neither complied with nor terminated, it will be necessary to pronounce that the exception is prejudicial.

2. Liability for *bona fide* obligations according to the legists

The Digest contains quite a lot of casuistry about liability concerning bona fide actions. This liability differed per action. When reasoning about this, the medieval legists made use of the 'rational' method of the universities, which was originally the method of accountants (*rationales*). They searched for an order behind the old texts. The first universities had been influenced to a considerable extent by Augustinian neoplatonism and searched for the notions underlying words. Behind liability, the legists saw a kind of morality. They were influenced by the moralists and canonists, according to whom *bona fide* meant 'according to the Christian way of life'. The first universities also conceptualised and systematised Christian morality.

The civil lawyers discerned different degrees of liability for bona fide obligations. Some legal acts only caused liability in the case of *dolus*. Then, there was a series of actions where liability was triggered by *culpa*, a notion which was read as 'fault' in the Middle Ages. In the context of bona fide actions that gave rise to liability in the case of *culpa*, they discerned *culpa lata*, *culpa leuis* and *culpa leuissima*. Finally, there were *bona fide* actions in which *dolus* and *culpa* did not play a role, namely if force majeure had been proved.

A. Dolus *and* culpa lata

Dolus (deceit, conscious misbehaviour) led to liability in the context of all actions. Derogation clauses were improper and were not taken into account. Even if the performance of an obligation was impossible, the debtor remained bound if the impossibility of the prestation was due to conscious improper behaviour on his part that was contrary to *bona fides* (*dolus malus*). *Fraus omnia corrumpit*: deceit undermines everything.

In the context of some actions, the debtor only became liable if he had committed a *culpa lata*. In Antiquity, this term indicated a serious disturbance of the public order; in the Middle Ages it indicated a major fault. Such major faults occurred when a suit was brought against a mandatory (D. 17.1.29*pr.*), when a pupil used the *actio tutelae* (action for guardianship) (D. 26.7.7.2) or when a suit was brought against a depository for nothing (D. 44.7.1.5). As long as they had not displayed gross negligence or scandalous foolishness, they were not liable and the claim was rejected. What was *culpa lata*? According to the Digest, it bordered on *dolus*. Ulpian provides a description in D. 50.16.213.2: *lata culpa est nimia negligentia, idest non intelligere quod omnes intellegunt* (*culpa lata* is gross negligence, this means not understanding what everyone understands). The civil lawyers also considered *crassa et supina ignorantia* (scandalous ignorance) as *culpa lata*. Malicious intent was, in other words, not necessary, but elements that played a role in the context of *dolus* usually also applied to *culpa lata*. Both notions went down in history together. In the Justinianic texts, the difference between liability for *dolus* and liability for *culpa lata* was only found with regard to delicts. This remained the same in the early modern *ius commune*. In the case-law concerning article 1150 of the Civil code, a major fault is still put on a par with intent. In the law of Belgium, the difference was only reintroduced in the twentieth century. Major faults are insurable; deceit is not. Liability for *culpa lata* can now be explicitly excluded.

B. Culpa leuis

Most bona fide actions led to the debtor being liable if the creditor proved a *culpa leuis*. He had to show that the debtor had not paid as much attention to his obligation as was expected of a good *paterfamilias*. Attention entailed more than a simple lack of negligence. It required a positive, caring attitude (*diligentia*). According to the civil lawyers, *culpa leuis* was the common degree of liability in Roman law. In the casuistry of the *Corpus iuris*, seventeenth-century lawyers began to see a difference between *culpa leuis in abstracto* (the care of a normal good *paterfamilias*) and *culpa leuis in concreto* (the care which a certain person gave to his own goods). The latter type of liability applied in the case of the *actio pro socio*: members of a partnership had to give the same care to the partnership's goods that they would give to their own goods (D. 17.2.72). In Roman logic, this was quite evident because *socii* co-owned the goods that had been contributed to the partnership. Here, one once again sees that the different distinctions that were made during the reception go beyond the Roman law itself.

C. Culpa leuissima

In some actions, the debtor became liable if there was a lack of utmost diligence (*exactissima diligentia*). This was the case, for example, for the person who borrowed a thing for use (D. 44.7.1.5). In this context, the glossators introduced the term 'liability on account of *culpa leuissima* (most minor mistake)'.

The *Corpus iuris* includes case-law in which the debtor was held liable without having committed any attributable fault. In this context, Roman law mentioned a duty of custody (*custodia*). The debtor of an action with a duty of custody was always liable when he lost the goods that had been entrusted to him. This was the case if the *actio commodati* was brought against a person who had borrowed something for use and lost it (Gaius 3.206). The laundry shop (*fullo*) or the person who mended clothes (*sarcinator*) had a duty of custody with regard to their customers' goods. If these customers claimed their goods back with the *actio locati* (the action for outsourcing) the judge always decided in their favour if the goods had been damaged or had disappeared (Gaius 3.205). Pledgees had *custodia* of pledged property. The manager of a warehouse (*horrearius*) had *custodia* of everything that had been entrusted to him (Labeo and Javolenus in D. 19.2.60.9). Shipmasters, liverymen and innkeepers had this duty of custody with regard to goods which they had received for safekeeping (with *receptum*, a receipt) and which were claimed back with the *actio de recepto* (D. 4.9.3.1). In the *Corpus iuris* the liability of shipmasters, innkeepers and liverymen was clearly a strict liability: they were also liable for damage done to property by third parties (D. 4.9.5.1). Laundry shops were liable for damage that had occurred through no fault of their own (D. 19.2.13: mice had gnawed at the clothes). However, the civil lawyers put these cases on a par with liability for *culpa leuissima*. They had learned from the canonists and the moral philosophers that no-fault liability was impossible. Someone had always committed some minimal fault. The careful innkeeper in whose inn luggage had been damaged had certainly failed to do something that could have prevented the damage. The controversial question was whether damage to property by third parties was to be borne, just as damage caused by theft, by all debtors who had a duty of custody (D. 19.2.40-41 and D. 13.6.19).

The doctrine of the glossators was well-received. This principle of liability for a minimal mistake was maintained until the nineteenth century. Savigny was the first to ignore it. In 1838, when he was Prussia's Minister of Justice, he pushed the Railway Act through Parliament. This Act provided for strict liability for organisers of rail traffic, who had to compensate all damage caused by the organization of rail traffic even if they had not committed any fault. The same liability would then be introduced with regard to industrial accidents. Employers who made use of new techniques were liable for damage caused by industrial accidents. The role of the employee in the accident was not taken into account. Savigny asserted that this was already possible in Roman law in the case of *custodia*. The German jurists who came after him began to call this type of liability 'Custodia-Haftung'. Some Pandectists still tried to catalogue it formally as a *culpa leuissima*. They were unsuccessful: strict liability became common in the nineteenth century.

*D. Force majeure (*uis maior*)*

In the Republic, shipmasters were always fully liable for damage to or the loss of goods that had been entrusted to them. Labeo changed this. If a shipmaster was the victim of piracy or shipwreck, he was granted an exception against the *actio de recepto* of D. 4.9. This was an early evidence of the awareness that 'ships must sail', a notion which would have a determinative influence on shipping law. Society benefits from efficient shipping. Later, the scope of this exception was expanded to include hoteliers and liverymen who had lost goods because of *uis maior* (D. 4.9.3.1). In this context, the term was mainly used to indicate natural disasters. In the Justinianic collection, one can find exclusion of liability in the case of *casus* (accident), *uis maior* (force majeure) or divine power (D. 19.2.25.6). The debtor who could prove that such elements had been present, was relieved of his obligation and everyone who had suffered damage had to bear his or her own loss.

Inst. 3.14.2 compares 'force majeure' with *dolus* and *culpa*. This comparison became the point of departure for the medieval doctrine of force majeure. According to Azo, force majeure began where guilt ended. In the *ius commune*, every debtor was relieved of his obligation if he could provide evidence of force majeure.

3. The fusion of civil law and canon law in the sixteenth century

Both the civil lawyers and the canonists received the Roman law of obligations. In the sixteenth century, their two traditions were fused in the sovereign councils on the Continent. From then on, all of the Roman texts were read in a different manner. The new doctrine of the sixteenth century became the basis of the law of obligations of the late *ius commune*. In the seventeenth century, obligations became a key issue in private law, a branch of law that was on the rise. The most important innovations in the early modern *ius commune* were the generalisation of good faith, the binding character of formless agreements and the establishment of the parties' intention as the source of obligations.

Bibliography. – Franciscus VIVUS, *Communes sententiae sive opiniones iurisconsultorum e iuris casarei et pontificii fontibus haustae*, Lyon 1566 shows the reader how far the fusion of canon law and civil law in the *ius commune* had progressed by the mid-sixteenth century. On the influence of the law faculty of Leuven in this domain, see L. WAELKENS, 'Was er in de zestiende eeuw een Leuvense invloed op het Europese contractenrecht?', in. D. TILLEMAN and A. VERBEKE (eds.) *Actualia Vermogensrecht*, Bruges 2005, p. 3-16.

Notabile. – From the sixteenth century onwards, the letter 'v' was used in Latin – see the words *Vivus* and *sive*. The humanists introduced the distinction between the vowel 'u' and the consonant 'v'. The old Latins wrote u and pronounced it as 'oo'. In some combinations, like *amne aduerso*, this sounded like 'w'. In uncial script, 'u' became the lower-case letter, while 'V' became the upper-case letter. This notation is common in editions of medieval juridical manuscripts. The humanistic differentiation between 'u' and 'v' was based on the contemporary pronunciation of Latin. In *incunabula*, this difference did not exist yet. In the sixteenth century, printers designed smaller letters that could be read more quickly, required less paper and were cheaper to typeset. On this occasion, the humanists had an upper-case letter fashioned for the 'u' and a small-case letter for the 'v'. This humanistic spelling remained common in editions of medieval manuscripts in the arts, but in the field of legal history it did not.

A. Good faith in all obligations

The canonists gave the Roman *bona fides* a new meaning. *Fides* was the Latin word for faith and *e bona fide* therefore meant 'according to the Christian way of dealing with one's fellow man'. Traders could be tough in their dealings with one another, but not heartless. In the ecclesiastical courts, they were always obliged to honour *charitas*. Consequently, *bona fides* became a duty of both debtors and creditors. Among the canonists, the expression came to mean 'good faith' or, in modern terms, 'reasonableness and fairness'. It no longer encompassed the judge's task of assessing obligations on the basis of all relations between the parties involved. In the thirteenth century Hostiensis wrote that *bona fides* was the opposite of *dolus* (deceit) and that all contractual obligations had to be bona fide.

In the sixteenth and seventeenth centuries, this generalisation of good faith could be found in the case-law of the Continental sovereign councils. In civil law, good faith began to apply to all obligations. The abovementioned interpretation of D. 44.4.2.3 as indicating that the *exceptio doli* could always be inserted into the *condictio* and the *actio ex stipulatu* led to good faith also being introduced for obligations arising from stipulation.

In the seventeenth century, when private and public law became two separate branches of law, good faith, originally an element of the law of obligations, was shifted to private law. Consequently, the requirement of reliable dealings no longer played a role in relations with the monarch. The generalisation of good faith in obligations ended up in the Code civil (art. 1134, paragraph 3) via the early modern *ius commune*. All obligations must be established properly, i.e. they must be characterised by a sense of public responsibility, reasonableness and fairness. The scope of good faith remained limited to private law in the nineteenth-century civil regimes. When one had dealings with the government under private law, good faith was required, but it did not exist within the public law. One did not, for example, act in good faith towards the *fiscus*. Today, some jurists are still promoting this Christian charity in public law, i.e. in dealings with the government. Hopefully, we can also expect charity from our government in return.

B. The enforceability of formless agreements (pacta sunt seruanda)

In Antiquity, *pacta* were agreements for which no action was provided. The *sedes materiae* is D. 2.14. Formless agreements were not enforceable. Those who wanted to conclude an enforceable contract had to make use of existing means. No one was bound to an agreement if it had not been cast into an enforceable form. These forms were the nominate contracts. The medieval civil lawyers called unenforceable agreements *pacta nuda* (naked agreements).

The *Corpus iuris* nevertheless mentions some situations in which consensual agreements became enforceable, for example the abovementioned consensual accessory clauses that could be enforced by means of the principal action, such as a *pactum fiduciae* or clauses ancillary to an agreement of sale. A *pactum* also became enforceable when one of the parties had performed his prestation. According to D. 2.14, this party was awarded an *actio praescriptis uerbis* by means of which he could enforce the performance of the other party's prestation. This was an *actio utilis* that was based on similar civil claims. Consensual agreements which became enforceable in this manner were called innominate contracts (*contractus innominati*).

The Romanists also mention *pacta praetoria* as an exception to the non-enforceable formless agreements, because this term occurs in the *Corpus iuris*. If a case involved a consensual 'receipt' of an innkeeper, a liveryman or a shipmaster (*receptum cauponum, nautarum et stabulariorum*) the praetors granted a remedy, namely the *actio de recepto*, by means of which entrusted goods could always be reclaimed. This action was not related to the actions which one had against these people on the grounds of *locatio conductio*. A consensual receipt, however, was not a *pactum* in the sense of D. 2.14. The same was true of *pacta legitima*: some agreements for which the Perpetual Edict did not provide an action were declared enforceable by the prefecture, for example promises of gifts, which gave rise to a claim in Justinian's time. Such a promise was not a *pactum* in the sense of D. 2.14 either. *Pacta praetoria* and *pacta legitima* were called *pacta uestita*, 'dressed agreements', by the civil lawyers.

In ecclesiastical law, the doctrine of *pacta* was revised thoroughly. Gratian's Decree (1139-1140), cited Matthew 5.34-37: "let your yes be yes and your no no, even when you are not under oath." A lie is just as bad as a false oath. This was also an argument to make every oral promise enforceable. The moral philosophers reflected on the value of a promise. In imitation of Augustine, the scope of the rule that one was bound to promises made to God was extended to include promises between people. In the ecclesiastical courts, the situation was clear from the thirteenth century onwards: *pacta, quantumcumque nuda, sunt seruanda* (agreements, no matter how nude they are, have to be executed). This formula can be found in the Decretals of Gregory IX (X. 1.35.1) – it had been taken from the text of a council of 348. The rule that *pacta sunt seruanda* became generally accepted in the ecclesiastical law in the Middle Ages.

The civil lawyers and the delegated royal judges, however, were of a different opinion. The canonists' principle was too inconsistent with Roman law. The first royal courts that did introduce the principle were the feudal courts. In the relations between a vassal and a liegelord, loyalty to one's given word played a role and regular agreements became enforceable: 'toutes convenances sont à tenir'. In the fourteenth century the commercial courts in the south followed suit. Bartolus, Baldus, Marianus Socinus and Salycetus wrote about the binding character of consensual agreements between traders. In the sixteenth century, the fusion of civil and canon law resulted in this principle becoming prevalent. The oldest municipal laws in which one can find *pacta sunt seruanda* are the laws of Freiburg-im-Breisgau (1520). *Pacta sunt seruanda* was first mentioned as a general principle of the law of obligations by Charles Dumoulin (Molinaeus, 1500-1566), who carefully observed the case-law of the Parliament of Paris, as well as by Matthias van Wezenbeke (Wesenbecius, 1531-1586) when he taught in Wittenberg. Strikingly, both these authors were notoriously anti-Catholic. In the aldermen's court of Antwerp, *pacta sunt seruanda* was applied from 1570 onwards. By 1600, the rule had become part of the *ius commune*. This remained the case in the Code civil, which included *pacta sunt seruanda* in article 1134, first subsection.

Bibliography. – Today, the basic work on the history of *pacta sunt seruanda* is R. FEENSTRA 'Die Klagbarkeit der pacta nuda', in: R. FEENSTRA and R. ZIMMERMANN (eds.), *Das römisch-holländische Recht, Fortschritte des Zivilrechts im 17. Und 18. Jahrhundert*, Berlin 1992, p. 123-144.

C. The clausula rebus sic stantibus

The canonists and moral theologians who so cherished the given word did leave open the possibility of departing from an agreement if circumstances had changed fundamentally. The medieval canonists taught that one was only bound by an agreement as long as the circumstances did not change (*rebus sic stantibus*). Gratian included this principle in his Decree (C. 22 q. 2c. 14 § 2). He quoted Augustine, who cited Cicero concerning this matter. According to Cicero (*De officiis* 1.10.31-32 and 3.25.94-95), one did not have to do what one had promised if this was no longer useful for the other party or if fulfilment of the promise resulted in more damage to the promiser than gain for the beneficiary. According to Augustine, one did not return a sword that one had received for safekeeping if the depositor had become insane. Johannes Teutonicus wrote a singular gloss about this passage of the *Decretum Gratiani*: according to Teutonicus, one did not have to return an object when it was no longer in the same condition. He referred to D. 46.3.38, but obviously misread this text. Thomas Aquinas was also of the opinion that a person could be excused if he did not keep his promise because personal and business circumstances had changed. Bartolus introduced this doctrine of the canonists in the *ius commune*. Jason de Mayno (1435-1519) built on this to state that the clause *rebus sic stantibus* was always presumed to be included in legal provisions, wills, agreements, oaths and civic statutes on oath.

Following Thomas Aquinas, the Spanish jusnaturalists defended the *clausula rebus sic stantibus*. Because their ideas were also disseminated in South-America, the *clausula* became common in the civil law of Southern America. In the nineteenth century, it was included in most of the South-American codes of law. In the Low Countries, this clause did not take root in the law of obligations. Grotius shot this idea down: he was of the opinion that there would be no law of obligations anymore if the *clausula* was introduced in a time when all markets were volatile and all values fluctuated widely. However, according to Grotius, the *clausula rebus sic stantibus* did have a part to play in the law of nations. It is still significant in this branch of law today. From the seventeenth century onwards, the clause lost its meaning in the *ius commune*. It does not occur in the European codifications of the nineteenth century.

D. The tacit termination clause

According to article 1184 of the Civil code, a party can demand that a contract be voided if the other party does not perform its prestation (tacit termination clause). In the Roman law of Antiquity a contract could not be set aside on the ground of the other party's non-performance. If no term of execution had been stipulated, one could, however, delay one's performance until the other party offered to keep his side of the bargain. See D. 19.1.13.8 and D. 21.1.31.8. This option was adopted by the early modern *ius commune* and ended up in art. 1612 of the Code civil. The Pandectists considered this waiting as a remedy at law with a discharging effect, namely the *exceptio non adimpleti contractus*.

In title D. 12.4, which deals with innominate contracts, the civil lawyers found the *condictio ob causam datorum* (reclamation of goods that had been given on account of a legal act). If a person had executed a consensual agreement, he could claim the counterperformance by means of an *actio praescriptis uerbis*. He could also claim back his own performance by means of this *condictio*. These measures did not exist for nominate contracts. Consequently, the civil lawyers did not accept the right to rescission of the agreement in the case of a nominate contract. The canonists, however, were of the opinion that one did not have to keep one's word if one's contracting partner did not live up to his: *frangenti fidem fides frangatur eidem*. Such a rule also existed in feudal law, where loyalty to one's given word was important. In the sixteenth century this rule made its way into the civil law. According to Charles Dumoulin the rule of *frangenti fidem* should be applied to all civil contracts. In the French civil law of the Early Modern Period, this became the tacit termination clause. One could ask the judge to set aside any contract which the other party did not perform. This rescission had an *in rem* effect: if ownership had already been transferred, the party which obtained the termination of the contract received its property. This party could revendicate the good.

E. Prejudice

In CTh. 3.1.1, a precedent of Constantine's chancellery mentions that an excessively low price never led to the termination of an obligation. The medieval jurists were familiar with this text and it was reproduced in the eighth-century epitomes of Alaric's Breviary. However, the Theodosian Code was not read in the law faculties, where the civil lawyers were confronted with C. 4.44.2 (also known as the *lex secunda*). This text contains a constitution of Diocletian of 285, in which the seller of a piece of land obtained that the rescission of the sale because not even half of the land's real value had been paid. The medieval jurists considered this to be a general rule, even though the constitution was contrary to D. 4.4.16.4 and D. 19.2.22.3-23. C. 4.44.2 tallied with medieval moral theology, which featured a doctrine of *iustum pretium* (just price). Thomas Aquinas was of the opinion that every transaction had to result in an equal benefit for both parties. According to the canonists, one always had to combat *laesio enormis* (prejudice) in legal actions. They took C. 4.44.2 out of its context and began to interpret it extensively. They granted a similar right to the buyer (in the Middle Ages, a buyer was already prejudiced if he had paid fifty percent too much) and extended the scope of the doctrine of prejudice to include almost all agreements.

The civil lawyers were somewhat bothered by C. 4.44.2 and sought to limit its scope. According to them, this rule only applied if one had not known the value of the property at the time of the sale. Otherwise, it was presumed that one had donated the rest of the value. Those who contractually waived the exceptions of Roman law also lost the benefit of C. 4.44.2.

In the Early Modern Period, the canonical doctrine of prejudice and the just price ended up in the *ius commune*. This doctrine, which seemed to be an acceptable principle within the ecclesiastical courts, acted as a brake on trade in the world of rising mercantilism. The Reformed jurists in particular inveighed against the broad interpretation of this text from the Code. In some regions, the scope of C. 4.44.2 was once again limited to the sale of land from the sixteenth century onwards. Nevertheless, the spectre of the just price continued to haunt jurists. For Lessius, who attempted to bring about a smooth fusion of canon and civil law around 1600, the just price was a central theme. According to him, the just price was the market price. He reduced the theme of prejudice to deviations from the market price caused by abuse of circumstances. In the meantime, the vision that obligations arose from the intention of parties (see below) had come into vogue in the *ius commune*. Prejudice became a case of vitiated consent. It continued to annoy jurists. Christian Thomasius (Halle, 1655-1728) called the *laesio enormis* of C. 4.44.2 *aequitas cerebrina* ('false equity').

Prejudice continued to exist within the *ius commune* until the period of codification. It was adopted in several codes of law, for example in articles 1674-1685 of the Civil code, where it is limited by all of the early modern restrictions: it only applies (1) to immovable goods, (2) if the prejudice amounted to more than seven twelfths of the value and (3) if it did not benefit the buyer. Today, prejudice is only found in the civil law of a small number of countries.

F. The causality of obligations

In the Code civil, every obligation needs a lawful cause in order to be valid. This 'causality' of all obligations also stems from the law of contract of the early modern *ius commune*.

In Roman law, the word *causa* meant 'conflict', 'legal fact' or 'legal act'. In the *Hermeneumata pseudodositheana*, booklets with Greek translations of Latin terms for tourists who visited Rome in Antiquity, one can find that this *causa*-lawsuit was called *aitia* in Greek. Because Roman law only applied in the case of conflicts, a fact or an action only became a legal fact or a legal action when a conflict arose. In other words: if one spoke of a legal act, one meant a conflict. A *causa donandi* was a (conflict about a) donation; a *causa promittendi* was a stipulation; a *causa mortis* was the legal fact that a person had died; and a *condictio sine causa* was a revendication on account of the absence of a legal act. In Antiquity, the causality of obligations did not exist. The validity of obligations did not depend on a prior fact or a prior legal act.

In the twelfth century, we find the term *causa finalis* in the writings of Johannes Bassianus (†1197). Here, it still means 'ultimate legal act'. In the gl. *'Origo' ad* D. 3.1.5 one can still interpret the expression in this manner. The causality of legal acts was never a theme for the glossators. In the Great Gloss, the meaning 'legal act' is never far away when the word *causa* occurs (see for instance gl. *'Causa' ad* D. 44.4.2.3 and gl. *'Causa' ad* D. 2.14.7.4). Around 1720 Hostiensis listed all the meanings of the word *causa* in his commentary on X. 5.1.18. This commentary never even hints at the causality of obligations or a *causa* that was at the basis of the validity of legal acts. Thomas Aquinas (1225-1274) was one of the first who understood the Aristotelian *aitia* as 'cause', but the first jurist who was influenced by this particular doctrine of *causa* was Baldus (1327-1400). In the sixteenth century, after the discovery of Greek culture, everyone would be familiar with Aristotelian logic. Henceforth, *causa* clearly referred to this new notion of causality.

At the beginning of the sixteenth century, causality was not yet part of the jurists' doctrine of obligations. Nicolas Everaerts does not mention a single word about it in his writings. The introduction of causality into the field of law was connected with *pacta sunt seruanda*. When the canonists' enforceability of consensual agreements was adopted into the monarchical case-law – and for the canonists *pacta nuda* were enforceable as soon as there was proof of the agreement's existence – the Continental Reformed jurists reacted against this 'papistical' law. According to D. 2.14.7.4, a *pactum* could be enforced under Roman law by means of an *actio praescriptis uerbis* if there was a *causa*, i.e. a legal act of the party that performed his side of the agreement. The early modern jurists, however, understood *causa* as a causal link with the other party's performance. *Do ut des*, I give so that you will give – after all, every legal transaction is entered into for a reason. The Reformed jurists also began to reinterpret D. 44.4.2.3, which was henceforth read as indicating that the action of a *stipulatio sine causa* could be invalidated by means of an *exceptio doli*. What was the 'cause' of a stipulation? For them, it was a counter-performance, an economic incentive. Donellus' *Commentaria de iure civili* offered the first systematical treatment of the principles of the law of contract. In this work, the scope of the *causa* for *pacta* was extended so that *causa* began to apply to all obligations. This *causa* was the Aristotelian *aitia* of the sixteenth century. The *causa efficiens* indicated the consent at the time of the conclusion of the obligation. The *causa finalis* was the most important cause: it was the economic interest that constituted the reason why the parties entered into an obligation. If these causes were not present, obligations were not enforceable. Consent and interest were actually the 'vest' by means of which the *pactum nudum* was transformed into a *pactum uestitum* – which was enforceable under the Roman law of Antiquity.

In short, the source for the causality of obligations is Donellus. In the works of his contemporary Cujas, one cannot find any mention of this causality. After Donellus, however, this causality was a common notion in his environs. Busius still wrote that the consensual pacts of the Catholics were dangerous because they led honest people to make thoughtless concessions. The requirement of causality ensured that no one would bind himself thoughtlessly. Grotius disseminated the idea that a valid obligation required a commitment on the basis of a reasonable cause.

Because of the causality of obligations, the conclusion of a contract meant that the obligations of both parties were linked to one another. This was the beginning of our synallagmatic contracts, i.e. contracts that involve mutual obligations.

Bibliography. – L. WAELKENS, 'De oorzaak van de causaliteit bij de contractuele verbintenissen', in: D. DAUWE, B. DE GRYSE, E. DE GRYSE, B. MAES and K. VAN LINT (eds.), *Aspecten van het middeleeuwse Romeinse Recht*, Brussels 2008, p. 669-679. DONELLUS' commentary can be found in his complete works: Hugo DONELLUS, *Commentaria de iure civili*, XII, in: *Opera Omnia*, III, Rome-Macerata 1893, col. 411-756.

G. Intention as the source of liability

In Roman law, obligations only arose through consensus in the following four cases: sale-purchase, rent-lease, partnership and mandate. Mere intention or willingness never led to legal ties. A tender was not binding, unless it was couched in a *stipulatio*.

The situation was different in medieval canon law, which was influenced by theology and moral philosophy. The theologians stressed the scope of *librum arbitrium* (free choice), which was propagated by Saint Paul. On the basis of their study of Augustine's writings, they developed the idea that one had to respect one's commitments towards one's fellow man just as one had to respect one's commitments towards God. In the Carolingian penitentials, one can discover the enormous importance of intent and the assessment of intent, as well as the conviction that everyone had to keep to his decisions in 'Trau und Glauben'. According to the canonists, consensual agreements were enforceable not because of the words, but because of the commitment expressed by these words.

The civil lawyers were looking at D. 2.14.1, where Pedius saw a *conuentio* behind every contract and Ulpian explained that this was a consensus between the creditor and the debtor. In addition, this was the first text of the title *De pactis*. This consensus was, therefore, one of the elements of an obligation. Bartolus turned it into a requirement: the debtor and the creditor had to reach an agreement about the *causa* (i.e., at that time, the type of legal act). If one party was under the impression that he was merely lending the object, while the other thought it was being given to him, no obligations arose.

In the Early Modern Era, consensus suddenly took centre stage. The canonists' precedents were adopted by the royal judges and theology exerted a considerable influence on the law. Since the Middle Ages, the theologians had attached great importance to the role of intention in the establishment of liability. According to them, intentions and consensus were also important in the law, as became evident in the context of donations and wills, stipulations and pacts and even in the case of transfer of ownership. At the end of the sixteenth century the theologians were called on to undermine absolutism. An important consequence thereof was that the civil lawyers adopted the theologians' primacy of consensus. The consensual agreements of the canonists were apparently established because the debtor and the creditor reached a consensus. After all, in the case of a strict *stipulatio*, the parties agreed before they began to formalise their deal. Was this prior agreement a *pactum* and the *stipulatio* the element that turned it into a *pactum uestitum*?

Grotius, who, as a jurist, theologian and poet, was especially sensible to the undercurrents of his time, distinguished three levels of intent around 1600: (1) the mere plan, (2) the societally or ethically binding intention that did not create a right, and (3) the binding intention that shows that one wants to grant a right to another party. The primordial importance of intent became common in the *ius commune* of natural law. Intent became the constitutive element of every obligation. In seventeenth-century Continental private law, all of the problems concerning the establishment of obligations were tested against the criterion of consensus. Old elements of Roman law which had nothing to do with this were reforged on the anvil of consensus. One of the consequences thereof was the development of the doctrine of vitiated consent. Deceit and violence, which had been aspects of the *exceptio doli* and the *exceptio metus*, and of the *actio de dolo* and the *actio quod metus causa*, respectively, suddenly became facets of the absence of consent. Error, a notion that originally concerned the specificity of a good that had been bought or sold, became a matter of vitiated consent. Even prejudice, which had been developed on the basis of the *lex secunda*, became a matter of vitiated consent in the seventeenth century. This is typical of the Continental law of obligations and contracts. Continental civil law has unambiguously opted for this type of law of obligations: see the case-law about article 1101 of the Code civil. In the eighteenth and nineteenth centuries, the English law of contracts was influenced by the *ius commune*, especially through the English translation of Pothier's work. The main reason for this influence was the facilitation of trade with Europe. It is comparable to the China's current reception of Western contract law for the purpose of furthering business relations. Nevertheless, freedom of consensus was not received in England. Keep this in mind when conversing with English jurists or when dealing with areas of law that are based on Anglo-American law.

From the sixteenth century onwards, all texts of Roman law were reinterpreted from the perspective of the freedom of choice of the *ius commune*. The jusnaturalists and the Pandectists considered the statement of intention as a central element of Roman law. The formal appearance of a legal act did not have any value in itself. It only had value as a declaration of intention. From Roman law, these jurists distilled a doctrine for interpreting legal acts. In this doctrine, declarations of intent became the building blocks of legal acts. What was the prevailing element when the declaration was open to more than one interpretation? In the dilemma between the theory of intent and the theory of declaration, the Pandectists usually opted for the supremacy of intent. Because the law of obligations only developed out of the Roman law at a late stage and these interpretations are so recent, the 'Roman' law concerning obligations sounds familiar to twenty-first-century Romanists. Many of them have no qualms about reading things in the *Corpus iuris* that are not really there. Does this mean that the current law of obligations is not, as everyone claims, Roman? No: it is Roman, but Roman law is reception.

Conclusion

Until well into the sixteenth century, all of the European countries seemed to be receiving the Roman law of obligation in a similar manner. The adoption of canon law into royal law on the European Continent but not in England had a determinative effect on the early modern *ius commune*. Consequently, bona fide obligations were brought to prominence together with the canonical interpretation of *bona fides*. In the early modern *ius commune*, Roman texts were reread and reinterpreted from this perspective. This explains why the Roman law of obligation seems so pleasant to Continentals. And why they think that, if the Anglo-American law of obligations is so different, it certainly does not derive from the Roman law... It is lucky that the Anglo-American jurists are proud of the 'indigenous' origins of their law of obligations.

§4. Obligations arising from delict

With regard to obligations arising from delict, Gaius and Justinian mention four actions in their Institutes: the *actio furti* (action for theft), the *actio legis aquiliae* (for damage), the *actio iniuriarum* (for injury and insult) and the *actio ui raptorum bonorum* (for robbery with violence). These are examples of actions which were granted in the civil law on account of facts.

1. Retaliatory actions

The actions for theft and *iniuria* already occurred in the Twelve Tables. In other words, they were part of civil law and not of criminal law. In the army, criminal law played a role when troops were endangered or discipline was undermined. These issues fell under the jurisdiction of the consuls. Behaviour that was detrimental to camaraderie among soldiers, however, was brought before the praetor and was a matter of civil law. When they got out of hand, conflicts concerning this camaraderie were dealt with during a formula procedure. The praetor imposed fines and withdrew civil rights. The formula did not provide for a compensation but for a retribution, a private punishment. Nevertheless, it was a civil law matter: the judgement was not pronounced by the army, but by a judge chosen by the parties.

In the civil law, the praetors developed this retaliation by providing 'penal' actions, of which there were a large number. By means of *actiones populares, ciues* could demand retribution from someone whose behaviour had annoyed them even though it had not harmed them. Every *ciuis* could, for example, summon a desecrator of graves before a judge, demand a civil fine from him and keep the money – if he won the case. When a *ciuis* saw that a person who was younger than twenty-five was deceived in public, he could claim a private fine from the deceiver by means of the *actio legis laetoriae* (192 BC). Other retaliatory actions could only be brought by the victims. Victims of extortion could be granted an *actio quod metus causa*, by means of which they could claim four times the extorted amount. The *actio ui raptorum bonorum* (the claim that was used in the case of violent robbery) was brought against every participant in an armed robbery and led to a private fine amounting to four times the value of the stolen goods. See D. 47.8.

A retaliatory action that would become important in the history of law was the *actio iniuriarium*. The word *iniuria* indicated any kind of unlawful conduct (D. 47.10.1). In the Twelve Tables, this was mentioned as a delict. *Iniuria* carried a fine of twenty-five asses. Centuries later, however, twenty-five asses was peanuts. Aulus Gellius, *Noctes Atticae* XX.1.13 recounts how a certain Veratius cuffed people in the street and had his slave pay each victim twenty-five asses. The plural *iniuriae* also included assault and battery. The breaking of bones by hand or with a stick carried a fine of three hundred asses if the victim was a free man and a fine of one hundred and fifty asses if the victim was a slave. The fine for the breaking of limbs was *talio*, as we have already seen above. In classical law, the *actio iniuriarium* was developed as a remedy at law that served as a retaliation for insults and injuries inflicted on a free person. The most important precedents concerning this action were collected in D. 47.10. Any injury that was illegally inflicted on a free man (this did not include self-defence or injuries incurred during a competition) gave rise to the *actio iniuriarum*, which was also granted in the case of insult, conscious defamation of someone else's character through self-satisfaction (the Greek *hubris*) beyond the level of tolerance (the former *iniuria*). At a certain time, even sureties received the *actio iniuriarum* against creditors who had sued them lightly (D. 47.10.19). The judge could freely determine the fine. Other than in the case of the *actio furti* and the *actio legis Aquiliae*, the damage was not a criterion (D. 47.10.17.2). The *actio iniuriarum* was exclusively penal, and was neither actively nor passively inheritable.

In the *ius commune* the *actio iniuriarum* was often used to retaliate manslaughter, assault and battery. The intent to insult was often presumed. The judge was free to determine the retaliation: the action led to an 'amende profitable'. This is the reason why, in the Middle Ages, people against whom an *actio iniuriarum* could be brought first tried to agree upon a reconciliatory amount in a settlement. In some medieval courts, the rates for retaliation were fixed. A famous example can be found in the laws of Aethelberth of Kent (601-604), which list retaliatory amounts. In the Low Countries, the action for injuries existed until well into the eighteenth century. It was used for both injuries and defamation of character. In American law, the reception of this action still plays a role, for example in the remedies at law that lead to car manufacturers paying millions of dollars to victims of accidents caused by construction defects, or tobacco producers paying equally large sums to surviving relatives of victims of lung cancer.

For the canon lawyers, retaliation was unacceptable because of the Biblical precept 'do no repay evil with evil'. For them, the key points were restitution and compensation. Because of their influence on the Continental law, retaliatory actions disappeared from the *ius commune* in the Early Modern Era. The canon lawyers also introduced the notion of guilt for all obligations arising from delict. For them, there was no liability without moral error, as we will see below.

Gratiani Decretum, C. 12 q. 2 c. 11 §1 – Addis etiam, quo augmento ea, quae furto de ecclesia abstulerunt, reddere debeant. Sed absit ut ecclesia cum augmento recipiat quod de terrenis rebus uidetur amittere et lucra de damnis quaerere.

You also ask with which additional charge they have to return what they took by theft from the churches. However, it should under no circumstances happen that the church receives back the earthly goods which it has lost with an additional charge and that she looks to derive profit from its damage.

Idem, C. 14 q. 6 c. 1. – Penitentia non agitur, si aliena res non restituatur. Si res aliena, propter quam peccatum est, cum reddi possit et non redditur, non agitur poenitentia, sed fingitur. Si autem ueraciter agitur, non remittitur peccatum, nisi restituatur ablatum, sed, ut dixi, cum restitui potest.

If another person's good with regard to which a sin has been committed can be returned and this does not happen, no remorse is shown. Instead, there is dissimulation. If the sinner acts sincerely, the sin is not forgeven anyway if, as I have already said, it is possible to return the good.

X. 5.36.9. – Si culpa tua datum est damnum uel iniuria irrogata, seu aliis irrogantibus, opem forte tulisti, aut haec imperitia tua siue euenerunt, iure super his satisfacere te oportet; nec ignorantia te excusat, si scire debuisti, ex facto tuo iniuriam uerisimiliter posse contingere uel iacturam [...].

If damage (*damnum*) or an insult (*iniuria*) has been inflicted on someone through your fault, or if you have helped others to do this – irrespective of whether it happened because of your incomepetence or negligence, you are legally required to give satisfaction and your ignorance does not exonerate you if should have known that your acts could propably result in injustice or harm.

2. The *actio furti* (theft)

Furtum is defined in D. 47.2.1.3: *furtum est contrectatio rei fraudulosa lucri faciendi gratia uel ipsius rei uel etiam usus eius possesionisue* (theft is the deceitful material appropriation of a good with the intent of benefitting either from the good itself, or from the use or possession thereof). Theft of use was, in other words, also punished. The Digest provides examples like the use of beasts of burden for a journey that was longer than that for which they had been rented. See Inst. 4.1.1. The definition of D. 17.2.1.3 which included theft of use was used in Germany until the nineteenth century in the context of the *condictio ex causa furtiua*, the private revendication of a stolen good. According to article 461 of the Belgian Criminal code, theft is the deceitful removal of a good that belongs to someone else, even if this good is only removed for use for a brief period. The latter element was added in 1964.

Furtum was dealt with by means of the *actio furti*. Traditionally, there was an important difference between *furtum manifestum* (when the thief was caught red-handed) and *furtum nec manifestum* (when the thief was not caught red-handed). The *actio furti manifesti* was used to claim a fine amounting to four times the value of the stolen good. According to the Law of the Twelve Tables 8.12, *furtum manifestum* was a *crimen capitale* which carried the punishment of *capitis diminutio*, i.e. a reduction of the thief's status of freedom. 'Red-handed' meant 'in public', or 'witnessed by enough people to be considered to be generally known'. A thief was still considered to have been caught red-handed if he was caught after a chase or during the search of a house into which he had fled. From the Twelve Tables onwards, the victim of a thief who had not been caught red-handed was only granted twice the value of the stolen goods. Providing proof was much more difficult in such cases. The victim had to substantiate that the thief had had the intention of illegally retaining the good or its use for himself.

This distinction between *furtum manifestum* and *furtum nec manifestum* would have important consequences in the history of law. In the classical era, the criterion for red-handedness was notorious proof, against which no appeal was possible. This rule was received. In some countries, there is still no possibility of appeal in the case of red-handedness. Consider, for example, the 'procédure des flagrants délits' in France, which also applies if the offender confesses. Another example is the punishment of crimes committed during a court session in Belgium. If offenders are caught in the act, there is no need for an investigation. This means also that it is impossible (for members of parliament, diplomats) to invoke immunity.

In the classical era, the *actio furti* was not only used to deal with non-red handed theft. The conscious acceptance of an undue payment was also considered theft (D. 13.1.18), as was the conscious retaining of goods that had been entrusted to one (D. 47.2.52.7). In the post-classical period, it became possible to bring the *actio furti* against those who handled stolen property or hid the perpetrator and the loot (C. 6.2.14). *Furtum* also included the illegal use of someone else's property (*furtum usus*, for example the hiring out of a horse that was stabled under one's custody).

The *actio furti nec manifesti* was originally reserved for the owner of the stolen goods. However, in the first century BC, this action was already awarded to anyone who had an interest in the non-disappearance of the good. This meant that the pledge creditor was granted the *actio furti* even in the case of a pledge without transfer. This was called *furtum possessionis*. In the classical law, there was a controversy about whether the pledge creditor could claim twice the value of the good or twice the value of the debt. The *actio furti* was also granted to those who had *custodia* of a good. However, if this person was insolvent, it was the owner who was granted the *actio furti*, not the custodian. This action was not granted to the ordinary creditors of a bankrupt company:

although these certainly had an interest in the debtor's assets remaining intact, they did not receive an *actio furti* if these goods were stolen.

The *actio furti* was a purely penal action: it was merely retaliatory. The entitled party could combine it with a remedy at law in order to get his good back. The owner could revendicate his good from the thief and from anyone who had acquired his good, while the possessor could combine the *actio furti* with his interdict. The owner was also granted a *condictio furtiua* against the thief himself, an action on account of unjust enrichment through theft (see below). It was, of course, impossible to combine two actions that aimed at the restoration of the assets of the claimant. The *exceptio longissimi temporis* could not be inserted into such actions. The revendication did not lapse (this can be derived from C. 9.37.8). But what about third-party acquirers – was there a time limit for claims against them? Such a limit for claims against *bona fide* third-party acquirers appeared for the first time in canon 39 of the Fourth Vatican Council (1215). From then on, the *ius commune* began to accept the opinion that a bona fide third-party acquirer of a stolen good had to be compensated. In the Early Modern Era, this rule was generally accepted in the *ius commune*. See article 2279 of the Civil code.

The *actio furti* was not admissible when brought by one spouse against the other if the couple was divorced or about to divorce. If one spouse withheld or alienated goods in the classical period, the praetor granted another action aimed at the restoration of assets, namely the *actio rerum amotarum* (the action for alienated goods), which became a penal action in the post-classical period.

In D. 47.2.93 one can read that theft was usually prosecuted *criminaliter* in Ulpian's day, which means that it came under criminal law. At that time, criminal law was part of the imperial law. Charges for theft were brought before an imperial judge, who started a *cognitio extra ordinem* with a governmental summons if appropriate. Nevertheless, the purely civil action still existed under Justinian. The *actio furti noxalis*, the action which was brought against a *paterfamilias* if his slave committed a theft, was also retained under Justinian. The bishops encouraged public prosecution. Christians were were advised not to make use of civil retaliatory actions.

In the Middle Ages, theft was dealt with by the higher (sovereign) justice. In towns and fiefs, the delegation of jurisdiction to feudal lords determined who prosecuted theft in which region. This was decided in the statute that was agreed on with the monarch. In the towns and fiefs which had not received higher jurisdictions, lawsuits concerning theft were brought before the representative of the monarch (reeve, bailiff). In some regions, the *actio furti* was still brought civilly.

The canon lawyers thought that theft had to be prosecuted publicly and that there was always a duty of restoration or reparation. This was derived from Augustine's idea that the sin of theft could not be forgiven if the stolen goods were not returned. This claim for the return of stolen goods was heritable both actively and passively. In the Netherlands, theft would never be considered as a private law matter after the *constitutio criminalis carolina* of 1532. In the Early Modern Period, all of the Continental royal councils adopted this canonical theory. The Spanish jurist Antonio Gomez (1501 – before 1572) was the first to defend that the private claim for restitution or compensation should be treated by the same judge as the criminal prosecution. In the early modern *ius commune* this led to the possibility of joining criminal proceedings as a civil party.

3. The *actio legis aquiliae* (torts)

Among their delictual actions, Gaius and Justinian mention the *actio legis aquiliae* to compensate damage.

The *lex aquilia* was enacted by plebiscite in 286 BC. It was on the grounds of this text that the praetors included the *actio legis aquiliae*, the aquilian action, in their edict. The case-law concerning this action was collected in D. 9.2, which is perhaps the most famous title of the Digest. In Antiquity, the *actio legis aquiliae* could be combined with other actions, such as claims arising from a contract, but not with other penal or repersecutory actions. Originally, the *actio legis aquiliae* would have led to retaliation; later it resulted in compensation. In the classical period, compensation became the most important aspect of this action, but it would have a retaliatory effect as well: if the defendant denied his guilt and it was established that he was the perpetrator, he had to pay twice the damage (*infitiando lis crescit in duplum*). This retaliatory aspect, which could not be inherited passively, disappeared entirely when the Roman law was received. Because of its mainly compensatory character, the *actio legis aquiliae* was easily brought into conformity with the ecclesiastical law and moral theology, which combatted every form of revenge or expiatory sums of money. This is why the *actio legis aquiliae* would form the basis of the early modern non-contractual law of compensation. Below, we will see that some aspects of the private fine were reintroduced in another way, namely through the compensation of immaterial or moral damages (compensation for pain and suffering).

Between Antiquity and the Early Modern Era, the aquilian liability, originally a closed and limited action, became a general, open action with liability for all damage done. The parallelism with *pacta sunt seruanda* (formless agreements are enforceable as well) is striking.

A. The contents of the lex aquilia

D. 9.2 teaches us that in Antiquity, the *lex aquilia* contained several chapters. Only the first and third of these are mentioned in D. 9.2. According to the first chapter, a person who illegally killed someone else's cattle or slaves had to pay the injured party the greatest value which the slaves or the cattle had been worth in the past year (D. 9.2.2*pr.*). This rule was inspired by the seasonality of prices. Even if the value of the cattle or the slave in question had diminished before the illegal killing, the greatest value in the past year had to be paid. The third chapter dealt with the burning, breaking or destroying of other property (*urere, frangere, rumpere*, D. 9.2.27.5). In such cases the greatest damage which the owner had incurred in the thirty days around the damaging of the property had to be compensated. According to some Romanists, these thirty days were the days before the damaging of the property, in analogy with the year in the first chapter; according to others, they were the thirty days after the damaging of the property, so that consequential damage was also included. This is all that the classical jurists knew about the old *lex aquilia*. Everything else that can be read in D. 9.2 is case-law about these scanty data.

B. Extension through the broad interpretation of principal conditions

In D. 9.2 *de lege aquilia* one discovers the power of a legal system without a legislator. On the basis of the limited data of the original *lex aquilia,* case-law created a magnificent institution.

In the classical period, the *actio legis aquiliae* was used to compensate all material damage that had been illegally caused by someone's actions. The medieval civil lawyers summarised these principal conditions of D. 9.2 in the expression *damnum corpore corpori iniuria datum.* Each of these elements was the subject of case-law, which was seized upon by jurists as a means of extending the scope of the *lex aquilia*:

- *damnum*: the classical jurists interpreted *urere, frangere, rumpere* broadly so that it applied not only to cattle and slaves, but also to other goods. *Rumpere* did not have to take the form of brutal destruction: a depreciation of the object's value sufficed. In this manner, the scope of the *lex aquilia* was expanded to include all damage to property. Then, this notion of damage itself was extended. Initially, only the market value of the damaged good or slave was taken into account. From Salvius Julianus onwards, the injured party's interests were taken into consideration as well. Consequently, damage that was incurred because one did not have an object anymore was also eligible for compensation. The person who had killed one race horse out of a team of four not only had to repay the horse itself, but also had to compensate the loss of value to the team (Inst. 4.2.10). It was not only the direct damage, but also the consequential damage that was taken into account.
- damage to property: the medieval Romanists called this *damnum in corpus datum* (damage done to a body); the humanists called it *damnum corpori datum.* In Antiquity and the Middle Ages, the point of departure of the action was material damage. In the case of such damage, one was also eligible for compensation for a loss of interest or for consequential damage. It was impossible to rely on the *lex aquilia* for every financial loss that was caused illegally. This was a sixteenth-century development.
- a perpetrator's actions (*damnum corpore datum*): this implied physical contact. According to the Roman sources, negligence or indirect damage did not give rise to the aquilian claim. In Gaius, we read that in his day, the perpetrator's actions could consist exclusively of words, for example if he persuaded someone to do something (Gaius 3.219; Inst. 4.3.16). In the late Empire, the judge sometimes granted an *actio legis aquiliae utilis* or *in factum* in the case of negligence or indirect damage (for example D. 9.2.7.8 and D. 9.2.8*pr.* about a doctor who neglected to follow up his patient properly after a successful operation).
- a close link between the perpetrator's actions and the damage: originally, this link had to be fairly direct. The person who cut the mooring rope of a ship only had to pay for the rope. This direct connection, however, came to be interpreted more and more broadly. In the classical period, the case-law already awarded an *actio in factum* based on the *lex aquilia* in order to allow a victim to claim compensation for the damage to a ship and its cargo that was caused because someone had cut the mooring rope (D. 9.2.29.5). Someone who incited a slave to dangerous actions which led to the slave's death had caused damage directly (Gaius 3.219).
- *iniuria* (unlawfulness): originally, this meant *dolus* (malice). In the case of an unfortunate accident, there was no *actio legis aquiliae.* Relatively soon, however,

liability for *culpa* (a non-permitted breach of the public peace) was introduced alongside liability for *dolus*. D. 9.2 makes it clear that negligence and carelessness played a part in the *actio leges aquilia*. According to Ulpian (in D. 9.2.44*pr.*), aquilian liability applied in the case of a *culpa leuissima* if a slave intentionally killed or caused damage with the knowledge of his master. In the Middle Ages, *culpa leuissima* became the norm and was understood in the same manner as in the context of contractual liability. Error, guilt and sin consequently played a role in aquilian liability. This explains why moral philosophers also treated this subject.

The jurists found another possibility to extend the scope of the *actio legis aquiliae*: the beneficiaries of this action. Originally, this action was only awarded to the owner. In the classical Roman law, this was extended to certain possessors, like the usufructuary and the usucapient. The *Corpus iuris* also mentions the borrower for use and the pledgee, but apparently they did not always receive the action. There was no clear link with the *custodia*.

Inst. 4.3.16. – Ceterum placuit, ita demum ex hac lege actionem esse, si quis praecipue corpore suo damnum dederit, ideoque in eum qui alio modo damnum dederit, utiles actiones dari solent: ueluti si quis hominem alienum aut pecus ita incluserit ut fame necaretur, aut iumentum tam uehementer egerit ut rumperetur, aut pecus in tantum exagitauerit ut praecipitaretur, aut si quis alieno seruo persuaserit ut in arborem ascenderet uel in puteum descenderet, et is ascendendo uel descendendo aut mortuus fuerit aut aliqua parte corporis laesus erit, utilis in eum actio datur. Sed si quis alienum seruum de ponte aut ripa in flumen deiecerit et is suffocatus fuerit, eo quod proiecerit corpore suo damnum dedisse non difficiliter intellegi poterit ideoque ipsa lege aquilia tenetur. Sed si non corpore damnum fuerit datum neque corpus laesum fuerit, sed alio modo damnum alicui contigit, cum non sufficit neque directa neque utilis aquilia, placuit eum qui obnoxius fuerit in factum actione teneri: ueluti si quis, misericordia ductus, alienum seruum compeditum soluerit, ut fugeret.

Translation MOYLE. – It is held that a direct action lies under this statute only when the body of the offender is substantially the instrument of mischief. If a man occasions loss to another in any other way, a modified action will usually lie against him; for instance, if he shuts up another man's slave or quadruped, so as to starve him or hit to death, or drives his horse so hard as to knock him to pieces, or drives his cattle over a precipice, or persuades his slave to climb a tree or go down a well, who, in climbing the one or going down the other, is killed or injured in any part of his body, a modified action is in all these cases given against him. But if a slave is pushed off a bridge or bank into a river, and there drowned, it is clear from the facts that the damage is substantially done by the body of the offender, who is consequently liable directly under the lex Aquilia. If damage be done, not by the body or to a body, but in some other form, neither the direct nor the modified aquilian action will lie, though it is held that the wrongdoer is liable to an action on the case; as, for instance, where a man is moved by pity to loose another's slave from his fetters, and so enables him to escape.

C. Extension in the case of the injuring or killing of free people

The *lex aquilia* did not contain any remedies at law that could be taken in the case of the injuring or killing of free people. For such cases, the *actio iniuriarum* was used.

In *Collatio* 1.11.2 we read that in a case concerning a deadly accident the court of appeal of Cordoba granted a compensation to the surviving relatives. The judgement, however, does not mention a legal basis. In the classical period such a compensation could not be claimed by means of an aquilian action. The aquilian action led to the payment of market value. D. 9.2 repeatedly states that the body of a free person could not be valued in financial terms and that, therefore, no compensation could be paid for damage to a body. In D. 9.2.5.3 and 9.2.6-7*pr.*, however, an important amendment to this principle was found. A free apprentice had become blind because of a blow which his master had dealt him. The boy's *paterfamilias* claimed compensation by means of the *actio legis aquiliae*. The medical costs did have a market value and could therefore be claimed back. The *paterfamilias* pleaded that his *familia* suffered a loss of income because the boy would not be able to work for his *familia* for some years and that this too had a market value. The judge ruled in favour of the *paterfamilias*. D. 9.2.13*pr.* contains a sentence by Ulpian that would have far-reaching consequences in the Middle Ages: a free man has an *actio legis aquiliae utilis* for himself; but he does not have the direct action because no one is considered to be the owner of his limbs.

From title D. 9.2 medieval jurists derived the rule that the killing and injuring of free people led to aquilian compensation. Not only D. 9.2.5.3 and D. 9.2.13*pr.* played a role in this context: so did D. 9.2.7.4, in which it can be read that gladiators – who were free people according to this text – were liable under the *lex aquilia* if they killed an opponent who had ceased fighting. The civil lawyers read the latter two texts as if the claim was brought by the victim himself or by his surviving relatives. These texts were extremely important because they allowed for the awarding of compensation in the case of bodily injury, so that it was no longer necessary to fall back on the retaliatory action on account of injuries. Which compensations could free people receive if they made use of the compensatory *actio legis aquiliae*? Apparently, they could receive compensation for medical costs and loss of income. Roffredus Benventanus (in Bologna until 1215) developed the latter aspect further in his *Libelli iuris ciuilis*. He extended 'loss of income' to include the income lost by surviving relatives when the victim died. The victim's life expectancy was found in Ulpian's life table (D. 35.2.68*pr.*), which was usually used to calculate superannuation schemes. The number of years which the victim had left to live were multiplied by his income. Roffredus' passage was included in Guillaume Durand's *Speculum iudiciale* and was thus disseminated widely. The moral theologians, however, found the new calculation inequitable. According to them, the lost income of a deceased person did not have to be paid to his heirs, especially not when they inherited the victim's sources of income. The criterion was that the person was dependent on the deceased and became needy because of the loss of income. For Thomas Aquinas, the judge only had to take the circumstances and the wealth – or poverty – of the parties into account when calculating the compensation on account of the injuring or killing of a person. Under the influence of Spanish scholastics, the jurists of natural law adopted the idea that it were not the heirs who had a right to compensation, but the people whose livelihood was threatened.

The importance of this discussion was that one could ignore the retaliatory *actio iniuriarum* and opt instead for the compensatory *actio legis aquiliae* if a free person was injured or killed.

How long did one still have to live according to the Roman law of Antiquity?

D. 35.2.68*pr.* – Computationi in alimentis faciendae hanc formam esse Vlpianus scribit, ut a prima aetate usque ad annum uicesimum quantitas alimentorum computetur eiusque quantitates falcidia praestetur, ab annis uero uiginti usque ad annum uicesimum quantum annorum uiginti octo, ab annis uiginti quinque usque ad annos triginta annorum uiginti quinque, ab annis triginta usque ad annos triginta quinque annorum uiginti duo, ab annis triginta quinque usque ad annos quadraginta annorum uiginti. Ab annis quadraginta usque ad annos quinquaginta tot annorum computatio fit, quot aetati eius ad annum sexagesimum deerit remisso uno anno: ab anno uero quinquagesimo usque ad annum quinquagesimum quintum annorum nouem, ab annis quinquaginta quinque usque ad annum sexagesimum annorum septem, ab annis sexaginta, cuiuscumque aetatis sit, annorum quinque. Eoque nos iure uti Ulpianus ait et circa computationem ususfructus faciendam. Solitum est tamen a prima aetate usque ad annum trigesimum computationem annorum triginta fieri, ab annis uero triginta tot annorum computationem inire, quot ad annum sexagesimum deesse uidentur. Numquam ergo amplius quam triginta annorum computatio initur. Sic denique et si rei publicae usus fructus legetur, siue simpliciter siue ad ludos, triginta annorum computatio fit.

Translation SCOTT. – Ulpianus says that the following rule should be adopted in making the estimate of maintenance to be furnished. The amount bequeathed to anyone for this purpose from the first to the twentieth year is computed to have lasted for thirty years, and the Falcidian portion of that sum shall be reserved. From twenty to twenty-five years, the amount is calculated for twenty-eight years, from twenty to thirty years, the amount is calculated for twenty-five years; from thirty to thirty-five years, the amount is calculated for twenty-two years, from thirty to forty years, it is computed for twenty years; from forty to fifty years, the computation is made for as many years as the party lacks of the sixtieth year after having omitted one year; from the fiftieth to the fifty-fifth, the amount is calculated for nine years; from the fifty-fifth to the sixtieth year, it is calculated for seven years; and for any age above sixty, no matter what it may be, the computation is made for five years. Ulpianus also says that we use this same rule in making the calculation with reference to the legacy of an usufruct. Nevertheless, it is the practice for the computation to be made for thirty years from the first to the thirtieth, but after the age of thirty years it is made for as many years as the legatee lacks of being sixty; hence the computation is never made for a longer time than thirty years. Finally, in like manner, the computation is made for the period of thirty years, where the usufruct of property is bequeathed to the State, either simply, or for the purpose of celebrating games.

D. The aquilian claim and unjust enrichment

'Unjust enrichment' also played a part in the evolution from the *lex aquilia* to the general action for damage which we know from the early modern *ius commune*.

For the glossators, the aquilian claim of D. 9.2 only played a role in the case of material damage. They struggled with the issue of compensation for bodily injuries inflicted on free people, but in the case of mere damage to the body they repeated the rule that body parts did not have a market value. The medieval moral theologians, however, linked the issue of damage to the body with the abovementioned duty of restitution and their notion of guilt (which we will treat below). For them, there was liability only in the case of *iniuria*, this *iniuria* was a *culpa* and *culpa* was a sin. Because sins could not be forgiven without reparation, i.e. without 'restitution', the extinguishing of the aquilian claim depended on the compensation. For the canon lawyers, this notion of restitution was a general tenet of delictual liability, which they also took into account in the context of unjust enrichment. This is why they connected both tenets with one another.

The civil lawyers were familiar with unjust enrichment from two passages from the *Corpus iuris*:

D. 50.17.206. – Iure naturae aequum est neminem cum alterius detrimento et iniuria fieri locupletiorem.	According to the law on which everyone can count because of his birth, it seems good administration of justice that no one becomes richer because of some one else's impoverishment and by acting against the law.
D. 12.6.14. – Nam hoc natura aequum est neminem cum alterius detrimento et fieri locupletiorem.	For it is equitable in the world of the living that no one is enriched by the damage he inflicts on another. [*Iniuria* is not mentioned here].

The civil lawyers then proceeded to link unjust enrichment with undue payment. In Roman law, there were a series of remedies at law that served to claim back undue payments. A good that had been transferred without a *causa* (legal act) was reclaimed by means of the *condictio indebiti* (revendication on account of undue payment, D. 12.6) or by means of the *condictio sine causa* (revendication because the prior legal act had not taken place, D. 12.17). If the payment was intended, but the legal act (i.e. the *causa*) did not take place, there was a *condictio causa data causa non secuta*. If it turned out that the *causa* was unlawful, the praetor granted a *condictio ob turpem causam*. Withholding an undue payment was seen as a *furtum* (D. 13.1.18). The glossators discussed the prohibition of enrichment together with the issue of undue payment. They saw this as a reason to interpret these *condictiones* broadly and established links with both the *actio de in rem uerso* (action to revendicate the enrichment) and the *actio negotiorum gestorum*. The latter action was used by authorised agents to revendicate costs about which no agreement was made, but which would result in an unjust enrichment of the beneficiary of the *negotiorum gestio*. Martinus de Gosia was the only glossator who pointed out that the duty of returning an unjust enrichment was a separate obligation, and not a principle to explain other obligations.

The canon lawyers emphasised the connection between undue payment and theft in Roman law. They interpreted theft from the perspective of the seventh commandment. In addition, they connected this with the abovementioned opinion of Augustine that no theft could be forgiven without restitution, extending this rule to include unjust enrichment as well as the reparation of damage. This amalgam was then developed into a theory about *aequalitas* and *inaequalitas*, i.e. distributive justice with its principle of equality which was disturbed by unjustified imbalances, or, according to the Dutch terminology of Grotius 'onevenheden' ('unevennesses'). For the thirteenth-century canon lawyer Hostiensis, *aequalitas* was still a principle of procedure which had nothing to do with compensations for bodily injury. In the text cited below, his contemporary Thomas Aquinas already assigns great importance to this disturbance of balance. He associates the duty of restitution with unjust enrichment and theft and, at the end of the fragment, with the compensation for bodily injury. With regard to this issue, moral philosophy would influence canon law. The Spanish Scholastics also integrated unjust enrichment and the disturbance of balance in their vision of aquilian liability.

THOMAS AQUINAS, *Summa Theologiae*, II IIae q. 62 art. 2 ad secundum. – Videtur quod non sit necessarium ad salutem quod fiat restitutio eius quod ablatum est [...]. Sed contra est quod Augustinus dicit: non dimittitur peccatum nisi restituatur ablatum. Respondeo: dicendum quod restitutio, sicut dictum est, est actus iustitiae commutatiuae, quae in quadam aequalitate consistit. Et ideo restituere importat redditionem illius illius rei quae iniuste ablata est: sic enim per iteram eius exhibitionem aequalitas reparatur. Si uero iuste ablatum sit, inaequalitate erit ut ei restituatur: quia iustitia in aequalitate consistit. Cum igitur seruare iustitiam sit de necessitate salutis, consequens est quod restituere id quod iniuste ablatum est alicui, sit de necessitate salutis. [...] Quando id quod est ablatum non est restituibile per aliquid aequale, debet fieri recompensatio qualis possibilis est. Puta, cum aliquis alicui abstulit membrum, debet ei recompensare uel in pecunia uel in aliquo honore, considerata conditione utriusque personae, secundum arbitrium probi uiri.

Translation FATHERS OF THE ENGLISH DOMINICAN PROVINCE, www.gutenberg.org. – It would seem that it is not necessary to restore what has been taken away. [...] On the contrary, Augustine says (Ep. ad Maced. cxliii): 'Unless a man restore what he has purloined, his sin is not forgiven.' I answer that, Restitution as stated above is an act of commutative justice, and this demands a certain equality. Wherefore restitution denotes the return of the thing unjustly taken; since it is by giving it back that equality is reestablished. If, however, it be taken away justly, there will be equality, and so therewill be no need for restitution, for justice consists in equality. Since therefore the safeguarding of justice is necessary for salvation, it follows that it is necessary for salvation to restore what has been taken unjustly. [...] Wherefore when that which has been taken cannot be restored in equivalent, compensation should be made as far as possible: for instance if one man has deprived another of a limb, he must make compensation either in money or in honor, the condition of either party being duly considered according to the judgment of a good man.

E. *The aquilian claim in the Early Modern Period*

In the sixteenth century, the fusion of civil and canon law also affected the aquilian claim. Once again, this fusion did not happen in the English law, where compensations for bodily injury were developed further on the basis of the *iniuria* and where the injuring of family members and personnel was treated under economic torts with loss of income.

On the Continent, the aquilian claim evolved to a considerable extent. By the end of the sixteenth century, the sovereign councils were applying new principles. Restitution was at the centre stage in sixteenth-century thought about unjust enrichment, theft and unlawful acts. In these three matters, the unjust imbalance played a part. *Iniuria* and *culpa* were also taken into account in the context of aquilian liability. Restitution was not only necessary in the case of corporal damage (*damnum*) but also as soon as someone received less than he was entitled to (*suum cuique tribuere* in Roman law, distributive justice in moral theology). Unjust enrichment and compensation for damage were treated together. From then on, one could not only receive compensation for injuries or death, but also for defamation, unlawful deprivation of liberty and damage to one's good reputation. This created a basis for compensation of moral damage, as well as damage to the body, even if this damage only consisted of an imbalance in the form of a scar or pain and grief. One could suggest that this was no longer a compensation but once again a retaliation... This extension of the aquilian liability can even be found in Donellus, who normally tried to bypass the canon lawyers. Grotius developed the *inaequalitas*, the inequality. A loss because of an undue payment, an illegal act or *negotiorium gestio* resulted in an action to compensate the enrichment. Grotius no longer fell back on the *condictio indebiti. Culpa* was at the centre stage. This error became the starting point of the obligation.

In the seventeenth century, the century that was important because of the *forum internum* and the development of the legal doctrine, the approach taken by Grotius was defended by Domat in France and by Pufendorf in Germany. Christian Thomasius pointed out that this entire institution to compensate damage had little left in common with the *actio legis aquiliae*, except its name. In 1794, the first code of law appeared that featured a general action for damages, namely the 'Algemeine Landrechte' for the Prussian states. In the eighteenth century, England once more looked at the Continent. Lord Mansfiled was won over to the Continental approach of restitution. However, the case-law did not follow his opinion; the doctrine of restitution was not extended to torts. In France, the case-law turned away from the fusion of enrichment without cause and aquilian liability in the eighteenth century. In Pothier's work, they are once again separate notions. In a similar vein, unjust enrichment and wrongful acts became separate institutions again in the Code civil of 1804, although the canon lawyers' had clearly left their indelible mark. In other civil codes, like the Dutch ones of 1809 and 1838, the action for compensation of damage and unjust enrichment stayed together.

4. Delictual liability

Just as contracts, obligations arising from delict only led to a result if the debtor was liable, i.e. if a tolerance threshold was exceeded. Just as in contracts, the liability for obligations arising from delict in Antiquity was developed per remedy at law. The medieval jurists tried to compose a conclusive doctrine in this context too. With regard to delicts, this doctrine was mainly determined by the canon lawyers.

A. Liability for public and civil delicts

The medieval delictual liability was analogous for obligations arising from delict and criminal law. According to the canon lawyers, all offences had to be prosecuted by the government (*omnia crimina publica sunt*). They only accepted liability arising from civil delicts if it was compensatory and not retaliatory.

The Roman criminal law is not discussed in this handbook. In the Republic, it was mainly a competence of the aediles; from the third century AD onwards, it was the exclusive competence of the imperial courts. In the sixth century, books 47-49 of the Digest, which are also known as the *libri terribiles*, were dedicated to criminal law. The following categories of offences are treated in these books:

- murder and manslaughter in many degrees.
- acts of violence, ranging from arson to assault and battery; theft which was prosecuted publicly came under this category. Because theft was usually prosecuted publicly in Justinian's day, the case-law concerning *furtum* can be found in D. 47.2.
- sexual offences: this included adultery.
- Forgery.
- political offences: betrayal, lèse-majesté, extortion by public servants, peculation, machinations, falsification of elections. Lèse-majesté carried the death penalty and was the basis for the persecution of Christians. By means of their *martyr* (testimony), martyrs confirmed that they considered God to be the highest authority. This was lèse-majesté. When the Roman law was received, the same legal ground was used to persecute heretics, who did not acknowledge the highest divine authority.
- various offences, such as abortion, which was made punishable by Antoninus Pius because the interests of the child and the father were not respected.

In the Middle Ages, the criminal law was received via its continued existence in the royal case-law after the fall of the Western Empire. Because of the continuous division of jurisdiction and the feudal lord's interest in this matter, it began to differ more from the Roman model than the civil law. It was once again unified in the sixteenth century, at the time of the rise of the nations. The criminal law of the early modern *ius commune* was influenced to a considerable extent by the doctrine of the canon lawyers.

After all, in the Middle Ages, the canon lawyers had had a strong interest in the criminal law which they found in the *Corpus iuris*. The ecclesiastical courts never had criminal jurisdiction, but reprehensible behaviour, correction and forgiveness had been food for thought for the moral theologians for centuries. The *libri poenitentiales* (penitentials) and the collections of canon law are evidence of the bishops' concerns about misbehaviour and criminality. In the aftermath of the Concordat of Worms, Gratian therefore tried to acquire criminal jurisdiction for the episcopal courts. His efforts failed, but because the matter featured in the *Decretum*, the canon lawyers did continue to study it. In the course of the twelfth century the famous canonical doctrine of guilt came into being. It became the basis of the Western criminal law and exerted a considerable influence on the monarchical criminal law in the Early Modern Era.

The compilers of the *Corpus iuris* clearly separated the criminal liability of books D. 47-49 from liability arising from civil delicts, such as the aquilian claim of D. 9.2. Nevertheless, one can find links between both matters in the Digest – links which also arrested the canon lawyers' attention. The person who killed a slave who committed burglary at night, was neither liable for the damage (D. 9.2.4) nor criminally liable (D. 48.8.). A mentally retarded person was neither liable for the damage which he had caused (D. 9.2.5.2), nor for parricide (D. 48.8.12). The sentence *quod non iure fit, iniuria fieri dicitur* can be found in both D. 9.2.5.1 and D. 47.10.1*pr.* Delayed reactions against violence were seen as revenge and could result in aquilian liability (D. 9.2.45.4) and criminal prosecution (D. 43.16.3.9). If a slave executed his master's order, the master was both liable under the aquilian law (D. 9.4.2*pr.*, D. 9.2.45.4) and criminally liable (D. 44.7.20, D. 50.17.153*pr.*).

Once they stopped hesitating to connect both matters, the canon lawyers also drew criminal principles from D. 9.2 alone. The right to self-defence, for example, was founded on D. 9.2.4. They derived from D. 9.2.8 that a person who led mules without being in control of them, was not only civilly but also criminally liable. They gleaned from D. 9.2.45 that the right to self-defence could not be invoked against a third party who was injured in the process and from D. 9.2.52.1 that people who had been incited to commit a criminal offence were not prosecuted. Our current theory of criminal law which has developed out of the canonical doctrine is therefore partly based on principles developed by the Roman prefecture in conflicts that concerned liability for torts. Conversely, criminal liability began to play a part in civil delicts. For the canon lawyers, only civil delicts that did not lead to retaliation were acceptable, i.e. only the rules for compensation of the *lex aquilia.*

The mixing of criminal liability and liability for torts was never reversed, so an entire series of principles of aquilian liability ended up in the general criminal doctrine in the early modern *ius commune*, while principles of criminal law made their way into our aquilian liability.

B. *Guilt and intent*

For the theologians, sin and the intent of going against the will of God were the central issues in moral philosophy. In their criminal doctrine, the canon lawyers wrote about *contemptus, crimen* and *delictum*. They adopted intent, the *animus* to commit a sin, as the criterion for liability. The point of departure in the legal texts became the word *culpa*, which meant 'blow', 'disturbance' or 'nuisance' and was often the Roman criterion for liability. The theologians and canon lawyers adopted this word, but understood it to mean ethical guilt or sin. In the context of sin, malicious intent took the centre stage. It began to play an essential part in delictual liability. A first justification for this was found in the texts from the Digest that dealt with insane persons and non-adults.

The *familia* of an insane person (*furiosus*) had to restrain him if he was dangerous (see D. 1.18.14). Otherwise, the burden of insane persons was to be carried by everyone. Those who suffered damage because of a *furiosus* had to bear the costs themselves. According to the *Corpus iuris*, the insane were not delictually liable for murder, parricide or private or public delicts – not even in the case of *damnum* (damage). Marcus Aurelius motivated this by means of pity; Modestinus was of the opinion that they had already been punished sufficiently by their own actions. Even Ulpian, who usually advocated harsh measures to protect society, stated that insane people were not responsible for their actions and could not commit a *culpa*. Delictual liability apparently required an intellectual element. Cf. Gaius: *nullum intellectum habent, non intelligunt quid agant.* However, insane people were liable for their actions during their lucid periods. In the case of judicial prosecution, some defendants simulated insanity in order to escape liability, but in *cognitio* procedures from Marcus Aurelius onwards, judges could consult psychiatrists in order to find out whether the defendant's dementia was simulated.

Subsequently, the canon lawyers looked at the texts about the delictual liability of children. Pliny mentioned that children were not crucified for nocturnal arson in the fields; Aulus Gellius writes that they were not turned in when they were caught stealing.

According to D. 48.13.7 and D. 47.21.2, the perpetrator's age was taken into account when his punishment was determined. Non-age resulted in mitigation. According to Mommsen, children were not liable under Roman law because they could not perform legal acts. The legal act, however, is a creation of the Pandectists. The classical law treated this problem casuistically. It turns out that the costs of nuisances caused by children were also borne by society rather than by the *familia*. Those who suffered damage because of children, bore the costs themselves. According to Labeo, children were liable for theft and *damnum iniuria datum* (D. 9.2.5.2). Ulpian added 'if the non-adult person is capable of *iniuria*'. When was one capable of deceit and dolose acts? According to Salvius Julianus, this could be assessed in a concrete manner. If children manifestly acted in a deceitful and malicious way, he assumed the legal fiction that they were adults. In the case-law, the rule was developed that non-adults were presumed not to be liable, but this presumption was refutable. People were liable for some Roman delicts without either *culpa* or *dolus*. One example was the carrying of forbidden weapons (*lex Iulia de ui armata*). Even children were liable if they carried such a weapon. For the canon lawyers, this was an argument to state that children normally did not act with *culpa* and *dolus*.

The canon lawyers found their intent in the Digest, in a series of criteria that determined liability in the case of offences. Sometimes, *consilium* was required, or *ops, dolus, culpa, casus*; in other cases, the act had to have been performed *sciens* or *dolo malo* in order to be punishable. The *lex cornelia de sicariis et ueneficiis* (D. 48.8) for example, stated that the intent to kill was determinative for the punishment of poisoning and robbery with murder. According to Salvius Julianus, this intent could be derived from the facts. If manslaughter was committed with a weapon, this was an indication of intent, while manslaughter with an accidental object did not necessarily indicate intent. Nevertheless, this exploration of psychological motives was not a common rule in Roman Antiquity. In the case of theft, the judge checked whether there was a thief, a stolen object and a victim. If something happened that was *iniuria* (illegal), the underlying intent was not assessed. The medieval canon lawyers, however, always read intent, i.e. the intent of acting in an unethical manner, into these preconditions for criminal liability.

C. From intent to liability

Delictual liability required guilty intent, i.e. an error. The same was true of aquilian liability. However, D. 9.2.44 stated that aquilian liability merely required a *culpa leuissima*: the slightest 'error' resulted in liability. Finding such an error was easy: one had always failed to do something that could have prevented the damage.

The criterion of error and intent also led to other applications. Mere *animus* without an attempt to commit the offence was not punishable under Roman law. D. 48.19.18 states: *cogitationis poena nemo patitur* (no one has to endure punishment for a thought). The medieval jurists based their doctrine concerning punishable attempt on this text. Dolose intent was only punishable if there had been an attempt at committing the offence. However, according to the medieval jurists, this rule did not apply to offences in which intent did not play a part, such as 'lèse-majesté'. The expression of a malicious intent towards the monarch was enough to be sentenced to the death penalty. The canon lawyers deduced from this that heretical ideas were punishable. Between punishment and impunity because of a lack of dolose intent, a doctrine of *impetus* was developed, which went back to a text by Marcian. In the case of inebriation or understandable anger (for example in the case of manslaughter of an adulterous wife) the punishment was mitigated (see D. 48.8.17). The irresistible urge to perform a certain act could lead to an absence of intent and therefore to impunity.

The matter of intent also led to criminal liability being an individual rather than a familial matter. A basis for this was sought in the old texts. If a Roman *paterfamilias* was sued for a delict committed by a member of his *familia*, the action was drawn up as a noxal action. The formula included the phrase 'unless you surrender him'. The *paterfamilias* had this choice and was therefore not delictually liable for family members in the early modern *ius commune*. If he paid, it was by his own choice. Individual liability also meant that population groups could not be proceeded against collectively. The early modern jurists found this rule in the works of classical authors who wrote about the desecration of temples in Asia Minor and the persecution of Christians. In the case of rebellions, only the instigators were prosecuted; Christians were sentenced individually. A community could not be held delictually liable (D. 4.3.15.1). When the Roman law was received, the scope of this rule was extended to include all groups. The criminal liability of associations is a twentieth-century invention. In the case of an *actio ui bonorum raptorum* (action on account of robbery by a gang), the victim could bring an action against each member of the gang. However, this was so because membership of a band of robbers was seen as *culpa*.

In principle, criminal liability ended when the perpetrator died. It was not transferred to his heirs. See Cicero, *De natura deorum* 3.38; Gaius 4.112; D. 48.19.20; D. 48.19.26.1. There were no lawsuits against corpses; the criminal judge did not enter into competition with the Final Judgement. However, judges occasionally forbade the burial of a person (sometimes at the request of his creditors). The noxal surrender of the body of a son or slave was also possible. Did aquilian liability also end when the person who was liable died? In the Middle Ages, the *sedes materiae* of this discussion was D. 9.2.23.8. In principle, the civil lawyers and canon lawyers were of the opinion that the aquilian action was not effective against the heirs, unless the unlawful act had resulted in the heirs' enrichment. This enrichment was linked to the restitution. In the Early Modern Era the doctrine of 'unevennesses' resulted in the heirs' obligation to compensate the damage.

Notabilia: the liability of those who committed suicide. – A Roman death sentence also implied a confiscation of goods. However, since the dead were not liable, one could escape criminal prosecution and confiscation by committing suicide. From Hadrian's reign onwards, this was no longer possible (D. 3.2.11.3). The Antonines were of the opinion that the goods of suicides fell to the *fiscus* (D. 48.21.3.1). The Roman *fiscus* also retained his rights to confiscate the offender's goods if the perpetrator died during appeal proceedings (D. 49.13.1; C. 7.66.3). C. 9.8.5.1 by Arcadius and Honorius (397 AD) treats a case of conspiracy in which heirs were held liable. The conspirators were sentenced to death and their goods were confiscated. Their sons were sentenced to *infamia* (reduction of their civil rights) and could no longer inherit property from their mother and grandparents; their daughters could only inherit the portion of their mother's estate that was reserved for them. None of the children could inherit from third parties, nor could they hold a public office. The civil lawyers saw this as an exception. In 399 the same emperors still emphasized the general rule, namely that guilt and penalty were personal and not to be transferred to the heirs (C. 9.47.22). Consequences that fell outside of the scope of the delict and put innocent heirs at a disadvantage were to be avoided wherever possible.

Bibliography. – On the development of criminal liability by the medieval canon lawyers, see L. Waelkens, 'Et si la responsabilité pénale du droit romain datait du douzième siècle?', in. J.-M. Carbasse and M. Ferret-Lesné (eds.), *Doctrines et pratiques pénales en Europe, Journées internationales de la Société d'Histoire du Droit, Montpellier 26-29 mai 2011*, Montpellier 2012, p. 87-95. After eighty years, Stephan Kuttner's work about the canonical doctrine of guilt is still equally masterly: S. Kuttner, *Die kanonistische Schuldlehre von Gratian bis auf den Dekretalen Gregors IX. Systematisch auf Grund der handschriftlichen Quellen dargestellt*, Vatican City 1935.

5. Obligations arising from quasi-delicts

In Antiquity, certain claims for damages were brought without the case involving *iniuria, dolus* or *culpa*. An example is the claim against a judge who had given an asserted unjust judgement (*actio de iudici qui litem suam fecit*, D. 44.7.5.4). Another example is the *actio de deiectis et effusis* (action on account of something that had been thrown or poured down) which is described in D. 9.3. This action was brought against any inhabitant of the floor of an apartment building from which something had been thrown onto the street. One did not necessarily have to have seen who had committed the act.

An important quasi-delictual action was the *actio de pauperie*. The case-law concerning this action can be found in D. 9.1. This action was used to demand a compensation for damage caused by domestic animals. Such animals were part of the *familia* (which was a community of people and goods), so the action was brought against the *paterfamilias*. According to Roman logic, this was an ordinary noxal action: it was brought against the *paterfamilias*, but he was acquitted if he surrendered the animal. His liability was specific. Domestic animals were a necessity in the Roman society. Everyone had to put up with the normal inconveniences they caused, including the normal damage which their normal behaviour could cause. The *paterfamilias* of the animal only became liable according to the *actio de pauperie* if an animal had caused damage that was inconsistent with its normal peaceful nature or which had been caused because the owner had not taken the precautions that were normally taken by those who kept an animal of this type.

The *actio de pauperie* (action for trouble caused by animals) was noxal in character, which meant that liability amounted at most to the value of the animal: even if the *paterfamilias* desired to refrain from surrendering the animal he could be sentenced at most to pay its value. If the animal died before it could be surrendered, the debtor was released from his obligation. If the victim was a free person, the calculation of the damage took into account the costs of treatment and the income forgone (D. 9.1.3). Some Romanists claim that the *actio de pauperie* was not a noxal action because it did not allow the defendant to choose whether he would surrender the animal or not, but this manifestly runs counter to D. 9.1.1.14.

A Mesopotamian clay tablet that is a millennium older details the case of an ox that had kicked someone in the hustle and bustle of a city. The owner did not have to pay damages because his animal had never reacted like this before. If the owner could not anticipate the animal's behaviour, he was not to blame. In other words: the

Mesopotamian criterion was different. This example illustrates that the central issue in the Middle East was the error of the owner rather than the behaviour of the animal. It was this Mesopotamian notion of guilt and error that Christianity and Judaism would bring to Rome. In the reception, it would play a role in the doctrine of compensation.

The *actio de pauperie* did not apply to wild animals. With regard to this action, Ulpian (D. 9.1.10) wrote that the damage caused by an escaped bear was not the consequence of abnormal behaviour and that his *dominus* stopped being a *dominus* as soon as the animal escaped. The *actio de pauperie* became inadmissible. For cases involving wild animals, the Digest and the Institutes referred to the edict of the aediles, i.e. to the criminal law: see D. 21.1.40-42 and Inst. 4.9.1. In the classical era, the emperor was the criminal judge, which meant that such complaints were lodged with his judges, i.e. with the same *cognitio* judges as the civil actions. Nevertheless, civil notions (such as *dominus*) did not play a role in these criminal proceedings. If a wild animal – and the Digest considered dangerous dogs to be wild animals – killed a free person in a public space, the criminal judge could sentence the person who was responsible for this death to pay two hundred *solidi* to the victim's relatives. In the case of damage to the body of a free person, the judge sentenced the person responsible to compensate the interest (*quanti res interest*, i.e. also the income foregone); in the case of damage to property he could have the person responsible pay twice the value of the damage. The person who was liable was the person who should have the animal under control, irrespective of whether it had escaped or had been on a leash. This procedure, in other words, resulted in the victim receiving more money than he would have received with the *actio de pauperie*. The normal burden of domestic animals was to be carried by the society, but not that of wild animals, because these were not necessary in this society. Compare with art. 1385 of the Civil code.

§5. Purchase-sale

The agreement of purchase and the agreement of sale (*emptio uenditio*) were consensual contracts in Roman Antiquity. The obligations which arose from these agreements were assessed *e bona fide*. Consensual agreements were flexible, because the obligations arose from the party's intent, which could be anything. And yet purchase-sale was consistent with the closed Roman system of agreements. It was a mutual agreement to exchange merchandise (*merx*) for a price (*pretium*). In the Digest, several important titles are dedicated to this issue. The contents of these titles were fused when the Roman law was received. The case-law about the object of the purchase agreement and the clauses pertaining to it was collected in D. 18.1. D. 19.1 is dedicated to actions on account of purchase and sale. Furthermore, book 21 deals with eviction, hidden defects and the *exceptio rei traditiae*. When the Roman law was received, the latter matters were integrated into the treatment of purchase-sale.

1. A consensual agreement with regard to specific objects

It is said that the consensual *emptio-uenditio* dates back to the 'real' agreement of purchase that arose from the transfer of the good, which was used in different regions in Antiquity. In the case of a real contract, the obligation of one party arose because of the other party's delivery. C. 4.19.21 details the case of a person who had paid (the handing over of cash money was considered to be a delivery; money was a *merx* as well) and claimed the delivery of an immovable good only on the grounds of that payment. According to the rescript that is mentioned here, Diocletian opposed real purchase-sales. According to some, purchases that were concluded by the payment of an advance (*arrha*) were a relic of the Greek purchase agreement – cf. the later possibilities of 'Barkauf', purchase by exchange and purchase by earnest-penny. The *mancipatio* is said to stem from such an old 'real' purchase-sale. The payment with a single coin (*nummo uno*), to which the later practice of tapping a coin against the scales still referred, made the obligations of the supplier binding, namely the additional stipulations (*nuncupationes*) and the guarantee against eviction (*auctoritas*). However, we should not invent a legal prehistory: legal history and its sources are difficult enough in themselves. Under Justinian, the *emptio uenditio* and the real purchase agreement with an advance and a deed of stipulation detailing obligations do seem to have coexisted. When the Roman law was received, it was mainly the *emptio uenditio* that became important for our current purchase agreements.

The *emptio uenditio* came into being originated when the praetor, probably between 250 and 200 BC, linked specific actions with this specific type of promise. The buyer was granted an *actio empti*; the purchaser was awarded the *actio uenditi*. An *emptio uenditio* was established as soon as a consensus was reached (orally, in writing, through letters or messengers, etcetera). It required neither earnest money nor a down payment (*arrha*). And yet an element of the real purchase and of the period of the swap agreements: the goods that were sold by means of *emptio uenditio* had to be individualised at the time of the conclusion of the agreement. The obligations were established by consensus about a price and specific merchandise.

A considerable part of the case-law that was handed down deals with the specificity of the merchandise. Every specific good could be traded by means of a purchase-sale. In the case of visible goods, there was no problem, but D. 19.1 contains judgements about more complex questions. Separate assets or a clearly defined capital, such as an inheritance or a share in an inheritance could be the object of *emptio uenditio*. Claims as well as servitudes could be sold by means of such an agreement. The good did not necessarily have to be specific at the time of the sale. It was enough that it could be specified in an unambiguous manner and could be valued at the time of the action. Wine for which the grapes were still on the vine could be sold by means of an *emptio uenditio* if it was certain which future wine was being sold, on which plot of land the grapes were growing and in which cellar the wine would mature. The proceeds of a planned fishing trip could also be traded by means of an *emptio uenditio*, for instance 'everything caught tonight at a specified price per fish'. Pomponius called this *emptio spei*, the purchase of a hoped-for object (D. 18.1.8*pr.*-1). The price, however, always consisted of money, despite the fact that the Roman case-law considered money to be a good. An exchange was not an *emptio uenditio*. The characteristic of specificity, which is older than the consensual nature of purchases, still plays a role in the current law concerning contracts that are established by consensus: cf. article 1585 of the Civil code.

It is clear that *emptio uenditio* could not be used to sell fungible goods. Supply agreements were not considered as sale agreements, unless the good was clearly specified. 'Deliver me X measures of wine every week' did not lead to *emptio uenditio*, but 'deliver me X measures of that wine Y from cellar Z every week' did (D. 18.1.35.7).

The words *e bona fide* featured in the *actio empti* of the buyer and the *actio uenditi* of the seller, which meant that the judge considered the complete legal relationship between the two parties, i.e. both of the obligations, if it came to a lawsuit. The buyer and the seller had to refrain from *dolus malus* (improper behaviour), such as insufficiently specifying the object of the sale. If there was insufficient specification, the proof of intent was to be delivered by the buyer. Compensation was only paid in the case of intent, see also article 1645-1646 of the Civil code.

D. 18.1.8. – Nec emptio nec uenditio sine re quae ueneat potest intellegi. Et tamen fructus et partus futuri recte ementur, ut, cum editus esset partus, iam tunc, cum contractum esset negotium, uenditio facta intellegatur: sed si id egerit uenditor, ne nascatur aut fiant, ex empto agi posse. 1. Aliquando tamen et sine re uenditio intellegitur, ueluti cum quasi alea emitur. Quod fit, cum captum piscium uel auium vel missilium emitur: emptio enim contrahitur etiam si nihil inciderit, quia spei emptio est: et quod missilium nomine eo casu camptum est si euictum fuerit, nulla eo nomine ex empto obligatio contrahitur, quia id actum intellegitur.

Translation SCOTT. – Neither a purchase nor a sale can be held to take place without property which can be sold; nevertheless, crops, and the yield of cattle can properly be made the object of purchase; and when the births have taken place, as the transaction is complete, the sale is understood to be concluded. If, however, the vendor contrived that the crops should not be raised, or the cattle not be born, an action on purchase will lie. 1. A sale is, however, sometimes understood to be contracted without property being the object of the same, as, for instance, where a purchase is made dependent upon chance; which occurs where fish or birds which are yet to be caught, or money to be thrown to the populace, is bought. A purchase is also contracted even if nothing happens, because it relates to the expectation. Where the purchase has reference to money thrown to the populace, and the purchaser is deprived by eviction, of what he had secured, no obligation on the ground of purchase will be incurred; for the reason that this is understood to have been the intention of the parties.

2. The obligations of the seller (the object of the *actio empti*)

A. Transfer

The seller had to deliver the goods in such a way that the buyer received possession and protection by means of interdicts (*uacuam possessionem tradere*). Unlike in the current law, he never had to grant the buyer ownership – not even under the post-classical or Justinianic law. Whether the buyer became the *dominus* of the good was not the concern of the seller. The buyer did not have a remedy at law against the seller if he had not received *dominium*. See D. 18.1.25.1. The seller's acquisition or non-acquisition of ownership depended on the position of the seller, the delivery, and retention of title. It could be stipulated that the transfer of *res mancipi* would happen by means of a mancipation, so that the buyer did not have to resort to *usucapio*.

In line with the reception, article 1604 of the Civil code mentions the obligation to transfer possession. Do not search for a profound explanation thereof in our unclear law of possession; it is a reference to the delivery. Article 1605 of the Civil code lays down the necessity of the transfer of the title of ownership when immovable goods are sold; article 2279 determines that with regard to movable goods possession is a title of ownership. In French and Belgian law, purchase in principle leads to the immediate transfer of ownership: article 1583 of the Civil code. Also see above about the *constitutum possessorium*.

*B. Guarantee against eviction (*euictio*)*

In the early Republic, the buyer who was sold a good by means of a *mancipatio* could bring the *actio auctoritatis* against the seller if a third party successfully claimed the good as his. This seller was then summoned as a third party to the suit in order to assist his former buyer. The seller who did not manage to secure the guarantee against eviction for his buyer, had to pay twice the selling price that the buyer had paid. In the oldest consensual sales agreement the guarantee against eviction was stipulated separately in a *stipulatio duplae (pecuniae)* (stipulation of the double amount).

The *actio empti* originally only granted a guarantee against a malicious eviction, so that the buyer did not have to wait until a third party claimed the good. He did have to deliver proof of the malicious intent. In the classical period, the buyer could use the *actio empti* to demand that the seller took the *stipulatio duplae,* under penalty of the immediate payment of the amount that could be obtained by means of the *stipulatio duplae*. This matter is treated in D. 21 of the *Corpus iuris*, among the actions of the curule aediles. Salvius Julianus was the first who saw the guarantee against eviction as an inherent obligation of the seller, which could be enforced by means of the principal action of the buyer, the *actio empti* (D. 21.2.8). Nevertheless, the idea was not adopted by the legists. The passage in the Digest dealt with the sale of a slave and was no longer of topical interest in the Middle Ages. In the *Corpus iuris* we can see that the *stipulatio duplae* also continued to exist. It could lead to better results than the *actio empti*, because the compensation that the latter could yield was limited to the real direct damage and the loss of profit (*lucrum cessans et damnum emergens*).

Selling someone else's good was a form of deceit according to the legists and the medieval legal practice. In the canon lawyer's work, one can read about the *euictio* (for example Hostiensis *ad* X. 3.17.3). In the Early Modern Period, when general good faith was put forward, the fixed guarantee against eviction nevertheless became a primary obligation, in imitation of this passage of Julian. This became the rule in the *ius commune* and eventually ended up in article 1603 of the Civil code. England stuck to the old system of the explicit guarantee.

In the case of the sale of a claim, the guarantee against eviction concerned the debt claim and not the solvency of the debtor: D. 18.4.4, see also art. 1693 of the Civil code.

C. Liability for the good that has not been delivered yet

The seller had the duty to take care of the good (*custodia*, D. 19.1.31*pr.* and D. 19.1.36). He was also liable for the theft of the goods, but received the *actio furti* against the person who had stolen the good from him (D. 47.2.14*pr.*). Nevertheless, the *Corpus iuris* clearly states that ultimately, the risk was to be carried by the buyer: *periculum est emptoris* (D. 18.6.8; Inst. 3.23.33a). If the good perished while under the seller's custody and without any *culpa* on his part, the buyer had to pay. By means of small compensation, he received the yield of the good from the time of the consensus onwards (*Fragm. Vat.*, 2; *Pauli Sententiae* 2.17.7).

Does this liability of the buyer dovetail with the abovementioned contractual liability? *Custodia* always led to liability in Antiquity, did it not? No, not in this case. This passage illustrates that there was no unified doctrine of liability in Antiquity. *Custodia* was not a legal concept that entailed specific consequences, but a regular word which was used to describe liability in the context of an action. The doctrine of liability was developed in the Middle Ages, an era of all-embracing philosophical thought.

The rule *periculum est emptoris* was adopted in the *ius commune* and in the Code civil. After 1804 the Pandectists returned to the texts that emphasised *custodia*. According to them, the risk was only transferred at the time of delivery. This rule was adopted into § 446.1.1 of the BGB.

D. Liability for hidden defects

The buyer had to keep his eyes peeled. *Ius ciuile uigilantibus scriptum*, the law is for those who are vigilant (D. 42.8.24). In the English law this became *caveat emptor* in the case of purchase-sale. In the Roman sources we find some aspects of the English attitude: do not promise too much; if the buyer expected to much it is his problem. If the buyer was of the opinion that a good was defective, he could only take action if the seller had guaranteed certain qualities (D. 19.1.13.14; D. 19.1.6.4) or if he could prove that the seller had maliciously and deceitfully withheld essential defects (Salvius Julian in D. 19.1.12.1).

Relatively early on, a specific regulation was developed for slaves and draught animals that were bought on the market in Rome. This regulation was not enforceable before the praetor, but before the curule aediles. This matter was treated in their edict, see D. 21.1. According to this edict, the seller was obligated to reveal the illnesses, physical defects and certain defects in character and noxal liability of slaves to candidate buyers. The buyer could also oblige the seller to provide a guarantee against defects in an obligation. This could be done until two months after the sale (six months for draught animals) before the curule aediles. If the seller refused to stipulate, the curule aediles granted the *actio redhibitoria*, by means of which the buyer could get his money back if he returned the good which he had bought. In the classical period the *actio redhibitoria* was aways granted to the buyer – it no longer required a stipulation. At that time, the same action also applied if certain qualities or the absence of certain defects were mentioned explicitly. In the same circumstances, the buyer was granted the *actio quanti minoris* before the aediles, by means of which he could receive a reduction in price for a year on account of defects, without having to return the slave or draught animal.

Yet another problem was the liability for hidden defects: defects which the seller did not know about either. In D. 19.1.13*pr.*-2 one can find the regulation that such defects could be settled with the action of the buyer. Under Justinian, the chancellery confirmed this. If the buyer could prove that the seller knew about the defects, the buyer received his entire interest by means of compensation: the damage he suffered as well as the loss of income. If the buyer could not prove this, or if the seller proved that he really had not known about the defects, the seller remained liable, but only for the difference in value caused by the defect. The seller was, in other words, liable for something that he did not know about. This is a societal choice. On the market, people met professional sellers who could settle claims for hidden defects with their overall turnover. Buyers on the other hand were left with the single defective good. The downside was that occasional sellers were also liable for hidden defects. This, however, did not lead to a complete compensation of the interest.

In D. 19.2.22.3, the medieval jurists read that the buyer and the seller could *circumscribere*, i.e. spin yarns concerning the purchase. The seller extolled the virtues of his goods and the seller could do the opposite without this being deceit. The civil lawyers focused on real deceit when they treated the matter of defects. If someone was deceived about the characteristics of a good, the *actio empti* could be used since it was an action *e bona fide*.

It is typical of the medieval legists that they adopted the entire regulation for slaves and cattle of the curule aediles for the regular purchase agreement. The *actio quanti minoris*, which could be used to acquire a reduction in price, and the *actio redhibitoria* for the return of the money and the merchandise became aspects of the regular purchase agreement. Justinian still treated these separately, but according to D. 21.1.1 these actions applied to all goods. In principle, a buyer could choose which action he would bring in the case of hidden defects. *Quanti minoris* and *redhibitoria* were typical of hidden defects. D. 21.1 describes what sellers had to mention or which guarantees they should have given when the sold slaves and animals. This title contains a list of ailments that led to reduction in price or restitution. The matter of real hidden defects, which neither the seller nor the buyer were obliged to know about, is not discussed here. From the case-law concerning defects, the civil lawyers derived that there was a guarantee by operation of law in the case of the sale of a defective good. These two actions from the edict of the curule aediles did have to be brought within a short term, hence the civil lawyers' conclusion that claims were brought within a short time in the case of hidden defects. If the lawsuit was initiated with the regular claim of the buyer, which was possible according to D. 19.113, this short term still applied.

In the Early Modern Period, Continental lawyers approached hidden defects from the viewpoint of good faith. The Roman liability of the seller for defects which he was not obliged to know about was a liability without fault. It could therefore not be brought up in the *ius commune*: there was deceit on the part of the seller, or he should have provided a guarantee. There was, however, an intensive debate about the question whether the aedilic actions and the *actio empti* had the same result for the buyer. The former actions expired after six months; the latter only after thirty years. Donellus and others came to the conclusion that the duty to provide a guarantee against hidden defects always expired after the short term of the aedilic actions. A large number of legal scholars, among whom were Molinaeus in the sixteenth century and Pothier in the eighteenth – to name only two scholars who had a great interest in case-law – indicated that the *actio empti* not only led to the dissolution of the purchase or the reduction of the price to which the aedilic remedies were limited (interpretation of D. 19.1.6.4), but also to an additional compensation for damage.

This short term for claims on account of hidden defects still exists. In commercial law, the short term is a question of fact to be decided by the judge. In the Code civil, this term was one year in the case of consumer purchase. The period of guarantee in the European union is currently two years. Guilt or deceit no longer play a role.

3. Clauses that can cancel a sale

The Romans did not consider the result of the *actio redhibitoria* to be a cancellation of the sale. The possibility to include conditions concerning the termination of the sale in a separate agreement (*pactum*) did exist. Because the actions involved were *bona fide* actions, these additional clauses could be enforced by means of the action for the principal agreement. Examples of such redhibitory clauses were:

- purchase on approval: D. 18.3.1;
- *in diem addictio* (assignment after a certain period of time): for an agreed upon time period, the seller retained the right to sell the good to someone else if he found a better buyer: D. 18.2.1, also see the right of repurchase in the Civil code.
- *lex commissoria* (clause of cancellation, the same term as the *lex commissoria* in the context of pledge); if the price had not been paid at a certain time, the purchase was cancelled: D. 18.3.1 and D. 41.4.2.3.

Was the purchase concluded and consequently cancelled if the condition was met, or was the purchase only concluded if the condition was met? In the terminology of the *ius commune*, this question ran as follows: were these clauses resolutive or suspensive? This matter was quite important in the case of the buyers' bankruptcy. If the sale had not been concluded yet, the seller could claim his goods back. Even if he had delivered them, there had been no transfer of ownership, in the absence of a valid title for transmission (*iusta causa traditionis*, see D. 19.3.6). However, if the purchase had taken place but could be cancelled, the successor in title of the buyer (the *emptor bonorum*) could even demand the delivery of the good if the seller had not yet delivered it. In such a case, the seller only had his *actio uenditi* (action of the seller), which was a regular claim that came in competition with the claims of the other debtors in the case of bankruptcy. The answer of the Roman jurists was that a purchase was a consensual agreement and that it was therefore the consensus that had to be considered. After he had heard all of the arguments and proofs, the judge had to assess whether the additional stipulations were resolutive or suspensive. In the former case, the seller was in hot water; in the latter case he was saved. Some classical jurists always gave an *in rem* effect to such a resolutive stipulation, so that the entire good was always restored to the seller. Under Justinian, this *in rem* effect became the rule. It was also adopted in the *ius commune*. We can find it in the Civil code, see art. 1664: the right of repurchase even applies against the further acquirer if the buyer had already resold the good to a third party.

4. Error (*error*)

Just like deceit (*dolus*), duress (*metus*), or prejudice (*laesio enormis*), error was not an example of vitiated consent in Roman law. One text from the *Corpus iuris* mentions error, deceit and duress (Inst. 4.13.1). the theory of vitiated consent, however, postdates the introduction of freedom of choice in the Early Modern Era.

In Roman law, error concerned the specificity of the good in the case of *emptio uenditio*. The principal texts were therefore found in D. 18.1. See especially D. 18.1.9, but also D. 18.1.11.1; D. 18.1.14 and D. 18.1.41.1. The case-law considered the object of the error. In the case of an error concerning the good, there was no purchase. If the error only pertained to the name of the good, the purchase had been concluded in a valid manner. An error concerning the raw material of the good resulted in interpretation. Ulpian was of the opinion that in a case involving such an error no sale had been concluded if the buyer considered the raw material to be essential (D. 18.1.9.2). The Digest merely sums up casuistry and does not offer a theory. The terms that can be found in the Digest are *error in corpore, error in nomine, error in sexu, error in substantia* and *error in materia*. The latter two terms pertain to error concerning the raw material. In the medieval conceptual thought, this terminology suddenly became important because people were searching for criteria in these 'concepts'. *Error in substantia* attracted attention because Thomas Aquinas had propagated the act-substance doctrine of Aristotle. According to him, a consensus that was based on an erroneous conception of elements that were considered essential could not lead to a consensual contract. In the Early Modern Era, this subjective criterion can be found in the works of the jusnaturalists like Grotius and Pufendorf. Pothier returned to the old meaning that the Digests gave to the word *substantia*: 'la substance de la chose' concerned the material or nature of the matter and a substantial error did not concern what the buyer had considered as essential. Pothier's idea was expressed in article 1110 of the Civil code. The nineteenth-century legal doctrine and case-law, however once again introduced the subjective criterion of Pufendorf (see for example Belg. Cass. 8 May 1905, *Pas.* 1905, I, 214; Belg. Cass. 3 March 1967, *R.W.* 1966-67, 1907).

D. 18.1.9. – In uenditionibus et emptionibus consensum debere intercedere palam est: ceterum siue in ipsa emptione dissentient siue in pretio siue in quo alio, emptio imperfecta est. Si igitur ego me fundum emere putarem cornelianum, tu mihe te uendere sempronianum putasti, quia in corpore dissensimus, emptio nulla est. Idem est, si ego me Stichum, tu Pamphilum absentem uendere putasti: nam cum in corpore dissentiatur, apparet nullam esse emptionem.

Translation SCOTT. – It is clear that the consent of both parties is necessary in all sales and purchases. But if they differ either as to the price, or as to something else connected with the sale, it will be incomplete. Therefore, if I thought that I was purchasing the Cornelian Field, and you thought that you were selling me the Sempronian Field, for the reason that we disagree as to the object of the transaction, the sale will be null and void. The same rule applies where I was under the impression that you had sold me Stichus, and you believed that you had sold me Pamphilus, who was absent; for when there is a disagreement with reference to the object, it is apparent that the sale is of no effect.

1. Plane si in nomine dissentiamus, uerum de corpore constet, nulla dubitatio est quin ualeat emptio et uenditio: nihil enim facit error nominis, cum de corpore constat.

1. If we disagree with reference to the name, but there is no dispute as to the object, the transaction of purchase and sale is undoubtedly valid; for a mistake in the name is of no consequence, when the property itself is agreed upon.

2. Inde quaeritur, si in ipso corpore non erratur, sed in substantia error sit, ut puta si acetum pro uino ueneat, aes pro auro uel plumbum pro argento uel quid aliud argento simile, an emptio et uenditio sit. Marcellus scripsit libro sexto digestorum emptionem esse et uenditionem, quia in corpus consensum est, etsi in materia sit erratum. Ego in uino quidem consentio, quia eadem prope ousia est, si modo uinum acuit: ceterum si uinum non acuit, sed ab initio acetum fuit, ut embamma, aliud pro alio uenisse uidetur. In ceteris autem nullam esse uenditionem puto, quotiens in materia erratur.

2. Hence, the question arises, where no mistake is made as to the object itself, but there is one as to the substance of which it is composed; as, for instance, if vinegar is sold for wine, copper for gold, or lead for silver or something else which resembles silver, whether there is a purchase and sale. Marcellus says, in the Sixth Book of the Digest, that, in this case, there is a purchase and sale, because the object was agreed upon, although there was an error with reference to the matter of which it was composed. I am of the same opinion, so far as the wine and vinegar are concerned; for, as they are very nearly the same thing, that is to say, the same substance, provided the wine becomes sour, but if it did not become sour but was so in thebeginning, that is, if it contained vinegar, it will be held that one thing has been sold for another. In the other instances, however, I think the sale was null, whenever a mistake was made with reference to the substance of which the articles were composed.

D. 18.1.11.1. – Quod si ego me uirginem emere putarem, cum esset iam mulier, emptio ualebit: in sexu enim non est erratum. Ceterum si ego mulierem uenderem, tu puerum emere existimasti, quia in sexu eror est, nulla emptio, nulla uenditio est.

If I think I am buying a virgin slave, when she, in fact, is a woman, the purchase will be valid; for there is no mistake as to her sex. If, however, I should sell you a woman, and you thought that you were buying a boy, for the reason that there is a mistake in the sex, the purchase and sale will be void.

D. 18.1.14. – Quid tamen dicemus, si in materia et qualitate ambo errarent? Ut puta si et ego me uendere aurum putarem et tu emere, cum aes esset? Vt puta coheredes uiriolam, quae aurea dicebatur, pretio exquisito uni heredi uendidissent eaque inuenta esset magna ex parte aenea? Venditionem esse constat ideo, quia auri aliquid habuit. Nam si inauratum aliquid sit, licet ego aureum putem, ualet uenditio: si autum aes pro auro ueneat, non ualet.

But what shall we say where both parties are mistaken as to both the substance and the nature of the object of the sale; as, for instance, where I think I am selling gold, and you think that you are purchasing gold, when, in fact, the metal is brass; or where, for example, two co-heirs sell a bracelet which is said to be of gold, at a high price to another coheir, and it is discovered that it is, for the most part, copper? It is held that this is a sale, because the bracelet contained some gold, for if the article is gilt, even though I think it to be gold, the sale will be valid, but where copper is sold for gold the sale will not be valid.

D. 18.1.41.1. – Mensam argento coopertam mihi ignoranti pro solida uendidisti imprudens: nulla est emptio pecuniaque eo nomine data condicetur.

You sold me a table plated with silver, with the understanding that it was solid, neither of us being aware that it was not. The sale is void, and the money paid on account of it can be recovered.

§ 6. *Locatio conductio*

Locatio conductio cannot be translated into a single English term. The current notions of rent, tenancy, contract of employment and contracting for work all came under this type of consensual contract in Antiquity. *Locare* means 'to place' or 'to put something at someone's disposal'; *conducere* means 'to take it along'. One could put a movable or immovable good, one's capacity for work or an assignment at the disposal of another person, who could take it with him. These different legal relationships were experienced as one single institution and were enforced by means of the same remedies at law (*actio locati, actio conducti*). The consideration consisted of the payment of a sum of money (*merces, pretium*). In the classical period, the jurists differentiated between several categories of *locatio conductio* and the different formulas used for each of these in the courts. Per category, the *bona fides* was interpreted differently. When the Roman law was received, the matter was subdivided. Johannes Voet (1647-1713) was the author of the threefold division into *locatio conductio rei* (of an object), *locatio conductio operarum* (of labour) and *locatio conductio operis* (of an assignment). This tripartition was adopted into the *ius commune* and the later codifications (see for example art. 1708-1711 of the Civil code). These designations are still used when we examine the old texts concerning *locatio conductio.*

According to some Romanists, *locatio conductio* originated from the relationships of patronage and expresses the relation between a strong lessor, employer or granter of emphyteusis and a weak renter, tenant or labourer. This interpretation, however, is a historism. The institution that determined the relationship of patronage was the *familia,* and in order to find out who was strong and who was weak, one has to know the prices of these contracts. However, no data about this prices were handed down. The different treatment of *honestiores* and *humiliores* in Roman law is a category of the criminal law and only originated from the second century AD onwards. We should not be too quick to transplant such an inequality onto other institutions of other periods.

1. *Locatio conductio rei*

A. *Definition*

This form of *locatio conductio* was developed in order to grant someone the enjoyment of a good upon payment. Besides the renter's own enjoyment, *locatio conductio rei* could also pertain to the proceeds of the good (for example in the case of subletting). The precise scope was evident from the agreement. All movable and immovable goods, including slaves and cattle, could be leased out. Someone who rented for agricultural purposes was a *colonus* (tenant farmer). In Antiquity, share farming (known as *colonia partiaria* in the Middle Ages) was considered to be a *locatio conductio*, even though medieval jurists saw it rather as a partnership.

Unlike government land, municipal agricultural lands (including *agri uectigales*) were perpetually leased to private parties by means of the *locatio conductio*, as Gaius 3.145 states. According to other jurists, such a long-term contract was an *emptio uenditio* rather than a *locatio conductio*. The lessee of municipal land, who, just like the concessionary of government land, traditionally enjoyed protection of possession against third parties, had a real action at his disposal, which he could bring against both the community and third parties (D. 6.3.1.1). This doubt as to whether a specific legal act should be qualified as an *emptio uenditio* or a *locatio conductio* indicates that these legal concepts were closely related. On the Continent, the importance of ownership resulted in a separation of the two notions, but in the early modern English law they were still intertwined. A current emanation thereof is hire-purchase.

On the basis of D. 43.18.1.3 (about renting a *superficies*) the medieval Romanists constructed a *locatio conductio ad longum tempus* (for a long time). According to the *exceptio longi temporis*, a long time was ten years. If the period stipulated for the agricultural lease exceeded ten years, the renter received a right *in rem*. This doctrine remained widespread until the end of the eighteenth century.

D. 43.18.1.3. – Quod si ait praetor 'si actio de superficie postulabitur, causa cognita dabo', sic intelligendum est, ut ad tempus quis superficiem conduxerit, negetur ei in rem actio. Et sane cause cognita ei, qui non ad modicum tempus conduxit superficiem, in rem actio competet.

Translation SCOTT. – When the Praetor says, 'If any other action having reference to the surface of the land is applied for, I will grant it, where proper cause is shown,' this must be understood to mean that if anyone has leased the surface of the land for a short time, a real action will be refused him. This action *in rem*, however, will lie in favor of him who has leased the surface of the land for a long time, after proper cause has been shown.

B. The parties' obligations

The lessor had to guarantee his lessee's quiet enjoyment under the tenancy agreement (*uti frui*) and maintain the rented good to that end. He was liable for hidden defects. He was always liable for eviction, even when there was neither *dolus* nor *culpa* on his part (D. 19.2.9*pr.*). The sanction was a complete compensation of the lessee's interest, which could be enforced by means of the *actio conducti*. This compensation included loss of income (*lucrum cessans et damnum emergens*).

The lessee had to pay the rent or agricultural lease, keep the good in his custody (the duty of *custodia*, see Inst. 3.24.5), maintain or preserve the rented good and give it back in a satisfactory condition. He was liable for *dolus* and *culpa* and by means of the *actio locati*, he could be obliged to pay full damages. Inst. 3.24.5 states that the renter had to show *exactissima diligentia*. According to some, in the late Empire, the *locatio conductio* of land to ordinary men also entailed personal servitude. When interpreting late imperial texts about the colonate one has to take the typical practices of that time into account. The leasing of land by means of *locatio conductio* was sometimes linked to the rental of services to the landowner. In addition, some land was exempted from land tax when it yielded grain for the *annona* (social security). In order to enjoy this exemption, agricultural lessors and lessees had to agree to grow corn for the *annona*. The lessors also agreed on commitments and facilities. In the Code, we even find an agricultural lessee who acted as a *peculium*-holder for his lessor. The data about the fiscal aspects of these matters, however, are too scarce to allow us to draw large conclusions.

There is no text that clearly identifies the person who bore the risk in the case of a purchase-sale. Sometimes the risk of unforeseeable situations was to be carried by the lessor, sometimes by the lessee. Examples that were also brought up in the *ius commune* are the liability of the lessor for leaking vessels (D. 19.1.6.4) and the risk of poisonous plants in a pasture, which was to be borne by the agricultural lessee (D. 19.2.19.1). The lessee's risk in the case of crop failure was shared with the lessor. In the case of such a crop failure, the imperial administration could cancel part of the price of the agricultural lease (*remissio mercedis*).

The duration of the agreement was stipulated, but could be extended tacitly (*reconductio tacita*, D. 19.2.13.11; cf. C. 4.65.16). In the case of unlimited duration, an equitable term of notice had to be respected. This is an important rule which still applies to all agreements pertaining to an exclusive partnership.

C. Position of the lessee in property law

The lessee did not have possession and therefore did not enjoy protection by means of interdicts. He merely kept the good with him (in Latin: *detinet*). He did not need protection of possession, because he could bring a claim against his lessor in the case of the slightest disturbance. The lessor then had to request the interdicts that were necessary to guarantee the interests of his lessor.

If the lessor sold the good, the Roman rentor did not have any means of defence. In the Roman law of Antiquity, the rule was 'sale ends lease' (*emptio tollit locatum*). The buyer could evict the lessee by means of a revendication or a possessory interdict. Of course, the lessee could then bring the *actio conductio* against his old lessor and receive a full compensation: see D. 19.2.25.1; D. 19.3.32 and C. 4.65.9. However, the *actio conducti* never resulted in the lessee being allowed to continue to live on the land. Even if the lessor had stipulated at the time of the sale that the lessee was allowed to stay on the land, the buyer was free to evict the lessee. He did not have a legal connection with the tenant. The seller could then claim the compensation which he had paid to his lessee from the buyer by means of the *actio uenditi* (D. 19.1.13.30).

Most of the medieval legal systems, by contrast, held the principle 'sale does not end lease'. They began to undermine the Roman regulation in every conceivable way. If the transfer of the good was based on a seizure of the rental good by the judge or the *fiscus*, the medieval legists were of the opinion that the tenant retained the quiet enjoyment of the rental good (interpretation of D. 19.2.33). In the case of share farming, they held that the rule 'sale ends lease' could not be applicable, because share farming was a kind of partnership where lessor and lessee jointly exploited land and divided the revenue. This was not a pure *locatio conductio*, so the tenant could not be evicted just like that. The civil lawyer granted tenants who had rented a good for more than ten years an *in rem* action on the basis of D. 43.18.1.3. This action could also be brought against the buyer of the good. Those who had rented a good for less than ten years were slipped a remedy at law by Bartolus. He advised the lessees to include two clauses in the rental agreement, namely that they would be allowed to continue to live on the land in the case of the sale, and that they held the good in pledge with regard to the claims of the seller. In this manner, they received an *actio in rem* which they could also bring against the buyer of the good (Bartolus, Commentary on the *Digestum Vetus, ad* D. 19.2.32).

Bibliography. – E.J.H. SCHRAGE, *Koop breekt geen huur, Enkele grepen uit de geschiedenis van het geleerde recht inzake de gevolgen van de vervreemding van een verhuurde zaak* [Rechtshistorische Cahiers, 7], Deventer 1984, with excerpts from the legal historical sources. English summary, see ID., '*Emptio (nondum) tollit locatum*', in: W. DE VOS (ed.), *Essays in honour of Ben Beinart*, III, Cape Town 1979, p. 1-13.

D. Remissio mercedis

The reduction of the rental price, the *remissio mercedis*, became an important institution when the Roman law was received. Its *sedes materiae* was D. 19.2.15.2. The term *deductio ex mercede* was used with regard to houses that were rented, but in the *ius commune* this term was a synonym of *remissio mercedis*. It pertained to major inconveniences that greatly reduced the habitability of the house. This issue was discussed in many twelfth-century sources and features in the works of most of the thirteenth-century authors. The reduction of the price of a rent or lease was justified on the basis of insufficient quiet enjoyment. A failed harvest or destruction by a storm were seen as a lack of *uti frui*, i.e. enjoyment, as well. Jacques de Revigny (†1296) made this lack measurable. He saw a connection with the prejudice of C. 4.44.2 and was of the opinion that the price had to be reduced if the lessee or tenant did not receive half of the normal benefit. This once again shows that *locatio conductio* and *emptio uenditio* were intertwined in this era's sense of justice. Among the canon lawyers, we find the same arguments: lack of enjoyment and prejudice. Thomas Aquinas treated *remissio mercedis* in his discussion of distributive justice. In the dramatic mid-sixteenth century, the period during which Rome would condemn emphyteusis because it did not provide the possibility of *remissio mercedis*, some jurists – including Guillaume Budé (1468-1540) – tried to link the institution to moral philosophy. The Spanish scholastics also approached the issue from the vieuwpoint of *inaequalitas*. The jurists did not follow their example. Donellus emphasized that this was old law and that, under tenancy law insufficient enjoyment gave rise to an assessment of the situation by the judge. During the great sixteenth-century crisis, Pius V's bull *Cum onus* (1569) condemned real rental agreements (with emphyteusis) and pointed out the fact that *locatio conductio* led to *remissio mercedis* in crisis situations. Grotius opposed *remissio mercedis*. In his view, the solidarity between lessor and lessee was tantamount to the lessor bearing the loss of his property's value and the lessee bearing the loss of the revenues of this property. For Grotius, there was no difference between agricultural lease and emphyteusis. In the late *ius commune* the typical notion of good faith of the Early Modern Era played a larger role on the Continent. The judge could assess the reasonableness and equity of the situation that had arisen between the lessor and the lessee. The *remissio mercedis* played a part in the *ius commune* until circa 1800. It was incorporated into the Code civil of 1804, but the Bürgerliches Gesetzbuch of 1900 no longer featured *remissio mercedis* because of the contractual freedom of parties.

2. *Locatio conductio operarum* (hire of services)

According to some, employment contracts were rarer than they are now because the Romans had slaves who did the work. One could even rent slaves by means of a *locatio conductio rei.* Nevertheless, Romans commonly hired services. By means of a *locatio conductio operarum,* one could permenantly acquire simple manpower as well as obtain specialised advice. In many circumstances a motivated day labourer or worker would have been cheaper than a slave. See D. 7.8.4*pr.* In either case, texts about employment contracts were handed down. Members of the equestrian or senatorial class could not conclude a *locatio conductio* for the remunerated provision of services. They worked for a *honorarium,* a free fee. This regulation was extended to all 'liberal' professions. In the *cognitio extra ordinem* these *honoraria* also became due and payable (D. 50.13.1).

Text. – Professors of philosophy and law cannot claim *honoraria.*

D. 50.13.1.4-5. – 4. An et philosophi professorum numero sint? Et non putem, quia non religiosa res est, sed quia hoc primum profiteri eos oportet mercennarium operam spernere. 5. Proinde ne iuris quidem ciuilis professoribus ius dicent: est quidem res sanctissima ciuilis sapientia, sed quae pretio nummario non sit aestimanda nec dehonestanda, dum in iudicio honor petitur, qui in ingressu sacramenti offerri debuit. Quaedam enim tametsi honeste accipiantur, inhoneste tamen petuntur.

Translation SCOTT. – 4. Are philosophers to be included in the number of professors? I do not think that they are, not because philosophy is irreligious, but because those who practice it should, first of all, scorn any mercenary labor. 5. Hence, the Governor of a province does not decide with reference to the remuneration of professors of the Civil Law, for their wisdom is considered to be something extremely sacred; but it should not be estimated by its value in money, or be dishonored where compensation is claimed by a person who ought to promise under oath to dispense instruction gratuitously. Still, contributions when tendered may honorably be accepted, which, however, would be dishonorable if demanded.

In the case of hire of services, the labourer was the *locator*, the employer was the *conductor.* The *actio conducti* served to enforce the performance; the *actio locati* to claim the wages. The risks with regard to the service were borne by the employer: if the service could not be provided and this was not due to the labourer, he received his wages (D. 19.2.38*pr.*; D. 19.2.19.9). Wages were also paid in the case of illness. This can be deduced from D. 8.1.15*pr.* and D. 12.4.5*pr.* In Dacian employment contracts, it was deemed necessary to detail that no wages would be paid in the case of illness. In the

Middle Ages, Azo wrote that illness was always at the expense of the employer. Most authors (Irnerius, the Gloss, Bartolus...), however, assumend that each person had to carry his own risk and that illness was a risk of the employee. Interruptions of work on account of weather conditions, defects of the materials to be used, the flooding of a mine, etcetera were at the expense of the employer.

In the Middle Ages and the Early Modern Period, employment relationships became less a matter of private law. During the French Revolution, the corporative system was abolished and there were attempts to return to the principles of the *locatio conductio*. They were incorporated into the Code civil in 1804.

3. *Locatio conductio operis (faciendi)* (contracting for work)

By means of the *locatio conductio*, one could contract work out (*locare*) and take it on (*conducere*). The legal concept was the same for small commissions - needlework, reparation or cleaning of clothes - and for larger ones such as the construction of building ranging in size from small to gigantic. The purpose was no longer to put labour at someone's disposal, but to guarantee a result.

The main obligation of the *locator* (client) was to pay the price. The *conductor* (contractor) was liable for *dolus* and *culpa*. Case-law show that the contractor was expected to show *exactissima diligentia* (extraordinary diligence, D. 19.2.25.7). He probably always had a duty of *custodia* with regard to the goods that were entrusted to him (this rule certainly applied to those who worked as a *fullo* or *sarcinator*). Contractors were also liable for ignorance (*imperitia*). They could not accept work that he could not complete and were liable for the work that they contracted out to third parties (D. 19.2.24) and for their employees (D. 9.2.27.9). The *ius* commune, in which liability required an error, the latter liability was called *culpa in eligendo*: an error made when selecting employees. Originally, the risk was always to be carried by the contractor. The *locatio conductio operis* was an obligation to guarantee a result. Later, a distinction was made: some risks were to be carried by the client - the destruction of an unifinished building by an earthquake, for example - while other risks, like a collapse that could technically have been avoided, were to be carried by the contractor. A lot of case-law dealt with transfer (*adprobatio operis*). Depending on the agreement, this could happen in instalments or at once.

There were specific liability rules for *locatio conductio operis* in the case of transport by sea, for example the regulation for general average (*lex rhodia de iactu*).

§7. Donations

Roman donations are discussed in D. 39.5 and C. 8.55. According to the traditional interpretation, in the classical period a donation was an agreement in which a good or right was transferred or a debt was taken over or remitted, and where the donator had an *animus donandi* and the beneficiary agreed to receive the donation. The *causa donandi* was said to have given a specific cachet to the transfer of ownership. This was said to have been a legal ground that only became valid when the beneficiary had accepted the donation. In Antiquity, however, the word *causa* always referred to a legal act. Delivery in other words already required a legal act in the Classical Period. The beneficiary only had a right of action if this legal act took the form of a *stipulatio.* From Constantine's reign onwards, the actual donation had to be recorded and the deed had to be registered. Under Justinian, a promise to donate something and the acceptance of that promise gave rise to obligations. In the Middle Ages this was interpreted as if the donation were a *pactum legitimum*, a consensual agreement that was made enforceable by Justinian. The obligation to register was preserved for larger donations (five hundred *solidi*). Promises to donate had to be registered as well.

In Antiquity, a series of measures limited donations because this legal act resulted in the impoverishment of the *familia*. The *lex cincia* (204 BC) imposed a maximum amount. Donations between spouses were void, unless they were added to the dowry. In the third century, the *patronus* was given the possibility to revoke a donation to a freed person on account of ingratitude. In the fourth century, the scope of this possibility was extended to the father; in the fifth century to the mother and other ascendants; under Justinian every donator could revoke his donation on account of gross misbehaviour.

Chapter VIII
Socio-economic law

§1. Food supply

Social security and socio-economic rights are not innovations of our own time. Today, there are more means than ever of taking care of the ill, the weak, the elderly, the unemployed and those in marginal social contexts, but care for the weaker has always touched jurists. Coexistence is a teamwork and jurists of all eras experienced the need to help the weak or to step in in times of need, even if it was only to avoid greater damage. In each period of legal history, we find measures that concern employment protection, poor relief, healthcare and food supply.

Protection of employment has already been mentioned briefly in the context of *locatio conductio*. Employment contracts were based on *bona fide* contracts. This was the framework within which jurists had discussions about sick leave and occupational risks. Not much is known about Roman healthcare. Nor does one find much information about the status of invalids – a rare example is CTh. 14,18. The Justinianic law provides care for orphans, the elderly and other needy people: it mentions several measures that enabled welfare work in institutions that were financed with 'pious' donations. These homes and hospitals can also be found in the Middle Ages. In the Scandinavian countries they were nationalised in the Early Modern Era; in the Reformed countries they were often 'municipalised'. In many Catholic countries, they were expropriated during the French Revolution. Their status has hardly been studied by the Romanists of the last few centuries. The Pandectists and their contemporaries demurely shifted the accent of their study of law to the liberal rights of individuals. Social care for family members was also an important issue in Roman law. In the Middle Ages we still find regulations that obliged landowners to provide minimal care for all of the people on their domain. In the Eastern European reception, traces of these rules remained present until the nineteenth century. Russian landowners still had to provide for their serfs, who were *familiares*. However, when the great Western nations began to combat the brutal slavery on the American continent and the islands, they were of the opinion that Eastern Europe had to abolish serfdom as well. For the landowners, this was an unexpected benefit, but for many people in these countries it was a dramatic social decline. It destabilised Russia for more than a century. This is another reason to avoid writing about social legal history at all costs.

We will nevertheless provide one short overview of an important socio-legal matter from Antiquity: the supply of free food for the needy.

1. In the Republic

The area surrounding Rome only had the agricultural capacity to feed fifty thousand inhabitants. From the fifth century BC onwards, trade in food was a concern for the magistrates. When the *ager romanus* grew, an eye was always kept of the supply of food. Many provincial grain traders received *commercium* so that they had access to the free market. During the Punic wars, the grain trade was of strategic importance: armies had to be supplied and the City could not be starved. After the fall of Carthage, the *aediles* took over the African grain trade and supplied Rome with enormous amounts of African grain. From then on, there was an offical grain market (*frumentum publicum*). Import quota and transportation were under the Senate's control. The *aediles* were in charge of the daily management of the grain trade. The curule aediles were given the authority to punish grain speculation and to impose sales quotas per district, as well as maximum prices. In the *municipia*, the municipal governments used muncipal means to perform these duties.

In the City, food supply was also essential in order to make wars acceptable. In the second century BC, the tribunes of the people pressed for elaborate grain laws. The *lex frumentaria* of C. Sempronius Gracchus (123-122 BC) was established under Hellenistic influence. The government had to guarantee the population that there would be a reasonably-priced supply of grain, had to buy grain itself when the market was disrupted and had to step in financially when there were shortages. From then on, a supported grain policy was developed, in which the quaestors, who managed the relevant budgets, played an important role. From then on the regulation of the grain trade also came under their edict. At the end of the Republic, the quaestor of Ostia played an important role in this matter.

In 57 BC, after new difficulties, care for the grain supply (*cura annonae*) was entrusted to Pompey for a period of five years. Originally, his task was to reorganise the free trade and stabilise the market by coordinating the interests of buyers and sellers throughout the Empire. Pompey published the expected grain yields per region in order to breathe new life into the free trade. In the same year, however, the tribune P. Clodius terrorised the Senate into organising the free distribution of grain for needy citizens. The idea that poor plebeians managed to force their government to provide free food is incorrect. There were no poor people among the members of the *concilia plebis*. Lists of the needy were drawn up and soon contained two hundred thousand names. From 56 BC onwards, the Senate paid the costs of the *cura annonae* to Pompey. After Pompey, Caesar appointed *aediles ceriales* who were responsible for the *cura annonae*.

2. In the Principate

In 22 BC, the *cura annonae* was entrusted to Augustus. At first, he continued to use Pompey's system. The *aediles ceriales* organised the distribution of grain via the *aerarium*. In the provinces of the Senate, a tax was imposed that obligated the provinces to deliver grain. Augustus, however, began to fund the distribution of the free grain himself, with the revenues of his imperial provinces, where grain was also levied as a tax. The emperor supervised the production in his provinces and the distribution in Rome. The transport of the grain to Rome was organised by chartering private transporters. This system would become the basic structure of the Roman social security. Initially, this practice was limited to the city of Rome. Many new laws were created in order to give the system an institutional basis.

A. Establishment of the prefecture for the distribution of grain

In 6 AD Augustus appointed a *praefectus annonae*, who was to monitor the free grain trade and the supplies. He was the only person who could grant export licenses for grain. He could seize means of transport, impose mandatory prices and bring criminal proceedings against cartels that had been formed with a view to influencing the grain prices (*lex Iulia de annona*, see D. 48.12.2). The Roman law combatted cartels: cf. C. 4.59.2. The *praefectus annonae* could exclude someone from the grain trade (D. 47.11.6.2).

The prefecture for the distribution of grain acquired its supplies of grain from the imperial provinces. In Egypt, he production of grain was supervised by the *praefectus Aegypti*. In most of the provinces, the governors organised the production of grain by means of measures in their edict. After every uprising in the grain-providing provinces, fields were expropriated for the benefit of the *fiscus*. The prefect of the *annona* also tried to keep the grain prices on the free market low. He had the same means to influence the market at his disposal as the *fiscus* – the fiscal supplies of grain, for example. Subsidising remained an exceptional measure, but it was used in 19 under Tiberius and in 64 under Nero. From Claudius onwards, the *praefectus annonae* was the only person who administered the free distribution of grain. The quaestor of Ostia was replaced by a *procurator*. The delivery of supplies to the armies also became the responsibility of the grain prefecture.

The office of *praefectus annonae* continued to exist until 538. In 222 Ulpian held it for a short period. The first *praefectus annonae* outranked the *praefectus praetorio*; later they were subordinate to him. From the fourth century onwards, they were subordinate to the *praefectus urbi*. In addition, a new prefect, the *praefectus annonae Africae* was established. He was based in Carthage.

B. The organisation of the transport of grain

Neither the *aerarium* nor the *fiscus* ever owned cargo ships. Between the production of grain in the provinces and the free distribution in the City, the transport by private shipowners made or broke the supply of grain. In the Republic the censors – and later the quaestors – concluded five-year transport contracts for the benefit of the army and the *frumentum publicum*. Only Pompey requisitioned ships. The normal method consisted of generating competition in order to keep carriage charges low, counteracting the formation of cartels by the shipowners, and granting privileges to those who wanted to sail for the *annona*. Claudius granted civil rights to those who had sailed a ship with a capacity of at least ten thousand bushels for the prefecture of the *annona* under a *locatio conductio operis* for six years (Gaius 1.32c; *Tituli ex corpore Vlpiani* 3.6). Nero granted a tax exemption to those who invested in grain ships. Hadrian and Antoninus granted exemption from *munera* (D. 50.6.6.5 and 9). These *munera* were based on the Roman tradition that influential people took up offices for free. This also happened in the *municipia*. In Hadrian's day these *munera* were financial contributions. Under Trajan, a ship-owner demanded to be exempted from a legitimate, obligatory guardianship because his involvement in the transport of grain meant that he already held enough public offices. The prefecture refused to grant an exemption in this case, but similar claims were accepted in later years (*Fragm. Vat.*, 236). Trajan granted shipowners exemption from the *lex papia poppaea*, which limited the inheritance rights of those who did not have three or four children.

The *praefectus annonae* issued the certificate by means of which one could collect these benefits. Constitutions about the granting of this certificate were developed. A lot of case-law concerned the problem of who received the exemption if the shipping company was a joint venture (*corpus*). Who was the *nauicularius* (shipowner) in such a case? Many people attempted to join such a *corpus*. In order to receive not just exemption from *tributum*, but also the status of *nauicularius*, one's investment in risk capital had to amount at least to the value of the equipment of a ship of ten thousand bushels. It were mainly the *municipia* who addressed the emperor to make a stand against these benefits.

The *praefectus annonae* could carry part of the risks involved in transport. If necessary, he concluded a contract of bottomry (*foenus nauticum*; a type of contract that, in the nineteenth century, was still included in art. 179 and following of the Belgian Commercial code). Labeo introduced the liability of the shipper in the case of force majeure. At a certain time, Claudius carried all shipping risks on behalf of the *annona*. However, in the case of general average, the right of Rhodos continued to apply (*lex Rhodia de iactu*, D. 14.2). General average is an institition that causes losses during a journey to be carried proportionally by the owners of the ship and the owners of the cargo. In the case of the general average or costs incurred to save the ship, the loss or costs were divided among the shipowner and the shippers in proportion to their share in the enterprise.

C. The promotion of large bakeries

Most people who were entitled to benefits had their bread baked by someone else or sold their grain to bakers. From Trajan onwards, the emperors tried to regulate the bakeries. Trajan granted civil rights to the bakers (*pistores*) who processed at least one hundred bushels (eight hundred portions) per day under the supervision of the *annona*. These *pistores* then received the same benefits as the shipowners who sailed for the *annona*. Like the shipowners, the bakers began to form *corpora* (groupings) in order to reach such a capacity and citizens also attempted to receive the status of *pistor*.

D. During the imperial crisis

From the assassination of Alexander Serverus to Diocletian, the *annona* functioned normally. However, the different interpretations of the sources conflict with one another.

It is said that Alexander Severus was responsible for large-scale government interference in the *corpora* of shipowners and bakers, and that he introduced a coercive system. There was a greater need for grain transport because there were more troop movements. However, the smooth functioning of the *annona* in these circumstances is the best proof that there was no coercive system. The fact that measures were taken against the *dardaniati* (profiteers in the grain trade, D. 47.11.6) shows that there were still opportunities for free grain traders. The pressure on the grain-producing regions did increase significantly in this period.

Aurelian (270-275) is credited with a reform of the system for the distribution of free food. Under his reign, the *annona* distributed olive oil, salt, wine and pork. A special tax (*anabolicum*) was established for the benefit of the *annona*. Was this the land of plenty for the needy? At the same time, historians ask themselves how the Romans managed to build the 'muro torto' around Rome under Aurelian. However, this wall and the changes to the *annona* can be linked: what passes for a reform of the *annona* in fact concerned the provision of temporary compensation and sustenance for the builders of the wall. There was, however one reform: the *annona* henceforth distibuted loaves of bread rather than grain so as to ensure that none of the public grain ended up with the free bakers. In this manner, the *annona* could reduce the amounts of grain it needed.

In this period, everyone who worked for the benefit of the *annona* as a *colonus* on *agri uectigales* received benefits at the expense of the municipalities. One can find texts about colonists and people involved in the *corpora* of ship-owners and bakers who were not allowed to resign from their office (for example CTh. 13.5.5.5 and 7). However, we should relativise what the historians have written about this issue. These measures mainly concerned the acquirement and loss of exemptions. The imperial courts were continuously pronouncing judgements about privileges and exemptions. Their constitutions were case-law!

E. The late Empire

Under Diocletian, the *annona* also delivered grain to other cities: Antioch, Nicomedia and, later on, Constantinople. In the latter City, the Roman system was adopted, albeit with only twenty-one public bakeries (*pistrinae publicae*) instead of the two hundred and seventy approved bakeries of Rome. Alexandria, Puteoli and Carthage also kept back some of the grain which was transited via their ports and distributed it locally. Grain was also donated to peoples of the federation. Parts of Italy were included among the production areas (*Italia annonaria*); exemption from taxes was granted to those who lived in Italy and produced grain for the *annona*. Henceforth, the imperial grain provinces bore the costs of transport themselves.

The *nauicularii* and *pistores* received more privileges than ever. Shipowners in the East no longer accepted any civil duties and ships could no longer be requisitioned (CTh. 13.5.7). The normal partners of the *annona* were no longer individual *nauicularii* and *pistores*, but large combinations (*corpora*) of shipowners and bakers, who often already acted as cartels – just like the corporations in the Middle Ages would. The privileges were granted to those who were members of these corporations. It was no longer just their investment that was exempted from *tributum*: all of their immovable goods were exempted as well if these immovable goods served as a collateral for activities for the benefit of the *annona*. The transfer of a corporation's assets that were burdened with a *functio nauicularia* or a *functio pistoria* was regulated. Goods that were pledged as securities of an approved *corpus* were exempted from *tributum*, but also continued to serve as collateral for the corpus after they were inherited. They could not be given away. If untaxed land that belonged to members of the *corpus* fell vacant, it fell to the *corpus* and not to the *fiscus*. It is said that *corpora* had their own goods in the second half of the fourth century. This sounds peculiar. A more logical conclusion is that they functioned as a *societas* or *curia*.

In the literature about Roman law, one finds the tallest tales about shipowners who had to sail unwillingly and poor bakers who were chained to their ovens for the benefit of the *annona*. This confusion is mostly caused by the historians translating *familia* as family and not as 'corporation' or 'structure of liability' (the meaning which the word has in C. 14.3.2). In addition, some authors are not sufficiently aware that the *annona* granted privileges as well as immunities and tax exemptions and that the prefecture did not continue to grant these if the beneficiaries transferred risks to others or alienated goods that were necessary for the privileged activity. Other causes of the confusion are the difficulty of the *Codex Theodosianus* and the fantasy of its readers.

CTh. 14.3.14. – Si cui pistoris filia nubserit ac postea is eandem dilapidatis facultatibus consortio putauerit eximendam, non alia lege adque ratione eundem ipsum pistoriae necessitati et corpori praecipimus adstringi, quam si eodem munere originis uinculo teneretur.

Translation PFARR. – If a daughter of a breadmaker should marry any man and afterwards, when her fortune has been squandered, he should suppose that she may be released from the guild, We command that he shall be bound to the compulsory duties and guild of breadmaking by the same law and reason as if he were held by the bond of birth status to such compulsory service.

Translation L.W. – If a daughter of a regulated baker had married someone and this man had thought to cast her off once her assets had been squandered, we decide that he himself will be forced to provide for the need of the bakery and for the *corpus*, according to no other law and for no other amount than that which she had to provide for that office at the beginning of the bond.

Explanation: one does not marry the daughter of a baker if it means being chained to the oven! However, it is understandable that someone who squanders pledged goods, must afterwards provide this collateral himself. A similar fanciful story about the marriage of bakers can be found in the classical interpretation of CTh. 14.3.12 (above, I, §4, 3, b).

In the fifth century, we find a series of strict decisions in the case-law concerning the transport of grain. Because of the decentralisation of power, the supervision of the *annona* had become more complex. We read about corruption: shipowners sold grain 'en route' and arrived with second-rate grain or less cargo. In the latter case, they invoked *iactus* (general average). Once the *annona* only accepted general average after an investigation during which some of the slaves among the crew were subjected to torture (C. 11.6.3). Later, the prefect of the *annona* had all of the shipowners who sailed for the *annona* pay his share in the costs of general average. Some shipowners used dilapidated ships in order to acquire exemptions and attempted not to set sail. The services of the *praefectus annonae* were sometimes corrupt. The internal activities of the prefecture in particular were subjects to strict measures. However, Rome never established the coercive economy that is described by many historians. It would have been highly remarkable if such an economy had been thought up in the fourth and fifth centuries and had not left any traces in the sixth-century *Corpus iuris*.

3. The reception

After the collapse of the Western Empire, the *annona* continued to function under the responsibility of the popes. Without the rich African provinces, however, the *annona* in Rome became much smaller. It was also decentralised. Gelasius I (492-496) determined that the local churches had to use a quarter of their revenues for the 'table of the poor'. Gregory the Great decided to spend a quarter of the Italian ecclesiastical revenues on this charity. The care of the *annona* became the responsibility of the bishoprics; the realisation of its tasks and the distribution of bread became a duty of all churches. In the Merovingian regions and later in the Carolingian areas, the bishops received the right to demand one tenth of the harvests for redistribution among the poor. This system spread to many other regions. The ecclesiastical tithes were a form of reception of the Roman *annona*. From the ninth century onwards, we find that local councils include provisions pertaining to the distribution of food: examples are the council of Paris of 829 (canon 31) and the council of Mainz of 846 (canon 10). In the Middle Ages, the table of the poor remained a principal task of the church. In the Protestant principalities, the ecclesiastical care of the poor was taken over by the civic and municipal authorities in the Early Modern Age. In the Catholic principalites, it remained an episcopal matter. When ecclesiastical goods were expropriated in the Netherlands during the French Revolution, the care of the poor also became the responsibility of cities and municipalities. This is the basis of the municipal Public Centres for Social Welfare in Belgium.

In Rome, the court of the *praefectus annonae* treated conflicts concerning tithes and the table of the poor until well into the nineteenth century. Today, the *annona* has been reduced to a small supermarket in the Vatican.

§2. Roman forms of partnership

Good company law generates trade and, consequently, prosperity. Everyone has entrepreneurial ambitions, but no one wants to be ruined. Company law stimulates these ambitions by limiting the risk of insolvency. Inscriptions and findings indicate that there were large Roman production and trade companies. This means that there must have been high-quality company law. Great business houses are always underpinned by company law. 'Wrong,' many Romanists say. They claim that trade was in the hands of filthy-rich Romans who could not go bankrupt. This is nonsense, of course. Real trade is conducted at daggers drawn by thousands of traders who go all out in the hopes of earning some money.

The science of Roman law refers those who want information about companies to the *societas*, the partnership of D. 17.2. This meagre title leaves most of our questions unanswered. In addition, other sources contain clear traces of other companies that are not mentioned in D. 17.2. *Societas*, which we have already discussed above, was the legal concept which determined the relations between citizens who agreed to co-own goods.

1. Limited partnerships?

In the Theodosian Code, one finds mentions of *corpora*, associations that were involved in production and transport. Their structure is not very clear. They seem to have been cartels of traders who attempted to reach the capacity that was required to work for the *annona*. In the case-law about *corpora*, one can find elements that suggest that they were more than traders organisations.

In the context of *corpora*, one finds stipulations that remind one of the *uniuersitas*. One example is the fact that goods that had a function in a *corpus* did not fall to the *fiscus* but to the *corpus* in the case of intestacy without heirs. On the other hand, one finds elements of the later limited partnerships. *Corpora* consisted of two kinds of partners. The *manceps* or *patronus* was the manager; the *corporati* were members. The manager acted independently. He and his entire *familia* were fully liable. If several managers worked together, they were each other's *socii*. The *corporati* transferred money or goods in fiduciary ownership to the manager in return for a share in the profits or a predetermined return on capital. The contributed goods became part of the *familia* of the managers. They had been transferred by means of a *pactum fiduciae* that determined the purpose for which the goods were earmarked. In the Theodosian Code, we find the term *dotis nomine*, 'as if it were a dowry'. This term denotes that these goods were earmarked and could only be used for a certain purpose. The *corporati* could not revendicate their goods with a simple *actio fiduciae* if they had contributed these goods by means of *fiducia*. *Socii* could withdraw at any time (C. 3.37.5 and Gaius 3.151), but *corporati* could not. They could, however transfer their rights vis-à-vis the manager during their life or after their death (through inheritance). If they had made goods available to the *corpus*, these could be transferred freely but remained earmarked for the same purpose.

Managers were appointed for five years: C.Th. 8.5.36; C.Th. 14.3.7. This term of appointment was related to the registration in the *lustra* (tax lists). After five years, there were two possibilities: the manager in question was replaced, or his term of appointment was renewed. If he was replaced, he transferred the goods in his *familia* that were earmarked for the association to his successor by means of a *mancipatio*. If a manager died, the earmarked assets remained part of his estate. However, they were separate from the other assets – ready to be transferred to a new manager. If one of the heirs took (some of) these separate assets, he became fully liable for obligations as manager. If an heiress *in manu* took (some of) these separate assets, her husband became liable as manager.

This partnership, which was established by means of a *fiducia* and has characteristics of a limited partnership, never disappeared. There are medieval texts about ship-owning companies that were organised in this manner. In his commentary on D. 17.2.7, Odofredus cites limited partnerships as if they were common.

Bibliography. – L. Waelkens, 'La liberté économique dans le droit romain du Bas-Empire, Réflexions sur le statut des boulangeries conventionnées d'après le Code Théodosien', in: *Liberté et pluralisme, Actes des Journées internationales d'histoire du droit d'Anvers (27-30 main 1993)*, Brussels 1995; see also *Imprenditorialità e diritto nell'esperienza storica, Erice 22-25 novembre 1988*, [Società italiana di storia del diritto,] Palermo 1992.

2. The *actio institoria*

In Roman law, the most common partnership by far was the limited liability partnership that was established on the basis of the *actio institoria*, which was part of the complex Roman civil case-law.

The *actio institoria* first appeared in business life in the third century BC. It functioned just like an *actio de peculio*, but was used for people who were not members of the *familia*. In a *praepositio*, a *paterfamilias* agreed on an amount to the extent of which he would cover the acts of a business manager. This manager could be anyone: a free man or a slave, a person with or without civil rights. The relation between the manager and the principal was usually a *societas*. This means that the goods which the *institor* acquired were co-owned by the principal. Internal conflicts between the principal and the manager were brought before the court by means of the *actio pro socio*. If there was no proof that the *societas* was based on consensus, the Roman case-law considered the relation between commissioner and manager to be a *locatio conductio*.

Through the *societas*, the *institor* acquired goods for the benefit of his principal's *familia*, who in his turn received the right to revendicate these goods. The typical characteristic of this manner of conducting trade was that the principal became directly liable for the debts of his *institor*, but that this liability was limited to the amount mentioned in the *praepositio*. If the *institor* failed to pay, his creditors formulated their *actio* as an *actio institoria* against the principal. Just as in the case of a *peculium*, the creditors could combine the *actio institoria* with an *actio de in rem uerso* if there were reserved profits.

If a manager died or resigned, a new manager was appointed. The *societas* between the principal and the *institor* devolved by operation of law. When the commissioner died, the relation with the institor was broken, but the regular laws of succession applied. The heirs could divide the assets and give up the business, or enter into a *societas*. All problems of succession could be resolved by means of a Roman will.

Inscriptions have been found that mention enterprises with thousands of employees and several branches in the Empire which were organised according to this system. Nevertheless, this matter was not treated systematically in the Digest. This out-of-date compilation which was drawn up for the dictator Justinian contained neither commercial nor financial law. A possible explanation is that these matters were considered as Constantinopolitan and that the compilers of the *Corpus iuris* were therefore of the opinion that they were not part of the legacy of the old Empire.

The *actio institoria* did not survive the fragmentation of the case-law in the West. The larger the jurisdiction, the greater the opportunities for exchange and trade, and the more problems pertaining to commercial and financial law. If a jurisdiction becomes smaller, commercial law is usually the first victim. There is no evidence of trade that made use of *peculium* and *institutio* in the early Middle Ages. In Constantinople, however, this legal concept did continue to exist. The word *pekoulion* regularly turns up in the Eastern sources. In keeping with the Roman legal tradition, trade with limited liability was based on this institution. In the twelfth century, the Venetian and Genoan trade firms adopted double-entry bookkeeping because the liability of *peculium* holders and *institores* was clearly registered in double-entry accounts. The *peculium* was discussed extensively by the civil lawyers. The *actio institoria* and the method of acting for third parties by means of an *institutio*, however, was only treated in passing. Apparently, this Latin term had not been handed down in trade circles.

The cities where merchant ships departed for Constantinople remained familiar with the Roman manner of conducting trade with limited liability. This method became important once again when Greek firms, which were still working with a combination of civil rights, limited liability and securities, arrived in the West in 1453. In the rough times of the sixteenth century, continental Europe experienced a major financial crisis. In trade and the mining industry, partnerships without capital were replaced with capitalised companies. Money that had been collected beforehand was the only thing that could convince the sixteenth-century sceptics. From then on, the rise of capitalism began in Central Europe. On the Atlantic side of Europe, companies without capital remained possible.

Bibliography. – J.-J. AUBERT, *Business Managers in Ancient Rome, A Social and Economic Study of Institores, 200 BC-AD 250*, Leyden-New York-Cologne 1994.

3. *Societas*

D. 17.2 and C. 4.38 are the traditional sources for *societas*. Titles D. 10.3 and C. 37 also deal with *socii* and *societas*, but many commentaries do not involve these titles in their treatment of *societas*.

In commercial law, *societas* was the legal concept by means of which two or more people who were *sui iuris* joined part of their assets or *familia* in order to reach a commercial goal. All of the assets which they devoted to the *societas* belonged to all *socii* in the same way and could be revendicated by each *socius*. The co-ownership that had been agreed upon was full ownership of the assets by each *socius*. The assets became part of the *familia* of every *socius*, albeit as assets that were earmarked for a particular purpose. *Socii* could agree that one of them contributed goods, while another contributed labour, or that the profits would not be divided equally. There was *custodia*-liability for the co-owned assets, but this only led to *culpa leuis in concreto*.

The *societas* meant very little for people who contracted with the *socii* and were not members of the *societas*. These contracting parties only acquired rights vis-à-vis the person with whom they had contracted. They possessed a stronger form of security because the common goods were part of the assets of every *socius*. By means of the *actio pro socio*, *socii* could obtain the offset of cash resources or floating assets from each other; by means of the *actio de communi diuidundo* they could withdraw from the *societas* and divide the goods. If the latter action was used, the entire legal situation that had grown between them (*bona fides, culpa leuis in concreto*) was taken into account. *Socii* were always fully liable towards each other, with their entire *familia* as security. No one could be obliged to continue to live in co-ownership with others. This rule also applied to *socii*: they could always demand division (C. 3.37.5 and Gaius 3.151).

Within a single trading firm, several *societates* could be combined. Several *patroni* or *mancipes* were each other's *socii*. All of the assets that were earmarked, including the contributions of the financial backers, were part of everyone's *familia*. They were co-owned: every *socius* could use this capital and was liable towards fellow contracting partners. When a *socius* resigned, the co-ownership with his fellow manager(s) was handeled as a *societas*. *Socii* separately or jointly appointed one or several *institores* of a new *societas*. If one *socius* appointed two *institores*, these *institores* were not *socii* of one another. Each of them brought in his assets individually according to his *praepositio*. The situation was different if several *patresfamilias* jointly appointed one *institor* or if the heirs of an undertaking jointly decided to let an *institor* continue to go about his business. They were each other's *socii*. The entire sum for which they were liable towards the contracting partners of the *institores* fell within the assets of each *socius*. If an *institor* did not pay, his contracting partners were free to decide against which of his principals they would bring a claim. This principal could then, in his capacity of *socius*, settle the affair with the other members of the partnership.

In large partnerships with many co-owners, people ran up against the inefficiency of the *societas* of D. 17.2. Every *societas* devolved when a partner died, i.e. every death put the future of the *societas* at risk. Every *socius* could demand the liquidation of the partnership. Gradually, case-law was developed about the latter problem. If, for example, a partner withdrew without having a serious reason to do so, his fellow partners could bring the *actio pro socio* against him (D. 17.2.14). However, the fact remained that claims could be lodged against every co-owner.

How could large business concerns like the Ateius firm be developed in these circumstances? This firm was the market leader in oil lamps, had eight thousand employees in Italy, Gaul and Dacia and must therefore have been able to withstand all issues of succession. The *Corpus iuris* does not provide an answer to this question. In the reception, one can find abbeys and shipowning companies which were structured like the abovementioned *uniuersitates*. They were led by a *curia*, the members (*curiales*) of which participated in law transactions. If a *curialis* died, his rights and obligations returned to the *curia*, which could appoint a new *curialis*. Every one of the *curiales* could enjoy limited liability if he appointed *institores*. Is it possible that this was the formula for transport by sea, the industrial bakeries that were regulated by the *annona* or the courier companies that worked for the government (C. Th. 8.5)?

§3. Means of payment and funding

1. Banks

Bibliography. – R. Bogaert, 'Het bankwezen in de Oudheid', in: *De Bank in Europa*, Antwerp 1991, p. 13-68; J. Andreau, *La banque et les affaires dans le monde romain (IVe siècle avant J.C. – IIIe siècle après J.C.)*, Paris 2001; P. Nardi, *Studi sui banchiere nel pensiero dei Glossatori*, [Quaderni di Studi Senesi, 44,] Milan 1979.

The *Corpus iuris* does not contain much information about the Roman bankers (*argentarii*). Two important archives of bankers are currently being published, namely those of the Jucundi in Pompei and the Sulpicii in Puteoli. It turns out that the Roman bankers had four activities:

- change: the testing and changing of minted money. Tested coins could be obtained in sealed bags – the seal mentioned the name of the banker and the value of the bag's contents.
- deposit banking: the safeguarding of deposits. Money that was deposited was a *depositum regulare* (full reserve banking); money on a current account (*ratio*) was a *depositum irregulare*, which could be used to withdraw cash for payments, or to make payments by means of transfers or cheques. In the latter case, the banker provided a proof of *depositum* (*receptum argentarii*), which the client could send to his creditor. The latter received an *actio recepticia* against the banker. In the post-classical era, the *receptum argentarii* was replaced with the system of *pecunia constituta*.

- investment banking: the provision of loans. Not much is known about this. Most of the Romanists consider *mutuum* as a loan and as the main legal act performed by bankers. According to the legal texts, however, a *mutuum* did not bear interest. In addition, the examples of loans that have been discovered do not mention stipulations concerning interest. There are three theories about the determination of the interest: (1) loans were issued at par, (2) the stipulations concerning interests were separate *pacta*, or (3) the interests were stipulated in separate *cautiones*. All three of these systems existed, but interest-bearing loans do not seem to have been a common practice for the *argentarii*. *Mutuum* was something for merchant bankers.
- merchant banking: the financing of trade. Bankers could become *socii* of a trading firm, so that their contributions became assets of the firm's partners. In addition, they traded and discounted claims, which were cast into the form of *pecunia constituta* (see below). Texts have been found that mention *argentarii* who conducted trade for third parties and bought and sold goods themselves. It was possible to have accounts with an *argentarius* that did not contain money but goods, for example grain. In this context, one can ask whether *mutua* were perhaps mutual contracts which detailed that a banker would buy goods for a trader and that the trader would buy these back at a higher price at a later time.

In medieval Western Europe, the Lombards and the Tuscans were the best-known bankers. They were engaged by the papal *camera apostolica* to collect the share of the ecclesiastical tithes that went to Rome. The money that had to be sent to Italy was used to finance trade: traders in the north received money to buy goods, as well as bills of exchange that detailed that they had to return a slightly larger amount in Italy. Azo teaches us that the medieval bankers mainly occupied themselves with negotiable instruments and in particular with the discounting of these instruments. This practice had its origins in the reception of *pecunia constituta*, which we will treat below. Regular interest-bearing loans were dangerous because they went against the ecclesiastical prohibition of interest and could therefore not be claimed before some courts. In order to temporarily lend out cash surpluses, Italian bankers often collaborated with Jewish brokers because the prohibition of usury, being an ecclesiastical law, did not apply to other religions.

In the fifteenth century, Greek merchant bankers settled in Lisbon, Venice, Genoa, Seville, etcetera. They financed the new trade flows of the Renaissance. In the Early Modern Era, Greek banking was mainly received on the Atlantic side of Europe, first in Spain and Portugal and then in the Netherlands and England. The combination of merchant banks and partnerships without capital is a striking feature of the wealth developed in seventeenth-century England. In addition, we see the rise of the regular interest-bearing loan under the influence of Greek immigrants. Just like the company law that underpinned this development, the financial law of this era has not been studied properly, even though such a study would be more than welcome in our time, which is characterised by the adoption of Anglo-American economic techniques.

2. *Pecunia constituta*

According to most of the Romanists, everything was paid in cash in Roman Antiquity. This, of course, is impossible. If aqueducts had had to be paid in coins, they would never have been built. 'Full reserve banking' does not seem to have been an option either:

there could never have been that many coins with the bankers. The imperial mint was a small administration. There were no cash flows that corresponded with the large trade flows of the old Empire – African grain in Rome, Italian amphora in Spain, Egyptian fish in Sagalassos... The supply of cash was relatively small, and the sources rarely mention transportations of money. Under Caesar, there was a liquidity crisis and no one was allowed to have more than fifty thousand sesterces in coins. This means that there were other means of payment and funding.

A first system of payment with documents was *receptum argentarium*. A debtor in Tongeren had to pay for goods from Trier. He deposited the money with a banker in Tongeren and received a receipt, which he sent to his creditor in Trier. This receipt gave the creditor a right of action against the banker or his agent in Trier. Any problems with the payment resulted in an *actio recepticia* before a court. The local agent in Trier paid out the debt in cash or kept the amount available for the creditor. The creditor in Trier could also give the receipt to his own banker, who then settled the matter with his colleage. If the first debtor deposited cash with his banker in Tongeren, this deposit was a *depositum regulare*, a regular deposit. He could, however, also deposit documents or receipts which he had received from another banker – in that case his deposit was a *depositum irregulare*. The third possibility was that the banker simply gave the debtor a receipt on credit and trusted that he would receive the money at some point. In this case, the debt was paid with scriptural money that did not exist. This is of course a foolish method. Every debtor dreams of paying with worthless money, and every banker dreams of his commissions on this money, but this practice results in the creation of artificial money and there is no banker who can keep this up. This method of payment was forbidden by C. 4.18.2.1. *Nota bene*: in the situation described above the normal method of payment would have been a *mutuum*; 'we will buy these goods for you in Trier and you will buy them from us in Tongeren'. In this manner, the bank had a collateral because it owned the goods in the interim.

A second common form of distance payment was the *permutatio*, which involved the swapping of rights of action. Cicero wanted to send a monthly allowance to his son who studied in Athens. He temporarily gave the rental income of an apartment in Rome to a Roman banker who was owed money by an Athenian banker. The Roman banker asked his Athenian colleague to deduce the money from this debt and to make it available for Cicero junior. The bankers employed correspondents and had current accounts with one another. They often found *permutationes* for their clients. The Senate made use of *permutationes* as well: by means of operating budget, it gave the governors drawing rights on local tax farmers.

Pecunia constituta was also used as a means of payment. The case-law concerning this method was collected in D. 13.5. This was the common method to create valuable papers and discount them with bankers or pay with them. Rights of action were abstracted and made marketable. We will treat the abstraction of these rights first. A debtor and a creditor definitively determined the debt in a *constitutum*. All possible controversies about this action were precluded, a fixed term for the payment was determined, notice of default was precluded, as were all possible limitations of liability, the specific rights of guardians and minors, stipulations concerning the choice of law, etcetera. The debt that was detailed in the document became a pure, incontestable debt. If someone demanded the payment of such a *constitutum* before the court, the praetor and the *cognitio* judge granted an *actio de pecunia constituta* instead of the action that was normally used for the original legal act. A debt that had been abstracted in this manner became marketable. It could be transferred without problems. The third-party acquirer who accepted a *constitutum* as payment acquired a *constitutum debiti alieni* (*constitutum* of another's debt). In the case of a legal conflict, the judge granted him the *actio de pecunia constituta* against both the previous holder and the original debtor of the *constitutum*. In this manner, one could pay debts with claims which one still had against third parties. If someone wanted cash, he could have his banker pay out a *constitutum*. The banker in question discounted interests and collection costs if neccessary and paid out the difference. The banker could then use the paper as a means of payment.

In comparison with the *receptum argentarium*, the *constitutum* had as a benefit that there was an economic activity which served as a security. It was not merely scriptural money. The *actio de edendo*, which could be used to obtain the right to inspect accounts, could also be employed to obtain the right to inspect the *constituta* held by bankers.

Pecunia constituta was used in the Middle Ages. In the twelfth century, the use of bills of exchange arrived in Genoa from Constantinople. The oldest bills of exchange that have been handed down state an amount in 'bezant'. Azo and Accursius mention *pecunia constituta* as one of the main tools of bankers. They emphasise the abstract character of this means of payment. What were Azo and Accursius writing about if not about the precursor of the bill of exchange? *Pecunia constituta* continued to be used in Constantinople and travelled to the Italian commercial cities via trade with the Levant. In Italy, *pecunia constituta* was used for trade with the north. Around 1400, the law relating to bills of exchange had become a matter for the commercial court. The link with the Roman *pecunia constituta* was no longer emphasised in legal education. Jurists like Dynus de Mugello no longer saw the connection between *pecunia constituta* and bills of exchange. The historians of the law pertaining to bills of exchange do not hark back to Roman practice either.

Bibliography. – L. WAELKENS, 'Pecunia constituta', in: A. GIROLLET (ed.), *Le droit, les affaires et l'argent, Actes des Journées internationales de la Société d'histoire du droit (Dijon, 30 mai-1er juin 2007)*, [= Mémoires de la Société pour l'histoire du droit et des institutions des anciens pays bourguignons, comtois et romands, 65,] Dijon 2008, p. 325-337.

Conclusion

1. Roman law is not a legal system

No one can ignore the fact that Roman law does not exist in and of itself. What we have before us are some works with old texts which we read from the perspective of a grand dream about Roman Antiquity which is part of our collective memory, the memory of Hegel's 'objektive Geist'. Departing from these texts and that dream, legal history went in all directions. Monarchs developed the Roman law in order to become emperors and motivate their soldiers. Bishops found means to realise their calling. Civil lawyers wanted to bring in a new order. The glossators thought they understood Roman law correctly and connected it with the feudal society. The commentators' Roman law provided the basis for a European *ius commune*. The sixteenth-century monarchs stimulated the study of Roman law that made them emperors within their own nation. The humanists preached a return to Antiquity and found typically sixteenth-century patterns of thought in Roman law. The School of Natural law used Roman law as a source for the private civil rights that protected people from monarchical absolutism. The doctrine of the seventeenth and eighteenth centuries boasted a new *ius commune* that counteracted absolutism. Savigny wanted to return to the real Roman law in order to undermine the misconceptions of the French Revolution. The Pandectists discussed Roman law because they were searching for a common civil law for Germany and continuously ran up against the *ius commune*. Were all of these scholars on the wrong track, guided by self-interest and suffering from a lack of vision with regard to the real Roman law? Luckily, the twentieth-century Romanists returned to the real classical Roman law. In a bourgeois era, they looked into Roman law and found the basis for our civil law, with marriage, ownership, obligations and torts – as if these already existed in pre-Christian times. Was the leading Romanist of the previous century, Max Kaser, also on the wrong track? The Romanists of our generation discovered the reception, walked the ways of canon law, looked for Roman influences in English law. Did they finally reach the truth and gain an insight into the real Roman law? No. The Romanists of the early twenty-first century attempted to reunify the European law and used Roman law as a means to that end. What was the matter with all of these jurists, who could not even assess the Roman law correctly? Nothing. They were legal scholars. Jurists do not want to explain the past, but ensure survival today and in the future. Every day, the science of law is looking to determine the course of society's ethics, which has shifted somewhat since yesterday. They have to know of this course in order to resolve conflicts in a societally acceptable manner. They do not stop thinking of the future when they look at the past. Does this mean that jurists are not scientists? Keep a close eye on other scientific disciplines and pay attention to how these scientists are also bending over backwards in order to manage to incorporate the past into the present. This is how science works.

2. Medieval jurists were not looking for 'rational' law

Does this mean that the reception of Roman law started because medieval jurists were looking for rational law in a time of degeneration? This is a classic position, but what is rational? Each period of Western history had its own brand of logic. The Roman *ratio* referred to calculations and bookkeeping and indicated a relatively concrete way of thinking. For early medieval people, the word 'rational' still referred to balanced Roman accounts. It is only in the thirteenth century that the Aristotelian *logos* was also translated into *ratio* and that people began to look for an absolute and transcendent notion in this new *ratio*. This *ratio* was adulated in the Renaissance, which saw an overwhelming reception of Greek thought. The Greeks' practical manner of thought was associated with Greek religious thought about a Christianity without a Pope. Early modern authors praised rational thought to the skies. It earned its credentials because it led to new prosperity and new chances of survival. Many people love rational thought and feel that their salvation depends on it. This however, is no reason to call the medieval hankering for Roman law a search for rationality.

There was, in short, no rational medieval Roman law. However, the Greek manner of thought was strongly marked by Roman societal thought, which had its own logic. Its coherence was inspired by the smooth functioning of society, as well as by the adherence to the rules that had led to the dominance of Rome, among others the civil freedoms. Maybe this is exactly what Roman logic is: this informal constructivism, this manner of granting everyone his rights and freedoms (D. 1.1.10) without undermining the Roman commonwealth.

And yet, medieval people were not looking for this kind of rationality in Roman law either. The medieval method consisted of using the Roman bookkeeping logic and the rediscovered Greek logic to reconcile *auctoritates* – authoritative texts – with one another and to arrive at a meaningful, harmonic overall picture of reality. The *auctoritates* themselves were not questioned. The texts of the *Corpus iuris* were authoritative. The question of why Roman law was received is not so much a question about the internal logic of Roman law, but rather a question about why it was so authoritative. And the answer to that question is simple: if you think that your neighbour's method leads to better results, you incorporate it into your own logic.

3. Roman law as Christian law?

Was Roman law received because it was Christian and the Justinianic collection was enacted *in nomine Domini Dei nostri Jhesu Christi*? How can we know this? How Roman is Christianity? How Christian is Roman law? When the first Christian theology was developed, the societal logic of the time was received. Traditionally, Western bishops opted to acculturate the Christian message to the Mediterranean Roman society. This is not detrimental to salvation history. The periods of exile had led to the acculturation of the chosen people to the Egyptian and Babylonian societies when these reached their apogee. Through several centuries of osmosis, *christianitas* and *romanitas* began to determine each other. The Latin stoic philosophy which was in the City's air played a part, as did politics. People listened to Tertullian under the African Severans, to the Eastern church fathers during the imperial crisis, and to Augustine's synthesis when the emperors tried to reconcile the East and the West. The fact that Christian doctrine and discipline became increasingly juridical in character is obviously due to the influence of the Roman tradition. Conversely, Christianity became important for the emperors' politics from the third century onwards. The reception of Roman law via the Christian community was manifest. The medieval reception was initiated by the bishops and the canonists. Matters such as procedure, administrative law, criminal law, the law of cohabitation or the law of wills were received via the canonists. The canonists' view on Roman law would once again have a large impact in the sixteenth century, when the ecclesiastical courts were nationalised. We will leave it to the reader to assess how Roman and Christian all of this was. In this book, we have considered the issue as a phenomenon related to the reception of Roman law.

4. Roman law as ideological law

The medieval reception of Roman law tied in with the interests of many people. The monarchs advocated a law in which the *princeps* of the people had received sovereignty (D. 2.1.2), the monarch created binding law at his own discretion (D. 1.4.1) and everyone could appeal against lower authorities. Because of the reception of Roman law, the bishops regained their autonomy, as well as the authority to manage ecclesiastical goods. Able-bodied men were guaranteed civil rights in a peaceful context. People intuited that Roman law served common interests. The medieval monarchs were legitimised by Roman principles; the bishops lived independently as they did in the Western Empire; the free warriors were forged on the anvil of Roman *ciuitas*. The ideology of the Roman texts dovetailed with the social substructure. When the second wave of reception struck the Continent in the Renaissance, every one once again felt that Greek civilisation revived the old Rome.

Two massive waves of reception originated in Constantinople. During the crusades, many people got to know this new Rome and desired to bring the splendour of Constantinople to the West. The reception of the Roman law of Constantinople held more appeal for the crusaders than overseas battles. The realisation that they were part of a common world implied the possibility of a *ius commune*. The old Italian cities and the Italian trade to which they were exposed were associated with ancient Rome. Only a concurrence of interests can explain that the university of Bologna boomed as soon as it began to study Roman law freely and in a scientific manner. The second massive wave of reception was caused by the capture of Constantinople in 1453. The immigration of thousands of wealthy Greeks caused a second confrontation. This time, the interests changed to absolutism, trade and free thought. The origination of a citizenry that became independent from monarchs and bishops was the consequence of the repercussions of this immigration. Once again, this wave of reception was associated with a rich Roman heritage.

5. 'Der Geist des römischen Rechts'

For centuries, Roman law continued to evolve in the formerly Roman provinces, and because of neighbouring territories' reception. The scientific approach of the Middle Ages was – to use the terminology of Hegel's 'Phänomenologie des Geistes' once again – an antithesis. The synthesis of Bartolism and the early *ius commune* became the thesis of the next wave. The sixteenth-century wave of reception was its antithesis. The science of law was once again confronted with the *Corpus iuris*. Roman law revived at the law faculties, where 'der Geist des römischen Rechts' was developed in early-modern legal doctrine. Jhering called this 'die Prädestination des römischen Rechts zur Kultur des Rechts'. Does this nineteenth-century rhetoric sound overly pro-Roman? Is the notion 'Roman' perhaps too closely associated with Roman Catholicism? Should we not ban all Roman law from the study of law? After all, we are now mainly receiving elements of Anglo-American law. Would it be better to replace the study of Roman law with the comparative study of Anglo-American law? These are interesting questions! Since the European Union has striven for the unity of the law, the common roots of English and Continental law have been laid bare. In this context, we encounter strange problems. This English law, which has been received in many countries, may very well be the true heir of Roman law; England may very well be the museum of Roman law. Is it not true that Anglo-American company and financial law resemble Roman law more closely than their Continental counterparts? Some good advice would be to examine this Anglo-American reception thoroughly and to consider Roman law from another angle in this context, because *nullum ius nisi romanum*.

Index of legal sources

Digesta

General index

www.ingramcontent.com/pod-product-compliance
Ingram Content Group UK Ltd.
Pitfield, Milton Keynes, MK11 3LW, UK
UKHW021846100926
8556IPUK00019B/1076

9 789462 700543